I0331703

City of Lyrics

Islamic Civilization and Muslim Networks

Carl W. Ernst and Bruce B. Lawrence, *editors*

Highlighting themes with historical as well as contemporary significance, Islamic Civilization and Muslim Networks features works that explore Islamic societies and Muslim peoples from a fresh perspective, drawing on new interpretive frameworks or theoretical strategies in a variety of disciplines. Special emphasis is given to systems of exchange that have promoted the creation and development of Islamic identities—cultural, religious, or geopolitical. The series spans all periods and regions of Islamic civilization.

A complete list of books published in Islamic Civilization and Muslim Networks is available at https://uncpress.org/series/islamic-civilization-and-muslim-networks.

City of Lyrics

Ordinary Poets and Islamicate Popular Culture in Early Modern Delhi

NATHAN L. M. TABOR

The University of North Carolina Press Chapel Hill

Set in Charis by Westchester Publishing Services
Manufactured in the United States of America

Library of Congress Cataloging-in-Publication Data
Names: Tabor, Nathan L. M., author.
Title: City of lyrics : ordinary poets and Islamicate popular culture in early modern Delhi / Nathan L. M. Tabor.
Other titles: Islamic civilization & Muslim networks.
Description: Chapel Hill : The University of North Carolina Press, [2025] | Series: Islamic civilization and Muslim networks | Includes bibliographical references and index.
Identifiers: LCCN 2025013926 | ISBN 9781469690216 (cloth) | ISBN 9781469690223 (paperback) | ISBN 9781469688299 (epub) | ISBN 9781469690230 (pdf)
Subjects: LCSH: Mushairas—India—Delhi—History—18th century. | Urdu poetry—Competitions—India—Delhi—History—18th century. | Ghazals, Urdu—India—Delhi—History and criticism. | BISAC: RELIGION / Islam / General | LITERARY CRITICISM / Poetry
Classification: LCC PK2168 .T34 2025 | DDC 891.4/39120980095456—dc23/eng/20250521
LC record available at https://lccn.loc.gov/2025013926

Cover art: *A Commotion in the Bazaar*, ca. 1750–60, by Nainsukh.
© Ashmolean Museum.

For product safety concerns under the European Union's General Product Safety Regulation (EU GPSR), please contact gpsr@mare-nostrum.co.uk or write to the University of North Carolina Press and Mare Nostrum Group B.V., Mauritskade 21D, 1091 GC Amsterdam, The Netherlands.

for Alisa Marlene

Contents

List of Illustrations, ix

Conventions, xi

Dramatis Personae, xiii

Prologue, 1

Introduction, 7
Delhi's Market for Speech, 1720–1750

1 At the Tomb of Delhi's Poet-Saint, 40

2 New Writers at the Queen Regent's Mosque, 80

3 Literary Discord and the Occupation of Delhi, 124

4 The Last Duel at Bedil's Grave, 171

Conclusion, 223
Networks, Competitions, and Accessing the Past

Acknowledgments, 237

Notes, 241

Bibliography, 287

Index, 321

Illustrations

Figures

0.1 Awḥadī teaching Shaiḳh ʿIrāqī, Amīr Ḥusainī, and Saʿīd Farġhānī, 35
2.1 The Ornament of Mosques, 83
2.2 Portrait of Nawwāb Amīr Ḳhān Bahādur Muḥammad Shāhī, 98
3.1 An elite woman holding a rose, 159

Map

F.1 Map of Shāhjahānābād and surroundings, circa late 1700s, xxii

Tables

F.1 Transliteration System, xi
F.2 Literary Figures and Their Distinctions, xiii

Conventions

All years appear according to the Gregorian calendar except for circumstances in which the Islamic lunar calendar (Hijri year) is required for dates for chronograms, in primary sources, and as linked with certain key events. In those cases, years are notated with AH (Anno Hegirae).

Excerpts from primary sources follow the transliteration scheme established for the *Journal of Urdu Studies* (*JUS*), found in table F.1. The *JUS* system affords consistency for representing Arabic, Hindi, Persian, and Turkish vocabularies that comprise Urdu's lexicon.

TABLE F.1 Transliteration System

ا	ā, a, i, u								
ب	b	پ	p	ت	t	ٹ	ṭ	ث	ṡ
ج	j	چ	ch	ح	ḥ	خ	ḳh		
د	d	ڈ	ḍ	ذ	ż				
ر	r	ڑ	ṛ	ز	z	ژ	z̲h̲		
س	s	ش	sh						
ص	ṣ	ض	ẓ						
ط	t̤	ظ	z̤						
ع	ʿ	غ	ġh						
ف	f	ق	q						
ک	k	گ	g						
ل	l	م	m						
ن	n	ں	ñ						
و	v, ū, o, au, w								
ھ	h	ہ	h						
ی	ī	ے	y, e, ai						
ء	ʾ	ۃ	t						
iẓāfat	-e	ىٰ	á						

Dramatis Personae

The poets, diarists, and noteworthy patrons presented in table F.2 appear alphabetically according to pen name. In the table for cases in which the pen name is unknown, individuals appear according to their title or given name. Occasionally, poets write under the same pen name (e.g., *Ḥashmat*) or cultivate names with etymologically parallel forms (e.g., *S̈ābit* and *S̈abāt*). In the text for those instances, I refer to the lesser-known versifier by their given name or title followed by the pen name (e.g., Bāqir *Ḥazīn*).

TABLE F.2 Literary Figures and Their Distinctions

Given name or title	*Pen name*	*Dates*	*Distinctions*
Najm ud-Dīn Shāh Mubārak	*Ābrū*	1683?–1733	Reḳhtah poet, associate of Ḳhwushgo, and student of Ārzū
Abū ul-Ḥasan	*Āgāh*	fl. 1730–50	Minor aristocrat and participant at Bedil's *ʿurs*
Imām ud-Dīn	*Aksīr*	1680?–1739	Medic, friend of S̈ābit, and casualty of Nadir Shah's massacre
Nāṣir ʿAlī Sirhindī	*ʿAlī*	1638?–1697	Influential ġhazal writer
Niʿmat Ḳhān	*ʿĀlī*	d. 1710	Mughal official, satirist, and maternal grandfather to Saudā
ʿAlī ul-Ḥusainī Gardezī	—	fl. 1740–60	Minor aristocrat and early reḳhtah taẕkirah writer
Muḥammad Nāṣir	*ʿAndalīb*	1694–1759	Sufi leader and informal student of Gulshan
Amīr Ḳhān, ʿUmdat ul-Mulk	*Anjām*	d. 1747	Mughal official, noted patron, and reḳhtah poet
Muḥammad	*ʿĀrif*	fl. 1740–50	Opium addict, reḳhtah poet, and student of Maẓmūn

(*continued*)

TABLE F.2 (*continued*)

Given name or title	*Pen name*	*Dates*	*Distinctions*
Sirāj ud-Dīn ʿAlī Ḳhān	*Ārzū*	1688–1756	Mughal official, tażkirah writer, reḳhtah poet, and student of Bedil
Niẓām ul-Mulk	*Āṣif*	1671–1748	High Mughal official and reḳhtah poet
Muḥammad ʿAṭāʾullāh	*ʿAṭā*	1681?–1725?	Professional soldier, reḳhtah poet, and student of Bedil
ʿAbd ul-Jalīl	*Aṭal*	1661–1725	Associate of ʿAṭā, grandfather of Āzād, and reḳhtah poet
Ġhulām ʿAlī	*Āzād*	1704–1786	Tażkirah writer, traveler, and teacher to Shafīq
Bhañwarī	*Babrī Rindī*	fl. 1710–40	Courtesan and student of Bedil
Bandah ʿAlī	—	—	See *Sabaqat*
Bāqir Ḥazīn	—	—	See *Ḥazīn*
—	*Bāsiṭī*	—	See *Sabaqat*
Rafīʿ Ḳhān	*Bāżil*	d. 1707/12	Gwalior-based poet and associate of Nāṣir ʿAlī
ʿAbd ul-Qādir	*Bedil*	1644–1720	Delhi's poet-saint
Burhān ul-Mulk	—	1680–1739	High Mughal official and patron to Wālih
Fażl ʿAlī	*Dānā*	fl. 1740–50	Associate of Saudā, reḳhtah poet, and student of Maẓmūn
ʿAlī Muḥammadī	*Dard*	1721–1785	Sufi leader, reḳhtah poet, mushāʿirah host in the 1740s
Dargāh Qulī Ḳhān	—	1710–1766	Diarist and minor official under Niẓām ul-Mulk
Muḥammad Jān	*Dīwānah*	d. 1738	Drug addict, reḳhtah poet, and associate of Muḳhliṣ
Shams ud-Dīn	*Faqīr*	1703–1767	Associate of Ummīd and Wālih; literary theorist
Ashraf ʿAlī	*Fuġhān*	1725–1773	Minor aristocrat, reḳhtah poet, and student of Ummīd
Gannā Begam	—	—	See *Minnat*
Gardezī	—	—	See ʿAlī ul-Ḥusainī Gardezī

TABLE F.2 *(continued)*

Given name or title	*Pen name*	*Dates*	*Distinctions*
Mīrzā Girāmī Hamadānī	*Girāmī*	d. 1743	Sufi leader, reḳhtah poet, and student of his father Qabūl
—	*Gulāb*	fl. 1730–50	Singer and courtesan with a preference for classical verse
Saʿdullāh	*Gulshan*	1664–1728	Sufi leader, student of Bedil, patron saint of performers
Qayām ud-Dīn	*Ḥairat*	fl. 1730–61	Secretary, tażkirah writer, and associate to reḳhtah poets
ʿAbd ul-Ḥakīm	*Ḥākim*	1708–1768	Visitor to Delhi during Nadir Shah's occupation, tażkirah writer
Mīr Ġhulām	*Ḥasan*	1727–1786	Tażkirah writer and reḳhtah poet
Muḥammad ʿAlī	*Ḥashmat*	1696?–1748	Professional soldier, student of Qabūl, and teacher to Tābān
Muḥtasham ʿAlī Ḳhān	*Ḥashmat*	d. 1750	Minor aristocrat, reḳhtah poet, and associate of Girāmī and Ḥātim
Sayyid Ḥātim ʿAlī Ḳhān	*Ḥātim*	fl. 1740–60	Minor aristocrat, originally from Jaunpur, student of Maẓmūn
Ẓuhūr ud-Dīn	*Ḥātim*	1699–1783	Minor official for Amīr Ḳhān and reḳhtah poet
Muḥammad ʿAlī	*Ḥazīn*	1692–1766	Exiled Iranian and frequent target of criticism
Muḥammad Bāqir	*Ḥazīn*	d. 1752	Reḳhtah poet and student of Maẓhar
Aḥmad	*ʿIbrat*	d. 1713	Musician and student of Bedil
Kishan Chand	*Iḳhlāṣ*	d. 1754	Secretary, tażkirah writer, and student of Qabūl
Muḥammad Ṣādiq	*Ilqā*	d. 1745?	Sufi leader, critic of Bedil, and student of Nāṣir ʿAlī
Inshāʾullāh Ḳhān	*Inshā*	1752–1817	Associate of Qatīl and reḳhtah poet
Zain ud-Dīn Ḳhān	*ʿIshq*	1705?–1785?	Associate of Ummīd and Maẓhar

(continued)

TABLE F.2 (*continued*)

Given name or title	*Pen name*	*Dates*	*Distinctions*
Durgā Dās	*ʿIshrat*	fl. 1750–60	Tażkirah writer
Shāh Walīullāh	*Ishtiyāq*	d. 1738	Sufi leader, reḳhtah poet, and student of Qabūl
Ibrahīm	*Istiʿdād*	fl. 1720–40	Former student and target of S̤ābit; later student of Matīn
Jān-e Jānān	—	—	See *Maẓhar*
Muḥammad Jaʿfar	*Jurʾat*	fl. 1720–40	Minor aristocrat, professional soldier, and associate of Gulshan
Abū Ṭālib	*Kalīm*	1581–1651	Iranian émigré and imperial poet laureate
ʿAbd ur-Raḥīm	*Kamgo*	d. 1718?	Associate of Sarḳhwush and student of noted Kashmiri writers
Muḥammad Yār	*Ḳhāksār*	fl. 1730–60	Shrine attendant and reḳhtah poet
Shukrullāh Ḳhān	*Ḳhāksār*	d. 1698	High Mughal official and patron to Bedil
Ḳhwājah ʿAbd ul-Bāsiṭ	—	fl. 1710-1770	Sufi leader, minor aristocrat, musician, later ustād to Bandah ʿAlī
Ḳhwājah Basant	—	fl. 1730–50	Imperial eunuch and early patron to Saudā
Bindrāban Dās	*Ḳhwushgo*	1678?–1757	Secretary, tażkirah writer, and student of Bedil
Fażlullāh	*Ḳhwushtar*	fl. 1680–1730	Son of Sarḳhwush, associate of Ḳhwushgo and Ārzū
Muḥammad Fāḳhir	*Makīn*	d. 1806	Saudā's main literary rival
Maʿnī Yāb Ḳhān	—	—	See *Shāʿir*
Abū'l-Faiẓ	*Mast*	fl. 1720–30	Student of Bedil and attendee at graveside gathering
—	*Masīḥā*	—	See *Ḥashmat*, Muḥammad ʿAlī
ʿAbd ur-Riẓā	*Matīn*	1692–1762	Iranian medic, S̤ābit's rival, and later teacher to Istiʿdād

TABLE F.2 (*continued*)

Given name or title	*Pen name*	*Dates*	*Distinctions*
Ḥabībullāh Jān-e Jānān	*Maẓhar*	1699–1781	Itinerant Sufi leader and rekhtah poet
—	*Maẓmūn*	fl. 1700–20	Bedil's domestic slave
Sharaf ud-Dīn	*Maẓmūn*	1689?–1735	Sufi, rekhtah writer, associate of Ābrū, and student of Ārzū
Gannā Begam	*Minnat*	d. 1775	Rekhtah poet, daughter of Ramjānī and Wālih
Mīr Muḥammad Taqī	*Mīr*	1723–1810	Tażkirah writer, rekhtah poet, and nephew of Ārzū
Zindah Rām Panḍit	*Mobad*	d. 1765?	Student of Girāmī
Muḥammad ʿAẓīm	—	—	See *Ṡabāt*
Muḥammad Shāh	—	1702–1748	Thirteenth Mughal emperor, ruled 1719–48
Muḥtasham ʿAlī Ḳhān	—		See *Ḥashmat*
Ānand Rām	*Muḳhliṣ*	1699–1750	Mughal official, tażkirah writer, and student of Bedil
Ġhulām Hamadānī	*Muṣḥafī*	1751–1824	Merchant, tażkirah writer, and rekhtah poet
Mīrzā Zakī	*Nadīm*	d. 1750	Iranian official under Nadir Shah and associate of Ummīd
Muḥammad Shākir	*Nājī*	1690?–1747?	Rekhtah poet and student of Ārzū
Sayyid Ġhulām Nabī	*Nasīm*	fl. 1720–40	Satirist and friend of Maẓmūn
Nāṣir ʿAlī Sirhindī	—	—	See *ʿAlī*
ʿĀlá Fiṭrat ʿAṭāʾullāh	*Nudrat*	fl. 1730–60	Religious cleric, tażkirah writer, and competitor of Saudā
Nudrat's Daughter	—	fl. 1740–50	Artist in dance, music, and calligraphy; poetry student of her father

(*continued*)

TABLE F.2 (*continued*)

Given name or title	*Pen name*	*Dates*	*Distinctions*
Nūr Bāʾī	—	fl. 1730–60	Delhi's top courtesan
Nūrullāh	*Nuzhat*	fl. 1710–30	Companion of Girāmī and student of Qabūl
Sharaf ud-Dīn	*Payām*	d. 1746	Associate of Mukhliṣ and student of Bedil
ʿAbd ul-Ġhanī Beg	*Qabūl*	d. 1727	Resident at Fīroz Shāh's fort and leader of the Qabuliyans
Qayām ud-Dīn	*Qāʾim*	1722–1793	Tażkirah writer, reḳhtah poet, and eventual student of Saudā
Muḥammad Ḥasan	*Qatīl*	1752–1817	Secretary, teacher to Muṣḥafī and Inshā, née Dīwānī Singh
Muḥammad Masʿūd	*Rāfiʿ*	fl. 1720–43	Minor aristocrat and participant at Gulshan's *ʿurs*
Rājā Roshan Rāy	—	d. 1744/46	Mughal official and patron to Girāmī
Ḳhwushḥāl	*Ramjānī*	fl. 1730–60	Famed dancer, one of Wālih's wives, mother to Minnat
Raḥmān Bāʾī	—	fl. 1730–50	Courtesan from a family of public criers
—	*Rindī*	—	See *Babrī Rindī*
Sayyid Saʿādat ʿAlī Ḳhān	*Saʿādat*	fl. 1740–60	Reḳhtah poet, Sufi from Amroha, and associate of Mīr
Muḥammad ʿAẓīm	*Ṡabāt*	1711–1748	Critic of Ḥazīn and student of his father Ṡābit
Muḥammad Afẓal	*Ṡābit*	d. 1739	Argumentative qaṣīdah writer and competitor to the Qabuliyans
Bandah ʿAlī	*Sabaqat*	1700?–1784	Mughal official, diarist, and student of Ṡābit, later known as Bāsiṭī
Muḥammad Māh	*Ṣadāqat*	d. 1736/1741	Rake, patron to Tanū, and associate of Ārzū and Ḳhwushgo
Niʿmat Ḳhān	*Sadārang*	d. 1746	Vocalist, associate of Ummīd, host of Gulshan's *ʿurs*

TABLE F.2 (*continued*)

Given name or title	*Pen name*	*Dates*	*Distinctions*
Muḥammad ʿAlī	*Ṣāʾib*	1592–1676	Iranian merchant, influential ġhazal writer
Najm ud-Dīn ʿAlī	*Salām*	fl. 1730–50	Reḳhtah poet, minor official, son of Payām, and associate of Mīr
Muḥammad Afẓal	*Sarḳhwush*	1640–1714	Associate of Nāṣir ʿAlī and former teacher to Gulshan
Muḥammad Rafīʿ	*Saudā*	1707–1781	Satirist and reḳhtah poet
Lachhmī Narāyan	*Shafīq*	1745–1808	Tażkirah writer, reḳhtah poet, from Aurangabad
Maʿnī Yāb Ḳhān	*Shāʿir*	d. 1745	Minor aristocrat, student of Bedil, and keeper of Bedil's relics
Muḥammad Ḥusain	*Shuhrat*	d. 1736	Imperial medic from Iran and associate of leading poets
Ḳhadījah Begam	*Sulṭān*	d. 1747	Isfahan-based poet with whom Wāliḥ fell in love; died en route to Delhi
Shukrullāh Ḳhān	—	—	See *Ḳhāksār*
ʿAbd ul-Ḥayy	*Tābān*	1715–1748	Reḳhtah poet and student of Muḥammad ʿAlī Ḥashmat
—	*Tanū*	fl. 1730–50	Singer and courtesan patronized by Ṣadāqat
Qizilbāsh Ḳhān	*Ummīd*	1678–1746	Iranian émigré, minor aristocrat, reḳhtah poet, and teacher to Fuġhān
—	*Uṭakkarlais*	fl. 1719–48	Reḳhtah poet famous for reciting nonsense poems
Sharaf ud-Dīn ʿAlī	*Wafā*	fl. 1740–70	Iranian émigré and associate of Wālih, Ārzū, and Ḥākim
ʿAbd ul-Aḥd	*Waḥdat*	1640–1715	Sufi leader and teacher to Gulshan, also called Shāh Gul
Shams ud-Dīn Muḥammad	*Walī*	d. 1707	Southern writer whose reḳhtah dīwān reached Delhi in 1720

(*continued*)

TABLE F.2 (*continued*)

Given name or title	*Pen name*	*Dates*	*Distinctions*
ʿAlī Qulī	*Wālih*	1712–1756	Iranian émigré, Mughal official, and tażkirah writer
Sulaimān ʿAlī Ḳhān	*Widād*	fl. 1730–60	Saudā's purported teacher
Aḥmad Yār Ḳhān	*Yaktā*	d. 1734	Mughal official and student of Bedil
Inʿāmullāh Ḳhān	*Yaqīn*	1727–1755	Reḳhtah poet and student of Maẓhar
Muḥammad Jaʿfar	*Zaṭallī*	d. 1713?	Satirist and reḳhtah poet
Zīnat ul-Bahjī	—	fl. 1730–50	Elite courtesan and noted singer
Zīnat un-Nisā Begam	—	1643–1721	Queen Regent (r. 1681–1707), builder of the Ornament of Mosques

City of Lyrics

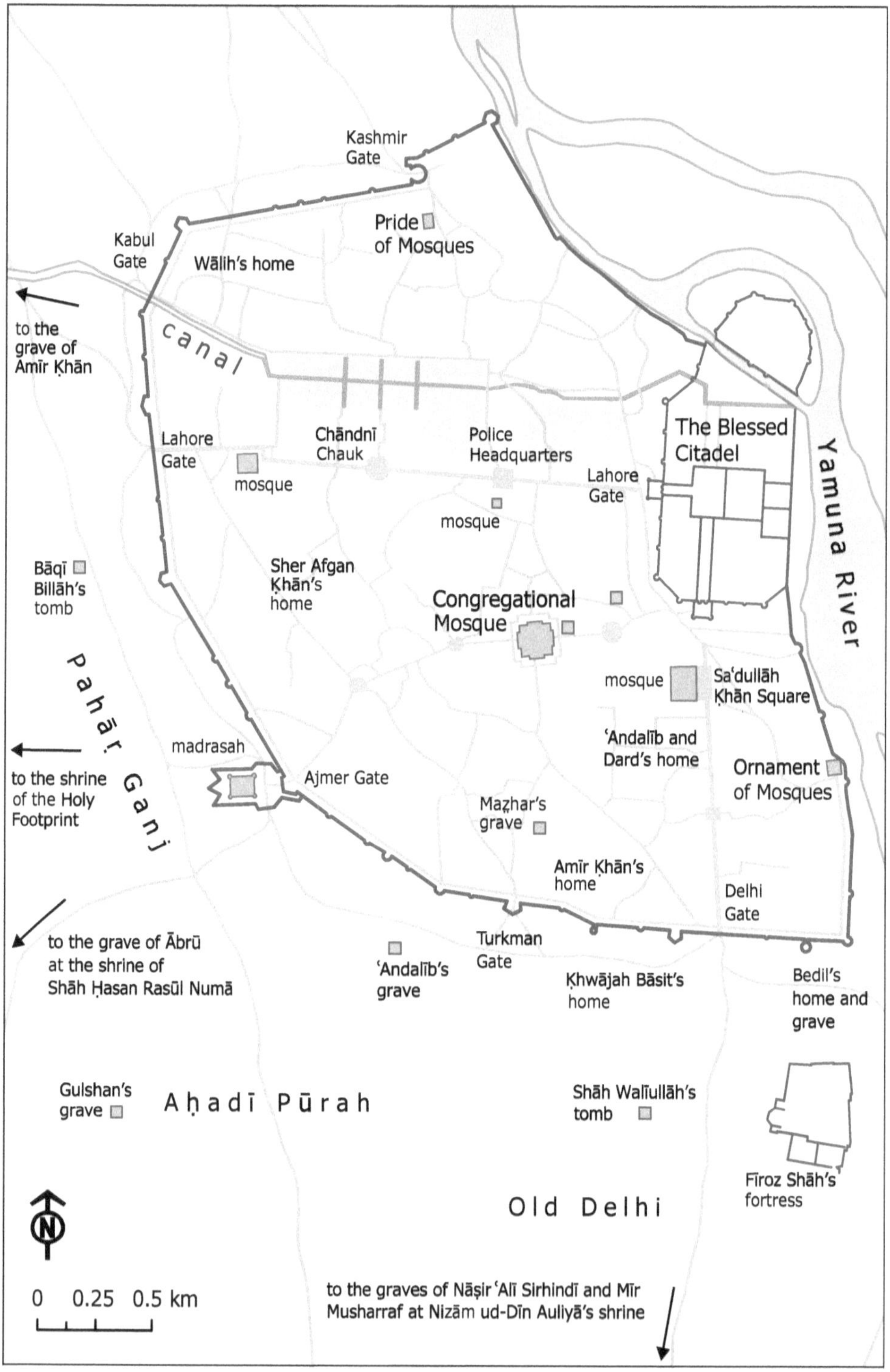

MAP F.1 A map of Shāhjahānābād and the surroundings, circa late 1700s.

Prologue

On a chilly Thursday evening in January 2018, roughly one thousand people crowded together under white plastic tents outside Delhi's Blessed Citadel, a seventeenth-century edifice otherwise known as the Red Fort. They had gathered there, in the middle of Delhi's walled city of Shāhjahānābād, to hear famous poets from across India recite hundreds of Urdu lyrics. The audience, largely from Muslim backgrounds, included rickshaw drivers, madrasah pupils, university students, tea sellers, religious clerics, bureaucrats, farmers, and a few local politicians. Since the early 1700s, Delhi has served as a haven for India's poets from a variety of educational and economic backgrounds to exchange ġhazals, a poetic form with immense cultural significance. With their strict formal conventions and deep historical resonances, these Urdu love poems and their performance have provided poets and audiences a means to access intricate social knowledge and display formidable artistic abilities. In South Asia, and across the Muslim world more broadly, the use and exchange of ġhazals demonstrate how verse, whether written, read, or recited, shapes the status of those who disseminate it, according to rhyme, refrain, and meter.

That night in 2018, poets presented hundreds of ġhazals as they came and went from the mic. Some sang their rhymes, and others spoke in delicately patterned cadences. As the night wore on, the audience dwindled to only a few hundred people remaining beneath the fluorescent pavilion lights. They sat huddled against the cold, sitting with family members and friends, men wrapped in leather jackets, shawls, and sportscoats, and about a dozen women in shawls, sweaters, and jackets.

On the stage, only ten poets remained of the thirty or so who had been there at the start. They sat on sofas that had been tightly covered with heavily starched white sheets. A three-foot-high saffron-colored candle flickered by the microphone into which poets presented verse. Most of these poets had already recited, but a few were preparing to take the mic for the first time and were listening keenly for the master of ceremonies (MC) to finally call out their names. The silent red sandstone ramparts of the citadel's Lahore Gate loomed behind the poets, partially obscured by the gleaming plastic sheeting of the tent. Affixed to it, a banner in English and Urdu announced the commemoration of January 26, India's Republic Day when the new constitution was adopted. The first such event was held in 1950 in one of the Red Fort's four-hundred-year-old throne rooms. Since then, Urdu poets have honored the Indian state with ġhazal performances in Shāhjahānābād.

In today's Urdu poetry gatherings, the best poets appear at the end of the night. Some audience members had been waiting for seven hours to hear their favorite reciters. To endure such a marathon of anticipation, audience members and poets alike sustained themselves with cups of tea, chewing tobacco, and other stimulants easily available in the bazaars just beyond the park surrounding the Red Fort.

Around 3:30 a.m., the audience and the poets were finally rewarded by the melodic recitation of Shabeena Adeeb, one of two female poets whose performances had been reserved until the gathering's end. From the crowd's enthusiastic cries of excitement, it appeared that they believed it had been worth the wait. Shabeena Adeeb is a top poet in the poetry performance circuits that include India's metropolises and country towns, the growing cities of Middle Eastern Gulf states (built by South Asian laborers), and destinations in the West wherever Urdu speakers live and can afford Urdu poets' fees and travel expenses.

Through Delhi's night air, the sound system's artificial reverberation effects carried one of Adeeb's most famous compositions. An audience member had requested the poem, passing the entreaty as a note to the stage. For ten minutes, Adeeb intoned the lines of her ġhazal, repeating phrases set to a minor-sounding scale:

> If you ignore my faults and come back, I will lay my heart in the open if you say so.
> Eid is about to come, and just now Delhi is being festooned. I, too, will decorate my home if you say so.
>
> Nations conquer through war, but men's hearts are won by love.
> There is hatred in your eyes, but I will turn it to desire if you say so.
>
> How can you say that this darkness won't end? How can you say the light will fade?
> By giving my heart's brilliance to the lamps, I can turn night into day if you say so.

Where did passion go? What happened to loyalty? You've now no
occasion to gift me marriage bangles.
With what love did you once say you'd give me the moon and stars
if I say so?

Listen up, those who badmouth others, look at yourselves.
You'll catch a glimpse of your own sins when I hold up a mirror
if you say so.

Everyone here is friends—there are no strangers. We've no need to
conceal things from our own.
But as for the ġhazal that mentions your cruelties, I can sing it
if you write it so.[1]

lauṭ āʾo bhulā kar ḳhaṭāʾeñ merī rāh meñ dil bichhā dūñ agar tum kaho
ʿīd āne ko hai shahr sajne lagā maiñ bhī ghar ko sajā dūñ agar
tum kaho[2]

jang se mulk jīte gaʾe haiñ sadā pyār se jīt letā hai dil ādmī
yih tumhārī nigāhoñ meñ nafrat hai jo is ko chāhat banā dūñ agar
tum kaho

kyā kahā yih andhere nah miṭ pāʾeñge kyā kahā roshanī ab nah ho pāʾegī
de ke dil kā ujālā chirāġhoñ ko maiñ rāt ko din banā dūñ agar
tum kaho

vuh junūn kyā hūʾā vuh wafā kyā hūʾī ab to chūṛī bhī lāne kī furṣat nahīñ
kis maḥabbat se kal tak yih kahte the tum chānd tāre bhī lā dūñ agar
tum kaho

dusroñ ko burā kahne wālo suno ḳhwud ko bhī to żarrā ek naẓar dekh lo
apne bhī ʿaib tum ko naẓar āʾeñge āʾīnah maiñ dikhā dūñ agar tum
kaho

sab yahāñ par haiñ apne paraye nahīñ aur apnoñ se kuchh bhī chhupāte
nahīñ
żikr jis meñ tumhārī jafāʾoñ kā hai vuh ġhazal bhī sunā dūñ agar
tum kaho

After repeating the final lines and thanking the audience, Adeeb stepped away from the mic. Between bursts of clapping, the crowd erupted with insolent shouts, urging her to return for another round of recitation. The

MC tried in vain to calm the audience then resignedly invited Adeeb back to the stage for an encore. "It's almost 4:00 a.m.," Adeeb protested jovially, "Don't you all have to perform your morning prayers?" After that, she sang her final composition.

For today's poets and fans, this kind of Urdu ġhazal performance is known as a *mushāʿirah*. At its heart, the mushāʿirah is a forum for the exchange of verse among performers, competitors, and listeners.[3] Three hundred years ago, Urdu-language poets and poetry fans attended poetry gatherings for many of the same reasons that they do today: to exhibit their mastery of poetic ideas and literary forms particular to Urdu poetry. These exchanges create connections between people, notably between those of distinct class backgrounds—high or low.[4]

There are also some distinctions separating today's Urdu poetry gatherings from those of the past. In the past, poets from varying class backgrounds did not present before imperial symbols of state power like the ramparts of the Red Fort or one of its throne rooms. Humble and elite poets alike gathered in Delhi's more everyday settings, such as in shrines, mosques, and coffeehouses. Before the mushāʿirah was linked with political power, its capacity to communicate literary ideals took shape through the urban sociability of the bazaar, what writers referred to as a "market for speech" or *bāzār-e suḳhan* in Urdu.

This book's tour of the early Urdu market for speech begins around 1720. We follow poets on an excursion through mushāʿirahs over a thirty-year period, during a time when a glut of silver and texts was pouring into India's cities and literary marketplaces. We learn how these material and intellectual changes impacted the valuation, assessment, and exchange of literature. We will survey the documentation of verse produced during this period to catch glimpses of diverse writers' social lives, conversations, and competitions as reflected in couplets they composed and as recorded in the notebooks they kept. Also, we will encounter a vast cast of characters, including figures such as Saʿdullāh Gulshan, a religious leader and a musician; Sharaf ud-Dīn Maẓmūn, a countryside wit; Gannā Begam Minnat, the daughter of a courtesan; ʿAṭāʾullāh Nudrat, a minor religious cleric; Muḥammad Rafīʿ Saudā, the spendthrift son of a merchant; and Ānand Rām Muḳhliṣ, a top imperial functionary and noted salon host. With them, we encounter other poets who were opium addicts, landed elites, dervishes, courtesans, merchants, and street singers and who traded and assessed ġhazals on equal footing with noteworthy authors.

In 1720, Delhi's guild of writers buried one of its own leading poets: ʿAbd ul-Qādir Bedil. As we will learn in chapter 1, Bedil emerged from a humble background to become a literary polestar, generously teaching Persian-language verse to many students for around forty years. After Bedil's passing, Delhi's commoners and elites soon began gathering at his grave annually to recite original poems, to seek Bedil's spiritual intercession, to receive donated food, and to purchase medicines sold by his tomb's caretakers. For a brief time, Bedil was Delhi's poet-saint. His former students and growing devotees maintained the recitation tradition until the late 1750s, but the last documented gathering at Bedil's grave occurred sometime in the late 1740s.

Chapter 2 takes us into the decade after Bedil's death, when poets drew fresh inspiration from a new poetry style referred to as *reḳhtah*, today known as Urdu. Said to be as piquant "as salt sprinkled in the wounds of the heart," reḳhtah mixed with the poetic imaginations of many Delhi writers.[5] One of them was Maẓmūn the Seedless Poet, whom we meet in chapter 2 at the Ornament of Mosques, a small, elegant edifice overlooking the Yamuna River. Maẓmūn's sharp intuition about literary style shaped new connections for reḳhtah writers who sought to establish networks, hierarchies, and innovative styles in competitions and interchanges. The poets at the Ornament of Mosques favored flexible language and ideas, writing in wordplays and teasing asides. They also found new methods for rerouting words of past Persian-language masters, and Maẓmūn himself presented a novel poem about the ringdove that reshaped literary style for subsequent Delhi poets.

After Maẓmūn's untimely passing, a new cohort of versifiers entered Delhi's gates. Chapter 3 introduces us to many of them in the halls of Amīr Ḳhān, a Mughal official who spent himself into serious debt to support poets. Delhi's literary scene grew increasingly cacophonous in the late 1730s as poets memorialized social and literary exchanges during a period of civic violence. Poetry with playful, multiple meanings circulated throughout gatherings in the 1730s, and a cohort of new writers—mainly high-born youth and Iranian immigrants—influenced Delhi's literary marketplace through their elite connections and flexible improvisations. Delhi's literary sphere, in a unique fashion, fostered a plethora of styles, including reḳhtah poetry, amatory lyrics, and clever poems composed to misdirect listeners. The literary sphere required all participants to follow these trends, and those who could adapt while maintaining distinct voices found welcome stages in public and semi-private salons. At the end of this 1730s period, the army of Iran's new emperor, Nadir Shah, occupied Delhi in March 1739, a moment that resulted in bloodshed and financial loss. As we will explore in chapter 3, the occupation fueled literary inspiration amid a polyphony of ġhazal styles.

The book's final chapter presents a series of literary duels that took place at Bedil's graveside salon in the 1740s, marking a moment where enmity produced shared literary values. ʿAṭāʾullāh Nudrat and Muḥammad Rafīʿ Saudā confronted each other with cutting insults to character and verse, while the grounds for their jousting were the poems of Bedil himself. As witnessed in these episodes, the poets of Delhi's literary market easily reordered what they considered prestige literary styles for the immediate demands of the performance setting. Poets' measure of literary delight emerged according to one-upmanship within a multilingual setting. The rough words of competitive ġhazal writing with its many styles pushed poets to seek virtuosity in their compositions that echoed words of enemies and favorite masters.

Similarly competitive inclinations to gather for the exchange of verse persist today across South Asia, the Middle East, and cities around the globe wherever Urdu speakers call home. The valuation and trading of poetry continue to shape the mushāʿirah's enduring relevance today, emerging in the 1700s as an institution by which people—courtesans, cooks, clerics, or even kings—defined language, ideas, and relational values. In the three decades covered by our tour, Delhi's poetry styles changed rapidly in ways that mirrored the material and political changes of India's early 1700s, signaling the expressive richness and social flexibility of urban settings. Delhi's poetry salons of the early 1700s reveal that verse created connections between members of various classes through the relational values of ġhazal composition. Reciters instantiated hierarchies but also provided means to reconfigure pecking orders by participating in contests over the ġhazal's style.

Our tour of early 1700s mushāʿirahs leads us into shrines such that of poet-saint Bedil, mosques such as the one in which Gulshan and Mażmūn resided, Delhi homes under military occupation, and into the heated literary duel of Nudrat and Saudā. Before we begin our excursion, we need to first establish the historical, urban, and literary boundaries of Delhi's market for speech as understood by its poets. In the book's introductory chapter, we will gain an understanding of how such borders framed poets' vision of Delhi's medieval past, defined poets' literary output, and, today, inform historical and literary methods employed for analyzing the thousands of couplets poets once recited in Delhi's mushāʿirahs from three hundred years ago.

Introduction

Delhi's Market for Speech, 1720–1750

City of Lyrics is a history of lyric poetry's social life in eighteenth-century India as told by those who sang, recited, and shouted verse in the mushāʿirahs of Mughal Delhi. For urban poets, the mushāʿirah was a marketplace or poetry bazaar (*bāzār-e suḳhan*), an apt conceit for popular literary settings, given the complex set of exchanges that took place between writers and fans involving cultural, embodied, and monetary forms of currency. Lyric poetry exemplified a speaker's worth in an economy composed of couplets circulated among competitive literary exchanges.[1] Poetry as a societal force, according to Shahzad Bashir, "bore a close relationship to the social status of all participants in the market, including matters pertaining to class, regional affiliation, and gender."[2] The stories shared by these littérateurs reveal how poets from across classes negotiated power as they participated in literary performances that defined social and literary hierarchies in Delhi's public square. Rapidly shifting poetic styles fueled Delhi's eighteenth-century mushāʿirahs to forge an unpredictable combination of political civility and linguistic audaciousness for those who spoke South Asia's many urban languages. The Urdu mushāʿirah has remained, and still functions today as, an institution for literary sociability for poets from multiple class backgrounds inspired by the competitive values of shared poetry recitation.

In the 1700s, mushāʿirahs were held in a range of settings—in poets' homes, courtiers' mansions, coffeehouses, gardens, shrines, and mosques. However, the most well-documented mushāʿirahs were those convened at one particular tomb.[3] Every year between 1720 and 1750, Delhi's poets recited poems in honor of ʿAbd ul-Qādir *Bedil* (The One Who Lost His Heart) (1644–1720), a literary figure who had taught many of them.[4] Born in the eastern city of Patna in 1644, Bedil was a Persian-language writer of immense literary talents and humble family origins. Despite being orphaned at a young age, Bedil became a wealthy poet in Delhi, the Mughal capital of India. Generous uncles provided young Bedil with his education, and travel gave him a breadth of experience across India's populist religions, but secure employment proved elusive to him. Only in his early forties, in the middle of the 1680s, did Bedil's literary virtuosity and carefully cultivated friendships finally secure him support from wealthy courtiers who funded his intellectual independence and, eventually, grand lifestyle. Bedil, in turn, instructed verse for a large cohort of writers who were much like himself: small-town intellectuals and other upwardly mobile people who worked in positions ranging from courtesans to clerics. After he died in the winter of 1720, Bedil briefly was thought of as Delhi's poet-saint by his students and fans based on the extent of his influence. To memorialize him, Bedil's students and hangers-on gathered every year to host a mushāʿirah at his former mansion, the site of his tomb. The annual mushāʿirah event lasted for about thirty years, during which time Delhi's expanding classes of ġhazal writers recited Bedil's poems and composed new lines inspired by his poetic forms. They also hosted hundreds of their own gatherings in locations scattered throughout the city.

In this period of history, India thrived under the Mughals, Indian rulers who descended from the house of Timur Gurkani (1336–1405), or "Tamerlane" in the Anglophone world. India's Timurid dynasty ruled South Asia from 1526 to 1857. But India's history in the "Age of Timurids" and afterward concerned more than conquest. The Timurid age inaugurated a period of creative ferment for Muslim thinkers networked with one another via a crosshatch of ideas, patronage, and travel. From this period, there emerged a dense set of relational and cultural connections maintained by the formal expectations of dynastic courts as well as the informal associations created through friendships and debates between intellectuals.[5] From the time of their emergence, the Indian Timurids maintained the intellectual traditions of their Turco-Mongolian ancestors by patronizing Persian-language poetry. Over the seventeenth century, particularly, elite Timurid men and women spent lavishly to support many writers, including Bedil, who ventured to Delhi and other South Asian metropoles.[6]

Yet, by the eighteenth century, many writers in India who produced Persian-inspired (or Persianate) verse were not materially connected, even tangentially, to the Timurid court. In fact, Delhi's literary sociability, created through the circulation of poems, found its most productive terrain outside of the court and the salons of Mughal notables. In fact, the greatest purveyors of poetry were new elites like Bedil, who came from a class comprising country-born clerics, mobile merchants, and upstart notables with local ties to South Asia rather than Greater Iran. Their involvement with intellectual life was distinct from yet motivated by the usual Timurid-era concerns for power that grew from competition and friendship.[7] In their pursuit of power, these newly elite men and women gathered to enjoy, write about, and recite poetry; these activities constituted a setting that Farhat Hasan refers to as the "contrastive publics" of early modern India, a cultural arena for communication between court and bazaar.[8]

Delhi in the 1700s served as a stage for these class-based trends in literary sociability. The capital's poetry scene increasingly followed the public demands of the commercial sphere, what Abhishek Kaicker calls a marketplace of satire and praise.[9] For example, lyrics recited in mushāʿirahs had value to the extent that they later dispersed via the tongues of both elites and commoners in the markets of Delhi. This ideal shaped the expectations of later poets who inherited the literary ferment of Delhi's streets and salons. As noted in the biography of Ulfat Ḥusain *Faryād* (The Complaint) (1804–1874) when recounting how his teachers remembered the scene: "The beauty of it was that in a mushāʿirah the most piquant verse would become famous throughout the city. Wherever you would look, the lyrics would be on the tips of tongues and at night continually sung in the bazaars. After a mushāʿirah and until the next event would occur, wherever you would look, from the elite (*ḳhāṣṣ*) to the commoners (*ʿawāmm*), the poetry gathering was being 'reviewed.'"[10]

In this passage by Faryād's biographer, Sayyid ʿAlī Muḥammad *Shād* (The Joyful) (1846–1927), the English-language word "review" describes the process by which the people of Delhi's bazaar assessed the merits of a particular mushāʿirah, like one casually would do today with a novel or a film.[11] The town square recalled by Faryād echoes what historian C. A. Bayly describes as the "Indian ecumene," a context of overlapping media and institutions in which urban elites and semiliterate classes circulated information. Bayly conceived of premodern India's public sphere as an arena for debate, manifested through recollection, poetry, and communal values associated with the marketplace.[12] The mushāʿirah was an integral aspect of this arena. Even as a memory, the literary sociability of Delhi's great and humble poets described here encompasses shifting interactions among classes of speakers in eighteenth-century India as they consumed lyric poetry and contested the styles, languages, politics, and behaviors expected with the mushāʿirah.[13]

The unique way that mushāʿirah poets recited and mingled together across Delhi's social divisions reshaped the city's affiliative boundaries. By wielding a single couplet—or merely a line—a poet from any social class had the potential to rewrite literary style and assert personal significance by upholding or overturning social and literary conventions that bridged past traditions and contemporary distinctions in unique and memorable ways. As a haven for "literary sociability," the mushāʿirah served as a crucible for the developing ways in which people interacted with one another vis-à-vis literature, with the attendant style, politics, and decorous behavior between groups and individuals shifting across different classes, places, spaces, and time periods.[14] Salon cultures in the medieval Islamic world, as noted by Samer Ali, focused on cultivating and performing shared forms of humanistic knowledge (or *adab* in Arabic and many other languages) for preserving past traditions and circulating new literature among Arab court poets.[15] The historian Helen Pfeifer demonstrates that forms of literary sociability in the Ottoman world involved participants' serious efforts to maintain group cohesion and social distinction while negotiating hierarchy and competition.[16] Emma Flatt echoes this idea in her examination of sociability, focusing on the material aspects of salon culture built through friendship and humiliation that shaped networks among Muslim courts of sixteenth-century South India.[17] Finally, Heidi Pauwels demonstrates how literary soirées in the eighteenth century emerged in western India's local courts to host Persian and Urdu verse as well as decidedly religious Braj Bhasha poetry about Hindu forms of devotion, further revealing the ubiquity of the mushāʿirah institution across time, places, and communities.[18]

For the last hundred years, artists and scholars have created many representations of Delhi's Urdu poetry gatherings seeking to capture aspects of the mushāʿirah's pasts. In the 1920s, the essayist Farḥatullāh Beg, in "Delhi's Last Candle" (*Dillī kī Āḳhrī Shamaʿ*), famously imagines a final imperial mushāʿirah that was attended by the Mughal court's poets. Beg's fantastical account is set in 1854 and was inspired by interviews he carried out with the city's oldest residents. His book inspired a series of subsequent plays, films, and novels.[19] Noting how lyric poetry recreated literary communities, the journalist Karīmī ul-Iḥsānī playfully suggests that a Mughal emperor's ghost must have been flying around the first post-independence mushāʿirah held in 1950 at the Blessed Citadel in Delhi.[20] ʿAlī Jawād Zaidī holds up the mushāʿirah as a mirror that reflected the socio-linguistic conditions of Delhi's literary community.[21] C. M. Naim highlights the sporting side of the mushāʿirah as a contest but also compares the contemporary event to a radio station in which the master of ceremonies acts as a "disc jockey" when selecting poets to come to the microphone to recite.[22] Frances Pritchett assesses the early nineteenth-century mushāʿirah as a workshop in which to hone literary artistry.[23] Lastly, Ali Khan Mahmudabad configures the nationalist mushāʿirah as a snapshot of the present that reflects the past by questioning notions of political belonging.[24]

Taken together, each of these approaches to the mushāʿirah's histories reveals that lyric poetry documents narratives about the past for Muslim cultures and societies. Indeed, the mushāʿirah of historical India and contemporary South Asia (and its diaspora) integrally reflects a sociability wedded to literature inspired by the Persian language, which had historically connected vast global regions.[25] Court historians writing in the premodern era used literary models, including lyric poetry, to frame what they witnessed.[26] Lyric poetry materially impacted those who consumed and circulated it within and beyond the gatherings. Delhi's townsfolk often uttered praise, devotions, and curses in meter and rhyme. This everyday use of verse comprised part of Delhi's public arena for literature governed by commerce and taste.[27] Public performers extolled histories, epics, and songs among Delhi's alleys. Sellers intoned the availability of their wares in florid phrases that echoed off the city's walls. While conversing with friends, a well-placed verse clinched a debate or cannily announced a veiled desire. These examples suggest how the historical ġhazal defined status and innovation for those who uttered its words, and how the mushāʿirah institutionalized this process over time to produce a polyphonic chorus of poets with diverse perspectives and conflicting aims. Thus, *City of Lyrics* returns to a metaphor that eighteenth-century poets employed to frame the mushāʿirah's literary sociability and history. For these writers, Delhi's mushāʿirahs and the many conversations and competitions born from them constituted a "market for speech" (*bāzār-e suḳhan*), consisting of interconnected and tumultuous spaces in which lyric poetry circulated as a volatile literary commodity avidly pursued by Delhi's poets.[28]

A Language That Was a City

Before it fell into ruin and eventually disappeared, Bedil's grave sat just outside the borders of both Shāhjahānābād and Fīrozābād, two cities attached to the wider metropolis of Delhi.[29] When Bedil was interred in 1720, Shāhjahānābād was still a new city, only recently completed in the 1650s under the Persian-speaking Turco-Mongolian Mughal dynasty. Fīrozābād was a medieval city established in the 1350s by the Persian-speaking Turkic Tuġhluq dynasty.[30] Bedil's former students, relatives, and admirers gathered between Shāhjahānābād's ornate gates and Fīrozābād's crumbling ruins on the poet-saint's death anniversary to read from his complete works at his tomb. Bedil's shrine also functioned intermittently as a commercial hub. As they did at any other of Delhi's hundreds of tombs, visitors contributed coins to caretakers for candles to light at the graveside; they bought medicines and, on certain occasions, availed hot food from the tomb's soup kitchen. Visitors who were trained in the art of poetry recited new verse modeled on the formal and thematic parameters of the dead poet-saint's ġhazals and those of ġhazal writers who preceded Bedil over Persian literature's millennium-long history. In this regard, Bedil's grave, situated between two cities, demonstrated how Delhi and its literary communities had been central for the development of Persian literature, both looking backward at earlier history and forward in time amid the ġhazals composed in the shrine's precincts.[31]

For the 1720–50 timeline traced by this book, the kind of literary and social history situated at Bedil's tomb falls within the category of "Persianate," a historical frame focused on Persian literature and language, including those traditions inspired by Persian-language values, disposition, style, and modes of comportment.[32] The historian Marshall Hodgson conceived the Persianate concept in the mid-twentieth century, and his foundational ideas have been critically developed by many scholars since. For instance, the historian Mana Kia reminds us that, over time, references to Persian rarely carried the connotation of an ethnic category or even a fixed geography, but rather referred simply to forms of association and hierarchy.[33] Literatures of the Muslim world broadly, and Persianate intellectual domains specifically, chart social and cultural history through shared linkages and negotiations that bridge geographies and religious traditions.[34] The concept of Persianate history encompasses both intellectual networks and material realms rather than being tied to specific places and peoples. Indeed, the first examples of the Persian language appear during the eighth century in letters exchanged by Jewish merchants from the area of Khotan in present-day China.[35] During the tenth and eleventh centuries, merchants, secretaries, and some poets used Persian to transmit the prized literary genres of the time—praise poems from Arabic traditions and epics from Greek, Sanskrit, and Old Persian. Crucially, the ways in which these early writers elected to use the Arabic script to convey Persian-language poetry further instantiated authors, texts, and ideas within an older imperial infrastructure connected by pen, ink, and cheaply produced paper.[36] Persian, in dialogue with Arabic literacy, opened new routes of social advancement for peoples who quickly mastered and expanded upon the Persian conventions required for professions connected to the state, including poets, accountants, courtiers, and courtesans.

By the thirteenth century, Muslim society entered a new global phase, poised for vast material and cultural expansions across the Afro-Eurasian landmasses.[37] Beginning in 1220, the Mongol empire and its successor states reordered societies through violent conquest, political patronage, and the commercial exchange of goods, people, animals, and ideas. Mercantile activity blossomed in entrepôts between the Black Sea and Beijing, and working-class guilds supported commerce, manufacturing, and information networks.[38] Yet, the Mongols and their inheritors also maintained the cultural traditions of the local dynasties they conquered. Regarding their faith, Mongol rulers converted to Islam and followed local Muslim religious leaders, thinkers, and mystics known as Sufis.[39] At imperial courts, Mongol emperors patronized literature in Persian (and other tongues), and their chancelleries maintained state documents in Persian.[40] Like Arabic before it and in concert with local tongues, Persian became a language of Sufi mysticism, literary art, and imperial bureaucracy, facilitating its spread across dozens of kingdoms from the Balkans to Bengal.[41]

As a center of commerce and trade since antiquity, India hosted Persian writers fleeing Mongol incursions, and, with their arrival, Delhi under the Tuġhluq dynasty became the Persian-speaking world's material and intellectual center for professional poets seeking patronage, distinction, and comradery.[42] In the late 1200s, it was as if Delhi's streets and civic structures had been built in metered language and poetic metaphor.[43] Melding poetic and architectural registers, the Persian-language poet Amīr Ḳhusrau (1253–1325) praised the city's "battlements formed like utterly silent tongues, / conversing with the moon and the heavens" (*kungur-e ū gashtah zabān-e jumlah tan / wa-āmadah bā māh samāʾ dar suḳhan*), as the ramparts protected a vast citizenry with a surfeit of knowledge in "science and literature" (*ʿilm-o adab*)—"there were more writers than one could count!" (*ahl-e qalam ḳhwud kih shumārad kih chand*).[44] By Ḳhusrau's estimation, the world's best littérateurs lived within the walls of Delhi: the poets were first class due to their excellent dispositions, and the secretaries among them could master any language to reproduce its poetic nuances and style.[45] Ḳhusrau also keenly attuned himself to the financial realities of the literary cityscape, purveying rare merchandise amid counterfeiters, cheats, and profiteers who unscrupulously engaged in "selling verse" (*suḳhan faroshī*) from "the shop of literacy" (*dukān-e suwād*).[46] Against the background of such corruption, Ḳhusrau painted himself as one who correctly followed past masters and ethically offered reputable wares in Delhi's "market for speech" (*bāzār-e suḳhan*).[47]

The purveyors of verse in Delhi's market for speech owed their literary sophistication, in part, to Delhi's linguistic diversity. Native speakers of the Muslim world's many languages made Delhi their home. In Ḳhusrau's time and in the 1700s, lyric poetry circulated via Turkish, Persian, Arabic, Hindi, and Sanskrit and other tongues spoken in Delhi's court, salons, bazaars, and alleys. Among these languages, the social parameters of lyric poetry's urban lives appeared most readily within the Persian-language's artistic and linguistic categories, as these registers championed inclusivity but also defined class hierarchies among its speakers. As Kathryn Babayan writes of Iran's Isfahan in the 1600s, professional writers established that "the very foundation of the city was contingent, in part, on the verbal."[48] Such an observation was certainly applicable to Delhi's urban domains over its history.

Following Isfahan's refashioning in 1598 Iran, the emperor Shah Jahan (r. 1628–58) commissioned his own new city in 1648 Delhi, calling it Shāhjahānābād. It was situated to the north of India's previous medieval capitals where Ḳhusrau once wrote and recited Persian poetry, growing to a population of over five hundred thousand.[49] Like the Tuġhluqs, the Mughals welcomed to Delhi a flood of Persian writers with multilingual backgrounds from the Caucasus, the Middle East, and Central Asia. Poets and secretaries under Shah Jahan's patronage built bulky monuments to vocabulary: dictionaries to assist composers of verse. In one such dictionary, "A Selection of Vocabularies" (*Muntaḳhab ul-Luġhāt-e Shāh Jahānī*) dedicated to the emperor Shah Jahan, the lexicographer ʿAbd ur-Rashīd (d. 1666) explains that he researched indispensable and frequent idioms found in spoken vocabularies (*bayān-e luġhāt*) and among noted books (*kutub-e muʿatabarah*). For ʿAbd ur-Rashīd, these expressions, whatever their provenance, deserved illumination because they were legitimated by poetic usages to be "understood by the public and approved by the elite" (*ʿāmm-fahm wa ḳhāṣṣ-pasand*).[50]

The story of the mushāʿirah in Delhi, as told by this book, recounts what transpired when a host of poets from Shah Jahan's city began to use common idioms in the cultivated speech of the ġhazal's concise love songs. The commercial sphere for literature, whether conducted via one of Delhi's local argots (Hindi, Hindvī, or Dihlavī) or in the Persian language (a transregional tongue), offered a dynamic arena for poets from across urban classes whom we have already assembled—sellers hawking their goods, braggarts in coffeehouses, storytellers shouting epics and tales, devotional singers wailing away at shrines, or mischievous littérateurs—but also for other kinds of producers, consumers, and sponsors of verse.[51]

For the intellectuals who traversed bazaar and salon, appropriate literary speech prospered on the everyday tongues of all types of eloquent people from across the high and low classes so long as they were residents of the city of Delhi, the Mughal cultural capital for contests of class and verse during the 1700s.[52] The writer Ẓuhūr ud-Dīn *Ḥātim* (The Arbiter) (1699–1783), a cannabis eater and frequent attendee of Delhi's mushāʿirahs, concisely described the everyday speech of Delhi (*rozmarrah-e dihlī*) by echoing ʿAbd ur-Rashīd's formulation: it, too, was "understood by the public and approved by the elite" (*ʿāmm fahm wa pasand-e ḵẖāṣṣ*). He added that such everyday speech was "held to be idiomatic by India's nobles and rapscallion littérateurs" (*mīrzāyān-e hind wa faṣīḥān-e rind*).[53] When broadly conceived, these two categories of local elites and clever authors constituted the core demographic of poetry gatherings.

From Delhi's nobility, staffed by sundry lords or *mīrzāyān*, came the elite group of poets who were usually educated in Persian and Arabic but were also native speakers of Delhi's local languages. They played roles in the literary sphere both as patrons and as participating poets or audience members. Ḥātim's second category of littérateurs, "the masses," comprising those considered newly elite, semi-elite or non-elite, encompassed a wider swath of Delhi's social classes, including poets who had secure patrons as well as those who did not—the freelancing, well-spoken wits of the bazaars and alleys. An early nineteenth-century survey of Delhi's languages, "The Ocean of Witticism" (*Daryā-e Laṭāfat*) coauthored by Inshāʾullāh Ḵẖān *Inshā* (The Expression) (1752–1817) and Muḥammad Ḥasan *Qatīl* (The Slaughtered) (1758–1817), attempted to sketch the parameters of Delhi's multilingual metropolis with specific registers and vocabularies from "rapscallion littérateurs."[54] Their work, completed in 1807, offered the first survey of Delhi's languages, condensing the linguistic brilliance of the royal horde's many citizens into a primer for Persian-educated poets.[55]

In a section of "The Ocean of Witticism" titled "solitary pearls" (*durdānah*), Inshā and Qatīl focus on how Delhi's citizens defined the boundaries and characteristics of the specific geographies in which they lived, citing localized idioms and accents used among the heterogenous mix of peoples who comprised the metropolis, including merchants, women, notables, rogues, mountainfolk, Afghans, and many others. As with many cities of the Muslim world, assorted commodities from across the globe entered Delhi's gates, and Delhi's poetic world intersected with these on material and linguistic levels.[56] Various classes of tradespeople trafficked these goods, and these merchants required their own distinct languages to gain advantage over competitors and to seduce customers. Indeed, the foundational demographic that Inshā and Qatīl first wrote about in their work were merchants (*dalālān*), although the authors occasionally describe merchants' idioms and nuances in disparaging terms.[57]

Linguistic nuance and playfulness facilitated exchange in bazaars, devotion in shrines, competition in salons, and distinction at the imperial court. The city center's few coffeehouses provided famously rich environments to hear verse, stories, and gossip uttered in Persian or Hindi languages from the lips of poets and coffee servers alike.[58] Meanwhile, in the bustling cattle market, horse traders conversed in their own codes and hand signals.[59] Within the alleys, in gymnasiums, and on the banks of the river, one could hear the rogues' tongue (*zabān-e luṭiyān*), an argot spoken by wrestlers, strongmen, and gigolos.[60] Certain members of the soldiery also spoke Turkic languages to varying degrees.[61] Between harem, symposium, and brothel, female poets of high standing and those working as professional beloveds cultivated distinct gender-based idioms and turns of phrase, registers later emulated extensively by male poets during and after the late 1700s.[62] The city's sizable population of northern folk spoke Kashmiri and Punjabi, and Delhi's neighborhoods had specific accents and jargons.[63] In mosques and seminaries, classical Arabic echoed through the halls. Lastly, immigrant merchants themselves spoke languages ranging from vernacular Arabic to Armenian, along with a smattering of diverse European tongues.[64]

Delhi's multilingual commercial realm was rich with bazaars, cafes, Sufi lodges, shrines, and poetry salons, while the literate and semiliterate people who traversed these settings placed immense value on the production and circulation of literary texts as a particularly dynamic aspect of market culture. For Inshā and Qatīl, it was as if the languages and phrases of Delhi's Urdu speakers formed a string of pearls that adorned the city.[65] But these precious embellishments did not belong solely to the elites. Littérateurs came from across the literate and semiliterate classes. Over time they increasingly formed connections to the commercial realm in some way. The unique literary languages of Urdu emerged from across the city's various neighborhoods and particularly from the scrappy world of the bazaar, marked by competition, eloquence, and occasional cursing.

Today, we use the term "Urdu" to indicate the precise and professional language of Delhi's early eighteenth-century bazaars and mushāʿirahs. But in the 1700s, during Inshā and Qatīl's time, the word *urdū* did not refer to a language at all. Rather, *urdū* (horde) was the local name for the city of Delhi itself. The townspeople called the newly built walled city of Delhi "The Exalted Horde of Shāhjahānābād" (*urdū-e muʿallá-e shāhjahānābād*) in honor of the military camp, or horde, of the founding emperor Shah Jahan (r. 1628–58).[66] In fact, the term "horde" comes to European languages from the Turkic word *ordā*, which refers to an itinerant court and military camp. Thus, the term *urdū* in the 1500s and 1600s invoked the pomp of the Mughals themselves and their nomadic ancestors (*ūrdū-e muġhal*) in the steppe lands with their "globe-trotting imperial army" (*urdū-e gīhān-pūʾī*) or their "victorious horde" (*urdū-e ẓafar qarīn*)—not a language.[67]

By the 1700s, the term *urdū* referenced more commonplace institutions: it invoked the neighborhood markets in Delhi (*bāzār-e urdū*), although there was perhaps still some sense that *urdū* was associated with the ruler's authority.[68] In the metropolis of Delhi, affectionally dubbed a camp, its denizens were well attuned to the various idioms and languages that built the public spaces they inhabited. And thus, wherever they ventured—from shrine to mosque to market—they simply spoke *zabān-e urdū*, the language of Delhi's urban landscape. According to Inshā and Qatīl, to be an *urdū-dān* (to use their term) was to know the city of Delhi, and thus the most important requirement of poets writing in this idiom was to be from Delhi itself—or at least to have descended from a Delhi resident, as was the case with Inshā.[69]

There is yet another twist to naming Delhi's poetic languages. During the early 1700s, poets referred to this stylish language of the horde as *reḳhtah* when it was employed in poetry. Mushāʿirah attendees from Delhi used the suggestive term *reḳhtah* to distinguish their local poetic language from Persian literary speech. As a verb, the literal meaning of reḳhtah (from the infinitive *reḳhtan*) is the action of mixing, scattering, throwing, spoiling, or casting something into a mold. But as a noun, reḳhtah refers to objects ranging from mortar, a fried egg, dice, or a wager with favorable odds.[70] For poets, the reḳhtah concept culminated in a type of highly original, impromptu verse extemporized in everyday language.[71] As noted by the historians Walter Hakala and Arthur Dudney, the various groups of poets reciting in salons understood the difference between Persian and reḳhtah as a stylistic distinction—meaning that these languages were each understood by poetry aficionados as conveying a unique tone, feeling, or new sets of suggestive meanings.[72] As elucidated by Ḥāfiẓ Maḥmūd Shīrānī nearly a century ago, unwieldly definitions of the word "reḳhtah" provide clues about how literary aesthetics and modes of circulation were changing during this time, as evidenced by Delhi intellectuals' shifting and multifold definitions and origin stories behind the term "reḳhtah" as a register for lyric poetry, commerce, and distinction.[73] Broadly, Delhi's writers understood reḳhtah to be two things: compositions that combined two or more languages, and effortless, improvised verses with engaging meanings, namely within poetry forms that transmitted love lyrics.

The Ġhazal

For poets in early 1700s Delhi, the rivalries, values, and associations produced by literature crystallized in the ġhazal, a precise poetic form that can be understood, in cursory fashion, as an arrangement of tiny love songs.[74] The term originates in the Arabic language (*ġhazala*, "to spin, to twist"), referencing poems or quips addressing flirtatious words to a love interest.[75] Lyricists today and in the past string together couplets with each two-line set voicing a unique erotic complaint spoken by a lover (*ʿāshiq*) to a neglectful beloved (*maʿshūq*), resulting in a form that is "highly conventional and highly flexible."[76] Writing ġhazals produces suggestive ideas conceived of through a relatively narrow set of themes that include singing, drinking, sadness, and destitution, coupled with praise of springtime, blossoms, and songbirds—metaphors that can be rerouted for political commentary, mystic insight, and literary dueling with competitors.

In the 1700s, Delhi's mushāʿirahs provided central spaces for circulating the ġhazal's formal conventions, musicality, and poetic imagery. Ġhazal performance in these gatherings offered a vibrant context for understanding both the ġhazal's dynamism as lyric poetry and the literary and social processes built into the ġhazal itself, such as hierarchy, association, and distinction.[77] Additionally, the ġhazal's end rhymes, refrains, and meters facilitated quick memorization, making it suitable for performance. The ġhazal's bound conventions, flexible conceits, and formal requirements encouraged versifiers to "break the fourth wall," calling out to the reader, competitors, influential authors, or even to themselves. Indeed, these couplets featured melodic recitation and self-reflexively called attention to the terms of their own production and circulation and the communities of fans, patrons, and critics who were crucial to shaping style. In the 1740s, the poet Mīr Muḥammad Taqī *Mīr* (The Leader) (1723–1810)—a student of one of Bedil's students—boastfully captured the performative possibilities harbored by the ġhazal, announcing self-referentially in a couplet:

When a singer recited one of Mīr's ġhazals last night,
at the assembly everyone's state reached ecstatic height.[78]

muṭrib ne paṛhī thī ġhazal ik mīr kī shab ko
majlis meñ bahut wajd kī ḥālat rahī sab ko

The ġhazal offered vast performative possibilities for styles that embraced everyday language or trafficked in highly complex ambiguity. Amatory registers that focused the ġhazal on love and loss remained immensely popular throughout the 1700s. Poets also composed ġhazals that expressed bragging, irony, and profanity. In this regard, the ġhazal, following Rebecca R. Gould's point, communicates cultural history and ideas unique to its own artistic and linguistic conventions.[79]

Across time, the mushāʿirah has served the ġhazal by "bringing together people from different backgrounds and for disseminating ideas and language."[80] The ġhazal in the 1700s also served the mushāʿirah. It did so by integrating the seemingly contradictory aspects of the ġhazal's bound conventions and flexible styles with everyday literary production. In the gathering space, the ġhazal was not simply about love per se. The ġhazal most centrally was and is about the ġhazal itself.[81] Nearly every word, idea, phrase, rhyme, and refrain in ġhazal couplets had to be legitimated actively by reference to another poem, a verse from a past writer that informed both new and old poetry. Links that poets conjured between past conventions and current practice gave the ġhazal the ability to reshape sensibilities among the writers who sang, documented, and judged each other's contributions in mushāʿirah spaces.

A network-based examination of the ġhazal reveals markedly flexible approaches to style for Delhi's many writers who rigorously pursued experimentation within the ġhazal's highly constricted form.[82] Lyric poetry created networks through personal and textual literary association and decorous comportment that defined popular culture across classes.[83] Delhi's eighteenth-century poets enjoyed the far-ranging pursuit of metaphor and originality built in dialogue with past masters, but they also relished the multifaceted pleasures associated with the exchange of ġhazals between reciters—socializing, one-upmanship, and song.[84] Ġhazals recited in eighteenth-century mushāʿirahs tell a complex story through their circulation by communities of fans, poets, and patrons, tracking social change and connections.

For mushāʿirah poets, the ġhazal's lyricism was a commodity to be praised, assessed, treasured, trashed, and, most significantly, traded.[85]

During the eighteenth-century emergence of reḳhtah poetry in Delhi's mushāʿirah scene, versifiers cultivated style and enacted sociability in contests over poetic meaning such that their seemingly effortless verse and language mixing sought to both undermine and uphold literary meaning through wordplay and incongruity. Composition that fostered these elements distinguished a poet's abilities and versatility within a closely competitive literary marketplace in which prestige grew relationally via wit, originality, and social appropriateness—even in playful violation of all these aspects. As Persian scholar Jane Mikkelson writes, lyric poems found in the urban Islamic world before 1800 or so formed "simultaneously the battleground, the stakes, and prize."[86] This is a description of a precious commodity, and like a commodity, the exchange of valuable lyric poems—the performance of literature and the assessment of it—played a central role in creating networks and associations among members of literate and semiliterate classes. For writers, audiences, and patrons, ġhazals contained multihued conceits that provoked competition and established hierarchies in early 1700s Delhi.

These routes for reḳhtah's unique urban sociability emerged through two main literary devices: emulation and misdirection. A 1740s poem by Mīr Taqī Mīr offers us an example of how emulation worked. Mīr, who also composed in Persian, noted the distinction of his own reḳhtah poetry in an emulative response to his senior colleague and competitor, the prominent Delhi-based poet Muḥammad Rafīʿ *Saudā* (The Frenzy) (1706/7–1781):

> Why not let reḳhtah remain silent, unenjoyable, and unimportant?
> You have become Mīr the Mad, but Saudā was always a total drunk.[87]

> *nah ho kyūñ reḳhtah be-shorish-o kaifiyat-o maʿnī*
> *gayā ho mīr-e dīvānah rahā saudā so mastānah*

In this verse, Mīr bragged that only poets such as Mīr himself and the eminent Saudā could bring a distinctive taste to reḳhtah composition, thus establishing them as masters, if in an offhand way. The source for Mīr's couplet—the lines it emulated—was, of course, a verse from Saudā himself that established the meter, rhyme, and thematic material for Mīr to echo.

Saudā's originating verse, in turn, contains a misdirection, a punning use of wordplay important in the mushāʿirah tradition. In his verse, Saudā eulogizes the passing of another Delhi poet: Sharaf ud-Dīn (d. 1735), who wrote under the unique pen name of *Maẓmūn*, a legal term for material or contractual collateral; a technical term for the contents of a letter (as in subject or topic); and a literary term for theme, trope, or signifier.[88] Saudā conjured each of these disparate meanings when he penned the following reḳhtah poem:

> He has up and gone, O Friends, the very source of good ġhazal writing.
> [Poetry's] "theme" left this world so Saudā remained a total drunk.[89]
>
> *binā hī uṭh gaʾī yāro ġhazal ke ḳhūb kahne kī*
> *gayā maẓmūn dunyā se rahā saudā so mastānah*

Here Saudā asserts that with the death of the influential poet Maẓmūn, it was as if poetic meaning itself had died. Maẓmūn projected a distinct voice in Delhi's new reḳhtah poetry scene, and Saudā playfully mourned Maẓmūn's passing with *īhām*, the very literary device for which Maẓmūn was most famous. The Arabic word *īhām*, when translated into English literary terminology, is *amphibology*—something that "hits twice"—a device in which ambiguous wordplay overrides singular meaning through misdirection.[90]

In Delhi's literary scene of the early 1700s, the misdirection of īhām was a crucial device for the ġhazal and central for the emergence of reḳhtah poetic style.[91] As wordplay, īhām simultaneously offered both obvious and obscure meanings to conjure new or "unbounded" themes (*maẓāmīn-e nā bastah*). When deployed as an aesthetic strategy for mushāʿirah poets, īhām marked personal innovation in an attempt to playfully twist thematic material (*maẓmūn-āfrīnī*) in ways that stretched prior conventions—just as discussed earlier in our analysis of Saudā's ġhazal performance. With that one word, *maẓmūn*, Saudā referenced Maẓmūn the poet, the idea of theme in a literary sense, and the very stakes of originality for all writers. Indeed, composers of īhām (called *īhām-goʾiyān*, "punsters" or "ambiguists") were considered among the most eloquent (*balīġh*) and entertaining (*laṭīfah-go*) of poets during the time of reḳhtah's emergence in Delhi, earning themselves opulent rewards at elite gatherings and gushing praise in the streets.[92]

Although its field for innovation was expansive, Delhi also imposed boundaries for originality, limits to poets' earning potential, and harsh critiques from competitors. As part of the city's rich linguistic setting, reḳhtah poetic styles quickly changed, and after 1750, īhām retreated from Delhi's gatherings, collected works, and patrons' preferences, sidelining Maẓmūn and his fellow "punsters" in later histories. Īhām's playful approach had flourished for nearly a century in Delhi's ġhazal scene, and well after the camouflaging approach of īhām faded, authors in Lucknow, a city to the east, still praised Delhi's unique contribution to the formation of reḳhtah style when reminiscing about Delhi's rich linguistic setting.

Even from its beginnings in the early eighteenth century, the mushāʿirah has been inseparable from the competitive sphere of marketplace economics. In this way, the mushāʿirah raises apparent contradictions between the integrity of literary aesthetics and their commodification. To wend our way through this problematic, the mushāʿirah's historical record must be carefully interpreted. Early eighteenth-century mushāʿirah chroniclers left ample clues for us about how these values were reconciled in the gathering's norms and language of the time. We can discover and unpack these oblique meanings by methodically reading between the lines of vast poetry and anecdote compilations left behind by literary chroniclers, especially in the way that they used parody and satire while recording memory and affect. Indeed, studying the performative history of how literary aesthetics were marketed in Delhi during the early 1700s poses an intriguing set of methodological and theoretical problems.[93]

Luckily, we have access to a detailed historical record documenting performed poetry's ephemeral setting, its circulation, and its consumption. This record was compiled in a piecemeal fashion and according to the picky, judgmental, and mischievous rationale of eighteenth-century Persian-educated polite society, requiring us to develop a specific theory and method for approaching it.[94] While offering us intriguing insights into networked Muslim societies, the raucous and sublime setting of Delhi's mushāʿirahs, which champion a Persianate transactional form of entertainment and delight when understood on its own discursive terms, can also expand and decenter Eurocentric notions of literary expression, consumerism, publicity, and popular culture.

Readers, Reciters, and Early Modern Sources

The story of eighteenth-century Delhi's popular literary culture emerges in part from anecdotal and gossipy accounts left behind by littérateurs who organized and attended Delhi's mushāʿirahs in the 1700s. For these chatty members of India's educated classes, the performance and assessment of Persian and Urdu ġhazals at mushāʿirahs created a distinct form of literary consumption that apprehended verse as a crucial urban commodity with its own system of market valuation. Poets of the early 1700s shaped Delhi's mushāʿirahs via three interrelated activities: gathering, reciting, and writing. Following the approach of the literary historian Sunil Sharma, these three interconnected processes constituted the indispensable means of production for Delhi's poets as they cultivated the city's premier form of literary sociability.[95] These three processes highlight the multidisciplinary nature of this book's project, engaging literary as well as historical registers.

Gathering is the first of the three processes we will discuss. Decorous modes of gathering were understood by people of various classes across the Muslim world as critical expressions of socializing and socialization. These types of gatherings could be categorized by the Arabic term *majlis*, meaning "assembly," which connoted an occasion for sitting among friends in diverse settings such as halls, courtyards, gardens, and mosques—we will be visiting these locales and more in the coming pages. The *majlis* has been an integral aspect of Islamic cultural history, facilitating hierarchy, debate, and conviviality.[96] Gatherings convened for many reasons, and the present work concentrates on those that convened specifically for reciting ġhazals, an event called *maḥfil-e mushāʿarah* or "an assembly for the exchange of poems." Besides verse, conversation, and competition, poets ingested substances such as coffee, cannabis, and opium and smoked hookahs loaded with tobacco. Notably, there are a few anecdotes of gatherings held among courtesans, India's female professional beloveds, who were often poets themselves. Additionally, many anecdotes valorize young men, and rumors of love affairs between novices and older poets circulated widely in Delhi's gatherings.

The second process examined here, recitation, shaped the sonic realm of the mushāʿirah; poets selected and performed certain verses by rhythmically intoning couplets or singing them. Recitation, like gathering, also enabled interaction between poets and poems.[97] Audiences expressed approval by shouting "Bravo!" (*āfrīn!*) and other stylized exclamations, such as those questioning a usage, pronunciation, or metrical issue. Through these interactive processes, the community of writers and their audiences elevated certain poems and poets above others, helping to guarantee their return, emulation, or memorialization.[98] Indeed, much of poetry's performance championed the aural realm. In the past and to this day, poets sing or rhythmically intone Persian and Urdu verse, reinforcing strict conventions for meter, end rhyme, and refrain that structure the ġhazal's amatory words according to almost musical registers. In Persian and Urdu verse, a refrain and end rhyme (*qāfiyah* and *radīf*), in addition to meter (*baḥr*), mark the formal elements of any poetic composition or competition, and they also bring alive the poetry, allowing us to hear recitations in the past.[99]

The last of the three processes considered in this book, writing, must be emphasized. Indeed, all interpretations of the other two mushāʿirah processes, gathering and recitation, are filtered through and ultimately dependent upon the writings left behind by participants. For the mushāʿirah's history and the social life of ġhazals in the past, writing was an integral process for both documentation and performance. Hence, the mushāʿirah's gathering and recitation space breaks down perceived dichotomies between the page and the voice.[100] These literary exchanges frequently took place via correspondence, including those that took place between members of the opposite sex attempting to maintain propriety. Additionally, poets penned emulations of poems inscribed by dead masters and their living colleagues. Further, the verse of living poets whose works were documented in writing before they had left the city to flee unrest or seek patronage elsewhere continued to orally circulate in Delhi's mushāʿirahs. In short, paper and pen were imperative aspects of salon sociability, as Persianate socio-literary contexts generated vast troves of written materials.[101] Besides documentation, the act of wielding a pen and shuffling papers in the salon space marked a performative type of cultured comportment. Members of a salon space marked their cultivation when an important verse or a moment in conversation or debate necessitated them to pause and extract a pen and diary from their pocket. Across paintings of salon scenes, the quill, pen box, and diary surface as important accoutrements among men, and occasionally women, of status gathering to recite.

The intellectuals of Delhi's literary scenes recorded verse and notable events in an array of different literary-focused types of written accounts, such as in edited collections of attendees' poems (*dīwān*), commonplace books (*bayāẓ*), and miscellanies (*majmūʿah*).[102] We learn from these sources about what poets recited, their arguments about these recitations, and the responses of audience members in attendance, including both the city's commoners (*ʿawāmm*) and notables (*ḳhawāṣṣ*). Sometimes diarists would note down information during the recitation itself; more often they would record verses and anecdotes afterward, either from memory or as relayed in rumor and gossip. Culled from these varied sources, the verses from these gatherings and the anecdotes about exchange or behaviors in the context of their performance wended their way into biographical anthologies or *taẕkirāt* (*taẕkirah*, sing.), works that preserved the entertaining, hierarchical, and contentious atmosphere of literary gatherings by recording in written form the vignettes that set the context for lyric poetry performed by versifiers.

The tażkirah is one of several primary methods of literary documentation employed across the Muslim world since the tenth century, and it remains a viable mode of history writing today.[103] Especially for historians seeking to understand Persian-educated societies, "There is no genre of literature more accessible and more rewarding of patient search than the so-called tażkirah literature."[104] Tażkirahs are genealogical texts that record, among other information, names, births, deaths, and locations where individuals dwelled in the past. Within their pages, tażkirahs also relay anecdotes about poets and mushāʿirah participants and samples of verse performed at particular gatherings. Often tażkirah writers peppered these accounts with their own criticism and bits of gossip to which they had been privy. The tażkirah constituted a deeply personal mode of writing inflected by conversation that addressed, in a piecemeal fashion, a public network of competitors and allies that could span cities and bridge regions.[105] In the 1700s, writers such as Kishan Chand *Ikẖlāṣ* (The Fidelity), a secretary from India's agricultural heartland, noted that participants in Delhi's market for speech understood poets to be like flower sellers:

With even your mention, O Rose Seller in the market of speech,
each and every petal turns a stylish color for you in the garden of speech.
Your qualities form the preface to the miscellany of beauty itself.
Indeed, your description is handmaid to the visage of speech.[106]

ai żikr-e tū gul farosh-e bāzār-e suḳhan
rangīn zi-tū barg barg-e gulzār-e suḳhan
auṣāf-e tū dībāchah-e majmūʿah-e ḥusn
tauṣīf-e tū mashshāṭah-e ruḳhsār-e suḳhan

Rather than casting away perceived limitations associated with consumerism in this uniquely Islamic source, we instead allow tażkirahs to speak for themselves. Even if descriptions of their subjects appear laudatory, fragmental, or partisan, they capture important local reminiscences.

In terms of their historiographic offerings, tażkirahs are inexorably tied to collective memory. This point is demonstrated by reviewing the word's connotations across languages, indicating how tażkirahs function as a multifaceted historical register that has a unique place among many sources for Muslim societies to access the past.[107] Marcia K. Hermansen and Bruce Lawrence provide a technical term toward this end, translating tażkirah as "memorative communication," a formulation advanced by Mana Kia in her theorization of the tażkirah as an assemblage or process that diagrams how memory develops among communities and collectives.[108] These broad definitions harmonize with approaches of scholars such as Katherine Schofield, who notes that eighteenth-century tażkirahs record histories of emotion at moments when communities scatter.[109] So too, Rian Thum's examination of Uyghur history writing since the 1700s explicates the tażkirah's crucial role within a popular manuscript tradition propagated through shrine visitations and devotional performances across Central Asia's Altishahr region.[110] Hence, tażkirahs both document history and produce varied, even disparate, modes of engaging with Muslim pasts based on contestable notions of memory.[111]

One example of the tażkirah's productive boundaries concerns its capacity to relay gender history, namely in the presentation of the poetry and biographies of educated women.[112] Across the vast corpus of tażkirahs written in Arabic, Persian, Urdu, Turkish, Uyghur, and other Muslim languages, most of the entries within a given work describe the activities of male poets, saints, or other notables. However, even early compendiums such as Farīd ud-Dīn ʿAṯṯār's *Anthology of Saints* (*Tażkirāt ul-Auliyā*) contain detailed accounts of foundational female poets.[113] The poet Sulṭān Muḥammad Faḵhrī (fl. 1497–1566), writing in Herat and Sindh in the 1550s, devoted an entire tażkirah to female poets, "The Wondrous Jewels" (*Jawāhir ul-ʿAjāʾib*), reflecting, as noted by the historian Maria Szuppe, the importance of female writers within literary and intellectual life during the early modern period.[114] We catch a glimpse of this social setting as depicted in a sixteenth-century folio by an anonymous artist showing an elite woman taking part in a gathering of Mongol-era court poets (see figure 0.1).

The tażkirah compilers of the eighteenth century continued to convey this norm while noting the class connections of the various women and their verse.[115] Over this period, women of lower classes began taking a greater role in many facets of Mughal society, gaining influence in the court or holding their own gatherings as singers and dancers among the musical salons of Delhi, a facet examined by Shivangini Tandon in her survey of tażkirahs.[116] Following her methodology for reading tażkirahs according to class relations, across our sources we find several women of non-elite or semi-elite classes, like the former courtesan Babrī Rindī, who likely contributed to the mushāʿirah at Bedil's grave, and a particular Kashmiri religious cleric's daughter who, apparently a poet in her own right, became the target of a satirist at the grave of Bedil in retribution for previous attacks on the satirist meted out by her father. Thus, we should not presume the tażkirahs and the memories they record to be wholly exclusionary, narrowly chronicling the interests of a few elite men, even though references to such subjects comprise most citations.[117] The instances in which female poets and their words reshape salon spaces should not be seen as exceptions but simply as further instances when they navigated the hierarchical and contentious literary marketplace in negotiation with male elites who controlled the dispensation of ideas.

Despite its chronological reach and voluminous cast of characters, much history writing has sought to denigrate or sideline the tażkirah. For instance, Ram Babu Saksena willfully wrote out "minor poets" from his history, which heavily relied on the tażkirah corpus, albeit his narrow reading of it. "Consequently, there was an abundance of Urdu poets who are unimportant and without any distinctive merit," writes Saksena before denigrating poets in the very sources he used: "The early [tażkirahs], especially those of [Mīr Taqī and Mīr Ḥasan], are full of their names and specimens from their compositions. They are not remembered and no mention of them could conveniently and profitably be made."[118]

Instead of following Saksena into this cul-de-sac, the reading strategy employed in *City of Lyrics* repositions the tażkirah based on the perspectives of so-called minor poets.[119] Importantly, there is virtually no secondary literature on the many minor poets whom we encounter in this book, allowing for their overlooked words and anecdotes to alter the scale and shape of Urdu and Persian literary history beyond its previous exclusions.[120] In addition to offering accounts of the lyric poems performed at mushāʿirahs, peculiar anecdotes about occurrences and exchanges of witticisms, and biographical information about the poets who performed, tażkirahs also relay details about the material and economic dimensions of the mushāʿirah, such as how poets searched for patronage and the sociable outcomes of these transactions central to the Persianate "poetic economy."[121]

The tażkirah was foundational to the documentation, enjoyment, and sociability of eighteenth-century Delhi's mushāʿirahs. Indeed, as the mushāʿirah's first historian ʿAlī Jawād Zaidī writes, "a sustained history of the mushāʿirah" appears most notably in tażkirahs.[122] Stefano Pellò theorizes this position further, framing the tażkirah and the mushāʿirah as wedded institutions that built urban "sociotextual" cohorts around class and shared values.[123] Indeed, among early 1700s mushāʿirahs, writing, or scribal practices more generally framed both salon conduct and documentation to the extent that pen and paper broke down perceived conceptual barriers between reciting and reading.[124] Poets kept a diary—called a *bayāẓ* or commonplace book—to record memorable verses.[125] Additionally, mushāʿirah organizers would loosely employ registers or diaries (*kitāb-e mushāʿarah*) in which versifiers wrote their compositions for future record, what the poet Asadullāh Ḳhān Ġhālib (1797–69) later called a "register of poems" (*ashʿār kā daftar*) and compared such a text compiled in a gathering to a "jewel treasury's door" (*dar-e ganjīnah-e gauhar*).[126] Poets' diaries were "speaking images of the mushāʿirah," such that readers could ascertain from them what the tongues of the nobles sounded like—their stuttering, choice of melodies, or the dynamics of their voices.[127]

Although a singular littérateur often claimed authorship, tażkirahs emerged collectively among a community of friendly allies and argumentative partisans (or argumentative allies and friendly partisans). Further, these texts contain an interesting performative element, perhaps hard to discern in their final edited form yet crucial to their production, compilation, and circulation: some components of tażkirahs could be produced on the spot, during the progress of an ongoing mushāʿirah gathering.[128] Indeed, this nexus of gathering, reciting, and writing among urban classes poses a productive methodological issue for understanding Islamic popular culture of the past. As many historians have demonstrated, scribal practices were integral to Islamic societies across classes, time periods, and regions.[129] The mushāʿirah spaces of early 1700s Delhi—even outside of rarefied environs of the imperial court and homes of nobility—were hardly unique with regard to the way that pen and paper featured as integral elements for poets regardless of class and social standing. In fact, it was pen and paper that allowed us to now "hear" the mushāʿirah's recitations. Concisely rendered and following the pioneering work of Kevin Schwartz, the tażkirah offers a detailed firsthand account of past Indo-Persian social networks.[130]

Analyzing Social Networks by Rhythm and Rhyme

To document the mushāʿirah networks conveyed by tażkirahs, I employ an "archeological" method for reading tażkirahs as an archive for recitations and exchanges among gatherings and coteries of the past.[131] In other words, the ways in which tażkirahs were written illustrate how eighteenth-century writers understood their relationships to their immediate communities, as writers culled memories, citations, anecdotes, and verse samples from friends, while also compiling lyrics from the recitations of students, colleagues, and patrons when they gathered.[132] Marveling at the thousands of biographic works produced in the early Muslim world, historian Shelomo

Goitein notes that "much time will be required before this enormous material can be critically sifted."[133] Such a statement is also true for early modern South Asia's trove of Islamic biographical data detailing the workings of a highly specialized literary economy. To sift through dozens of prefaces, many hundreds of capsule biographies, and hundreds of thousands of verse samples requires analyzing such material according to poets' own sociable processes that recorded these facts in the first place. In other words, we need to follow the steps of past writers themselves (*tatabbuʿ*), seeking implicit and explicit clues for a record of who gathered, how poems were recited, and what types of information (mainly verse, anecdotes, and biographical information) were diarists and poets motivated to record.

Significantly, taẕkirahs bear an explicit imprint of the gathering space, so the key to unlocking the mushāʿirah's recitations is in the very words mushāʿirahs circulated, in the literary speech of its participants. Bindrāban Dās *Ḳhwushgo* (The Eloquent) (1678?–1757), Bedil's student and biographer, distinctly captured firsthand perspectives due to the fact that, as Ḳhwushgo explicitly stated, he encouraged poets to inscribe the verses they recited at his mushāʿirahs directly into his diary, a work that formed the basis for his taẕkirah.[134] So too, Ġhulām Hamadāni *Muṣḥafī* (The Qurʾān Binder) (1751–1824), a poet who, although over a generation removed from Bedil, regularly hosted gatherings over his long career and developed taẕkirahs from his regular mushāʿirahs, most notably "The Valley of Orators" (*Riyāẓ ul-Fuṣaḥā*), compiled circa 1806. These two texts provide an important clue for reengineering what went on in gathering spaces: taẕkirahs, in part, were drafted within the boundaries of the mushāʿirah. If all poems were, as we will see, emulative, and mushāʿirahs were ubiquitous, the verse samples within taẕkirah may have remnants or echoes of the shared elements by which all poets composed. This is especially the case since emulations also followed the same formal structures, the aural elements that give ġhazals their musicality.

From this perspective, the taẕkirah comes alive when considering its method of assemblage as also a constituent in representing the past.[135] To perform this task for Urdu-language verse requires reading across taẕkirahs, commonplace books (*bayāẓ*), and dīwāns, carefully unearthing parallel ġhazals shared between poets, an approach advocated by mushāʿirah historian ʿAlī Jawād Zaidī.[136] For over a century, Urdu-language scholars such as Farḥatullāh Beg have already performed some of these efforts, noting parallel lines in their prefaces to the edited collections of eighteenth-century poets.[137] Other poets, the so-called minor writers, either compiled no dīwān, assembled one for it to disappear, or produced a collection that sits ignored somewhere in an archive. For these minor poets, only selections of their oeuvre remain among a few ġhazals preserved in the tażkirah corpus—only by dint of their memorable recitations in mushāʿirahs.[138] Few though these poems may be, that they were often invariably recited in a mushāʿirah produces stronger connections for reconstructing gatherings of the past. By linking so-called minor poets' ġhazals with their contemporaries' words, the ġhazals of purportedly minor poets provide intriguing connective strands from which we can pull the 1700s mushāʿirahs further into focus.

Reading the tażkirah corpus according to its own logic of documentation within a community of poets requires both historical and literary approaches, a foundational methodology for early modern poetry and its writers innovated by Paul Losensky and his history of literary emulation in Safavid and Mughal poetry in which "poetic voice" serves to illustrate the past.[139] His approach focuses on the "network of imitations" that surround the ġhazals of all poets no matter their status.[140] As Losensky states, Mughal-era writers "honed their skills by replying to masterpieces of the past," allowing poets to "demonstrate their mastery of the tradition and to display their refinements of and departures from the model."[141] Poets, when displaying their influences, paid close attention to both content and form: noted metaphors or phrases paid tribute to past masters, and formal elements such as prosody and rhyme revealed connections between versifiers. Delhi's poets of the 1700s referred to this as *tatabbuʿ* or "following" in the footsteps of past masters, competitors, and colleagues by writing recognizable emulations.[142]

Beginning in the 1300s, Persian ġhazal writers focused on complexity (*takalluf*) and emulation through following a pattern (*tatabbuʿ*) within the formation of literary style, factors that also impacted later reḳhtah poetics. The historian Maria Subtelny provides a foundational assessment of how complexity and imitation produced socio-literary networks in the Timurid courts of 1400s Central Asia and Iran, writing, "The composition of imitational poetry was not an end in itself, however, it also served an important function, for it was the means by which a poet established himself within the collective Persian literary tradition."[143] What was true of Subtelny's fifteenth-century context also applied to the eighteenth-century Delhi mushāʿirah scene, as our ġhazal marketplace comprised "an intricate web of interrelationships and interdependences between poets of different generations and distant localities," to again quote the from Subtelny's description of early Timurid literary culture.[144] Instead of looking for connections among distant geographies, as Subtelny productively guides us to do in her account, our mid-1700s Delhi context allows us to discover how the formation of literary style also occurred at the local level, centered within a neighborhood mosque.

Thus, evidence of the association and competition among poets—their networks built in metaphor and the rhythm of poetic speech—can be found by comparing the rhyme, refrain, and meter of ġhazals composed among groups of coeval poets and via the lineages of their past influences. Significantly, all verse performed within mushāʿirahs of the 1700s adheres to these emulative rules, and analyzing the rhyme, refrain, and meter of poems in tażkirahs and collected works reconstructs mushāʿirahs beyond the few anecdotes that remain in writings from the eighteenth century.[145]

All new and emulative poems presented in gatherings of the 1700s took shape according to a shared *ṭarḥ*, a model verse that provides all the formal elements by which to compose a ġhazal: the end rhyme (*qāfiyah*), refrain (*radīf*), and meter (*baḥr* or *wazn*).[146] Collectively, rhyme, refrain, and meter are called the "grounds" or "earth" of a poem (*zamīn-e shiʿr*). The formal requirements of Islamicate poetry—its rules for repetition and prosody—necessitate in-depth study and explication beyond the scope of this introduction or even this book. Yet, for the purposes of our mushāʿirah history, it is important to understand a few basic facts about each element of the *ṭarḥ*. End rhyme (*qāfiyah*) is the foundational repetitive element in Islamicate verse, established first in Arabic poetry in late antiquity to be adapted for Persian and Urdu in the medieval and early modern periods, respectively. The end rhyme caps off all lines requiring repeated syllables, albeit depending on the form.

After the end rhyme comes the refrain (*radīf*). This takes the form of a repeated word or phrase at the end of a line after the end rhyme. The refrain or *radīf* represents perhaps the most aurally recognizable element for new initiates, which makes each poem highly distinct and represents Persian and Urdu's particular contributions to the specialized rules of Islamicate poetic practices. End rhyme is required for all verse, but the refrain is not. For instance, Arabic poetry does not generally use refrains. The ġhazal repeats the *qāfiyah* (required end rhyme) and *radīf* (the optional refrain) in both lines of its first couplet. This is called the *maṭlaʿ* or "opening." After that, only the second line of subsequent couplets requires a rhyme and, if the poet uses one, a refrain. Thus, the ġhazal's rhyme scheme appears as AA, BA, CA, DA, and so on. In the final couplet, called the *maqṭaʿ* or "ending," readers encounter the poet's *takhalluṣ* or pen name, a branding device that often elicits wordplays or offers a chance for the poet to boast of her own abilities or to name-drop competitors and admired poets from the past.

Meter (*baḥr* or *wazn*) is complicated. In Arabic, Persian, and Urdu, meter is quantitative whereby the number and lengths of syllables matter greatly. Counting and assessing syllable length is usually associated with classical languages as opposed to modern English prosody that focuses on stress. Thus, in a Persian or Urdu ġhazal, each word has a measurable number of consonant and vowel patterns (or metrical feet) that are scanned as either long, short, or a combination thereof called "overlong." In the mushāʿirah, poets listened closely to their own compositions and those of others, scanning each line for the precise number and pattern of required long or short syllables that fit into precast metrical forms. There are sixteen established forms, and each of these meters has its own variations in terms of the number of metrical feet and combinations of short, long, and overlong syllables therein. However, only a few of these permutations have wide usage within their respective Arabic, Persian, or Urdu literary traditions.

Conveniently, the meters have their own names (e.g., *hazaj*, *ramal*, and *rajaz*), and their specific syllable lengths and patterns that can be represented, according to their metrical feet, in Arabic mnemonic words (*tafāʿīl*), Persian onomatopoeic words (*ta tan tan tat)*, or with macrons and breves (˘ ¯ ¯ ˘)—a system established for Greek and Latin poetry. Thus, *hazaj* (lit. "trilling") in four metrical feet per line, one of the most frequently used meters in Persian and Urdu poetry, paradigmatically appears as *mafāʿīlun mafāʿīlun mafāʿīlun mafāʿīlun* according to the Arabic system, sounds like "*ta tan tan tan* | *ta tan tan tan* | *ta tan tan tan* | *ta tan tan tan*" according to the Persian onomatopoeic approach, and in the classical system of macrons and breves appears as: ˘ ¯ ¯ ¯ | ˘ ¯ ¯ ¯ | ˘ ¯ ¯ ¯ | ˘ ¯ ¯ ¯ .[147] For specialists in the past and today, this information, especially as it relates to meter, is just a drop in poetry's oceans, but for new initiates into Delhi's poetry scene, it is important to know that these formal elements comprise everyday literary practices for poets reading, writing, and reciting in the early 1700s or today, and the *ṭarḥ* or "base" acts as a shorthand model by which to access these detailed compositional parameters.[148]

When versifiers gathered to recite and jot down notable ġhazals, the new verses treaded the "grounds" (*zamīn*)—the end rhyme, refrain, and meter—first established by the *ṭarḥ* and thereby "followed" (*tatabbuʿ*) the approach of a past master or clever contemporary. Nāṣir ʿAlī Sirhindī, an adept ġhazal writer of the late 1600s who eventually settled in Delhi, stated, "The test of a poet is the ġhazal's *ṭarḥ*" (*imtiḥān-e shāʿir ṭarḥ-e ġhazal ast*).[149] Nāṣir ʿAlī's description of emulation—the test of the poet—provides the historical grounding of the mushāʿirah as it both created links among contemporaries and facilitated dialogue with writers of the past whose words legitimated literary traditions long after these writers' physical demise.

I follow Nāṣir ʿAlī's advice and utilize the ġhazal's formal elements to test poets' words, finding parallel couplets that linked coteries of poets within Delhi's mushāʿirah scene through the words of past masters whom all poets attempted to emulate. Nāṣir ʿAlī proved his words by penning *ṭarḥ*-based emulations of compositions from Muḥammad ʿAlī *Ṣāʾib* (The Mark) (1592–1676), a superstar ġhazal writer of the previous generation.[150] Namely, Nāṣir ʿAlī demonstrated his admiration for Ṣāʾib in an "imitative quotation" or *taẓmīn*, a tribute ġhazal that followed Ṣāʾib's inviting rhyme, commanding refrain, and popular meter. While all poems cited in this book adhere to prosody rules, only in this instance are a ġhazal's formal requirements detailed according to their full technical parameters.

In Nāṣir ʿAlī's tribute to Ṣāʾib, the ġhazal's end rhyme is *-ārast*, the refrain is *ba-bīnīd* ("Look!"), and the meter is called *hazaj muṡamman akhrab makfūf maḥżūf*, paradigmatically represented as *mafʿūl mafāʿīl mafāʿīl faʿūlun*, by the Arabic system, or *tan tan ta* | *ta tan tan ta* | *ta tan tan ta* | *ta tan tan* (¯ ¯ ˘ |˘ ¯ ¯ ˘ |˘ ¯ ¯ ˘ |˘ ¯ ¯). Adding his own words to Ṣāʾib's seductive line that established the compositional formalities, Nāṣir ʿAlī composed:

My heart is wounded by just one desert thorn. Just look!
While his eyelash is occupied, what option is there? Just look!

. . . .

O ʿAlī, my chest bled because of Ṣāʾib's verse:
"How did that thorn catch in the rosebud's shirt? Just look!"[151]

dil zakhmī-e yak bādiyah khār ast ba-bīnīd
tā ān miẕhah mashġhūl chih kār ast ba-bīnīd

. . . .

khūn gasht ʿalī sīnah-am az miṣraʿ-e ṣāʾib
dar pairahan-e ġhunchah chih khār-ast ba-bīnīd

Thus, Ṣāʾib's lines, as it invoked the image of the thorn, a catchy refrain, and musical rhythms, wounded Nāṣir ʿAlī through their sharp stylishness. He had no choice but to follow Ṣāʾib's form, quoting him and adding his own harmonious words to the mix.

In observing Nāṣir ʿAlī's connection to Ṣāʾib, the taẕkirah writer Khwushgo stated that Nāṣir ʿAlī conducted a mushāʿirah in absentia with the master (*ġhāʾibānah ba-mirzā [ṣāʾib] mushāʿarah dārad*), adhering to all the technical formalities required of ġhazal writing.[152] This fastidiousness would have greatly pleased Ṣāʾib. That is, Nāṣir ʿAlī's skilled emulation of Ṣāʾib made it seem as if they were sitting face to face exchanging lines in a parallel fashion. Nāṣir ʿAlī was so skilled at following Ṣāʾib's style that he earned the title of "The Second Ṣāʾib," even in Ṣāʾib's hometown of Isfahan.[153]

Yet, the lineage of imitative quotation between Ṣāʾib and Nāṣir ʿAlī did not begin with Ṣāʾib, for Ṣāʾib himself stated in the final couplet of his own ġhazal:

It was that very ġhazal from my dear Awḥadī that went:
"For the sightless, what kind of springtime is this? Just look!"[154]

īn ān ġhazal-e awḥadī-e mā-ast kih farmūd
ai be-biṣarān īn chih bahār-ast ba-bīnīd

Ṣāʾib cited the source of his original homage, a line from a classical-era poet named Rukn ud-Dīn Awḥadī Marāġhaʾī (1271–1338) (see figure 0.1), a versifier famous for his elegies and lyrics.[155]

Awḥadī composed a ġhazal with the following opening and closing couplets, setting the model (and thereby establishing the rhyme, refrain, and meter) for his literary descendants, including Ṣāʾib and Nāṣir ʿAlī:

For the sightless, what kind of springtime is this? Just look!
There is no rosebush, and yet its roses bloom. Just look!

. . . .

It is not easy to compose a commentary on Awḥadī's words.
Leave the poetry to him. Is this even a poetry competition? Just look![156]

ai mardum-e kūr īn chih bahār-ast ba-bīnīd
gulban nah wa gulhāsh babār-ast ba-bīnīd

. . . .

sharḥ-e sukhan-e awḥadī āsān natawān guft
shiʿr-ish bahilīd īn chih shiʿār-ast ba-bīnīd[157]

Despite the ubiquity of emulation in mushāʿirahs and the literary world at large, the performative links among new poems, poets, and the legitimating words of literary masters are often submerged, hidden among the poems

FIGURE 0.1 *Leaf with Miniature of a Gathering of Poets*, 1550. Rare Books and Special Collections, McGill University Libraries. MSP leaf 30.

themselves. Occasionally, taẕkirah writers depict a set of exchanges or moments of emulation when groups of poets constructed new poems based on a *ṯarḥ*. These instances provide the basis for depicting what transpired in literary gatherings—visions of victories, defeats, and delights. Yet, the reader and mushāʿirah historian want even more evidence to substantiate how these verses were formulated and written as part of exchanges. In an anachronistic fashion, some historians of the Persianate world mourn that few records exist for depicting mushāʿirahs in realistic detail; there were no audio-recording devices or stenographers to capture every word.[158] These are strange pronouncements that ignore the auditory and scribal means that gathering participants used to record mushāʿirah verse. In other words, the *ṯarḥ* and the poems on which they are based solve the "mechanical reproduction issues" that previous historians have cited as impediments to knowing what went on in gatherings.[159]

Appropriately, digital humanities approaches augment such a methodology outlined by Nāṣir ʿAlī and Ḳhwushgo, something that has already begun in the hands of Frances Pritchett for the works of foundational Urdu-language poets Ġhālib and Mīr.[160] The process for assessing mushāʿirah connections in Persian-language compositions differs slightly. A significant portion of the vast corpus of Persian-language poetry exists in digital format through ganjoor.net, an open-source "web-based miscellany of works by Persian-language poets."[161] This platform provides a means to search by poet (*shāʿir*), meter (*wazn*), and end rhyme (*qāfiyah)* from among a millennium of Persian verse to compare such elements.[162] However, searchable online repositories are only a tool and can in no way substitute for archives that preserve manuscripts toward providing larger contexts within which to read embedded verse. Neither can they replace the work of previous scholars from Afghanistan, India, Iran, Pakistan, and other places besides whose research makes critical editions available to scholars worldwide.[163] Instead, current digital humanities approaches offer a channel by which to find tentative intertextual connections to be verified using the same methods poets and readers of the past employed to cultivate affinities in verse: carefully following (*tatabbuʿ*) the thematic and formal connections between poets across time.

As we recall, Ḳhwushgo, the taẕkirah writer and crucial mushāʿirah documentarian, named this process of exchanging verses with dead masters a "mushāʿirah in absentia" (*mushāʿarah-e ġhāʾibānah*).[164] Indeed, these current digital humanities approaches help to elucidate the values and methods of reading and reciting Islamic literature of the past. By sifting through anecdotes and verse samples to fit together shards of verse in parallel meters, end rhymes, and refrains, this book reconstitutes recitations between literary competitors and reconstructs the delight of exchanging poetic speech to foreground the production of friendships and rivalries within settings bound by decorum and hierarchy—in other words, the historical sociology of Islamic literatures based on their networks.[165]

Conclusion

The three processes at focus in this book—gathering, reciting, and writing—shaped how versifiers within Delhi's mushāʿirah circuits transmitted poetry and stories about the sociability cultivated in Bedil's salon and those of his inheritors, creating a form of commemoration that preserved delight, hierarchy, and contestation. Through its discussion of these skills, *City of Lyrics* provides a cultural history of salon-based poetry so that the reader learns to relish its arguments, quips, and the technical aspects of its verses. Indeed, reading poetry and anecdotes in this fashion serves to produce an alternative history of Urdu literature that pivots on its sociability. The bounds of acceptable conduct and speech among Persianate verse networks were formed through the poetry itself and participants' memories of an anecdotal literary past. Delhi's writers who maintained salons created incomplete and informal networks in which an expansive if contentious notion of sociability flourished. A fine-grained depiction of these interchanges, critiques, and competitions—the public realm of poetic composition—presents an intuitive historical narrative to counter the canonical paradigm that focuses on great poets and singular authors. Thus, to write a history of the mushāʿirah is to revive the gossipy and critical setting of Delhi's literary society as recorded in a partisan and fragmentary way.

The mushāʿirah's history illustrates literary sociability, namely its competitions and friendships, as shared among writers in early 1700s Delhi, and it charts poets' social networks constructed in the ġhazal's formal aspects, revealing how literary information builds its social settings. In this regard, Urdu literary history is not confined to a singular interpretative register, nor is it bound to one language. Instead, it is based on the associations and arguments produced in the performance of poetry and among its attendant modes of comportment. One might think of *City of Lyrics* as a kind of Anglophone taẕkirah about the mushāʿirah of the 1700s, enjoyed by the general reader and relished by specialists. Inspiration for the title comes from Malikzādah Manẓūr Aḥmad's collected essays entitled "The City of Speech" (*Shahr-e Suḳhan*) that presents the verse samples and prose portraits of mushāʿirah celebrities of the late twentieth century.[166] The infectious milieu of the contemporary era, Malikzādah Manẓūr's concept of a "city of speech," mirrors that of the past, and as a researcher and reader, I delighted in the historical anecdotes from taẕkirahs, pursuing such depictions for their enjoyment and complexity. Writers, whatever their era, recorded mushāʿirah accounts for very immediate and human reasons—to earn a patron's attention and wealth, to create literary distinction, or to entertain an audience of peers. The translations of gatherings' verses and their discussions transport the reader into the world of the mushāʿirah as an entertaining realm originally conducted in multiple languages among Persian-educated classes.

The economic and ethical values defined by the eighteenth-century mushāʿirah continue to shape the largest platform for poetry on the planet: the current mushāʿirah. For Urdu, Hindi, and Persian speakers, the term mushāʿirah is synonymous with the singing and recitation of verse to the delight and entertainment of listeners. Across the regions of South Asia and the Middle East today, people congregate for all-night performances of recited poetry. They gather in small-group settings or at large festivals with thousands of listeners. During mushāʿirah events, audience members encourage or heckle poets while sipping cups of tea, jostling to request verses, recording recitations on cell phones, or jotting down favorite couplets. Often, listeners memorize verses, committing them to heart for a later occasion. Such memorized verses, recordings, or scribblings then circulate in cheaply printed books, bootleg video CDs, or cassettes sold in the markets found in nearly every city across India and Pakistan. At the time of this writing in 2025, individual users shared among themselves recordings of novel performances captured on multimedia cell phones and uploaded onto the internet through platforms such as YouTube. Since 2015, the YouTube channel Mushaira Media has captured over half a billion views of its recordings of poets reciting verse across India, Pakistan, and the Middle East.[167] In short, there is a surplus of recorded Urdu poetry, circulating on the internet and traded between enthusiasts' cellphones. India's vast market of consumers continue to reshape global tastes, including literary ones.

Indeed, competing over poetry became the motivating form of association across which this Indo-Muslim literary network was elaborated, connecting Persian-speaking poets and literacy aware poetry aficionados across regional, linguistic, and class divides. *City of Lyrics* therefore offers insight into how literary performance and appreciation contributed to the articulation of a distinctive multiregional, networked culture prior to the modern era. Many of the same concerns about literary ethics, presentation, originality, and delight that arose in the early 1700s at focus in this book still inform the contemporary mushāʿirah's distinctive forms of aesthetics and sociability.

1 At the Tomb of Delhi's Poet-Saint

On Wednesday, December 4, 1720, Delhi's most famous living writer ʿAbd ul-Qādir *Bedil* (The One who Lost his Heart) died at his home after coming down with a fever in late November. Though breaking temporarily during a late-night poetry gathering on December 3, Bedil's temperature again climbed, driving the poet into fainting fits. Bedil's biographer, quoting an appropriate poem, alluded to the inevitability of fate despite the joys of frivolity while commenting on Bedil's concerns over finances: "My love, there is many a rogue in the gambling house who / laugh at all the credit and cash of this world and the next" (*jānān ba-qimār ḵhānah rindī chandand / bar nisyah-o naqd-e har do ʿālam ḵhandand*). The next morning, around 9:30 a.m., Bedil's condition took a turn for the worse, and the poet's phoenix-like soul "animated with everlasting life and having winged away from the nest of his corpse, cast its shadow among the denizens of the high empyrean heaven."[1] In accordance with Muslim rites, on the very same day, Bedil's face was turned toward Mecca, and his remains were laid to rest under a plinth that the poet himself had plotted in his mansion's courtyard ten years earlier. Even in death, Bedil's ability to disseminate his writing did not end. When his body was lifted from the deathbed for burial, a few scraps of paper with two poems written on them slipped from beneath a pillow.[2]

To mark the occasion of his death and the majesty of his literary achievements, Bedil's students kicked up a flurry of poetry writing at the site of Bedil's tomb during an annual event to commemorate his passing. From 1720 until 1760 or so, Bedil's former students recited thousands of poems at the poet-saint's posthumous mushāʿirah, a yearly salon over which, some of them believed, Bedil's spirit continued to preside from beyond the grave. This type of event is called an *ʿurs* in Islamic terminology (lit. "wedding day"), held to memorialize a union with the divine. From a broad perspective, the annual memorial event at Bedil's grave was celebrated according to unitarian religious practices as led by charismatic men and women, the living and dead saints who led guilds, seminaries, shrines, and empires in the early modern period. At the grave of Delhi's poet-saint, an atmosphere of sociability coalesced around the commercial ventures of the tomb caretakers and the enjoyment of verse. Devotees came to light candles, buy medicines, and seek Bedil's saintly protection for themselves and their children, while enjoying hot food prepared on site and distributed free of cost. This literary sociability drew in many different types of participants, including Bedil's students, other poets traveling from near and far, and diverse congregants from both elite and common classes who understood their attendance at the gathering as a pilgrimage to the departed charismatic teacher.

This chapter considers the popular image of the poet-saint Bedil from the view of his students, whose words garnered attention and controversy in Delhi's mushāʿirahs. Bedil's tomb and its institutions represented both an intellectual and a material inheritance for his students, fans, and devotees, providing a seemingly confounding social space in which literary association, religious intercession, and commercial enterprise existed in tandem. The diversity of Bedil's sociable world has been considered by the literary historians Ḳhalīlullāh Afẓalī, Mahduḳht Pūr Ḳhāliqī Chatrūdī, and Mariyam Ṣālhī-e Nayā, who note that Bedil self-consciously restructured his authorial voice throughout his life to address different audiences based on their social positions, and in his old age he concerned himself with the puzzle of how a wide variety of audiences (*anwāʿ-e muḳhāṯabān*), most notably including commoners, could relish his words.[3] Prashant Keshavmurthy notes that Bedil's works circulated beyond purely elite settings to include the Sufi hospice.[4] Indeed, Bedil's afterlife thrived due to Islam's popular realm as cultivated at shrines and by charismatic leaders. The ritual elements that later developed at his grave both augmented and rerouted some aspects of Bedil's self-fashioning for commoners, notably as Bedil's posthumous image conformed to commercial and devotional ideals expressed among Delhi's bazaars and Sufi shrines.

As we will witness, the posthumous image of Bedil encompasses various class perspectives that emerged from multiple sources, including the poet-saint's own accounts of his words and deeds, first-person records from his students and colleagues, and the myriad legends and anecdotes that continued to grow with his popular image after his death—all three registers comprising, to a degree, malleable narratives that could buttress the artistic, mystic, and economic facets of Bedil's tomb and texts. These perspectives framed how the inheritors of his intellectual and material lineages, including Bedil's biographer Bindrāban Dās *Ḳhwushgo* (The Eloquent) (1667/78?–1757) and many others, understood Bedil's mundane relationships and his salon-based sociability, thereby depicting a diverse milieu of writers with changing goals and strategies for developing their own distinct authorial voices. With its uneven social aspects, and with its attending poets burying their disparate memories of the poet-saint in its precincts, Bedil's tomb encouraged classes of new elites to pursue language experiments by strategically moving between styles, idioms, and social registers.

These intertwined and seemingly contradictory modes of autobiography, biography, and legend shaped how Delhi's poets understood the literary life and salon conduct of their poet-saint Bedil. With his humble beginnings and enormous stature, Bedil powerfully influenced how poets perceived the norms of early eighteenth-century mushāʿirah networks to mark a change in Delhi's literary society, which proved significant to the historiography of the mushāʿirah. Throughout its duration between 1720 and 1760, this salon constituted the era's most prestigious literary event. Thus, the apex of Delhi's literary life took place, surprisingly, not at the court as might be expected, but instead, among common pilgrims praying for a saint's intercession amid the recitations of argumentative poets with varying literary abilities and conflicting poetic goals. We turn now to meet these poets.

The Bumblebee, the Swordsman, and Other Congregants

As Bedil's biographer Ḳhwushgo noted of the posthumous mushāʿirah, "Every year a poets' gathering occurred, and the entirety of the city's witty-minded ones congregated," at the shrine, where "a fine gathering (*majlis*) would be organized." Ḳhwushgo also prayed, "May the eye of discord remain far from this stylish congregation" (*majmaʿ-e rangīn*).[5] For approximately forty years, between 1720 and roughly 1760, the evil eye indeed seemed to be turned away from the annual gathering, a notable accomplishment considering how mushāʿirahs tended to encourage both discord and bonhomie among their congregations of variegated attendees. Writers in eighteenth-century Delhi noted how poets from all over India, including Hyderabad, Gujarat, the Punjab, and other regions, visited the celebrations at Bedil's grave in mid-1700s Delhi. Along with the elites who recited poetry, devotees from many backgrounds lit candles, received donated meals, and purchased elixirs said to be of Bedil's invention. We have no record providing the names of these humble pilgrims to the poet-saint's grave. For those documenting this popular literary event, they were simply commoners (*ḳhalāʾiq*) who benefited from the tomb as a shrine built and maintained by Bedil's inheritors, both his relatives and former students. Curiously, even many of the elite poets whom taẕkirah writers identified as attending the grave festivities likewise remain unnamed. We know only that there were many of them.

Among these later forgotten littérateurs in attendance at Bedil's posthumous gatherings was a woman known within Delhi's bazaars as *Bhañwarī* (The Bumblebee) (fl. 1710–40). But, in poets' circles, this Bumblebee was known by a different nickname, Babrī Rindī, a reference to her pen name of *Rindī* (The Debauchery) and the rakish way in which she cropped her bangs (*babrī*). Once a student of Bedil, Bhañwarī was a talented singer, dancer, and courtesan, hailing from a class of professional women who were marginalized in some sources but who were crucial to intellectual life as poets and political actors.[6] In one of her surviving couplets, which circulated until the early 1800s, Bhañwarī cautioned herself and her audience to be on guard against the seductive and chaos-inducing aspects of the beloved's eyes: "O Rindī, when stepping away from faith and fortitude and soul, / beware! For the beloved's eye is one hundred times more calamitous" (*rindī zi-pai burdan īmān-o dil-o jān / hushdār kih ṣad gūnah balā ast dar ān chashm*).[7] Babrī Rindī's poem plays on the conceit that the only thing worse than renouncing religion is falling in love with the mere eyes of the beloved.

We will continue to witness, especially in chapter 3, how courtesans shaped public taste by singing favorite verses and by crafting their own emulations, carrying forward new ideas in dialogue with other contenders. The recitations of lyrics like those sung by Bhañwarī were staged in front of the various relics that once belonged to Bedil, including his sword and his unusually large walking stick. These two items were both kept in the possession of a former student of Bedil's known as Gul Muḥammad *Shāʿir* (The Poet) (d. 1745), more widely known by his courtly title Maʿnī Yāb Ḵhān or "The Ḵhān of the Capture of Meaning," so named for his prowess with metaphor.[8]

Muḥammad ʿAṭāʾullāh *ʿAṭā* (The Gift) (1681?–1725?) was another important attendee of Bedil's gathering. He was a student of Bedil who cut a distinctive figure within the living poet-saint's salon and among posthumous gathering activities. ʿAṭā's verse and stories help illustrate the stakes of the mushāʿirah's history. After moving to Delhi from the countryside town of Amroha around 1700, ʿAṭā gained a reputation as a skilled swordsman in the streets and as a witty poet in the salon space. Ḵhwushgo observed of ʿAṭā, "He was a dear fellow due to his charming antics and he would even take heads off [with his humor]." Here, Ḵhwushgo played with the idiom "to take heads" (*sar zadan*) in allusion to the dual sharpness of his sword and verse.[9] ʿAṭā himself spliced stories of his swordsmanship skills into his lyrics. In Bedil's diary under the heading "From 'The Gift *ʿAṭā*' came the gift of eloquence" (*bah ʿaṭā shud ʿaṭā suḵhan dānī*), Bedil recorded a favorite poem from his student that commented on the beloved's sharp glances: "Due to the narcissus that kept scattering heads in every direction, / the eye of the garden turned to devouring itself" (*zi-nargis kih har sū sar afgandah bīsh / nigāh-e chaman gasht charān-e ḳhwīsh*).[10] With no lovers left to stare at it, the narcissus, which itself appears like an eye lined with kohl, captures the gaze of the entire garden.

With his striking words and notable personality, ʿAṭā served as an entertaining mushāʿirah celebrity, even after his death, in the eyes of many writers throughout the 1700s. Yet, athletic and literary distinctions also garnered controversy for ʿAṭā within Bedil's orbit. Once, a rumor circulated among Bedil's students about ʿAṭā's professional misconduct, prompting the poet-saint himself to temporarily prohibit ʿAṭā from attending the private gatherings at his mansion. According to a colleague who harbored enmity for ʿAṭā, Bedil purportedly had learned that ʿAṭā concocted a scheme to write ġhazals for others to recite in their own names at the poet-saint's mushāʿirah, a business decision that Bedil deemed to have breached the bounds of literary ethics.[11] Accordingly, several European scholars accused ʿAṭā of having a bad character and writing pornographic verse.[12] Perhaps for these reasons, ʿAṭā's name is absent from foundational Urdu histories of the nineteenth century.[13]

These popularized rumors of his blunders and indiscretions overlook much from ʿAṭā's story and his role in shaping the public life of Delhi's lyric poetry. In fact, over the course of his literary career, ʿAṭā masterfully negotiated multiple shifting demands, including those of his teacher Bedil, the literary marketplace, and the mushāʿirah space itself. To do so, he frequently altered his poetic voice, writing first classically styled verse, then poetry in the "New Style" (*ṭarz-e tāzah*), and finally parodies and reḳhtah compositions. Bedil himself encouraged his student ʿAṭā to cultivate these stylistic distinctions within his compositions, but ʿAṭā's adeptness in advancing such controversial and perhaps enviably rapid shifts led some competitors within Bedil's cohort to relish and magnify ʿAṭā's purported downfall. One faction elevated ʿAṭā's verse, and another held it as doggerel. Yet, these rumors of his poor conduct and overuse of obscenity need not push ʿAṭā to the margins of literary history. Anecdotes concerning controversies over colorful figures like ʿAṭā, and socially marginal figures such as Bhañwarī, reveal the complexities of the social requirements placed upon literary society of the time and the necessity of preserving the precarious and transitory space of the poetry gathering. The arguments and discord that erupted from poets' gatherings, and the ways that boundaries were opened and closed to incorporate both novel verse and unusual figures, were important aspects of popular literary culture and, thus, are worthy of preservation through textual and material means.

Bedil's Student ʿAṭā

Around 1700, ʿAṭā, then in his early twenties, departed from his provincial town and came to the "Exalted Horde" of Delhi (*urdū-e muʿallá*).[14] ʿAṭā was not from the kind of prestigious background favored by Mughal elites (Arab, Iranian, Turk), but instead descended from a family of Indian Shīʿī converts from the Doab region of North India. In his hometown of Amroha, ʿAṭā acquired a suitable education under a respected local Qur'an reader (a certain Qāẓī Muḥammad Munawwar), whose recommendation secured him employment under the imperial official Sāqī Muḥammad Mustaʿidd Ḳhān (d. 1724).[15] But when ʿAṭā arrived in Delhi as a young man, his verse was out of step with the reigning literary mode. He wrote in the classical style (*ṭarz-e qadīm*), avoiding the highly complex approach (*ṭarz-e tāzah*) associated with Bedil. A rakish poet named Muḥammad Afẓal *Sarḳhwush* (The Heady) (1640–1715), who preferred the new style, in 1707 recorded an earl mention of ʿAṭā. At a gathering, ʿAṭā recited a ġhazal that Sarḳhwush, perhaps disappointedly, found to be clean and simple verse (*shustah wa ṣāf*) in the classical style:

> I have seen a fairy, but to whom inclined am I?
> My blood is racing, but whose sacrifice am I?
>
> I have no idea where my anxiety has taken me.
> Though I have lost myself, in whose heart am I?
>
> Like a bubble, I shattered without a sound.
> O ʿAṭā, whose wine glass am I?[16]
>
> *parī dīdah-am māʾil-e kīstam*
> *bah ḳhūn mī tapam bismil-e kīstam*
>
> *nadānam kujā burdah ḥairat-e mārā*
> *zi-ḳhwud raftah-am dar dil-e kīstam*
>
> *nadārad shikastam ṣadā chūn ḥabāb*
> *ʿaṭā shīshah-e maḥfil-e kīstam*

According to the mushāʿirah celebrity Sarḳhwush, ʿAṭā's early poem, although simple, adhered to the conventions expected from those who preferred the registers from the time of Amīr Ḳhusrau, developing metaphors within the older bounds of social and literary acceptability.

When ʿAṭā first encountered his teacher Bedil after 1707 or so, the poet-saint had entered a relatively comfortable yet internally contradictory phase of his career. After his circuitous rise to prominence, Bedil had fashioned himself as both a lord of speech and a religious ascetic: at once a king seated upon a literary throne and a dervish cultivating poverty for spiritual gains. A very large man, Bedil appeared as a Sufi ascetic (*qalandar*) with a completely shaved face and head. He strolled through Delhi hoisting his purportedly seventy-pound staff, incongruously nicknamed "The Maiden."[17] Bedil had also acquired fabulous wealth from his unique writing talents and ability to navigate India's increasingly competitive Persian-language economy that started to favor upwardly mobile "new elites" from the countryside such as himself.

Like his student ʿAṭā, Bedil was born in a regional city. In his birthplace of Patna in present-day Bihar, Bedil obtained Persian and Arabic language training under two devoted uncles, Mīrzā Ẓarīf and Mīrzā Qalandar, who supervised Bedil's education after his father passed away when Bedil was four years of age. As a young man, Bedil had traveled around the eastern reaches of India before leaving Patna for good in 1664, after what little borrowed fortunes he had dried up.[18] Bedil married five years later, after which time he attempted to serve as a soldier for a Mughal prince jockeying for the throne. When this venture failed, Bedil left the imperial service and continued his writings and Sufi ramblings across north Indian locales.

After another decade or so of traveling between Delhi, Agra, Mathura, and the Punjab to compete with poets, to search for knowledge, and to fulfill patrons' demands, Bedil's career as a poet finally gained traction. During this middle phase of his career, Bedil mailed frequent letters to his maternal cousins ʿIbādullāh and Rūḥullāh back home in Patna, conveying good news about the completion of his latest works or providing comfort for a tragedy ʿIbādullāh experienced.[19] Bedil also complained about not having an audience of like-minded poets and readers for his verse, implying that "like a pearl in the sea, I am alone in a crowd." Precious though he might be in those turbid waters, Bedil still needed to survive, and at the end of the letter, he noted that "worldly complaints emanated from the pocket." He was asking his brothers for financial support. "Due to [these] details as revealed in [my] gloominess, a brief charitable payment [would] lessen the vexation," he pleaded with ʿIbādullāh.[20]

The letter, although written in florid prose and embellished with several ornate apologies, reveals that during his early years, Bedil's financial position remained insecure, occasionally burdening his cousins in Patna. But this changed around 1670, when Bedil began to associate with the poet and courtier ʿĀqal Ḳhān Rāzī (d. 1696/97), a governor to the crown lands of Delhi under Emperor Aurangzeb (1658–1707). In addition to supporting Bedil financially and becoming his confidant, Rāzī introduced Bedil to his son-in-law, the nobleman Shukrullāh Ḳhān *Ḳhāksār* (The Abject) (d. 1698), who, in 1680, became Bedil's most generous benefactor, and whose sons continued to patronize Bedil after Shukrullāh Ḳhān's death.[21] Around 1684, evidence of the new patron's generosity took shape in a mansion worth around five thousand rupees. Bedil's stately abode was nestled in a neighborhood on Delhi's *gużar ghāṭ*, a ferry landing outside the walled city at Delhi Gate. Shukrullāh Ḳhān also presented Bedil with a stipend of two rupees per day.[22]

For ʿAṯā, Bedil's student from Amroha, the poet-saint's grand lifestyle in Delhi must have seemed sumptuous. When on the road, Bedil traveled with an extensive baggage train, and when in Delhi, he paraded through the city's bazaar on his horse, staging spectacles of elitism. Bedil also avidly and ostentatiously consumed luxury goods, seeking expensive horses, foreign musical instruments, and eyeglasses. On one occasion, Bedil requested that sixty enameled hookahs be sent to his house to enhance his salons.[23] However, Bedil constantly worried about his reproductive health, his capacity to produce an heir, and his ability to secure finances enough to support a large polygamous household. He married four times.[24]

Despite Bedil's appetite for luxurious living, ʿAṯā likely bonded with his teacher Bedil through their shared predilections for pursuits associated with lower classes and provincial life upon their eventual meeting. For instance, Bedil allowed himself a cannabis habit, indulging in a drug strongly associated with the lower echelons of society.[25] Like ʿAṯā, Bedil enjoyed the martial arts, particularly wrestling, a prominent urban profession also associated with the lower classes. Strongmen worked as bone setters or local toughs in addition to demonstrating their skills in public wrestling competitions.[26] That a lofty, highly philosophical poet such as Bedil would stoop to a commoner's profession, even if just for show, might seem remarkable at first glance. Bedil's great regard for fitness, leading to his physical prowess, had been inspired by his uncle and childhood teacher in Patna, Mīrzā Qalandar, who also cultivated a robust exercise regime.[27] Bedil's biographer Ḳhwushgo, too, eulogized Bedil's strength: the poet-saint could outrun horses and push over walls while packing on a large girth gained by consuming vast quantities of food. Bedil's daily calisthenics incorporated thousands of squats, which enabled him to develop his grappling abilities (*kushtī kardan wa maṣāraʿah justan*) so that the poet-saint could instantly knock down an opponent. Bedil was also known for practicing his wrestling throws on horses.[28] Decades later, other taẕkirah writers called Bedil the "Wrestler of Speech" (*pahlawān-e suḳhan*) in reference to his appearance and physical talents.[29] At one literary encounter, a student referred to Bedil and his competitor as two elephants about to fight.[30]

To maintain his standard of living as a wealthy dervish, Bedil required patrons who would compensate and reward him for writing verse. Yet, maintaining a relationship with a patron was complex. Any link between earning silver and writing poetry—however necessary—was thought to somewhat adulterate literary speech. For Bedil, the possibility for patronage was further complicated by the fact that the poet-saint famously abhorred writing panegyrics for wealthy donors—thus abnegating a sure method for income. Instead, Bedil cannily cultivated his relationships with patrons by appealing to their pride and referring to them as his literary equals. In fact, Mughal nobility who funded poets' careers were themselves contenders among the literary classes, often producing noteworthy verse, commentaries, and compendiums. Were Bedil to have claimed to be teaching those who were paying him, a patron's literary output would be denigrated and his ego bruised, thus jeopardizing the relationship. Those who spread rumors about Bedil crossing this line earned the poet-saint's wrath. An actual dervish named Shāhid publicly breached the delicate balance Bedil had struck by suggesting that the poet-saint was a teacher to his patrons. In a letter to a friend, Bedil referred to Shāhid as "an atheist, an ungrateful monkey, sponger of leftovers, a fat and stupid bear, a descendant of ape lineage, and a tweezer for pubic hair," before cursing "the prattle from his filthy mouth" for even suggesting that Bedil provided literary instruction to the notables who supported him financially.[31]

ʿAṭā encountered a similarly boisterous salon atmosphere at Bedil's home by the riverside boat launch where Bedil held late-night gatherings for the city's musicians, Sufis, fellow poets, patrons, and sundry listeners. Such parties, according to attendees, reverberated with loud verse-singing and the exchange of witticisms, jokes, and anecdotes. Set amid drinking and tobacco smoking, these indeed were raucous affairs, with poets booming their recitations loudly enough to be heard in the alleys outside Bedil's home. Bedil recited poetry in a high, declarative singing voice, as witnessed by several writers who noted his musical abilities. Two of his students were also musicians: the dancing girl *Bhañwarī* (The Bumblebee), whom we met earlier, and Aḥmad ʿIbrat, a fiddle player upon whose death Bedil cried for days.[32] One of the compositions Bedil enjoyed singing was a famous "increment" poem (*mustazād*) by a classical-era poet named Ibn-e Ḥusām (d. 1356), who had settled in India late in life. "May your shape not be restricted by the confines of clothes," Bedil warbled in praise of a young man's attractive figure, "unless they are resewn / from a fresh tulip into a robe to fit your measurements, and from the rosebud—your hat" (*andām-e tū dar band-e qabā sharṭ nabāshad | illā kih badozand / az lālah-e serāb bah qadd-e tū qabā rā | w-az ġhunchah-ī kulāhī*).[33] These images conjure the tumescence of springtime buds (*lālah-e serāb*), comparing the budding flowers (*ġhunchah-e kulāh*) to a well-proportioned young man's state of arousal.[34] These suggestive lines likely caused a delightful start from Bedil's audience.

A humorous anecdote about Bedil's salon space survives from Ḳhwushgo's pen in which a poet usually aligned with Urdu literary history implicitly satirized Bedil by making fun of the poets of the Mughal court. Ḳhwushgo documented a colorful visit from Jaʿfar *Zaṭallī* (The Prattler) (1658?–1713), perhaps the most famous versifier of Delhi's bazaars, whose surviving compositions display performative, technical, and rhetorical flourishes based on his talent for turning the linguistic nuances of the street into withering political commentary on imperial politics. Like ʿAṭā, Zaṭallī earned an income writing satires and panegyrics for wealthy patrons, showing up at their doors with an invective in one hand and a eulogy in another—a hustle ʿAṭā himself would soon pursue.[35] According to this custom, Zaṭallī presented to Bedil a *maṡnawī* that he had written in praise of the poet-saint that also denigrated the verse of two court poets patronized under previous emperors: "What is the verse of imperial poets ʿUrfī and Faiẓī? Before you, each is a stupid owl" (*chih ʿurfī chih faiẓī bah pesh-tu push*).[36] He only presented the first line when Bedil stopped him, saying, "Oh, you've really honored me in coming here. But your humble Bedil is not worthy to hear epic poems usually reserved for only the true masters." Bedil was perhaps well aware of Zaṭallī's employment tactics, and he gave the writer two coins from his purse for writing the poem before sitting silently. Ḳhwushgo noted that "several of the gathering members, and especially me, made it known that if Zaṭallī had been compelled to recite the verse's second line, well-knowing what the rhyme would be, people would have been delighted, but [Bedil] refused."[37]

ʿAṭā likely encountered another character in Bedil's household who deserves mention: an enslaved man whom Bedil nicknamed *Maẓmūn* (The Theme). Bedil often summoned Maẓmūn in a loud voice to refresh the coals in the gathering space's hookahs set out for the many attending guests. While we do not know much about the poetic gleanings of Maẓmūn himself, Bedil's student Ḳhwushgo circulated a legend that the Iranian poet Ḥakīm Zulālī Ḳhwānsārī (d. 1615), a famous "new writer" of narrative poems, learned the trade of poetry (*kasab-e suḳhan*) in the presence of master poets while changing out the hookahs in the mushāʿirahs of ʿAbdullāh Hātifī (1454–1520).[38] Given the vociferous and frequent recitations among Bedil's gatherings, perhaps Maẓmūn, too, contracted verse abilities while adding new coals to the hookahs of Bedil's guests. However, the only literary reminder of Bedil's house servant (*ġhulām*) came from Ḳhwushgo, who memorialized Maẓmūn with poem built in double entendres: "Since Bedil's station is upon the throne of eloquence, / meaning is his mistress and *Maẓmūn* (The Theme) is his slave" (*bedil kih taḳhtgāh-e faṣāḥat maqām-e ū ast / maʿnī kanīz-e ū ast-o maẓmūn ġhulām-e ū ast*).[39] With his hefty staff, several wives, stable of horses, and collection of musical instruments, Bedil spent his remaining years there. Yet, by his own fanciful claim, he lived out these thirty-six years like an ascetic.[40]

Bedil's Instruction

While no tażkirah record exists depicting interchanges between Bedil and ʿAṭā, we can discern hints about the nature of their literary relationship by studying the two poets' parallel emulations. Another associate of Bedil whose relationship with the poet-saint yields insight into Bedil's character is the diarist Aʿẓmatullāh Ḥusainī *Beḳhabar* (The Uninformed) (d. 1730), who recorded several intriguing anecdotes about his own encounters with Bedil in salons. Beḳhabar was from an influential family based in Bilgram, a small town to the east of Delhi, and was likely an early, and notable, participant in later salon activities at Bedil's grave. On one trip to Delhi, he also escorted his relative, the poet and chronicler Ġhulām ʿAlī *Āzād* (The Liberated) (1704–1786), a teenager at the time of their journey.[41]

Beḳhabar's accounts reveal facets of the poet-saint's conduct and his understanding of stylistic distinction within the salon space, aspects of which were reflected in Bedil's general approach to his students.[42] In his diary, Beḳhabar recorded an anecdote in which Bedil provided friendly instruction to him during a mushāʿirah. Referring to himself in the third person, Beḳhabar wrote, "This humble servant once had the chance to run into [Bedil] where I found him to be truly the perfection of creation, of taste, of humility, and of delight." In his diary entry, Beḳhabar recounted the way he introduced himself to Bedil as a poet who wrote "proper verses about joy and indigence; there's been not another word on my tongue." To which Bedil responded with great ceremony: "Sir, after a time I have benefited from similarly stylish people (*ham-rang*) as yourself." Beḳhabar noted that he, himself, then proceeded to entertain the gathering by presenting three ġhazals, reading them aloud at his turn according to his rank (*ba-maqām-e ḳhwud bah ḳhwāndah shud*).

Beḳhabar began by reciting a snappy poem in the presence of the aged Bedil. The ġhazal referenced the salon space itself and, by design, attempted to elicit a chuckle from the salon attendees. "When the ending lines of a poem appear grand, the beauty of the first verse is demeaned," Beḳhabar intoned. He continued: "At the party, my low status pulls the rug from under the elites sitting on it" (*buland uftad chū maqṭaʿ past sāzad ḥusn-e maṭlaʿ rā / kashad pāʾīn-e maḥfil qadr-e man bālā nashīnān rā*).[43] This verse was well suited to the mushāʿirah space as it married stylistic form with thematic content. Beḳhabar implicitly commented on his own humble yet potentially dynamic place in the gathering by elaborating on the relationship between the opening verse (*maṭlaʿ*) and closing verse (*maqṭaʿ*) of the ġhazal, two important formal components integral to lyric poetry undergirding all performative recitations in the mushāʿirah context, even today.

At one level, Beḳhabar utilized the poetic device of opposite and same (*mutaẓādd wa muṭābaqah*) to foreground the role of the *maṭlaʿ* as the dawning or rising of the ġhazal itself, and the *maqṭaʿ* as the pause or cutting-off of the ġhazal, a quality further reflected in the contrasting of the words *buland wa pusht* and *bālā wa pāʾīn*—synonyms for high and low. Beḳhabar, in an ironically self-deprecating manner, called attention his low position in the hierarchy of the gathering. The poems themselves referenced the stratified nature of the event. Thus, the delight of the line stemmed from its performative tension with the words and context in which the verses were uttered aloud. Beḳhabar confirmed that he recited the lines, and, as the second line itself states, we are to assume he "brought down the house" (*pāʾīn kashīdan*)—another idiom implied in this meta-discursive verse—with his clever rhetoric. However, Bedil did not comment on this enlivening couplet: Beḳhabar recorded no praise from Bedil's lips.

Instead of lauding him, Beḳhabar noted that Bedil nitpicked an idiom Beḳhabar used in a different verse. During the mushāʿirah, Bedil objected to Beḳhabar's final couplet, in which Beḳhabar aimed to misdirect the audience through wordplays on various Persian-language idioms. Addressing himself in the second person, the junior poet recited, "I was unknowingly bled to death, O Beḳhabar, empty handed. / Even the rags I wear had to be counterfeited" (*ḳhūn shudam beḳhabar zi-dast-e tihī / jāmah-e faqr rang bāyad kard*). Beḳhabar's lines attempted to stretch exposition and image by using Persian idioms to further enhance his allusions to fate, poverty, and deception.[44] The conceit centered on the lyric's speaker, a hapless lover who was so poor that the only way he could bring any color into his life was by spilling his own blood to dye his rags so that even they appear counterfeit. But the language may have seemed overwrought, as someone in the audience called out to Bedil, "Mīrzā Ṣāḥib, I don't understand the aesthetics of this line." To which Bedil responded, "In poverty, only God destines the station where you stand. In short, this line is uninformed (*beḳhabar*); 'wealth remains in an empty hand'" (*daulat pāʾindah dar dast-e tihī-st*).

Thus, Bedil corrected the themes Beḳhabar attempted to enhance by suggesting an idiomatic Persian-language usage. In this mushāʿirah anecdote, Bedil rectified Beḳhabar's fumbled colloquialism by reining in the younger poet's daring use of stock phrases. Bedil did not object to the multiple meanings. Instead, Bedil further highlighted Beḳhabar's shortcomings with a double entendre on Beḳhabar's pen name, meaning "uninformed." Although this might seem harsh to contemporary readers, Bedil's critique probably came across as jocular to attendees, as this type of nitpicking opprobrium was part and parcel of the mushāʿirah ethos.[45] Bedil's fault-finding of a canny verse was interesting indeed for another reason as well, since, as we will see, there is evidence that, in his youth, Bedil himself may have differently assessed such feats of literary daring in a mushāʿirah.

BEDIL'S FIRST MUSHĀʿIRAHS

Bedil's own memories of former gatherings survive in his mystic autobiography "The Four Elements" (*Chahār ʿUnsur*). One anecdote Bedil recounts about his youth offers a more well-rounded depiction of his own salon verse and comportment when compared to how persnickety the figure of Bedil appears in Beḳhabar's story. In his autobiography, Bedil documented his early exposure to complex new literature in a salon hosted by his uncle

Mīrzā Ẓarīf in the city of Cuttack, Orissa.[46] Throughout "The Four Elements," Bedil casts himself as a miracle worker with innate poetry abilities. He extemporizes poems on mysticism and dreams himself interacting with respected teachers.[47] One episode captures Bedil as a teenager sitting at the margins of a local poetry gathering. The anecdote centers on his exchange with Ḥusain *Wālih* (The Astonished) (1582?–1664?), a writer in the new style (*ṭarz-e tāzah*) from the city of Herat.[48]

Wālih recited a narrative poem (*maśnawī*) about literary speech in which he argued that style (*rang* in literary terminology) and delight mattered above all else in the pursuit of capturing meaning:

There is no magic in artless beauty,
  stuffed with the mere rags of conversation.

If the gathering is filled with the beloved's voice,
  and if solitude is a mirror of the beloved's secrets,

without style (*rang*) this sedition turns common.
  But if style appears, what a typhoon there shall be!

Speech is a springtime, so do not ask the mere rose.
  So too with the roar of drunkenness—do not consider only wine.

Wherever speech blossoms like the rose, prick your ear.
  Make astonishment your homeland and remain still.[49]

chih saḥr ast īn ḥusn-e be-rang-o bū
  kih bālīdah dar kiswat-e guftagū

agar bazm labrez-e āwāz-e ū ast
  wa gar ḳhalwat āʾīnah-e rāz-e ū ast

bah be-rangī īn fitnah sāmān kunad
  agar rang gīrad chih ṭūfān kunad

suḳhan naubahār ast az gul mapurs
  hamīn shor-e mastī ast az mul mapurs

bah har jā suḳhan gul kunad gosh bāsh
  bah ḥairat watan sāz-o ḳhāmosh bāsh

Here, Bedil asserts that for Wālih, a poet who "arrayed metaphor with the new style," poetry was more than just the sum of its parts. That is to say, the delight of literary speech—likened to a storm, the springtime, and revelry—comes from the nuance of style as it develops themes such as of the rose and wine.

The conversation at Mīrzā Ẓarīf's gathering then veered off course when a jokester (*shoḳh*) brought up the overly clever conceits of "New Writers," as if to chide Wālih and imply that he was placing form over meaning with his "variegated poems" containing alternating diacritics.[50] Upon hearing this, the young Bedil, according to his own account, stepped forward to mediate, first crafting a ġhazal that utilized the complex new style, earning him cheers from the mushāʿirah circle. "The treasurers of the wealth of literary devices poured jewels of equity from the chests of their admiration," Bedil noted of their praise. Adolescent though he was, Bedil then closed the gathering with another ġhazal that echoed the sentiment of Wālih's concluding line (*bāsh* "Be!), as the young poet assuredly issued an edict to express literary speech within stylish registers. In the poem, Bedil plays on the double meanings carried by the names of famous poets to amplify his idea of newness:

Bang upon stillness! Be a poet off every nook and corner!
Shock your vision with the theatre of secrets (*asrār*)![51]

While praise for the banquet of meaning has turned exceedingly common,
until you also acknowledge the abundance (*faiẓ*) of the poet Faiẓī, refuse nothing.

Here, every breath again manifests the poet Jāmī's cup (*jām*) in its hand.
So, be a friend to the quality of that beauty unburdened.

From the ancestors, other than literary speech, nothing else is heard.
Thus, when it comes to poetry, be equitable toward all approaches.

It is difficult to raise an objection with the genealogists of poetic meaning.
Thus, speak with the power of the poet Anwarī, and dwell in the mysticism of the poet ʿAṭṭār.

But the hero of the tale must pass away into endless sleep. The End.
You are not worthy of existence until I say to you, "Arise!"

"If other than the songs of the departed nothing is worthy of certainty,
then we, too, must have already left ourselves. Fool, be vigilant!"[52]

bar khamoshī zan zabāndān-e dar-o dīwār bāsh
chashm-e tū ḥairān-e tamāshā-khānah-e asrār bāsh

niʿmat khwān-e maʿānī sakht ʿām uftādah ast
tā tū ham faiẓī barī iqrār be-inkār bāsh

jalwah īn jā har nafs jāmī digar dārad bah kaff
maḥram-e kaifīyat-e ān ḥusn-e be-takrār bāsh

az salaf ham juz sukhan chīzī digar nashanīdah'ī
pas kalām az har kih bāshad munṣif-e aṭwār bāsh

rafaʿ-e inkār az nisb-joyān-e maʿnī mushkil-ast
go bah qudrat-e anwarī dar maʿrifat-e aṭṭār bāsh

tābiʿ-e afsānah rā dar khwāb bāyad murd-o bas
qābil-e hastī nah-ī tā goyīmat bedār bāsh

juz nawā-e raftagān gar nīst manẓūr-e yaqīn
mā ham az khwud raftah-īm ai be-khabar hushyār bāsh

Bedil's poem emphasizes the importance of literature as representing a singular enduring link to the ancestors, such that attempts to reignite delight and originality had to be routed through the past by conforming to styles established by the progenitors. As Bedil sums up, "Don't mix the colors of autumn with a blooming rose garden, and don't cloud meaning's mirror with opaque colors."[53] For the pubescent Bedil, as it was for any writer participating in the era's recitational spaces, it was only well-hewn poetic speech, echoing the triumphs of past masters and recited aloud, that could perpetuate the salon's ideals of transitory delight and sociability.

These daring values may have faded in importance for Bedil by the time of his old age; his ideals may have been tempered over the years by the atmosphere of contentious contemporary literary debates to the extent that he had become more wary of some kinds of stylistic poetic speech. Thinking back to the scene with Bekhabar recounted earlier, instead of relishing Bekhabar's daring idioms, Bedil had responded to Bekhabar's lines by voicing a stiff set of poems that markedly lacked the spark struck by the youthful Bedil through his recitation at Mīrzā Ẓarīf's gathering. "O Bedil, you completely bowed your body. But to what end?" Bedil recited, addressing himself in the second person, "You humbly reached the ground, but did not stoop to the threshold" (*bedil hamah tan ḥalqah shudī lek chih ḥāṣil / dar khāk nashistī wa bar ān dar nah nashishtī*).[54] While nimbly cast, Bedil's austere lines lack delight. The couplet from Bedil's lips provided a momentary appraisal of the mushāʿirah in which the speaker's staged humility betrays literary inability or aloofness brought on by an insult. The elder poet's iciness was plain to the other attendees. The mushāʿirah closed with one attendee citing lines by the classical poet Ḳhāqānī Shirvānī (1122–1190), although Beḳhabar does not note who uttered them: "My neighbor heard my crying and said, / 'Well, the evening has come again for Ḳhāqānī!'" (*ham-sāyah shanīd nālah-am guft / ḳhāqānī rā digar shab āmad*)—a fitting conclusion to an evening of poetry recitation when Bedil was in a serious mood.[55]

Bedil's Favorite Poems by ʿAṯā

Bedil recorded several poems by his student ʿAṯā in his diary. Intriguingly, the poems he chose to document from his student's oeuvre reveal little to nothing of Bedil's stylistic impact. Instead, the lines reveal a shift in ʿAṯā's voice as he moved outside the classical register. Under Bedil's tutelage, ʿAṯa turned toward īhām, the playful style of misdirection favored by Delhi's poets in the early 1700s, and the young poet likewise gravitated toward Sufi devotional verse. In one couplet, ʿAṯā states, "Anyone can get some wisdom from an old sage. / But my sage, O Wine Drinkers, will be the Sage of Jām" (*rasad har kas az faiẓ-e pīrī ba-kām / buwad pīr-e mā mai-kashān pīr-e jām*). ʿAṯā proclaims his alliance to the foundational Sufi thinker Aḥmad-e Jām (1049–1114), a famously strong Sufi from Iran, while playing on the associations with drinking implied in the poem.[56]

In another devotional verse, ʿAṯā asserts his preferences for song-based forms, writing a quintain praising Ḳhwājah Ġharīb Nawāz, otherwise known as Muʿīn ud-Dīn Chishtī (1143–1236), the founder of the Chishti Sufi order in India:

I am a humble servant, burning with anguish.
Please favor me with kindness!
Instead, you slaughtered me with a wink and a flirt.
Such is the lord of kindness who favors his servants.
    I am the stranger, and you are host to strangers.

. . . .

I recognized you from the first.
I went door to door looking for you.
I searched and I found you.

I have made this gift of ʿAṯa, your servant
I am the stranger, and you are host to strangers.[57]

bandah-e ʿājiz-am ba-soz-o gudāz
bandah-e ḳhwīsh rā ba-luṭf nawāz
kushtī āḳhar marā ba-ʿishwah-o nāz
īn shah-e mihrbān bandah nawāz
mā ġharībam-o tū ġharīb nawāz

. . . .

mā zi-awwal shanāḳhtīm turā
dar ba-dar gashtah kāftīm turā
just-o jū kard yāftīm turā
īn ʿaṯā bandah sāḳhtīm turā
mā ġharībam-o tū ġharīb nawāz

Under Bedil's guidance and in Delhi's competitive literary market, ʿAṯā refashioned his literary voice several times over the course of his career as a poet of Delhi's salons and streets. These stylistic shifts and the assessments that ʿAṯā's friends and competitors made of them reflect how ʿAṯā's poetry shaped the salon space at Bedil's home, and how these verses impacted the poet-saint himself, ʿAṯā's fellow students, and members of the wider community that memorialized ʿAṯā's poetry and his connections to the poet-saint. Ḳhwushgo recalls ʿAṯā's demonstration of his strategic shifts in style through a ġhazal that ʿAṯā recited in Bedil's salon:

Your intoxicated eye comes to me in a vision.
It would appear like a glass of wine in my vision.

One night, the memory of his face caused a typhoon of tears.
My eyes drank in an ocean in their vision.

His hair and his turban at this length and breadth
would appear like a mountain and a desert in my vision.[58]

chashm-e mastish āmadam tā dar naẓar
mī numāyad jām-e ṣahbā dar naẓar

shab ba-yād-e rūʾish az ṯūfān-e ashk
dīdah-e mā dāsht daryā dar naẓar

resh-o dastār kih bā īn ṯūl-o ʿarẓ
mī numāyad koh-o ṣaḥrā dar naẓar

In this ġhazal from Bedil's mushāʿirah, ʿAṭā experimented with the imaginative approach (*ḳhayāl-bandī*, lit. "thought binding") favored by poets of the early sixteenth century by emulating a poem of Mīr Jalāl Muḥammad *Asīr* (The Prisoner) (1620–1648), one of the most important "thought-binding" poets still popular in India in the early 1700s and beloved by Bedil himself.[59] ʿAṭā's ġhazal features the same meter, end rhyme, and refrain—"my vision," and themes contained in Asīr's original poem:

I get drunk when those dark eyes come into my vision.
  What flirt would make such a show dance across my vision?

. . . .

My eyelashes would usually rain down red ochre.
  But the blank page, white as a cloud, is a desert in my vision.[60]

mastam-o ān chasm-e shahlā dar naẓar
  shoḳh mī raqṣad tamāshā dar naẓar

. . . .

mishq bārān mī kunad miẕhagān-e man
  kāġhaż-e abrī ast ṣaḥrā dar naẓar

ʿAṭā skillfully expounded on Asīr's themes to the delight of Ḳhwushgo and others at Bedil's mansion. By adopting the refrain—"my vision"—from Asīr's originating verse, ʿAṭā expanded metaphors associated with the dark, intoxicating eyes of the beloved and the endless tears shed by the ġhazal's speaker, who could weep blood-filled oceans of grief while gazing deep into a bottle of wine.

Verse Politics

The year of Bedil's death, 1720, came just one year after several political events of great significance that also found their way into the poetic expression of the time. In 1719, Mughal politics significantly shifted. This was the year that saw the new emperor, Muhammad Shah (r. 1719–48), secure his place on the throne. His rule came after a period of imperial unrest culminating in the assassination of the king Farruḳh Siyar (r. 1713–19). Historians of Mughal India have perpetuated two seemingly contradictory narratives to account for the socioeconomic and cultural import of these events. One of these narratives asserts that the era of Muhammad Shah engendered broad growth in artistic and cultural realms. The other narrative associates his epoch with the degradation of socioeconomic and political life, ideas that were supposedly echoed by innovative poets of the period, who professed anxiety about the rot brought in by the age.[61]

Recent scholarship amply demonstrates that the late Mughal social structure during this period indeed experienced significant changes. These shifts were marked, most notably, by the breakdown of divisions between the elite and commoners toward the creation of more accessible social institutions.[62] Indeed, people of the bazaar, from the lowest strata of Delhi's society up through the laboring professionals and guild members, were impacting Mughal society to a greater degree than previously documented on many fronts. Among them, new elites brought with them their own varied notions of sovereignty, respect, and history. Thus, at a moment of popular political change led by bazaar politics in the eighteenth century, versifiers who were a product of and witnessed the marketplace's fluctuations continued to echo the idea of an inclusive market for speech within their gatherings and writings.

Beginning in the sixteenth century, Persian writers began to represent literature as something to be weighed and assessed by elites and commoners alike, and this trope was taken up by the poets at focus in our 1720–60 chronology. In one anecdote, ʿAṭ̤ā successfully responded to the following Persian verse from the imperial pretender and prince Kām Bak̤hsh (1667–1709): "My bed is the earth, and funeral pastries served as my pillows" (*bistaram k̤hak-o k̤hisht bālīn ast*). ʿAṭ̤ā deferentially answered with proper courtly etiquette: "May I be sacrificed for you," before idiomatically completing the line: "But this is only one fate that has befallen my head" (*yakī az sar gużasht-e man īn ast*).[63] In another instance, ʿAṭ̤ā memorialized the emperor Aurangzeb (r. 1658–1707), redeeming the emperor's previous military defeat. In the 1650s, Aurangzeb failed to reconquer Kandahar from the Safavid incursion led by Shāh ʿAbbās II. As if single-handedly defeating the Safavid king through the power of his words, ʿAṭ̤ā recited in honor of Aurangzeb:

Because I am united with the warrior Aurangzeb,
  I went and confronted ʿAbbās the Second [in Kandahar]
I carve my drinking goblets from stone
  and I turn the [Safavids'] Qizilbash soldiers into shattered *pāshās*.[64]

ba-aurang ġhāzī chū yak dil shawam
  ba-ʿabbās raftah muqābal shawam

surū-hā ba-sangam tarāshā kunam
qizilbāsh rā pāsh pāshā kunam

Like his student ʿAṭā, Bedil also weighed in on Mughal imperial politics. In 1719, the year before he died, Bedil feared losing his own life due to a skirmish that took place in a mushāʿirah as the fog of war took hold in the salon. This involved Bedil's confrontation with Aʿẕmatullāh Ḥusainī Beḳhabar, the minor poet and diarist we met earlier who documented his instructive encounter with Bedil at a salon. The confrontation between Bedil and Beḳhabar began when Bedil wrote a chronogram commenting on the assassination of the emperor Farruḳh Siyar (r. 1713–19) by Ḥasan ʿAlī Ḳhān (d. 1722) and Ḥusain ʿAlī Ḳhān (d. 1720), courtiers from the Barhah clan of Sayyids who were effectively running the Mughal state. Bedil memorialized the year of Farrukh Siyar's killing when he wrote:

You saw all that they did to the noble king.
They inflicted one hundred tortures upon him for nothing.
I sought the date from Wisdom, and she said,
"They were treasonous to the mere scent of salt."[65]

dīdī kih chih ba shāh-e girāmī kardand
ṣad jūr-o jafā zi-rāh-e khāmī kardand
tārīḳh chū az ḳhirad bajustam fardmūd
sādāt bū-e namak ḥarāmī kardand [1131 AH]

Bedil's words employ the idiom of biting the hand of one who feeds you—that is to say, being disloyal to the one who gives you salt (*namak ḥarāmī kardan*). In other words, the courtiers violated the shāh's every hospitality. This was a gutsy accusation for Bedil to make against a political establishment with the power to kill a king.

Beḳhabar, Āzād's relative and Bedil's competitor, had a different view. Deftly intervening in Bedil's dialogue with "Wisdom" personified, Beḳhabar wrote a response contesting Bedil's position:

It is proper what they did to the mad king,
since it was completed on the doctor's orders.
According to the Hippocratic oath, Wisdom drafted history as a prescription:
"The Sayyids gave him the necessary medicine."[66]

ba shāh-e saqīm ān chih shāyad kardand
az dast-e hakīm har chih āyad kardand

baqarāṯ ḵhirad nusḵhah-e tārīḵh nawisht
sādāt dawā-īsh ān chih bayād kardand [1131 AH]

In the chronogram, Beḵhabar alludes to classical medical practices that used salt to treat illnesses, justifying the killing most likely because his family had garnered the Sayyids' support after the emperor's death. While in Bedil's eyes, the Sayyid brothers were perfidious as they spat on their rewards, Beḵhabar found their deeds therapeutic for the Mughal polity.[67] Beḵhabar's relative Āzād Bilgrāmī assessed this intriguing disagreement some decades later, noting that in gatherings, "quarrels would arise in a flash between the two factions" arguing about the assassination; "one party considered it just and one group thought it evil," alluding to the split being sectarian in nature.[68]

After these bold and challenging poems captured popular attention, Bedil was so afraid for his life that he left his mansion and grand lifestyle in Delhi for Lahore, where he remained for a year and a half.[69] What must it have been like for Delhi's poets to see their most revered literary leader flee the city in 1719? Was it understood as a major upset or just another argument that ran its course in the contentious salon circuit? I found no information from the taẕkirah record that could help us answer these questions. As the historian Sayyid Ahsanuzzafar points out, we get only a glimpse of Bedil's anxiety about the matter from a few letters. So too, an influential governor opportunely invited Bedil to shift to Hyderabad in the South.[70]

Bedil eventually returned to Delhi after the Sayyid brothers were defeated, but within less than a year, he was dead. After 1720, Delhi's poets no longer could hear Bedil singing erotic poetry, neither did they see him practicing his daily rounds of squats and pushups. Yet, Bedil's poetry was still recited from the tongues of his students, in the same gathering space that circulated his other products, notably medical concoctions he supposedly invented. The poet-saint's former students inherited Bedil's sociable legacy in literary and material forms, to be memorialized in a tomb and on paper in a weighty tome of his verse kept by the grave, from which they recited at each anniversary. Both elites and commoners convened at the posthumous salon. Among the commoners were those devotees who sought the poet-saint's intercession by praying over his bones, as they would at any of the shrines dotted throughout Delhi's neighborhoods. Thus, some attendees treated Bedil's tomb, texts, and salon itself as a public gift (*ṣalā-e ʿāmm*), secured through the power of a pious land endowment.

Securing Literary Inheritance

Upon his death, Bedil's family, students, and colleagues labored to preserve the poet-saint's intellectual and material inheritance. Burying the poet-saint in the mansion's courtyard, a decision that Bedil himself had decreed, secured both material property and literary heritage, turning a private gift that a patron had made to Bedil into the public gift of a shrine with commercial potential. Within Muslim societies, the *ṣalā-e ʿāmm* or public gift consisted of presenting food, water, or any other means of sustenance for public benefit. Shrine attendees distributed food to the hungry and ladled out water into a passerby's cupped hands from a stand. Among writers at the time, the term *ṣalā-e ʿāmm* also appeared in reference to parties and gatherings of elites throughout Delhi—these exclusionary gatherings were also cast, perhaps contradictorily, as "public gifts."[71]

Soon after his death, Bedil's surviving relatives, most likely his remaining wives, secured the poet-saint's shrine property as a type of pious land endowment, known as a *waqf*, to maintain the inheritance of Bedil's persona, property, and texts.[72] The historian Chanchal B. Dadlani describes how elite women such as Bedil's relatives played an instrumental role in shaping the civic environment through land endowments in Delhi's early 1700s.[73] Across the Muslim world, shrines and associated kinds of real estate were considered important sites for accruing capital, preserving inherited property, and serving the ritual needs of often multi-confessional communities. But legal steps had to be taken to secure such shrines' pious import, earning potential, and provisions for long-term maintenance. These legal steps were necessary because the Islamic system governing at the time referenced the Qur'an, primarily in *Sūrah un-Nisā* ("The Women"), as the primary reference point to stipulate how estates were to be divided proportionally among immediate heirs.[74]

In turn, the sole religiously legitimate method to avoid splitting up property, and to secure greater inheritance for some family members—usually women—was to establish a legal hindrance (the meaning of *waqf*) whereby mosques, shrines, tombs, graveyards, public kitchens, baths, and any land associated with them could be held in trust for individuals, for institutions, or for the public. For instance, Muslim women in sixteenth-century Jerusalem set aside pious endowments for a soup kitchen that achieved long-lasting social and material standing.[75] Non-Muslims also utilized *waqf* for material and political aims.[76] Poets, too, established *waqfs* for their graves and for whatever infrastructure was built around them, including soup kitchens.[77]

The tomb of the Persian-language poet Saʿdī in Shiraz, an Iranian city with many poets' mausoleums, hosted a soup kitchen that was popular among the elite and commoners alike.[78]

Provisions afforded through *waqf* could likewise apply to transportable items, like horses, slaves, weapons, or—as concerns us here—books.[79] Poets' collected works had long represented a key material dimension of Islamic piety and occult beliefs, witnessed most profoundly in the bibliomancy practices associated with the poet Shams ud-Dīn *Ḥāfiz* (The Keeper of the Qur'an) (1315–1390). Like Ḥāfiẓ's shrine in Shiraz, Bedil's shrine was also a pilgrimage destination (*ziyārat-gāh*) erected to host all-night gatherings for those seeking the poet-saint's intercession (*muʿtaqidān*).[80] Bedil's student Ānand Rām *Mukhliṣ* (The Loyal) (1699–1750) hinted at other parallels between Bedil and Ḥāfiẓ by quoting a couplet from Ḥāfiẓ's dīwān that referenced the ritual importance of books: "Never would he die, he whose heart has been revived by love. My durability has thus been proven in the account book of the world" (*hargiz namīrad ān-kih dil-ish zindah shud bah ʿishq / ṡabt ast bar jarīdah-e ʿālam dawām-e mā*).[81] Ḥāfiẓ's dīwān was perhaps the most famous ritual text used for prognostication, whereby readers asked a question, randomly opened a page from Ḥāfiẓ's works, and pointed to a verse for a cryptic answer.[82]

Later in the 1700s, other poets' tombs across Delhi emerged as protected endowments, further cementing the emulative textual, spiritual, and material processes used to institutionalize urban literary traditions as public gifts. The tombs of Bedil's former students ʿAndalīb and Saʿdullāh Gulshan (Naqshbandi adherents who are central figures in chapters 2 and 3) became important pilgrimage destinations in the late 1700s and still stand protected in Delhi through *waqf* provisions; also, the Iranian émigré Muḥammad ʿAlī *Ḥazīn* (The Grieved) (1692–1766), featured in chapters 3 and 4, donated his lands to the Shīʿī population of Varanasi for a mosque, some shrines, a graveyard, and later his own tomb, all comprising an area known today as the *Dargāh-e Fatmān*.[83]

While legal stipulations dictated that a local judge should administer pious endowments, Bedil's grave remained under family control. Specifically, it was managed by Mirzā Muḥammad Saʿīdullāh, the son of ʿIbādullāh, Bedil's maternal cousin in Patna, from whom Bedil frequently sought financial support during the uncertain years of his professional development. Bedil's nephew Saʿīdullāh oversaw the ritual and commercial aspects of the tomb for at least twenty years, as first documented by Bedil's student and biographer Ḳhwushgo, and later the diarist Dargāh Qulī Ḳhān (1710–1766) around 1739.[84] Hence, Bedil's tomb and text formed a nexus point to legitimate literary gatherings and verse singing during this period.

Text and Ritual at the Grave

Bedil's complete works, personal effects, tomb, and mansion (perhaps the most valuable portion of the poet-saint's estate) all constituted part of a *waqf* complex created for his heirs, including any of his surviving spouses and his extended family; none of Bedil's children survived to adulthood. The *waqf* complex also served the interests of his former students, but this aspect of the gift was legitimated through the public-facing aspect of the shrine institution. Amid the activities of candle lighting and the bustle of a small medicine market, the caretakers of Bedil's tomb prepared and served food to devotees, providing their own form of a public gift at the shrine.[85] The food dispensary at Bedil's grave inspired one reciter to craft a poem at the gathering in the late 1730s, proclaiming: "Since the day that pain and suffering over you became my guests, / the main dish I serve is a salt-rubbed kabob: my heart" (*ġham-o dard-e tū az ān roz kih mahmān-e man ast / dil namak sūd kabāb ast kih bar ḳhwān-e man ast*).[86] None of the diarists who visited the grave noted what type of food the dispensary served, only that it was a hot preparation (*ṯaʿām-e puḳhtah*).[87] The verse, uttered by a student in attendance at the graveside mushāʿirah, alluded to the soup kitchen by referencing kabobs made from lamb heart, a delectable treat. But in the context of pining for his object of affection, the poem's speaker can only serve up his own heart, salted to stave off melancholy and roasted in the flames of love to satiate the ravenous emptiness left by rejection.

Sufi practices in early modern South Asia revolved around the circulation and reception of texts that had various degrees of mundane and extraordinary uses such that devotees recited or sang verse for ritual contemplation and religious expression. Further, within this "literacy-aware society," books were tied to charismatic individuals.[88] At Bedil's posthumous mushāʿirah and among the gatherings of his inheritors, readers and reciters relished their engagements with poetry works and stories, providing clues for how Bedil's former students and graveside devotees understood the role of Bedil's verse and sociability within a Sufi recitational setting. Bedil's student and biographer Ḳhwushgo described the setting as a "colorful congregation" (*majmaʿ-e rangīn*) in which, advancing poet by poet, "each recited a ġhazal from [Bedil's] collected works and then presented a jewel of their own."[89] As we will soon see, among them was Bedil's student ʿAṯā.

Another former student wrote, "Having gathered upon that hallowed ground (*ḳhāk-e pāk*), [the poets of the city] would strike up inviting conversation (*ṣuḥbat-e garm*) and would sing magical verses in recitation."[90] The poet-saint's ġhazals were recited from an autograph copy of Bedil's complete works (*kulliyāt*) that was stored at the grave. Its pages were rumored to hold 99,000 couplets and to weigh nearly twenty-five pounds.[91]

Whatever the book's girth might have been, its title page exhorted readers to use the collected works for their own ethical enrichment:

> O mirror-natured one, you provide guidance
> in this business of morality, never revealing a fault.
> But my collection of thoughts is a public resource (*ṣalā-e ʿām*)
> Peruse it and seize a portion of solace.[92]

> *ai āʾīnah ṭabʿ tū irshād pażīr*
> *dar kasb-e fawāʾid nanumāʾī taqṣīr*
> *majmūʿah-e fikr-mā ṣalā-e ʿām ast*
> *sairī kun wa qismat-e tasallī bar gīr*

The mirror-natured one invoked in Bedil's verse could be interpreted as both God and as an object of affection. The mirrors of the heart, an important Sufi trope, provided inner direction by reflecting God's wisdom. In contrast to the interior mirrors of the heart, Bedil's literary works (a collection of ideas or *majmūʿah-e fikr*) addressed the public (*ʿāmm*) by offering themselves up as something any reader or listener could consider, implying that the book was itself a mirror reflecting higher realities.[93]

Nevertheless, Bedil's collected works circulated at the posthumous mushāʿirah were not employed for bibliomancy in the same way as Ḥāfiẓ's dīwān was used. Bedil's collected works proffered a kind of mystical aid, parallel to but distinct from the occult-oriented use linked with Ḥāfiẓ's dīwān, which was consulted for individual bibliomancy. Sitting in public trust at the tomb, Bedil's collected works were directed toward Delhi's population at large, to be read aloud for cultivating piety within everyone in earshot, including commoners and elites alike. Bedil's opening verse in the graveside book urged readers to peruse the collection of poems (*majmūʿah-e fikr*) to find any amount of consolation (*qismat-e tasallī bar giriftan*). Touting its general usefulness, Bedil called his text a public resource or *ṣalā-e ʿāmm* for achieving spiritual or literary solace.[94]

Twenty years after Bedil's burial, Muḥammad Nāṣir *ʿAndalīb* (The Nightingale) (1694–1759), an inheritor of the poet-saint's literary scene, circulated

Bedil's public gift poem. A Sufi leader who was well connected within the intellectual network of Delhi's Naqshbandi brotherhood, ʿAndalīb wove Bedil's original quatrain verses into his own poetry at a gathering sometime in 1739. At the memorial of his "professed teacher" (*pīr-e baiʿat*), the final leader of the Naqshbandi brotherhood Muḥammad Zubair (d. 1739), ʿAndalīb paired his plain-spoken quatrain with Bedil's opening lines from the tomb-side collected works, augmenting the public gift motif:

In the pot, I have not cast oil and honey.
    Neither have I sifted black musk nor saffron.
If you want the correct flavors, then taste
    the water and salt (*āb-o namak*) I have stirred together.

O mirror-natured one, you provide guidance
    in this business of morals, never revealing a fault.
This collection of my thoughts is a soup kitchen (*ṣalā-e ʿāmm*).
    Drink of it and be satiated with a portion.[95]

dar deg nah roġhan-o ʿasl reḳhtah-īm
    nī mushk nah zaʿfrān dar-ū beḳhtah-īm
gar żāʾiqah-e darust dārī bachashī
    āb-o namakī baham bar āmeḳhtah-īm

ai āʾīnah ṭabʿ tū irshād pażīr
    dar kasb-e fawāʾid nanumāʾī taqṣīr
majmūʿah-e fikr-mā ṣalā-e ʿāmm ast
    sairī kun wa qismat-e tasallī bar gīr

ʿAndalīb's verse provided interesting food for thought, indeed. His simple lines comprise only the bare elements of a recipe, salt and water (*āb-o namak*), perhaps derived from the tears of a weeping devotee. When mixed with Bedil's headier lines, the concoction became a dish worthy of a public gift through which the listener could obtain spiritual sustenance.

Besides reading it for wisdom, devotees had an additional use for Bedil's collected works. Remarkably, they weighed their children against the book. They first set the child and the hefty tome on one side of a large scale, and then they would place jewels and coins on the other side until the scales were balanced. The riches would be donated to the tomb's caretakers.[96] The practice of donating according to a human weight was associated with the Mughal court, specifically a ceremony that began during the reign of

Humayun (r. 1530–40) and continued among his descendants, whereby on both the emperor's solar and lunar birthdays amounts of precious metals and robes of honor equivalent to his majesty's weight were distributed to commoners.[97] The emperor Jahangir (r. 1605–27) observed that the weighing ceremony (*jashn-e wazn*) was of Hindu origin, called *tulādān*.[98] At Bedil's grave, the ritual, which made a playful spectacle of donation, served to symbolically express the profound value placed on both the book and the child. But unlike the soup kitchen, which required the expenditure of time and money to feed the shrine's visitors, the ritual involving the book and the children brought wealth to Bedil's shrine and its proprietors to be used toward their collective maintenance.

Another notable commercial venture associated with the shrine was observed with scorn by a diarist around 1739. In the courtyard lit with candles and crowded with attendees, Bedil's nephew Saʿīdullāh sold medical concoctions purported to be of Bedil's invention. It seems that Bedil must have considered the two-rupee daily allowance from his patron to be insufficient; rarely did the bureaucratic finance offices of royals ever fully remit agreed-upon stipends. Bedil developed his practice of manufacturing various kinds of medicines that were sold throughout the city to supplement his income. After Bedil's death, the formulas, reproduced by his nephew Saʿīdullāh, remained for decades similarly popular throughout Delhi.[99]

In his youth, Bedil had cultivated an interest in amulets and healing practices, which he studied at the same time as he began composing verse. Although he claimed to have renounced occult medical practices in his mid-twenties, Bedil later in life resumed concocting and selling medicines, perhaps motivated by the many expenses generated by his large household.[100] Indeed, the local medicine market of Delhi was immensely profitable. North of Bedil's home and near the imperial mosque at a piazza called Saʿdullāh Ḳhān Square, the city's denizens bought a wide variety of pills and electuaries, with crowds of men seeking correctives for sexual dysfunction, masturbation suppressants, and remedies for venereal diseases.[101] Bedil himself was familiar with such aphrodisiacs. Before he passed away, his material and physical requirements had expanded with three additional wives coming under his care after his first marriage. Ḳhwushgo noted that Bedil occasionally ingested powdered arsenic (*zarnīḳh-e kushtah*) to improve sexual performance in his old age.[102] In fact, procreation may have been a point of anxiety for the poet-saint as, in his late sixties, he produced his one and only son, presumably with a much younger wife. Sadly, this child died.[103] With no direct heirs, Bedil's literary, sociable, and material estates were thus preserved as a public gift for the throngs of pilgrims and poets who visited his tomb and kept his mushāʿirah going.

The Students' Arguments

Soon after his burial, there emerged a cohort of dissenters who argued over Bedil's place within Delhi's literary pantheon. Ḳhwushgo's home witnessed a flurry of poetry recitation when he hosted ʿAṭā and many other controversial figures linked to Bedil as students, fans, or critics. Although Ḳhwushgo did not specify its frequency in his writings, from his notebook it is apparent that a regularly scheduled mushāʿirah was held on a fixed day—likely monthly—when Ḳhwushgo hosted the city's poets, great and humble alike, claiming that nearly one hundred poets would come to his home. After eating and drinking together, they would recite ġhazals one by one, presenting paper copies of favored compositions to the senior poets present.[104] The view from Ḳhwushgo's gatherings depicts the uneven terrain associated with Bedil's words and memory, forming a milieu that debated Bedil's literary position.

For instance, one poet with sharp opinions about Bedil refused Ḳhwushgo's invitations. This was Muḥammad Ṣādiq *Ilqā* (The Infusion) (d. 1745?), a poet famous for his sharp opinions and Sufi ideals. Ilqā was a descendant of former Hindus who had converted to Islam at some point. In Delhi, Ilqā busied himself providing Islamic education for Hindu boys, cultivated his talents for crafting chronograms and solving puzzles, and enjoyed drinking at poetry recitals.[105] Ilqā's overindulgence in spirits likely caused him to audaciously comment on a colleague's long gray hair, finding it unbecoming and not suitable for a poet. The insult was met with the response that Ilqā's beard was no better than the pubic hair on the testicles of rapscallions.[106] Ḳhwushgo tried to reason with him, but the poet kept refusing on various pretexts and closed the matter by saying that as opposed to hosting a mushāʿirah, Ḳhwushgo's money would be best placed in Ilqā's hands so he could spend it on booze and prostitutes (*sharāb wa shāhid*)—the true aims of any poet by his accounting.[107] In sum, Ilqā was a proper dervish who would have clearly been a welcomed and entertaining presence at a recital but whose behavior could also earn scorn or breed contention.

Indeed, besides having fakir-like tendencies, Ilqā also held some sharp opinions about poetic style, influenced by his friendship with a revered poet from the previous generation. This was Nāṣir ʿAlī Sirhindī (1638/39?–1697), the most famous ġhazal writer of the late seventeenth century, whose notoriety still shaped Delhi in the 1720s. As in the case of Bedil, Nāṣir ʿAlī's fame, within his lifetime, reached as far as Iran, Central Asia, and—so it was rumored—even Baghdad.[108] Nāṣir ʿAlī Sirhindī also possessed an infamously rakish nature and was devoted to booze and prostitutes. "Now he was a poet," Ilqā mentioned to Ḳhwushgo on one occasion when bemoaning the lack of talent in their literary scene, "but he passed away. Bedil possessed some understanding of literary speech, but he, too, is now dead."[109] Although Ḳhwushgo records no reaction, Ilqā's statement may have been a startling one for Ḳhwushgo to have heard, considering Ḳhwushgo's reverence for the poet-saint. Ilqā's faint praise of Bedil likely was motivated by an occasion when Ilqā lampooned a ġhazal from a Mughal official. To ameliorate this injustice, Bedil and other noted poets composed responses to the official's poem, thereby legitimating the official's words in the face of Ilqā's jokes.[110] Whatever the case, Ilqā's invocation of the two poets alluded to a growing popular lore about purported literary contests between Bedil and Nāṣir ʿAlī.

In line with Ilqā's views, chroniclers often cast Bedil and Nāṣir ʿAlī as literary competitors.[111] Beginning in the 1680s, diarists depicted interchanges between Nāṣir ʿAlī and Bedil that sought to position them as opposites. In one such interchange, the two poets debate semiotics. Bedil recited a ġhazal that went, "The mirror of my state was not reflective. / With these many manifest words, I remained hidden like [their true] meaning" (*nashud āʾīnah-e kaifiyat-e mā ẓāhir ārāʾī / nihān māndīm chūn maʿnī bah chandīn lafẓ-e paidāʾī*). Nasir ʿAlī objected to Bedil's utterance, stating, "Doesn't meaning depend on the word? Wherever an utterance is manifest, its meaning should undoubtedly be clear." Bedil had a quick rejoinder, and smiling, he quipped, "You think that a meaning is dependent on the word, but an utterance is not that much." Bedil continued, "Meaning is 'that from which it comes' (in Arabic *min hethu hiya hiya*) and never arises from a word itself."[112]

One reason that chroniclers and poets framed Bedil and Nāṣir ʿAlī as literary opposites concerned their distinct professional lives. While Bedil propagated a mystical self-conceit and avoided writing panegyrics for pay, Nāṣir ʿAlī lived as a journeyman writer, seeking patrons in North India, Kashmir, and the Deccan. For high nobles in these locales, he wrote panegyrics and held poetry recitals, and from them he also received fabulous rewards. Nāṣir ʿAlī was a wily contender in the writers' market Bedil famously abhorred despite his own humble beginnings.[113]

Yet other anecdotes cast Nāṣir ʿAlī as the victor in literary competitions. A set of legends narrated Bedil's first meeting with Nāṣir ʿAlī. Many of Bedil's "ruined" students with "twisted understandings" of literature had begun appearing before Nāṣir ʿAlī. After several such encounters, Nāṣir ʿAlī pointedly asked Bedil, "My friend, tell me: how many more [literary] themes (*maẓāmīn*) have you slaughtered today?"[114] Another legend recorded in the 1740s held that Bedil came to visit Nāṣir ʿAlī and shared with him a couplet that went, "Never throw any hard stones at the shaiḳh / For there might be a bottle sleeping under his arm, you lush" (*mazan bar shaiḳh sangī-e saḳht dastī / kih mīnā dar baġhal ḳhuftah ast mastī*). Nāṣir ʿAlī said to the poet-saint, "You've composed an excellent second line!" Bedil responded, "Why don't you write a tribute (*taẓmīn*) in a couplet based on the first line?" Bedil was urging the poet to compose a new poem by incorporating the first line of the couplet. True to his character, Nāṣir ʿAlī issued a biting response: "It is not acceptable that I compose a tribute on one of my own hemistiches."[115] Not only was Nāṣir ʿAlī refusing to honor Bedil's poetry, but he was also accusing the poet-saint of plagiarism, claiming the delectable line as his own.

However, chroniclers have likely overstated the depth of the contention between Bedil and Nāṣir ʿAlī. Bedil recorded a vast amount of Nāṣir ʿAlī's poems in his notebook, calling him a "King in the Realm of Literary Speech" (*malik-e mulk-e suḳhan*), and the poet-saint wrote a chronogram memorializing Nāṣir ʿAlī's passing.[116] To cast doubt on the consistency of the animosity between other purportedly warring pairs, even the controversial character Ilqā was later identified by historians as a direct student of Bedil.[117] Despite professing sharp opinions about Bedil's poetry, Ilqā attended the graveside festivities and composed at least one poem modeled on Bedil's own verse, a form selected at random from the poet-saint's collection when it circulated in the gathering. In the battlefield language of the salons, Ilqā intoned:

> I landed such a strike upon generosity with only two hands—
> I have never been wounded, drinking the luster of someone's blade with two hands.[118]

> *zadīm sīlī zad bar karam zi-bas bah do dast*
> *naḳhwurdah-īm chū zaḳhm āb-e teġh-e kas bah do dast*

Bedil's verse, as selected from the graveside collected works, set the formal aspects for Ilqā to model in terms of its rhyme, refrain, and meter. Bedil's verse recited from his collected works ran:

He never says a prayer for anyone, raising his two hands—
unless it's for the wine carafe, smashed at the two hands of the nightwatchman.[119]

ijābatī nadamīd az duʿā-e kas bah do dast
magar sabū shakanad gardan-e ʿasas bah do dast

Few verses in the Persian ġhazal corpus end with the striking refrain "with two hands" (*bah do dast*), an image linked with fate that appears evocative but constricting at the formal level. Ilqā's verse presents the image of drinking water from one's own two cupped hands, calling to mind the act of generosity from whoever poured the liquid. But false generosity is dangerous, especially from a newly sharpened sword shimmering like water. Bedil's two-handed verse, in contrast, plays with several idioms. The image of two hands being raised usually calls prayer to mind, but such a posture is never adopted by the cruel beloved, who only raises his hands to say a prayer for the jugs of wine broken under the truncheons of morality police.[120] As the 1700s progressed, and Delhi's literary society branched out in various directions, poets magnified the relational aspect of Bedil in their verse, as the poet-saint's posthumous gathering both preserved memories of Bedil and reflected the changing tastes of those poets and former students who maintained the salon space they once shared with him.

Satirizing the Poet-Saint

Like that of his teacher Bedil, the financial status of ʿAṯā waxed and waned over his career. For a time, ʿAṯā cultivated an image of indigence, just like his teacher Bedil did, claiming to be satisfied with two eggs per day. Referencing these brushes with economic ruin, ʿAṯā stated in a verse with a pun on his name, "It is inauspicious to leave a 'gift' (*ʿaṯā*) at the door of poverty. / May you keep learning, keep considering, and keep recognizing this" (*ʿaṯā dar muflisī ke ṭok rahtā / samajhte būjhte pahchānte raho*).[121] Yet, in contrast to his teacher, who always dealt judiciously with his patrons, ʿAṯā wittily and sarcastically confronted those who would support his literary career. Ānand Rām *Mukhliṣ* (The Loyal) (1699–1750), another student of Bedil with a close connection to ʿAṯā, noted this and denounced ʿAṯā's means of professional advancement, stating, "From among each one of these hapless people of high status, [ʿAṯā] earned a salary by insulting them or by [writing] a few satirical lines."[122] Like Zaṭallī, ʿAṯā's ability to pen satires of noted men proved profitable, garnering him enough income to maintain a land grant and to buy a mansion in his hometown of Amroha (123 km east of Delhi) while also keeping up a middling palanquin in Delhi. Muk̲hliṣ hinted at the perfidy of ʿAṯā's transition from panegyrist to satirist, noting the irony when ʿAṯā lampooned an official who had formally vouched for him—this official was Sāqī Muḥammad Mustaʿidd K̲hān, the emperor's court historian.[123]

Thus, the final phase of ʿAṯā's literary development was marked by satire and the unique registers of the bazaar, leading later historians to link the satires that expanded ʿAṯā's fortunes with those of Zaṭallī, his more famous contemporary.[124] For a time, ʿAṯā traveled through Delhi's streets in a litter carried by servants. These kinds of displays propped up ʿAṯā's social position, and he soon gained entrance into the courts (*darbārs*) of various lords. ʿAṯā's status as a notable elevated his position in Bedil's salon, where ʿAṯā's witticisms and satires were enjoyed and encouraged. Unlike the poet-saint's attitude toward Zaṭallī, Bedil welcomed ʿAṯā's satires into the gathering space, on one occasion praising ʿAṯā for writing a satire about the poet-saint himself. Bedil stated, "ʿAṯā earns the right to satirize me because of his emulation and discipleship to my poetry," and then scribed the satire into his own diary.[125] Thanking Bedil for this gesture, ʿAṯā then composed a quatrain to memorialize the event:

Bedil, the lord of the spheres, the perfection of every craft,
  from the recesses of his eye, glanced upon me.
By means of the favored pen box and diary,
  He granted me the rank of vizier in the kingdom of speech.[126]

bedil shah-e iqlīm kamāl-e har fan
  az goshah-e chashm tā naẓar dāsht ba-man
az rū-e ʿināyat-e qalam-dān-o bayāẓ
  farmūd marā wizārat-e mulk-e suk̲han

ʿAṯā's quatrain perpetuated the conceit shared among Bedil's followers that the poet-saint was a lord in the domains of literature.

In contrast to the praise they earned from Bedil, ʿAṯā's satirical poems were resented by Muk̲hliṣ and also alienated others in Bedil's circle. Indeed, Muk̲hliṣ once used ʿAṯā's satires as a pretext to slander ʿAṯā and degrade his literary style. Muk̲hliṣ judged ʿAṯā's writings as "from a world of tumult (*az ʿālam-e shahr āshob*) written about men of standing (*arbāb-e taḥrīr*)" and crushingly panned them as nothing more than "hodgepodge writings" (*khichaṛī nāmah*)—that is, meaningless as gruel of boiled lentils and rice.[127] In the early 1700s, the most damning insult poets slung at each other was the accusation of meaninglessness. Poets could stomach allegations of plagiarism, of butchering an idiom, or of having poor taste. In contrast, accusations of meaninglessness implied that writers' words lacked all distinction and thus failed to achieve recognition within Delhi's market for speech. In chapter 4, we will analyze some particularly heated performances of these kinds of damning allegations as indicative of the power struggles in salons or on paper that emerged over this period.

Indeed, rather than reflecting a purely objective assessment of ʿAṭā's style, Mukhliṣ's withering assessment of ʿAṭā's verse as meaningless preceded from a personal conflict that erupted between the two men at a mushāʿirah. The incident occurred in Mukhliṣ's own home where ʿAṭā recited a few verses in light meters on classical themes, paper copies of which he then entrusted to Mukhliṣ to be cited in Mukhliṣ's taẕkirah. But while there, ʿAṭā irked Mukhliṣ by flirting with Muḥammad Sharaf ud-Dīn *Payām* (The Message) (d. 1745/46), a young writer whom Mukhliṣ treated as a confidant and held in high regard for his literary accomplishments and their shared delight in frequenting Delhi's coffee houses.

To apprehend the larger meaning of Mukhliṣ's attack on ʿAṭā's verse, we must understand more about Payām's literary persona and how he figured in this vignette. For one thing, Payām's poems, which Mukhliṣ assiduously copied, were strikingly complex. In the style of the "New Writers" (*tāzah-goʾiyān*), Payām had once recited a couplet that generated some skepticism among other writers for its daring use of a classical theme, which he rerouted with a repeating wordplay that sought to trick listeners. In this case, the joke was on his own pen name: "Will my addled brains spill out of my ear canal? / The lamenting cry of 'I am Payām!' has still not been heard" (*maġhz-e majnūn zi-rah-e gosh bīrūn khwāhid rekht / nālah-e zār-e payām-am nah shanīdah ast hanūz*).[128] The poem, with its gory central image, alluded to the legendary lover Majnūn, who went mad and became the target of children who pelted him with stones, presumably hitting him hard enough to cause an acute cerebral herniation. Alluding to this image, the poem casts its speaker as having gone so crazy that he has lost all sense of himself.

Taken with Payām's literary style, ʿAṭā complimented the young poet's fresh ideas (*tāzagī*) and devised a double entendre of his own on Payām's name, "The Message."[129] ʿAṭā stated, "Even kisses sent by 'Message' (*payām*) are not bereft of freshness (*tāzagī*)." In kind, Payām quickly improvised a response wordplay on ʿAṯā's name, "The Gift." "O Friends, pay no heed to 'the Gift'; it was presented out of impertinence (*nā-durūstish*)."[130] While it would not necessarily have been considered obscene, it does reflect the normative (yet ridiculed) homoerotic sentiments of urbane society propagated by men of standing during this time before this type of wordplay would begin to fall from favor by the late 1750s.

This teasing and flirtation with Muḳhliṣ's dear friend Payām irked Muḳhliṣ, prompting him to refer to ʿAṯā's reḳhtah compositions as a "hodgepodge" (*khichaṛī nāmah*). Muḳhliṣ's condemnation of ʿAṯā's poetry was not shared by Bedil nor among Bedil's students. For example, Ḳhwushgo noted that such "compositions had earned the attention of Ānand Rām Muḳhliṣ, the pulse-taker of subtle discernment (*nabẓ-dān-e bārik bīnī*)," deferentially alluding to Muḳhliṣ as an overly critical medical technician. Ḳhwushgo found ʿAṯā to be an "ornament of gatherings" (*zīnat ul-majlis-hā*), displayed in his "zesty behavior" (*ḥarakāt-e namkīn*) and inclination toward humor and satire.

In his final stylistic shift, ʿAṯā embraced the flirtatious registers that caused Muḳhliṣ to damn him with accusations of meaninglessness, embracing idioms of the bazaar—the stylish phrases of ruffians (*lūṯiyān*) and young rakes (*bāñkah-hā*) whose unique language was the literary register of the streets and, increasingly, the salon.[131] Taking up the homoerotic themes from Muḳhliṣ's gathering and his flirty speech with Payām, ʿAṯā composed in the eloquent tongue of mischievous rakes who dipped into both Hindi and Persian grammars:

A beard is not suitable for a rake who is a mere boy.
 It is nothing more than a spider's web and is quite lacking.
On my face have grown some twisting mustaches,
 and in the eyes of the young rakes they are like a scorpion's stinger.[132]

ḍhārī nabuwad lāʾiq-e ān bāñkah kih chhū ast
 īn jālā-e makkaṛ hamah hech ast wa ṭharū ast
bar chahrah-e man yih ḳham nikāle muñchheñ
 dar dīdah-e bāñka-hā chū ḍāñk-e bichchhū ast

Echoing a theme from his Persian composition about the beloved's hair and turban being like dramatic landscape, ʿAṯā's unique style twisted the image of the beloved, usually a young man with a slight beard, to instead refocus on the sweaty street fighters strutting around with curled mustaches. According to the historian Dānish Faiẓān, ʿAṭā comported himself like one of Delhi's stylish rakes (*bāñkah-hā*), and from this position, ʿAṭā crafted a distinct literary voice through his "roguish poetry" (*shiʿr-e rindānah*) that the people of Delhi still recited in the streets as late as 1806.[133]

Cultivated in Bedil's salon, such distinctions propelled ʿAṭā's voice into the records of subsequent writers who still heard ʿAṭā's poetry and legends of his prowess in the salon and on the streets throughout the eighteenth century.[134] Nearly fifty years after ʿAṭā's death, Mīr Ġhulām Ḥasan (1727/28?–1786), a mushāʿirah host and tażkirah writer, recorded a famous song (*tarjīʿ band*) from ʿAṭā as an example of his "lovely original thoughts that had thus established his individual style" (*ṭarz-e ḳhwud*).[135]

When my yell crashes like thunder,
  it splits a lion-like chest down to the liver.[136]
The stars in the night sky no longer glimmer.
  Because of me Rustam's heart palpates with terror.
[In the field, the enemy thrashes hand and foot,
  like a caged chickadee that gives a flutter.][137]
I shall send the demons into a dizzying whirl,
  when I draw from my waist the dagger.
And when [the hero] Bhīm sees my fine figure,
  at that moment this couplet on his lips will quiver:

"Of all the rakes, only you are the Imām!
  In all the tumult, only you are the leader!"[138]

naʿrah-e man chū raʿd gar kaṛakad
  sīnah-e sher tā jigar taṛakad
bar falak shab namī ṭapad anjum
  dil e rustam zi-sahm dhaṛakad
[dast-o pā mī zanad ʿadū dar ran
  ham chū pidṛī kih dar qafas phaṛakad]
kiñkaroñ ko lage chakāchauñdhā
  bandah kar kattī az kamar saṛakad
saj mārā agar bah bīnad bhīm
  dar īn bait az labish phaṛakad

dar hamah bāñkahā imām tūʾī
  lashkar ārāʾī dhūm dhām tūʾī

Indeed, ʿAṯā's stylized uses of language in the salons prompted Bedil to bestow a grant in the domain of poetry to ʿAṯā, even though some students like Muḵhliṣ objected to ʿAṯā's bold voice.

But honor bestowed by the poet-saint could also be taken away. Muḵhliṣ gleefully noted ʿAṯā's downfall in Bedil's salon: ʿAṯā was forbidden from attending the poet-saint's gathering after Bedil discovered that ʿAṯā had ghostwritten ġhazals for others to recite in their own names.[139] ʿAṯā presumably did this for money, and when Bedil discovered it, the poet-saint proscribed the practice from happening further and eventually prevented ʿAṯā's entrance to his parties.[140] Sadly, we have no examples from the poems-for-profit scheme that Muḵhliṣ accused ʿAṯā of hatching, and Ḵhwushgo avoided mention of the profiteering. But plagiarism and ghostwriting were common occurrences in a society where poetry was sung in the streets and patrons paid handsomely for a few verses. The career of ʿAbd ul-Jalīl Bilgrāmī, one of ʿAṯā's colleagues, underlines that although most poets achieved little fame in their lifetimes and garnered only a few passing nods from the court, many hustled their wares in the literary marketplace, demonstrating that multilingual poetry could be "leveraged for material gain" despite its seemingly marginal status.[141] Poets took whatever means they deemed necessary to distinguish themselves and achieve status and fame among their peers, patrons, and the wider public.

Indeed, most of the poems that survive from ʿAṯā's oeuvre are those written in the vernacular style developed late in his life. One of ʿAṯā's most famous couplets spread via tażkirahs compiled across India, including the South. In it, ʿAṯā's couplet combines imagery from both wrestling and swordsmanship, lamenting, "Alas, in the battle of beauty with you, the trick of your eye is like a dagger. / It is as if under your eyelash there is hidden a trick of a glance, like a deer" (*ai dar nabard-e ḥusn-e tū kaṭṭī pachhāṛ-e chashm / zer-e mizẖah nihuftah chū āhū pachhāṛ-e chashm*).[142] ʿAṯā deployed the Hindi word for a wrestling trick or maneuver (*pachhāṛ*) to augment the power of the beloved's eyes, which are said to be both like those of a gazelle (*āhū chashm*) and capable of throwing everything into turmoil.[143] In this case, ʿAṯā also developed a metaphor involving a wrestling move (*āhū pachhāṛ*) to elaborate on how a throw might knock one's competitors off their feet.[144] Fittingly, in his later years, ʿAṯā took up residence near the shrine of the Holy Footprint, a location where wrestlers would gather for contests.[145] One of ʿAṯā's colleagues, the poet ʿAbd ul-Jalīl Bilgrāmī (1661–1725) who was also a fan of Bedil's verse, teasingly composed a reḵhtah couplet about ʿAṯā's purported retirement, implying that he was defeated on the fields of battle and poetry: "When he heard his friends' tumult, / the cowardly fucker went and skulked in his hut" (*jab sunā dhūm dhām yāroñ kā / jhopre meñ ḍabak rahā buṛchod*).[146]

A DISHEARTENED APOLOGY

While Muḳhliṣ delighted in ʿAṭā's ejection from the poet-saint's salon, he neglected to note in his taẕkirah that Bedil eventually forgave ʿAṭā for his literary profiteering. In a self-abasing letter, Bedil begged ʿAṭā to return: "I am a total dirtbag (*tūdah-e ġhubār ālūdāh*). That is, I am a heap of earth (*āmāj*), exposed for the pleasure of your target practice." Bedil's faithlessness in accusing ʿAṭā of literary profiteering rendered the poet-saint worthy to be shot full of arrows, in other words, a heap of earth with a bull's eye affixed to it. Bedil further wrote, "Because of such wretches like me (*ḳhāksārān*), standing on the way of destitution and in the stumbling footsteps of mute Bedouins, my chest has been stitched up with bristling arrows of anxiety (*nāwak ḳhār ḳhār*), and my mirror of hope has been caught in the mesh of expectation. May I not hide my heart in shame, suspecting your vindictive arrows have been loosed (*kīnah kashī tīr*); and even under the taut accusation of faithlessness (*tang tuhmat-e be-wafāʾī*), may I not turn my face from your pointed shafts."[147]

Bedil expressed his contrition in terms familiar to ʿAṭā, a professional soldier with a steady hand for the sword and, so it would seem, good aim with bow and arrow. Further expounding on ʿAṭā's favorite martial images, Bedil continued, asking for mercy in the face of having violated the bounds of proper salon conduct, "The time is now to wash away the dust of vexation on this sorry one with the moisture from the dripping mercy of your bow and to illuminate the troubled carpet of this paraplegic (*zamīn-gīr*) with the lamp glow of your bow curves (*shamaʿ ḳhānah-e kamān*)."[148]

As the letter from Bedil is undated, it remains unclear when ʿAṭā resumed attending the living Bedil's gatherings. Whatever the case, Ḳhwushgo noted that ʿAṭā remained an indispensable entertainer during the posthumous mushāʿirah's first years in the 1720s. At an early death anniversary, likely on October 11, 1725, ʿAṭā read a chronogram memorializing Bedil: "ʿAbd ul-Qādir Bedil left" (*ʿabd ul-qādir bedil raft*, 1138 AH). ʿAṭā noted that the hemistich's meter was the same as that of a famous children's poem for building vocabulary.[149] When ʿAṭā himself died around age forty, to be presumedly buried at the shrine of the Holy Footprint where he retired, Ḳhwushgo mourned the loss, noting that "a light in the gathering for Bedil's death anniversary dissolved."[150]

Conclusion: Gathering for the Present and Preserving the Past

After Bedil died, poets continued to gather in his name to commemorate his verse and maintain his unique style of sociability. But the posthumous mushāʿirah also became a stage to voice arguments, utter bad language, masquerade others' verse as one's own, or duel with competing versifiers. The tomb's history demonstrates how in early eighteenth-century society, seemingly informal institutions like the mushāʿirah were tied to more permanent fixtures and spaces within Delhi's urban environment. As we will see, mushāʿirahs emerged out of a variety of tombs and mosques as well as types of *waqf*, including properties maintained for private or public benefit. Activities in these contexts demonstrate how public institutions overlapped with each other in spaces appropriate both for provisioning of material needs, such as Bedil's posthumous soup kitchen and apothecary's stand, and for furthering social distinction, as evidenced in the mushāʿirah and book rituals. Commercial ventures and shrine rituals wedded literary production to place, forming the linguistic building blocks of Delhi's tombs and mosques.

In this demanding arena offered by Bedil's shrine, the goals of visitors were myriad and contradictory—to earn a name, attract a patron, best a competitor, exchange gossip, consume intoxicants, purchase medicines, flirt with younger poets, brag about personal accomplishments, nitpick another's verse, test a new theme, delve into transcendental religious experiences, or share a verse with friends over a meal. Connections within these literary networks that crosshatched within the salon space become most clear when we examine them according to the terminology and values that littérateurs participating in these networks used to map their communities. As in the case of Bedil's shrine and the gathering it hosted, material economies and literary economies overlapped. The terrains of literature as social facets of urban life intersected with material inheritance.

This fact was not lost on Bedil, his family, or his students—all of whom inherited Bedil's figurative and geographic poetic real estate. One of Bedil's students, Sirāj ud-Dīn *Ārzū* (The Wish) (1688–1756), who will soon appear in the next chapter, noted the connection between literary and material property in a poem, further elaborating the idea that poetry has its own terrains: "It is a calamity to seize conceits from the original ideas of neighbors. / In poetry's grounds where has the law of eminent domain ever been applied?" (*balā-st aḳhż-e maʿānī zi-fikr-e ham-ṭarḥān / zamīn-e shiʿr kujā ḥaqq-e shufʿah dāshtah ast*).[151]

For Delhi's literary community, regular mushāʿirahs recurrently held in particular places institutionalized the preservation of literary knowledge, binding it to urban geography. However, despite being fixed to particular places and times, mushāʿirahs such as these usually lasted for a much shorter interval than the decades-long match at Bedil's posthumous gathering.

Ġhulām Hamadānī *Muṣḥafī* (The Qur'an Binder) (1751–1824), a taẕkirah writer and salon host, claimed the distinction of being the last person to observe the remnants of Bedil's gathering space, as he noted in his taẕkirah "Necklace of the Pleiades" (*ʿIqd-e S̱uraiyah*), a survey of post-1720 writers active during the reign of Muhammad Shah (r. 1719–48). By the early 1780s, the mansion that had once hosted the posthumous gathering, sheltering Bedil's tomb, had crumbled to ruins. Apologizing to his readers for breaking his narrative's chronological cohesion, Muṣḥafī notes, "Though it is not proper to mention [Bedil] in this taẕkirah . . . necessity dictates that if a few of his poems and particulars be written down it will prove beneficial."[152] Muṣḥafī was forced to contend with Bedil's celebrity to legitimate his own literary inheritance among his writings and salon conversations in 1770s Delhi, still benefiting from the traces of the erstwhile salon scene cultivated at Bedil's grave and from the poet-saint's former students who hosted gatherings of their own.[153]

By 1820, a police constable writing about Delhi's monuments noted that the tomb was only a rumor, and he could find neither remains of Bedil's mansion nor the grave; only the memory of the epitaph on the gravestone had survived the ravages of time: "The poet Saʿdī of Shiraz once wrote, / 'O Bedil, what can be said of a John Doe?'" (*pesh az īn guft ṣaʿdī-e shīrāz / be-dil az be-nishān chih goʾīd bāz*).[154] These purported last words encourage us to ask a similar question: What can the poems of long-dead poets tell us about the conversations, conduct, and compositions of Delhi's salons in the early 1700s?[155] Unlike the epitaph on Bedil's grave, the many poets who gathered and recited verse provide a historical record of the conversations and competitions that occurred in the multifaceted market for speech in Delhi, especially in their playful language.

2 New Writers at the Queen Regent's Mosque

For about eighty years, Delhi's poets convened regularly on the land where ʿAbd ul-Qādir Bedil lived, died, and was interred. From about 1680 to 1720, poets gathered there to exchange verses with the living poet-saint. After Bedil died in 1720, regional poets crowded yearly around the mansion's tomb for the next four decades or so to commune with the poet-saint at his annual graveside commemoration. Although they were the most famous and long-lived literary events in that precinct of Delhi, the poetry gatherings on Bedil's land were not the only mushāʿirahs taking place in the immediate vicinity during these years. Rather, at some point in the decade or so before Bedil's passing, another gathering had sprouted up nearby, about one kilometer north of Bedil's tomb.

In the scenic environs of this small mosque known as the Ornament of Mosques (*Zīnat ul-Masājid*) (see figure 2.1), a close-knit group of poets regularly congregated to quaff cannabis-laced drinks and joke with each other while reciting new compositions.[1] Two poets who lived at the Ornament of Mosques served as hosts for these gatherings: Saʿdullāh *Gulshan* (The Rose Garden) (1665–1728), a former student of Bedil; and Sharaf ud-Dīn *Maẓmūn* (The Theme) (1689?–1735), a more distant literary descendant of Bedil who had taken instruction from one of the poet-saint's students. The reader should not confuse Sharaf ud-Dīn Maẓmūn with the man enslaved by Bedil and with whom the poet shared a nickname. Coupled with our preceding analysis of the poet-saint and his gatherings, the lives, verse, and sociability of Gulshan and Maẓmūn provide us with further layers of insight into Delhi's mushāʿirah culture. In particular, by comparing the legacies and fluctuating renown of Gulshan and Maẓmūn, we can explore how local context and shared circles for performance and debate conditioned the production and assessment of style in Delhi's mushāʿirah culture. Taken together, stories about Gulshan and Maẓmūn demonstrate the decisive impact that factors such as time, place, and companionship wielded on the development of individual and collective poetic style. Stories that take place at the Ornament of Mosques further show how Delhi's mushāʿirah circles perpetuated a permissive form of literary sociability that allowed poets new methods for repurposing spaces and verse.[2]

The first decade of Bedil's posthumous salon (1720–30) coincided with important stylistic shifts among Delhi's poets. In the early 1700s, middling courtiers and regional aristocrats with growing wealth steadily accrued intellectual influence, and the cultural platforms they generated rerouted the trajectories of various literary classes who defined language and style. No longer did literature's shape and direction remain solely in the hands of those with high imperial connections. As witnessed with Bedil's struggles in the late 1600s, professional writers had to strive for a steady income, relying on a wider variety of notables than previously available to fund their careers. To an extent, this resulted in a more general dispersal of both wealth and ideas.

Sharaf ud-Dīn Maẓmūn had a playful assessment of the changes wrought by Delhi's expanding market for speech. Punning on his own name, Maẓmūn proclaimed, "The market for themes is flush with counterfeit goods. / Whoever calls himself a poet now opens a shop" ([*adānī*] *jins se maẓmūn kā hai bāzār garm / jo ko*ʾ*ī shā*ʿ*ir kahātā hai so ab khole dūkān*).[3] Indeed, new literate classes from peripheral settings were influencing Delhi's literary marketplace, as witnessed in Bedil's student ʿAṭā, who hailed from the provincial town of Amroha. Indeed, Delhi's great and humble poets alike adopted flexible understandings of literary style to legitimate poetic speech, collectively generating new interpretive repertoires among versifiers, patrons, and literary consumers. During Delhi's 1720s and 1730s, Bedil's acolytes and the novices studying under them found fertile terrain for cultivating new ideas according to the dynamic and daring language of the bazaar. Writers willing to adopt vernacular registers impacted hierarchies through crafting literary style and distinction to expand both how poets conducted themselves in salons and the verse that grew out of their competitions.

Saturday Night at the Ornament of Mosques

One Saturday night during the mid-1720s, Bedil's biographer Bindrāban Dās Ḳhwushgo memorialized the Ornament of Mosques in a ġhazal recited during one of the weekly Saturday-evening mushāʿirahs hosted by his old friend Gulshan. Ḳhwushgo captured the bounds of the mosque's seductive environment in a couplet:

> If you want to take in the air and water of the rose bed of poetry—
> go see the environs of [Zīnat un-Nisā] Begam's mosque on the bank of the Yamuna's waters.[4]

agar āb-o hawā-e gul zamīn-e shiʿr k̤hwāhī bīn
fiẓāʾī-e masjid-e begam-e kanār-e āb-e jamnā rā

In K̤hwushgo's mind, aspects of the rarified milieu such as its riverine setting, the mosque's cloud-like domes, and the gushing words of salon reciters conjured up a famous verse that Shams ud-Dīn Muḥammad *Ḥāfiz* (The Keeper of the Qur'an) (1325–1390) penned centuries before when describing Shiraz. In 1350s Iran, Ḥāfiẓ established the meter, rhyme, and theme that, centuries later, would inspire K̤hwushgo's poem:

Hey barkeep, pour the rest of the wine! After all, in heaven you will not find—
Shiraz's rose-lined promenade on the bank of the Ruknābād's waters.[5]

badih sāqī mai-e bāqī kih dar jannat nak̤hwāhī yāft
kanār-e āb-e ruknābād-o gulgasht-e muṣallā rā

The Ornament of Mosques (*Zīnat ul-Masājid*) sat on the edge of the Yamuna, where the riverbanks' cool breezes and greenery transported poets to the equally enticing gardens of Shiraz, Iran. In the early 1700s, elite women were reshaping Delhi's geography, and this particular mosque was named for Nawwāb-e Qudsiyah Zīnat un-Nisā Begam (1643–1721), the uniquely unmarried second daughter of emperor Aurangzeb (r. 1658–1707) who was also Queen Regent (*pādshāh begam*) to her father.[6]

Zīnat un-Nisā Begam commissioned the prayer hall in 1710 as one of her numerous architectural projects and intellectual pursuits.[7] Local legend held that unused funds meant for the Queen Regent's dowry were instead used to build the edifice.[8] With its name at once invoking its founder and its considerable beauty, the Ornament of Mosques became a significant location for mushāʿirahs when at least two poets of note took up residence within its precincts soon after its construction. The Ornament of Mosques' graceful architecture and halcyon environs offered an inviting setting for Delhi's poets, who utilized the area as a space to hone their creative abilities. At the Ornament of Mosques, poets' imaginations were spurred on by the mosque's delicate domes, its view of the Yamuna River, and the intoxicants they consumed on the mosque premises.

Indeed, the Queen Regent's Ornament of Mosques itself soon became a distinctive theme in poets' compositions, offering a familiar local touchstone for Delhi's poets.[9] K̤hwushgo's friend and frequent guest Najm ud-Dīn Shāh Mubārak *Ābrū* (The Honor) (1683/85–1733) likewise memorialized the locale, taking K̤hwushgo's themes a step further. Ābrū was, foremost, a

FIGURE 2.1 *Zīnat ul-Masājid* (An Image of the Ornament of Mosques), *Delhi,* 1820–25. British Library, London. *Naqshah-e,* Add. Or. 550.

champion of *īhām*, the ubiquitous wordplay of the 1720s and 1730s that misdirected readers with familiar and unfamiliar word associations. Ābrū grew famous as a literary "sensualist" (*ḥusn-parast*) when he released a poem in reḳhtah that described the intimate attributes of the beloved.[10] Thus, Ābrū memorialized the Ornament of Mosques by extracting a theme out of a familiar locale for Delhi poets, playing with the Ornament of Mosques and its multiple meanings. Ābrū recited, "Though the mosque prayer niche of his dyed eyebrows is but ornamentation, / why wouldn't such a trifle appear to him as *zīnat ul-masājid*, the adornment of all mosques?" (*miḥrāb-e abrūān koñ wasmah hu'ā hai zewar / kyuñ kar kahīñ nah un koñ ab zīnat ul-masājid*).[11] Ābrū's architectural metaphors delineate a beloved's eyebrows as perfectly arched and incongruously standing like idols before all worshippers in a mosque. But the reference to Delhi's Ornament of Mosques expands the conceit of the beloved's eyebrows as an architectural feature according to local terms that only Delhi's poets recognized and appreciated as a familiar sight.

As the other resident of the Ornament of Mosques, Ābrū's close friend Sharaf ud-Dīn Maẓmūn would also have relished the metaphor and the wordplay. Although Maẓmūn shared a residence at the prayer hall with Gulshan and the two poets socialized and performed within overlapping circles, they each forged qualitatively distinct paths toward distinguishing themselves and gaining renown within the spans of their respective lifetimes. In short, Gulshan shunned as uncouth the competitive aspects of Delhi's mushāʿirah scene in which poets distinguished themselves via exhibiting prowess with cutting language, while Maẓmūn heartily embraced the boisterous expressive milieu.

Local Geography and Literary Distinction

At the Ornament of Mosques, Gulshan and Maẓmūn hosted scores of poets over the period they dwelt there. Versifiers from within Ḳhwushgo's circle gathered there for feasts, enjoying meals donated by nearby grandees and imbibing elixirs mixed with cannabis. Gulshan eked out a meager living from a "hodgepodge (*khichaṛī*) of fixed donations appointed for mosque dwellers (*masjidiyān*)," but, according to one of his devotees, Gulshan's meager income barely afforded him candles.[12] Despite his relative poverty, Gulshan maintained connections to members of several elite literary circles in the city, including notables of the court, musicians who traversed between public shrines and courtly performance spaces, and highly respected poets such as Bedil and his student Sirāj ud-Dīn *Ārzū* (The Wish) (1688–1756), a premiere poet, taẕkirah writer, and literary theorist. Gulshan's Sufi moral code demanded that he shun the material trappings of these domains, but such cultivated indigence did not stop him from generously hosting disciples. Bedil's student Ārzū warmly narrated a time when Nāṣir ʿAndalīb and he visited Gulshan at the Ornament of Mosques on the final day of Ramẓān, the holy month of fasting. Although weak due to abstention from food and water during the daylight hours, Gulshan still managed to host Ārzū and ʿAndalīb, inviting them to join him on the patchwork blanket he kept on the floor of his dwelling and to engage in lively conversation.[13] After sunset prayers, a noblewoman who lived nearby arranged food to be sent to the three poets, and they ate well.

On other occasions, Gulshan made vegetarian accommodations for his guests who required it. For example, Gulshan's Hindu disciple Ḳhwushgo abstained from meat and select foods held to be polluting according to upper-caste Hindu standards.[14] Gulshan's wide social circle, like that of his teacher Bedil, encouraged Hindu discipleship in markedly Islamic terms. The relaxing setting and need for inspiration prompted poets across faith traditions to indulge in stimulating comestibles at the mushāʿirahs of the Ornament of Mosques. The young poet Ẓuhūr ud-Dīn *Ḥātim* (The Arbiter) (1699–1783) admitted to drinking cannabis-laced drinks and wrote three poems praising the coffee and tobacco he also consumed there.[15] Further, Ḳhwushgo reminisced about another occasion when poets gathered to consume cannabis drinks at the Ornament of Mosques, which had prompted a conversation about the various literary themes suggested by the Hindi words for cannabis.[16]

Zīnat un-Nisā Begam had established the Ornament of Mosques in 1710 under a *waqf* endowment to serve as a public benefit and later the site of her tomb (see figure 2.1). Women with means often secured mosques, shrines, and other pious spaces through such endowments to significantly shape the social geography of the city. As we recall, this was the case for the relatives who established Bedil's tomb as a *waqf*, most likely his female dependents among them. The Ornament of Mosques served as a space for public interaction for many years. In Maẓmūn's time, it was called the Lady's Mosque (*masjid-e begam*). By the nineteenth century, it came to be known as the Maiden's Mosque (*kuñwārī masjid*). Today, the building is known as the Cloud Mosque (*ghaṭā masjid*) due to its white marble domes.[17]

As we learned from our consideration of Bedil's shrine, sites associated with devotion or pious endowments represented important public spaces within the Islamic urban fabric and were thus crucial for generating the kinds of group cohesion that took shape at mushāʿirahs. At the Ornament of Mosques, donated food was distributed among the worshipers who appeared for devotional readings and Qur'an recitation, as was the case at Bedil's shrine and hundreds of others spread throughout the metropolis. Zīnat un-Nisā Begam established the Ornament of Mosques as a type of public good (*ṣalā-e ʿāmm*) directed at civic piety. As discussed in chapter 1, the inheritors of these *waqf* spaces, including those who used and inhabited them, repurposed *waqf* properties like mosques and shrines for myriad purposes in ways that mirrored changes in the composition of Delhi's populace and its patterns of sociability. Like shrines, mosques formed important sites for poetry exchange that, depending on context, surpassed or circumvented the pious intent of *waqf* builders.[18] Ḳhwushgo, an upper-caste Hindu, was clearly at home in Gulshan's pious dwelling. In this regard, mosques constituted part of Delhi's urban geography for poets of this period. They were edifices established in dialogue with Muslim norms whose spaces were also shaped by modes of interpretation and use determined by the arguments and gatherings of poets no matter their religious affiliations.

The environs at the Ornament of Mosques were not always as serene or stimulating as poets' praise of it would indicate. This was especially true for poet-in-residence Gulshan, whose sensitive ears would become the stuff of legends. At one point, Gulshan shared a wall in his mosque dwelling with one of the city's Kashmiri merchants (*bāzāriyān-e kashmīrī*) who would beat his children and, as one anthologist put it, "curse them with the foul language associated with those of his class." Vexed by the children's screaming, Gulshan urged the Kashmiri to stop the abuse, but the man persisted in beating the children, sometimes heightening his discipline to intentionally trouble Gulshan. At the end of his wits, Gulshan decorously said to the merchant, "My dear, may my house be a blessing for you. I shall go somewhere else." The merchant, sensing that Gulshan was hinting that he, instead, should relocate, responded, "If you want me to leave my home, then give me the amount of 5,000 rupees." This was a significant sum—the same cost of Bedil's lavish mansion in the 1680s. In shock, Gulshan responded, "Brother, my rank does not permit me to possess such wealth." Around the same time, Gulshan was due to visit his patron ʿInāyatullāh Ḳhān (d. 1726), an important nobleman connected to the court.[19] Gulshan explained the situation to the courtier, who sent the sum to the merchant at once.[20] While seemingly untroubled with the well-being of the children, Gulshan expended great effort to relocate the merchant and the merchant's family to spare his sensitive ears the strain of the Kashmiri's rough language and his children's crying.

The poet Sharaf ud-Dīn Maẓmūn is the second major figure centered in this chapter. Like Gulshan, he lived in the chambers below the mosque's plinth, keeping up appearances as a Sufi-minded ascetic. Besides Gulshan's circle, the mushāʿirahs at the Ornament of Mosques also hosted an overlapping cohort that included Maẓmūn's friends. These were poets now held to be foundational voices in Urdu literature's early history: Ẓuhūr ud-Dīn *Ḥātim* (The Arbiter) (1699–1783), Shams ud-Dīn Ḥabībullāh Jān-e Jānān *Maẓhar* (The Spectacle) (1699–1781), Najm ud-Dīn Shāh Mubārak *Ābrū* (The Honor) (1683/85–1733), and Shākir *Nājī* (The Elect) (1690?–1744/47?). Later writers memorialized their gatherings or concocted apocryphal legends about their interchanges.

Ābrū and Maẓhar, even in South India in 1751, were still celebrated for the acerbic words they exchanged, likely in the precincts of the Ornament of Mosques. One anecdote has Ābrū intoning a verse, "Among Delhi's poets, only one has 'Honor'" (*dihlī ke shāʿiroñ meñ ik ābrū huʾā hai*). Hearing this first line, Maẕhar decided to turn it into an insult making fun of the fact that Ābrū had only one eye: "But since he lost one eye, he has been dishonored (*be-ābrū*)" (*jāne se ek chashm ke be-ābrū huʾā hai*). Ābrū heard Maẕhar's wordplay with his pen name and said, "After a search, I will wring some meaning from this simple style." Ābrū then issued this scalding retort: "So what if my eye is blind by the Creator's hand? / As long as there is there is 'Honor' (*ābrū*) in this world, Jān-e Jānān Maẕhar is nothing more than pubic hair" (*kyā huʾā ḥaq ke kiye se kūr merī chashm hai / ābrū jag meñ rahe to jān-e jānān pashm hai*).[21]

Unlike Gulshan, Maẓmūn and his cohort were not averse to the harsh language of the public square. Besides penning memories of abusive words such as these in their taẕkirahs, these poets also scripted remnants of such rough gatherings in their dīwāns. The writings compiled by this group of poets are linked together through meters, end rhymes, and refrains shared among their compositions.[22] Before considering their words and assessing the impact past masters had on their respective styles, we will establish our societal context by turning to Gulshan and Maẓmūn's respective biographies.

Gulshan's Story

Saʿdullāh Gulshan was born in the southern Indian town of Burhanpur around 1665 into a family of well-connected Muslim converts.[23] Little is known of Gulshan's first twenty-two years in the South, except that he accompanied his father on a pilgrimage to Mecca. Afterward, he journeyed between Surat, Ahmadabad, and Aurangabad, cosmopolitan centers of Persianate culture and literary production where Gulshan developed his abilities as a poet and his status as a Sufi leader grew. In 1687, when Gulshan was said to have arrived in Delhi, India's literary economy was thriving under Shah Jahan's son, the emperor Aurangzeb ʿĀlamgīr (d. 1707).[24]

Among his many reasons for coming to Delhi, Gulshan's devotion to ʿAbd ul-Aḥd *Waḥdat* (The Unity) (1640–1714/15) provided his greatest draw. A native of Sirhind, Waḥdat resided in the neighborhood around Fīroz Shāh's fortress, a fourteenth-century ruin just outside the walled Mughal city and today known as Feroz Shah Kotla. This was an important locale for mushāʿirahs hosted by a group linked to the Kashmiri poet named ʿAbd ul-Ġhanī Beg *Qabūl* (The Acceptance) (d. 1727), as discussed in chapter 3. Waḥdat, who descended from the religious reformer Ahmad Sirhindī

Mujaddid (The Renewer) (1564–1624), functioned as a charismatic Sufi leader for the Naqshbandi brotherhood, a lineage that had begun to increasingly shape Delhi's literary scene. Waḥdat's devotees called him *Shāh Gul* (The Lord Rose). Based on Gulshan's association with Waḥdat, Gulshan's later teacher, Bedil, bestowed the pen name of "The Rose Garden" upon Gulshan. Bedil perhaps reasoned that only a lord of roses (*shāh gul*) could cultivate such a rose garden (*gulshan*).[25] Gulshan's alliance with the influential Naqshbandi brotherhood and his connections with influential people across India, including those in Gujarat, the South, Delhi, and the Naqshbandi headwaters in Punjab, put him in a unique position to witness and transmit the gossip and lore that comprised an anecdotal history for Delhi's versifiers.

Many of the stories about Gulshan within the Urdu literary canon are simply legends. Yet, the most important verifiable aspect of Gulshan's public character concerns his role as a mushāʿirah host. Every Saturday at his home in the Ornament of Mosques, Gulshan invited poets to gather and recite their verse.[26] In the lower rooms of the edifice, Gulshan counted himself as among the humble mosque dwellers (*masjidiyān*) of the city but, as mentioned earlier, still managed to host at the mosque his students and friends with food suitable to both Muslim and Hindu religious inclinations.

Gulshan's choice of residence was quite deliberate. Anecdotes about him reveal his connections to various wealthy patrons who likely could have funded his maintenance in a more conventional home. But dwelling at a mosque provided Sufi cultural capital for residents, allowing them to advertise their indigence while also alleviating housing costs. While poetry remained important to him, Gulshan trained his focus on mystical thought. With this, Gulshan had deep links to the musical traditions cherished by Delhi's Sufi brotherhoods and provided musical training to a cohort of his own students. Gulshan's well-known singing abilities further connected him to Sufi devotional traditions crucial for the cultivation of India's popular Islamic mysticism.

Poets dubbed Gulshan the "Amīr Ḳhusrau of the Age," a title referencing the eponymous poet and Sufi thinker Yatīm ud-Dīn Ḳhusrau Dihlavī (1253–1325), who was renowned for his poetry and musical skills.[27] Gulshan cultivated a warm friendship with the innovative court singer, poet, and lutenist Niʿmat Ḳhān *Sadārang* (The Ever Delightful) (1670–1748), whose musical style was associated with Sufi singers.[28] Gulshan too was likely familiar with Delhi's Islamic music styles, and such musicians later memorialized Gulshan at his tomb. About himself, Gulshan composed a couplet reflecting on his pen name while also noting his musical abilities: "My reed pen is the portrait maker of his one hundred delightful meanings. / Though I write as 'The Rose Garden,' a nightingale-like nature is appropriate for me" (*kilk-e man ṣūrat kash-e ṣad maʿnī-e rangīn-e ū ast / gar kunad gulshan taḳhalluṣ bulbul-ṭabʿam rawā-st*). With a voice as cultivated as his pen, Gulshan likely could sing his own verse with some skill.[29]

A Heady Ġhazal Scene

Prior to entering the orbit of the poet-saint Bedil, Gulshan retained close, although ambivalent, connections with Delhi's noted literary celebrities of the 1680s and 1690s. Gulshan's personal conflicts with noted mushāʿirah celebrities of the age provide us with some clues as to why Gulshan's dīwān fell from favor. Prior to his relationship with Bedil, Gulshan's literary inclinations primarily took shape in dialogue with the leading ġhazal composers of Delhi's 1690s literary scene. During this period, Gulshan attached himself to the contentious mushāʿirah circles propagated by two immensely popular writers, Nāṣir ʿAlī Sirhindī (1638/39?–1697) and Muḥammad Afẓal *Sarḳhwush* (The Heady) (1640–1715).[30] Based on Gulshan's own accounts, as recorded by others, the relationships Gulshan forged within this milieu often had a fraught quality.

Gulshan's colleagues Nāṣir ʿAlī and Sarḳhwush were associated closely with one another. As the premier ġhazal writer of the era, Nāṣir ʿAlī's fame had ignited in India's cities and spread to Isfahan and Samarqand.[31] Sarḳhwush, known as Nāṣir ʿAlī's greatest friend and admirer, had compiled an important tażkirah that magnified Sarḳhwush's position as a generous mushāʿirah host. A long-haired rake with a mischievous air, Sarḳhwush was famed as a skilled ġhazal writer known even among Isfahan's circles. Sarḳhwush resided at the edge of Saʿdullāh Ḳhān Square, a raucous market at the center of town that was alive with trinket sellers and astrologers.[32] Sarḳhwush inscribed a witty salutation on the front door to his home where he hosted Delhi's writers: "If you have come, the door is open. If you did not come, then the right [to enter] is unnecessary."[33]

When Gulshan arrived in Delhi in the late 1680s, he visited Sarḳhwush's home for poetry instruction, and, over the course of about eight years, he learned the craft from Sarḳhwush. But Gulshan was sensitive to the harsh language favored by the mushāʿirah celebrity Sarḳhwush and his raucous circle of friends, including Nāṣir ʿAlī. According to the few anecdotes that survived via various tażkirahs, Gulshan shunned their obscenities and bragging. In his tażkirah "The Words of Poets" (*Kalimāt ush-Shuʿarā*), Sarḳhwush himself first noted that in the time he instructed Gulshan, he described his student as a "young man with a free disposition and generous spirit." At some point, he amended these words after Gulshan revealed his thin-skinned disposition, describing Gulshan as having an "upstanding nature" (*durust ṭabʿ*).[34] This was perhaps a disappointing aspect of Gulshan's character for Sarḳhwush, given the latter's penchant for mischievous conduct.

In one story told to Ḳhwushgo that illustrated this nature, Gulshan once accompanied Sarḳhwush to Bedil's home to meet the poet-saint. Sarḳhwush and Bedil had been apart for various reasons, and, when they arrived, Sarḳhwush said to Gulshan and the other companions, "Do you two want to see some elephants fight?" (*hawas-e tamāshā-e jang-e fīlān dārīd*), in reference to Sarḳhwush's impending verse exchange with Bedil. Sarḳhwush, excited by the potential literary duel, then dashed off this line that he recited for everyone there, "By the grace of God, I have plucked the pubic hairs from this world and the next! / I have grabbed one and how firmly I have seized it" (*az fażl-e ḥaqq zi har do jahān rum giriftah-īm / yak dargiriftah-īm-o chih muḥkam giriftah-īm*).[35] This sort of ribald parlance was common in Sarḳhwush's mushāʿirah circles. Another time, a poet visiting one of Sarḳhwush's gatherings expressed the opinion that his host's long gray hair was ugly and "ill-suited for a poet." Sarḳhwush responded that his guest's beard was "no better than the pubic hair on the testicles of rogues."[36]

Sarḳhwush revered Nāṣir ʿAlī, a leading ġhazal writer of the 1600s, calling him "the Pride of India" (*ābrū-e hindustan*), and he often quoted Nāṣir ʿAlī's verse in poetry gatherings.[37] For instance, during a mushāʿirah, Sarḳhwush recited these lines in praise of Nāṣir ʿAlī:

> In the lands of speech, the world conqueror shall be ʿAlī!
> In the ways of the heart, he is a saint, O ʿAlī *pīr* ʿAlī!
> When it comes to the poetry of ʿAlī, no one can match his verse.
> Just as no one's penmanship can match that of the calligrapher Mīr ʿAlī.[38]

> *dar mulk-e suḳhan buwad jahān-gīr ʿalī*
> *dar mashrab-e dil walī ʿalī pīr ʿalī*
> *bā shiʿr-e ʿalī namī rasad shiʿr-e kasī*
> *zi-ānsān kih ḳhaṭ-e kas ba-ḳhaṭ-e mīr ʿalī*

At another mushāʿirah, Sarḳhwush heard someone reciting from one of Nāṣir ʿAlī's *maśnawī*s, but the poet in question misquoted the lines. Nāṣir

ʿAli's original verse went, "O God, cast the essence of the rose's fire into my breath / Throw sparks into the cottonfield of my bones" (*ilāhī żarrah-e wardī ba-jān rez / sharar dar panbah zār-e ustuḳhwān rez*)—a striking and complex couplet that expanded the theme of a cottonfield that easily catches fire.[39] But the ignorant poet fouled up the line, reciting instead, "O God, cast flashes of pain into my body / Throw sparks into the soft meadows of my hair" (*ilāhī żarrah-e dardī ba-tan rez / sharar dar panbah zār-e mū-e man rez*).[40] Sarḳhwush laughed and improvised a response, much to the embarrassment of the ignorant poet:

> Why make this request of God, my dear?
>   Even I could have done this exact job.
> For I could light up a handful of grass,
>   and I would burn off the hair on your head and your beard too.[41]

> *chirā īn ḥājat az ḥaq ḳhwāhī ai yār*
>   *tavānam kard man īn qadr kār*
> *kih musht-e ḳhas ba-ātish bar furozam*
>   *hamah mūʾī-esar-o reshat basozam*

In stark contrast to his teacher Sarḳhwush, Gulshan despised Nāṣir ʿAlī and his poetry. This was the case even though Gulshan and Nāṣir ʿAlī shared similar religious inclinations in their devotion to the Naqshbandi brotherhood, which was based in Nāṣir ʿAlī's hometown of Sirhind, North India. When comparing Nāṣir ʿAlī with Gulshan's revered teacher Bedil, Gulshan pronounced that Nāṣir ʿAlī, "having renounced [literary] advancement, conspired to turn fate in whatever amount he could."[42] By Gulshan's estimation, these unfortunate inclinations of Nāṣir ʿAlī were a product of "a melancholy temperament" and a tendency to "beat the drum of 'I' and nothing else."[43]

In fact, Gulshan was often offended by Nāṣir ʿAlī's character. Two surviving anecdotes depict what may have spoiled whatever companionship Gulshan and Nāṣir ʿAlī once had. While traveling on the road between Lahore and Delhi, Gulshan was struck by a fit of poetic inspiration. Stopping the caravan, Gulshan planted himself in the shade of a tree and vowed to sit there until his composition was finished. Nāṣir ʿAlī, who was also in the caravan, approached Gulshan when he completed his poem and embraced him so closely that their chests rubbed together, urging him to keep the caravan going in a decorous but needling manner: "You are so far away," Nāṣir ʿAlī said to Gulshan, "I myself have become quite weak and am now making preparations for my final voyage" (*safar-e vāpasīn*).[44]

Additionally, Gulshan gossiped to Ḳhwushgo about a time when Nāṣir ʿAlī scandalized him. It happened when Gulshan and old friend were paying a visit to Nāṣir ʿAlī with a young boy accompanying them. Nāṣir ʿAlī took one look at the youth (*amrad*) and said, "Might I bite your lip?" Gulshan's friend was offended by this and left. The next day, Nāṣir ʿAlī loosely apologized, sending Gulshan's friend a line by the poet Muḥammad ʿAlī *Ṣāʾib* (The Mark) (1592–1676): "At the slightest pretext of warmth, dewdrops turn their backs on the rose. / In friendship, why would someone be this faithless?" (*bah andak rū-e garmī pusht bar gul mī kunad shabnam / chirā dar āshnāʾī īn qadr kas be-wafā bāshad*).[45] Nāṣir ʿAlī's poetic apology via Ṣāʾib was ambiguous indeed. It would seem Nāṣir ʿAlī still wanted to bite the young man's lips.

Gulshan's opinion of Nāṣīr ʿAlī perhaps impacted later anthologists such as Ḳhwushgo, who revered Gulshan as his Sufi master. Ḳhwushgo wrote that Nāṣīr ʿAlī "generally had rough manners with people, in fact he even used to insult them."[46] On one occasion, Nāṣir ʿAlī was visited by the poet Rafīʿ Ḳhān *Bāżil* (The Munificent) (d. 1707/12?) from Gwalior during a time while he was having a gathering with his students and friends. In a mushāʿirah, Bāżil recited a line from his compositions: "'I had a heart but gave it away. There was a soul, so I offered it up. / The thing that the beloved wants is my patience—I don't have that [to give]" (*dil dāshtīm dādīm jān būd ʿarẓ kardīm / chīzī kih yār ḳhwāhad ṣabr ast ān nadārīm*). Deriding him for employing a tired trope in his poem, Nāṣir ʿAlī said, "Sir, now recite from your own work and cease this boasting," causing the other listeners, probably Nāṣir ʿAlī's hangers-on, to chuckle.[47] Whatever Gulshan's assessment of this behavior might have been, Nāṣir ʿAlī's personality and his verse were immensely important topics in salon conversation throughout the 1700s. By dint of his frankness, charisma, and true aim, Nāṣir ʿAlī's style of literary critique proved especially impactful as poets looked for parameters to guide their habitual questioning of each other's originality and propensity to level harsh accusations of purported plagiarism at competitors.

Similarly to the way Gulshan rejected Nāṣir ʿAlī's ribaldry, the sensitive poet likewise recoiled from Sarḳhwush's boldly hued words. The breaking point between Gulshan and Sarḳhwush came when Sarḳhwush composed a quatrain that he recited in Gulshan's presence. Sarḳhwush intoned:

As it is, there are four verified wise men.
  Ibn ʿArabī is the first of them—so it's rumored.

Then [come] Maulānā Rūmī, Ṣaḥābī Astarābādī, and Mullā Shāh.
The fifth, by God, is God's wonder Sarḳhwush![48]

chār-and zi-taḥqīq kamā hiya āgāh
ibn ʿarabī awwalishān dar afwāh
pas maulvi-o ṣaḥābī-o mullā shāh
panjam sarḳhwush ġharībullāh allāh

This poem greatly offended Gulshan. "We five are all sages," Sarḳhwush jokingly explicated for Gulshan, "I suppose there could be others—Quṭb ud-Dīn Baḳhtiyār Kākī and Niẓām ud-Dīn Auliyā, for instance. But the rest were not sages, simply mere ascetics" (*zāhid*). Gulshan was not amused by Sarḳhwush staging himself among the greatest thinkers of the age. Gulshan admonished his former teacher: "Now this pridefulness that I hear from you is quite tasteless and while I would normally ignore it, you've really gone down a bad road now." Angrily turning to depart from Sarḳhwush's presence, he warned, "You and I are not going to meet up for some time." Thereafter, he ceased visiting Sarḳhwush's home in Saʿdullāh Square. After a few days, Sarḳhwush approached some of Gulshan's friends, gently inquiring, "Would it be possible to meet with Gulshan sometime?" Sarḳhwush explained, "I read him a verse that he did not like and now he has ended our meetings, saying I've taken a bad road. Would you all be arbitrators for me? If I could have guessed that I might have been rude (*be-adabī*), what other way would there have been to make Gulshan unhappy?" Hearing about Sarḳhwush's good-humored joke, Gulshan's anger dissipated when he learned of his former teacher's concern.[49]

Sarḳhwush then issued an indirect apology to Gulshan, cast in the subtle style particular to well-mannered society of the period. Gulshan had presented a poem he wished to have answered: "Like a ruby, I hold both fire and water in one vessel" (*bah yak paimānah chūn yāqūt dāram āb-o ātish rā*). Sarḳhwush fittingly responded: "Only to the extent of gentility did I tame [my] refractory nature" (*zi-bas bā narm ḳhūʾī rām kardam ṭabʿ-e sarkash rā*).[50] Their later verse exchange further reflected Sarḳhwush's conciliatory gesture toward the delicate Gulshan, as he announced the fresh taming of his recalcitrant tendencies. This interchange repaired the relationship to an extent, and Gulshan soon left for Gujarat. Yet, after returning to Delhi, Gulshan shifted his allegiance from Sarḳhwush to Bedil, turning to the poet-saint as his main teacher. By Sarḳhwush's estimation, Bedil and Gulshan were of the same character in their preference for mystical thought. But this time, Gulshan no longer appeared to Sarḳhwush as a young man with a free disposition and generous spirit, but rather as a disappointingly "straightlaced" novitiate.[51]

Maẓmūn's Story

Maẓmūn's disposition contrasted strikingly from that of Gulshan, his housemate. Our "Seedless Poet" maintained a carefree disposition, buoyed by the mischievousness prized among some of Delhi's poets. For possibly as long as two decades, Maẓmūn shared a residence with Gulshan at the Ornament of Mosques. Yet, contemporary anthologists oddly do not connect these two figures, nor have any current historians of Urdu literature elaborated on the significance of their geographical, literary, or social overlaps. Indeed, I was unable to find any historical documentation of Gulshan and Maẓmūn interacting, trading poems, or sharing meals, even though they socialized in near-identical circles and inhabited the same building. Whatever the case, Maẓmūn was an entertaining fixture in Delhi's mushāʿirah scene. His memory remained alive until the late 1800s, most notably through the efforts of the modern Urdu historian Muḥammad Ḥusain *Āzād* (The Liberated) (1830–1910), who recounted an anecdote about Maẓmūn that he learned from his own teacher, the Mughal poet laureate Muḥammad Ibrāhīm *Żauq* (The Distinction) (1790–1854).[52]

Maẓmūn was likely born in Gwalior, but he grew up in the village of Jājau, a small town south of the old Mughal capital of Agra.[53] As a boy, he likely witnessed a crucial battle fought near his hometown during a 1707 succession struggle.[54] As a teenager, Maẓmūn quit Jājau not long after the imperial upset and came to Delhi, remaining there until his early death sometime in his forties. Maẓmūn's compendium-writing peers did not document the details of his educational background. Yet, we do have evidence for Maẓmūn's noted lineage via his descent from the Sufi Chishti brotherhood through the saint Farīd ud-Dīn Masʿūd (1179–1266), also called Bābā Farīd. Maẓmūn indicated this in the rhyming double entendres he composed based on his ancestor's nickname of "The Treasury of Sugar" (*Ganj-e Shakkar* or *Shakar Ganj*).[55] "Why shouldn't I make such sweet-lipped beloveds my disciples?" inquired Maẓmūn. "After all, Bābā Farīd [a Treasury of Sugar] is my gramps" (*kareñ kyūñ nah shakkar laboñ ko murīd / kih dādā hamārā hai bābā farīd*). The conceit in these lines ventures in several directions. The terms for sweet-lipped (*shakkar lab*; *shīrīn lab*) provide well-hewn allusions to the seductive words of the beloved. Maẓmūn's poem implies that the speaker had access to a whole treasury of sweet words through his ancestry. In another famous verse, also using wordplay, he stated, "Give Maẓmūn a treat with that sweet lip. / Afterall, he is the son of [Bābā Farīd], the Treasury of Sugar" (*lab-e shīrīn se de maẓmūn ko mīṭhā / kih hai farzand vuh ganj-e shakkar kā*).[56] These confectionary double entendres and Sufi connections, so it would seem, allowed Maẓmūn to outpace even a champion seducer in competitions of alluring and delightful speech. Such lines would have offended the sensitive Gulshan as they situated noted Sufi masters in profane contexts. Indeed, as we learned earlier, Gulshan decried similarly erotic conceits in his encounters with various mushāʿirah celebrities from the preceding generation.

The clever Maẓmūn, on the other hand, had no compunctions about planting flirty words on Sufis' tongues. Indeed, Maẓmūn's racy wit earned him a noted place in Delhi's mushāʿirah scene, where he was famous for his easygoing manner, his jovial sociability, and his "incredibly enthusiastic and intimate association" (*ġhāʾiyat garm-josh wa chaspān-e iḳhtilāṭ*) with fellow poets who relished his verse and character firsthand.[57]

Maẓmūn's most famous verse would have emphatically addled Gulshan's sensibilities in its double entendre confounding grammar and sexuality: "Although the wine house is packed with acts of impropriety, / but once you've actually seen the madrasah that's where you find actives and passives" (*mai kade meñ gar sar-ā-sar faʿl-e nā maʿqūl hai / madrasah dekhā to vāñ bhī fāʿl-o mafaʿūl hai*).[58] The couplet deploys terminology for the active and passive voice as it applies to Arabic grammar to comment on the infamy of religious schools where instructors would take liberties with their young male students.

Maẓmūn was a master of misdirecting meaning. That is, he composed according to the playful misdirection of double entendre or *īhām*, the dominant stylistic approach among both Persian and reḳhtah composers of the period. The poetic misdirection of īhām generated chuckles among mushāʿirah listeners, but it also distinguished literary genius within the pecking order of poets. In an īhām-based poem composed about himself, Maẓmūn stated, "In this world, [poetry's] theme (*maẓmūn*) certainly has become famous / ever since you released a *ṭarḥ* of double entendres" (*huʾā [to] jag meñ maẓmūñ shuhrah t[e]rā / ṭaraḥ īhām kī jab señ nikālī*). Here, *ṭarḥ* means the model verse by which all others compose.[59] Indeed, upon Maẓmūn's words about the "actives and passives" of the madrasah, his colleagues Nājī and Maẓhar each composed responses to this famous poem, utilizing Maẓmūn's delightful form (*ṭarḥ*) full of double meanings. Nājī compared the beloved's face to the sunflower (*suraj mukhī ka phūl hai*), and Maẓhar imagined the beloved's touch to be like the moonlight in the shape of a flower (*chāndnī kā phūl hai*).[60]

Maẓmūn's poetic skills blossomed under mentorship of those from Bedil's circle. Ārzū, a student of Bedil, helped nurture Maẓmūn's distinct reḳhtah voice, instructing the junior poet for almost thirteen years.[61] Comparing him with his other reḳhtah students, Ārzū marveled that Maẓmūn was an "unparalleled master in the art of reḳhtah composition" and assigned Maẓmūn the nickname of "The Seedless Poet" (*shāʿir-e bedānah*), jesting about the younger poet's appearance. In his thirties, Maẓmūn had suffered an inflammatory disease of the sinuses that caused his teeth to fall out over some years. Like a seedless grape or some other pipless fruit, Maẓmūn's head was empty of teeth and thus, "The Seedless Poet" sprouted up under his teacher's teasing.[62] Toothless or not, Maẓmūn the Seedless Poet disseminated his verse across other congregations besides those of his teacher, including Ḳhwushgo's regularly convened mushāʿirah. In a draft of Ḳhwushgo's taẕkirah that he had been editing, Ārzū noted attendance of a certain Miyāñ Maẓmūn at Ḳhwushgo's mushāʿirah. There, Ārzū also alluded to Miyāñ Maẓmūn's friendship with Sayyid Ġhulām Nabī *Nasīm* (The Zephyr) (fl. 1720–40), a secretary from a rural town who also studied with Ārzū and frequented Muḳhliṣ's and Ḳhwushgo's homes where he composed lampoons for their entertainment. This "Miyāñ Maẓmūn" was likely our Seedless Poet.[63] Anthologist Qāʾim Chāndpūrī, who witnessed Maẓmūn's conduct in salons on several occasions, described the poet's excursions to mushāʿirahs lasting "until the last day at the end of road," when he continued "to remain a guest of the noblemen within the circle of the gathering" (*ḥalqah-e majlis*).[64]

The Associations of a Seedless Poet

Despite his frequent trips to salons, Maẓmūn's dīwān was quite meager, consisting of only 200–300 verses. In reference to the paucity of his literary output, Maẓmūn confesses, "Just like an invalid lets out a complaint due to the pain in his heart / Even Maẓmūn writes a poem in this same way from time to time" (*dard-e dil se jis ṭarḥ bīmār uṭhtā hai karāh / is ṭarḥ ek shiʿr maẓmūn bhī kahe hai gāh gāh*).[65] Slim though it was, Maẓmūn's dīwān traveled well beyond Delhi, ending up in the hands of the Hyderabad-based anthologist and poet Lachhmī Narāyan *Shafīq* (The Merciful) (1745–1808), who commented on its ġhazals.[66] Maẓmūn's verse collection has yet to resurface, but a substantial selection from it remains accessible in Shafīq's

"Garden of Poets" (*Chamanistān-e Shuʿarā*), the tażkirah he completed in 1761 while still a teenager.[67]

As noted in other tażkirahs cited by Shafīq, Maẓmūn had three documented students. One of these, Muḥammad *ʿĀrif* (The Mystic) (fl. 1740–50), was an opium addict who lived in the vicinity of Delhi Gate and attended literary gatherings of the 1740s with some frequency.[68] Another student, Faẓl ʿAlī *Dānā* (The Wise Man) (fl. 1740–50), garnered more attention than ʿĀrif due to his jovial character, odd appearance, and wider association among leading reḳhtah writers of the 1740s. With his dark complexion, Dānā sported a great beard and wore a black cloak that reached his knees. Such affectations earned Dānā ridicule from reḳhtah poets who teased him for looking like one of the black bears from springtime parades.[69] Maẓmūn's third student, a certain Sayyid Ḥātim ʿAlī Ḳhān (fl. 1740–60) from Jaunpur, was mainly remembered for a poem he penned about modern love.[70] Like their teacher, these three poets regularly visited mushāʿirahs. But like most poets of the age, Maẓmūn's three students likely never assembled dīwāns.

A thin dīwān and a scanty load of students did not stop Maẓmūn from gaining notoriety within elite patronage circles and a lasting impact. Maẓmūn came under the patronage of the Mughal official ʿUmdat ul-Mulk Amīr Ḳhān (d. 1747), a third-level paymaster and governor of Allahabad from 1743 to 1746 (see his illustration in figure 2.2). Amīr Ḳhān also supported Maẓmūn's teacher Ārzū, along with Ḳhwushgo and many other Persian-language poets of this period.

Like many patrons of the time, Maẓmūn's supporter Amīr Ḳhān was also a poet, writing under the pen name *Anjām* (The Result). He kept a large mansion at the southern edge of the walled city.[71] In 1747, Amīr Ḳhān was killed by an "unmanly angel of death," who stabbed Maẓmūn's patron by the orders of competitors at court.[72] Until this unfortunate end, Amīr Ḳhān was the premier literary patron of his early eighteenth-century era, though he also famously mismanaged his finances. Maẓmūn secured a small salary from Amīr Ḳhān, but this sum was insufficient for his livelihood.[73] The early reḳhtah chronicler Mīr Ḥasan noted an anecdote in which Maẓmūn petitioned the Mughal courtier for employment. Amīr Ḳhān, this time in his capacity as a government official, accepted Maẓmūn as an employee but quickly thereafter became preoccupied with other affairs and forgot to release Maẓmūn's salary.[74] This caused Maẓmūn to become taciturn (*besuḳhan*), and he began to doubt that he would even receive his salary. Steeling himself, the Seedless Poet took the liberty of improvising a highly deferential poem, which he recited before his heedless patron: "The

FIGURE 2.2 *Nidhā Mal, Amīr Ḵhān, ʿUmdat ul-Mulk, Seated on a Terrace*, 1740–45. Private collection, courtesy Francesca Galloway Ltd.

nobility has the misfortune to hear my petition. / But this servant would never bring such speech upon his tongue, so to speak" (*ʿarẓ-e ḥāl apne se haiñ ahl-e sharāfat be-naṣīb / nahīñ sukhan rakhte zabān ke bīch goyā yih najīb*). Amīr Khān, being an expert judge of character, immediately instated Maẓmūn's salary and reimbursed him the backpay he was owed, according to Mīr Ḥasan.[75]

The figure of Maẓmūn and his verse have received some scholarly attention by twentieth-century Urdu literary historians such as Jamīl Jālibī, Ġhulām Ḥusain Żū'l-Faqār, and Ḥasan Aḥmad Niẓāmī. In his analysis of our Seedless Poet's literary contribution, Jālibī comments that Maẓmūn's style owed much to the *īhām-goʾī* mode of his colleague Ābrū, at times appearing derivative of Ābrū.[76] In a more generous assessment, Żū'l-Faqār focuses on Maẓmūn's sociability among his contemporaries, noting that although Maẓmūn wrote little, he wrote eloquently (*kam-go the lekin khwush-go the*).[77] Niẓāmī echoes these sentiments while centering his consideration on the uniqueness of Maẓmūn's misdirections.[78]

In terms of his contemporaries and the generations who came directly after them, the poets of Delhi's literary scene fondly remembered Maẓmūn and continued to write emulations of his verse. In 1778, nearly half a century after Maẓmūn died of his recurring sinus infection, a diarist coopted one of Maẓmūn's poems into an anecdote about The Seedless Poet's passing. The day he died, according to this tażkirah writer, Maẓmūn's friends gathered at the foot of his bed at the Ornament of Mosques and began giving loud speeches about the pains of the Day of Judgement. Just before breathing his last, Maẓmūn opened his eyes and uttered a final verse: "O Preacher, do not scare Maẓmūn with the tumult of the Final Gathering. / He already endures the shock of separation [from the beloved]. The Apocalypse is nothing!" (*shor-e maḥshar setī wāʿiẓ nah ḍarā maẓmūn ko / hajr ke ṣadme uṭhātā hai qayāmat kyā hai*).[79] The anecdote strikes a Sufi tone with a saintly Maẓmūn uttering a couplet utilizing the familiar theme of the beloved's sublime beauty being like Armageddon. While entirely apocryphal, the episode reveals the respect even later anthologists afforded the poet, citing a famous line from his oeuvre to cast him as an eloquent mystic.

Based on evidence from a variety of sources, Maẓmūn emerges as an important poet for writers of his period by dint of his verse and mushāʿirah conduct. This significance is demonstrated by poetry memorializing him, the many anecdotes about him in tażkirahs, and the surviving verse samples across compendiums. Such an assemblage contrasts with the diminished image of Maẓmūn we have today. Aside from the exceptions in works like those mentioned above by Jālibī, Żū'l-Faqār, and Niẓāmī, Maẓmūn surfaces, at best, as a footnote in contemporary histories, where he is usually marginalized among more well-known examples and listed as just another *īhām-go* poet, simply an ambiguist.

Aside from evidence based on his verse and the way his contemporaries valued him in their remembrances, Maẓmūn's material connections to Delhi and the Mughal hierarchies also encourage us to reconsider his historical importance. When Maẓmūn arrived in Delhi, likely around 1710, he chose the Ornament of Mosques as his first and only home in Delhi. This sublime setting on the banks of the Yamuna River was also the erstwhile dwelling of Sufi leader and occasional poet Gulshan, who hosted the weekly poetry gathering attended by Ḳhwushgo, Ārzū, and many others. The location of Maẓmūn's residence and its connection to various poetry circles are important factors to consider for understanding his role in mushāʿirah history and for accessing the overlapping networks of poets, patrons, and literary lore in mid-1700s Delhi.

We also can understand Maẓmūn's position more clearly when we study it in comparison to Gulshan's life course and the way he has been remembered. According to period historians and those who came later, Gulshan's importance to literary circles of the time hinged on two factors: his networks of associations and his reputation for piety related to his Sufi practices. As regards the first element of Gulshan's distinction, for the poets of Ārzū and Ḳhwushgo's generation, Gulshan's prestige emanated from his former association with Bedil, Sarḳhwush, and Nāṣir ʿAlī—the premier Persian-language poets and Delhi-based salon hosts of the late 1600s and early 1700s at the end of Aurangzeb's reign. As for the second element fostering Gulshan's status, Urdu's first historians revived Gulshan's posthumous notoriety in the 1750s by assigning him the role of the Sufi preceptor who supposedly inspired all reḳhtah composition with a miraculous line. As will be discussed ahead, this latter facet was a fabrication, doubted by Delhi's writers nearly from its first appearance.

In turn, we can trace Maẓmūn's personal history and understand his impact by connecting evidence left from Ārzū and Ḳhwushgo's generation with stories that emerged within and after the 1740s burgeoning reḳhtah scene. Notably, Maẓmūn's reputation survived the criticisms meted out by later versifiers to his generation—for example, the 1750s critique of poets such as Mīr Muḥammad Taqī *Mīr* (The Leader) (1725–1810), who downgraded the influential circles that once gathered at the Ornament of Mosques. As Ġhulām Ḥusain Żū'l-Faqār observes, Maẓmūn's reserved eloquence and wide circles of association secured his place within mushāʿirah circles and, therefore, among the favored writers of Yaqīn and Saudā, two of the reḳhtah composers who memorialized him in couplets.

Maẓmūn's verse and connections bridged networks among reḳhtah writers of the 1720s and 1730s within whose verse and prose he was often memorialized. Inʿāmullāh Ḳhān *Yaqīn* (The Certainty) (1727–1755), a celebrity poet of the 1740s, composed a ġhazal quoting Maẓmūn's own famous lines to welcome the Seedless Poet back from beyond the grave and into the mushāʿirah. To do so, Yaqīn recast Maẓmūn's verse into his own in tribute (*taẓmīn*) to a poem of Maẓmūn's that caught Yaqīn's ear with a wordplay:

> Like a wretch does, quit endlessly praising those boys.
> By those words, Maẓmūn, your theme becomes religious doctrine.[80]

> *gadā ho kar kiyā mat kar itī taʿrīf laṛkoñ kī*
> *kih un bātoñ sitī maẓmūn tirā uṣūl jātā hai*

Popular culture at the time championed homoerotic imagery. Even so, a man who went running after attractive young men to excessively praise their good looks risked spoiling his own character. Yaqīn composed his tribute poem in praise of Maẓmūn's lines while echoing Maẓmūn's original meter, rhyme, and refrain. Yaqīn chided himself in verse:

> Like Yaqīn keeps doing, stop endlessly praising boys.
> Otherwise, a Maẓmūn-like beloved emerges from those words.[81]

> *yaqīn ho kar kiyā mat kar itī taʿrīf laṛkoñ kī*
> *kih un bātoñ sitī maẓmūn sā maḥbūb jātā hai*

Instead of praising mere unschooled boys, Yaqīn's conceit asked the poet to choose better objects of literary inspiration, perhaps the inventiveness found in the words of an influential poet like Maẓmūn.

Reconstructing Gatherings

Fifty years after the end of Gulshan's and Maẓmūn's gatherings, Ẓuhūr ud-Dīn *Ḥātim* (The Arbiter) (1699–1783) still cherished fond memories of the times they spent together in the salon at the Ornament of Mosques. By the 1780s, Ḥātim stood at the end of a fruitful career, having generated a reḳhtah dīwān that he continuously edited and a Persian one as well. In the 1770s and early 1780s, Ḥātim frequented the home of the young writer and host Ġhulām Hamadāni *Muṣḥafī* (The Qurʾān Binder) (1751–1824) where in evening mushāʿirahs he recited verse and, as Muṣḥafī put it, "recounted memories of former times."[82] In his younger days, Ḥātim had been a hard-drinking rake working as a mercenary, admitting, "Look at what this age has become when even Ḥātim gave up the booze. / Yet, in recollection of those fresh green-faced ones he now takes only cannabis" (*dekh ṭaur is daur kā ḥātim ne kī tark-e sharāb / yād kar kar sabz-rū koñ vo to ab pītā hai bang*).[83] Later, Ḥātim lived in what Muṣḥafī referred to as the "lap of luxury," having ingratiated himself to Delhi's princes and dignitaries, including Amīr Ḳhān (d. 1747), whom we met earlier as a significant Mughal official with a long payroll of poets.[84]

Throughout his long career, Ḥātim had weathered social unrest on the political front and stylistic upsets in the literary realm, which he adapted to by rapidly shifting his modes of expression across his Persian and reḳhtah compositions. Through all of these changes, Ḥātim cultivated a senior position among younger versifiers while still imagining himself to be young at heart.[85] Ḥātim's close friends called him "Ḥātim the Second" because he had reinvented himself several times.[86] At Muṣḥafī's mushāʿirah, other poets teased Ḥātim, assigning him a range of playful appellations. Despite being the subject of humor, Ḥātim had secured a position for himself as an influential teacher. At one mushāʿirah, Mīr Taqī Mīr teasingly called Ḥātim "the Nursemaid of Poets" because of all those he had trained.[87] Historian ʿAbd ur-Rashīd ʿAṣīm reveals that, beginning with the sixteen or so disciples he had nurtured during his lifetime, Ḥātim's line of literary descent numbered into the hundreds, with subsequent poets in his line writing verse well into the mid-twentieth century.[88]

For the young writer and salon host Muṣḥafī, Ḥātim called back to a distant but intriguing time, an epoch rife with what Muṣḥafī perhaps idealistically referred to as "nights of serious matters" (*amr-e ḳhaṭīr shab-hā*). In Muṣḥafī's words, poets like Ḥātim, who were "trustworthy acquaintances and agreeable friends" (*āshnā-e ṣadiq wa yār-e mawāfiq*), could act as candles lighting Muṣḥafī's lonely way through "the desert of hesitation" (*badīyah-e taraddud*) as the young writer sought to document and reconstruct the gatherings at the Ornament of Mosques that occurred decades before his birth.[89] In a chronogram written on Ḥātim's death, Muṣḥafī expressed his reasons for providing so much detail about and praise for the elder poet's perspective, bringing his particulars out of obscurity: "Fate, with the swipe of an eraser, scraped away the mark of [Ḥātim's] lifetime from the page of the world."[90]

Like Muṣḥafī, I rely on the context and chronology provided by Ḥātim's written teachings to reengineer the gatherings at the Ornament of Mosques and other locales. Ḥātim was one of the few poets to draft a dīwān that noted when he wrote a ġhazal, for whom it was composed, and the precise meters used for each verse. Ḥātim suggested how his biography and his verse overlapped: "With a different rhyme and in another ġhazal, O Ḥātim, / I provide commentary and testimony of my particulars" (*muḳhtalif qāfiyah se aur ġhazal meñ ḥātim / apne aḥwāl kā ham sharḥ-o bayān rakhte hain*).[91] These were crucial details for students who had no teacher; having a teacher was a luxury available to only a minority of versifiers. So too, few poets had the financial means or significant influence to attract disciples, let alone to assemble their own collected works. Many junior writers had to seek options for learning aside from devoting time and money to becoming the mentee or acolyte of a living teacher. Fortunately, given the diffusion of recited poetry in a literacy-aware society like India, coupled with the relative ubiquity of paper, learning verse could occur aurally by picking up snippets from a range of poets or textually by cribbing from others' notes or libraries. Educated poets in India with access to books utilized the verse examples and idioms found in dictionaries, verse manuals, and other literary guidebooks to educate themselves about literary composition.[92] There was a burgeoning market for teachers crafted out of paper in the form of different kinds of how-to manuals.

Ḥātim's contribution to this market for paper teachers was his dīwān titled *Dīwānzādah*, perhaps translated as "The Descendant of Collection." In this uniquely named text, Ḥātim offers an edited version of his first volume of verse, which he subsequently referred to as "The Old Collection" (*Dīwān-e Qadīm*). Ḥātim's reasons for editing his older poems, and recomposing them in some cases, were myriad, but among them was to educate and instruct novices (*mubtadiyān*) like Muṣḥafī while leaving a kind of "inventory of traces" to account for some of his authorial choices.[93] Because of this, Ḥātim's *Dīwānzādah* recorded a great deal of context about its composition. Ḥātim explained that he "presented an abridgement of a notebook draft" (*baṭarīq-e iḳhtiṣār sawād-e bayāẓ namūdah*), also implying a shortcut in black and white. Indeed, the work's notations were designed to "lessen any vexations of reciters and copyists" (*ḳhwāndigān wa naql-nawīsān*) to allow beginners some instruction in the formal elements Ḥātim noted in the book, and to make explicit and fix in written form some subtleties governing relational conventions among poets.[94] Based on Ḥātim's intricate descriptions of his *Dīwānzādah*, the work appears as a condensed biography of his poetic output and its generation, in other words a "taẕkirah of one."

As a source of salon-based poetic speech, Ḥātim's *Dīwānzādah* contribution is quite vast, despite the text's intended status as an abridgment. For each poem that he included, Ḥātim consistently noted the year in which he wrote the poem, the name of the meter he used, and the meter's mnemonic syllables. Also, by including details on how he himself emulated other poets in composing specific poems, *Dīwānzādah* offered guidance for reḳhtah composers on how to precisely emulate the poetry of past masters and colleagues according to their accepted parameters of meter, rhyme, and refrain. In other words, by using the book to publicly rehearse the relational and technical intricacies of how he composed his poems, Ḥātim's *Dīwānzādah* provided a prosthetic teacher for those poets who had no master of their own, as had been the case for Ḥātim himself.

For mushāʿirah historians, the *Dīwānzādah* provides crucial metadata. Ḥātim classifies the poems included in the *Dīwānzādah* into several categories, labeling them, for example, as those he wrote at someone's request (*farmāʾishī*), those he wrote in response to a colleague or competitor (*jawābī*), and those he wrote according to a form (*ṭarḥī*). Ḥātim's contextual categories allow us to overhear what poets like Maẓmūn, Nājī, Maẓhar, and even their teacher Ārzū recited at the Ornament of Mosques in dialogue with Ḥātim. Indeed, in the first half of the *Dīwānzādah*, which consists of ġhazals composed between 1718 and 1735 or so, Ḥātim communicates the impact that Maẓmūn's circle of poets had on him by assiduously noting which of his ġhazals were composed in response to something recited or written by versifiers from among this tightly knit circle.

In this chapter, I rely on the tiny autobiographies that accompany verses that Ḥātim emulated from Maẓmūn in his *Dīwānzādah* to reengineer select gatherings at the Ornament of Mosques. The few poems by Maẓmūn that remain scattered among taẕkirahs that Ḥātim drew upon to emulate in his *Dīwānzādah* tell the mushāʿirah's history because they link up to parallel poems composed by those among the cohort, including Maẓhar, Nājī, and Ābrū, who joined Maẓmūn at the Ornament of Mosques. In 1723, Ḥātim recited this couplet at the Ornament of Mosques:

> For friendless Ḥātim, without you, who else is there?
> There is no one else since you will not be mine.[95]

> *ḥātim-e be-kas kā tujh bin kaun hai*
> *kaun hai jo gar nah hove tū mirā*

With this verse, he was in fact answering a prior poem by Maẓmūn praising the magic of reḳhtah composition. Maẓmūn had written:

Whoever escaped from being under another's spell,
they were bewitched by that reḳhtah of mine.[96]

nahīñ chalā afsūn kisī kā jin upar
reḳhtah is ko huʾā jādū mirā

To account for the wordplay in Maẓmūn's second line, a self-deprecating translation could read, "It seemed a mess to him, that magic of mine." For Maẓmūn, Ḥātim, and the friends who joined them, the only book that contained magical reḳhtah verse was the dīwān of a poet new to Delhi's literary sphere—Shams ud-Dīn Walī Muḥammad *Walī* (The Saint) (1667–1707) whose story is foundational to understanding reḳhtah's early history and the unique mushāʿirahs held at the Ornament of Mosques.

A Legendary Dīwān and Its Reception

At Muṣḥafī's salon, Ḥātim reminisced admiringly about the poetry collection of a versifier named Shams ud-Dīn Walī Muḥammad *Walī* (The Saint) (1667–1707), a southern poet who was, according to Ḥātim, "among the first to have written a dīwān in *reḳhtah*."[97] Ḥātim further recounted that Walī's dīwān reached Delhi in 1720 or 1721, the second year in the reign of the emperor Muhammad Shah.[98] Ḥātim's assertion, in 1780, was the first historical mention of precisely when this important text reached Delhi. Yet, it was a secondhand report in the words of an aged poet during the twilight of his literary career. This setting may provide some reason to doubt the veracity of the information, but a few details may encourage their acceptance as facts, especially considering how dramatically Walī's dīwān impacted those reciting verse at the Ornament of Mosques.

In fact, Shams ud-Dīn Walī's literary style took Delhi by storm. His poems were said to have "flowed off the tongues of the humble and great alike" (*zabān-e ḳhwurd wa buzurg jārī gashtah*).[99] Indeed, poets in Maẓmūn's home made Walī's words echo off the stone walls of the Ornament of Mosques as they recited them, assessed their beauty, and wrote verses of their own following Walī's innovative routes. In doing so, poets at Maẓmūn's gatherings rehearsed the process of *tatabbuʿ*, treading in Walī's footsteps. Enjoying the challenge, Maẓmūn emulated several of Walī's poems, choosing one with a particularly difficult end rhyme within its Hindi vocabulary. Walī's demanding phrases considered the magic of the beloved's tangled tresses:

To my core, O Shameless One, I'm enchanted by your veil
—as if I've seen the spell of your tresses that entangles my heart.[100]

mujh ghaṭ meñ ai nigharghaṭ hai shauq tujh ghunghaṭ kā
dekhe soñ laṭ gayā dil terī zulf kā laṭkā

Using Walī's meter and end rhyme, Maẓmūn adroitly echoed the theme while matching the assonance of Walī's Hindi vocabulary, using words ending in hard consonants:

Though snake charms instantly stop the heart,
from which conjurers did your tresses learn a spell [to ensnare my heart]?[101]

afsūn-e mār jhaṭ paṭ lete haiñ dil ko aṭkā
kin sāḥiroñ se sīkhā zulfoñ ne terī laṭkā

As if in a mushāʿirah with the living Walī, Maẓmūn attempted to push the theme of the heart-stopping power of the beloved's magical tresses along new twists of meaning in rhyming Hindi vocabulary.

Operating as a distinctive cohort, Maẓmūn and his friends wrote hundreds of ġhazals modeled on the words of Walī that furthered their own new ideas. In a song closing his dīwān, Ābrū praised Walī's verse for allowing Ābrū to achieve his own literary success:

Walī, in the art of *reḳhtah*, is the master.
How, indeed, shall Ābrū respond to this exhortation?

By composing verse through following [Walī] in emulation,
it might bring some benefit to your imagination.[102]

walī reḳhte bich ustād hai
kahe ābrū kyūñkih us kā jawāb

walekin tatabbuʿ kahnā suḳhan
kare faiẓ soñ fikr meñ kāmyāb

In addition to this lavish praise poem, some members of Maẓmūn's cohort offered tempered praises or even criticism of Walī's poems, including Ābrū, who boasted that he himself had accomplished prophet-like literary miracles (*aʿjāz*) while Walī's were mere saintly wonders (*karāmat*).[103] Within the gatherings at the mosque, Ḥātim more exuberantly cheered Walī's saintly position, stating,

Even though Ḥātim is no small thing in the comfort of his heart,
  Walī is, indeed, the saint (*walī*) in this world amidst all poetic speech.[104]

ḥātim bhī apne dil kī tasallī koñ kam nahīñ
  garchih walī walī hai jahān meñ suḳhan ke bīch

Ḥātim later cut this couplet from his edited works. Ditching his praise of Walī, Ḥātim edited the end of the ġhazal by expanding it into a verse set (*qiṭʿah*). Rather than belaboring the concept of the saint (*walī*), Ḥātim now cast himself as a messiah:

I say to you all if there is a fair judge [among you] then let him see
  every type of delight sits amidst my poetic speech.
For thirty years, Ḥātim's tumult has echoed in India.
  He is the Second Coming amidst the craft of reḳhtah composition.[105]

kahtā hūñ sab se hai koʾī munṣif so dekh le
  sab ṭarḥ kā mażāq hai mere suḳhan ke bīch
ḥātim kā shor tīs baras se hai hind meñ
  ṣāḥib qirān hai reḳhtah-goʾī ke fan ke bīch

Nearly two centuries later, twentieth-century Persian-language scholar Ḥaidar Ibrāhīm Sāyānī echoed eighteenth-century fans of Walī when he compared Walī's reḳhtah compositions to ornaments for sale in a shop, stating, "The jewels of Walī's creative intricacy (*nāzuk ḳhayālī*), elaboration of situations (*muʿāmalah bandī*), advancement of meaning [*maʿnī āfrīnī*], and flights of imagination (*ḳhayālāt kī buland parwāzī*), that he prepared in the market for speech (*bāzār-e suḳhan*), are still gazed upon by the world today, and in every assessment, there is a new luster to behold."[106] The terms used by Sāyānī to describe the facets of Walī's jewels in his version of the market for speech are each widely accepted concepts for specific rhetorical techniques employed by Persian and Urdu poets in the past and in the present. The terms "elaboration of situations" (*muʿāmalah bandī*)—that is so say, depictions of encounters that had been previously authorized by classic poets—and "advancement of meaning" (*maʿnī āfrīnī*)—again, meanings that had first been legitimated by classic poets—remained particularly important points of contention among Urdu poets well into the nineteenth century and continue to form arenas of intellectual inquiry for contemporary literary historians.[107] That Walī's unique style has continued to propel literary and historical debates from the 1720s until today testifies to his poetic impact, which deserves further examination.

The particulars of Walī's life are nearly unknown. Anecdotes about his salon conduct or notable style have yet to appear in any anthology. Even his patrons' identities remain opaque, although Walī's praise poems link him with the Qadri Sufi order.[108] We do know that this poet, the so-called "father of reḳhtah" (*bābā-e reḳhtah*), was likely born in the southern city of Aurangabad, spending time in Burhanpur and Surat before going on pilgrimage to Mecca in Arabia and finally passing away back in India at Ahmadabad.[109] Contrary to legends about his time in Delhi, Walī's travels likely never took him to the imperial capital and its gatherings. The chronologies of this lore do not line up, and in their propaganda, Delhi's first reḳhtah writers used the apocryphal story of Walī's travels to Delhi to exaggerate their city's influence on Walī. Hence, it is most likely that instead of Walī's charisma, it was purely his verse that reshaped poetic speech among Delhi's mushāʿirahs. In comparison, as we learned in the previous chapter, it was both the verse and the personalities of Bedil and his some of followers, as fixtures in the mushāʿirah circuits, that shaped literary sociability of the early 1700s. If Walī was the father of reḳhtah poetry among these early gatherings, he was a physically absent one. Walī, in absentia, reworked the connections and tastes of Delhi's mushāʿirahs only inadvertently through his written verse.

Over the 1720s and 1730s, the earliest reḳhtah poets of Delhi filled their notebooks and later dīwāns with emulations of Walī's notable lyrics. Ḳhwājah Ḳhān *Ḥamīd* (The Glorious) (fl. 1730–50), a taẕkirah writer from Aurangabad in Walī's southern region, noted that Walī's "dexterity of imagination was astonishing and his pleasant dīwān reveals the basis for a particular style" (*rangīnī ṭarḥ namūdah*).[110] Another writer in Delhi described Walī's dīwān verse as "the ornament of the pages of night and day and a hoop in the ears of the verse singers of the age."[111] In asserting that Walī's verse "outshone the sun itself," Qayām ud-Dīn *Qāʾim* (The Steadfast) (1722–1793) invoked a wordplay on Walī's given name, Shams ud-Dīn (the Sun of the Faith). With Ḥamīd's being the earliest, these assessments only began to take shape nearly three decades after Walī's dīwān purportedly arrived in the Mughal capital and over two decades after Gulshan died.

Gulshan's Poems

While Delhi's poets at the Ornament of Mosques grew enamored with Walī's verse over the 1720s and 1730s, legends clouded the genesis of Walī's literary inspiration. In the 1750s, a story emerged that the impetus for Walī's daring literary style originated with Gulshan, perhaps within the precincts of the Ornament of Mosques. But this famous legend, now a treasured element of Urdu literary lore, did not, as we might presume, hatch from Gulshan's circle. Nor did this now canonical story mention Gulshan's housemate Maẓmūn, one of the most compelling reḳhtah poets of the era when Walī's dīwān reached Delhi.

The tale linking Gulshan and Walī proceeds as follows: Sometime in 1700 or 1701, the forty-fourth year of the emperor Aurangzeb's reign, a poet named Walī traveled to Delhi from his native land in the South, said to be Aurangabad or Ahmadabad, and once in the capital, he presented his Persian poems in Gulshan's salon. Walī's performance would have presumably occurred on a Saturday night at the Ornament of Mosques. When Walī recited samples of his Persian verse, Gulshan was said to have suggested that Walī instead employ his native tongue, a southern language called Deccani, to write poetry according to Persian conventions of meter and metaphor. One of Delhi's earliest commentators on the reḳhtah scene in Delhi, Mīr Taqī Mīr, who did not reach Delhi until 1737 at the earliest, reported that Gulshan said the following to Walī: "All these topics (*maẓāmīn*, sing. *maẓmūn*) that have turned out to be useless in Persian: employ them in your reḳhtah. Thus, when you are called to account [on the Day of Judgement], there will be no argument with the determination [of your fate] due to the righteousness of [your] fame." We discern in these lines an amusing nod to Walī's pen name of "Saint."[112]

Despite the popularity and allure of this pervasive legend, Gulshan likely never met Walī at a mushāʿirah in Delhi, if he even met this former student of Bedil at all. By the 1780s, other taẕkirah writers raised doubts about this tale, writing of it, "truth or falsehood, its fate weighs upon the teller's neck."[113] Purnima Dhavan and Heidi Pauwels show that although the taẕkirah-based stories about Walī are evocative and intertextual, it is a difficult task to assess the truth claims of Walī and Gulshan's meeting from these writings, especially considering that some chroniclers make no attempt to prop up Gulshan's salon as the site for Walī's inspiration.[114] Other contemporary scholars postulate that Walī and Gulshan met a decade prior, between 1688 and 1693, and not in Delhi, but rather in Ahmadabad, where Walī was supposed to have traveled later in his life, or in Gulshan's southern hometown of Burhanpur.[115] These latter guesses hinge on the timings of Gulshan's travels and the moment he first came to Delhi, ranging from twenty to forty years before he died in 1728. Walī was said to have died in 1707, presumably in Ahmadabad, Gujarat, where a grave purported to be his was located until its state-sponsored destruction in 2002. Another question concerns the time frame for the dīwān's completion: If Walī and Gulshan did meet in 1700, how did Walī so quickly compose his entire reḳhtah oeuvre in a mere seven years? This was a task usually completed over several decades and refined over a lifetime. Certain references in Walī's dīwān imply strongly that he was already composing reḳhtah verse before 1700. For instance, writing in 1834, Garcin de Tassy noted that Walī's verse offers a few chronotopes, notably one that referenced the siege of Fort Satārā in present-day Maharashtra: "Your tresses have blockaded the pearl in your ear, / Just as when India's Imperial Army laid siege to the Fort of Satārā" (*liyā hai gher tujh zulfāñ ne tere kān kā motī / magar yū(ñ) hind kā lashkar lagiyā hai jā satāre koñ*).[116] The conquest was over by April 21, 1700.[117]

We must temper our assessment of Walī's influence with an understanding of how other Delhi poets contributed to the inception and growing popularity of reḳhtah verse. From this vantage point, the poetry recited at the Ornament of Mosques and the networks built there show us that Maẓmūn's circle harbored super-fans of Walī who emulated him, as Ābrū stated, but they also responded to verses that Walī composed in emulation of the Persian-language poets that he loved from India, Isfahan, and Kashmir. That is, besides the influence of Maẓmūn's circle of reḳhtah-writing friends, the words of poets from Isfahan and Kashmir reshaped the stylistic and emulative choices poets made at the Ornament of Mosques. Secondly, the ġhazal-based social networks at the Ornament of Mosques diminish Gulshan's purported contribution to literary history. Based on the anecdotes about this space and verse known to have been recited in the 1720s and 1730s at the mosque, Gulshan had little to no documentable impact on the competitive and delightful sociability that the mischievous Maẓmūn and his circle of friends cultivated at the Ornament of Mosques. In fact, the prudish Gulshan likely shunned the raucous words that this circle of cannabis drinkers hurled at each other, while Walī's boasting and conversational tone found a friendly crowd among Maẓmūn's friends. Had Walī and Gulshan met, their tastes in poetry would have caused them to clash.

Before we consider further the toothsome verse from Maẓmūn (a toothless poet), we turn to Gulshan's style and influences. Gulshan's connection to Bedil brought him into the company of some of the master teacher's other students, such as the taẕkirah writer and mushāʿirah host Ḳhwushgo, and, later, Ārzū, while also securing Gulshan's place within the influential gathering circles of the early eighteenth century.[118] As evinced by his few surviving verses recorded in taẕkirahs, Gulshan's literary style did not change considerably when he switched teachers.[119] Under both Sarḳhwush and Bedil, Gulshan shaped his ġhazal writing according to the masters of the 1600s, most notably Muḥammad ʿAlī *Ṣāʾib* (The Mark) (1592–1676), the most influential ġhazal writer of the seventeenth century and early eighteenth century. Ṣāʾib was independently wealthy and traveled to India between 1625 and 1632 before returning to his adopted hometown of Isfahan. Two of Gulshan's surviving couplets from his early career with Sarḳhwush reveal Ṣāʾib's direct influence, as Gulshan matched meter, rhyme, and refrain to Ṣāʾib's hits, adding to the many emulations Ṣāʾib's poems produced throughout the Persian-educated world.[120]

Under Bedil's tutelage, Gulshan composed a ġhazal in dialogue with Jalāl Muḥammad *Asīr* (The Prisoner) (1620–1648), a literary contender with Ṣāʾib in Isfahan who also influenced Delhi's poets.[121] In a playful mood, Bedil likely suggested that Gulshan compose something based on a particular ġhazal from Asīr because it referenced Gulshan's pen name: The Rose Garden. Asīr wrote:

> The winds, from Rose Garden to Rose Garden, draw my madness,
> and with the blood of a rainbow, make rose-colored waves in my goblet.[122]
>
> *hawā gulshan bah gulshan mī kashad dīwānah-e mā rā*
> *zi-ḳhūn-e tūbah mauj-e gul kunad paimānah-e mā rā*

Perfectly echoing Asīr's meter, rhyme, refrain, and metaphors, Gulshan's response rang:

> O God, to my madness, grant the intoxication of heartache.
> Like a wound, with my blood overflow my goblet.[123]
>
> *ilāhī nashāʾ-e dardī-e dil dīwānah-e mā rā*
> *chū zaḳhm az ḳhūn-e mā labrez kun paimānah-e mā rā*

At the formal level, Gulshan's contribution was a perfectly competent, if staid, emulation of Asīr's meter, rhyme, refrain, and "fresh" themes.

Gulshan's most famous couplet, however, deserves special attention. This verse about the beloved's exceedingly long eyelashes presumably took shape under Bedil's instruction, as it bears the poet-saint's penchant for complexity. The eyelash couplet became an object of ridicule in the hands of reḳhtah composer Muḥammad Rafīʿ Saudā during a gathering at Bedil's grave in the 1740s. Gulshan composed this eyelash poem based on the meter, rhyme, and refrain established by Rafīʿ ud-Dīn Muḥammad *Wāʿiẕ* (The Preacher) (1618?–1693/94), an Iranian "New Writer" of Isfahan whose fame spread in India over the late 1600s and early 1700s.[124] Wāʿiẕ developed a Romeo-and-Juliet-like theme by alluding to the ill-fated lovers Majnūn and Lailá:

My heart is like Majnūn, and like Lailá—those flirty looks of his.
But the ropes on Lailá's tent are those long eyelashes of his.[125]

dilam majnūn-o lailá ān nigāh-e ʿashwah sāz-e ū
ṭanāb-e ḳhemah-e lailá ast miẕhagān-e darāz-e ū

Rather than comparing the lover's long eyelashes to Lailá's tent ropes, Gulshan opted to compare them to a famous book on metaphysics and its commentary. Following the meter, rhyme, refrain, and long-eyelashes metaphor established by Wāʿiẕ, Gulshan applied to his most (in)famous ġhazal a line thick with heady allusion:

Only with onehundred exactitudes are you able to fathom the meanings of those flirtations of his.
An entire commentary on the metaphysics of the eye are those long eyelashes of his.[126]

ba-ṣad diqqat tawān fahmīd maʿnī-hā-e nāz-e ū
kih sharḥ-e ḥikmat ul-ʿain ast miẕhagān-e darāz-e ū

The delight in these lines stems from Gulshan's use of complex literary double entendres, the wordplay of *īhām* (misdirection or amphibology), that presents familiar and unfamiliar word associations. In the poem's second verse, Gulshan makes clever reference to a specific metaphysic manual and its commentary found in madrasah curriculum: *The Philosophy of the Source* (*Ḥikmat ul-ʿAin*, lit. "the knowledge/wisdom of the eye/source/wellspring") by Kātibī ul-Qazwīnī (1204–1276), an important philosopher, logician, and astronomer from Iran. Qazwīnī's work proved to be highly influential, and one of Qazwīnī's intellectual inheritors, Ibn Mubārakshāh ul-Buḳhārī (d. circa 1340), wrote a widely circulated commentary (*sharḥ*) on it, simply known as "A Commentary on the Philosophy of the Source" (*Sharḥ-e Ḥikmat ul-ʿAin*).[127]

A translation of Gulshan's verse that accounts for these multiple meanings reads, "Only with onehundred exactitudes are you able to fathom the meanings of those flirtations of his. / Indeed, just like Ibn Mubārakshāh's commentary on Kātibī ul-Qazwīnī's 'The Philosophy of the Eye' are those long eyelashes of his." That Gulshan's most famous verse warrants such a long explanation attests to its convoluted if cunning exactitude. Gulshan's contemporaries found enjoyment in a two-line elucidation of the metaphysics of the beloved's trichomegaly. Within Gulshan's lifetime this line was famous among Delhi's writers. Kishan Chand *Ikhlāṣ* (The Sincerity) (1690?–1754?) considered the fame of this line in his work "The Eternal Spring" (*Hameshah Bahār*), published in 1727—roughly the same year Gulshan died.[128]

In late 1727, Gulshan contracted dysentery or perhaps overdosed on China root, an increasingly popular drug in the post-1500 period and a common treatment for syphilis in Europe.[129] Whatever the case, he became too sick to care for himself at the Ornament of Mosques, and in mid-December 1727, his student Muḥammad Nāṣir *ʿAndalīb* (The Nightingale) (1693/94–1759) brought Gulshan home with him to Pahāṛ Ganj, a neighborhood outside the southwestern quadrant of the walled city. Gulshan remained bedridden in ʿAndalīb's home for twenty-one days, and on January 4, 1728, Gulshan finally succumbed to his illness in the presence of Ārzū, Ḳhwushgo, ʿAndalīb, and ʿAndalīb's seven-year-old son ʿAlī Muḥammadī who later became the famous Naqshbandi leader and poet known as Ḳhwājah Mīr *Dard* (The Agony) (1721–1785).[130]

Aside from poets such as these, the city's musicians also mourned Gulshan's death. Gulshan's friend Niʿmat Ḳhān Sadārang began leading a commemorative assembly at Gulshan's grave every Sunday evening.[131] On Gulshan's death anniversary (*ʿurs*), which occurred on 21 *Jumādá ul-Awwal* according to the Hijri calendar, dancers and musicians maintained a lively gathering late into the night in commemoration of Gulshan as a poet-saint for the city's performers.[132] Gulshan's grave, situated just south of Pahāṛ Ganj in the district of Aḥdī Pūrah, also served as a destination, among other tombs, for dancers and singers during the city-wide pilgrimage for Basant, the late January/early February holiday marking forty days before the start of spring.[133] This tradition continued for over a decade. In 1739, a visiting southern official noticed that on the seventh day of Basant, dancers gathered as a group around "the grave of a respected gentleman buried in Aḥdī Pūrah"—this being the grave of Gulshan.[134]

For Delhi in the 1740s, Gulshan was the poet-saint of professional performers. Gulshan's annual commemoration, the spring festivities, and the weekly musical soirees at his tomb cemented his respect among the city's guilds of performers and poets, befitting his title "The Amīr Ḳhusrau of the Age."[135] Like Amīr Ḳhusrau, Gulshan has been given outsized credit for shaping Indo-Muslim literary and music cultures. But unlike Ḳhusrau, a prodigious writer, Gulshan authored few literary works, and those received scant attention. In fact, one chronicler noted that "after [Gulshan's] death, no one had much inclination to study his collected works."[136] That Gulshan's poems were nearly forgotten by the 1750s—perhaps a startling realization both for contemporary consumers of Urdu's literary lore and for his devotees and fellow Bedil-students who sang Gulshan's praises over the 1720s and 1730s. Gulshan's literary notoriety was a product of his contemporaries' adulations, namely the former students of Bedil who revered Gulshan for factors other than his literary acumen.[137] In the 1740s and 1750s, those of Bedil's acolytes who still remembered Gulshan began to pass away, and new memories of Gulshan's salon arose to disseminate Walī's dīwān of stylish reḳhtah verse.

Maẓmūn's Followers

In comparison to Gulshan, Maẓmūn had a far greater impact on Delhi's literary scene and therefore the historical styles of early reḳhtah known today. Indeed, not a single verse of Gulshan's remains extant in tażkirahs to prove Gulshan's reḳhtah influence among contemporaries. Gulshan's purported impact was apocryphal, and even doubted by chroniclers in the era Gulshan's legends first circulated. Maẓmūn's influence, however, has been muted by time and historical framing.

Those who emulated Maẓmūn in gatherings, such as Ḥātim, enable us to catch a glimpse of Maẓmūn's style as it affected versifiers who visited him at the Ornament of Mosques. The evidence for Maẓmūn's distinction and influence comes from the dialogues and emulations his verse produced and those whom he also followed. During the early modern period in which Maẓmūn wrote, all new verse, without exception, arose from models and ideas first legitimized by past versifiers. Later Persianate poetry, even in reḳhtah, made use of these same images, ideas, and formal elements. The figures whom poets chose to emulate and how they utilized their verses set the boundaries of their literary communities on the page and within the geography of the city, delineating a variety of alliances to past masters and their preference for new- or old-style poetry. These links are found in formal elements and imaginative ideas. Emulation of the meter, rhyme, and refrain in the words of noted masters established connections between poets and instantiated stylistic allegiances among peers who also enjoyed and judged new and old verse.

The earliest record of Maẓmūn's cohort exchanging poems leads us to a gathering that took place around 1718/19 (1131 AH) where we find a group of rambunctious versifiers weaving into their compositions idioms and ideas cultivated from Delhi's streets and reminiscent of the robust language used by Bedil's student ʿAṭā, as described in chapter 1. For instance, Maẓmūn presented a theme complaining about the neglectful beloved, using metaphors about the heat of anger and the chill of sadness in well-known Hindi phrases that easily translate into similar English-language idioms:

I used to think that those beauties would get hot under the collar
because of me.
Instead, my heart went cold as soon as they snowed me.[138]

maiñ jāntā thā ḳhūbān garmī karenge mujh soñ
dil sard ho gayā hai jab se paṛā hai pālā

Ābrū responded to Maẓmūn's words, composing a ġhazal of ten couplets that ended with these lines in which he bragged about his verse:

Ābrū's verses became the envy of the pearls.
With the brand of my pen name, I made them into a string of pearls,
my dear.[139]

ashʿār ābrū ke rashk-e guhar hūʾe haiñ
dāġh-e suḳhan señ us ko lū lū hūʾā hai lālā

As if calling to a local merchant (*lālā* in Hindi), Ābrū used the brand of his pen name (*dāġh-e suḳhan*) to turn raw pearls into decorations threaded for ornamenting the beloved's neck.

Ḥātīm, twenty years old at the time, also contributed a ġhazal to this gathering. His verse ended with lines praising street fighters who could defeat the competitor for the beloved's affections:

When Ḥātim's boys who bring the hurt showed up,
they triumphed over everyone, even the headstrong rival.[140]

zor āwarī soñ laṛke ḥātim ke pās āʾe
jo hai raqīb sarkash sab ko diyā hai bālā

Reḳhtah gave these Persian-educated poets a way to introduce the bragging, erotic, and clamorous language of the bazaar into Persianate forms as they sought new meanings and images. Judging by the poems just reviewed, Ḥātīm's boys were indeed bringing their best skills to the battlefield of verse at the Ornament of Mosques. The method we use for assessing and reconstructing their spirited exchanges involves using the same methods they employed to compose imaginative verse: echoing the meter, rhyme, and refrain of past masters and contemporary competitors. In other words, we follow in the footsteps (*tatabbuʿ*) of Maẓmūn's friends as they emulated and enjoyed notable poems.[141]

Maẓmūn's cohort enshrined two important past masters, referring to them when setting the tone and style of their exchanges at the Ornament of Mosques. The first of these was the Persian-educated poet Shams ud-Dīn Walī Muḥammad *Walī* (The Saint) (1667–1707), an absent father of reḳhtah about whom little is known. Despite the mysteries surround him, Walī's verse indelibly reshaped Persianate style when his famous dīwān reached Delhi in 1720 or 1721. The second figure was Muḥammad ʿAlī *Ṣāʾib* (The Mark) (1592–1676), an Iranian poet who, like Walī, probably never came to Delhi or may have briefly passed through the city, but whose words rang from the lips of nearly all Persian and reḳhtah composers in the city's mushāʿirahs. Ṣāʾib earned his position as the champion ġhazal composer of the middle 1600s after traveling between India and Iran where he garnered support from the leading literary patrons of the age. Nearly all the poets who vied for attention and fame in the mushāʿirahs of the 1700s read and emulated Ṣāʾib. Walī himself emulated Ṣāʾib's couplet in which the speaker put the beloved to sleep with his sad tales:

> In the veil of a story, I composed for him such a long description of my current state,
> it only brought heaviness to his eyes, as if falling asleep bit by bit.[142]
>
> *zi-bas dar pardah-e afsānah bā ū ḥāl-e ḳhwud guftam*
> *girān gashtam bah chashmish hamchū ḳhwāb āhistah āhistah*

Walī used this same idea, but he shifted its focus to the image of the beloved arriving in a dream:

> O Walī, in my heart appears an image of the beloved without a care.
> For this is how he appears before my eyes, as if a dream and bit by bit.[143]
>
> *walī mujh dil meñ ātā hai ḳhayāl-e yār be-parwā*
> *kih jyūn ankhiyāñ maneñ ātā hai ḳhwāb āhistah āhistah*

Across Delhi in the 1720s and 1730s, both Ṣā'ib's and Walī's poems earned emulators of their Persian and reḳhtah lines on the "bit by bit" refrain.[144]

Maẓmūn's Last Recital

The year that he died, sometime in 1734 or 1735 (1147 AH), Maẓmūn recited one of his most influential ġhazals at the Ornament of Mosques.[145] With his missing teeth, some of the Seedless Poet's consonants had softened, but he could still convey a striking couplet. Mumbling his words, Maẓmūn recited:

> Freedom from arrest will never be an option for this headstrong one.
> Even from my corpse the collar around my neck will never fall, O Ringdove.[146]
>
> *giriftārī se is sarkash ko āzādī nahīñ hargiz*
> *mū'e se bhī nah niklegā yih ṭauq-e gardan ai qumrī*

The verse called to the ringdove, a familiar figure within the Persianate vernal lexicon held to be an eternal prisoner of love with a ring of dark feathers around its neck. Maẓmūn chose to emulate a ġhazal that had influenced mid-1600s writers from Kabul to South India and from Isfahan to Bengal. But he chose to write his version in reḳhtah. Ḥātim had also developed the theme about the coloring on the ringdove's neck, urging it to beware of the seductions of the garden:

> Don't keep flying to the cypress to give so much of your heart, O Ringdove.
> Now you are only pilloried, but next your neck will be cut, O Ringdove.[147]
>
> *itā bhī mat lagāve sarv se jā jā man ai qumrī*
> *abhī to ṭauq hai par ab kaṭegī gardan ai qumrī*

The speaker of this poem lauds the ringdove for being eternally fettered, a far better fate than being slaughtered—another risk when falling in love someone with a seductive cypress-like figure. Due to its scent and shapely form, the cypress tree was another perennial image in Persianate poetics.

Nājī took theme of the ringdove and his attachment to the cypress in a different direction. Instead of alluding to the ring of dark feathers on the bird's neck, he concentrates on the somber, gray color of its coat:

After that elegantly dressed cypress waltzed into the garden, you were totally cheated.
That's why your coat is the same as that of a drab pigeon, O Ringdove.[148]

vuh sarv-e jāmah zeb ā kar chaman meñ chhal gayā tujh koñ
tabhī to fāḳhtāʾī hai terā pairāhan ai qumrī

The humble ringdove approaches the kingly cypress hoping to be given a similarly ornate mantle. Instead, he is left with a coat the color of ashes. Other participants at the Ornament of Mosques, namely Ābrū and Maẓhar, did not contribute to the gathering. Ābrū, who had written many verses emulating Maẓmūn, had died two years before in 1733, after being kicked in the head by a horse.[149] Maẓhar's Persian dīwān and the remnants of his reḳhtah oeuvre bear no mark of his attendance.

Sadly, the remaining lines of Maẓmūn's ġhazal are lost. Nājī's and Ḥātim's complete ġhazals survive in their collected works. Yet, it was Maẓmūn's vision that prompted his circle of poets to string together words on the suggestive theme of the ringdove as housed in the refrain of his verse. Maẓmūn's inspiration was not prompted by Walī or even Gulshan. Rather, it originated from lines composed in Kabul or South India, or perhaps on the road in between, from the lips of Ṣāʾib and Maʿṣūm, two poets who journeyed from Isfahan to India.

THE FLIGHT OF THE RINGDOVE

Muḥammad ʿAlī Ṣāʾib left his home in Isfahan around 1625 and set off for India.[150] His first stop was in Kabul, where he met a certain poet named Mīr Maʿṣūm *Maʿṣūm* (The Innocent) (d. 1642).[151] Both Ṣāʾib and Maʿṣūm came under the generous patronage of Kabul's governor Ẓafar Ḳhān *Aḥsan* (The Most Excellent) (d. 1662) and subsequently followed Aḥsan to South India on military campaigns after 1628. Ṣāʾib remained under Aḥsan's patronage until he returned to Isfahan in 1632, likely staying for a short period with Aḥsan in Kashmir. The path of Maʿṣūm's story is less clear, though it appears he parted ways with Ṣāʾib and Aḥsan in 1632 to take a position with Mīr Muḥammad Bāqir Aʿẓam Ḳhān, an Iraqi nobleman appointed to the governorship of Bengal that same year. Ṣāʾib later composed a closing couplet memorializing his time with Maʿṣūm, writing that he would befriend no one else among versifiers.[152] Maʿṣūm's career becomes untraceable at this point. Aʿẓam Ḳhān's governorship in Bengal quickly terminated in 1635, but Maʿṣūm presumably remained there until his death in 1642.

Maʿṣūm managed to release a dīwān that circulated among the literati of Mughal India until at least the mid-1700s and eventually reached Iran, his verse remaining of interest until the 1680s in Isfahan's coffeehouse scene.[153]

The inspiration for Maẓmūn's reḳhtah ġhazal calling to the ringdove originated from an exchange between Ṣāʾib and Maʿṣūm. It is impossible to say who dreamed up the suggestive verse ending with "O Ringdove." Maʿṣūm, who is often cited within later taẕkirahs for crafting the verse, composed a suggestive foundation for the theme in the image of the collar on the ringdove's neck:

You have a collar of ermine, and mine is of iron, O Ringdove.
Tell me whose beloved cypress is more pitiless, yours or mine, O Ringdove?[154]

tū az sinjāb dārī ṭauq-o man az āhan ai qumrī
bagū sarv-e tū be-raḥm ast yā sarv-e man ai qumrī

Indeed, the ringdove, with a downy collar closed by the cypress, is in a better position than the lover speaking in the poem. The lover pining for the beloved with a shapely cypress-like form has been punished with an iron clasp around his neck.

Ṣāʾib took the themes in another direction, melding sight and sound to form the collar on the ringdove's neck:

The cypress of the rose garden no longer endures the wrath of your complaints, O Ringdove.
From the black ashes, smear a collar of silence on your neck, O Ringdove.[155]

nadārad sarv-e īn gulzār tāb-e shewan ai qumrī
banih az surmah ṭauq-e ḳhāmushī bar gardan ai qumrī

According to humoral medicine, a voice, especially when enunciating complaints, could generate immense heat. Ṣāʾib brought this idea into his variation on the theme of the ringdove's collar. In this case, the ringdove sang with such fury that he burned the garden down, causing the cypress to flee. The ashes that remained formed the substance of the dark ring around his neck and silenced him because no beloved cypress remained to which he could warble.

With Aḥsan's 1632 appointment to his new post of governor, the ringdove poem found its way to Kashmir, where it flourished via two local poets. One of them, Mīrzā Dārāb Beg *Joyā* (The Inquiring) (d. 1706), a descendant of an Iranian immigrant from Tabriz, had supposedly met Ṣāʾib as a boy. Nevertheless, Joyā's career only began to flourish in the 1670s and 1680s during the later reign of Mughal emperor Aurangzeb (r. 1658–1707), long after Ṣāʾib returned to Isfahan. Joyā admired Ṣāʾib's verse, which circulated among the literary cliques of Kashmir, and added his own variation within the themes established by Ṣāʾib and Maʿṣmūn. Joyā's ġhazal appears in his dīwān, with an opening that reads:

With the chain that love bound to my feet, O Ringdove—
only a mere link has been slipped around your neck, O Ringdove.[156]

zi-zanjīrī kih ʿishq andāḳht bar pā-e man ai qumrī
fatād āḳhir turā ham ḥalqah-yī bar gardan ai qumrī

In this case, the ringdove and the ever-suffering lover are wedded together. While an entire chain suitable for human form fetters the lover's feet, a tiny link at the end slips around the neck of the ringdove.

Joyā's influence reached beyond Kashmir via his students, notably those who left the mountains for Delhi's literary scene. This included ʿAbd ul-Ġhanī Beg *Qabūl* (The Worthy) (d. 1725), a noted mushāʿirah host with an extensive following who lived within the precincts of Fīroz Shāh's fortress and who championed the "unsatisfied misdirection" (*īhām-e nā tamām*) of the early 1700s. But a poet with a fainter voice named ʿAbd ur-Raḥīm *Kamgo* (The Taciturn) (d. 1718?) brought the ringdove theme to Delhi in the 1690s and recited it before Sarḳhwush, Gulshan's former teacher and the most important mushāʿirah impresario of the age. But rather than developing his own theme, Kamgo paraded Joyā's imaginative verse as his own when he visited Sarḳhwush's home in Saʿdullāh Ḳhān square while seeking poetry instruction.[157] Sarḳhwush enjoyed the verse and noted it down in a diary. Kamgo's word-for-word plagiarism later appeared in Sarḳhwush's widely circulated taẕkirah, "The Words of Poets" (*Kalimāt ush-Shuʿarā*). Kamgo did not last long in Delhi's poetry scene, leaving for the Deccan sometime around 1715, but his theft from a fellow Kashmiri had lasting consequences. Sarḳhwush's writings found their way into the hands of the mushāʿirah host and poet Ānand Rām Muḳhliṣ, who reproduced the lie of Kamgo's authorship.[158]

This brings us to the era in which Maẕmūn resided at the Ornament of Mosques, enjoying the scenic setting of the riverside prayer hall. Delhi knew and cherished Ṣaʾib's works, and this particular verse from the Iranian ġhazal superstar, held to be "worthy of poets whose nature enjoys complexity," was arguably the single most important ġhazal used by Persian and reḳhtah writers of the 1720s and 1730s to develop their compositional abilities.[159] That Maẓmūn wrote an entire reḳhtah composition on a beloved Persian verse marked an accomplishment among his circle of friends, Nājī and Ḥātim. In fact, between 1734 and the late 1740s, five other poets within the Delhi mushāʿirah scene wrote variations on the ringdove poem established in the 1630s by Maʿṣmūn and Ṣāʾib: the poet Ḥakīm Shaiḳh Ḥusain *Shuhrat* (The Fame) (d. 1736) contributed to the form; Ānand Rām Muḳhliṣ composed a version that was supposedly a favorite of the emperor Muhammad Shah; Muḳhliṣ's colleague Qizilbāsh Ḳhān *Ummīd* (The Hope) (d. 1746) wrote an engaging ġhazal following the ringdove refrain; and the Iranian poet Muḥammad ʿAlī *Ḥazīn* (The Grieved) (1692–1766), who emigrated to India in 1737, composed a version of this poem.[160] Ḥazīn's version earned a critical response from Ārzū when the Delhi-based salon host accused Ḥazīn of stealing a theme from Ṣāʾib.[161] It also caught the attention of Saudā's rival, the Kashmiri cleric ʿAṭāʾullāh *Nudrat* (The Rarity) (fl. 1730–50).[162]

Beyond Delhi, Ṣāʾib's return to Iran brought the ringdove verse into the competitive circles of Isfahan's writers. Rafīʿ ud-Dīn Muḥammad *Wāʿiẓ* (The Preacher) (1618?–1693/94), a colleague of Ṣāʾib, wrote a variation on it, and roughly a century later the poet Mīr Sayyid ʿAlī *Mushtāq* (1689–1756) composed a version of the ringdove poem.[163] Maẓmūn the Seedless Poet had tapped into something rich when he recited his final famous ġhazal at the Ornament of Mosques. He knew about the literary inheritance of Ṣāʾib, seeing how this influential ġhazal writer still reshaped the ġhazal. Maẓmūn tested his mettle on a verse that even his teacher Ārzū could not match.[164] Nājī, also one of Ārzū's reḳhtah students, successfully followed Ṣāʾib's steps in a ringdove ġhazal. In Nājī's final couplet, he closed the matter:

> Since you are no one's friend, you should study wailing from Nājī.
> Indeed, this game of love is an exceedingly difficult art, O Ringdove.[165]
>
> *jo tū maḥram nahīñ to sīkh le nājī setī nālah*
> *kih hai is ʿishq-bāzī kā nipaṭ mushkil fan ai qumrī*

Indeed, the game of verse was a difficult art, further complicated by linguistic choices, modes of stylistic distinction, and a heavy inheritance bestowed on all writers from ġhazal masters of the past. For a twenty-nine-year-old Saudā, Maẓmūn's death was a calamity. It was as if the science of poetry itself had died: "Friends, the source of good ġhazal writing has up and left. / The poet Maẓmūn left this world, and only Saudā remained—a total drunk" (*binā hī uṭh gaʾī yāro ġhazal ke ḳhūb kahne kī / gayā maẓmūn dunyā se rahā saudā so mastānah*).[166]

Conclusion

Other gatherings in more publicly accessible spaces also emerged in the early 1700s. Yet, the Ornament of Mosques hosted a crucial contingent of poets and verse that reshaped our understanding of the mushāʿirah and the early years of reḳhtah poetry's developing literary scene. Gulshan sat as a charismatic figure within the intellectual, social, and music circles of Delhi's educated classes, but his contributions to the Persian literary style of the time were few. As we will see in chapter 4, only two poets, the daring writer Rafīʿ Saudā and the Kashmiri cleric Nudrat, emulated Gulshan's poetry in the 1740s. Yet, Gulshan likely produced not a single reḳhtah composition. The stuffy or even thin-skinned aspects of his character force us to reconsider his role as projected via legends and stories of reḳhtah's entrance among Delhi's mushāʿirahs. Instead, Maẓmūn's verse and anecdotes present a more revealing picture of Delhi's salon-based literary sociability, especially as there are simply more examples of his verse preserved in taẕkirahs. The striking language of the bazaar, its braggadocio and idiomatic quips, made for a fresh and seductive means by which Persian-educated writers could craft new ideas. While reḳhtah in the salons of Delhi relied on these local idioms, literary practice still linked the words of reḳhtah poets to the larger Persianate world. Reḳhtah poets emulated one another, but they also followed in the well-trodden paths of the premier writers of the age who were famous not just in Delhi but across regions such as Iran, Kashmir, Bengal, and the Deccan.

Despite the city's public performers who venerated his grave, Gulshan's influence faded, and few anthologists memorialized his verse. In contrast, Maẓmūn's literary influence remained intact, preserved among the hundred or so lines scattered across the writings of the influential taẕkirah writers of the mid-1700s and those who followed. Historians, poetry fans, and Delhi's public in general each cultivated differing and occasionally overlapping practices to commemorate local celebrities from among the city's saints, poets, and performers. Shrine spaces and compendiums each provide access points to memories imbued with associations of the past devotion or entertainment. Maẓmūn's impact on literary style was arguably far bolder than that of Gulshan. However, later taẕkirah records reversed the relative weight of Gulshan's and Maẓmūn's legacies. Gulshan's Sufi connections made him a better candidate for the type of history memorialized at shrines and recorded in compendiums, writings that vaunted his charisma, such as it was, and downplayed his verse. In contrast, Maẓmūn's commemoration appears implicitly in the many delectable verses memorized for diary and taẕkirah entries and poets' emulations.

For the literary communities in Delhi's mushāʿirahs, a single couplet could stand as a memorial, linked with anecdotal delights or linguistic authority. Each of these verses has its own story, miniscule biographies about the literary speech of Delhi's streets and bazaar, as preserved in the stylistic linkages that structured the tiny love songs of Delhi's mushāʿirah space. Maẓmūn's salon-based instincts impacted the styles of later writers who emulated him, notably Saudā and Yaqīn. Maẓmūn's favorite verse with the ringdove refrain later influenced Persian-language poets connected to the highest levels of the imperial court. These connections grew denser as the ranks of Delhi's reḳhtah poets expanded after Maẓmūn's passing. We now turn to the close-knit settings in which Delhi's clever reḳhtah composers impacted the city's larger contingent of Persian writers, as mushāʿirahs continued during a military occupation in the wake of a mass killing.

3 Literary Discord and the Occupation of Delhi

By the late 1730s, new voices, urban violence, and divergent literary values seeded poetic and social change in Delhi's gatherings to produce clashes of style and collisions of meaning. Several distinct approaches to poetry thrived in tension with one another, even within the ġhazals of single authors who performed in Delhi's mushāʿirahs during this cacophonous phase. Amid the city's increasing literary clamor, on February 24, 1739, Iran's new emperor, Nadir Shah (r. 1736–47), defeated the Mughal army just north of Delhi at Karnal, capturing the emperor. Nadir Shah reached Delhi on March 19, 1739, after settling the terms of Mughal surrender, and his military began a three-month occupation of the city. During this time, Iran's emperor exacted payments from the Mughal treasury and punitive taxes from Delhi's elites. But before Nadir Shah acquired these riches, Delhi's commoners forcibly demanded their own political exactions.

In response to the humiliation of their emperor, Muhammad Shah, a group of Delhi's non-elite locals rose up to kill hundreds of Qizilbash soldiers in the streets under cover of night. They had been emboldened by rumors about the invading emperor's assassination, but Nadir Shah was very much alive and retaliated against them by ordering a massacre of the common folk the next morning and afternoon. The city's poets witnessed this five-hour-long bloodshed yet neglected to include much elaboration of the violence in their verse. These omissions occurred despite the fact the occasion of Bedil's annual posthumous gathering coincided with the months of tense occupation, as did many other regular gatherings.[1]

Even in the midst of political tumult, particularities of urban geography and class enabled the continuation of Delhi's market for speech. The violence meted out by the visiting emperor's troops erupted in the central corridor of the city, well away from Bedil's grave and other favored gathering spaces near the fortress of Fīroz Shāh. So too, the Qizilbash troops were instructed to target only the commoners, rather than the elites and associated classes who comprised the majority of those who gathered to exchange verse. Among the thousands of Delhi's commoners who perished, only a few

Mughal notables lost their lives, among them two mushāʿirah poets and their families who died from wounds suffered in the chaos.

Such a resounding silence is especially perplexing considering that the occupation brought with it new poets to Delhi's flourishing literary community who were distinctly well-positioned to observe and comment on the political violence. Even during the occupation, traveling writers joined gatherings, visited shrines, and penned new verse of their own, motivated by wealth, connections, and a chance to impact Delhi's ġhazal scene. Notable Iranian poets who trekked to Delhi before, during, and following Nadir Shah's occupation include Muḥammad ʿAlī *Ḥazīn* (The Grieved) (1692–1766), ʿAlī Qulī *Wālih* (The Astonished) (1712–1756), and Qizilbāsh Ḳhān *Ummīd* (The Hope) (1678–1746).[2] Indian literary figures from outlying towns also appeared: Mīr Taqī Mīr and ʿAbd ul-Ḥakīm *Ḥākim* (The Ruler) (1708–1768). Versifiers who reached Delhi during this phase encountered a polyphony of poets' voices and a plethora of contrasting styles. Newly arrived poets formed close friendships with Delhi's veteran versifiers, and also found enemies among them, and some became teachers for young Delhi notables eager for instruction. Iranian émigré Ummīd joined the ranks of well-connected local mentors such as Jān-e Jānān *Maẓhar* (The Spectacle) (1699–1781), a Naqshbandi adherent, and Muḥammad ʿAlī *Ḥashmat* (The Magnificence) (1696?–1748), a famous writer of *īhām* or "misdirection." Newcomers like Ummīd also found their ways to the courtesans' quarters where elite public performers wrote and sang amatory styles of verse (see figure 3.1). There, women such as Gulāb (The Rose Water) (fl. 1730–50), Raḥmān Bāʾī (fl. 1730–50), and Tanū (The Delicate) (fl. 1730–40) distinguished themselves in the old style of ġhazal writing favored by lyricists from the distant past and by Ṣāʾib, a perennial favorite.[3]

Written in subtle metaphor and complex wordplays (notably īhām), the poetry that emerged during this phase of political unrest and urban change produced a rich literary narrative about Delhi in the 1730s and 1740s.[4] Seeds planted in the city's gatherings in the late 1730s resulted in a blossoming of taẕkirah writing that culminated in the 1750s. In assessing the effluence of poetry and related writing produced during this phase, we discover that the political and economic changes occurring in Delhi during and after the occupation, which might have hindered poets' gatherings, in fact appeared to be a boon. As we will see from our survey of the verse in circulation during this time of change, discordant voices produced new and original ideas. From these writings and memories, we find a moment when early modern society embraced multiple meanings in its verse to craft new networks and connections.

An Aggrieved Entrance

The spring of 1734 found Muḥammad ʿAlī *Ḥazīn* (The Grieved) (1692–1766) standing by the Persian Gulf waters of Port Abbas deciding the direction to which he should flee. As a young man, Ḥazīn had left behind his beloved hometown of Isfahan, with its resplendent garden parties and verse singing, to widen his education by traveling across Iran and Iraq. An increasingly restive Iran, pummeled under the violence of a regime change, had made Ḥazīn's sea voyage unavoidable. Accompanying the political tumult, dangerous rumors circulated that Ḥazīn himself had orchestrated the assassination of a governor appointed by Nadir Shah.[5] On the cusp of monsoon winds shifting toward India, even the port city Ḥazīn was leaving had grown tense under competing factions.[6] Roughly a decade later, his new dīwān of 1743 would capture this moment of springtime trepidation, mourning the homeland he would soon leave:

> Cloudy weather desires a moistened melody. Strike up a song!
> Like the spring breeze, February's clouds are swift footed, O Ringdove.[7]
>
> *hawā-e abar ḳhwāhid naġhmah-e tar nālah-yī sar kun*
> *nasīm-āsā sabuk sair ast abar-e bahman ai qumrī*

Ḥazīn's verse, following in a form favored by Maẓmūn in chapter 2, implied that the ringdove's song hailed the coming spring on the wake of late winter clouds.

During the previous spring, Ḥazīn had first left Iran at forty-one years old, when he had traveled to Oman for a few months before returning to his home country. Now, a year later, Ḥazīn could not decide in which direction to set his sails. An English ship captain Ḥazīn met at the port argued against India, advising Ḥazīn to travel toward Europe. Ḥazīn ignored this and opted for India, landing in Sindh, where he immediately deemed the local weather disagreeably intemperate and began searching for better climates. After three years of shuffling between equally uncomfortable towns and fighting constant illness, Ḥazīn arrived in Delhi by March of 1737, incidentally in the company of a young Āzād Bilgrāmī.[8]

In Delhi, Ḥazīn found a welcoming host in top literary patron Amīr Ḳhān and accepted an invitation to stay at his haveli in the walled city's southern edge.[9] Word of Ḥazīn's arrival traveled fast. Among the first of Delhi's poets to greet him was Mīrzā *Girāmī* (The Honored) (d. 1743), infamous as an obstreperous reciter. Girāmī traipsed to the doors of Amīr Ḳhān's residence with a street performer's flair and an entourage of about fifteen followers. This group was known as the Qabuliyan Contingent, so named for ʿAbd ul-Ġhanī Beg *Qabūl* (The Worthy) (d. 1727), an influential poet from Kashmir who prized īhām, and Girāmī, the son of Qabūl, was its marshal.[10]

With his outsized ego and a diary tucked under his arm, Girāmī attended mushāʿirahs across Delhi dressed as a dervish (*qalandar*). His red yogi's sarong (*lungī-e jogiyān*), teased-out beard, and unitarian attitudes toward everyone from Jews to Zoroastrians caused others to assume he was an atheist. Famous for loudly singing his verse, a notably complex verse circulated among writers' diaries and found emulators among Girāmī's colleagues for its vibrant use of īhām's synesthetic misdirection: "May colorful verse be harmonious to the ears of those with no tongue. / Indeed, people fill the ears of lunatics with cinnabar" (*bah gosh-e be-zabānān shiʿr-e rangīn āshnā bāshad / kih pur sāzand az shanjarf mardum gosh-e māhī rā*).[11] The lines alluded to medical treatments whereby cinnabar, that is mercury sulphate normally used to treat ocular pain, could be poured into the ear to relieve diseases. Yet, the poem simultaneously conveyed the idea that stylish or colorful verse (*shiʿr-e rangīn*) could function as medicine for those whose hearing had been lost, perhaps even restoring the ability to speak through pen, inkwell, and ink—the latter another product of cinnabar.

Hoping to impart similar verse to Ḥazīn's ears, Girāmī stood in the alley below the mansion and let out "a cry that rang in the heavens" to welcome Ḥazīn.[12] In fact, whether in the street or at the mushāʿirah, Girāmī was known for being inordinately loud. In the manner of his father Qabūl, he shouted "*āfrīn*" (bravo!) such that "its force was an earthquake suddenly heard throughout the city."[13] Girāmī's boisterous welcoming of Ḥazīn did not have the desired effect on the newcomer, displeasing its target. The Isfahan-schooled poet, who had grown up listening to poetry recited calmly in gardens, had not yet accustomed himself to Delhi's rambunctious ġhazal scene. It was a shock. As we recall with the careers of versifiers like ʿAṭā in chapter 1 or Maẓmūn in chapter 2, street-smart poets with unruly musical abilities like Girāmī formed an important constituency among versifiers in Delhi.[14] In response to Girāmī's bellowing greeting, Ḥazīn recoiled from his visitors but eventually rallied to oblige Girāmī and his followers with an impromptu mushāʿirah.

Ḥazīn held vocal music in high esteem, and when he eventually established himself in Delhi, Ḥazīn dazzled his listeners with songs based on his staid notions of ethical listening habits—very different from Girāmī's vocal antics. Ḥazīn had developed a keen ear and vocal abilities during his youth, when the young poet attended performances of ġhazal singers who deeply impacted him. At an impromptu garden mushāʿirah in Isfahan, a famous calligrapher with "talents in music and singing" named Maulānā ʿAlī Kosārī Iṣfahānī presented verse that sent the teenage Ḥazīn into "out-of-body raptures" when he heard Kosārī sing, "Tonight, come to the garden so that we might fill our cup. / You light the candle and the rose, and I'll act like the moth and the nightingale." (*imshab bayā tā dar chaman sāzīm pur paimānah rā / tū shamaʿ-o gul rā dāġh kun man bulbul-o parwānāh rā*). For Ḥazīn, these words were "melodies of a second miracle" equal to the Prophet David's psalms.[15] In one of his surviving treatises, Ḥazīn outlined his aural predilections in line with Islamic orientations of ethical listening, which he and other writers at the time and after understood as a set of self-cultivation techniques. The ethical listeners could imbibe pleasant melodies and poems that allowed one to escape worldly and spiritual hindrances while also elevating an awareness of the soul. Ḥazīn cautioned that this sublime state could only be attained if the listener abstained from dervish-type behaviors such as drinking, excessive weeping, ecstatic dancing, or rending one's clothes.[16] As we recall, these were aspects of behavior embraced by Girāmī and his Qabuliyan retinue. In contrast, Ḥazīn associated verse singing—and the complicated connections it produced between the ear and the heart—with poetry gatherings centered on lyrics about love.

When Ḥazīn first encountered Girāmī at the home of Amīr Ḵhān, Girāmī's Qabuliyan greeting and the rustic verse, which he likely presented in a street singer's style, shocked Ḥazīn, who sank into a corner before allowing Girāmī and his Qabuliyans to host an informal recital of some kind. Ārzū, who narrated this episode, noted that when Ḥazīn's turn for recitation came, he must have read ġhazals in "a tortured voice" (*āwāz-e ḥazīn*)—a well-placed eponymous double entendre illustrating the poet's encounter with this outlandish contingent.[17]

The Ambiguists

By the time Ḥazīn reached Delhi, it was those who could adapt and master such high levels of improvisation and creativity who found the warmest welcome in the city's booming ġhazal scene. Hence, Ḥazīn's ability to tolerate and adequately respond to Girāmī's bellowing welcome and invitation to exchange verse can be interpreted as a kind of rite of passage for the Iranian newcomer into a dimension of mushāʿirah culture that was new to him—and not exactly matching his predilections for more subdued verse performance.

Girāmī, like his father Qabūl before him, prized noisy, complex, and quick-witted words. Bedil's student Ārzū described Girāmī and his cohort as seeking "unbounded words" and "fresh meanings" with which to compose verse in Persian and reḳhtah, "as if in another tongue, like Hindi or French."[18] Ārzū also created the exonym by which Girāmī and his cohort were known: "The Qabuliyan Contingent" (*firqah-e qabūliyah*), so coined when Ārzū described Ḥazīn's first meeting with Girāmī. This moniker, too, was an īhām, which made his group sound like a religious sect, as in "The Qabuliyan Persuasion."[19] In building their own communities through the development of īhām, Qabūl and his son Girāmī advanced a popular form of literary sociability to "draw breath into the words of the masses" through "joyful interaction, roguish behavior, competitive elegance, and winning of hearts" (*ḳhwush ḳhalq wa rind-mashrab wa maʿrakah ārā wa maqbūl-e dilhā*), thus producing one of the most publicly impactful styles in use among mushāʿirah poets of the early 1700s.[20]

The origins of these abilities lay in Kashmir, where ʿAbd ul-Ġhanī Beg Qabūl's skills blossomed into what was a wellspring for īhām-styled poetry. The mountainous region had long been a center of trade, ideas, and production of luxury goods, and under the Mughals it became a favorite vacation spot for emperors and a retirement destination for courtiers and poets, many of whom lie in the "Tomb of Poets" (*mazār-e shuʿarā*), which has since disappeared.[21] Qabūl's style stemmed from the free-spirited poet Muḥammad Tāhir Ġhanī (1630–1696), who kept his distance from courtly patronage circles but still grew popular across the Persian-speaking world within his lifetime due to his unique voice that featured īhām.[22] While Ġhanī may have imparted his īhām style to Qabūl, tażkirah writers record Qabūl's mentor as Mīrzā Dārāb Beg *Joyā* (The Inquiring) (d. 1706), a fan of Ṣāʾib whom we briefly encountered in the previous chapter as a writer of ring-dove poems.[23] Upon moving to Delhi around 1710, Qabūl secured patronage from top-ranking nobles, the last of these an imperial medic from Iran named Muḥammad Ḥusain *Shuhrat* (The Fame) (d. 1736) who often attended Ḳhwushgo's gatherings.[24]

In Delhi, the homebase of the Qabuliyans was south of Shāhjahānābād in Fīroz Shāh's fortress (*Fīroz Shāh Koṭlā*), a crumbling medieval-era edifice erected in the 1350s during the Tuġhluq dynasty.[25] There, Qabūl hosted mushāʿirahs that drew in a diverse contingent of students across a wide range of backgrounds and tastes.[26] The locale also housed a diverse cohort of Naqshbandis, followers of Delhi's foremost Sufi order. Foremost were Shāh ʿAbd ur-Rahīm ʿUmarī (1644–1719), who had established a madrasah in the Fīroz Shāh neighborhood, and his son Quṭb ud-Dīn Aḥmad (1703–1762), better known as Shāh Walīullāh Dihlavī, who shouted homilies to Delhi's masses in the 1730s.[27] ʿAbd ul-Aḥd *Waḥdat* (The Unity) (1640–1714/15) also lived in the fortress's precincts, where he hosted mushāʿirahs and taught his student Saʿdullāh Gulshan (1664–1728), the Bedil disciple from the Ornament of Mosques in chapter 2.[28] *Waḥdat*'s grandson Shāh Walīullāh *Ishtiyāq* (The Yearning) (d. 1738), another elite Naqshbandi, stayed in the fortress neighborhood and became a student of Qabūl.[29] The poet Jān-e Jānān Maẓhar (whom we also met in chapter 2) occasionally resided in the Fīroz Shāh neighborhood, though he also stayed in mosques and shrines throughout the city.[30] Ḳhwājah ʿAbd ul-Bāsiṭ Akbarābādī (fl. 1710–70), a lesser-known Naqshbandi poet who also led musical assemblies across Delhi, likewise resided nearby, just outside the city walls between Turkman and Delhi Gates.[31] Only two noisy Naqshbandi poets situated themselves well away from the Naqshbandi center at Fīroz Shāh's fort: ʿAndalīb and his seventeen-year-old son Mīr Dard who lived in the neighborhood of Pahāṛ Ganj until 1739 when the Iranian occupiers' violence forced them to seek refuge within the walled city in March of that year.

Ḳhwushgo referred to Qabūl as the "Advocate of Īhām" (*murawwij ul-īhām*)—also connoting "Master of Deception"—and documented around twenty or so noted students from many religious communities, reflecting Qabūl's unitarian religious views.[32] A Persian-educated Hindu secretary named Kishan Chand *Iḳhlāṣ* (The Fidelity) (d. circa 1748 or 1754) learned verse under Qabūl and in 1727 compiled a taẕkirah titled "The Eternal Spring" (*Hameshah Bahār*) that documents with vernal-themed īhāms the guidance Qabūl provided for him and other students. Iḳhlāṣ wrote that Qabūl "turned the grounds of literature (*zamīn-e suḳhan*) verdant, he watered the oceans of poetry (*baḥr-e shiʿr*), the roses of metaphor (*gul-hā-e maʿānī*) opened under his blossoming nature, and the miraculous notations from the irrigation of his moistened pen cleansed the hardened dust from the hearts of his poetry students."[33]

Iḳhlāṣ kept close contact with others in the Qabuliyan cohort such as Muḥammad ʿAlī *Ḥashmat* (The Magnificence) (1696?–1748), a good-looking Kashmiri and influential reḳhtah poet who purportedly dressed in women's clothing, and Ḥashmat's student ʿAbd ul-Ḥayy *Tābān* (The Luminous) (1715–1748), also a reḳhtah poet who died young of alcoholism.[34] Ārzū was likely an informal student of Qabūl, as evinced by his frequent meetings with

Qabūl throughout the 1720s, so noted in Ārzū's tażkirah where he also cited no fewer than 105 of Qabūl's couplets.[35] This connection resulted in Ārzū's incorporating many īhāms into a dīwān he completed in 1727.[36] When Qabūl died, Ārzū elegized that "poetry itself congealed under the freeze of an ice market."[37] Finally, Mukhliṣ documented one occasion in which he obtained a selection of Qabūl's favorite poems and noted Qabūl's impact on Ikhlāṣ's work during a gathering. Mukhliṣ also coined the Sufi-sounding double entendre "Qabuliyan Lineage" (*silsilah-e qabūliyah*), noting Qabūl's distinction.[38]

Qabūl composed verse laden with īhām's misdirection that playfully employed what he and subsequent tażkirah writers termed *īhām-e nā tamām* (unsatisfied amphibology or incomplete amphibology), a method by which a poem could simultaneously and equally withstand two radically different interpretations.[39] As Qabūl himself stated, "The poem that does not carry two meanings (*maḥmil*) is worth nothing more than a camel's hump" (*shi'rī kih nabāshudish do maḥmīl bā kūz-e shutur buwad barābar*).[40] For poets, the word *maḥmil* (litter or basket) connotes a poem's capacity to hold meaning. For camel drivers, it refers to the goods carried on an animal's back. Thus, a poem with one saddle for its meaning was no better than a common pack animal according to Qabūl. Qabūl's ideas about īhām differed markedly from prior accounts of Persianate double entendre as a literary device. Classical Persianate literatures held that īhām possessed both distant meaning and near meaning: a poem's associations could misdirect the listener or reader toward the more obvious idea, while the distant idea held greater validity.

In contrast to the classicists, Qabūl instead advocated that īhām should not be judged according to relative distance, whether near or far, but rather that all meanings contained within īhām should be equally attainable. In other words, īhām should remain unending, incomplete, or unsatisfied—*īhām-e nā tamām*.[41] Though referenced by Ārzū in his 1746 work "The Justice of Speech" (*Dād-e Sukhan*), the concept appears to have little application beyond the literary circles linked with the Qabuliyans.[42] Despite īhām constituting a dominant aesthetic among rekhtah poets of the early 1700s in particular, curiously, we find no mention within modern scholarship of Qabūl or the Qabuliyans, the most notable purveyors of this aesthetic in the early 1700s. As noted by contemporary literary historians such as Shamsur Rahman Faruqi, Frances Pritchett, and Ḥasan Aḥmad Niẓāmī, rekhtah composers considered īhām in terms similar to Qabūl's notion of the concept but instead focused on the near-far dichotomy found in classical texts.[43] Only Jamīl Jālibī hints at the influence of Qabūl's Persian words on reḳhtah composition when considering a reḳhtah couplet purportedly authored by Qabūl as recorded in a taẕkirah completed in 1830s Lucknow.[44]

The Qabuliyans bear within them some of the divisions that also characterized Delhi's literary community in the early 1700s. While the Qabuliyans cultivated playfulness and a sharp sense of style (*rang*), they also harbored confrontational streaks that alienated other audiences. In one anecdote, hangers-on in Amīr Ḳhān's court who found īhām-laden verse unpleasant crafted their own response to Qabūl. Employing an idiom for something completely worthless, they countered Qabūl's famous axiom about the camel's bier with the following line: "The poem formed with its meaning on two bases is worth nothing more than a camel's fart" (*shiʿrī kih bināʾ shudish do maḥmil bā gūz-e shutur buwad barābar*). For some audiences, popular verse filled with īhām sounded inordinately unpleasant, as they could pose auditory issues. Homophones, distant associations, and vernacular speech could potentially alienate those who found such verse overly clever or who were not privy to whatever conceit a pun-writing poet deployed. However, the mischievous Qabuliyans would likely have delighted even in this insult to Qabūl, because it unwittingly produced its own auditory and scribal wordplays: the term they used for the camel's flatulence (*gūz-e shutur*) is a near homophone for the term for a camel's hump (*kūz-e shutur*). So too, period scribal conventions present *gūz* and *kūz* with identical lettering, thereby removing potential barbs from the intended insult.

Delhi's Loudest Poets

In the decades after his death, Qabūl's style of incomplete īhām flourished in the hands of his students. Ishtiyāq wrote emulations based on verse from Maulānā Rūmī's *Dīwān-e Shams* (circa 1247), while also gravitating toward reḳhtah to compose emulations of Ābrū.[45] Iḳhlāṣ maintained his connections to the Qabuliyans through his fellow students' pupils, for instance, socializing with ʿAbd ul-Ḥayy Tābān (d. 1748), who learned verse under the Qabuliyan poet Muḥammad ʿAlī Ḥashmat (d. 1748).[46] But it was Qabūl's son Girāmī who most vigorously maintained the public face of the Qabuliyan Contingent. Girāmī did so while instructing his own students in poetry, notably in the verse of Ḥāfiẓ.[47] In the late 1730s, Girāmī secured patronage from Rājā Roshan Rāy (d. 1746), an official serving under the Grand Vizier Qamar ud-Dīn Ḳhān (r. 1724–48).

Girāmī's career took a populist turn at this stage, and he began to cast himself as a "protector of the common people" (*muʿtaqad fīyah un-nās*) who could perform miracles, "making things appear in his hands with types of tricks and deceptions" (*qabīl-e shuʿbadah wa nīranjāt*).[48] Although some believed in his mystical powers, Delhi's high society (*dihlaviyān*) regarded Girāmī with suspicion, judging his religious populism, entreating tactics, and jovial manners to be a means of ensnaring people, particularly Delhi's young men (*naujawānān-e dihlī*).[49]

But this sort of infamy proceeded Girāmī's own design. As one writer noted, Girāmī aimed to make himself the center of attention (*ul-ʿain-e mushāhadah*) by any means, and he did so by setting to melody the strikingly original verse he recited at mushāʿirahs.[50] As an expert in popular music, Girāmī preferred the company of street singers to poets, and he himself enjoyed performing as a musician.[51] Girāmī sometimes performed at the garden tomb of Mughal governor Mīr Musharraf, which was located south of the Old City near the shrine of Niẓām ud-Dīn Auliyā (1238–1325). On Musharraf's annual death anniversary, his son Mirzā Kallū patronized hundreds of singers and dancers who performed for late night drinking parties.[52] In one of the porticos on the grounds, Girāmī led poetry recitations with his students, loudly singing verse amid the dancing and music—a sight that bemused Ḳhwushgo in the 1720s but caught the critical eye of Dargāh Qulī Ḳhān in the late 1730s.[53]

But songs could enliven a gathering or ruin the atmosphere. One writer coined the maxim, "The poetry of the preacher and the clerk takes orders from the singer" (*shiʿr-e munshī wa mullā ḥukm-e khwānandagī-sāz dārad*), meaning that literate clerics and secretaries, who were understood to be middling writers, required melodic voices to brighten their otherwise dim verses. So too, public singing could detract from a performance, making poets appear illiterate. Stories about illiterate verse singers filtered from Isfahan's coffeehouses into the works of Delhi writers. By the 1750s, reḳhtah documentarians explicitly noted the semiliterate poets who would sing charged erotic verse among sex workers or chant lyrics in gangsters' argot in the marketplace.[54] Girāmī was willing to hazard the risks of a fallen reputation that went with street life and public verse singing because it strengthened his populist persona.

Girāmī found welcoming comrades among other equally vocal poets who composed in working-class speech registers, gravitated toward young men, and courted literary controversy. Girāmī's poems attracted Jān-e Jānān Maẓhar, the peripatetic Naqshbandi, who recorded one couplet from Girāmī and three poems from Qabūl in his diary.[55] Additionally, Maẓhar and Girāmī wrote parallel response poems, following a model offered by

Nāṣir ʿAlī.[56] However, both Girāmī and Maẓhar shared a predilection for singing poetry. In Maẓhar's case, vocal dexterity and mischievousness (*shoḳhī wa shor ṭabīʿat*) caused him to set his reḳhtah compositions to melodies (*mutarannum sāḳhtah*) in gatherings, as Muḳhliṣ observed of him, "Wherever my lord would enunciate his rose petal-scattering knowledge of poetry, it was as if an eloquent-tongued nightingale had loosed its chirping after having alighted at the top of a thicket of rose bushes; or it was as if he was a moth who fell into the flaming tongue of the intensity of his own poetry recitation for the amusement of those with their faces illuminated by the candles of the gathering."[57] Maẓhar's high-spiritedness brought him into contact with many important mushāʿirah poets, most notably Inʿāmullāh Ḳhān Yaqīn, a popular versifier who exemplified the rising younger generation in Ḥātim's gatherings.[58]

Maẓhar's connection to Yaqīn provoked rumors in the 1740s that Maẓhar purportedly fell so deeply in love with the younger poet that he began ghostwriting verse for him.[59] In this vein, Ḳhwushgo related a time when Maẓhar "gave himself over to the affections of a young man" despite his otherwise admirable observance of Naqshbandi tenets. Eventually, this unnamed young man grew distant, and for six months, Maẓhar holed himself up in one of the mosques he called home, even digging a grave so he could be buried alive out of his grief. After hearing his wailing over this burial place, Maẓhar's friends circulated a rumor that someone had suddenly died and required the plot, hoping Maẓhar would cease his mourning to make room.[60]

While Maẓhar's romantic life is debatable, his literary connections to other poets in Girāmī's orbit deserve further inquiry. Maẓhār and Girāmī's circles overlapped with the Iranian-born poet Muḥammad Riẓā *Ummīd* (The Hope) (1678–1746) who, like Ḥazin, arrived in Delhi around 1737. Rather than journeying to Delhi from Iran, Ummīd arrived from South India. Sometime between 1701 and 1707, about thirty years prior to his Delhi sojourn, Ummīd had established himself with a land grant (which he thought measly), a courtly title of "Qizilbāsh Ḳhān" (acknowledging his Turkoman roots in the Qarāmānlū tribe), and the well-earned trust of his patron Niẓām ul-Mulk Āṣif Jāh (1671–1748), the governor of the South who subsequently brought Ummīd to Delhi.[61] Like Ḥazīn, Ummīd studied Persian letters in the Safavid capital of Isfahan, but, being fourteen years senior to Ḥazīn, Ummīd learned ġhazal writing under very different circumstances, studying with two of the most radical poets in Isfahan: the high Safavid official Ṭāhir Waḥīd (d. 1698) and the middling accountant

ʿAbd ul-ʿĀl Najāt (d. 1714). According to Iranian tażkirah writer Wālih (whom we will soon meet), Waḥīd and Najāt "spilled literature's blood" with their particular styles.[62] Ironically, a legend grew that Ummīd's words saved him from death after taking part in a local rebellion around 1723.[63] Ummīd's entertaining verse convinced Niẓām ul-Mulk to free Ummīd from prison, likely saving him from execution.[64]

Like Girāmī, Ummīd possessed musical abilities to understand the finer points of Indian-language songs (*nuktah-e naġhmāt-e hindī*), and while he sang them well, an Iranian accent still clung to his Hindi even after decades of living in India.[65] Despite the Persian lilt to his songs, Ummīd also grew close with Delhi-based musicians such as singer and lutenist (*bīn-nawāz*) Niʿamat Ḳhān *Sadārang* (The Evergreen) (d. 1746) and Nūr Bāʾī (fl. 1730–60), the top courtesan of her day. As a court singer, Sadārang survived several violent imperial upheavals to popularize a singing style call *ḳhayāl* (idea, reflection, imagination, specter), a new musical approach blending vernacular song forms with the classical ones that had been favored by the Mughals since the sixteenth century.[66] Nūr Bāʾī, Sadārang's student, sang ġhazals in the *ḳhayāl* style extraordinarily well and was among the wealthiest independent women of Delhi. Quickly, legends grew around Ummīd's relationship to each of these performers: in his tażkirah of the 1770s, Muṣḥafī described Ummīd and Sadārang as connected by a "spiritual pact" (*muttaḥidah-e rūḥānī*), dying within moments of each other.[67] Reḳhtah tażkirahs drafted in the 1760s and 1770s painted anecdotes about Nūr Bāʾī's besting Ummīd with her witty asides.[68] Like the elite ġhazal singers, Ummīd moved with ease across Delhi's upper echelons and among the common people, visiting gatherings, the court, and local shrines where a mixture of Delhi's elites and lower classes congregated, tending more to his "entertaining poets, song, and style" (*shuʿarā nawāzi wa rāg wa rang*) than to his land holdings.[69]

Upon his arrival in Delhi, Ummīd also circulated in the top literary salons where he struck new friendships with Ārzū and Muḳhliṣ and rekindled connections with Shams ud-Dīn *Faqīr* (The Fakir) (d. 1769), whom Ummīd first met in South India, and Zakī Nadīm (d. 1750), an old friend employed by Nadir Shah.[70] Later on in the 1740s, there was a growing demand for nuanced Persian-language dictionaries, and Ummīd quickly became a source for lexicons by the poets Muḳhliṣ (*Mirāʾt ul-Isṭalāh*), Lālah Ṭek Chand Bahār (*Bahār ul-ʿAjam*), and ʿĀlá Fiṭrat ʿAṭāʾullāh Nudrat (*ʿAin-e ʿAṭā*), the latter a Kashmiri poet whom we will meet in chapter 4.[71] Most importantly, Ummīd was just as eager to be shaped by Delhi's ġhazal scene as he was effective in shaping it. Maẓhar and a Delhi-based poet named

Zain ud-Dīn Ḳhān *ʿIshq* (The Love) (fl. 1705/10–1785), who came to India as a child, were both inspired by a verse from an earlier recension of Ummīd's dīwān, and they each composed responses to Ummīd's ġhazal (which was first inspired by superstar Ṣāʾib). As Maẕhar writes, "As soon as my utterly tattered heart came to its senses, the beloved slipped from hand. / Like the snare as soon as it gains awareness, its prey slipped from hand" (*tā ba-hosh āyad dil-e ṣad chāk yār az dast raft / dām tā az ḳhwud ḳhabar gīrad shikār az dast raft*).[72]

So too, Girāmī had a hand in shaping Ummīd's words in a ġhazal that featured his famous antinomian values. He wrote a couplet with a particularly unique refrain on "the heart." Girāmī considered a Sufi image of the Kaʿbah as the heart:

Upon the commoners streaming toward His Kaʿbah,
He became a guest in the recesses of the heart.[73]

jūyand bah kaʿbah-ish ḳhalāʾiq
mihmān shudah ū bah ḳhānah-e dil

In a parallel composition, Ummīd responded with a couplet in the same meter, further reflecting the theme:

Islam is to be found in neither the church nor in Mecca.
I am annoyed by these excuses of the heart.[74]

dar dair-o ḥaram nadārad islām
tang āmadam az bahānah-e dil

With his expressions of unitarian religious themes, the Qabuliyans found a welcome partner in Ummīd, who had much more in common with Girāmī than Ḥazīn had with the Qabuliyans. Instead of being confused by loud poets or demoralized by rowdy behavior, Ummīd himself contributed to the hubbub of Delhi's literary scene when he arrived in 1737. Ḥazīn, on the other hand, retreated to Lahore after a year's stay in Delhi, hoping to return to Iran. He never did. Instead, Ḥazīn traversed between Delhi and Lahore at least three more times between 1739 and 1742, before resigning himself to Delhi until 1748 after which time he resettled in Varanasi. In the intervening years, Ḥazīn publicized his true estimate of Girāmī and his greeters when he penned a screed against the Qabuliyans' Kashmiri ancestry, praying, "So that another Kashmiri is not birthed from this wretched world, / may the whores be barren as mules and Satan celibate" (*tā namī zād zi-dunyā-e danī kashmīrī / kāsh īn qaḥbah satarwan bud-o iblīs ʿazab*).[75]

Girāmī inherited from his father a tendency toward belligerence—a proclivity that both Ārzū and the southern traveler Darāgh Qulī Ḳhān noticed and perhaps appreciated. Ārzū found the father and son's "style and bearing . . . indeed contrary (*muḳhālif ṭarz wa ṭaur*)."[76] When Dargāh Qulī Ḳhān described Girāmī's tendency to visit gatherings with a notebook of his poems safely tucked under his arm, he pointedly noted that Girāmī's book contained the weapons for the blood sport that mushāʿirah recitation had become.[77] In turn, Girāmī bragged about his own verse and precious diary in an ambiguous couplet: "May the of blood of lovers be on that gleaming white neck of his. / Like white pages of a diary in which colorful meaning is found" (*ḳhūn-e ʿushshāq bar ān gardan-e sīmīn bāshad / chūn bayāẓī kih darān maʿnī-e rangīn bāshad*).[78]

Carrying around a notebook containing only one's own poems marked an oversized ego.[79] Dargāh Qulī Ḳhān observed that Girāmī had such a high regard for his own poems that the poet would defend his verse to the point where the veins would pop out of his neck. Girāmī would cheer allies and taunt enemies during gatherings, causing salons to "exceed the bounds of even a debate" (*bah sarḥad-e munāẓarah mī rasānad*).[80] This show of belligerence was a tactic that Girāmī had learned from his father, as Qabūl required his students to militate against competitors and champion their own verse forcibly in mushāʿirahs.

Muḳhliṣ described Qabūl as using mushāʿirahs to enact "great disputes" (*daʿwā-e bulandī*). Following this conceit, some of Qabūl's most lethal munitions were the poems he composed for his students. Indeed, as part of their training, Qabūl required his students to recite verses composed by Qabūl in their own names with the goal of defeating the opposing side in cheering matches.[81] The chief enemy of Qabūl and his students was one Muḥammad Afẓal *Ṡābit* (The Proven) (d. 1739), a noted writer of panegyrics who, like Qabūl, also composed poems for his own students to perform.[82] Ārzū described Ṡābit as a poet who was "equally at peace and at war." Relatedly, Qabūl's student Iḳhlāṣ wrote that Ṡābit's "tongue was quite serious."[83] Ḳhwushgo, more generous than his juniors Ārzū and Muḳhliṣ, found among the verses Ṡābit once recited at Bedil's shrine a couplet in emulation of the poet-saint himself: "The Imam, who is the path of salvation, is like a lamp, / as if with a red candle when a stream of blood poured from his nose" (*imām rā kih barāh-e hidāyat ast chirāġh / chū shamaʿ-e surḳh rawān gasht jū-e ḳhūn zi-dimāġh*). The verse painted an image of Ḥusain's martyrdom during the battle of Karbala. The lamp of salvation appears to bleed, mourning the death of Ḥusain. Ḳhwushgo recorded the couplet and Ṡābit's words of performative humility. "If one of my poems might have seemed careless in your view," pleaded Ṡābit, "please cross it out from the manuscript."[84] Ḳhwushgo meant for his words to be taken ironically: Ṡābit was just as serious as the lofty words of his poem.

In the blood sport between Ṡābit and Qabūl, one public battle produced a chain of casualties that continued to wreak havoc beyond its initial skirmish. The trouble began around the year 1721, when Ibrahīm *Isti'dād* (The Talent) (fl. 1720–40), a young poet of Arab descent, for unknown reasons, decided to discontinue his study under Qabūl and instead apprenticed himself to Ṡābit.[85] Isti'dād studied with his new teacher for about thirteen years before he had a disagreement with Ṡābit over a verse Isti'dād had composed comparing the martyred grandson of the Prophet Husain ibn 'Alī (d. 680) to a plumbline. When Isti'dād recited this verse in front of another poet named 'Abd ur-Riẓā *Matīn* (The Unyielding) (1692–1762), an Iranian who immigrated to India around 1712, Ṡābit accused his student of plagiarizing the couplet.[86] Ṡābit marched Isti'dād to the center of town to present his case before a deputy to the police chief Ḥājī Fūlād Ḳhān, demanding the student return the poems Ṡābit had composed for him.[87]

To his dismay, Ṡābit learned then that the law did not extend to plagiarized verse and had to seek retribution by his own devices. This inspired him to write a four-hundred-line qaṣīdah titled the "The Shooting Star" (*Shahāb-e Ṡāqib*), in which he detailed the episode, claiming that the thieving student had been set right and Ṡābit's reputation as a talented poet had been preserved.[88] For 436 couplets, Ṡābit mercilessly finished each line with rhymes on Isti'dād's pen name and gestured toward Matīn—the aforementioned poet in the audience for Isti'dād's fateful recitation—as also being a plagiarist.[89] Taẕkirah writers held the poem indicting Isti'dād and Matīn to be among Ṡābit's most notable compositions, even though it sprang from a distant battle with Qabūl.[90] Ṡābit even acknowledged Qabūl's posthumous impact on the episode with a wordplay on his old sparring partner's name:

> Were [Isti'dād] to recite a fine and fresh ġhazal in his own name,
> not a soul would remember his ideas.
> Since you do not steal from Qabūl or me, why not take
> testimony from the poets Ārzū or Payām or Fā'iẓ?[91]

> *banām-e ḳhwud ġhazal-e ḳhūb tāzah-ish mī ḳhwānad*
> *naẕar bah īn kih ḳhayāl-ish kasī nadārad yād*

agar qabūl nadārī zi-man chirā nakunī
zi-ārzū-o payām-o fā'iẓ istishhād

Ṡābit's namedropping implied that since Isti'dād could no longer plagiarize from his former teachers in Qabūl or Ṡābit, he could gather misappropriated literary "evidence" from the poets Ārzū and Muḥammad Sharaf ud-Dīn *Payām* (The Message) (d. 1745/46). As we will see, Payām, a close associate of Mukhliṣ, composed a famous verse set that memorialized Nadir Shah's violence that would ultimately take Ṡābit's life in 1739, ceasing his arguments with the Qabuliyans.

The Occupation

Muḥammad 'Alī Ḥazīn returned to Delhi from Lahore in February 1739 after failing to find safe passage out of India via the overland caravan routes as an invading army marched toward India. Thus, Nadir Shah again forced Ḥazīn back to India, but this time as the Iranian king advanced toward Lahore with his Qizilbash soldiers after their conquest of Kabul. At the time of his second arrival in Delhi, Ḥazīn was no longer able to stay at the home of Amīr Khān, the poetry patron and Mughal official who, two years previously, had first welcomed him. Amīr Khān was now stationed about 120 kilometers to the north in Karnal along with Muhammad Shah and other officials who were all busily preparing for military confrontation with Nadir Shah.[92]

On his return to Delhi, Ḥazīn instead ensconced himself at the Kabul Gate-area residence of 'Alī Qulī *Wālih* (The Astonished) (1712–1756), who shared Ḥazīn's Isfahan birthplace.[93] The two Iranians had first encountered each other in 1734, at Port Abbas, both en route to India. Wālih, a Safavid courtier, was leaving a failed love affair with his cousin, the poet Khadījah Begam *Sulṭān* (The Emperor) (d. 1747). Wālih hoped to marry Sulṭān, but her mother had decided to wed the poet to an official in Nadir Shah's court, seeking family ties with the new political order. In the wake of his heartbreak over Sulṭān, Wālih became subject to gossip at Isfahan's gatherings, prompting his exile to India.[94]

In contrast to Ḥazīn, whose travails and indecision delayed his trip from Port Abbas to Delhi, Wālih was eager to reach Delhi where possibilities for securing patronage and status awaited him. In the five years since their first meeting in 1734, Wālih had cultivated a name for himself as a poet of some stature in Delhi with a wide circle of friendships within the city's dense literary networks. While Ḥazīn remained distracted by planning his elusive route home, Wālih's background and failed love affair with Sulṭān had ceased to be an item of gossip and shame. A Delhi poet named Shams ud-Dīn Faqīr (d. 1769) had chronicled the romance of Wālih and Sulṭān, broadcasting details of Wālih's heartache in epic poetry. Sulṭān attempted to join Wālih in India, but she died en route.[95] At some point, Wālih married the well-connected courtesan Ḳhwushḥāl Ramjānī (fl. 1730–60), their union producing the polydactyl reḳhtah poet Gannā Begam *Minnat* (The Grace) (d. 1775?).[96]

Importantly, the formerly heartbroken Wālih secured patronage from India's wealthiest governor, Burhān ul-Mulk (1680–1739), whom Wālih followed on February 13, 1739, to Karnal where he witnessed his patron's preparations, confusion, and competitions with other military elites there as they readied the Mughals' defenses against Nadir Shah's troops. On February 24, 1739, Nadir Shah's forces defeated the Mughal army, which Wālih captured in a poem:

On that side, the Qizilbash soldiers, like the beloved's eyes,
all carry spears upon their piebald rides.
On this side, the Indian soldiers in full chainmail
are like crows tangled up in snares.[97]

az ān sū-e qizilbāsh chūñ chashm-e yār
hamah nezah-dārān-e ablaq sawār
az īn sū-e zirih posh-e hindī tamām
zāġhī kih pechīdah bāshad bah dām

Himself trapped, the Mughal emperor Muhammad Shah agreed to symbolically submit to Nadir Shah, promising to pay financial penalties with terms that allowed him to continue his rule as India's emperor. Wālih offered his aside that a clever bird when snared goes tame once in hand.[98]

To help save face of the state's nobility and facilitate treasury payments, Muhammad Shah agreed to host Nadir Shah as a guest in Delhi: the conqueror now appeared as an invitee. His imminent arrival was marked by the quickly approaching occurrence of two important holidays, both coincidentally falling on the same date of March 21, 1739: the Eid holiday, Feast of Sacrifice on 10 *Żū'lḤijjah*; and Nowruz, the Persian New Year on the vernal equinox of 1 *Farwardīn*. The two emperors agreed to celebrate these occasions together in Shahjahanabad. Also, rapidly approaching on March 24 was Holi, the spring holiday celebrated by elites and commoners alike in Mughal Delhi with colorful dyes and intoxicants in the town squares, rendering a public festival with potential for conflict. As the holidays drew near, Wālih remarked at the wonder of seeing two emperors moving toward Delhi, "a mere arrow's flight between them." Nadir Shah arrived on Thursday, March 19, 1739, and at Friday services the next day Nadir Shah's name was read aloud across the city's mosques to cement his position as ruler.[99]

Importantly, the Mughal state structure remained intact, as did the social and economic routes needed to fund poets and host literary gatherings. The ability to preserve these elements of Delhi's intricate political and artistic infrastructure during a time of great tumult was made possible, in part, because the Persian-educated elites from Iran who converged on Delhi during Nadir Shah's incursion shared with Indian elites a language and a cultural understanding of how to ceremonially and materially reconfigure hierarchy. This allowed the two parties to negotiate a balance of domination and respect through political theater in which both could secure their own footing and maintain state power.[100]

Despite the state's efforts to preserve the appearance of a seamless transition, the impact of Nadir Shah's conquest was felt quickly throughout India.[101] Nadir Shah's two-month residency at the Blessed Citadel within Muhammad Shah's main palace augmented the social spaces of Delhi's mushāʿirahs. New poets visited among the gatherings, including those who came to Delhi from many directions as part of the tumult wrought by Nadir Shah. These newcomers recited verse crafted for Delhi's audiences while experimenting with old couplets within the dense networks of competitions and emulations that structured the city's ġhazal scene. Ḥazīn was among them, but not for long because by May of 1739 he again left Delhi in an effort to return to Iran via Lahore.

Connections facilitated by shared language, modes of comportment, and family ties brought Iranian elites comfortably into the salons of Delhi's notables. For example, Wālih's brother, who worked for Nadir Shah's bureaucracy, facilitated Ḥazīn's third return to Delhi in the autumn of 1739, after the governor of Lahore grew irritated with Ḥazīn for some unknown reason.[102] Other new residents of Delhi who hailed from across Iran and other regions were eager to exchange verse. The mushāʿirah scene churned out many new verses from these émigrés well into the late 1740s. Some of them remained for several years to make noticeable, if brief, impacts, such as Zakī *Nadīm* (The Confidant) (d. 1750), an official from Nadir Shah's government ministry who remained in Delhi for nearly two years after his patron's departure. Nadīm became fast friends with the eminent Iranian-born teacher

Qizilbāsh Ḳhān Ummīd; the two were "sociably harmonious" according to Muḳhliṣ's conceit referencing Ummīd's musical talents, and they together visited several gatherings across the city, where they quizzed poets about their Turkish language abilities.[103]

Yet, the ease the emperors' respective elites had with each other in Delhi's mushāʿirah circles was divorced from the political aspirations of the city's commoners, who protested Nadir Shah's military occupation. Early in the morning of March 22, 1739, an armed conflict took place that left as many as twenty thousand commoners dead, as recounted in Abhishek Kaicker's recent work, which offers a keen socio-political analysis of Nadir Shah's entrance to Delhi and its aftermath. Kaicker's interpretation overturns long-standing narratives about connections between notables and their subjects by tracing how Mughal elites with strong familial and social ties to Iran and Central Asia negotiated Nadir Shah's supremacy through ceremony, exchange, and violence. Importantly, Kaicker contextualizes how Delhi's population reacted to Nadir Shah's occupation, showing that it was mainly commoners who fomented sharp expressions of resistance as they sought to assert ideas of popular sovereignty developed over previous decades in intellectual and material registers. Kaicker's reading brings to light how remnants of a markedly non-elite political discourse shaped power at the civic level.[104]

On the night of March 21, men from the city's working classes and Mughal soldiery had begun killing the occupier's red-hatted soldiers based on a rumor that Nadir Shah had been assassinated and emboldened by this false news of the victor's death. Delhi's commoners and soldiers launched their attack on the Qizilbash Turkoman, who staffed Nadir Shah's military seeking to restore Muhammad Shah's sovereignty. Reports of the killings reached Nadir Shah throughout the night, but the conquering emperor purportedly did not believe this news, thinking his commanders were inventing these stories as a pretext to sack the city for their own material gain.[105]

On the morning of March 22, Nadir Shah discovered the truth of these bloody accounts. After dodging a bullet intended for him that instead struck a commander, Nadir Shah rode to a mosque adjacent to the police headquarters and called for a massacre (*ṣadā-e qatl-e ʿāmm*), giving his troops permission to slaughter Delhi's commoners in the squares normally bustling with sellers and other marketplace professionals.[106] As Kaicker notes, Nadir Shah's directives did not call for a "general killing" (*qatl-e ʿāmm*) in the literal sense, but rather a targeted, violent civil intervention designed explicitly to subdue Delhi's common folk. In the open markets across the walled city and in provisioning bazaars outside the ramparts to the west, the Qizilbash troops killed thousands of people from Delhi's working classes and torched homes in the downtown area. They left behind city neighborhoods filled with bodies piled in the streets, wreckages of burned-out homes, and destroyed market wares. Among the multitudes of slain commoners, only fourteen elites perished.[107]

These elites came from the same demographic as those who visited poetry gatherings. Delhi's privileged mushāʿirah patrons largely belonged to the classes of landed notables or were connected to Mughal aristocrats through patronage and family. So too, poets such as Wālih and Muḳhliṣ, who occupied high positions as state functionaries, were able to witness the violence firsthand while keeping safe due to their class status. Thus, mushāʿirahs persevered in the weeks that followed, facilitated by the fact that the city's geography protected its extant mushāʿirah circles. From charting the residential locations of notable mushāʿirah hosts, we see that the southeast areas of the city hosted the top literary gatherings. Since the Qizilbash violence mainly occurred at the city center and its connected markets, this southeast section largely remained unscathed. Areas that survived destruction simply due to being outside of the business districts targeted by the Qizilbash include neighborhoods in Wakīl Pūrah (Muḳhliṣ and Ārzū's locale), those around Aḥadī Pūrah (the location of Gulshan's tomb), and those surrounding Fīroz Shāh's fortress in the Old City. Other areas gained protection when elite residents paid marauding troops to keep away. This is how the Ornament of Mosques and Amīr Ḳhān's home, both located near Delhi Gate and Bedil's grave, stayed out of the path of destruction.[108]

The home of ʿAndalīb and his son Dard was near the impacted district of Pahāṛ Ganj, and the two Sufis sought sanctuary in the home of ʿAndalīb's disciple Mihrparwar Begam (1684?–1744) inside the walled city, where they ultimately remained after 1739.[109] Others were less fortunate. Living near one of the city's downtown markets, Afẓal S̤ābit and his friend Ḥakīm Imām ud-Dīn *Aksīr* (The Antidote) (1680?–1739) were wounded in the chaos. Aksīr died within three days, and S̤ābit held on for a few weeks. Theirs are the only two documented fatalities among known mushāʿirah poets.

Coded Verse

Questions persist about why Delhi's poets who continued to gather during Nadir Shah's three-month occupation did not memorialize more details about the slaughter of commoners. Such a lacuna was especially ironic as poets increasingly composed in reḳhtah, a literary style with linguistic markers illustrative of lower-class identity. Yet, writing verse in everyday speech did not always indicate affiliations with the commoners targeted by Qizilbash troops. In what survives from his notebook, southern traveler Dargāh Qulī Ḳhān provided only exceedingly brief descriptions of the occupation's impact. Reporting from Delhi, Ḳhān observed that elites held fewer parties than usual, and even those celebrations had grown dimmer. Otherwise, Dargāh Qulī Ḳhān writes nothing about the military defenses and political negotiations he had been tasked with helping to conduct on behalf of Muhammad Shah during the time of Nadir Shah's incursion, nor did he note the thousands of lower-class people whose bodies lay in the streets for months.[110]

Other poets offered only a bit more detail about Nadir Shah's time in Delhi, and sometimes their scanty accounts were phrased in grisly terms. Ārzū, who called Nadir Shah a scourge worse than poison, noted rumors of cannibalism, citing a story he heard about a yogi who consumed his mother's corpse.[111] Ḳhwushgo wrote that "the Qizilbash army, having brought down India's head, streamed channels of blood [in Delhi] with the slaughter of commoners," but otherwise says little else.[112] Muḳhliṣ described the events of 1739 in great detail, but only conveyed an elite perspective on the events that was focused tightly on securing his family's safety and carefully recording the amounts of money extracted from him and his fellow elites by Nadir Shah's military and Mughal political functionaries. Also, by his own admission, Muḳhliṣ maintained social obligations to local associates and friends, consorting with them during gatherings for "gossip and poetry" (*gap wa shi'r*).[113]

Ḥazīn, who cast himself as a refugee from Nadir Shah, provided a perfunctory description of the New Years' day violence in his autobiography, noting its tragedy but also inflating the number of Qizilbash dead.[114] Mīr Taqī Mīr, still a teenager at the time, mourned only how he lost his allowance upon the death of Samsām ud-Daulah, his patron killed during the confrontation with Nadir Shah's troops at Karnal a month before the Delhi massacre.[115] Wālih blamed the commoners for their own deaths, according to his account—another elite view. It was customary for the Qizilbash troops to be highhanded and oppressive (*shitlāq*) with people, and the commoners of Delhi, whom Wālih dismissed as among the most ignorant in the world, had, according to Wālih, responded heedlessly with their own violence in kind, as if sealing their own fates. Wālih, who had watched a three-month decline in Burhān ul-Mulk's health from two battle wounds sustained at Karnal and a gangrenous leg that caused his patron to faint at court, wrote his narrative explicitly to laud his deceased patron despite the Mughal military failures. According to Wālih, if Burhān ul-Mulk had lived, none of the Nowruz violence would have happened.[116]

Such brief but informative assessments of Nadir Shah's occupation leave questions remaining about the persistence of literary sociability during the occupation and after the violence on March 21–22. To answer these, we require an approach that deploys literary analysis to understand how mushāʿirah poets memorialized the event by casting it as a theme in their ġhazals. Following Arthur Dudney's assessment of eighteenth-century verse and social history, such a literary historical perspective allows us to consider mushāʿirah poetry about the massacres through "a deep engagement with literary aesthetics and the critical tradition" as utilized by ġhazal writers composing between March and April of 1739. That is, rather than searching for a social history in verse at the expense of literary aesthetics, we adopt an approach that focuses on the literary aesthetics of emulation and competition in order to produce a history of the event based on writers' concerns for convention.[117] Such an approach is especially important when considering the variety of styles and voices poets at the time could deploy. We are not attending to the work of these poets in order gauge their ability to reify generic categories in service to a new theme—Nadir Shah's conquest—but rather to understand how deploying conventions allowed them to forge intertextual, and therefore social, connections in a time of crisis.

I note the dearth of rigorous first-hand accounts detailing the fatalities and injuries suffered by Delhi's working classes not to damn the mushāʿirah poets for being hardhearted or aloof. In many ways, these poets were bound by the constraints of their social positions and also by the socio-aesthetic conventions regulating the themes that were appropriate for them to address in their poetry. Therefore, mushāʿirah poets documented the violence in Delhi through the ways they knew best—by creatively emulating the words of past masters and recent innovators. For instance, a frequently cited verse about Nadir Shah's exactions, penned by the young poet Tābān, reveals how poets' political views turned the crisis into a theme. In yearning tones, Tābān's verse recounts how the Mughals' precious Peacock Throne was carted away on a baggage train headed for Iran in May of 1739 as part of the spoils of the conquest: "O Tābān, my heart, scarred by Nadir Shah's hand, / has lost any intention to go and snatch the Peacock Throne" (*dāġh hai hāth se nādir ke mirā dil tābān / nahīñ maqdūr kih jā chhīn lūñ taḳht-e ṭā'ūs*).[118]

Here, the conceit concerns a defeated lover who wanted to regain the Peacock Throne, but Nadir Shah, in the personage of a cruel beloved or wily competitor, had damaged the lover's heart to the point that he has lost his will to accomplish such a daring task. In these frequently cited lines, Tābān repurposed some of the details about the political upset in service of literary convention in a way that might counter outsiders' expectations. Constraints such as those that guided Tābān's telling, rather than repressing creativity, proved themselves productive to the poetry scene. The emulative expansion and dense trading of verse prompted by poetic attempts to narrate Nadir's conquest in ġhazal form generated new methods of interpreting the event to circulate ideas about its impact.[119] The persistence of verse exchange during the conflict and the possibilities for composing it introduced competing factions that both cemented tropes about the event and revealed how different registers of public poetry were used to memorialize the violence.

Despite his anxiety about protecting his loved ones and property, Muḳhliṣ still exchanged verse with friends during the occupation, and in these gatherings, he peppered his own poetic recitations with the words of Bedil, Delhi's poet-saint, and Muḥammad ʿAlī *Ṣā'ib* (The Mark) (1592–1676), the preeminent poet of the Persian world and one of Delhi's best-loved ġhazal writers. Mourning the violence that had taken place in Delhi, Muḳhliṣ composed a memorial merging the suffering of the lover with the scene of a devastated city:

> In its occupation, my heart turned up with all sorts of colorful bruises—
> just as if it were Delhi, a great city now with all its lamps put out.[120]

> *dil sar-o kārish bah rangārang dāġh uftādah ast*
> *ham chū dihlī shahr-e ḳhūbī be-chirāġh uftādah ast*

This couplet closely follows Ṣā'ib, utilizing Ṣā'ib's rhyme and meter, but also offers a new take on the theme of discord as manifested from darkness.

Written one hundred years previously, Ṣā'ib's couplet had considered the darkness in the lover's heart to be like rust that builds up at the center of a metal decanter, comparing the hue also with the base of a lamp where light does not reach:

Wine cannot not polish the rust at the heart of its own decanter.
Even at the lamp's base, it turns out there is only inky blackness.[121]

bādah zang az dil-e mīnā natawān-ast zidūd
tīrigī lāzimah-e pā-e chirāġh uftādah ast

Muḳhliṣ took Ṣā'ib's darkness theme and applied it to the discord of the city while implicitly acknowledging a Hindi proverb about the obliviousness of authorities: "under the lamp there is darkness" (*diye tale andherā*).[122]

Other associates of Muḳhliṣ who gathered during the occupation also tried their hand at elaborating the theme of the massacre's devastation by utilizing similar processes of emulation and meaning making. In his memoirs, Muḳhliṣ notes a reḳhtah ġhazal penned by his dearest friend Payām, a student of Bedil whose creativity in reḳhtah was crucial to its early scene in Delhi.[123] After comparing Nadir Shah's invasion with Timur Gurkani's sack of Delhi in 1398, Muḳhliṣ recommends that his reader should consider two of Payām's reḳhtah couplets "that demonstrate new style and balance," required of any emulation:

Those Delhi boys, with hats askew,
put an end to every lover.
Not a single lover comes into view,
after the hatted ones' mass murder.[124]

dillī ke kaj kulāh laṛkoñ ne
kām ʿushshāq kā tamām kiyā
ko'ī ʿāshiq naẓar nahīñ ātā
ṭopī wāloñ ne qatl-e ʿām kiyā

The image of a young man with his hat foppishly askew (*kaj kulāh*) has long persisted as a famous trope, first employed by Delhi poets Amīr Ḳhusrau (1253–1325) and Ḥasan Sijzī (1253–1338) several generations prior to Timur's attack.[125] Payām's couplets on the *kaj kulāh* appear in reḳhtah taẕkirahs, evidence of a place in literary memory, and they promote Payām's importance as a ġhazal contender and literary authority.[126] Importantly, Payām's frequently cited *kaj kulāh* verse was itself a tribute (*taẓmīn*) emulating the Deccani words of Shams ud-Dīn Muḥammad Walī (d. 1707), an approach he often used in his verse.[127] Examples of Payām's sharply honed emulative abilities appear in the Persian quatrains he modeled after Rūmī and recited at Ḳhwushgo's home. We also witness Payām's emulative skills in his few reḳhtah compositions that survive in which he emulates Ābrū, a poet he likely encountered at the mushāʿirahs of Ḳhwushgo or Ārzū.[128] Payām contextualizes the killing of commoners by re-deploying the amatory mode that Walī had established over half a century previously, but this time Payām invokes this lovelorn poetic tone in service of heralding a sudden social and political change. The poem Walī penned over half a century before Payām reads as follows:

"My two eyebrows, so cute and askew like me,
 the new moon said to them salaam in salutation."
Then with a sidelong glance, the flirt gave a wink—
 that brought all his lovers to completion.[129]

do bhūʾāñ ham soñ kyūñ nah hoñ bāñkī
 māh-e nau ne jise salām kiyā
ġhamzah-e shoḳh ne bah nīm nigāh
 kām ʿushshāq kā tamām kiyā

Walī depicts the beloved as a young man with his hat askew (*kaj kulāh*), wishing even his arched eyebrows would be just as rakish (*bāñkī*) as his hat. Walī also cites the new moon, which, for Payām writing in March 1739, would have been associated with the Eid holiday that had just passed.

Payām's tribute may appear overly subtle, perhaps to the point of obfuscating the violent event. But poetry aficionados in 1739 Delhi would have appreciated the nod to Walī, as the southern-born poet had many fans who were likely to recognize the conceit and Walī's words. Invoking a ġhazal from Walī was an appropriate technique through which Payām could effectively comment on the magnitude of an event that devastated Delhi's commoners and convulsed urban landscape. Indeed, the magnetism of Walī's *kaj kulāh* is such that his charms break up marriages, thereby destroying the social fabric of the city, as do other attractive youth whom we catch glimpses of throughout the Persianate literary canon. Payām set into motion a variation of this familiar literary figure by reenvisioning the ġhazal's elusive youth as the red-hatted Qizilbash soldiers laying waste to Delhi, an association made more powerful because the Turkish mercenary also served as a classical example of the beloved.[130]

The ambiguities of Persianate literary conventions provide a range of possibilities for interpreting couplets recited during this time as commentaries on Nadir Shah's massacre of Delhi's commoners. In the weeks that followed the violence of March 21–22, 1739, Mughal and Iranian authorities extracted vast wealth from the city's notables and ordered the executions of hundreds of people, according to contemporary accounts. Even if it was from their likely sheltered vantage points, the city's poets witnessed the violence and oppression meted out during this phase. For example, news of the dismembered corpses of the Qizilbash soldiers who were killed in the initial fracas in Pahāṛ Ganj likely circulated among the mushāʿirah poets. From within the poets' own strata of society, some officials committed suicide in the aftermath of the chaos. ʿAlīmullāh Ḳhān, the police chief's son, slit his wrists, and another official took poison to end his life.[131] These tragedies can easily find analogues within the stock images of Persian literature. They are overdetermined and therefore ambiguous, capable of citation in gatherings outside of the months of occupation. Were it not for the fastidious recordkeeping and careful emulations of poets like Muḳhliṣ and Ḥātim, it would be nearly impossible to draw conclusions about particular couplets' social meaning.

As we know, Ḥātim's circles in 1739 were growing increasingly crowded with recent émigrés to Delhi who were jostling to find their places among the city's senior literary masters, young poets, and the Qabuliyans. Ḥātim's secretarial abilities shine through in his work in the way that he diligently noted time-markers within his couplets alongside the carefully recorded context of each ġhazal he crafted at a mushāʿirah exchange, for a patron, or in response to a competitor. Indeed, between April 21, 1738, and March 28, 1740—the span comprising the years 1151 and 1152 AH when Nadir Shah-impacted salons were to have occurred—Ḥātim participated in twenty-four gatherings in which he produced at least one composition. Gatherings were held on a regular basis, either monthly or weekly.[132] Between March 20 and May 16, 1739, Ḥātim likely found the time to attend at least ten gatherings even with his busy schedule performing kitchen duties for Amīr Ḳhān.

In a ġhazal dated 1739 (1151 AH), Ḥātim wrote, "Why wouldn't there be, O Ḥātim, a general massacre in Jahān[ābād]? / This year Nowruz was colored red when it came" (*kyoñkar nah qatl-e ʿām ho ḥatim jahān meñ / nuurūz is baras kā paṛā thā bah rang-e surḳh*). Ḥātim composed these lines for a mushāʿirah held between two New Years' celebrations: March 21, marking the Persian New Year on 1 Farwardīn, and April 10, 1739, when the Islamic New Year began on 1 Muharram 1152 AH, according to the Hijri calendar.[133] So too, on Ḥātim's fortieth birthday in 1741/2 (1154 AH), Tābān and Saudā gathered with Ḥātim to compose ġhazals with refrains of "in between" (*ke bīch*).[134] On one occasion in 1739/1740 (1152 AH) an informal student of Ārzū named Muḥtasham ʿAlī Ḳhān Ḥashmat (d. 1750) provided a verse with the refrain "it's spring" (*hai bahār*).[135] This grabbed the attention of many poets besides Ḥātim.[136] Maẓhar wrote a version that emerged as one of his most popular reḳhtah ġhazals inscribed across commonplace books and taẕkirahs.[137] Muḳhliṣ, who wrote little in reḳhtah, followed the refrain, and his engaging version reached the ears of writers in the South.[138] Finally, Saudā, still new to the reḳhtah scene, composed a ġhazal in the form, stating in a final couplet, "No sooner had I said adieu to Saudā, when I began to feel some pity. / This one was utterly possessed, and now suddenly it's spring!" (*ab ḳhudā ḥāfiẓ hai saudā kā mujhe ātā hai raḥm / ek to thā hī dīwānah tis par ātī hai bahār*).[139]

Mushāʿirahs after a Massacre

Thus, we turn to a gathering likely held in late March of 1739 with six poets: Maẓhar, Ḥātim, Muḥammad Bāqir Ḥazīn, Tābān, Saudā, and their patron Amīr Ḳhān, at whose home the mushāʿirah likely occurred. Maẓhar was the most senior poet within the group, making him the likely candidate for establishing the model upon which these six poets composed, and Muḥammad Bāqir *Ḥazīn* (The Grieved) (d. 1752) was one of his earliest protégés.[140] The exchange between these six poets reflects a literary community built out of a close-knit group of poets eager for suggestive models when reḳhtah writers were still few. Such inclinations were driving poets to gather and emulate each other in the wake of Nadir Shah's New Year's massacre. The gathering produced memorable verse that was recorded in diaries, edited for taẕkirahs, and cited across literary histories into the twenty-first century. Indeed, such memorable verse also serves excellent documentary purposes for discovering poets whose collected works were never compiled or whose manuscripts have since disappeared. This forum at Amīr Ḳhān's house produced evocative ideas tied to the violent events and new literary knowledge elaborated through trading poetic themes via emulation. Maẓhar's opening line survives in several taẕkirahs, providing a foundation:

> Give me enough respite so that I might depart, Fowler.
> For too long have I dwelt in the shade of this garden.[141]

> *itnī furṣat de kih ruḳhṣat hoveñ ai ṣayyād ham*
> *muddatoñ is bāġh ke sāye meñ the ābād ham*

According to Persian literary convention, the bird catcher (*ṣayyād*) is one of many oppressors, and the lover, singing like a nightingale, often begs him for freedom. Bāqir Ḥazīn echoed his teacher's theme in his opening couplet:

The rose season already happened. Why would you see me happy?
Do something, Fowler! It's not as if I am about to be set free.[142]

faṣl-e gul to ho chukī kyā dekh hoñge shād ham
kuchh kar ai ṣayyād nahīñ hone ke ab āzād ham

Bāqir Ḥazīn's verse turns the conceit around: the fowler has no reason to latch the door to the cage as the nightingale/lover has no reason to sing. Springtime roses, the object of the nightingale's inspiration, have already dropped their blooms.

Amīr Ḳhān responded in an opening couplet often attributed to him in early reḳhtah tażkirahs in which the courtier displayed his famous wit. In his version, the nightingale voluntarily submits to the fowler:

Since I have the sinking feeling that I will never be free,
Lowering my face in submission, shall I then go to the garden
[and say], "Hey Fowler, I am here!"?[143]

ab yahī aḥsās hai jo hargiz nah hoñ āzād ham
phir chaman meñ jā'eñ kyā muñh le ke ai ṣayyād ham

Amīr Ḳhān cleverly uses the Hindi idiom for showing obedience (*muñh meñ lenā*) in this couplet to voice the nightingale's capitulation to his capture.

Ḥātim's couplet on the theme employs several idioms, echoing the Persian phrase, "a clever bird when snared goes tame once in hand"—that same phrase, as we recall from earlier, that the Iranian Wālih chose to describe the emperor resigned to Nadir Shah's victory:

You will only let me go when I have withered to bones in my cage.
Now what will you do with me, Fowler, a mere fist full of feathers?[144]

sūkh kar kāñṭā hū'e pinjre meñ tab chhoṛe hai tū
ab kahāñ jāveñ yih le kar musht-e par ṣayyād ham

Like Bāqir Ḥazīn, Ḥātim also flips the conceit onto its head. The captured nightingale goes tame in hand, but only because he has wasted away, leaving the fowler nothing but feathers.

Within this closely knit group of versifiers, ideas and formal parameters produced evocative couplets during each composition, allowing the formal parameters to propel the images in new directions. Saudā combined these approaches to produce another take on the theme of the oppressive fowler in his opening and closing couplets.

I'm already bursting at the seams with sorrow for the garden, Fowler.
Give me enough respite to be free even a smidgen from the rose.

. . . .

Listen Madman, your verse has become like fetters for a maniac (*saudā*).
Indeed, it is not as if from your prison that I am about to be set free.[145]

ḳhānah-pur dard-e chaman haiñ āḳhir ai ṣayyād ham
itnī furṣat de kih ho leñ gul ṭuk āzād ham

. . . .

ai janūn miṣraʿ tirā saudā kī hai zanjīr-e pā
qaid se terī nahīñ hone ke ab āzād ham

Saudā's rose was more oppressive than the fowler's snare because the nightingale grows tired of singing for blooms in the garden all throughout the springtime. Saudā's last line exemplifies the creative emulative processes by which poets generated meaning through redeploying evocative images and quoting ideas or phrases to acknowledge local or distant links. Saudā praised the words of his fellow poets, capturing specific phrases and emulating them for the purpose of capturing new ideas (*maẓmūn bandī*). The production of couplets like those of Saudā constructively bound together the cohort of poets and their shared process of meaning making.

Following Saudā's ideas, Tābān's opening line also considers the fowler as an oppressive figure, but this time introduces the idea of the nightingale's plea for freedom:

Even after letting out one hundred types of sighs and complaints,
I can never ever be free from this very cage.[146]

sau ṭarḥ gar kareñge nālah-o faryād ham
is qafas se to bhī ho sakte nahīñ āzād ham

No matter how complex the nightingale makes his song, the fowler always keeps him caged according to literary convention. Bāqir Ḥazīn expanded on this topic, framing the nightingale's crying as a complaint against injustice:

Alas, in the end there is no escaping from this high-handedness.
He just up and took my heart, and I increasingly complain.[147]

kuchh nah āḳhir chal sakā hā'e in zabar-dastoñ sitī
le gaye dil ke ta'īñ karte rahe faryād ham

Addressing the fowler or perhaps the cruel beloved, now the poet speaks of a captured heart and complains against his oppressor's highhandedness.

Ḥātim's opening verse considers this theme by evoking the dark image of oppression, albeit in ironic terms, as would be expected among ġhazal writers:

To whom could I possibly bring complaints of your oppression
when you are the very one from whom I seek justice?[148]

kis kane le jā'eñ terī ẓulm kī faryād ham
tujhī se tere sitam kī chāhte haiñ dād ham

Ḥātim considers the multiple associations of injustice as darkness, the same theme invoked in Muḳhliṣ's emulation of Ṣā'ib that considers Delhi grown quiet after the massacre. Tābān echoes this theme of the lover's complaints against injustice while adding gory images:

Even after murdering me, you shall chop my corpse into pieces.
I seek my justice from my killer.[149]

ba'd mere qatl ke bhī lāsh ke tukṛe kare
chāhte haiñ apne us qātil se apnī dād ham

Following Ḥātim's theme, Tābān merges criminal and judge in his oppressive figure. Even in death, the poet cannot seek justice for his murder because the beloved responds only by dismembering him. Saudā picked up the idea of slaughter by alluding to the Feast of Sacrifice (*'īd-e qurbān*), which began on March 21, the day before the massacre was ordered:

Certainly, slit some throats, but also allow some time for necking.
Since it's the Feast of Sacrifice, allow me to give you glad tidings![150]

żabḥ to kartā hai ṭuk furṣat gale lagne ke de
'īd-e qurbān tujhe de le mubārak bād ham

Saudā's verse utilizes a Hindi phrase for friends pressing their necks together in an embrace (*galā lagnā*) in reference to the religiously sanctioned method of slaughtering an animal for the Eid celebration by slitting its throat (*żabḥ karnā*).

Amīr Ḳhān also conjures up the severed throats of sacrificed animals in his ġhazal, crafting an īhām into his pen name of *Anjām* (The Result):

Because I kept my head, my dignity was preserved as a "Result" (*anjām*).
That is, I thankfully did not squirm beneath the headsman's blade.[151]

sāth apne sar ke thā anjām pās-e tamkanat
shukr hai taṛape nah zer-e ḳhanjar-e jallād ham

Falling on the wrong side of an uprising or coming into disfavor of the emperor put courtiers at constant risk of a beheading, as was the fate of several officials on Nadir Shah's orders after the uprising.

Tābān considers violence and the oppressor's instruments in two couplets. The first reflects Amīr Ḳhān's ideas, but in Tābān's hands, the lover makes a voluntary sacrifice:

Having already given up my head, I wander love's roads.
Now I never fear the headsman's blade.

ham apne sar de phirte haiñ rāh-e ʿishq meñ
kab tirī talwār se ḍarte haiñ ai jallād ham

Execution has no meaning for the headless lover, who must contend with far more perilous dangers of love while traveling on its roads. Tābān also introduces a new oppressor to the ġhazal exchange: the phlebotomist standing ready with his fleam to let out the lover's melancholia-infected blood:

If one opens my carotid artery only then will I escape from insanity.
This is the very type of phlebotomist I search for.[152]

khol deve gar rag-e jān ko to saude se chhuṭeñ
ḍhūñḍte haiñ is ṭarḥ kā ab koʾī faṣṣād ham

Tābān paints an image of the lover committing suicide while trying to cure his madness through bloodletting.

Ḥātim likewise elaborates the theme of melancholia with an invocation of Majnūn, the famed lover driven to madness from his unrequited connection to Leila:

On land and sea, you find the fame of my mania.
When it comes to the passions of lovers, I am Majnūn's teacher.[153]

baḥr-o barr meñ hai hamārī shuhrat-e dīwāngī
ʿāshiq ke kām meñ majnūn ke haiñ ustād ham

Tābān's lover may have threatened to kill himself out of madness, but Ḥātim's speaker has plumbed such depths of melancholia that he could instruct Majnūn in the deserts where he dwells.

Bāqir Ḥazīn closes his ġhazal with a similar invocation, writing an īhām on his own pen name over the saintly tomb of Majnūn:

Why wouldn't Lord Majnūn's soul be pleased with me?
For, I have made the desert of love grief's abode—Ḥazīn-*ābād*.[154]

kyūñ nah hoveñ shād ham se ḥaẓrat majnūn kī rūḥ
ʿishq ke ṣaḥrā ko rakhte haiñ ḥazīn ābād ham

Bāqir Ḥazīn offers a clever īhām in the Qabuliyan style, as it worked in several directions. The poet makes Majnūn's traditional abode of the desert simultaneously the abode of grief: "Ḥazīnville."

Always a poet to champion his hometown, Ḥātim closes the exchange with a couplet that returns to the image cited by Payām and Walī: the young man reigning over the city with his devastating handsomeness.

Having given my heart to Hindustan's Hindu boys and its premier city,
why should I completely abandon Shāhjahānābād, Ḥātim?[155]

hind ke [hindū] bachoñ se dil lagā kar aur shahr
kyuñkih jāveñ chhoṛ ḥātim shah jahāñ ābād ham

Indeed, Ḥātim remained in Delhi through Nadir Shah's occupation and the chaos it produced, also weathering more sieges in the late 1750s and early 1760s.

Murdering a Doctor

In a brief two-year span from 1737 to 1739, members of Ḥātim's circle cultivated broad ties with the Qabuliyans and the students of Ummīd and Maẓhar, resulting in a closely knit group of poets with overlapping influences and inclinations connected through the emulative network considered here. A shared practice in a mushāʿirah and the shared experience of the occupation of Delhi enabled this cohort of poets to produce an ambiguous set of compositions in late March 1739 that somewhat guardedly gestured toward the events that brought chaos and destruction to their town. The goal of such an interchange was not to document the event so much as ambivalently chart its occurrence through metaphor, binding topics according to the shared vocabulary of Persianate convention and imagery.

A close reading of verse produced during this period reveals connections vital for understanding the impact of language and literature in mediating the event. This process of close reading generates even further evidence. For example, by closely reading a verse, the taẑkirah writer Shafīq Aurangābādī was able to ascertain the unfortunate end of Ṡābit, the Qabuliyans' main literary rival. Delicately treading around the ignominy of his dying during a massacre of commoners, taẑkirah writers refrained from detailing the specifics of his passing and obfuscated the years of his death, but Shafīq Aurangābādī settled these contradictions decades later in his taẑkirah by closely reading one of Ṡābit's final compositions, a qaṣīdah written in memoriam for his friend Ḥakīm Imām ud-Dīn *Aksīr* (The Antidote) (d. 1739).[156]

By 1739, Ṡābit had retreated from the competitive sphere of salons and the political setting of the court. With his finances likely spent, he lived with his friend the medic and occasional poet Imām ud-Dīn Aksīr, whose residence was located close to the walled city's central markets.[157] The year before, Ṡābit's student, a certain Bandah ʿAlī, helped to compile Ṡābit's dīwān housing the composition of his words about the conflict with Istiʿdād, Matīn, and the Qabuliyans.[158] But at this stage, his battles were over. Matīn had left for Lucknow in 1735, and Qabūl had been dead for over a decade. In the home of his friend Aksīr, he "donned a faqir's cloak" to focus on studying hadith and writing about the tragic events of Karbala.[159] By early May of 1739, Ṡābit too had died. His last literary act was to compose an elegy for Aksīr who had preceded him in death by a matter of months. Both were casualties of the chaos brought about when Nadir Shah ordered his troops to massacre Delhi's commoners in the walled city's downtown.

Taẑkirah writers produced conflicting dates and accounts of Ṡābit's passing. Ḳhwushgo mentioned Aksīr's literary abilities and the medic being a subject of a qaṣīdah by Ṡābit, but he provides no details about Aksīr's end. Regarding Ṡābit, Ḳhwushgo and Muḳhliṣ were similarly silent, and Ārzū only hinted at the argumentative poet's end by writing, "the skies will have turned a thousand times before another writer like this is born!"[160] Regarding the year of his death, documentarians produced three different dates: Jān-e Jānān Maẓhar related to Āzād Bilgrami in a letter that Ṡābit died June 13, 1737; Wālih, who knew Ṡābit's son, recorded 1738, as did chronicler Muʿtamad Ḳhān. Ḳhwushgo noted 1739 as the year of Ṡābit's end.[161]

Ḳhwushgo's date is the correct one according to Shafīq Aurangabādī, writing twenty years later at a distance from the contentious Delhi ġhazal scene and violence of 1739. As Shafīq wrote, the Qizilbash "bloodletters, having destroyed [Aksīr's] house, inflicted wounds on the doctor, his son, Mīr [Ṡābit], and their companions."[162] Aksīr and his son, Mīr Mubārak Ḳhān, died three days later, on March 25, 1739, according to Shafīq. The precise fate of the companions and Ṡābit remains unclear in Shafīq's words, only implying that Ṡābit held on for some months. Shafīq's clue for this detail emerged from Ḳhwushgo, who noted that Ṡābit stayed at Aksīr's home and wrote a qaṣīdah in praise of his host.[163] It was filled with deep expressions of loss and medical terminology:

For the dark fates of love's madmen, alas!
  The night of horrors has stopped the heavens.

. . . .

In this age, under the influence of scarcity and ignorance,
  no one consults the medical guidance of Galen.

. . . .

In short, the world's temperament has turned utterly corrupt,
  unless Ptolemy provides treatment.
With the highest virtue and lordship, Dr. Imām ud-Dīn is
  better than Plato and Dioscorides.

. . . .

To rebuff the disease in the errors of novices' poems,
  the etchings of his ink pen performed like black licorice extract.[164]

zi-baḳht-e tīrah-e saudāʾiyān-e ʿishq afsūs
  giriftah-ast falak rā tamām shab-e kabūs

. . . .

dar īn zaman kih zi-taʾṡīr-e fuqr-o nā-dānī
  kasī rajūʿ nadārad ba ṭibb-e jalīyānūs

. . . .

ġharaẓ kih gashtah mizāj-e jahān basī fasād
  magar ʿilāj kunad ūstād-e biṭlīmūs
suphar-e faẓl-o sayādat ḥakīm imam ud-dīn
  kih hast bih zi-falāṭūn-o dīsqūrīdūs

. . . .

ba-dafʿ-e ʿillat-e shiʿr-e saqīm-e nau-mashqān
tarāshah-e qalamish kard kār-e aṣl us-sūs

To settle the debate on Ṡābit's end, Shafīq resorted to a close reading of Ṡābit's final composition, perhaps ignored among commentators because Ṡābit's combat with the Qabuliyans overshadowed the qaṣīdah for Aksīr. Ṡābit's love of serious verse and Aksīr's medical background were two overlapping categories evidenced in the technical terminology from the world of Greek medicine. For each couplet, Shafīq provided a commentary to prove that it was, in fact, an elegy for Imām ud-Dīn Aksīr, who suffered fatal wounds in the violence on March 22, 1739. Shafīq's analysis revealed that literary companionship between the two men shaped meaning-creation within the poem.

Whatever treatments he wrote about, they were of insufficient help to Ṡābit, and he died in May 1739, around the time Nadir Shah left Delhi. So too, tażkirah writer Durgā Dās *ʿIshrat* (The Pleasure) (fl. 1750–60) provided his own conclusion on the debate: Ṡābit died "in the year 1152 AH (1739) during Nadir Shah's enslavement of Delhi."[165] Ṡābit had one son who survived the events of 1739, the poet Muḥammad ʿAẓīm *Ṡabāt* (The Resolute), and like Girāmī with Qabūl, Muḥammad ʿAẓīm carried on his father's combative approach and serious words in poems of his own and in attacks on Ḥazīn, who had just made his second entrance to Delhi to hide out in Wālih's home, waiting to make a final attempt to return to Isfahan via Lahore. Ṡābit's ignominious end in May of 1739, wounded in the home of his friend at the hands of Qizilbash soldiers, was respectfully omitted in his colleagues' histories. But before Nadir Shah left Delhi in the wake of a baggage train loaded with wealth and the imperial Peacock Throne, there was a wedding.

The Ġhazal Singers

Sitting in an audience hall at the Blessed Citadel, the courtesan Nūr Bāʾī had choices to make.[166] Due to her status as the most famous courtesan in Delhi, Nūr Bāʾī had been asked to sing verse at the wedding of Naṣrullāh Mīrzā, the younger of Nadir Shah's two sons. Together, Nadir Shah and Muhammad Shah had arranged royal nuptials to take place in Delhi on April 6, 1739, a mere two weeks after Nadir Shah's massacre of the city's commoners. The wedding promised to cement the conclusion of their battles while

FIGURE 3.1 Kalyān Dās, *Portrait of a Lady Holding a Rose*, circa 1740. Johnson Collection, British Library, London. J.60,22.

vouchsafing their future compacts. Naṣrullāh Mīrzā was to wed a bride whose pedigree on her father's side descended from Delhi's founder Shah Jahan (r. 1628–58) and on her mother's side boasted a connection with Aurangzeb (r. 1658–1707). The wedding festivities were to last three days and with entertainments that included elaborate fireworks, a menagerie with elephants and other beasts, the requisite luxuries of cloth, jewels, and wines, and a performance from the city's top courtesan.[167]

Despite the fanfare, the wedding transpired in a tense atmosphere. Outside the walls of the palace and beyond the riverbanks where servants lit fireworks and Nūr Bāʾī was preparing to sing, the city was still raw from the Iranian occupation. It would prove resilient, but on that day, the corpses of Delhi's commoners still lay rotting in the streets, their bodies yet to be collected for cremation regardless of faith. Inside the palace, the weighty terms of surrender hung heavily around the necks of Muhammad Shah and the wedding attendees. They were bracing under the demands of exactions given to the victorious Iranians, representatives of whom were celebrating along with them at this royal wedding.[168]

As an additional note of tension, the wedding fell on the eve of the Islamic calendar's new year. It was within the first ten days of Muharram, the time of year that Shīʿī Muslims dedicated to commemorating the tragic assassination of the Prophet's grandson, on the battle plains of Karbala, Iraq, in 680 CE. Although Nadir Shah himself was not Shīʿī, he was mindful of this anniversary because nearly all his Qizilbash soldiers were. Disregarding his soldiers' customary practices, Nadir Shah forbade them from singing traditional mourning songs in the days after his son's wedding, perhaps worrying that these expressions of grief would further exacerbate the overwrought environment of the tense city. Several of Nadir Shah's soldiers ignored these orders and were punished with hangings.[169]

As part of a liminal class of artists with elite political connections, Nūr Baʾī was familiar with the intricacies of these dynamics and dramatic events. She was Delhi's best-loved courtesan, and her network of associates, including colleagues and clients, kept her apprised of the news while she traveled freely through Delhi's streets performing at the salons. According to accounts left behind by taẕkirah writers among the fans who followed her, Nūr Baʾī was fluent in Persian, proficient in reciting reḳhtah verse, and unmatched in her dancing and singing skills.[170] She learned the latest vocal music sung in shrines, private gatherings, and the imperial court that perpetuated both Hindi and Persian amatory lyrics from devotional traditions and the past masters, including everyone from Saʿdī to Amīr Ḳhusrau.

As she prepared to recite at the fraught wedding of Nadir Shah's son, Nūr Bāʾī had a wide repertoire of songs from which to choose. She knew that in order to be successful, she would have to select words that would appeal to the widest possible number of these diverse wedding guests who had varying tastes and backgrounds. Perhaps more importantly, she had to please each of the two emperors who were both her patrons now. Professional performers like Nūr Bāʾī made their mark by expertly allowing the nuances of the situation to guide their choices about the verses to sing. To aptly select music, Nūr Bāʾī had to take into account time, place, and companions, and her understanding of the competitive verse marketplace.

On the one hand, Nūr Bāʾī could choose to perform compositions preferred by the īhām masters among Qabuliyans and the reḳhtah composers who once ventured to the Ornament of the Mosques. She could choose to feature poetry in the complex style favored among elite pen pushers like Ārzū and Muḳhliṣ, Bedil's former students. Nūr Bāʾī also could select verses that exemplified older modes favored by some of the recent Iranian immigrants such as Ḥazīn or Wālih, or the image-conjuring verse preferred among senior émigrés like Ummīd who had come to India decades prior. With a wide array of options to choose from, Nūr Bāʾī had to sing something that would speak to the many tastes among her audience, the socially charged situation, the performative erotic requirements, and the male elites with demands for her sexual labor.[171]

To address the competing demands, Nūr Bāʾī chose from the top hits of the day—verses favored by all these groups. She sang Ṣāʾib's couplets:

Heart Stealer, you have seductively conquered me again.
  Now what's left of my heart for you to come and take again?

Bring the wine, take a drink, clap your hands, stomp your feet!
  It's not as though you have come to the winehouse to perform
    prayers again?[172]

dilrubāyānah digar bar sar-e nāz āmadah-ī
  az dil-e mā chih bajā māndah kih bāz āmadah-ī

mai badah mai bisitān dast bazan pāī bakūb
  baḳharābāt nah az bahr-e namāz āmadah-ī

By many accounts, Nūr Bāʾī's performance at the royal wedding was a smashing success. The admiration she drew tempted Nadir Shah to later seek her services in a more intimate setting after the wedding. Nūr Bāʾī accepted the proposition and provided personal entertainment for this man with no molars who inhaled his food and frequently dyed his hair to appear more virile.[173] After that encounter, an acquaintance had the temerity to ask Nūr Bāʾī what their tryst was like. To negotiate the power imbalance implicit in both the question and the sexual exchange with Nadir Shah, Nūr Bāʾī answered with a double entendre, drawing on her wit and knowledge of military terminology to note both the violence that had occurred only weeks prior and her own position as being subject to sexual aggression of elite men: "The general massacre even had come inside my breach."[174] Sex and the suggestion of erotic ideals were part of the job for courtesans such as Nūr Bāʾī, who used ambiguity such as this to meet the prurient and literary demands of audiences across the capital.

As Nadir Shah prepared to depart from Delhi in May 1739, he dreaded the prospect of leaving Nūr Bāʾī behind. Delhi's favorite courtesan spurned the request of the invading emperor to depart in victory with her from the city. Meanwhile, only a few years after Nadir Shah left, yet another poetry style took hold among Delhi's purveyors of speech, challenging courtesans and bearded versifiers alike to master its cadences. The cacophony of Delhi's poetry scene harbored a type of amatory verse associated with the classical style that, by the nineteenth century, would overtake the complex trends dominating Delhi's mushāʿirahs. Notably, Ḥazīn was an early champion of this classically flavored verse style in his own semi-public performances.

But the most famous singers of amatory ġhazals in the style of old masters were the city's courtesans, a group of female poets who, like Nūr Bāʾī, entertained with a variety of forms overlapping with male poets but with some aspects associated specifically with the female gender, such as dance, certain vocal styles, and unique modes of professional comportment. By the 1720–50 period examined in this book, educated, performing women like Nūr Bāʾī built audiences and shaped the mushāʿirah scene based on this classical/amatory approach. In fact, during the occupation and in the years immediately afterward, such amatory verse with classical themes surfaced in the recitations and writings of poets as they attempted to understand the harrowing events of March 1739 and further propel the market for speech.

Romantic Favorites

After his third return to Delhi in late 1739 or early 1740, Ḥazīn's musical abilities began to flourish in his own gatherings, prompting one diarist to title the émigré the "Candle in the Gathering of Brilliant Utterance."[175]

Dargāh Qulī Ḳhān, a courtier from Hyderabad whose views have woven their way throughout this book, visited salons at Ḥazīn's home and found a sumptuous setting.[176] Ḥazīn had his central courtyard rinsed and scrubbed to the point that it presented a "radiance of a polished mirror."[177] Carpets were then laid out on the courtyard's central raised plinth. Ḥazīn's band of poets and hangers-on sat on this elevated spot to recite and discuss verse. While attending one of Ḥazīn's gatherings, Dargāh Qulī Ḳhān recorded a few couplets from one of Ḥazīn's ġhazal-singing performances in his diary:

When the candle's flame from the heart continuously flared out,
it's as if lovers' burning sighs, one after another, fled out.

There is no gem that I cast, countless, upon the earth.
However, ruby-colored tears, by the hundreds, from my heart
I let out.[178]

shuʿlah-e shamaʿ musalsal zi-dil āyad bīrūn
āh-e jān-e soḳhtagān muttaṣil āyad bīrūn

īn guhar nīst kih nashumardah bah ḳhāk ashānam
ashk-e gulrang bah ṣadd ḳhūn-e dil āyad bīrūn

These two couplets adhere to an amatory style favored by writers from the classical era—the so-called ancients. But in the performance that Dargāh Qulī Ḳhān witnessed, listeners also would have recognized another famous ġhazal, whose thematic material, meter, rhyme, and refrain originated from Ṣāʾib, the superstar writer of the past universally appreciated by Persian and reḳhtah poets. Ṣāʾib's verse illustrates enduring nature of the yearning lover's tear filled with blood from his heart:

A bloodied teardrop from any of this water and clay never leeched out.
For this is the rose that from the desert-edge of the heart grew out.[179]

ashk-e ḳhūnain nah zi-har āb-o gil āyad bīrūn
īn gul az dāman-e ṣaḥrā-e dil āyad bīrūn

Such amorous verse was particularly suitable for song and in musical gatherings with percussion, plucked strings, and dancers. In Delhi during the early 1740s, Ḥazīn's performances mirrored those of the premier ġhazal singers of Ṣāʾib's verse, Delhi's courtesans.

Across the Islamic world, courtesans constituted a class of urban professional beloveds available for hire to provide entertainment, companionship, artistic instruction, and sometimes sexual intimacy. As discussed by historian

Katherine Schofield, such professional entertainers of Delhi came from classes termed *kanchanī*. These same professional singers were sometimes identified as *ḍomnīs* or "auspicious singers" within European and Persian sources or *ṭawā'ifs* in Indian sources.[180] The backgrounds and statuses of Delhi's courtesans varied greatly. Some of these courtesans were enslaved or indentured in their roles as entertainers, while others were brought up from childhood into their respective traditions through a familial connection.[181] The status of courtesans also depended on the arenas in which they performed—the harem, the private salon, the court, or among shrines.

Although many elite historical accounts of courtesans cast them according to static literary tropes, later writings show that eighteenth-century female entertainers experienced dynamic forms of mobility, class standing, visibility, and wealth afforded through shifting social and artistic values during that time. Professional elites such as Nūr Bā'ī negotiated their high positions through hosting noblemen, accepting sumptuous gifts, and riding through the streets in fancy litters perched upon the backs of elephants, the usual conveyance reserved for Delhi's wealthiest male citizens. Other professional public women shaped public space according to visceral logics. Famous dancers such as Ramjānī and Kālī Gangā were among the famous dancers of Delhi's 1730s and 1740s, and the noted performer and conversationalist Ad Begam attended gatherings in striking sartorial choices, wearing nothing on her legs but painted patterns resembling ornate cloth.[182]

Delhi's courtesans also shaped the market for speech through their curatorial capacities in selecting which songs and poetry they would perform in gatherings and before the notables who attended mushā'irahs. Like Ḥazīn, courtesans such as Nūr Bā'ī catered to the city's tastes by singing Persian poetry that addressed the amatory ideas favored by Ṣā'ib and other old style ġhazal composers. Gulāb (The Rose Water) (fl. 1730–50), a noted poet who could send listeners into dreamscapes of sight and sound, sang verse in gatherings that triggered synesthesia in her audiences: the listeners reported that from her melodies emanated perfumes. She chose a complex ambiguous couplet from Ṣā'ib's dīwān: "By which mirror-faced beloved shall one be obliterated? / This world and the next are merely a house of mirrors because of the beloved's face" (*maḥv-e kudām-e ā'īnah-sīmā shawad kasī / ā'īnah ḳhānah-ī ast do 'ālam zi-rū-e dost*).[183] In this poem, the beloved, with a mirror-like face, sees only himself in the world, so the poem references both the infinitude of reduplicated reflections when placing two mirrors in front of each other (like the heavens and the ocean) and the cruel beloved who tricks the lover with a hall of mirrors.[184]

One courtesan versifier stands out within Dargāh Qulī Ḳhān's diary: Raḥmān Bā'ī (fl. 1730–50), a poet who likely participated in the festivities at Bedil's grave. Raḥmān Bā'ī was from a Muslim caste whose members functioned as professional musicians and reciters (*ḍhāṛhī*) in military, courtly, and civic settings.[185] Appended to her capsule biography, Dargāh Qulī Ḳhān added a couplet that was likely from Raḥmān Bā'ī's own compositions:

His sideburns are not work of the painter Mānī, and they are not
a sketch by the artist Bihzād.
Indeed, this black ink drawing is the excellent work of nature's
ustād.[186]

ḳhaṭish nah kardah-e mānī nah naqsh-e bihzād ast
kih īn siyāh qalam kār-e ḳhūb-e ustād ast

The conceit in this ġhazal revolves around the deep black color of the beloved's sideburns (*ḳhaṭṭ*, which also refers to marks on a page), drawn not by famous painters but by either a lowly artist with only pencil and paper or perhaps God Himself. Whether the verse belonged to Raḥmānī Bā'ī or Dargāh Qulī Ḳhān, its emulative connections reveal an intriguing social network as the couplet likely originated from Bedil's ʿurs gathering during the annual reading sessions from his complete works.

Evidence for the Bedilian origins of Raḥmān Bā'ī's verse appears in the poet-saint's dīwān in lines that established their formal parameters. As considered in the couplet quoted by Dargāh Qulī Ḳhān, Bedil's version in the first and final couplets held evocative and contradictory images produced through the theme of the artist:

Where are there drawings that have not covered desire in the paints
of yearning?
The mere thought your hair-thin waist lies in the pen of the artist
Bihzād.

. . . .

You seek salvation. Instead, choose silence, Bedil.
On the safe road, silence is the ustād.[187]

chih naqsh-hā kih nah bast ārzū bah pardah-e shauq
ḳhayāl-e mū'ī-e miyān-e tū kilk-e bihzād ast

. . . .

najāt mī ṭalabī ḳhāmushī guzīn bedil
kih dar ṭarīq-e salāmat ḳhamoshī ustād ast

Besides harboring an outline of Bedil's impact, the couplet quoted in Dargāh Qulī Ḳhān's diary was also a tribute (*taẓmīn*) from Qabuliyan poet Muḥammad ʿAlī Ḥashmat, as the last line quotes words from a couplet Ḥashmat composed. Ḥashmat's verse was released sometime prior to 1727 under his previous pen name of *Masīḥā* (The Messiah), and it followed the punning style of his teacher Qabūl:

Masīḥā glanced upon your sideburns and then with wounded heart responded,
"See, this black ink drawing is the excellent work of a true ustād."[188]

ḳhaṭ-e tū dīd masīḥā wa guft bā dil resh
kih īn siyāh qalam kār-e ḳhūb-e ustād ast

Here, Ḥashmat's īhām hinges on the word for wound (*resh*) and beard (*resh*), producing a humorous īhām about the appearance of the beloved. Instead of the poet with a wounded heart speaking, the beloved's newly sprouted beard announces that the young man's peach fuzz has gone, rendering him a man and therefore unavailable for seduction. Raḥmān Bāʾī's version refocuses the amatory nature of Ḥashmat's second verse by name-dropping the visual artists Mānī and Bihzād, characters associated with classical-era poetry.

Between the emulation of Bedil and the tribute from Ḥashmat, courtesans like Raḥmān Bāʾī exhibited noteworthy abilities to shape Delhi's ġhazal scene. Courtesans composed their own verse by innovating upon ideas and forms that circulated among gatherings. The courtesan Tanū (The Delicate) (fl. 1730–40) maintained her connection to mushāʿirah circles through her patron Muḥammad Māh *Ṣadāqat* (The Sincerity) (d. 1741), a rakehell from Ārzū's and Ḳhwushgo's gatherings and occasional contributor to Delhi's ġhazal scene. Tanū sang a striking couplet that notably expanded upon classical images associated with love and sacrifice. The Sufi poet Faḳhr ud-Dīn ʿIrāqī (1213–1289) states in a couplet:

What life I had palpitated at the beloved's door.
My worn-out heart is like a chicken at slaughter.[189]

ʿumrī batapīd bar dar-e yār
ḳhastah jigar chū murġh-e bismil

ʿIrāqī's couplet offers the trembling dance of a slaughtered chicken, perhaps sacrificed at a threshold to ward off the evil eye, to illustrate the lover's erratically thumping heart.

In Tanū's contribution, likely a song performed in a gathering of her colleagues and an all-male clientele, she expounds on the sacrifice metaphor to express a moment of profound matrimonial ambivalence reflected in a mirror:

I left this world, but longing never left my heart.
  I am as if a mirror. My appearance is my slaughter.[190]

raftīm-o naraft ḥasrat az dil
  chūn āʾīnah-īm jalwah bismil

In weddings, the first moment in which bride and groom glimpse each other, called "manifestation" or "splendor" (*jalwah*), is highly ritualized, and occurs when a mirror is placed on top of the Qur'an and the bride and groom are bid to gaze into it together to find one other's face. In this poem, dualities created in the mirror during the wedding festivities signify the liminal space of the lover as a bride just after she has taken vows and is about to leave her natal home.

Ḥazīn himself respected the formal patterns used by Delhi's courtesans. Utilizing Tanū's meter in an emulatory fashion, Ḥazīn composed a *maṡnawī* called "In Remembrance of Lovers" (*Tażkirat ul-ʿĀshiqīn*) that eulogized the men most important to the poet. In a wine song spoken to a barkeep that comprises its opening section, Ḥazīn's poem invoked similar bridal imagery as voiced by Tanū:

So that my mirror manifests purity
  and reflects that heart-stealing face,
make [the tavern] as the beloved's bridal chamber,
  pass over the mirror and leave behind a reflection.[191]

tā āʾīnah-īm ṣafā pażīr
  ʿaks-e rukh-e dilrubā pażīr
gardīd chū jalwah gāh-e dildār
  āʾīnah gużār-o ʿaks bagużār

Ḥazīn's words reflected Tanū's images: the poem's speaker casts himself as a bride in the liminal space of newly wedded couples, looking into a mirror and waiting to see the reflection of the important men in his life.[192] As witnessed here and in other histories of the Muslim world's courtesans, performance and composition of amatory words inspired by classical authors required poets to perform gendered roles that were decidedly feminine or at least linked to courtesans.[193] For this elite class of women who were expected to display their erotic identities, the ġhazal acted as a route to project distinction and authority. Thus, amatory words, when performed before elite audiences, required poets of both male and female gender to enact decidedly feminine comportment when seeking patronage.[194]

Notably, Dargāh Qulī Ḳhān describes Ḥazīn's ġhazal performances with the same idioms he used to illustrate the literary, aural, and performative nuances of the many courtesans he visited, registers Ḥazīn had first learned as a young boy growing up in Isfahan. Dargāh Qulī Ḳhān writes about Gulāb, Delhi's famous singer of Ṣāʾib's verse, that "contemplation of her stylish gesticulations (*ḥarakāt-e rangīnish*) brings the qualities of wine to bear."[195] Similarly, in Dargāh Qulī Ḳhān's formulation, Ḥazīn adopts the role of an elite performer who entertained his audience with a "well-spring of nightingale-like ġhazal recitation" such that his "delicate gesticulations (*ḥarakāt-e laṭīfish*) were perfect for beauty and elegant utterance."[196]

Conclusion

The violence of 1739 brought writers together, but it also inaugurated a phase in which Delhi's ġhazal reciters and singers began to further distinguish themselves amid an abundance of competing registers, including classically amatory, ambiguously complex, and local reḳhtah styles. This process of differentiation was made especially stark when Ḥazīn released a controversial and influential dīwān in 1743, filled with couplets in popular forms by past masters, and it soon caused controversy.

The Qabuliyans' lineage faded despite their enticing contributions to Delhi's literary sphere, leaving few to defend "incomplete īhām" that was once prized in the streets and at mushāʿirahs. With his elite connections, Girāmī survived the events of 1739, maintaining his performances and arguments while meeting his obligations to his students until he died several years later. In 1743, his father's student Ḥashmat composed an elegy for Girāmī with a chronogram at the end:

In mourning of him, by my authority,
  words of justice left my tongue.
My heart burned and, thus, composed the year of his death:
  "A wondrous rogue exited this world."[197]

dar mātam-e ū wilāyat-am rā
ḥarf-e inṣāf bar zabān raft
dil soḳht-o guft sāl-e wafātish
rindī-e ʿajabī az īn jahān raft [1156 AH]

Ḥashmat's end came six years later during Awadh governor Safdar Jang's failed attack on rebelling chiefs in the district of Rohilkhand.[198] Ḥashmat's famous abilities with the sword and spear did not save him, and his star pupil Tābān mourned him in a long elegy ending with a chronogram:

For your wretched Tābān, with wounded liver,
while considering the chronogram, there was stressful impediment
when my gaze fell upon the last line.
From "then" a voice from beyond provided this correction.
Oh, Ḥashmat is a martyr! Woe is me![199]

terā tābān ġharīb-o ḳhastah jigar
fikr-e tārīḳh meñ thā ḥadd muẓṭarr
miṣraʿah-e āḳhrī pah kī jo naẓar
kad se hātif ne us ko dī yih ḳhabar
hāʾe ḥashmat shahīd wāwelā [1161 AH]

While Ḥashmat's death gives the appearance that the Qabuliyan lineage had met its end, Girāmī instructed a productive student named Zindah Rām Panḍit *Mobad* (The Fire Priest) (d. circa 1765), a Kashmiri Hindu who found success in Delhi and later Lucknow. Mobad's Qabuliyan *kulliyāt* traces its author's career as a Persian-language poet through qaṣīdahs, an extensive corpus of ġhazals, and chronograms. Mobad was a child prodigy under Girāmī, completing a junior dīwān in 1737 while still a youngster enthralled by Girāmī's playful charisma, clever verse, and combative posturing. Alluding to the chase and delight in hunting for meanings, Mobad composed a couplet that closed his collection of youthful ġhazals:

Wherever there is stylish meaning, it waits as prey for me.
Upon the pages of time, such speech holds memory for me.[200]

har jā kih hast maʿnī-e rangīn shikār-e mā-st
bar ṣaḥfah-e zamānah suḳhan yādgār-e mā-st

Mushāʿirahs occurring between 1737 and 1742, with their intensive search for meaning, created dynamic settings for recitation and writing. The violence Qabuliyans and their colleagues witnessed in 1739 and the thick interchanges of ġhazals among Delhi's reciters produced "battles of words" that served to distinguish versifiers "from the shadow of beastliness" in poetry's crowded gathering spaces, to follow the Qabuliyan ideals of the young Mobad.[201] As we will see, dueling and arguments in mushāʿirahs produced wild and untamed words, but they also produced counter-intuitive connections between fellow poets on the hunt for new poems.

4 The Last Duel at Bedil's Grave

Between 1720 and 1750, Delhi's versifiers sharpened their aptitude for crafting new aspects of ġhazal-writing in ways that stimulated the literary marketplace. As we have seen, poets tested and reshaped the boundaries of acceptable literary style by emulating past and present masters in public settings, such as salons for poetry recitation and dīwāns for copying and memorization. Their forays into the terrains of meter and rhyme brought possibilities for productive friendships but also for new enmities, a tendency witnessed within Delhi's local centers for poetry recitation. The gathering at Bedil's graveside, which we visited in chapter 1, during its 1720–25 period represented a site in which notable poetic rivalries took shape. We now turn to the 1740s, when the gatherings at Bedil's grave continued to mirror Delhi's wider literary scene and served as yet another site for the verbal wars roiling among the city's competitive ġhazal writers.

Poets and mushāʿirah performers of the 1740s have left behind rich anecdotes recounting the increasingly restive nature of Delhi's poetry scene. For example, in the late 1740s, Mīr Taqī Mīr (1723–1810) inherited from Mīr Dard the management of a monthly mushāʿirah. In Mīr Taqī Mīr's account, Dard had transferred the gathering to him because it had become terribly unruly and Dard no longer wanted to handle it himself. Perhaps the mystically inclined Dard had assumed that Mīr Taqī Mīr's more worldly temperament was better suited for the challenging managerial task. Commenting more generally on the mushāʿirah milieu, Ġhulām Hamadānī Muṣḥafī (1751–1824), a taẕkirah writer, poet, and salon host, asserted: "In my experience, these [literary] gatherings usually last no longer than a year before discord and conflict break them up."[1] The unruliness alluded to by Mīr and Muṣḥafī often stemmed from the fervency of poets launching attacks on one another over the originality and coherency of their fellows' verse. Even so, Mīr Taqī Mīr seemed to embrace the boisterous gathering he had inherited, and he increased its frequency from monthly to weekly.[2]

By 1750, taẕkirah writers' notebooks were rife with accounts of poets accusing one another of committing plagiarism or of otherwise failing to sufficiently develop original and meaningful verse. Indeed, one of the most damning accusations that could be propelled by one poet against another was the idea that the poet had produced nonsense. Mīr became particularly infamous for this kind of condemnation in his 1751 tażkirah in which he derided his fellow poets and their reḵhtah gatherings, dismissively referring to such gatherings with the sardonic neologism *murāḵhatah*—mushāʿirahs for the exchange of reḵhtah poems. By 1750, regular reḵhtah-focused gatherings had been occurring for three decades. They were no longer novel at that point. Mīr's clever term did reference an innovation in the socially combative setting of Delhi's ġhazal scene. He used *murāḵhatah* to dismiss the mushāʿirahs of poets he reviled, notably those of Muḥammad Yār *Ḵhāksār* (The Abject) (fl. 1730–60), a humble attendant at the shrine of the Holy Footprint. Indeed, Mīr refrained from referring to his own rambunctious gathering as a *murāḵhatah*.[3]

Nonsensical verse represented an ultimate failure, especially given that successful poets demonstrated acumen by stretching the meaning of a familiar poetic trope by mixing it with novel stylistic features. Such verse, whose stylistic features exceeded the boundaries of its own coherency, was said to be "empty" (*pūch*), composed of words that betrayed their own meaning. On top of this, a spate of plagiarism accusations erupted during the restive 1740s, tarring the careers of noted ġhazal writers Yaqīn, Maẓhar, and, as discussed below, Ḥazīn.[4] So too, poets attacked each other with accusations of unseemly behavior in the gathering or denunciations of sodomy, cuckoldry, and loutish comportment in other settings.[5] For instance, rumors swirled around Mīr that he was erotically involved with an older man, while Jān-e Jānān Maẓhar (1699–1781) was accused of falling in love with his younger students.[6] Likewise, Mīr Ḥasan scribed memories of the poet Uṭakkarlais (fl. 1740s–60s) uttering lewd nonsense lyrics to professional female dancers who likely shot back their own retorts.[7] Indeed, Delhi's poets employed the same set of metrics to assess the personal integrity of a poet and the value of his words: illogical or unmetrical verse indicated faults in poets' personalities.

With these concerns in mind, our final chapter turns to Bedil's grave in the 1740s to examine a duel between two poets, ʿĀlá Fiṭrat ʿAṭāʾullāh *Nudrat* (The Rarity) (fl. 1730–60) and Muḥammad Rafīʿ *Saudā* (The Frenzy) (1706/7–1781). During a heated period between 1743 and 1747, these two versifiers hurled biting couplets at each other with a level of verve and élan that makes this exchange stand out to the mushāʿirah historian. In this especially vigorous poetic exchange of insults and accusations, Nudrat stated about his fellow poet Saudā, "This black-faced imbecile is a madman incarnate. / Nature rendered his form like that of an elephant" (*hast saudāʾī mujassam īn siyah rūʾī laʿīn / paikarish ustād-e qudrat fīl āsā reḳhtah*). Saudā responded to Nudrat by aptly extending the proboscisian injury while lacing it with the insult of uxory: "Indeed, your nose is not an inch less than that of an elephant's trunk. / Sometimes it clutches you wife's skirts, sometimes her sleeve" (*nāk to ḳharṭūm se hāthī ke terī kam nahīñ / pakṛe gah jorū kā dāman us se to gah āstīñ*).[8] Saudā continued the pachydermian theme set by Nudrat, devising another poem in which he described Nudrat's wife as a giant and beastly prostitute who babbled refrains in mock Kashmiri language. Saudā also cast Nudrat's daughter as a literary hack with an inflated sense of importance.[9] But at the center of the insults traded at Bedil's grave was a conflict over originality: they accused each other's verse of a monstrosity bred from animalistic imitations that, devoid of the human spirit of intelligent creativity, produced empty noise, hence lacking all meaning.

Nudrat's and Saudā's barbed exchanges demonstrate how by the 1740s Delhi's literary marketplace had become incendiary with competitions in a setting that thrived on the complexity borne from the friction of heated intertextual references. Nudrat and Saudā adroitly dialogued with past masters—a basic skill required in their literary guild. Yet, as public duelists, they enfolded an additional element into their artistry: knowledge of the competitive social milieu of Delhi's ġhazal-writing scene also informed their emulations and provided thematic material for their compositions. In other words, the duel of Nudrat and Saudā demonstrates that the highly localized literary rivalries of Delhi enfolded themselves into the performative nuances of the ġhazal itself, wedding social context to a lyric poem.

Importantly, such lampooning and ribald verse were integral for the Persianate world, as aptly demonstrated in the scholarship of historians such as Ricardo Zipoli, Paul Sprachman, Domenico Ingenito, and Ḳhwājah Ḥamīd Yazdānī.[10] The Urdu canon embraced impropriety as well, a subject discussed by Shamsur Rahman Faruqi.[11] In the specific setting of Delhi's early 1700s, Abhishek Kaicker shows that highly personal attacks were common facets of the various genres of parody and satire that inflected literary speech.[12] Hence, in the case of Saudā and Nudrat's duel, the context is markedly intimate, in the sense that we have evidence of two living poets addressing each other in front of peers and critics who witnessed them trading creatively curated affronts.

The confrontational and comparative nature of the mushāʿirah encouraged poets with seemingly opposing styles, like Nudrat and Saudā, to challenge one another in service of defining meaning for lyric poetry. As these dialogues generated ideas, the enmities receded to reveal highly productive connections between poets in a face-off to demonstrate the crucial nature of "empty and meaningless" words for Delhi's 1740s literary community. The accusations of meaningless verse that Nudrat and Saudā aimed at each other occurred precisely because they each found so much meaning in the literary values they shared, which were overdetermined not only by parallel rhyme, meter, and metaphors but also by immediate memories and associations particular to times and places linked with Delhi's mushāʿirah scene.

Colorful Words at a Pilgrimage

On an early spring evening sometime between 1743 and 1747, amid burning candles and the poet-saint's relics, attendees at Bedil's annual gathering caught a Kashmiri poet erupting into a slew of idiomatic profanity.[13] Voiced in Persian and proclaimed in perfect meter, his curses slandered the poet Saudā's reḳhtah verse circulated at an earlier occasion. We hear the last half of the ġhazal as it echoed in the shrine:

At her every evacuation, Saudā's melancholy mother had to visit
a veterinarian.
Each treatment prescribed was an enema to her behind with reḳhtah.
The pharmacist, when presented with the prescription, said to her,
"Why not shove a few hundred sycamores and minarets up there
as well?"[14]

bahar dafʿ-e mādah-e saudā pai-e baiṭār raft
nusḳhah-e ḥuqnah pasish bahr-e mudāwā reḳhtah
guft ʿaṭṭārī bah ū chūn nusḳhah-e ḳhwud rā namūd
ṣad chanār-o ṣad manārish ham dar ānjā reḳhtah

The poet who proclaimed these words was Nudrat, and he wanted those assembled to know that Saudā's reḳhtah poems had no place at Bedil's tomb. Nudrat also strongly implied that reḳhtah itself lacked originality to the point of sounding like the noise of animals. In other writings, Nudrat had clearly expressed his opinion that literary speech (*suḳhan*) existed exclusively in two languages: Persian and Arabic.[15] Reḳhtah poets like Saudā were prattling beasts.

At the center of the insults were conceits propelled by the misdirection of *īhām*, honed to points that would have impressed wordplay artists considered in previous chapters. Nudrat began his diatribe with an īhām that pilloried Saudā's mother and Saudā's pen name with the medical term for black bile (*saudā*), which causes melancholic madness and difficulty in the lower intestine. The double meaning allowed Nudrat to paint an image of Saudā's melancholic mother (*mādah-e saudā*) suffering from such severe constipation it necessitated medical intervention. The course of treatment, as imagined by Nudrat, provided him the angle to expertly deploy a classic Persian idiom of abuse: telling someone to shove sycamores and minarets inside themselves, as attested in period dictionaries.[16] But the coup de grâce was Nudrat's accusation that Saudā's words were empty of style:

To silence him, only a binder's knife can cut his tongue from his tome—
for he has torn away the binding of composition and dictation with his reḳhtah.

. . . .

No sooner was there an empty verse then its nonsensical style ruined your achievements.
Wherever you find a reḳhtah writer, his heart has been shredded with reḳhtah.[17]

saifah bāyad kard az jildish zabān rā be-suḳhan
zi-ān kih ū shīrāzah-e inshā wa amlā reḳhtah

. . . .

rang-e muhmil dast-gāhī reḳht tā az bait-e pūch
būd har jā reḳhtah go'ī dilish rā reḳhtah

By ending each sentence with the word "reḳhtah," Nudrat animated the detestable characteristics he applied to Saudā's authorial persona. With his running wordplay on "reḳhtah," Nudrat reduced Saudā's literary efforts to nothing more than "couplets of nonsense" (*bait-e pūch*). To be empty of style in the literal sense of *pūch* was perhaps the most damning curse for Delhi's writers, given that cogent dialogue with past masters established literary authority, originality, and future lineage.[18]

Not to be outdone, Saudā's rejoinder compounded Nudrat's sentiment and hurled it back at his rival through rhymes and further criticism of empty, indistinct style. Saudā recited:

Unlike everyone else, doggerel doubles your understanding, you pimp.
But this is idiocy so just march off to Kashmir at once.
But in regard to Saudā, you rodeo goat, it was from your pen that

No sooner was there an empty verse then its nonsensical style
ruined your achievements.
Instead, wherever there is reḳhtah composition, one's heart is itself
like reḳhtah.

āp ko dūnā nah auroñ se samajh aʿe bhaṛwe pūch
ḳharīyat is meñ hai kar kashmīr ko jaldī se kūch
ḥaq meñ saudā ke tire ḳhāmah se ai ḳhiṭṭah ke qūch
rang-e muhmil dast-gāhī reḳht tā az bait-e pūch
būd har jā reḳhtah-goʾī dilish rā reḳhtah

Just as Nudrat had ridiculed Saudā's reḳhtah, here Saudā returns the insult by ridiculing Nudrat's Kashmiri roots. Saudā accomplishes this by citing combat sports popular in the Mongol, Central Asian, and Kashmiri regions in which mountain goats were made to butt heads.

Bedil's Words as Weapons

If we were to rewind to an earlier point in this duel, back in time before the point at which Nudrat calls Saudā a chattering rooster, and then even a bit further back, we may be surprised to hear neither the words of Nudrat nor Saudā, but rather those of a third, posthumous participant. Indeed, we would hear the words of Bedil himself echoing around his own tomb. Someone—perhaps Nudrat, Saudā, or another participating poet—had dug out the tomb's well-worn copy of Bedil's complete works to present a ġhazal by Bedil, following a custom that we witnessed in chapter 1. This copy of Bedil's works was kept in the care of poet Maʿnī Yāb Ḳhān, and by that point in the 1740s, it had been appreciated by hundreds of poets over a twenty-year period.

The originating ġhazal by Bedil provided the form and a few of the suggestive metaphors that both Nudrat and Saudā repurposed to use against each other in their duel. At an evening mushāʿirah marking the anniversary of the poet-saint's death, participants sat in a circle around Bedil's grave and recited the chosen ġhazal, with its first two couplets defining the formal and imaginative bounds of Nudrat and Saudā's duel. In Bedil's words:

What are these heavens that kicked up such a tumult among creation—
when an overturned glass spilled red wine over the black earth?

Hundreds of times, my trails of dust have left the desert of the possible—
until fate concocted its plan under the impossible name of the
phoenix.[19]

chīst gardūn k-īn qadr dar k̤halq ġhoġhā rek̤htah
sar nigūn jāmī bah k̤hāk-e tīrah ṣahbā rek̤htah

gard-e mā ṣad bār az ṣaḥrā-e imkān raftah-and
tā qaẓā rangī barā-e nām-e ʿanqā rek̤htah

Within the intertwined images of its first two couplets, Bedil's ġhazal offers a contemplative Sufi vision of fate and asceticism. In the first couplet, an overturned glass in the tavern sacrifices its contents to the earth, sending the drinkers into a frenzy for the spilled wine. In the second couplet, the speaker embraces his exile to the desert, kicking up sand and dust in pursuit of the colorful phoenix (*ʿanqā*), a mythical bird whose mere shadow brings good luck.

Nudrat recasts Bedil's ideas in his own literary form. In the place of red wine, Nudrat substitutes black bile. Instead of a multihued phoenix, Nudrat conjures black crows. Instead of the colorful desert, as we will see, Nudrat dumps heaps of trash. Then, following the meter, rhyme, and refrain established by Bedil, Nudrat transposes terms from Bedil's dīwān to consider tumult of a different sort, the uproar of the audience around the grave reacting to recitations. In another stanza of the same poem, Nudrat cites the performative setting of their exchange, further slandering Saudā according to his cursed and animal-like nature:

As if a crow who tonight eats the brains of the audience,
this total imbecile at the gathering cast noise and tumult with rek̤htah.[20]

chū kulāġh imshab kih maġhz-e sāmaʿān rā mī k̤hwurad
īn laʿīn dar bazm ṭarḥ-e shor-o ġhoġhā rek̤htah

The sublime abstraction of Sufi thought first conjured by Bedil turned to concrete literary insults according to the immediate demands for originality cultivated in Delhi's mushāʿirahs. The auspicious phoenix, according to tradition, is a selfless bird that eats dry bones. In contrast, the crow, who is often positioned opposite the phoenix in ġhazal convention, represents an unlucky bird devoid of sweet songs who pecks out the eyes and tongue of the poet.

Saudā was not to be defeated. Either on that same evening or the next one, Saudā recited his own composition, an emulative piece that carefully quoted each of Nudrat's Persian couplets. Saudā did so through crafting a quintain, a literary structure that required inspirational material to produce a tribute (*tażmīn*) that blended recognizable lines with new composition. Following the same meter, rhyme, and refrain as Nudrat did earlier, Saudā's emulative quintain turned Nudrat's Persian-language insults against the Kashmiri cleric who uttered them while changing the context in which they were recited to the competitive and rich social setting of the city's premiere mushāʿirah.[21] In front of the audience at Bedil's grave, Saudā intoned:

Upon going to the *ʿurs* for Mīrzā Bedil, with such severity
you recited utter nonsense that night.
Then everyone, both good and bad, had this to say about you,
  "As if a crow who tonight eats the brains of the audience,
  this total imbecile at the gathering cast noise and tumult."[22]

ʿurs meñ jā mīrzā bedil ke taʾīñ bā shadd-o mad
shiʿr-e nā-mauzūn-o pūch us rāt ko paṛhtā thā jad
kahte the sun sun ke tere ḥaqq meñ sab yūñ nek-o bad
  chū kulāġh imshab kih maġhz-e sāmaʿān rā mī k̲hwurad
  īn laʿīn dar bazm ṯarḥ-e shor-o ġhoġhā rek̲htah

By turning Nudrat's words against himself and exploiting the double meaning of the term "rek̲htah," Saudā defends the rek̲htah verse that Nudrat had attacked. Indeed, mushāʿirah poets at the time were keenly critical of anything they perceived to be nonsense verse with incorrect meter, and accusations of such failings were frequently made. The crows and bile traded between Nudrat and Saudā were evidence of not just their enmity against one another but also of the original methods the two innovative poets were using to distinguish their words in an increasingly crowded literary sphere with growing competitions.

At Bedil's grave, poets were expected to produce strikingly original verse following the formal and thematic parameters set by Delhi's poet-saint himself, but these verses were often rerouted for the impromptu demands of a particular mushāʿirah performance. For example, Bedil's Sufi words from the same poem echoed at the tomb:

Alas for this greed wandering in madness that by striving for desire
  endured to bear the dust of the earth, tossing it upon the division of
    this world and the next.[23]

āh az īn ḥirṣ-e junūn-jaulān kih az saʿī-e amal
  k̲hāk-e dunyā burdah bar farq-e ʿuqbā rek̲htah

Instead of casting the dust of the world at the edge of an unknowable abyss in a fit of maddening love, Nudrat and Saudā threw poetic filth digested from their performed enmity and heated emulations. At the tomb of Delhi's poet-saint, Nudrat stated about Saudā:

> In the dungheaps, famine has broken out due to him gobbling up all the shit.
> To hide his theft, in his toilet shirt he covered his tracks with reḳhtah.

> *dar mazābil qaḥṯ uftādast az guh ḳhwurdanish*
> *ḳhāk dar pairāhan-e bait ul-ḳhalā-hā reḳhtah*

Saudā flung back Nudrat's highly idiomatic insult, splattering Nudrat's words in the face of their original speaker:

> The people have said about you, from Kashmir to Ethiopia,
> that you are indeed an animal never found to be clever.
> But the rarity of Nudrat is that his appearance is both human-and crow-like.
> In the dungheaps, famine has broken out due to him gobbling up all the shit.
> To hide his theft, he covered his tracks in his toilet shirt.[24]

> *log kahte haĩn tujhe kashmīr se le tā ḥabash*
> *jānwar haĩ ek jis ko so nah pahuñche ko dakash*
> *tis pah nudrat kih shakal ādmī wa zāġh wash*
> *dar mazābil qaḥṯ uftādast az guh ḳhwurdanish*
> *ḳhāk dar pairāhan-e bait ul-ḳhalā-hā reḳhtah*

At Bedil's grave, Delhi's mushāʿirah networks coalesce: Nudrat and Saudā, from opposing stylistic camps, chose poetic forms that mirror each other. Besides Nudrat's insult and Saudā's remix as noted above, both poets selected famous meters and rhymes authored by noted Persian writers, demonstrating that even opposed contenders with differing agendas converged in their emulations as directed by the mushāʿirah's need for exchange and the taẕkirah's thirst for confrontation.[25]

The Duelists

In its broadest outline, the conflict between Nudrat and Saudā at Bedil's grave appears as a tit-for-tat set of intertextual exchanges, with each poet competing to produce the cleverest metaphors, and with each fortifying his position with reference to the words of past masters. Whether friendly or contentious, these elements of competitive exchange and emulation constituted prerequisites for any mushāʿirah exchange. Further, the connections among the two contemporary poets Nudrat and Saudā, and their literary master Bedil, were substantial and highly public, easily recognizable to poets across Delhi's literary scene. As avid consumers of Bedil's words, Delhi's 1740s poets were familiar with the distinctive refrain of "reḳhtah" that Nudrat and Saudā borrowed to frame their exchange.[26] To gain a broader context for the characters fueling the mushāʿirah's contentious dynamics in the 1740s, we briefly consider the biographies of these dueling poets.

The Rarity

ʿAṭāʾullāh Nudrat has received little scholarly attention since the 1700s. What we know of him can be derived from brief considerations of his combat with Saudā depicted in three taẕkirahs, which were each drafted in the nineteenth century. Nudrat likewise makes some appearances elsewhere: as a marginal figure in modern scholarship centered on Saudā, as a minor player in some recent literary histories about competitions, and in one recent taẕkirah about Kashmiri writers.[27] The aspect of Nudrat's life and work that has been afforded the most detailed attention is an episode of his purported plagiarism concerning a dictionary, yet even this was relegated to a footnote in a story focused mainly on Ārzū.[28]

As gleaned from these sources, Nudrat's biography is exceedingly brief. While his competitors often referenced Nudrat's Kashmiri identity, Nudrat gestures to that background only once, in an oblique reference to Kashmir's laughing fields of saffron—also a common poetic trope.[29] Since Nudrat was an accomplished prose writer, we can surmise that he was highly educated in Persian and Arabic, reserving Hindi and Kashmiri for daily life, and likely was employed as a religious cleric or secretary, earning enough to maintain a modest household. Nudrat married at least once and had a daughter whom he schooled in poetry and philosophy. We may derive this information from a sestet (six-lined verse), which we will examine closely, filled with references to classical prose works in Arabic in which Saudā sarcastically ribs Nudrat's daughter.

Nudrat developed a "classical"-sounding amatory voice through writing emulations of Shams ud-Dīn Muḥammad Ḥāfiẓ (1325–90) and Muḥammad ʿAlī Ṣāʾib (1592–1676). Nudrat acknowledged these two past masters explicitly by name in his ġhazals and implicitly by writing tributes (*taẓmīn*) in their highly recognizable forms.[30] Along with these older figures, Nudrat also paid close attention to his contemporaries. He was drawn to engaging with important lines produced and disseminated by members of Delhi's ġhazal-writing community, and, as we will see, he tested his mettle along with his peers by composing in concert with famously "fresh" (*tāzah-goʾī*) poems that had been circulating in Delhi for decades. A notable example can be found in Nudrat's response to a difficult verse by Aḥmad Yār Ḳhān *Yaktā* (The Unique) (d. 1734), a poet who had attended Bedil's graveside gatherings and went deaf to the point that poets had to shout their verse at him. Yaktā had successfully completed a couplet that incorporated a difficult form with polyvalent images:

> Until the plans for world conquest were drawn in lines iridescent like a peacock's feather,
> the day, bright as Greeks, poured the army of night, black as Ethiopians, to the brim of the goblet, as if at the boundaries of Russia.[31]

> *tā ḳhat̤t̤ish t̤arḥ-e jahān girī t̤āʾūsī reḳht*
> *lashkar-e zang chū rūmī bah sar-e rūsī reḳht*

These multivalent lines conjure up the image of wine's iridescence reflecting at the top of dark liquid in a small cup (*rūsī*), while any plans for world conquest were drowned in armies of alcoholic images. Nudrat responded with equally complex images that incorporated wordplay on his own pen name "The Rarity," in a final couplet that marked his accomplishment in this difficult form:

> O Nudrat, among hypocrites it is rare to have clarity on inner purpose.
> When cast upon the mirror, color appears iridescent like a peacock's feather.[32]

> *nudrat az ahl-e riyā ṣāfī-e bāt̤in e mat̤lab*
> *rang bar āʾinah hamchūn part̤āʾūsī reḳht*

According to poetic convention, a mirror can be a fickle object, reflecting the changing styles of hypocritical poets standing in front of it or projecting the intentions, whatever they might be, of whoever else may gaze into it. Allegedly, many versifiers attempted compositions in Yaktā's form, but Nudrat's imaginative consideration of it is the only one that I have yet discovered.

Nudrat's intellectual blossoming occurred between 1748 and 1752 when numerous Delhi poets saw important taẕkirah projects to completion. These include releases by Ānand Rām Mukhliṣ, ʿAlī Qulī Wālih, and Sirāj ud-Dīn Ārzū, for Persian writers, and the humble reḳhtah tażkirahs of Mīr Taqī Mīr and ʿAlī ul-Ḥusainī Gardezī, the first authors to document the growing reḳhtah crowd. Before the releases of their well-known tażkirahs, Nudrat presented a highly original historical work of his own. In 1736/37 (1149 AH), Nudrat finished his untitled tażkirah that surveyed writers across a nine-hundred-year span.

Nudrat's tażkirah was distinct in that it focused only on writers from the distant past and those recent writers who wrote in the old style. This was a shockingly new perspective, especially in comparison to the prevailing methods for tażkirah writing of the era, which favored either comprehensive or highly localized approaches. Nudrat's frame offered an early iteration of what was later called "the literary return" (*bāz gasht-e adabī*), a conservative approach to writing Persian literary history that turned its back on writers from India and Central Asia—no matter that Persian speakers in India outnumbered those in Iran seven to one.[33] Nudrat's tażkirah presaged this turn three decades ahead of Iranian thinkers adopting the "literary return" lens. After 1800, this "literary return" ethic became the dominant narrative for Persian literary history.

In his preface, Nudrat declared his alliances by stating that new writers (*tāzah-goʾiyān*) produced words that opposed the craft of meaning making (*maʿnī ṭarāz-e muḳhālif*), conspiring with "the old magician Fate" against the classical writers to dominate literary aesthetics. To correct this error, as he himself tells us, Nudrat had composed a work that considered poets in chronological fashion to uphold the old style of the ġhazal, avoiding such writers who hid literature's "beauty marks behind a veil of avoidance and neglect."[34] In other words, Nudrat distinguished himself by composing a highly selective literary history. While in their previous projects, tażkirah writers and their contemporaries sought to document a capacious vision of literary society no matter their stylistic allegiances, Nudrat advocated only one: the classical approach.

In 1765, about thirty years after Nudrat completed his singular tażkirah, the Iranian littérateur Luṭf ʿAlī Āżar Begdili (1722–81) composed "The Fire Temple of Āżar" (*Ātishkadah-e Āżar*), which modern scholars consider to be the first tażkirah that addressed Persian literary history in the same manner as Nudrat. Begdilī's tażkirah was later co-opted by nineteenth-century Iranian literary critics advocating the narrow frame of the literary return.[35] Yet, Nudrat's tażkirah, drafted around 1737, appears to be the first to innovate this intellectual shift. Hence, it may be argued that it was Nudrat, a minor poet from Kashmir, rather than the Iranian Begdilī, who drafted the first example of a tażkirah that sought to limit the conceptual scope of Persian literature by geography or style. While Nudrat's words may alter our understanding of Persianate conservativism's history, Nudrat's tażkirah is incomplete, with only half of his survey surviving. The manuscript cuts off in a discussion of the classical-era poet Maulānā Rūmī, still an immensely popular ġhazal writer for Delhi's littérateurs.[36]

The Frenzy

Muḥammad Rafīʿ Saudā has received far more consideration than his rival Nudrat as a poet and literary figure. Over a period of 250 years, students and fans of Saudā's verse have buttressed Saudā's position as a foundational reḳhtah versifier, as documented in tażkirahs, modern histories, and critical editions of his words. Although he gained most of his renown from reḳhtah verse, Saudā was also a contender in the Persian language. Curiously, far less has been written about Saudā's Persian-language prose and verse output than his reḳhtah material even though Persian was the dominant tongue of the time. In his 1967 dissertation, Mohammad Shamsuddin Siddiqi produced a critical edition of Saudā's oeuvre (minus the *marśiyahs*), which formed the basis of the heavily censored version of Saudā's works he later released with Majlis-e Taraqqī-e Urdū, Lahore.[37] The printed version from Lahore also extirpates all of Saudā's tributes. Thus, Siddiqi's nearly comprehensive dissertation remains the best accounting of Saudā's complete works based on careful comparison of Saudā's dīwān among various manuscript copies.

Despite the long durée of studies devoted to Saudā, this famous poet's biography is only slightly more detailed in comparison to that of Nudrat. Particulars about Saudā's life can be gleaned from tażkirahs drafted after 1750, sources consulted in previous studies by Jamīl Jālibī, Shaiḳh Chānd, and Ḳhalīq Anjum—twentieth-century scholars who have contextualized Sauda's oeuvre. These authors agree that in the 1740s, Saudā was still in the early stages of his career, quickly rising to earn the title of "The Poet Laureate of Reḳhtah" (*malik ush-shuʿarā-e reḳhtah*) by 1750.[38] In comparison to his contemporaries, who began reciting at mushāʿirahs in their early teens, Saudā was a late arrival, entering Delhi's market for speech in his late twenties after purportedly burning through his inheritance.[39] It was due to this elite background that Saudā, like Nudrat, acquired a high level of education in Persian, Arabic, and other literary training available to Delhi notables.

Saudā's father, Muḥammad Shafīʿ, was a successful merchant from Bukhara who married into the state hierarchy with a betrothal to the daughter of the court poet and humorist Niʿmat Ḳhān-e ʿĀlī (d. 1710). It can be surmised that Saudā grew up with a Persian vernacular as one of his mother tongues and that he likely heard stories of his maternal grandfather's literary exploits ridiculing Mughal officials.[40] Taẕkirah writers list several poetry instructors, with Ārzū and Ḥātim as the most recognizable of Saudā's rumored teachers, although they were most likely only senior associates who had provided Saudā some guidance rather than dedicated mentorship.[41] While all of Saudā's teachers' identities are uncertain, later historians allude to Saudā's main poetry instructor as Sulaimān ʿAlī Ḳhān *Widād* (The Affection) (fl. 1730–60), a Persian writer from Delhi who later moved to Lucknow in the 1750s, just as Saudā eventually did after 1757.[42]

Saudā completed an initial copy of his dīwān in 1760, around the time he left Delhi for the east, and it details his literary and personal connections, a theme the historian Nasīm Aḥmad further elaborates in his 2001 critical edition of Saudā's ġhazals.[43] After he left Delhi, Saudā composed relatively fewer ġhazals, instead devoting more of his efforts toward long forms and a new clutch of Shīʿī elegies (*marṡiyah*) supported by generous patrons who paid vast sums for such works. Hence, Saudā ended up devoting the largest constituent of his dīwān to a hoard of qaṣīdahs, *maṡnawīs*, quintains, and sestets. Among these long-form poems, Saudā's satires distinguished his position. In this, he continued the traditions of his maternal grandfather, the humorist Niʿmat Ḳhān-e ʿĀlī, as Saudā cited in a couplet.[44] The targets of Saudā's satire were limitless: officials, fellow poets, colleagues' daughters, competitors' wives, animals, and even himself. Saudā's views on literature appear flexible and adaptive in comparison to Nudrat's constricted vision of the literary world; this expansiveness was perhaps due to the variety of influences in Saudā's successful career and his precipitous rise to prominence.

Writing in his later years, Saudā stated that "the world of poetry has thousands of styles (*rang*)" and that a "forceful nature" (*ṭabʿ-e jabr*) does not produce "stylish meaning" (*maʿnī-e rangīn*) for verse.[45] At differing stages in their careers, with seemingly disparate styles, Nudrat and Saudā appear to illustrate two different literary trajectories, and their opposing viewpoints were never to meet again as time progressed. Moreover, the mushāʿirah tradition at Bedil's grave closed soon after their confrontation, while the enmities in their words lived on, fixing them as bitter contestants in a battle for stylistic ascendency. In a moment that belies this unchanging frieze of the two poets endlessly locked in artistic combat, at a later date, Saudā rhetorically asked: "What purpose is there to slander another's verse as weak or muddled when, based on one's familiar style (*rang*), it may not be amenable to one's particular taste?"[46]

A History of Hostilities

Despite the fiery creativity it generated, the call-and-response battle between Nudrat and Saudā did not immediately garner literary inquiry. It took nearly a century before it caught the sustained attention of a Lucknow-based author named Saʿdat ʿAlī Ḳhān *Nāṣir* (The Victor) (1774?–1871?), the first tażkirah writer to consider the critical and historical implications of the exchange.[47] Frances Pritchett offers a careful analysis of Nāṣir as a foundational Urdu historian, elucidating his scrupulous attention to lineage, his vast collection of anecdotes and verse, and his diligent reading of previous tażkirahs, most importantly that of Muṣḥafī.[48] Nāṣir proudly claimed to be an intellectual descendant of Saudā and thus dedicated his 1845 tażkirah, aptly entitled "The Elegant Tażkirah of Jolly Battles" (*Tażkirah-e Ḳhwush Maʿrakah-e Zebā*), to his revered teacher: "Saudā's chain flows from my breath. / One now remains in this atelier, Nāṣir, it is I" (*jārī hamāre dam se hai saudā kā silsilah / nāṣir ab is gharāne meñ bāqī haiñ ek ham*), Nāṣir announced in the preface.[49]

Fittingly, the tażkirah began with the duel between Nudrat and Saudā, establishing the literary foundation for what Pritchett has aptly termed "elegant encounters," combats fought through the exchange of ġhazals.[50] Rather than putting Saudā's ability on display, Nāṣir opens his tażkirah by featuring the skills of Nudrat, whose talents to create original verse according to mid-eighteenth-century values glimmered across the wordplay of two lines:

> That lowly Rafīʿ, indeed, must be at war entirely with himself.
> On his own frenzied head Saudā foolishly spewed his bile of reḳhtah.[51]

> *ḳhwud bah ḳhwud dar jang bāshad ān rafīʿ-e pusht qadr*
> *bar sar-e saudāʾī-e ḳhwud az jahl ṣafrā reḳhtah*

Nudrat's jabs are familiar and cutting products of complex and clever mushāʿirah performances of early 1700s Delhi as they pillory Saudā's given name, Rafīʿ, short for "The Exalted of the Faith" (*rafīʿ ud-dīn*), by referring to him as lowly (*pusht qadr*). Nudrat then parodies Saudā's pen name, which holds several meanings: love frenzy, valuable goods, or black bile. Nudrat opted for elaborating the last and lowliest of these associations, while blackening Saudā's pen name with the verb *reḳhtah*, also the name of Saudā's preferred literary mode that was, by the 1740s, growing in importance. In Nudrat's formulation, this lowly Rafīʿ named Saudā attempted to battle his literary betters but only spews bile upon himself.

Why would Nāṣir open a tażkirah lovingly dedicated to Saudā with an insulting couplet? While few tażkirah writers would open by deriding past masters, Nāṣir's aim was to memorialize literary battles and, thus, auspiciously begins with an insult of Saudā to illustrate his intellectual ancestor's emulative abilities and mastery of both Persian and reḳhtah. He then immediately quotes Saudā's clever reḳhtah response that flipped Nudrat's insult on its head.

From the judge to the sheriff, everyone knows, even the chancellor on up,
O Envy of the Moons, that the cause of this battle is with your camp.
Then you villainously declare about me, you pimp,
  "That lowly Rafīʿ, indeed, must be at war entirely with himself.
  On his own frenzied head Saudā foolishly spewed his bile."[52]

qāẓī aur koṭwāl se le jānte haiñ tā bah ṣadr
jang kā mabdā tire ghar vuh rashk-e māh-o badr
phir mujhe kahtā hai ai bhaṛwe tū yih az rāh-e ġhadr
  ḳhwud bah ḳhwud dar jang bāshad ān rafīʿ-e pusht qadr
  bar sar-e saudāʾī-e ḳhwud az jahl ṣafrā reḳhtah

Saudā performed his feats of reversal for seventeen stanzas, one for each of Nudrat's couplets, displaying a kind of verbal dexterity we already witnessed at Bedil's grave. In Saudā's response to Nudrat, he combines Persianate themes ("envy of the moons") with popular terms of abuse (pimp or *bhaṛwā*) while detailing classes of city officials to establish a grounded context in which he placed his verse.

Nāṣir provides readers with Saudā's couplet and his longer stanza as evidence of Saudā's victory over Nudrat. After this, Nāṣir continues his tażkirah by elaborating his claim that Nudrat fled Delhi after the defeat. This makes for an enticing story, but one unlikely to be true since other poets in Delhi's mushāʿirah scene suffered far more ignominious defeats and never left the city. However, Nāṣir neglected some specifics, never mentioning, for instance, the fact that the duel took place at the graveside gathering; nor does he outline the lineage of Saudā's rival Nudrat. The gaps could have appeared because Nāṣir believed that his audience was already familiar with the context and required no further elaboration. More likely, however, Nāṣir was not aware of the confrontation: Bedil was no longer Delhi's poet-saint, and his tomb was lost sometime between 1780 and 1820. While the grave was gone, and with it literary memory, Saudā's rejoinder, transmitted via Nāṣir's taẕkirah retelling of this "jolly battle," met the high literary standards of nineteenth-century Lucknow's ġhazal-writing poets who relished the idea of building up a reḳhtah register inspired by versifiers from the previous generation.

Stanzas from Saudā's battles with Nudrat at Bedil's grave reveal how mushāʿirah debates, enmities, and memories continued to frame the historical record, even as the momentum of these episodes slowed after the 1740s. By 1780, Bedil's salon was only a memory, and by 1820, the tomb itself had disappeared with no trace of the vibrant mushāʿirah contests that had taken place there. What lasted beyond Bedil's self-crafted Sufi identity and beyond the institution cultivated by his students was the memory of Nudrat and Saudā's harsh words that still informed notions of the past founded through literary distinction built on contentiousness.

Saudā's Tributes

In the 1760s, literary historian Lachhmī Narāyan *Shafīq* (The Merciful) (1745–1808) presented his own interpretation of the episode, aligning Saudā's goal within the complex and competitive networks of ġhazal emulations. Within his discussion of Saudā's biography, Shafīq cited a four-line stanza in which Saudā gestured toward the duel while depicting Nudrat as a self-congratulatory buffoon:

Though he relishes his satires of Saudā,
He should let them be. There are repercussions for this idiot.
For when the pimp cannot even scan the meter of his own verse,
He will instead go around lampooning others—this is the rarity of Nudrat.[53]

gar hajw pah saudā kī use raġhbat hai
hone do kih gedī ke taʾīñ rajʿat hai
mauzūn nah kare shiʿr ko apne bhaṛwā
kartā phire hajw auroñ kī yih nudrat hai

In the quatrain presented by Shafīq, Saudā cursed Nudrat as a panderer who sold meanings through whatever hackneyed verse he could craft: offensive words directed at his competitors. Saudā derided Nudrat's lack of originality, claiming that since his rival lacked the talent for dreaming up new meanings on his own, he could only generate new ideas by contemplating the faults of his literary betters. Yet, Saudā's verse should not be interpreted as intending to critique literary lampooning in general, because Saudā himself perfectly exemplifies this art in these four short lines.

After recording Saudā's stanza in his tażkirah, Shafīq proceeds with a commentary broadly elaborating some of the central ideas expressed in the gravesite battle, expanding first on the crucial importance of satire to create meaning. To illustrate this point, Shafīq quoted a quatrain from Tarāb Ġhubār (fl. 1710s), a Persian-language poet of the South who, like Saudā, also reversed an insult to create meaning. Shafīq depicted Ġhubār responding to a qaṣīdah meant to ridicule him with a witty quintain pronouncing that due to that lampoon people now understood his faults as raised to the level of artistic speech.[54] Indeed, the poetic register emerging in Delhi's mushāʿirahs applauded the capacity of poetic barbs to expand literary knowledge. Shafīq's point was that such clever reversal also applied to Saudā's creative invectives.

The second topic Shafīq addressed in his commentary concerned the wider context of literary conflicts brewing in 1740s Delhi. For this, Shafīq cited other quintains Saudā wrote in tribute (*tażmīn*) to the ġhazals of both rek̤htah and Persian authors, including those of Saudā's contemporaries Mīr Taqī Mīr, Tābān, and Yaqīn. But most significant was Shafīq's mention of Muḥammad ʿAlī Ḥazīn, the Iranian émigré poet we met in chapter 3, who was fast becoming an infamous literary figure in 1740s Delhi. Shafīq claimed that one notable tribute Saudā wrote was for Ḥazīn. It comprised nineteen stanzas with no closing couplet (*be-maqṭaʿ*), and it was a satire. In the 1740s, there began to emerge a phenomenon of critiquing Ḥazīn, yet it is unlikely that Saudā participated in this collective badmouthing. As noted by a contemporary scholar of Saudā, Mohammed Siddiqi, Saudā's purported satire of Ḥazīn has not survived—if it ever existed at all.[55]

In citing the missing tribute that Saudā had supposedly scribed to satirize Ḥazīn, Shafīq provided a valuable clue: Hazin and his newly released 1743 dīwān played roles in structuring the combative verse that Nudrat and Saudā hurled at each other at Bedil's grave. This key encourages us to attune our ears to the extent to which Ḥazīn—a poet who wrote in the classical style but was also, as we shall see, hailed as the "Leader of the

Moderns"—played the role of a crucial stylistic influencer in the story of Nudrat and Saudā. We can trace this in the shared emulations between Nudrat, Saudā, and, surprisingly, Ḥazīn. Saudā venerated Ḥazīn, stating that except for the superstar Ṣā'ib, "such a vigorous (*zabardast*) poet has not returned in Iran, Central Asia, or India." Saudā elaborated his praise of Ḥazīn in reḳhtah poems as well, stating that Persian speech was unrestricted and stretched from Saʿdī to Ḥazīn.[56]

Saudā possessed a strong aptitude for composing insulting quintains in reḳhtah as inspired by Persian verse, composing reḳhtah tributes to the verses of Persian authorities from his contemporary 1740s period, namely Nudrat, and from near-contemporary masters such as Bedil (1642–1720) and Nāṣir ʿAlī (d. 1697). Casting his imagination further into the past, Saudā also creatively composed quintains from the verses of two important Timurid-period poets. The first of these was ʿIṣmatullāh Buḳhārī (d. 1426), who wrote for the emperor Shāhruḳh Mīrzā (r. 1405–47) and his courtiers in Herat, Afghanistan. The second was Abū Ṯālib Kalīm Kāshānī (1581–1651), a contemporary of Ṣā'ib who ventured to India where he became the Mughals' poet laureate (*malik ush-shuʿarā*) under Shah Jahan (r. 1628–58). By composing Persian quintains modeled after Buḳhārī and Kalīm, Saudā projected an image of himself as both a satirist and a contributor to Persian literary history, albeit one crafting verse from the decisive stance of a reḳhtah composer, a position in which he took great pride. Additionally, Saudā crafted lampooning Persian quintains from the verse of three important figures: classical-era poet Saʿdī Shīrāzī (1210–92); Shīʿī devotional poet Kamāl ud-Dīn Muḥtasham Kāshāni (1528–88); and Muḥammad Fāḳhir *Makīn* (The Anchored) (d. 1806), Saudā's main literary rival in Lucknow after 1760.[57] The three poems Saudā wrote in tribute to the compositions of these figures appear in addition to the mixed-language quintains and sestets that we witnessed Saudā slinging at Nudrat in Bedil's posthumous mushāʿirah.

Although the satirical quintains of Saudā rightly deserve attention, Saudā's "serious" quintains—those that were not designed to skewer anyone—also reveal important aspects of Saudā's ability to craft dialogue with past masters and otherwise distinguish himself in the competitive literary marketplace. Foremost, Saudā's non-satirical quintains also mark him as a capable participant in the wider Persianate linguistic sphere, one who—just as journeymen poets had been doing since the twelfth century—sought inspiration and new meanings from past masters. Citing taẕkirah writer (and Gulshan's competitor) Afẓal Sarḳhwush (1640–1714) as his source, in his later essay on literary criticism "Warning to Egoists" (*ʿIbrat ul-Ġhāfilīn*), Saudā quoted Nāṣir ʿAlī's famous dictum: "The test of the poet is the ġhazal's *ṭarḥ*" *(imtiḥān-e shāʿir ṭarḥ-e ġhazal ast)*.[58] To this end, Saudā chose peculiar forms from the Persian-language literary tradition to prove his abilities as a reḳhtah-writing poet. For instance, he followed parameters from a famous poem by Iranian versifier Nidāʾī Yazdī (circa 1520s), a composer of Shīʿī devotional poetry often cited across taẕkirahs.[59] Another example from Saudā's emulations is a tribute to Kalīm in a rare and difficult form that Ṣāʾib had previously attempted.[60]

By the 1740s, Saudā had already developed a sophisticated aptitude for choosing Persian forms to model his own verse on that would prove engaging enough to satisfy his artistic inclinations. Many Persian ġhazals featured forms that could be easily emulated in reḳhtah by writers of the middle 1700s, as witnessed at the Ornament of Mosques and through the pens of Qabuliyan descendants. By exhibiting their prowess with such forms, writers fixed themselves within a larger pantheon of versifiers stretching beyond Delhi and reaching into the distant past. In this vein, Saudā constructed one quintain on a ġhazal from Bedil that opened with a couplet that could be interpreted as wordplay on Saudā's name:

For the desert I have no desire, and for the garden no excitement.
Wherever I strut, I whip up the spectators into a frenzy.

nah bā ṣaḥrā sarī dāram nah bā gulzār saudāʾī
bah har jā mī ravam az ḳhwīsh mī joshad tamāshāʾī

Saudā remixed Bedil's couplet by assembling three reḳhtah lines that slandered the nightingale and the parrot, with the final line echoing Bedil's idea of the spectacle:

I'm not some nightingale, content with the rose in this mere garden, Brother.
I am definitely not a parrot whose heart gets carried away on the garden's breeze.
I am a pyrotechnic peacock! Yet, how did spring arrive?
For the desert I have no desire, and for the garden no excitement.
Wherever I strut, I whip up the spectators into a frenzy.[61]

nah bulbul hūñ kih is gulshan meñ ser-e gul mujhe bhāʾī
nah ṭūṭá hī kih dil merā fiẓāʾ-e bāġh le jāʾī
maiñ hūñ ṯāʾūṣ-e ātish-bāzī kaisī hī bahār āʾī

nah bā ṣaḥrā sarī dāram nah bā gulzār saudāʾī
bah har jā mī ravam az ḳhwīsh mī joshad tamāshāʾī

In this verse, Saudā played with an old and venerated form, one that had originated among the eleventh-century qaṣīdahs of Nāṣir Ḳhusrau and Sanāʾī, two poets considered as "classical" writers from the old style. Dozens of poets followed the evocative scheme offered by this form, including thirteenth- and fourteenth-century poets Maulānā Rūmī and Saʿdī, who each were considered "medieval" poets central to the canon. Mughal court poets of the 1500s and 1600s also closely followed this meter and rhyme, namely "new writers" such as Kalīm and, most notably, Ṣāʾib.[62] The form, in its basic constituents with a straightforward meter and inviting end rhyme, proved suggestive for nearly a millennium's worth of writers, including a wily reḳhtah poet like Saudā.

But there were also immediate reasons for Saudā to follow this tried-and-true model for his tributes. Based on what we know of Saudā's admiration of Ḥazīn, it is unsurprising that Ḥazīn also appears within the lengthy train of poets composing in this form. In line with Bedil's theme of a spectacle wrought in avian metaphors, which Saudā also developed, Ḥazīn stated in his poem's penultimate couplet:

The is no sanctuary for the fate of the bird of my glances.
So long as every loop of your tresses is a snare for spectators.[63]

namī bāshad rihāʾī qismat-e murġh-e nigāh-e man
buwad har ḥalqah-e zulf-e tū tā dām-e tamāshāʾī

Here we have evidence that, by composing quintains that emulated Ḥazīn's ġhazals, Saudā facilitated a mushāʿirah exchange with Ḥazīn, the newest literary celebrity to break into Delhi's ġhazal scene of the 1740s.

In another quintain, Saudā built ideas on the words of Kalīm that also appear in Ḥazīn's 1743 dīwān. In a form with a refrain of "the heart," Saudā addressed himself to Kalīm, stating:

May it leave this world, this heart and the loyalty of the heart.
If there is one love, then the heart can be consoled.
But with a mere wink of the eye, the heart falls ill.[64]

jāʾe dunyā se yih dil aur wafā-dārī-e dil
ek dil hove to ho saktī hai ġham-ḳhwārī-e dil
ġhamzah-e chashm hī thā bāʿiṡ-e bīmārī-e dil

Saudā then quotes Kalīm as responding with the following couplet:

The bend of a tress is yet another trap to ensnare the heart.
Yet it cannot contain a single hair because of the excess of the heart![65]

ḳham-e zulfī ast digar dām-e giriftārī-e dil
kih dar ū mūī nagunjīdah zi-bisyārī-e dil

In these lines authored by Saudā and Kalīm, the heart is posed as a liability, prone to diseases from love and a mere glimpse of the beloved's alluring hair. Kalīm offers a "mind-bending" (*ḳhayāl-bandī*) image of the beloved's hair being a trap that cannot hold even itself due to all the other hearts it has already ensnared.

Ḥazīn also had composed in this form, and his opening and closing couplets as well as his themes, meter, and rhyme share features with the compositions of Saudā and Kalīm:

If love becomes a beloved as a result of my weeping heart,
only then shall I grasp the tip of his tress with help from the heart.

. . . .

Do you not hear the complaints of the heart rent into one hundred pieces, Ḥazīn?
Have you no memory of the time when you excelled at the consolation of the heart?[66]

ʿishq agar yār shawad az aṡar-e zārī-e dil
sar-e zulfī bah kaf āram bah madadkārī-e dil

. . . .

nashanūī nālah-e zār-e dil-e ṣad-chāk ḥazīn
yād-e ān roz kih būdat sar-e ġham-ḳhwārī-e dil

A fourth participant in Saudā's exploration of Ḥazīn's style was none other than Saudā's sparring partner Nudrat. In a markedly complex ġhazal, Nudrat opened with a difficult and evocative couplet that considers the same themes that Kalīm, Saudā, and Ḥazīn had voiced:

Dreams come to my eyes like tears, by way of the heart.
But now my lustful eye has only incapacity due to a sickness in the heart.[67]

khwāb chūn ashk zi-dīdah rawad az bārī-e dil
chashm-e rāġhib natawān dāsht zi-bīmārī-e dil

In this verse, Nudrat considered how the heart conjured fruitless dreams before the lover's eyes only to have them dashed away by the pain inflected by the same disease-prone organ. These resonances demonstrate that, as an integral aspect of their dueling, Nudrat and Saudā were developing a shared voice by following both an old master, Kalīm, and a new authority, Ḥazīn, who had recently arrived in Delhi. Saudā produced another quintain on a form from Ḥāfiẓ that also shared a connection to Ḥazīn and Nudrat by dint of its inviting pattern and rhyme scheme.[68]

From these exchanges, we can witness the range of stylistic and compositional resonances that matched with patterns used by Delhi's ġhazal writers of the 1740s. Highly intertextual emulations shaped influence—even for reḳhtah composers like Saudā. Following Shafīq's point about the crucial importance of satire, enmities indeed generated meaning, but with them, shared emulations produced substantial literary connections that legitimated individual style within a web of versifiers—even among poets at odds with each other. As we soon examine in closer detail, Nudrat and Saudā shared positive opinions about Ḥazīn and welcomed his entrance to Delhi's ġhazal community. The emulations that converge within and across the verses of Nudrat, Saudā, and Ḥazīn demonstrate how poets' literary experiences were shaped by immediate associates and creativity conjured by both the mushāʿirah institution itself and by the broad requirements placed on poets to compose new words based on previous forms, especially famous patterns from noted masters.

Leader of "The Moderns"

As we recall from chapter 3, Ḥazīn's repeated attempts to return to Iran from Delhi between 1737 and roughly 1741 complicated his position in Delhi's poetry scene, distracting him from full participation in gatherings and diluting his ability to navigate a maze of personal and artistic boundaries. Ḥazīn resignedly settled in Delhi from 1742 until 1748, but there is little evidence of him visiting premier mushāʿirahs during this six-year period. Instead, Ḥazīn installed himself as a polestar for the city's poets to encircle. The émigré poet hosted sumptuous gatherings, much as Delhi's courtesans did, in which he was the central performer of amatory verse emulating Ṣāʾib.

At the conclusion of his six-year stay, Ḥazīn left Delhi for the final time in 1748, heading to Varanasi. Soon after his departure, some of Delhi's littérateurs began circulating anecdotes depicting Ḥazīn as a gracious host who eagerly invited guests to recite their verses at his home.[69] One such story was eventually recorded in the 1845 edition of Saudā's dīwān. It told of Saudā's visiting Ḥazīn to present a reḳhtah verse about a weathercock to which Ḥazīn responded with only a modest degree of praise.[70] Saudā also could have encountered Ḥazīn in person at one of Delhi's elite gatherings, most likely through the two poets' shared association with Amīr Ḳhān.

In contrast to his agreeable stories, Ḥazin also earned the scorn of a vocal faction within Delhi's ġhazal-writing community who accused the émigré poet of plagiarism, errors in usage of idiom, and writing unmetrical lines. All of these accusations were leveraged as signs of poor character and evidence that Ḥazīn had violated literary decorum. Hence, littérateurs who scribed details of pleasant encounters between Ḥazīn and other poets were likely motivated to do so partly in defense of Ḥazīn's character. Like many Delhi poets of his time, Ḥazīn incited a share of controversy through his participation in literary discussions about ġhazal politics, remarks that informed the stakes of Nudrat and Saudā's interaction.

As recounted in taẕkirahs, one episode that played a role in sullying Ḥāzīn's reputation took place when he inadvertently insulted a circle of writers formerly led by S̤ābit, a recently deceased poetry master and particularly argumentative poet. As we recall, S̤ābit met an unfortunate end in May of 1739, due to wounds he sustained during Nadir Shah's massacre of Delhi's commoners. Ḥazīn may have been unaware of S̤ābit's demise, especially considering that many writers were loath to explicitly discuss the matter due to class-based concerns analyzed in chapter 3. After S̤ābit died, his son, the poet Muḥammad ʿAẕīm *S̤abāt* (The Steadfast) (1711–48), assumed his father's legacy by sustaining S̤ābit's combative approach.[71] During Ḥazīn's remaining years in Delhi, Muḥammad ʿAẕīm maintained his father S̤ābit's enmities from decades past, while also preserving stories and legends that were passed down to him from his father. This proved helpful for taẕkirah writers. For example, Muḥammad ʿAẕīm provided information about Delhi's literary scene to Ḥazīn's friend Wālih, furthering S̤ābit's serious views of literature.[72]

The story of Ḥazīn's unfortunate encounter with S̤ābit's circle hinges on his interaction with a poet named Bandah ʿAlī *Sabaqat* (The Anticipation) (1700?–1784), a highly placed Mughal official and S̤ābit's foremost student.[73] Bandah ʿAlī hailed from a Central Asian family of Panipat-based Naqshbandis. Bandah ʿAlī had inherited his title of Sher Afgan from his maternal grandfather, the former governor of Multan. Adding to this distinction, Bandah ʿAlī had married the daughter of Roshan ud-Daulah (1681–1736), a hapless imperial official, also from Panipat.[74] Ṡābit proudly stamped his star student's name on his papers to advertise this elite connection, including on the final draft of his dīwān completed in 1738 under Bandah ʿAlī's supervision.[75]

With Ṡābit's passing in 1739, Bandah ʿAlī found himself in need of a new teacher.[76] Ṡābit's old friendships with the poets Aksīr and Shuhrat, Iranian émigrés like Ḥazīn, likely prompted Bandah ʿAlī to seek instruction from Ḥazīn when he finally settled down.[77] As noted years later by Muṣḥafī and Muḥammad Ḥasan Qatīl, Bandah ʿAlī attended one of Ḥazīn's ġhazal performances, bringing with him a copy of his own dīwān from which he presented a few of his poems written in the style of Iranian "new writers," including Bābā Fiġhānī Shīrāzī (d. 1519), Mīrzā Qulī Mailī Mashhadī (fl. 576–1614), and Muḥammad Ḥusain Naẓīrī Nīshāpūrī (1560–1612). After listening to Ṡābit's most prized student recite some of his couplets, Ḥazīn declared that Bandah ʿAlī's dīwān required a scrubbing "from tip to tail."[78]

This report of Ḥazīn's words was likely an overstatement on the part of both Muṣḥafī and Qatīl. Writing years after the event, Bandah ʿAlī simply mentioned that Ḥazīn had provided him with a few corrections. However, by his own admission, Bandah ʿAlī reacted to Ḥazīn's critique by ceasing ġhazal composition altogether and drastically declaring that he had "washed his dīwān in water."[79] This statement played upon a common taẕkirah trope about poets defeatedly dumping their collected works into ponds and rivers.[80] Whatever the case, Bandah ʿAlī retreated from the competitive mushāʿirahs and gave up his pen name, taking the title Bāsiṭī in devotion to his new master Ḳhwājah Bāsiṭ whose daughter he later married, presumably as a second wife. For the rest of his life, Bandah ʿAlī severely restricted his literary ambitions to composing only quatrains—a form favored for its brevity and ease—and drafted a loose collection of verse rather than attempting to work on another dīwān of his own. Bandah ʿAlī was content to maintain commonplace books with carefully organized verse but no commentary, save for a few of his own biographical details.[81]

Soon after Ḥazīn's fateful encounter with Bandah ʿAlī, the rumor began circulating that Ḥazīn had not limited himself to providing Bandah ʿAlī corrections but rather had used the occasion as a platform to critique the verse of Bandah ʿAlī's departed teacher Ṡābit. Wālih and Ārzū circulated gossip that after reading over one of the late Ṡābit's lines in correspondence with Bandah ʿAlī, Ḥazīn had immediately responded that the couplet in question was plagiarized, declaring, "The theme in this verse is from another poet that [Ṡābit] has stolen."[82] Ḥazīn's accusation against Muḥammad ʿAẓīm's father reached Muḥammad ʿAẓīm himself who began plotting retaliation. As we remember from chapter 3, Muḥammad ʿAẓīm's eminent father Ṡābit had often embroiled himself in conflicts over students. Perhaps recalling against his father's territorial behavior and perhaps harboring a certain sensitivity toward accusations of verse theft directed against his father, Muḥammad ʿAẓīm began assembling a case against Ḥazīn by declaiming that nearly five hundred couplets from Ḥazīn's latest dīwān exhibited plagiarisms of either the purposeful or inadvertent variety. Muḥammad ʿAẓīm gathered ammunition for these accusations by cross-checking Ḥazīn's verse against those from other poets' dīwāns and tażkirahs, volumes likely housed in Ārzū's library. The full accounting was lost, but Ḥazīn's friend Wālih recorded a portion of Muḥammad ʿAẓīm's evidence in his voluminous tażkirah, corroborating Muḥammad ʿAẓīm's perspective that Ḥazīn had, in fact, ignominiously lifted poetry from past masters.[83]

From this and other stories, a narrative emerges that Ḥazīn, with his lordly attitude and sloppy compositions, had rightfully earned the scorn of Delhi's ġhazal writers. We find records of his detractor's accusations within the pages of Ḥazīn's fourth and final dīwān. The previous three of Ḥazīn's collected works were lost, and this last poetry collection, released in 1743, was compiled by Wālih Dāġhistānī (1712–56), Ḥazīn's friend, occasional host, and fellow émigré. Ḥazīn's fourth dīwān caused a clamor within months of its publication, generating both negative and positive reviews. His new dīwān echoed the forms and ideas from classical writers such as Rudākī, Saʿdī, and Amīr Ḵhusrau, to name a few, and the expansion of meaning from "new writers" like the Mughal court composers Kalīm and Naẓīrī, the ġhazal luminary Ṣāʾib, and Bedil, who had been Ḥazīn's senior contemporary—all names cherished across Delhi.

Ārzū's Attacks

Despite his period of absences and purportedly aloof nature, Ḥazīn's fourth dīwān bears a strong stamp of Delhi's impact, a marker that he shared with Nudrat and Saudā. While the previous section provided some examples of resonances between Ḥazīn and Saudā's work, it is also possible to find intriguing examples of how Ḥazīn and Nudrat invested in overlapping themes and forms. One example of this concerns the participation of both Ḥazīn and Nudrat in a revival of the ringdove theme first popularized in Delhi by Maẓmūn's reḵhtah recitations considered in chapter 2:

Freedom from arrest will never be an option for this headstrong one.
Even from my corpse the collar around our neck will never fall, O Ringdove.[84]

giriftārī se is sar kash ko āzādī nahīñ hargiz
mū'e se bhī nah niklegā yih ṭauq-e gardan ai qumrī

The famous ringdove poem, formerly recited by 1720s reḳhtah writers following Maẓmūn, again flew through Delhi's mushāʿirahs in 1741 when Muḳhliṣ composed a couplet on this difficult form in Persian. It caught the attention of the emperor himself when the recently arrived Iranian courtier Qizilbāsh Ḳhān Ummīd shared Muḳhliṣ's composition with the emperor Muhammad Shah and Amīr Ḳhān. Ummīd enthusiastically noted its difficult form before reciting Muḳhliṣ's ringdove poem for the high officials:

You have brought the apocalypse upon my head with your wailing, O Ringdove.
And after all that you wish to dwell in the garden with me, O Ringdove?[85]

qayāmat bar saram āwardah-ī az shewan ai qumrī
tū ḳhwāhī baʿd az īn dar bāġh būdan bā man ai qumrī

The emperor enjoyed the couplet so much he expanded Muḳhliṣ's land holdings and gave him a cash gift. Perhaps emboldened by this, Ummīd himself composed in the form, following Muḳhliṣ:

You have killed me in the rose garden with your wailing, O Ringdove.
Now besides iron fetters, my blood is on your neck, O Ringdove.[86]

halākam kardah-yī dar būstān az shewan ai qumrī
bajā-e ṭauq ḳhūn-e man turā dar gardan ai qumrī

Thus, in 1741, the ringdove poem, previously traded between reḳhtah poets, had returned to its Persian origins, winging from the Ornament of Mosques into the throne room of the Blessed Citadel via Muḳhliṣ's words in Ummīd's memory or diary. Although the form had more distant origins in a 1620s exchange between Iranian writers Ṣā'ib and Maʿṣum while on the road to India, renewed interest in the verse and the cash reward it generated during the early 1740s pushed others to try and extract new meanings from this form.

Two of these poets eager to prove themselves via the ringdove theme were Ḥazīn and Nudrat. Ḥazīn's ġhazal followed the aural ideas in the wail of the ringdove as considered by Mukhliṣ and Ummīd, stating in the first couplet:

By no means may your lament give affection to the lip bringing
complaints against me—
while your wailing tears at the collar of my patience, O Ringdove.[87]

mabād az nālah-at mihr az lab-e faryād-bardār-am
garībān mī darad ṣabr-e marā īn shewan ai qumrī

Ḥazīn's ġhazal in the ringdove form caught the attention of others in Delhi's literary circles, most notably Ārzū, who quickly turned into a leading enemy of Ḥazīn. This was perhaps a surprising development given the diversity of Ārzū's experiences as a writer, his usually even-handed nature with fellow poets, and the fact that others from his circle, namely Saudā and Khwushgo, held more generous views of Ḥazīn. For reasons that remain unclear, Ārzū's harsh assessment of Ḥazīn grew even more severe over the 1740s, culminating in a passage within Ārzū's 1750 tażkirah, "A Miscellany of Delicacies" (*Majmaʿ un-Nafāʾis*), in which Ārzū derides Ḥazīn as a beggar posturing as a king.[88]

Ārzū expounded his most infamous critique of Ḥazīn in a 1744 screed called "The Admonition of Egoists" (*Tanbīh ul-Ġhāfilīn*). In this work, Ārzū's main criticism of Ḥazīn concerns the Iranian's deployment of metaphor. While arguing that to accurately capture poetic themes and develop their meanings required use of proper language and reliance on past convention, Ārzū adumbrates hundreds of examples from Ḥazīn's couplets from his fourth dīwān that exhibited authorial failures on these fronts, including a couplet from Ḥazīn's version of the ringdove ġhazal. Ārzū cites Ḥazīn, stating,

Among us prisoners, know that this ease of mind is our only prize.
For on your neck, you have no burden of an iron collar, O Ringdove.[89]

miyān-e mā asīran īn sabuk-sārī ġhanīmat dān
kih bar gardan nah dārī bār-e ṭauq-e āhan ai qumrī

Ārzū lambasted Ḥazīn's attempt at the ringdove form by stating that the term "among" (*miyān*) was not appropriate because it distorted the term "ease of mind" (*sabuksārī*, lit. "light-headed"), making what was intended to be an abstract noun with an infinitive suffix (*yā-e maṣdar*) appear as an adjective with a second person singular suffix (*yā-e khiṭāb*). According to Ārzū's close reading, the term "this ease of mind" (*īn sabuksārī*) appeared as

"You are an airhead." To preserve the intended meaning, Ārzū argued, a different construction was needed to avoid any ambiguity and preserve the meter. Instead of "prisoners" (*asīrān*), Ārzū advocated that Ḥazin use the term "captured ones" (*giriftārān*). Thus, Ārzū's correction to the first lines appears as, "Among captured ones like us, know that ease of mind is our only prize" (*miyān-e mā giriftārān sabuk-sārī ġhanīmat dān*). But he did not stop there.

Ārzū then accused Ḥazīn of thematic plagiarism. He attempted to shore up his argument by citing the original couplet written by Mīr Maʿṣum that had inspired over a century of emulations from Persian poets across India and eventually reḳhtah writers at the Ornament of Mosques. The couplet from the 1620s reads as follows:

> You have a collar of ermine, and mine is of iron, O Ringdove.
> Tell me, whose beloved cypress is more merciless, yours or mine,
> O Ringdove?[90]

> *tū az sinjāb dārī ṭauq-o man az āhan ai qumrī*
> *bagū sarv-e tū be-raḥm ast yā sarv-e man ai qumrī*

Some poets grew uneasy with Ārzū's picayune criticism and, in their own taẓkirahs, began voicing their skepticism about his broadsides against Ḥazīn. For instance, Wālih characterized Ārzū's attack on Ḥazīn as unjust, and Ḥākim Lāhaurī opined that Ārzū's critique was generally tyrannical.[91] Āzād Bilgrāmī considered Ārzū's points in detail before presenting counterevidence of his own to buttress Ḥazīn's position. Embellishing his remarks by quoting verse about overly zealous critics, Āzād obliquely labeled approaches like Ārzū's as nitpicking.[92] Saudā, who respected Ḥazīn's position as a master poet, also criticized Ārzū for his excess. As Saudā noted, "producing objections to a master who possessed Ḥazīn's level of achievement" was "exceedingly difficult." It was only a poet like Ārzū, "from a class of poets known to be not even a bit inferior to [the court writers] Abū'l Faẓl and Faiẓī," who was able to make "any progress in exacting obsessive corrections," Saudā wrote over a decade after the release of Ārzū's tirade.[93] Saudā damned Ārzū with great praise.

NUDRAT'S DEFENSE OF ḤAZĪN

Along with the chorus of defense voiced by famous ġhazal composers and taẓkirah writers, at the end of the 1740s, Ḥazīn's most ardent support came from outside this eminent crew. It came instead from Nudrat, the Kashmiri poet who emulated Ḥazīn's verse throughout his own dīwān, and who also composed a tribute to Ḥazīn based on the ringdove form. Nudrat adopted a self-consciously imaginative approach in his ringdove experiment, especially in opening and closing lines that illustrate his aspiration to craft words distinguishing his position in Delhi's literary sphere:

Since you do not coo like a dove before the cypress of the garden,
    O Ringdove,
  perhaps you fantasize about the splendor of my cypress, O Ringdove.

. . . .

The parrot beak at the tip of Nudrat's rare pen draws a feathery script.
  My every hemistich shall be like a cypress in the garden of speech,
    O Ringdove.[94]

chū kūkū mazanī bar rū-e sarv-e gulshan ai qumrī
  magar dārī ḳhayāl-e jalwah-e sarv-e man ai qumrī

. . . .

kashad manqār-e ṭūṭā ḳhaṭ bah pesh-e ḳhāmah-e nudrat
  buwad har miṣraʿ-man sarv-e bāġh-e guftan ai qumrī

Ḥazīn creatively maintained the traditions of classical writers, "a conservative freshness" as Jane Mikkelson notes when considering Ḥazīn's own avian-themed references. Nudrat followed a similar trajectory, using idiomatic ideas in service of complex meanings related to ringdove themes such as horticultural imagery.[95]

Nudrat's valorization of Ḥazīn also appears in his prose. In 1749, purportedly after twenty years of work, Nudrat completed a dictionary project titled "The Source of the Gift" (*ʿAin-e ʿAṭā*), released a year after Ḥazīn fled Delhi for Varanasi. In his preface, Nudrat outlines his rationale for writing the dictionary: "The Source of the Gift" considered old and "modern" literary devices for poets who "have hoisted and shall continue to hoist the standard of discernment and emulation (*taṣaffuḥ wa tatabbuʿ*) within wisdom's valley of synthesis and metaphor (*maʿrifāt-e marakkabāt wa istaʿārāt*)."[96] Nudrat announces his intention to establish the boundaries of literary speech by examining the words of noted masters and settling scores on Ḥazīn's behalf by offering correctives for previous dictionaries, notably the work of Ārzū. For new phrases, Nudrat conducted research among "the language knowers from the lands of Iran," leading him into further association with Ḥazīn. Nudrat dedicated his dictionary to Ḥazīn with gushing praise, describing Ḥazīn as "the desire of the refuge of perfections with lineage of a sage who discerns the mysteries of speech, the holder of the humanity's perfections, 'Leader of the Moderns' (*qidwat ul-muta'akhkhirīn*), Shaikh Muḥammad ʿAlī Ḥazīn."[97]

Nudrat's dictionary clearly announces a political position. As he states in the preface, Nudrat had assembled the work to forcefully critique Ārzū's 1734 lexicon "Sirāj's Vocabulary Lamp" (*Sirāj ul-Luġhat*), a project Ārzū also titled according to his given moniker "Lamp of the Faith" (*Sirāj ud-Dīn*). Nudrat decried Ārzū's dictionary for inaccurately reflecting contemporary phrases and argued that rather than constituting an original dictionary in its own right, Ārzū's work should actually be considered a compilation of other scholars' works. Nudrat summarily stated that Ārzū simply attached his own name to more worthy dictionary projects such as "Burhān's Conclusive Proof" (*Burhān-e Qāṭiʿ*, Deccan, circa 1652) and "The Dictionary of Qūsī" (*Farhang-e Qūsī*, Iran, unknown dates). Ārzū's dictionary, in Nudrat's eyes, contained "camel cats" (*shutur gurbah*), absurdities to which Nudrat voiced strong objection.[98]

Entries in Nudrat's dictionary reflect a preference for classical writers from Iran, but several contemporary examples appear in citations from verse by the famous "new writers" Nūr ud-Dīn Muḥammad Ẓuhūrī (d. 1616) and Qizilbāsh Khān Ummīd (d. 1746), the Iranian émigré with innovative literary values who had only recently died in Delhi.[99] Nudrat's dictionary quickly earned a critical response from Ārzū in his 1750 taẕkirah *Majmaʿ un-Nafā'is*. Ārzū accused Nudrat of plagiarism, claiming that "The Source of the Gift" repurposed much of Ārzū's "Sirāj's Vocabulary Lamp." In poetry, Ārzū also compared Nudrat's verse to menstrual blood and claimed that religious functionaries like Nudrat did not have the fecundity to produce a dīwān, let alone a worthy line of poetry.[100] Yet, Nudrat closely followed the words of past masters and contemporary Indian versifiers to compose worthy and engaging words in emulation of the best mushāʿirah verse circulating throughout Delhi, words that, as we might expect, intersected with the poems of Ṣā'ib and Ḥazīn. As we will discover, Nudrat's verses also entwined fruitfully with those of Saudā beyond the incident at Bedil's grave, impacting the boundaries of Delhi's mushāʿirah verse in a multiplicity of ways.

An Argument over Nothing

At the time of their altercation, Saudā was quickly becoming a famous satirist. Eager to share his own vision of this rising figure, Nudrat pulled no punches in his assessment of Saudā's visage:

In this world, even an ostrich does not appear to share your style.
Only the Almighty could cast such a form in the world's creation in reḳhtah.

. . . .

His nose is like a trunk and his teeth jut from his lip like an elephant's.
There's even dirt on his head, tossed up as an elephant does in reḳhtah.

dar jahān ham rang-e tū nāyad shutur murġhī padīd
rang-e īnjād-e jahān tā ḥaqq taʿālā reḳhtah

. . . .

bīnī-ish ḳharṭūm-o dandānish chū pīl az lab bīrūn
bar sar-e ḳhwud ḳhāk z-īn rah-e pīl bālā reḳhtah

In response, Saudā skillfully reversed each one of these couplets, casting creative reformulations of those same insults back on to Nudrat's head:

A Kashmiri's nose resembles an elephant trunk, so the scholar says.
And jutting from the lip, one will find his greedy teeth.
If someone inquires about the mark of your appearance, I simply say this:
"His nose is like a trunk and his teeth jut from his lip like an elephant's.
There's even dirt on his head, tossed up as an elephant does."[101]

nāk kashmīrī kī ho ḳharṭūm sī ai żū funūn
lab se bāhar tere dandān-e ṭamaʿ ko dekhūn hūñ
jo koʾī pūchhe nishān tujh shakal kā maiñ yūñ kahūñ
bīnī-ish ḳharṭūm-o dandānish chū pīl az lab bīrūn
bar sar-e ḳhwud ḳhāk z-īn rah-e pīl bālā reḳhtah

Some of the images were sourced from Bedil's dīwān, albeit reformulated into profanity. This should come as no surprise for those who remember that the context for Saudā and Nudrat's exchange was Bedil's graveside *ʿurs* (death anniversary) in which poets customarily selected verses from the poet-saint's collected works (*kulliyāt*) to read aloud and emulate in spontaneous compositions of their own. The tirades about tossing dirt on heads that Nudrat and Saudā exchanged between themselves were inspired by one of Bedil's sober Sufi couplets in which the poet-saint relays his longing for union with the beloved:

For an eternity, I have been adrift from your unique embrace.
  How long must I search, a handful of dust cast into the sea?[102]

az azal gum-gashtah-e āġhosh-e yaktā-e tū-ām
  tā bah kay jūyam kaf-e ḳhākī bah daryā reḳhtah

While Bedil invoked the image of casting dust into the sea to describe searching for oneness with God, Nudrat and Saudā irreverently twisted the trope into one of an elephant tossing up dirt onto its own head, and then used this as the jumping off point for a sustained consideration of how each other's faces resembled those of animals.

Even before this extended exchange of poetic mockery at Bedil's grave, Nudrat and Saudā had on a prior occasion already traded verse that was likewise influenced by Bedil's words. By investigating this prior exchange and other crossing points between Nudrat and Saudā that preceded their famous battle, we can deepen our appreciation of the complexity of these two poets' personal and poetic connections. This earlier poetic dialogue took place at some unknown date, perhaps the night before the duel between Nudrat and Saudā at focus in this chapter. The incident began when an unnamed attendee at Bedil's ʿurs opened the poet-saint's *kulliyāt* and selected a ġhazal for the attending poets to emulate. The one he chose was written in an exceedingly famous form emulated across Iran and India. Among the clusters of burning candles and assembly of medicine buyers, the ġhazal's opening lines resonated:

My imagination is a phoenix. Of fakirs, ask nothing.
  The whole world knows my story and I am nothing.[103]

ʿanqā sar-o bargīm mapurs az fuqarā hech
  ʿālam hamah afsānah-e mā dārad-o mā hech

The opening imagery of Bedil's couplet offers a set of imaginative contradictions with the high-flying phoenix typifying the imagination of the speaker, despite his lowly position as a fakir begging for alms.[104] Inspired by this recitation from Bedil's complete works, Saudā composed his own ġhazal following the same form and themes. In its final two couplets, Saudā's tribute in reḳhtah recorded the formal aspects of the poem by citing Bedil:

To Saudā I once said, "I heard about your fame.
  But what I saw of you, utter wretch, amounted to nothing."
Saudā responded, "Don't you remember that disheartened line from
  Bedil?

[It's the one that goes:] 'The whole world knows my story and
I am nothing.'"[105]

saudā se kahā maiñ kih tire shuhrah ko sun kar
dekhā jo tujhe āye to ai be-sar-o pā hech
bolā kih tujhe yād hai vuh miṣraʿ-e bedil
ʿālam hamah afsānah-e mā dārad-o mā hech

In this conceit about a speaker mocking his own performed humility, Saudā demonstrated his characteristic wit and prodigious ability to reroute old lines for new meanings. Instead of being a wretch, Saudā craftily positioned himself as a figure whose renown approached that of Bedil: the poet-saint paragon whose spirit was still strongly impacting compositions by Persian writers and the growing cohort of reḳhtah composers. At that moment, the poet-saint's grave still remained a key hub for literary sociability, albeit in a different style than could have been envisioned by Bedil. The kind of intimate verse exchange now rehearsed at Bedil's grave rearticulated the poet-saint's forms and ideas in accordance with larger-scale socioeconomic and linguistic changes occurring in Delhi's literary sphere. While Bedil described his own imagination as flying high like a phoenix, Saudā regenerated this description, framing it, in an act of defiance and distinction, as an imaginative response to a competitor or perhaps to Bedil himself.

The couplet in Bedil's guiding form that ended with the refrain of "nothing" was well known by writers in the 1740s, including Ḥazīn, who had recently revived it in his controversial 1743 dīwān. Ḥazīn's contribution to this dialogue over "nothing" opened with a couplet that experimented with Bedil's oppositions, but instead of juxtaposing humble beggars with soaring phoenixes, Ḥazīn focused instead on the collapse of high- and low-class distinctions in the beloved's bedroom eyes:

In your seductive gaze, the beggar and the sultan are nothing.
But are you even aware that my heart is also nothing?

. . . .

The glass of acceptance has been shattered for its drunkenness.
Debauchery has no concept of pain and pleasure—nothing.[106]

ai dar naẓar-e nāz-e tu sulṭān-o gadā hech
āyā ḳhabar-at hast zi-ḥāl-e dil-e mā hech

. . . .

paimānah-e taslīm shikastah ast ḳhumārish
rindī kih nadārad ḳhabar az dard-o ṣafā hech

In these couplets, we find another instance of Ḥazīn taking cues from Delhi's contemporary literary scene. Yet, in distinction to Bedil, who infused the ġhazal's form with his characteristic Sufi puzzles and contradictions, Ḥazīn's rehearsal of the "nothing form" followed the amatory routes for which he was best known.

By writing ġhazals, poets inscribed highly personalized contexts and connections across social settings; in this way, styles of friendship and comportment (*adab*) manifested themselves through specific instances of literary exchange in Delhi and across the early modern Islamic world.[107] For Ottoman writers, love poetry constructed mediated ideals about personal relationships in urban settings, as discussed by Walter Andrews and Mehmet Kalpaklı.[108] Under the Safavids, conceptions of Isfahan took shape through acts of collecting verse and paintings. As described by Kathryn Babayan, such texts linked locality, speech, and visual repertoires of urban belonging, with the ġhazal constituting a particularly crucial means of mediating sociability (*ṣuḥbat*) for Isfahan's locals.[109] As defined by neighborhoods, shrines, and mosques, locality shaped poets' urban identities, and their exchanges occurred—and often were pointedly represented as occurring—in specific space and places around the city, during precise moments in time, and among known associates. So too, specific couplets were attached to the personae of particular writers, tying the way they were remembered to distinct events and anecdotes about the recent past.

As Jane Mikkelson has demonstrated, Delhi's poets, specifically Ḥazin and Bedil, closely followed previous ġhazal composers, most notably Ṣāʾib, in setting conceptual and material boundaries for poetic style. In turn, Ṣāʾib, Bedil, and Ḥazīn each deployed metaphor in their lyrics to signal respective preferences for old or fresh ideas while also mapping their local and pan-regional affiliations; in this way, each subsequently defined anew the Persianate world of the past according to "interconnected matters of style, geography, literary criticism, and poetics."[110] So far in our exploration of mid-1700s gatherings, we have witnessed many instances of how these processes took place at the scale of neighborhoods, rather than regions, and among minor contemporaries, rather than noted masters. In mid-1700s Delhi, the poets considered here—who knew each other intimately and understood one another's limitations and tics—demonstrate through the verse they exchanged how literature mediated many dimensions of personal association.

This firsthand quality of poetic exchange made the production, assessment, and representation of particular verses deeply personal. The ways in which Delhi's poets emulated highly contextualized ġhazals, as examined in this book, demonstrate the processes by which localized literary networks actuated competitions, sociability, and memories linked with specific couplets or even whole compositions. While focusing on the immediate needs of performance and competition for writers who met face to face, the literary-historical approach to interpreting ġhazals from their socially positioned frames developed in our analysis leads to important insights into how extended lineages from past masters took shape for individual poets.

Empty Meanings

To understand how the verses and figures of past masters mediated and were mediated by the relationship between Nudrat and Saudā, this grounded historical literary approach prompts us to first examine how both earlier and contemporaneous poets exacted emulations related to the figures on whom the dueling poets staked their claim in their famous 1740s battle. To begin, in its final couplet, Ḥazīn's version of Bedil's "nothing form" directs our interpretation with its nod to Muḥammad Ḥusain Naẓīrī Nīshāpūrī (1560–1612)—the form's originating composer. Just as Saudā did for Bedil in the final couplet of his own nothing-form ġhazal, Ḥazīn invoked Naẓīrī with a tribute (*tażmīn*) and a double entendre:

> The clamor of Hazīn's grief is from his complaint about Naẓīrī.
> Were it not for the echo, the mountain would cry out nothing.[111]

> *ġhoġhā-e ḥazīn ast zi-faryād-e naẓīrī*
> *bāngī kih nabāshad nakunad koh ṣadā hech*

Ḥazīn's contribution praised Naẓīrī for writing brilliant verse that still echoed in gatherings well after Naẓīrī's death. Ḥazīn's tribute emerged in his quotation of the final line from Naẓīrī's ġhazal:

> It's because of you that my murmuring is in the style of Naẓīrī.
> Were it not for the echo, the mountain would cry out nothing.[112]

> *az tū-st kih īn zamzamah bā ṭabʿ-e naẓīrī-st*
> *bāngī kih nabāshad nakunad koh ṣadā hech*

A strikingly original poet, Naẓīrī had honed his skills in top literary circles across Iran and later in India, before eventually accruing enough wealth to settle down in Ahmadabad. Even many decades after his death, his fame still drew eighteenth-century poets to visit his grave in Gujarat.[113] Naẓīrī's later popularity can be attested in the words ʿAbd ul-Ġhānī Qabūl, the "misdirecting" founder of the Qabuliyans who composed a ġhazal on this pattern. As recorded in Ārzū's tażkirah, only one of Qabūl's couplets survives:

Like a signet ring upon which a prayer is engraved—
on my verse besides the name of God there is nothing.[114]

mānand naginī kih duʿā-yī ast bar ān naqsh
dar ḳhānah-e mā nīst bajuz nām-e ḳhudā hech

For a ġhazal built on "nothing," the thematic possibilities were endless. Saudā had likely read Qabūl's dīwān, citing lines from the famous ambiguist in his later criticism.[115] Frequent emulations from well-known writers such as Ḥazīn, Bedil, and Qabūl cemented the importance of Naẓīrī's pattern for Delhi's ġhazal composers. When Bedil's version of the poem rang out at the Delhi graveside gathering, it pricked the ears of several attending poets besides Saudā. One of them was Nudrat, and he imbued the opening line of the responding ġhazal he composed with amatory words in the classical mode he often preferred:

Like his mouth, the promises of that bright-faced one are nothing.
Like his hair-thin waist, agreements all are nonsense, and fidelity is nothing.[116]

mānand-e dahān waʿdah-e ān mihr laqā hech
chūn mūʾī miyān ʿahd hamah pūch-o wafā hech

Nudrat's composition in the "nothing form" reveals that Nudrat and Saudā exchanged literary ideas in their more conventional compositions before their famously belligerent mushāʿirah at Bedil's grave. This history of trading verse was predicated on the great degree of overlap between the two poets' social and literary spheres of influence. Nudrat and Saudā both pored over Ḥazīn's dīwān when it was released; both poets were well acquainted with Ārzū's intellectual output; both nurtured a deep understanding of Persian-language literary history in terms of its stylistic developments over time; and both actively participated in Delhi's ġhazal scene.

The record of their compositions in this shared "nothing form"—Nudrat's in Persian and Saudā's in reḳhtah—not only evinces a dialogue that predated combativeness but also suggests that these two poets had a history of composing extremely similar ġhazals. Like Nudrat, Saudā also opens his version of his "nothing form" ġhazal in an amatory style:

> Neither the glance nor the eyebrow nor the charisma nor the
> flirtations—nothing.
> Even the moon is a roulette ball for you, but otherwise nothing.[117]
>
> *nah chashm nah abrū nah karishmah nah adā hech*
> *māh gend hai bāzī kī tere us ke sivā hech*

In several different turns of phrase, Nudrat and Saudā echo each other's themes, each informed by the masters who first deployed similar ideas. For instance, both poets developed auditory themes that were first offered by Naẓīrī, elaborated on by Bedil and quoted by Ḥazīn, by invoking the sound of the caravan bell, a prominent motif throughout Islamicate literatures.[118] Nudrat wrote in Persian:

> Nudrat, what righteous words do you divulge from your empty
> brains?
> Like a hollow drum, the result is the clang of a bell or something.[119]
>
> *nudrat suḳhan-e ḥaq chih barāyid zi-tihī maġhz*
> *chūn ṭabl-e tihī ḥāṣilī az bāng-e darā hech*

Instead of considering the caravan bell's "clang" (*bāng*), Saudā, in reḳhtah, described it as having a voice that calls out to the lover noting the finitude of existence:

> The caravan of life is so fast paced that within it
> even if listeners wish to hear it the caravan bell's clang is nothing.[120]
>
> *kyā qāfilah-e ʿumr-e sabuk-rav hai jis meñ*
> *chāhe jo sune sāmiʿah-e āwāz-e darā hech*

In other arenas, Nudrat and Saudā explored new territory on the theme of the lover's heart, a well-established topic, but one perhaps arbitrarily avoided by Naẓīrī, Bedil, and Ḥazīn in their contributions. Nudrat opted for a complex image from the perfumery trade, comparing a bleeding heart in the beloved's clenched fingers to a recently harvested gland from a musk deer, an organ that could itself appear like a tightly balled fist. Nudrat wrote:

While the blackness of your tresses was like a musk bladder filled
with blood,
In your fist the heart of this wretch is nothing!

saudā'ī-e zulf-e tū buwad nāfah-e pur-ḳhūn
dar musht chih dārad dil-e īn be-sar-o pā hech

In his turn, Saudā ruminated on the aural associations produced by the lover's breaking heart:

The moment you smash a glass a sound escapes.
But the lover has a heart that once shattered the sound is nothing.

shīshe ko bhī toṛo to nikaltī hai ek āwāz
'āshiq hī kā vuh dil hai kih ṭūṭe to ṣadā hech

These verses make clear the extent to which Nudrat and Saudā shared overlapping tastes in their compositions, each following pathways established by past masters and charting new routes of their own. This perspective draws our attention to the high degree of similarity that can be found between the approaches of the soon-to-be dueling poets, each attempting in their respective verses to extract new ideas from the same themes and well-established form.

Yet, Saudā would soon stretch his emulation of Bedil past its breaking point, picking up a barbed idea from a couplet by Bedil that considered the image of the bubble:

Since the clothing of the mystery is a bubble-like puzzle,
in the end, besides the knot on the cloak, I figured out nothing.[121]

z-īn kiswat-e 'ibrat kih mu'ammā-e ḥabāb ast
āḳhir nagushūdīm bajuz band-e qabā hech

Riding Bedil's Sufi aspirations, the bubble verse conjures spatial metaphors and nothingness in an effort to capture the contradictions of existence. The speaker of the poem conveys the difficulty he finds in expressing how a bubble-like costume might exist, so much so that its wearer only reached as far as undoing one knot of its mystery. Yet, opening the knot of a bubble, popping it, produces only air—nothing.

Saudā repurposed Bedil's Sufi puzzles, taking the idea of the bubble's emptiness as a negative marker and applying it both to Bedil's poem itself and to those of his rival Nudrat. At Bedil's gathering, Saudā, in reḳhtah, chided Nudrat's self-importance while simultaneously insulting Bedil and Nudrat's respective verses:

Do not puff up this poem so much, as if it were a bubble.
Your poem is such nonsense that besides air it is nothing.[122]

is jāmah pah itnā nah aphir bulbule kī ṭarḥ
jāmah yih tirā pūch hai to ġhair-e hawā hech

With this couplet, Saudā fatefully set in motion his fight with Nudrat, especially in the way he deployed the frequently cited and damnatory word signifying empty speech: *pūch*, rendered as nonsense. Saudā coopted the spatial aspect of the term by comparing Nudrat's unoriginal poems to bubbles, reversing the Sufi values of Bedil: they were empty of meaning and full of air. His dismissal of poems, and of Nudrat himself as a kind of stuffed shirt, set the tone for the forthcoming exchanges between the two poets, as played out in the series of derogatory quintains they aimed at one another at Bedil's grave.

Saudā's and Nudrat's dīwāns provide us with alternative routes toward understanding their story as one of shared artistic inclinations, in contrast to material found in emulations and the information provided by the thin taẕkirah framing of their competition at Bedil's grave as a clashing of opposite forces. The mushāʿirah setting and comparisons between their verses provide evidence that Nudrat was an important, and until now unnamed, influence on Saudā's literary style and production. The tastes and inspirations shared by Nudrat and Saudā were generated by a dense literary matrix that overdetermined the style and substance of the ġhazals produced by them as well as other poets in Delhi's literary milieu.

For poets of 1740s Delhi, the ġhazal's originality proved fickle and difficult to master, a fact compounded by the boisterous environment of mushāʿirah competitions that drew poets into close, sustained, and heated exchanges. Emulative overlaps, which can be pictured as tributaries crossing in poets' dīwāns, muddy the taẕkirah-based narratives about Nudrat and Saudā's enmity and complicate the nature of their fight. Shafīq's original reading of Saudā's lampoons pointed us toward the primary function of literary production and exchange, rightly emphasizing how enmity, just like any other relational exchange in the literary world, generated meaning in lyric poetry. The weapons poets crafted and deployed for literary duels were complex and defined by the immediate needs of a literary sociability that thrived on admiring rivalries, intimate enmities, and sparks of stylistic distinctions that emerged from the frictions of close encounters.

Layers of Satire

We remember Saʿdullāh Gulshan (d. 1728) from chapter 2 as a Naqshbandi Sufi musician, a denizen of the Ornament of Mosques, and an occasional attendee at the Qabuliyans' gatherings. On one occasion in 1722, Gulshan memorably used the poet-saint's ʿurs mushāʿirah as a stage for chiding Muḥammad Murād (d. 1727,) a fallen Mughal official who occasionally appeared at the courtyard tomb to recite his own verse. Seeing Murād, Gulshan gave a start. During a pause in the recitations, he turned to address Murād by his courtly title, asking, "My esteemed Iʿtiqād [Ḳhān], have you had a moment to think up some poems lately?"[123] Gulshan's words, although seemingly innocuous, were clever and cutting. Only a few years prior to this incident, Murād had fallen on the losing side of a political shakeup; as a result, he was imprisoned and stripped of his wealth. Under emperor Farruḳh Siyar (r. 1713–19), Murād had climbed the Mughal hierarchy, and had gained riches and responsibilities indicative of a courtier with power and influence. But, when the Sayyid brothers captured Delhi in 1719, Murād's good fortune ended abruptly. They blinded and throttled Murād's patron, then seized Murād's wealth and land holdings before ordering his imprisonment. Now free in 1722, only Murād's title remained of his former status. Literary elites like Gulshan teasingly addressed him as Iʿtiqād Ḳhān Farruḳh Siyar Shāhī, including the last appellation (Farruḳh Siyar Shāhī) as a jeering reminder of Murād's fall.

No longer supported by an emperor, Murād perhaps indeed found himself with more time to devote to poetry.[124] Well aware of Gulshan's stinging implications, Murād began to intone lines from the "Rose Garden" (*Gulistān*), a well-known didactic text in the Persianate world by Musharrif ud-Dīn Saʿdī of Shiraz (1210–92). Murād recited: "When the day for fools finally came . . ." (*ba-nādānān chunān rozī rasānad*). Hearing this Gulshan gestured for Murād to join the circle around Bedil's grave. Taking his place among the group, Murād completed Saʿdī's couplet: "Only the philosopher continued be puzzled" (*kih dānā andar ān ḥairān bamānad*).[125] In the verse, Murād mitigated the memory of the humiliation he suffered during the 1719 struggle for the throne by turning to an old theme: while fools unwittingly succeeded in whatever they attempted, the wise inevitably failed.

Just then, the poet Abū'l-Faiẓ *Mast* (The Intoxicated) (fl. 1720s) chimed in with his own interjection. Like Gulshan, Mast was another former student of Bedil who attended the poet-saint's posthumous gatherings and frequented the circuit of mushāʿirahs hosted by fellow acolytes.[126] Not to miss his chance to compound the venerable theme in Murād's verse, Mast responded with a rejoinder also from Saʿdī, "The alchemist toiled and died from his grief, / but the fool found treasures among the ruins" (*kimiyā gīr bah ġhussah murdah ranj / ablah andar ḳharābah yāftah ganj*). Murād and Mast had chosen concluding poetry from an instructional story in the "Rose Garden" that told of how kings should conduct themselves. The banter was a gesture to the controversial political problems that led to Murād's own fall from imperial circles.[127]

For more than three decades after this incident, poets continued gathering at Bedil's resting place to recite the poet-saint's verses and to offer their own compositions. Yet, by the end of Muhammad Shah's reign in 1748, there were already major shifts occurring in Delhi's literary scene heralding the wane of Bedil's annual mushāʿirah. By that year, the reḳhtah literary community of Delhi, which had started out by championing īhām, distanced itself from that equivocal style. By 1748, Ḥazīn already had left for Varanasi, and by 1750 Nūr Bāʾī had relocated to Murshidabad, inaugurating what would soon become a flood of eastward-bound departures.[128] This literary exodus from Delhi was caused by several interrelated factors. Between 1753 and 1761, the capital suffered under further invasions and occupations, events that leveled the locales popular for poetry gatherings. These devastating events of the middle 1700s damaged much of the southern portion of the city, including Wakīl Purāh, Fīroz Shah's fortress, and likely Bedil's former home and tomb. While these sites that once hosted Delhi gatherings crumbled, other cities with wealthy local elites began patronizing Delhi's poets, raising new establishments for the Persianate world's market for speech in Lucknow, Patna, Varanasi, and other cities mainly to the east of Delhi.

The absence of documentation of the ʿurs event in reḳhtah taẑkirahs of the 1750s signals that festivities around Bedil's grave had begun to fade or had become of diminished interest to reḳhtah poets. For these reasons, the duel between Nudrat and Saudā at Bedil's grave that took place sometime between 1744–47 proved to be among the last of the documented recitations to have taken place at the poet-saint's death anniversary. The institution's demise coincided with Bedil's students reaching the ends of their respective careers. Ḳhwushgo, who recorded the anecdote about Gulshan teasing

Murād, along with many other literary vignettes considered in this book, had recently left Delhi for the east in 1743, following his patron Amīr Ḵhān who had been appointed as Allahabad's governor. Ḵhwushgo never returned.[129] Mast faded into oblivion. In 1745, Maʿnī Yāb Ḵhān died unexpectedly from overexerting himself in bed; he had famously served as the caretaker for Bedil's complete works and other literary artifacts at Bedil's tomb. Muḵhliṣ died in 1750.[130] Ārzū, an important actor at the grave, left Delhi in 1754, providing further evidence for the gathering's end. By the early 1750s, Gulshan's poems, too, along with his witty comments, were nearly forgotten. Wālih Dāġhistānī observed in his taẕkirah that no one read Gulshan's dīwān any longer.[131] Today, Gulshan's dīwān is largely neglected, although pieces of its are accessible in taẕkirah verse samples and fragments preserved in diaries.[132] Although Gulshan's literary status receded soon after his 1728 death, the poet's influence as a religious figure continued. About a decade after his death, Gulshan chiefly became known as a municipal saint whose ʿurs attracted public performers for musical assemblies every spring.[133]

Despite these shifts in his status, one couplet by Gulshan continued to garner attention and imitation for several more decades, and it soon worked its way into Nudrat and Saudā's famous mid-1740s duel:

> Only with one hundred exactitudes were you able to fathom the meanings of his flirtations,
> since his long eyelashes are a commentary on the wisdom of the eye.[134]

> *ba-ṣad diqqat tawān fahmīd maʿnī-hā-e nāz-e ū*
> *kih sharḥ-e ḥikmat ul-ʿain ast miẕhagān-e darāz-e ū*

The imagery and allusions that Gulshan employed in his famous couplet were notably complex, even according to the standards of the poet's literary peers who trafficked in such multilayered conceits. In 1727, the year before Gulshan died, Kishan Chand Iḵhlāṣ noted in his taẕkirah that these opening lines from a ġhazal by Gulshan were "famous among versifiers."[135] This helps us estimate that the famous couplet was probably written before 1726, after Gulshan had spent several decades studying under Bedil. The couplet's metaphysical convolutions seem markedly Bedilian. The fact that Gulshan's earlier teacher, Sarḵhwush, failed to record this couplet in his taẕkirah "The Words of Poets" (*Kalimāt ush-Shuʿarā*) further ties the couplet to Bedil's mentorship. Finally, the appearance of these lines in the taẓkirah of Bedil's star pupil Ḳhwushgo offers another thread connecting Gulshan's famous verse to Bedil's influence.[136]

The significant complexity and insider references found in Gulshan's eyelash couplet are due partly to its substantial intertextual connotations. Firstly, in his phrase "philosophy of the eye" (*ḥikmat ul-ʿain*) Gulshan alludes to "The Philosophy of the Source" by Najm ud-Dīn ʿAlī bin ʿUmar Kātibī ul-Qazwīnī (1204–76). Qazwīnī was an important philosopher, logician, and astronomer from Iran who secured patronage under the early Mongol Ilkhanate (fl. 1260–1335). One of Qazwīnī's intellectual inheritors, the scholar Ibn Mubārak Shāh ul-Buḳhārī (fl. 1354), wrote a widely circulated commentary (*sharḥ*) on Qazwīnī's "Philosophy of the Source," called "A Commentary on the Philosophy of the Source" (*sharḥ-e ḥikmat ul-ʿain*), which became a crucial text in madrasah curricula across the Muslim world.[137] A literal rendering of the second line of Gulshan's couplet reads: "His long eyelashes are just like Buḳhārī's commentary on Qazwīnī's *Philosophy of the Source*."

Old Words in New Barbs

Although Gulshan's couplet was sober in tone, two decades later Saudā deployed it in a lampoon of Nudrat's daughter in the contest at Bedil's grave, a facetious move demonstrating how Delhi's poets could, through skillful manipulation of a single verse, quickly reroute taste and authorial associations in Delhi's Persian and reḳhtah literary scene. In a biting sestet that he recited as part of their marathon battle, Saudā gushingly praised the accomplishments of Nudrat's daughter, repurposing august lines into ridicule to recite:

> Maulvī [Nudrat] is raising a daughter bestowed with love and faith.
> Even the perfection of Nūr Bāʾī could be her skillful handmaid.
> But perhaps the length of her long tresses shall be abbreviated.
> A mere gesture of her eye's glance is her enchantment.
> Only with one hundred exactitudes could you begin to fathom the meanings of her flirtations,
> since her long eyelashes are "A Commentary on the Philosophy of the Eye."[138]

rakhe hai maulvī duḳhtar kih dīn-o dil niyāz-e ū
faẓīlat nūr bāʾī kī kanīz kār-sāz-e ū
maṭawwal ko kare hai muḳhtaṣar zulf-e darāz-e ū

ishārāt-e nigāh-e chashm hai jādū ṭarāz-e ū
ba-diqqat mī tawān fahmīd maʿnī-hā-e nāz-e ū
kih sharḥ-e ḥikmat ul-ʿain ast miẕhagān-e darāz-e ū

Saudā began the verse innocently enough, seemingly commending Nudrat for the care and regard that he heaped upon his unnamed daughter. By the second line, the poem's sarcastic intent manifests itself by musing that Nudrat might consider employing the famous courtesan Nūr Bāʾī as his daughter's servant. Later in the poem, Saudā describes Nudrat's daughter as a skilled calligrapher and an accomplished musician, further illustrating the lengths Nudrat, as a middling secretary and religious functionary, went to provide a broad education for her comparable to Nūr Bāʿī and other elite women.[139] In yet another stanza, Saudā describes Nudrat as an overweening father bragging about his daughter's accomplishments. Again, deploying Gulshan's couplet as a refrain, Saudā recited:

Since we keep hearing how accomplished she is in the art of poetry,
had Bedil been here then he would have learned from her!
If she were to instruct an ignoramus like me what would result?
To even understand a verse about the beloved's eyebrow is tough work.
Only with exactitude could you possibly understand the meanings of her flirtations,
since her long eyelashes are "A Commentary on the Philosophy of the Eye."[140]

sunā jātā hai fann-e shiʿr meñ bhī itnī hai qābil
sabq us se paṛheñ is waqt hoñ gar mīrzā bedil
agar vuh dars de ve ham se nādān ko to kyā ḥāṣil
samajhnā maṭlaʿ abrū kā us ke sakht mushkil
ba-diqqat mī tawān fahmīd maʿnī-hā-e nāz-e ū
kih sharḥ-e ḥikmat ul-ʿain ast miẕhagān-e darāz-e ū

Through his brief allusion to the poet-saint, Saudā's lampoon of Nudrat's daughter using Gulshan's famous couplet leads us to surmise that the composition likely circulated at Bedil's grave or within settings that appreciated the conceit. To get the joke, poets had to be acquainted with Bedil's circle of famous students, Nudrat's educational regime for his daughter, and Nudrat's collection of poems. The reference to Bedil, specifically, addressed an audience familiar with the poet-saint's importance and with the previous rounds of Nudrat and Saudā's competitions.

Little has been written about this poem, except for one brief mention of its refrain in a small survey of Saudā's Persian tributes by Muḥammad Sharaf ʿĀlim.[141] Besides the intertextual connections already noted here, there are a few clues by which we can assess Saudā's composition within Delhi's market for speech. At the time, Nudrat's unnamed daughter was likely unmarried and around thirteen years of age, when poets began composing worthwhile verse. She was still under Nudrat's care, since she was referenced as his daughter as opposed to someone's spouse, as would have been the case following a wedding. Among the elites, brides were generally around fourteen years of age at the time of betrothal.[142] The way in which Saudā muted his insults in the poem suggests that he knew his words could likely reach the tender ears of an accomplished girl child, further illustrating women's participation in the market for speech even in ribald competitions.

The historical record preserves incidents in which women circulated compositions and literary responses through letter writing. For his heckling of adult women, such as Nudrat's wife, Saudā resorted to his usual bawdy language, as found in a quintain with a refrain in which he casts Nudrat's wife as a streetwalker summoned from Delhi's Kashmiri neighborhood and asks us to imagine her speaking in mock Kashmiri dialect.[143] The late seventeenth-century writer Sher ʿAlī Ḳhān Lodī repurposed an exchange from an earlier Timurid tażkirah to present a witty dialogue between Lady Attūnī and her husband, the panegyrist Mullā Baqāʾī. Lodī also presents anecdotes in which the Mughal queen Mihr un-Nisā Nūr Jahan (1577–1645) exchanged poems with noted poets and courtiers, correcting the versifier Kalīm's usage of a metaphor, for example, or besting her brother-in-law, the governor of Bengal Qāsim Ḳhān Juwainī (r. 1628–31).[144]

The story of Gulshan's couplet relayed here references a third category of women mushāʿirah poets: the offspring of professional writers, such as Nudrat's daughter, who were raised from childhood by their literary parents to become skilled poets in their own right. As briefly noted in the last chapter, Wālih Dāġhistānī and his wife, the courtesan Ramjānī, raised their daughter Gannā Begam *Minnat* (d. 1775?) to be a skilled poet in reḳhtah and Persian verse.[145] Later tażkirah writers held that Saudā was one of her instructors.[146] Besides training his daughter in poetry composition, Wālih also described many examples of women poets in his 1750 tażkirah, although he occasionally expressed disdain for India's women poets, whom he sometimes panned as a class of writers who lacked sufficient acuity in Persian. In other instances, Wālih somewhat inconsistently records his admiration for Persian-writing female poets of India. He wrote praise of the poet Kāmilah, who circulated a famous eulogy for the Mughal poet laureate Faiẓī.[147] On another occasion, Wālih described the poet Bībī Zāʾirī as being so accomplished in verse that among men's literary battlefields she "seized the ball of rhetoric and skill in the crook of poetry's polo stick."[148]

Wālih's entire career and identity as a topic of literary inspiration was owed to his legendary failed love affair with the poet Ḵhadījah Begam *Sulṭān* (The Emperor) (fl. 1720–1747), for whom he composed many lines of poetry, with whom he exchanged many letters, and from whom he recorded lines in his taẕkirah.[149] One couplet from Sulṭān alludes to the participation of women in the literary sphere as mediated by paper: "You are like me, O Sulṭān, having never inhabited this plane. / Only in world after world of books am I present" (*sulṭān chū manī nabūdah dar dahr / ʿālam ʿālam-e kitāb ḥāẓir*).[150] Paper was the primary means by which elite women participated in the realm of public poetry exchanges. However, some evidence suggests that courtesans, semi-elite women of a class who ventured into the public, participated in person at Bedil's gathering. As discussed in chapter 1, Bedil's student Bhañwarī likely visited the festivities, as did the courtesan Raḥmān Bāʾī whose writings suggests she was composing emulations of the poet-saint at the annual festivities.[151]

In the final stanza of his composition, Saudā mischievously suggests that Nudrat's daughter was in on the joke when he cast Nudrat's daughter in the role of reciting her father's verse to ridicule him.

In short, what can I say, Saudā, about all this learning and perfection?
Would she even be able to recite a verse by this preacher, having
corrected it?
God only knows, is the verse unmetrical or this daughter of his?
Either she is being sly with him or she simply thinks he is an ass.
Only with exactitude could you possibly understand the meanings
of her flirtations,
since her long eyelashes are "A Commentary on the Philosophy of
the Eye."[152]

ġharaẓ maiñ kyā kahūñ saudā kih us faẓl wa kamāl ūpar
nahīn paṛh saktī shiʿr-e maulavī hargiz vuh mauzūn kar
ḵhudā jāne vuh nāmauzūn hai yā un kī hai yih duḵhtar
adā kartī hai un se yā unheñ vuh jānatī hai ḵhar
ba-diqqat mī tawān fahmīd maʿnī-hā-e nāz-e ū
kih sharḥ-e ḥikmat ul-ʿain ast mizhagān-e darāz-e ū

Saudā pictured Nudrat's daughter reciting verse from her father's dīwān in an exaggerated manner to amplify its metrical failings. To counter this position, the stanza could also be read as implying that Nudrat was ghostwriting verse for his daughter to present as her own, as was done by Ṡābit and Qabūl in the 1720s. In this case, her recitations were pictured as betraying both her own and her father's clumsiness with meter.

It was certainly possible that Nudrat's daughter could have attended the gathering and heard Saudā's poem about her in person, but it was more likely that she encountered the poem in written form or heard it recited by her father from his memory. She likely would have appreciated its humor because the refrain also appeared in her father's own dīwān.

In the same meter, with matching rhyme and refrain, Nudrat had composed a ġhazal that followed Gulshan's ideas about the long eyelashes of the beloved. In the first two couplets and the final one, Nudrat recited:

> To the extent that his flirtatious glances are the erasure of his own beauty
> only by welcoming flirtations to himself would he receive any relief.
> It is possible to thread his two eyebrows at a distance of two bow lengths.
> For lovers, the Prophet's Night Journey is the length of the beloved's eyelashes.
>
> . . . .
>
> When I planted my desiring eye on his favors, Nudrat,
> a branch on the palm tree of hope grew to the length of his eyelashes.[153]

> *zi-bas kih maḥw-e ḥusn-e ḳhwud nigāh-e ʿishwah-sāz-e ū*
> *bah istiqbāl-e nāz-e ḳhwīsh mī āyad niyāz-e ū*
> *tawān bar qāb qausain-e do abrūʾīsh naḳh kardan*
> *shab-e miʿrāj-e ʿushshāq-ast mizẖagān-e darāz-e ū*
>
> . . . .
>
> *az-ān chashm-e ṭamʿ bar altifāt-ish dūḳhtam nudrat*
> *kih shāḳh-e naḳhl-e ummīd-ast mizẖagān-e darāz-e ū*

Picking up Gulshan's complexity, Nudrat stacks another layer of classical allusions to prophetic imagery in the Night Journey and hopeful palm trees.[154] In the first couplet, Nudrat presents the contradictions of the beloved's self-conceit: he flirts with no one else but himself, even though such egotistical behavior is unbecoming. In the second and final couplets of the ġhazal, Nudrat develops Gulshan's image of the beloved's impossibly long eyelashes according to ideas taken from the Qur'an and stories of the

Prophet. In the Qur'an, a verse from "The Star" describes the distance between God and the Prophet Muhammad as a span "within two bow-lengths away or closer" after his ascent to heaven following the Night Journey (*miʿrāj*) from Mecca to Jerusalem.[155] The beloved's eyebrows have the arch of bows according to poetic convention. In this case, threading the eyebrows or stringing them up with a bowstring is only possible because the extent of a prophetic journey for lovers is the mere length of the beloved's eyelashes. The final couplet alludes to a Shīʿī hadith about the Prophet in which one of his companions asks the Prophet why he walks around with date pits in his pockets, dropping them in the earth. The Prophet replied, "They are palm trees, Lord willing" (*naḳhl inshā allāh*).[156]

Conclusion

Saudā's impish experiments with the eyelash couplet in his famous duel with Nudrat aptly demonstrate how poets marshaled intricate forms of intertextuality to shape the mushāʿirah setting on a hyperlocal scale. Due to limitations in the historical record, it is impossible to ascertain whether Nudrat's eyelash couplet was written before or after Saudā's lampoon. Based on available evidence, we can only assign an approximate date to Nudrat's dīwān—the sole source in which his eyelash couplet appears. We can safely surmise that Nudrat's dīwān must have been released shortly after the 1742/43 completion of Ḥazīn's dīwān. Thus far, we have based our retelling of Nudrat and Saudā's exchange on the idea that Nudrat wrote his eyelash emulation before Saudā's mocking version, yet it is possible that these two events may have occurred in reverse order. Perhaps after Nudrat heard Saudā's poetic pillorying of Gulshan and Nudrat's daughter, Nudrat composed his own, serious emulation of the eyelash verse to preserve the couplet's dignity and, by extension, that of his daughter.

In whatever order its verses were written, the location of the duel at Bedil's grave imbues the couplets with resonances that echo memories of the versifiers who wrote in the form or were schooled under those who attempted its unique parameters. The approach to literary publics advanced throughout this book posits a close relationship between place and memory; through its application we demonstrated how Bedil's grave and a series of other significant Delhi locales created associations for the city's poets via the accretions of literary meaning layered upon these sites over the years as poets continued to use them for recitation and exchange of verse. To access the particular ideas and sociability associated with literary spaces, poets formulated a ġhazal-based map of the city through which to access sites such as Bedil's grave, the gatherings at Fīroz Shāh Koṭlā, the rooms of Amīr Ḳhān's residence, and the courtyard at the Ornament of Mosques. When gatherings ceased to occur in a given neighborhood, home, or monument, the associations and memories of poets and places as bound by verse to these locales became more difficult to access for historians who were not able to attend those events in person.

In contrast, for Delhi's poets who were part of these localized networks, the sites remained redolent, accessible, and productive, reactivated in the memory of those who attended them with mention of a neighborhood or a time where an exchange occurred even after the gatherings associated with that site came to an end. To gain access to mid-1700s gatherings, today's historians must rely only on a series of texts. As we recall from the book's introduction, the kinds of primary source texts available to us include the taẕkirah, which provides a sketch of poets' literary memories; the dīwān, which offers an edited collection of a given poet's oeuvre, albeit with less direct access to poetic contexts which inspired composition or compilation; and diaries and commonplace books that contain a variety of less formally composed information about poems and their contexts. By closely reading the ġhazal while attending to the significant contextual cues provided by these primary source texts, historians can forge new connections between these texts, revealing more information about the urban niches that harbored poets' associations, recitations, and memories.

My analysis of the performative intertextual links discussed throughout this book provides evidence that notions of originality changed at a remarkably rapid rate for Delhi's ġhazal poets who attended mushāʿirahs, released dīwāns, and read new verse from across the Persian-speaking world. By more fully appreciating the velocity and magnitude with which these changes took place, literary historians can better understand how and why Urdu emerged as a literary language in Delhi. The story of Saudā's "eyelash poem" provides an example of the speed at which Delhi's poets could reappraise and reassign meanings to verse. In choosing Gulshan's couplet to compose upon, Saudā drew on public knowledge about literary style and mushāʿirah politics, gossip he heard, or an event he himself had witnessed. He knew about Gulshan's association with Bedil and likely had heard the recollections of many poets about Gulshan's presence at the tomb-side festivities. Saudā probably likewise had heard gossip about Gulshan's disillusionment with Sarḳhwush, his former mentor whom he left in favor of Bedil. Saudā was also aware of Nudrat's dīwān. We can surmise that, at the very least, Saudā knew that Nudrat's dīwān contained a ġhazal emulating Gulshan's most famous couplet. These links show us how emulation and interchange within the mushāʿirah setting built literary memory.

Saudā's and Nudrat's respective virtuosities relied on the ammunition of useful facts that they would store away about other poets, coupled with the knowledge of how to deploy emulative and intertextual skills at several levels. Nudrat and Saudā's face-off reminds us of Rebecca R. Gould's point about the communicative aspect of the ġhazal, as first cited in this book's introduction. Lyric poetry, even in translation, relays cultural norms particular to its own expressive capabilities and formal conventions. For Gould, ġhazals bring together seemingly incommensurate ideas and contexts, a context apparent in the war between Nudrat and Saudā as they hurled curses at each other while giving implicit, intertextual nods to the poet-saint Bedil.[157] Building on Gould's idea, we witness that the ġhazal, when situated historically within the mushāʿirah, demonstrates its position as a kind of historical "hypertext," harboring a socio-aesthetic complexity that cannot "conveniently be presented or represented on paper."[158] Recovering the data from poets' emulative networks—in this case the coarse poems of Nudrat and Saudā—provides evidence for a social history implicitly documented in lyric poetry and its multifaceted performance context.

Yet, for ġhazal writers of early 1700s Delhi, the associations linked with specific ġhazals were obvious considering that ġhazal performance and competition was highly entertaining and memorable. Delhi's successful mushāʿirah poets displayed abilities to understand and satisfy the immediate needs of their audiences and to properly route any meaningful references that emerged from the setting in which they performed. In other words, they enfolded the highly competitive ġhazal scene into itself, implicitly preserving memory of a literary past tied to locality and competition. The ġhazal, after all, as we argued in the Introduction, mainly is about the ġhazal itself, but within its lines also lurk the contexts of its production, circulation, and delights that governed the instincts of mushāʿirah poets and the memories of the communities in which they performed.

To access these memories and performance contexts, one must read across ġhazals through networks of meaning tied to time, place, and companions.[159] One final example drives this point home. Nearly every citation of couplets recited at Bedil's grave can be traced back to the ritual of reading aloud from the poet-saint's collected works during his annual ʿurs mushāʿirah, a fact witnessed by Dargāh Qulī Ḳhān in chapter 3 when he attended Delhi's gatherings during and after Nadir Shah's occupation. An often-cited poem from Ārzū that had been composed sometime before 1728 still echoed among mushāʿirahs of the early 1740s and found its way into Qulī Ḳhān's diary. Ārzū recited:

Since they endure so much pain of a hangover, alone in the grave—
it is fitting that the wine drinkers' tombstones are of grape-jasper.[160]

zi-bas burdand bā ḳhwud dar laḥd ham ranj-e maḳhmūrī
sizad lauḥ-e mazār-e maikashān az yashm-e angūrī

Ārzū's famous verse followed the rhyme and thematic material from Bedil's works. In a poem with these evocative lines, Bedil wrote:

The beloved is with cup in hand, and I am dead drunk—
sighing from tyranny of neglect, complaining about separation.[161]

dil-dār qadaḥ bar kaff mā murdah zi-maḳhmūrī
āh az sitam-e ġhaflat faryād zi-mahjūrī

The track of these emulations continued into the words of Tābān, the young reḳhtah composer from the circle of Qabuliyans whom we met in chapter 3. Tābān presented a reḳhtah verse in Ārzū's meter, echoing the rhyme and thematic images established by Bedil's poem. The opening lines of Tābān's ġhazal reflect these two overlapping streams of influence:

The treatment for those with injured heart is your glances' intoxication.
Indeed, there is benefit for a wound in grape wine.[162]

ʿilāj-e dilfigārān hai tirī ankhiyoñ kī maḳhmūrī
kih ḥad nāfiʿ hai zaḳhmī ke taʾīñ ṣahbā-e angūrī

In turn, Bedil, Ārzū, and Tābān each developed the theme of drunkenness, and their poems share connections through shared rhyme and meter. Tābān's form connected him to Ārzū, an informal teacher who influenced his words, and thereby, by extension, to Bedil and the graveside gatherings. These associations were clear to fellow poets. Mention of a metaphor and recitation of a rhyme conjured memories of mushāʿirahs that were always already present in a couplet. Such associations may easily be lost to present-day readers, but with careful literary excavation we can conjure the voices from the past and shout "*vāh vāh*" (bravo) along with long-deceased poets while imaginatively situating ourselves among them in the mosques, homes, and tombs where their cheers also once rang.[163]

Conclusion

Networks, Competitions, and Accessing the Past

Although mushāʿirah poetry has remained popular since the 1700s, Urdu poetry connoisseurs today are sharply critical about the confrontational and commercial aspects of the mushāʿirah's market for poetic speech. This deviates significantly from the attitudes of their predecessors who recognized, despite some ambivalence, the commodification of verse as constituent to its formation. In 2009, a now-defunct literary magazine asked its readership, "Is the mushāʿirah the reason for Urdu's cultural decline?" A chorus of middle-aged men responded "yes," asserting that the mushāʿirah had been cheapened by market forces, mass media, and Bollywood's influence on susceptible poets, such as those who cultivated glamorous appearances in the style of movie stars and set their verses to film songs' melodies.[1]

In the opinion of such magazine editorializers, these factors turned the once pristine mushāʿirah into an unruly arena of doggerel that appealed to the masses' basest emotions and populist political leanings. These and other fans of Urdu poetry figured the mushāʿirahs of the past as holding a transcendent aesthetic and ethical integrity, housing an ideal form of Urdu literature somehow shielded from politics and money. Depending on whom you ask, the period upon which these idealized mushāʿirah are projected shifts. For many, the gatherings of the nineteenth century proffered the ideal mushāʿirah, often imagined with imperial poets Ġhālib and Żauq reciting before a burning candle. For others, the post-independence period of the 1950s or the gatherings of the 1980s represented its apex. Against these imagined ideals, some of the magazine's surveyed readership critiqued today's poetry gatherings, their sponsors, and, most of all, their poets for the commercialization promoters and audience members brought to the events. These contemporary mushāʿirah critics, in sum, voiced ambivalences about lyric poetry's ease of circulation among less worthy classes.

Yet, the hierarchical yet inclusivist tendency of the mushāʿirah in the past was an integral constituent within Indo-Persian literary consumption and sociability, in addition to a frank grappling with its mercenary aspects. Poets of the early 1700s embraced the challenging sociability of the mushāʿirah's market for speech, attempting to meet the demands of popular and elite preferences while also adapting to rapidly changing style. Past versifiers thrived in a context that modern consumers today reject. Yet there may still be faint flickers today illuminating Urdu mushāʿirah's earliest history across time.

As it unfolded throughout the book, Delhi's writers gathered each year on Bedil's death anniversary to read verse from his collected works while elaborating literary ideas of their own. As we surveyed in this book, the stylistic and social developments at Bedil's graveside between 1720 and 1750 influenced and reflected larger shifts in literary sociability occurring within Delhi's mushāʿirah scene. These were changes that occurred in terms of social class and literary style. Over its thirty-year duration, Bedil's ʿurs mushāʿirah distinguished itself as a particularly dynamic and competitive space, even among the dozens of other poetry salons proliferating across Delhi at that time, such as those taking place at the Ornament of Mosques, Fīroz Shāh's fortress, and other celebrated locales featured in these pages. Between 1720 and 1750, Delhi's literary gatherings blossomed across a multitude of other spaces, such as at the abodes of poets and patrons and at shrines scattered across the city—all nourished by the words of new elites venturing to the Mughal capital. The mushāʿirah, implicitly, welcomed lettered and semi-lettered classes to gather, recite, and record ġhazals that framed memory and competition.

Between 1720 and 1750, new elites like Bedil, ʿAṭā, Maẓmūn, Ḥātim, and Saudā developed Delhi's mushāʿirah scene in a highly competitive multilingual literary setting. These poets and dozens of others cultivated a milieu of confrontational sociability by which they and their competitors were obliged to perform complex feats of originality, deftly welding new ideas together with tributes to past masters and references to one another's verse. Their newly minted ġhazals circulated in the city's open market for poetry, and the most successful among them circulated in recitations and diaries to redefine taste and language in Delhi. The market for speech imbued ġhazals with social capital; poets leveraged the gains gleaned by their verse to negotiate greater material rewards from wealthy patrons and, most importantly, secure notoriety in each other's eyes.

Through formal and informal channels of exchange, the circulation of ġhazals generated and strengthened associations for literate classes such as shared reputation with patrons, reverent ties with past masters, and heated rivalries with peers. But this was an uneven terrain. After public recitation at gatherings, couplets by writers of all ranks were repeated from memory not only by versifiers across various salons but also by a quotidian cast of characters, including would-be poets, shopkeepers, and coffee-house habitués, who passed along what they heard in streets and bazaars. Couplets also circulated in written form, such as in the diary entries of poetry aficionados and in copies of the formal dīwāns or taẕkirahs released by literary notables.

The dissemination and exchange of poetry established an urban social network etched in rhyme and meter for members of Delhi's literate classes, extending centuries back in time and stretching widely across the city's precincts. Through hints left behind within and between the ġhazals they exchanged with peers, eighteenth-century Delhi versifiers provided a means for today's historians to reconstruct various aspects of their gatherings. As demonstrated in each chapter of this book, poets encoded clues about the context, tone, and company at a given gathering in the way they retained and reworked formal elements in the ġhazal couplets exchanged with peers and past masters. By piecing together corresponding shards of meter, rhyme, and refrain scattered across diaries and dīwāns, and coupling these with anecdotes dotting chronicles and taẕkirahs, we recovered various layers of information about whom poets exchanged verse with, what they argued about, how they sounded and comported themselves, and what qualities they valued in the contentious and canorous mushāʿirah space.

The mushāʿirah-positioned view of the ġhazal's circulation provides a class-based perspective of literary history. To compete in a fast-paced ġhazal scene, Delhi's mid-1700s writers hastened to improvise new ideas and stylistic innovations to meet the demands of shifting tastes, fluctuating demographics, and shrinking patronage opportunities. Not all poets could face these difficulties, but the new elites that could reshaped Delhi's language economies through their opinions of poems by past masters. The city's literary salon culture pitted Delhi's living poets against each other while also calling another group of participants to the fore of competitive spaces—poets in absentia. Indeed, absent or dead poets from across the Persian-speaking world participated actively in Delhi's mid-1700s gatherings. When Delhi's secretaries, courtesans, or rural Sufi leaders invited the past masters they enjoyed into the salons through voicing key phrases or couplets associated with them, these absent figures authorized the language of the mushāʿirah. Invoked through emulative verse, the masters in their ghostly forms materialized in full force to legitimate metaphors, dare novice poets to one-up an image, and lament the perennial shortcomings of verse in ways that poets across the ages took personally to heart. When chosen for emulation at a mushāʿirah, a historical couplet authored by a particular master signaled shared social and artistic loyalties among versifiers who accepted the challenge of composing on its form. But these choices also demarcated class distinctions. The chosen verse offered poets a testing ground on which to demonstrate their skills and provided the means to establish and rework hierarchies among poets, both present and absent, through impromptu creative performance.

Our literary historical account of ġhazals in the context of their recitation and circulation reveals that the production and assessment of lyric poetry in Delhi's eighteenth-century mushāʿirah circuit was reliant on social context and connections between poets living and dead. Even for versifiers such as Nudrat and Saudā, who believed that they were conveying highly divergent values through their respective verse, the mushāʿirah context forced warring poets into similar postures and a "narcissism of small differences" based on how the salon's rules of poetic engagement mandated competitors to engage in overlapping emulations with one another and heed the same contemporary stylistic trends. This dynamic process of forging relationality and meaning making in close competition with worthy peers was practiced not only among the eighteenth-century poets in Mughal India considered in this book, but on a far wider scope; Persian-educated elites and semi-elites from Europe to Southeast Asia also traded poems authorized by past masters to establish linguistic hierarchies. As threaded throughout this book, Marshall Hodgson's "Persianate culture" concept sets the groundwork for understanding the myriad ways that concerns for hierarchy characterized Persianate public and literary social settings across many geographies.

Mushāʿirah poetry in early modern Delhi charted a highly localized history about the powers of literary speech. Hence, locality emerges in this book as a vital node for understanding how Delhi's poets defined taste and literary alliances. We saw how poets and their works bound themselves explicitly to specific neighborhoods, shrines, private homes, and public gathering spaces. Among our examples, Bedil's grave provided the most vivid case for how a salon space also served as a memorial, a meeting place, and a workshop for forging new verse associated with its particularities of place. Our work framing literature as an outgrowth of a spatially situated social practice in Mughal-era public culture demonstrates how the embedded production of sung, recited, and scribed ġhazals gave rise to a network of interlinked spaces constituting a popular literary marketplace with a flexible yet consequential ethos and code of behavior mirroring that found in the cacophonous world of the bazaar.

Charisma and networking were necessary ingredients for the making of successful mushāʿirah hosts, performers, documentarians, and, most crucially, for the verse itself. Buttressed by the status of their venerable mentor, Bedil's former students were highly significant actors the literary processes of networking with fellow notables during the three decades considered here. Between 1720 and 1750, the status of poets such as Muḳhliṣ (d. 1750), Ārzū (d. 1756), and Ḳhwushgo (d. 1757) each rose as patrons and historians in Delhi's market for speech; their names are among those most frequently cited in literary documentation of their peers. These three stars of Bedil's literary progeny hosted significant gatherings of their own and recorded their perspectives on the public literary history of their times in their respective taẕkirah projects, which together nearly frame the thirty-year expanse of this book's history. In addition to this triad of Bedil's stellar students, literary history was also made and documented by many so-called minor students of Bedil, such as the courtesan Babrī Rindī (fl. 1720–40) and the rapscallion ʿAṭā (d. 1724) considered in chapter 1, who each demonstrated sharp instincts for distinctive verse. The careers of Rindī and ʿAṭā illustrate how the competitive sociability formed in Delhi's gathering spaces held flexible notions of literary speech which could crucially encompass diverging registers, languages, and ideas.

The principal players we chose to visit in our tour across Delhi's middle 1700s mushāʿirah terrain were not the city's most famous versifiers. Rather, the routes we treaded followed so-called minor poets, allowing us to trace the significant and underappreciated contributions they made to a volatile literary market. Each of our supposedly minor poets presented an inviting emulation or significant turn of phrase that rerouted our journey through the market for speech and thereby Delhi's literary history as recorded in taẕkirahs, dīwāns, diaries, chronicles, and commonplace books. Influential past masters of 1600s such as Walī and Ṣāʾib continued to impact the ġhazal, but it was Maẓmūn the Seedless Poet and his adroit reḳhtah abilities and appreciation for complex Persian literature that greatly influenced a junior entourage at the Ornament of Mosques, demonstrating that even minor writers shaped ġhazal conventions from below.

As such, the scenes of poetry exchange featured in our sojourn contrast strikingly with the standard sketch of the mushāʿirah that was popularized by early twentieth-century historians but still enshrined today. In this ideal-type gathering, as epitomized by Farḥatullāh Beg's novella "The Last Candle of Delhi," poets with perfectly kept beards and erect spines sat staidly in carefully orchestrated circles, passing a candle to one another like a talking stick as each politely took his turn to perform.[2] As opposed to this peaceful image, evidence gathered in this book indicates that poetry salons were fueled by a flexible sense of comportment, which at times celebrated discord as much as order, and which welcomed unrestrained floods of verse, which were sometimes released heatedly and considered peripheral by canonical standards. However spitefully flung about, the impassioned words of dueling poets held great social significance and evinced remarkable virtuosity, especially given that they were often composed on a spur-of-the-moment basis by poets scrambling to defend their dignity. The supposedly minor versifiers who take center stage in this book provide the most effective guides for accessing distant mushāʿirahs of the past. Poets such as Ḥātim, Nudrat, Maẓmūn, Girāmī, and ʿAṭā incorporated a wide range of forms, styles, and modes of comportment into their recitations through the emulations they performed, enabling us to reconstruct remote branches of Delhi's poetry networks from clues left behind in their often-overlooked mushāʿirah-based poetry.

We have lost access to the majority of those ġhazals composed at Bedil's grave or at other locales we visited in this tour of Delhi's mushāʿirahs. Some were not written down, and the texts sheltering others were not preserved. Likewise, we can no longer physically visit many of the legendary sites in which these poems were composed and recited. The exact coordinates mapping the poet-saint's tomb have been lost for two and a half centuries. Amīr Ḳhān's mansion, featured as a site where multitudes of famous poets took the stage in chapter 3, no longer stands. The Ornament of Mosques remains intact, although now hemmed in by densely packed buildings that block its view over the Yamuna River. It might still yet offer an inviting setting for exchanging verse. Fīroz Shāh's fortress stands as an archeological site contested by modern religious reformers and, according to some Muslims who use it as a place for prayer, houses a bureaucracy of *jinns* (spirits) who might be willing to help convey their appeals to the divine.[3] Even so, we would no longer be likely to find noisy Naqshbandis there, reciting verse with Qabūl's "unsatisfied īhām." When poets ceased gathering in a certain location, the impression of the literary styles they developed in that context began shifting from living memory to pages of taẕkirahs or diaries. This transposition from gossip, rumor, and conversation to writing altered the shape and scope of poets' distinctions. The immediacy of the embodied and localized mushāʿirah was condensed into rhetorical conventions that, although preserving the text, provided only glimpses of the context for shouted, sung, and debated verse.

The absence of gathering spaces for poetry recitation in present-day Delhi leads one to wonder whether something of the mushāʿirah's history that may have been preserved through situated reiteration has been erased. This is especially the case when considering that the dominant, mass-mediated iteration of the mushāʿirah today is no longer structured by rhyme, refrain, and meter. Looking back, contemporary mushāʿirah audiences classify the early modern gatherings centered in this book as *ṭarḥī mushāʿare* (patterned mushāʿirahs), a categorization that emerged only in the late nineteenth century. The concept *ṭarḥī mushāʿarah* now indicates a kind of gathering in which poets presented verse according to a set of shared formal parameters as defined by the *ṭarḥ* (base, model, sketch) that oriented all recitations. For example, the ring-dove motif grounded the compositions of many poets who exchanged verse structured upon it in dialogue with one another.

Nearly every couplet presented in our tour of Delhi's gatherings would fall under this *ṭarḥī-mushāʿarah* classification. Yet, for the eighteenth-century poets we befriended in this book, the *ṭarḥī-mushāʿarah* note would be dismissed as an empty signifier, needlessly marking the unmarked, because all poetry in their tradition would be composed this way. In the 1700s, the *ṭarḥ* almost ubiquitously offered a shared starting point for poets to compose upon, but its presence in a gathering in no way differentiated poetry composed according to a singular modality for crafting verse. As late seventeenth-century poetry master Nāṣir ʿAlī Sirhindī noted, "the test of the poet is the ġhazal's *ṭarḥ*."[4]

Despite the many stylistic shifts that occurred in Delhi's salons over the thirty-year period considered in this book, the use of the *tarḥ* remained constant, and this practice continued late into the nineteenth century. Despite the *tarḥ*'s omnipresence over the course of the mushaʿirah's most formative decades, its use is nearly absent from salon exchanges across the Persianate world of today. As documented by Ali Khan Mahmudabad, the use of the *tarḥ* declined beginning in the late 1800s.[5] Indeed, *ṭarḥī mushāʿarahs* occur only in a minority of specialized, small, and less popular gatherings, known as *nashisteñ* (sittings) in Urdu. These contemporary *ṭarḥī mushāʿarahs* occur only in places where Urdu is spoken, including South Asia and in cities across the Urdu-speaking diaspora from Dubai to Dallas.[6] In South Asia, these include affairs held for specific occasions such as mushāʿirahs convened for Sufi saints (*manqabatī mushāʿare*) or to praise the Prophet (*naʿtiyah mushāʿare*). In these cases, a model verse (*ṭarḥ*) circulates among invited poets who craft compositions beforehand to then read aloud in a shrine space in front of an audience at an auditorium, or simply at a private residence. Examples of these can easily be found on YouTube and sometimes also can be observed virtually in real time in correspondence gatherings taking place on message boards as poets post their responses.

Despite the ṭarḥ's absence and other significant differences, today's mushāʿirah still invests significant power in words. The contemporary Persianate market for speech is still buffeted by meaning's fluctuating value as conveyed via recited words, decorously presented amid mushāʿirah poets who themselves circulate, record, and critique the verse they consume. Literary styles and poets' clashes come and go, but some remnants of the ethos of Delhi's mid-1700s gatherings continue until today, propelled by the institution's unique form of popular literary sociability that emerged in the times and places covered by this book.

That most contemporary Urdu poets no longer follow formal aspects so closely lead some to declaim that there is a recession of literary style and loss of literary knowledge in Urdu poetry and poetics. When I was discussing my interests in the mushāʿirah and its unique form of competitiveness at a conference, a senior scholar of Urdu literature told me it seemed that I was intrigued by ugly poetry. That might appear to be the case, considering the nontraditional approach that I take in this book with Urdu and Persian verse and its performance, studying intricately crafted devotional poetry and highly technical defensive verse alongside what might be akin to spontaneous, rhymed dirty jokes. In my response to that comment, I mentioned that I found mushāʿirah verse socially significant and therefore intellectually fulfilling. Indeed, wide audiences still enthusiastically value what today's Urdu poetry salon has to offer.

The mushāʿirah scene today forms the beating heart of contemporary Urdu literary entertainment. It is a crowded field with a global impact. On stages across South Asia, the Middle East, and beyond, conveners inaugurate events by ceremoniously lighting candles before mushāʿirah performers who sing, shout, and recite poetry for audiences of thousands. Mushāʿirahs also continue to be performed within intimate settings with only a few dozen people present. Within this varied landscape, technology has proven instrumental in broadening the mushāʿirah's impact. Announcers introduce poets on public address systems, and audience members use recording technologies to document verse, which they then circulate widely on cell phones and websites. Before the internet age, mushāʿirah poetry was disseminated via optical discs, cassettes, and CDs. Circulation via television, radio, and newsprint continues.

The mass-mediated aspect of the contemporary mushāʿirah and the role of technology in broadcasting its verse give the appearance that everything has changed in the poetry salon between the middle 1700s and today. This view is compounded by the *ṭarḥ*'s absence and an associated loss of shared meter, rhyme, and refrain in mushāʿirahpoets' exchanges. Yet a closer analysis demonstrates strong continuities bridging mushāʿirahs across time. For example, the mushāʿirah institution today churns out couplets at a rate that would be met with delight and awe by the early modern taẕkirah writers we met in Delhi. Historians such as Ḳhwushgo, Ārzū, and Muṣḥafī measured their subjects' dīwāns according to quantities, recording how writers produced tens of thousands or hundreds of thousands of couplets in their collected works, a mark of literary accomplishment gauged in economic proportions.

Evidence compiled in this book decisively overturns the dominant narrative about the evolution of modern Urdu poetry, and the economic dimensions of the mushāʿirah specifically. Such stories about how the mushāʿirah changed through time usually begin in the nineteenth century. They trace a trajectory in which the mushāʿirah tradition moved from the Mughal court to the public square through the printing press and other mass-mediated technologies that circulated ideas in colonial India, a setting considered by C. A. Bayly.[7] The career of patron, writer, and printing press proprietor Karīm ud-Dīn Maġhfūr (fl. 1840–60) is often broached to illustrate this process of transformation. Despite having a personal distaste for poets, Karīm ud-Dīn hoped to host regular poetry gatherings at his shop, and then to release a weekly imprint of the verses produced and recited there.[8] So too, newspapers such as *Dihlī Urdū Aḳhbār* (The Delhi Urdu News) and Lahore's *Koh-e Nūr* (The Mountain of Light) released models (*ṭarḥ*) for poets to emulate, while publishing poems by local writers and popular poets of the past. In this telling of its history, Urdu literature, and mushāʿirah poetry specifically, acquired their modern forms through colonial intervention and technological change—a story no different than that told about many other performance traditions. This narrative, however, neglects to consider the dynamics of the premodern marketplace in which patrons, poets, and documentarians wedded together literature with capital, a fusion closely considered by Shahzad Bashir and Abhishek Kaicker in their respective works about the early modern Persianate world. As Bashir notes, taẕkirahs captured methods for assessing verse. For Delhi in the 1700s, literary production became tied to the glut of New

World silver buttressing the Indian economy, as noted by Kaicker, a facet compounded by fewer options for patronage.[9]

For the wider Persian-speaking world, a vast literary marketplace fueled by millions of couplets circulated on cheap and readily available paper, among public performers, via the steel-trap memories of master poets, and through the voices of everyday minor poets who worked as merchants, clerics, and secretaries. In this regard, the dominant idea that the mushāʿirah moved its center from its starting place at the court to the public square can be reversed. The first Mughal emperor to host an institutionalized mushāʿirah that included elements of the salon culture we have witnessed in this book was Shah Alam II (r. 1760–1806). His court adopted a tradition initially propagated in Delhi's public square, within and across the mosques, coffeehouses, shrines, and streets of the city. Indeed, the mushāʿirah did not move from the court to the public square, but rather the Mughal court incorporated selective aspects of a preexisting raucous, shared literary marketplace into its rarified and exclusive interiors.

Thus, when critics complain about the commercialization of the mushāʿirah or condemn its poets for pandering to popular sentiment, they are unwittingly criticizing features of the institution that have perennially been deemed as the primary marker of the mushāʿirah's success—the currency and popular appeal of its verse. The mushāʿirah began as a popular platform governed by an appetite for originality and incessant demand for new material. Today's Urdu market demands that poetry be produced at near industrial scale for a marketplace of discerning consumers. But instead of tażkirahs, the verses circulate on files traded between cell phones and corresponding websites that host recordings (YouTube most notably). Through these means, memory cards, cell phones, and virtual platforms house an exponentially expanding archive of popular Urdu poetry that is exhaustive in its ambition for documentation. In this rhizomatic digital archive, recordings of large stadium-sized mushāʿirahs with world-famous poets appear alongside videos of small, informal gatherings with versifiers only recognizable as poets to those who attended the event. Curiously, digital media and the miniaturized technology that carries such data share much in common with tażkirah writing of the past: just like digital documenters of today, tażkirah authors sought to capture the totality of a popular literary marketplace that accounted for a variety of conflicting tastes, a diversity of style, and a similarly crowded arena of poets.

As it was centuries ago, the advent of a popular verse can still suddenly challenge the terms of literary taste for consumers. One line of poetry that resonates deeply with audiences can potentially upset established hierarchies of distinction. In this regard, there is no need for an entire dīwān to establish a poet's reputation. Few mushāʿirah poets today have them. In fact, over time, only a minority of poets produced dīwāns, a fact reinforced by the thousands of now largely unknown poets whose names and a mere line or two appear in taẕkirahs of the 1700s and before. That something so emotive and enjoyable can be so easily accessed in miniature form—only two lines at most!—draws our attention to how mushāʿirah literature both instantiates hierarchies and breaks them down. In the performance setting of the contemporary mushāʿirah, Urdu speakers refer to the instance in which a poet's novel verse upstages more familiar recitation as "to loot the mushāʿirah" (*mushāʿarah lūṭnā*). Although always on the lookout for something new, adoring fans in mushāʿirah performances also demand to hear the hits, the well-known lines requested through shouts or a note passed on to the stage. Good poets oblige their audiences by reciting well-loved lines to uproarious cheers but also challenge them to welcome new verse.

As it was in the mid-1700s, the sheer volume of the work produced by today's mushāʿirah poets exceeds the capacity for containment by any systematic organizational schema. We find that most popular verses produced today, like many delightful compositions of the past, fail to find secure homes in the Urdu and Persian literary canons. The mushāʿirah, as a popular stage for literature across time, produces texts and connections that do not fit neatly into conventional categories of modern literary history and thus possess an ephemeral quality. The YouTube sphere of Urdu poetry, like the taẕkirah tradition of the early modern era, does not conform to canons as formulated in the nineteenth century, even though YouTube has become so crucial for Urdu literature documentation, teaching, and entertainment. Yet, just like the way that many mushāʿirah poets in the contemporary era fail to secure lasting fame, many of the minor mushāʿirah poets of Delhi's 1700s find no place in the contemporary Urdu canon. For the 1700s poets, this lack of popular recognition today relates not only to the fact that they wrote in Persian but also to the way their work eludes neat authorial boundaries. Indeed, Persian poets of Delhi's 1700s are also absent from the Persian canon even though Indian writers comprised the overwhelming majority of pen pushers and composed the largest trove of texts during that era.

Throughout this book, we witnessed how mid-1700s Delhi poets innovated variations in style to convey multifaceted literary identities and ideas about belonging and association. Poets in the middle 1700s framed their ideas about belonging according to emulations of past masters, contemporary allegiances to noted teachers, and regular associations with friendly competitors and contentious colleagues. These were processes by which distinction formed a foundation for a highly localized sense of literary exchanges that were framed in hierarchies of accomplishment and in dialogue with a wider knowledge of the Persianate literary past. Like their predecessors centuries earlier, mushāʿirah poets in the contemporary era continue to voice multiple aspects of South Asian Muslim identity through their verse, yet they tend to convey identarian ideas in more overt and explicit terms, as demonstrated by the recent work of literary historian Ali Khan Mahmudabad. For early modern mushāʿirahs, poets' political identity emerged as a means of expressing distinction outside of conventional realms of hierarchy. While Persianate cultures in general and Indo-Muslim culture specifically champion notions of hierarchy in dialogue with the past, the public realms of Urdu and Persian's literary sociability complicated collective rankings through individual means of promoting distinction.

In contrast to the relatively inclusive scope of Delhi's 1700s poetry salon, Muslim minorities from lower classes are more readily excluded from metropolitan stages in the highly elite realms of conventional mushāʿirahs today. But they are the consumers we must focus on. Local media companies capture mushāʿirah performances by lower-status poets and release them on to YouTube and subscribers' cell phones. This produces an alternative archive of Urdu literature that remains largely untapped due to the class bigotries that prevent literary historians from acknowledging local mushāʿirah couplets as rising to the level of literature. This lacuna among elite consumers is particularly odd from a marketing perspective. Indeed, the lower-class demographic of Muslims comprises the bulk of mushāʿirah audiences and poets today, as madrasahs in towns and cities across India have maintained Urdu and Persian curricula, many times for members of the lower classes. Locals with these common and profound educations in the Islamicate humanities would be the ideal demographic from which to expand the circulation of contemporary Urdu poetry. They should be leading the routes of Urdu style and charting its history, not excluded from it.

The exclusions we find in literary history today are related. That is, class and style differences create perceptual barriers for elite consumers, prompting Urdu literary historians to misrecognize past connections and therefore misunderstand mushāʿirah-influenced literatures. Prevailing wisdom argues that due to the absence of sonic recording technology in the past, we cannot know what went on in early mushāʿirahs. Perhaps, also, it is implied with this approach that Islamicate historical practices were not sufficiently attuned to capture tonal dimensions of conversations, recitations, and other performative aspects of intellectual life—the kind of social history well documented in European accounts of its own early modern salon culture.[10] Yet, the dominant narrative about premodern salons also argues that mushāʿirahs were ubiquitous, a facet romanticized by India's intellectuals of the late 1800s and early 1900s. Indeed, noted poets in the middle 1700s hosted weekly gatherings, and an eager Delhi poet could visit a mushāʿirah every night of the week—their quantities of ġhazals produced at scale certainly demonstrate this fact.

Just like gatherings today, mushāʿirahs of the past generated thousands of couplets every year. The pen wielders of the past were eager documentarians in the literacy-aware society of India in which paper, ink, and quill were also abundant. The voice and the page formed a continuum in a process for capturing mushāʿirah-based memories in couplets and anecdotes, producing a surplus of love lyrics that flooded collected works, diaries, and histories written by the Persian-educated elites of Delhi. Thus, the contradiction should be apparent: to recover a complex multi-dimensional record of what went on in gatherings, we turn to the sources that captured couplets on the page. Tażkirahs and dīwāns, as demonstrated here, provide such evidence, but the scribal practices and adept memories of poets serve as the basis for such texts.

These exclusions continue to appear contradictory in the current mushāʿirah scene. For the Urdu literary world today, it is damning to be called a mushāʿirah poet (*mushāʿare kā shāʿir*), an appellation that implies a versifier seeks public approval instead of literary depth. Such a label is highly contradictory because it places little value on poets and their words, stations held to be at the pinnacle of Islamicate verbal arts.[11] Further, by reaching millions of listeners, today's Urdu mushāʿirah currently does more than any other institution to promote literature and language across the planet, reaching deeper and wider than any university, website, cultural foundation, or academic book. The poetry salon today, as it did in the past, achieves this hold on the globe by perpetuating the abiding aesthetic value that poetry be "understood by the public and approved by elites" (*ʿāmm fahm wa ḳhāṣṣ pasand*). Through their literary speech and character, today's mushāʿirah poets continue to exemplify the hierarchical yet inclusive form of sociability at focus in this book. A verse recited in an auditorium, heard from a recording, or read aloud from someone's notes conjures for the consumer both the delight of linguistic play and the emotional pull of memory.

Why would a skilled craftsman who produces words with such artistic and emotional depth be valued so little, such that the moniker "mushāʿirah poet" itself currently constitutes an insult? Why wouldn't those who produce the largest poetry platform on the planet be granted a higher status in the dominant imagination? A clue to unpacking this mystery was provided to me one evening in 2012 when I was visiting Muzaffarnagar, a city about one hundred kilometers north and east of Delhi. My two hosts, deliberately unnamed mushāʿirah poets, drew me into a debate with them in the back of a rickshaw as we pulled away from the mushāʿirah we had just attended. They were arguing about how to define the difference between fame and popularity. The concerns they expressed over boundary formation in shaping distinction and style seemed to correspond with the preoccupations of poets in the middle 1700s.

One stated, "Poets can rest their whole careers on one couplet." To illustrate, he recited a famous line by one of the top mushāʿirah poets of the day:

> Allah, may the blessings of my subsistence never depart.
> For two days, there has not been a single guest in my home.

> *allāh mere rizq kī barkat nah chalī jāʾe*
> *do roz se ghar meñ koʾī mihmān nahīñ hai*

On the other side of me, the second poet responded, "You don't even need a couplet. You can grow famous on merely one line." My sense was the two poets in the rickshaw were dismissive of such popular verse but also envious of the fame that the humble, yet evocative lines recited by the first poet had garnered for its author. Mushāʿirah poetry still generates power for those who compose and circulate it, and mushāʿirah poets continue crafting an artistry that builds meaning on the metered speech of past masters while linking itself to charisma and memories of place. As a famous mushāʿirah poet notes in one line:

> The havelis of the past even now are not derelict.

> *māẓī kī ḥawelī abhī vīrān nahīñ hai*

We still require the artistic and memorable words of mushāʿirah poets to shape taste as they did in the past, producing a couplet that could rewrite histories through uncharted routes and distant connections. Indeed, there are more than a few hopeful candles lit for the hundreds of mushāʿirahs happening today across South Asia and the Middle East, linking poets to each other and to the past through the contentious and profitable exchange of verse.

Acknowledgments

My initial interest in Urdu mushāʿirahs arose from attending them as a language student in Lucknow, India, and over the years I've accrued many debts while researching and writing about this vast and complex tradition. While traveling between Lucknow, Muzaffarnagar, and Delhi, friends and mentors such as Syed Asghar Wajahat and Rehman Musawwir shared with me their writings, friendship, and wisdom. My interests in the performed mushāʿirah brought me to focus on Muzaffarnagar, where the city's poets and aficionados educated me on the competitive and delightful boundaries of contemporary Urdu poetry. These include Tanveer Gauhar, Rifat Jamal, Avtar Narayan Kaul, I. H. Najm, Husain Ahmad Qasmi, Kaleem Qasmi, Ashok Sahil, Abdul Haq Sahr, Kavyitri Khushboo Sharma, Ayaz Ahmad Talib, and Saleem Tyagi.

As my project morphed from an ethnographic into a historical study, I relied on advice and encouragement from Kamran Ali, Samer Ali, Katherine Butler Schofield, Indrani Chatterjee, Kathryn Hansen, Syed Akbar Hyder, Gail Minault, Farina Mir, Afsar Mohammed, C. M. Naim, Francesca Orsini, Carla Petievich, and Frances Pritchett, whose guidance and scholarship have informed my approach to Urdu literature's pasts while encouraging my pursuit of topics at the margins of the discipline. From the University of Texas at Austin, friends and colleagues pushed me toward new avenues in the study of South Asian language, history, and social linguistics. Dean Accardi, Asiya Alam, Gregory Maxwell Bruce, Charlotte Giles, Namrata Kanchan, Peter Knapczyk, Mathangi Krishnamurthy, Elliot McCarter, Daniel Majchrowicz, Timsal Masud, Raisur-Rahman, Mubashir Rizvi, John Schaefer, and Nikki Seifert continue to be fantastic peers although we are now scattered far beyond the Lone Star State.

Over the past decade, conferences, research trips, symposiums, and hundreds of emails connected me with colleagues who have generously tolerated my quirky approach to South Asian history and literature. These include David Boyk, Shounak Ghosh, Sara Grewal, Usman Hamid, Emma Kalb, Pasha M. Khan, Razak Khan, Mana Kia, Baqar Mehdi, Daniel Morgan, Thomas Parsa, Heidi Pauwels, A. Sean Pue, Yael Rice, Zahra Sabri, Kevin L. Schwartz, Richard Williams, and James White. Most notably, Max Bruce, Purnima Dhavan, Arthur Dudney, Walter Hakala, and Peter Knapczyk have open-handedly shared with me many of their insights on history and literature in the eighteenth century as it framed the Mughal world.

At Western Michigan University, local medievalists and fellow early modernists have supported my development as an educator on and researcher of the premodern world, contributing their perspectives from European contexts through gatherings at the Medieval Institute and the International Congress on Medieval Studies. These include Robert Berkhofer III, Marion W. Gray, Marjorie Harrington, Mallory Heslinger, David Kutzko, Natalio Ohanna, James Palmitessa, Larry Simon, Anise Strong, and Susan Steuer. Beyond the Medieval Institute, I am thankful to have supportive colleagues in the Department of History whose work and conversations have taught me a tremendous amount, including David Benac, Andrea Berto, Amos Beyan, Linda Borish, Sally Hadden, Mitch Kachun, Evan Kutzler, Ángela Pérez-Villa, Lewis Pyenson, Michael Nassaney, Eli Rubin, John Saillant, Bill Warren, Victor Xiong, and Takashi Yoshida. I am also grateful to Carla Koretsky for her consistent encouragement and support. The curiosity about the Islamicate past expressed by my WMU community has provided an enticing welcome for me into the mix of medieval studies and history at WMU.

Colleagues from the Great Lakes Adiban Society have fostered a welcoming community of Midwestern scholars focused on premodern Islamicate literatures. Connecting those of us in Michigan, Illinois, and Indiana, the rigorous approaches of these scholars to language and history have inspired me at our annual workshops and panels at the International Congress on Medieval Studies where I have benefited from adiban-based input on various writing that eventually culminated in this book. The adiban include Samer Ali, Yoni Brack, Cameron Cross, Shahla Farghadani, Kaveh Hemmat, Franklin Lewis, Chad Lingwood, Paul Losensky, Karla Mallette, Michael Pifer, and Jennifer Tobkin. Among the adiban, Shaahin Pishbin deserves special thanks for directing me to ʿAṭā's references in Bedil's diary.

Financial support for research on this project has been furnished by the WMU History Department Burnham-Macmillan Endowment, the Wenner-Gren Foundation, and United States Department of Education Fulbright Program. Access to manuscripts, catalogues, and imaging were key for both the early and later forms of the project as it took shape. Mette Vorraa at the Bodleian Libraries helped me secure imaging of Ummīd's dīwān. At the British Library, Ursula Sims-Williams, Dorian Leveque, and Andrew Gough facilitated my visits and helped with references and manuscript imaging. Jake Benson of the John Rylands Research Institute and Library answered my questions regarding the digital offerings he has catalogued and made available. Imtiaz Ahmad at Khuda Bakhsh Oriental Public Library facilitated my access to *guldastahs*, tażkirahs, and other Persian and Urdu holdings. Nizamuddin Dihlavi at the Kutubḳhānah-e Anjuman-e Taraqqī-e Urdū played an important role in securing rare Urdu and Persian print materials. Charlotte Giles at the Library of Congress supplied images and reference information for several rare *bayāẓs*. The University of Michigan Library generously provided me access to databases and its vast collection of Persian and Urdu holdings. At WMU's Waldo Library, Julie Hayward secured out-of-the-way sources from various US libraries and endured my late returns. The talented Jason Glatz patiently redrew multiple drafts of a Delhi map to help me reconstruct a city long since disappeared.

The Islamic Civilization and Muslim Networks series at the University of North Carolina Press was my top choice for this project, first recommended to me by A. Sean Pue. I am indebted to the series editors Bruce B. Lawrence and Carl W. Ernst for supporting what they called my "provocative approach" to a unique group of poets from Delhi's alleys and salons. Senior executive editor Mark Simpson-Vos has been a key advocate of *City of Lyrics*, providing direction, patience, and humor. I am grateful to Thomas Bedenbaugh, Valerie Burton, Madge Duffey, Cate Hodorowicz, and Tara Jordan for assistance with the many details of finalizing this project. Copyeditor Katherine Dhurandhar and production editor Mary Ribesky carefully attended to the manuscript's challenging typographic terrain. David Boyk brought his attention to detail and deep linguistic knowledge to the book's proofs, making an involved task delightful. Finally, I give special thanks to the anonymous reviewers for their criticisms, suggestions, and direction that have improved the work in ways I could not have foreseen.

Comfort in the form of food, travel, companionship, and meaningful distractions came from friends and family members scattered between California, India, Morocco, Michigan, Long Island, and Texas. They include Samer Ali, Zarinah El-Amin, Eric Archer, the Birdseed Salesmen, Linda Borish, Summer Davis and Michael Ashburn, Dawud Clark and Zakiyyah Hajj, Mark Crain and Hazel Gómez, Souad Eddouada, James Gavan, Mitch Kachun and Karen Libman, Todd Kuchta, Irma López and Benjamin Jones, George and Barbara Marsh, Bill Meyer and Clara Lawrence, Jodi Hope Michaels and Natalio Ohanna, Ann Miles and Rich McMullen, Rich and Sue Munda, Hafiz Nauman Akbar, Sonya and Norman Perkins, Stephen Williams, Helen Yee and Matthew Fries, the Pandey and the Ziai families of Jaipur, my parents Jeanette Tabor and Douglas Tabor, and, finally, my brother Blaine Tabor—I could not have done this without his love and friendship.

There are three final people who, in their own ways, shaped this project from its inception. In Lucknow, Shiba Iftikhar introduced me to Farḥatullāh Beg's *Dillī kī Āḳhrī Shamaʿ*, guiding me through this unique novella and informing my love for translating and recasting mushāʿirah anecdotes. Syed Akbar Hyder has been a steadfast supporter of my work from our first meeting at UT Austin, and he has offered me a crucial model for writing about South Asia in a way that takes risks and considers new narratives. Were it not for his suggestion to study the mushāʿirah there would be no "city of lyrics" in my own scholarship, and I think of him with every translation I attempt. Alisa Perkins and I began talking about Muslim cultures in India and Morocco during our first date, and we have kept this conversation going as we've moved between dozens of cities across two continents over nearly twenty years of marriage. Our love continues to grow as we find new connections.

Notes

Prologue

1. Namokaar Channels Pvt Ltd, "11 January 2018 || Shabeena Adeeb || Lal Quila Mushaira || All India Republic Day || Urdu Academy," YouTube, accessed May 1, 2020, https://youtu.be/o4snMwTvGoQ?si=cAkNXFxpCwZoTQdx&t=690.

2. One variation of the second line frequently recited by Adeeb goes, "The [Hindu] Festival of Lights has come, and every street was festooned. I, too, will decorate my home if you say so" (*ā'ī dīpāvalī saj ga'ī har galī maiñ bhī ghar ko sajā dūñ agar tum kaho*).

3. Throughout the book I refer to mushāʿirahs as gatherings, salons, assemblies, and poetry competitions. The Arabic-language word *mushāʿarah* is a reciprocal noun that in Persian and Urdu connotes gathering together for recitation to battle one another, cited in *Luġhatnāmah-e Dihḳhudā*, comp. ʿAlī Akbar Dihḳhudā (Tehran: Mu'assisah-e Luġhatnāmah-e Dihḳhudā, 2020 [1399 SH]), s.v. *mushāʿarah*, https://dehkhoda.ut.ac.ir/fa/dictionary/detail/340730?title=%D9%85%D8%B4%D8%A7%D8%B9%D8%B1%D9%87; *Farhang-e Āṣafiyyah*, comp. Sayyid Aḥmad Dihlavī, 4 vols. (Lahore: Maṭbaʿ-e Rifāh-e ʿĀmm Press, 1908), s.v. *mushāʿarah*.

4. For a discussion of rural mushāʿirahs as they connect classes today and in the past, see Tabor, "Local Apocalypse."

5. Muṣḥafī, "Taẕkirah," fol. 2b.

Introduction

1. For a the mushāʿirah as a poetry contest, see Naim, "Audience Interaction," 108. Cf. "tournaments of value" in Appadurai, "Politics of Value," 22–23, 59nn5–7.

2. Bashir, *Market in Poetry*, 73.

3. On Bedil's tomb and its gatherings, see Tabor, "Heartless"; Keshavmurthy, "Circling the Shrines"; Ḳhalīl, "ʿUrs." For Bedil's biography, see ʿAbd ul-Ġhanī, *Life of Bedil*; Hadi, *Mirzā Bedil*; Ahsanuzzafar, *Mirzā Bedil*; Siddiqi, "Bīdel." For discussions of Bedil's literary contributions in wider contexts, see Keshavmurthy, *Persian Authorship*; Mikkelson, "Parrots and Crows"; Mikkelson, "Flights"; Schwartz, "Transregional Poet."

4. As in the case of ʿAbd ul-Qādir *Bedil* (The One who Lost his Heart), poets were primarily known by a nom de plume or *taḳhalluṣ*, and this tradition is maintained in the present text. The first occurrence of a poet's *taḳhalluṣ* appears italicized followed by a parenthetic gloss to provide non-specialist readers with access to the variety, color, and creativity of pen names, a convention established in Bruijn, "Name of the Poet," 45–46.

5. Binbaş, *Intellectual Networks*, 3–15. For early Timurid impact on India's multilingual setting, see Orsini and Sheikh, *After Timur Left*.

6. On Mughal court poetry and its patronage, see Losensky, *Welcoming Fighānī*, 137–45; Sharma, *Mughal Arcadia*, 54–58, 99–100, 143–55; Hasan, *Mughal Poetry*; ʿAbd ul-Ġhanī, *Persian at the Mughal Court*; Ahmad, "Ṣafawid Poets." Shiblī Nuʿmānī claimed that literary culture of the 1600s, in particular, promoted the mushāʿirah, noted in *ʿAjam*, 3:17.

7. Alam, *Political Islam*, 168–89; Alam, *Crisis of Empire*, xxxiii–xxxv. See also, Chandra, *Parties and Politics*, 6. For a review of the intellectual turn in eighteenth-century historical studies, see Parthasarathi, "South Asia," 553–55.

8. Hasan, "Forms of Civility," 99–105. Also, Hasan, *Paper, Performance*, 64–65. Jamal Malik frames the mushāʿirah (circa 1700s) as a consensus-building institution of "alternative modernity" in "Muslim Culture," 239–42.

9. Kaicker, *The King and the People*, 133.

10. Shād ʿAẓīmābādī, *Ḥayāt*, 165–66. In nineteenth-century Lucknow, if Mirzā Ḳhwānī Nawāzish recited a ġhazal "in a mushāʿirah with a special glance or gesture, the lines would keep circulating orally for a time as people would recite the poem and praise it," as noted in Masʿūd, *Marṡiyah Ḳhwānī*, 2. On reciters outpacing poets, see Khan, *Broken Spell*, 258.

11. See "bazaar-style information economy" in Appadurai, "Politics of Value," 43–44.

12. Bayly, *Empire and Information*, 190–99.

13. Instead of widening its scope, my approach to the Persianate engages writers in a specific time and place, delimiting "vertical" geographical frontiers and widening "horizontal" social boundaries. For horizontal geographies and vertical social frontiers, see Green, "Introduction," 1.

14. For sociability as a "play-form" of association and ethics, see Simmel, "Sociability," 255, 260–61. For comparative early modern European contexts, see Lilti, *World of the Salons*, a revisionist history of the French "salon" that focuses on how sociability produces power, and Schellenberg, *Literary Coteries*, which considers material enactments of Anglophone sociability.

15. Ali, *Literary Salons*, 25–27, 32–36, 104–5.

16. Pfeifer, *Salons*, 8, 18, 40.

17. Flatt, *The Courts*, 109–14. On the "Persianate flowering" of the 1500s, see Hodgson, *Venture*, 2:315, 490, 511 and 3:349–350.

18. Pauwels, "Soirées," 4–5, 9–10, 11.

19. Beg, *Āḳhrī Shamaʿ*, 46–47. For a translation, see Qamber, *Last Musha'irah*. For other historical fictive settings, see Mir, *Murder*; Faruqi, *Kaʾī Chānd*, 251–58; Faruqi, *The Sun*, 315–20; Faruqi, *Sawār*, 207–10.

20. Sarvar Taunsvī, *Mushāʿare*, 11. For Iḥsānī's mushāʿirah reporting, see *Āl Inḍiyā*.

21. Zaidī, *Tārīḳh*, 75.

22. Naim, "Audience Interaction," 112–13. See also "umpire" in Bashir, *Market in Poetry*, 17.

23. Pritchett, *Nets of Awareness*, 77; Pritchett, "Long History 2," 870, 892–94.

24. Mahmudabad, *Poetry of Belonging*, 19, 38.

25. Zaidī, *Tārīkh*, 31, 49–58.

26. For early modern India, see Kaicker, "Promises and Perils"; Busch, *Poetry of Kings*.

27. Kaicker, *The King and the People*, 123–34; Umar, *Urban Culture*, 45–47.

28. C. A. Bayly in *Empire and Information*, 196, notes that the market metaphor applied to the whole Mughal empire according to Tassy, *Histoire*, 1:136.

29. For a history of eighteenth-century Delhi, see Umar, *Muslim Society*, 593–637. On Delhi's political structure legitimating language, see Hakala, *Negotiating Languages*, 97. For Islamic cities and geographies, see Jayyusi et al., *City in the Islamic World*.

30. Blake, *Shahjahanabad*, 11; Jackson, *Delhi Sultanate*, 155.

31. Dudney, *Delhi*, 133–37.

32. Hodgson, *Venture*, 2:293.

33. Kia, *Persianate Selves*, 45–53, 196–98.

34. Flatt, *The Courts*, 3, 12–15. See also Eaton, *Persianate Age*, 10–11.

35. Zhang, "Judaeo-Persian," 114–16. For Jewish communities in Ghazna and Bamiyan, see Haim, "Early Judeo-Persian," 106.

36. On scribal cultures and paper in the Islamic world, see Bloom, *Paper before Print*, 46–89; Shatzmiller, "Adoption of Paper."

37. For Islam as first global culture, see Cook, "Islam."

38. On the Mongol exchange, see Favereau, *The Horde*, 164–205.

39. On the Mongol state and Sufi brotherhoods, see Deweese, "Islamization," 123–25; Rahimi, "Consolidation," 312, 317–18, 325. Regarding popular Islam in urban working classes, see Karamustafa, *Unruly Friends*, 8–13, 23–28; Ridgeon, "The Felon, the Faithful and the Fighter."

40. Guha, "Perso-Indian World," 448–49. For the ġhazal's "conquest" of the qaṣīdah, see Keyvani, "Mongol Qaside," 291–92. For a revisionist approach, see Evilsizor, "Poetry and Patronage," 336–37.

41. For "Balkans-to-Bengal" defined by circulation of Ḥāfiẓ, see Ahmed, *Islam*, 19–71. For Arnold Toynbee in 1939 demarcating Persianate realms stretching from the "Ottoman Pashalyq of Buda" to the "Hindu Empire of Vijayanagar," see *Study of History*, 5:514–15. For the China-based British consul Rutherford Alcock in 1880 declaring that the Russian frontier spanned between the "Bosphorus to the Bay of Bengal," see Vambéry, "Russia's Influence," 482. For geography defined by the "Ganges to Bosporus" (circa 1818) in the context of Rūmī's popularity, see Hammer-Purgstall, *Redekünste Persiens*, 164, as discussed in Schimmel, *Triumphal Sun*, 388.

42. Beyond Delhi, earlier iterations of *bāzār-e sukhan* appear in the *Shāhnāmah* when Firdausī (940–1025) mourned, "There is no buyer for this effort" (*hamīn ranj rā kas kharīdar nīst*), in Firdausī, "Shāhnāmah," fol. 5b. The poet Labībī (d. after 1038) conceived of "the market and price of poetry" (*bāzār-o qīmat-e sarwād*), Ṭūsī, *Luġhat*, 107–8; Injū Shīrāzī, *Jahāngīrī*, 1:1031. See further discussion in Lewis, "Reading," 57. Early qaṣīdahs (circa 1060–1141) note poets' ambivalence toward the *bāzār-e sukhan* concept, notably in Azraqī Haravī, *Dīwān*, 41; Sanā'ī Ġhaznawī, *Dīwān*, 253. My thanks to Cameron Cross and Samuel Lasman for pointing me

toward medieval sources advertising the *bāzār-e suḳhan* concept. On pre-Mongol-era poets of India, see Ḥusain, *Early Persian*; Sharma, *Indian Frontier*, 33–38.

43. On shared Tuġhluq and Mughal visions of language and architecture, see Sharma, "City of Beauties," 73. Ḳhusrau's purported lines in scribed inside Delhi's Red Fort, "If there is a paradise on this earth / It is right here, it is right here, it is right here" (*agar firdaus bar rū-e zamīn ast / hamīn ast-o hamīn ast-o hamīn ast*) are discussed and translated in Kinra, *Writing Self*, 137.

44. Ḳhusrau Dihlavī, *Qirān*, 33–34, 40. For a seventeenth-century description of Delhi echoing Ḳhusrau, see Kinra, *Writing Self*, 137–38. For Ḳhusrau's biography within Delhi's longer cultural history, see Dudney, *Delhi*, 63–82.

45. Ḳhusrau Dihlavī, *Dībāchah*, 27, 28. For discussion of Ḳhusrau's *Dībāchah*, see Gabbay, *Islamic Tolerance*, 20–40. For its partial translation, see Borah, "Nature of Persian."

46. Ḳhusrau Dihlavī, *Dībāchah*, 72, 76.

47. Ḳhusrau Dihlavī, *Dībāchah*, 80.

48. Babayan, *City as Anthology*, 4.

49. Moosvi, *Trade in Mughal India*, 131.

50. Tattavī, *Muntaḳhab*, 8. For Ḳhusrau's praise of poetic language that reaches commoners and elites, see *Dībāchah*, 17. Cf. "comprehensible to the popular understanding (*ʿāmm-fahm*) and approved by the educated (*ḳhāṣṣ-pasand*)," in Steingass, Preface, v.

51. On the multilingual Persianate commercial sphere, see Bishara and Chatterjee, "Persianate Bazaar." On the various meanings of Hindi, see Farooqi, "Hindi of Urdu."

52. Alam, *Political Islam*, 182–86.

53. Ḥātim, *Dīwānzādah*, 1975, 39.

54. On Inshā and Qatīl sharing everything like brothers, see *Daryā*, 1850, 4–5. Further examples of Qatīl's intellectual generosity seeding others' scholarship are found in Muṣḥafī, "Taẕkirah," fols. 2b–3a.

55. For Urdu translations from ʿAbd ul-Ḥaqq's heavily edited 1916 Persian edition of *Daryā-e Laṭāfat* by Sayyid Inshāʾullāh Ḳhān Inshā, see Kaifī Dihlavī, *Daryā*, cited in Hakala, *Negotiating Languages*, and ʿUrūj, *Daryā*, cited in Lelyveld, "*Zuban*." For an accessible manuscript version of *Daryā-e Laṭāfat* housed at Princeton University Library and available online, see Inshā and Qatīl, "Daryā," 1825, https://catalog.princeton.edu/catalog/9974812783506421.

56. For commerce in Delhi, see Blake, *Shahjahanabad*, 55–57, 104–21. On Mughal trade, see Gupta, "Trade"; Guha, "Rethinking the Economy." On economic decline in the 1700s, see Richards, "Seventeenth-Century Crisis," 635–38. On language and trade, see Tandon, "Friendship," 170–71; Deshpande, "The Marathi Kaulnāmā," 601–5; Alam, "Regional Change," 221.

57. Inshā and Qatīl, *Daryā*, 1850, 24–34.

58. Dargāh Qulī Ḳhān, *Muraqqaʿ*, 62; Muḳhliṣ, *Mirʾāt*, 570–71. See also Kaicker, *The King and the People*, 27–29, 135–37; Hakala, "Coffee in Eighteenth-Century Delhi."

59. Rangīn, *Faras-Nāma*, 42–44.

60. For the words of public “strongmen” (*lūṭiyān*), see Mīr, *Nikāt*, 72, 140–43; Dargāh Qulī Ḳhān, *Muraqqaʿ*, 77–78; Qatīl, *Sharbat*, 30–31, 35; Inshā and Qatīl, *Daryā*, 1850, 116–17, 157–59, 469–70. For a discussion of these registers, see Pellò, “Conversion,” 230–31. For a popular narrative poem composed in *zabān-e lūṭiyān*, see Najāt Iṣfahānī, *Masnawī*.

61. Chatterjee, “Quest for Selfhood,” 77–82; Ḳhān, *Ṭahmās*, 301–2.

62. Inshā and Qatīl, *Daryā*, 1850, 170–83. For reḳhtī, see Naqvī Allāhābādī, *Tārīḳh-e Reḳhtī*; ʿAbbāsī, *Reḳhtī*; Petievich, “Rekhti”; Vanita, *Urdu Rekhtī*. Also, Ḥasan, *Begamātī Zabān*.

63. Inshā and Qatīl, *Daryā*, 1850, 27–38.

64. For Armenians in Delhi, see Ghougassian, Haghnazarian, and Aslanian, “Julfa.” For a bibliography of European travelers’ accounts of Mughal India, see Mukhia, *Mughals*, 182–83.

65. In their exploration of “the lands of poetry” (*zamīn-e shiʿr*), Inshā and Qatīl depicted the literary sciences as comprising “seven continents” with each “continent” chapter comprising domains, provinces, cities, and even a garden.

66. Faruqi, *Early Urdu*, 26. For period definitions of reḳhtah cited by Faruqi, see Mīr, *Nikāt*, 23; Mīr, *Remembrances*, 132–33. For a description of the mobile imperial camp, see Kinra, *Writing Self*, 131–35.

67. For the definition of *urdū* as “camp,” see Gilchrist, *Oriental Linguist*, 99. For a poetic invocation of the imperial army, see Wālih Dāġhistānī, *Taẕkirah*, 3:1137. For the exiled tribes of Israel (*urdū-e banī isrāʾel*) as referenced in a nineteenth-century Persian translation of the Bible, see *Qāmūs-e Kitāb-e Muqaddas*, 3rd, comp. James H. Hawkes (Tehran: Intishārāt-e Asāṭir, 2015 [1394 SH]), s.v. *urdū*. For the Old Turkish definition, see *Drevnetiurkskiĭ Slovar′*, comps. V. M. Nadeliaev et al. (Leningrad: Izdatel′stvo “Nauka,” 1969), s.v. *ordu*.

68. See *ūrdū-e bāzār* and see the extensive discussion in Shīrānī, *Maqālāt*, 1:10–44, esp. 29–30. See also Lelyveld, “*Zuban*”; Bailey, “Urdu.”

69. For Inshā’s childhood excursion to Delhi, see Inshā and Qatīl, *Daryā*, 1850, 38–39. For Muṣḥafī on the language of the horde (circa 1780), “That is to say, [Muṣḥafī] is an educated speaker in the language of the *urdū*” (*yaʿnī kih hai zabāndān urdū kī vuh zabān kā*), see Muṣḥafī, *Kulliyāt*, 1:107. Further discussion in Faruqi, “Long History 1,” 806. I have slightly modified Faruqi’s translation.

70. Expansive modern definitions of reḳhtah appear in *A Comprehensive Persian-English Dictionary, Including the Arabic Words and Phrases to Be Met with in Persian Literature*, comp. Francis Joseph Steingass (London: Routledge & K. Paul, 1892), s.v. *reḳhtah*; *A Dictionary of Urdu, Classical Hindi, and English*, comp. John Thompson Platts (London: Oxford University Press, 1968), s.v. *reḳhtah*; *Luġhatnāmah-e Dihḳhudā*, comp. ʿAlī Akbar Dihḳhudā (Tehran: Muʾassisah-e Luġhatnāmah-e Dihḳhudā, 2020 [1399 SH]), s.v. *reḳhtah*, https://dehkhoda.ut.ac.ir/fa/dictionary/detail/168932?title=%D8%B1%DB%8C%D8%AE%D8%AA%D9%87.

71. See period definitions in Ārzū, *Dād*, 7; Mīr, *Nikāt*, 3, 123–24; Yaktā, *Dastūr*, 3–6; Ḥātim, *Dīwānzādah*, 2011, 106; Ābrū, *Dīwān*, 1967, 240nn1; Ḥamīd Aurangābādī, *Gulshan*, 4–6. The poet Muḥammad Ṭāhir Ġhanī Kashmīrī (d. 1668) describes a “reḳhtah line” in his poem, “Even though the gathering of my imagination is unlit,

there is no problem. / For a line of reḳhtah is a candle that is not of this world" (*be-chirāgh-ast agar bazm-e ḳhayālam ġham nīst / miṣra'-e reḳhtah shama'ī ast kih dar 'ālam nīst*) in Ġhanī Kashmīrī, *Dīwān*, 53. For explication of this couplet and further definitions of reḳhtah, see Muḳhliṣ, *Mir'āt*, 657; Bahār, *'Ajam*, 2:1135.

72. Dudney, *Persian World*, 168, 211–13; Hakala, *Negotiating Languages*, 100–107. On the development of pre-1700s reḳhtah, see Bangha, "Poetry in Mixed Language."

73. Shīrānī, *Maqālāt*, 1:1–9.

74. Persian and Urdu literary historians debate the question of the ġhazal's unity or disparateness. Both approaches are contingent on context and methodology. In the early modern world, most poets never completed a dīwān, and a majority of littérateurs accessed verse from reciters' memories and anthology-based materials, which almost never recorded a ġhazal in totality. These include commonplace books (*bayāẓs*), diaries (*safīnahs* or *jungs*), and biographical compendiums (*taẕkirahs*), which themselves circulated in a piecemeal fashion and on readily available paper in the hands of partisan writers with disparate tastes and opinions.

75. *Arabic-English Dictionary of Qur'anic Usage*, comps. Elsaid M. Badawi and Muhammad Abdel Haleem, (Leiden: Brill, 2008), s.v. *ġh-z-l*. Its early history appears in Lewis, "Transformation of the Ghazal," 127–30.

76. Meisami, *Court Poetry*, 241. Also noted in Sharma, "Generic," 143. The ġhazal's two lines (*miṣra'*) comprise a distich (*bait*), with each line having the same syllable length.

77. Lewis, "Reading," 108–11.

78. Mīr, *Kulliyāt*, 1983, 1:451. On metaphor and meaning in Urdu and Persian ġhazals of the 1700s, see Faruqi, *Urdū Ġhazal*, 20–23. On ġhazal singing, see Brookshaw, "Melodious Tunes," 92–93; Manuel, *Cassette Culture*, 89–104; Kugle, "How a *Ghazal* Lives," 605–7. On similar "poems about poetry" or "meta-ġhazals," see Andrews and Kalpaklı, *Age of Beloveds*, 90–106; Grewal, "Ghazal as 'World Poetry,'" 26–27, 34; Lewis, "Transformation of the Ghazal," 135–36. For an explication of Mīr's poem, see Faruqi, *Shor-Angez*, 2006, 3:502–8; Frances W. Pritchett, "*muṭrib ne paṛhī thī . . .* ," "A Garden of Kashmir: The Urdu Ġhazals of Mīr Muḥammad Taqī Mīr," accessed June 13, 2024, https://franpritchett.com/00garden/09c/0930/0930_01.html.

79. For "lyric translatability," see Gould, "Russifying the *Radīf*," 264–66. For arguments over the Urdu ġhazal's nature as a discursive text, see Pritchett, "Classical Ghazal"; Russell, "Ghazal Rejoinder."

80. Mahmudabad, *Poetry of Belonging*, 64.

81. Julie Meisami refers to this process as the "third dimension" to ġhazal composition whereby deployment of conventions creates new meanings as opposed to the elements themselves, as noted in *Court Poetry*, 241.

82. On Urdu ġhazal craft and creation of meaning, see Pritchett, *Nets of Awareness*, 77–122; Petievich, *Assembly of Rivals*, 1–12; Shiblī Nu'mānī, *'Ajam*, 5:69–119.

83. For circulation in the context of Persianate literary style and its formations, see Schwartz, *Remapping Persian*, 57. On circulation in social networks, see Latour, *Actor-Network-Theory*, 36, 211–12; Appadurai, "Politics of Value," 54.

84. On the central role of exchange in creating value, see Appadurai, "Politics of Value," 3–16. On lyric poetry's role in shaping social history outside Islamic settings, see Cohen, *Social Lives of Poems*; Ikegami, *Bonds of Civility*; Fox, *Real Country*.

85. For a nineteenth-century version of literary analysis according to economic metaphors, see Ṣābir, *Tażkirah*, 1:13–18. Also cited in Pritchett, "Long History 2," 883–84. Cf. "linguistic marketplace" from discourse analysis in Rossi-Landi, *Language as Work*; Smith, *On the Margins of Discourse*.

86. Mikkelson, "Parrots and Crows," 527. Also noted in Dhavan and Pauwels, "Crafting Urdu," 8.

87. Mīr, *Kulliyāt*, 1983, 1:138. For *be-shorish*, see "without tumult" in Frances W. Pritchett, "*nah ho kyūñ reḳhtah* . . . ," "A Garden of Kashmir: The Urdu Ġhazals of Mīr Muḥammad Taqī Mīr," accessed September 8, 2021, https://franpritchett.com/00garden/00c/0084/0084_04.html. Also, Faruqi, *Shor-Angez*, 2006, 1:345–47.

88. For a detailed consideration of *maẓmūn* development and theorization, see Pritchett, *Nets of Awareness*, 106–22.

89. Saudā, *Dīwān*, 343; Āzād, *Ḥayāt*, 64. For a similar sentiment on Saudā's death, see ʿĀshiqī ʿAẓīmābādī, *Tażkirah*, 1:775. For other *īhām*s with *maẓmūn*, see Dudney, *Persian World*, 224.

90. Informally, *īhām* can mean "pun" or "double entendre," though homonymic joking associated with the former and risqué asides linked with the latter limit *īhām*'s connotations. I favor the terms "wordplay" and "misdirection" for *īhām* more generally, saving "pun" or "double entendre" for occurrences of those phenomena. In my translations, I incorporate dual meanings where feasible, but others provide alternate translations in the notes. For consideration of *īhām* in Arabic-language literary theory, see Bonebakker, "Tawriya." Amīr Ḳhusrau innovated the use of *īhām* in 1200s Delhi, as noted in Ḳhusrau Dihlavī, *Dībāchah*, 56–58. Also, Losensky and Sharma, *Bazaar*, lii–liii.

91. The poet, mushāʿirah host, and tażkirah writer Muḥammad Afẓal Sarḳhwush (introduced in chapters 1 and 2) explicitly linked Ġhanī Kashmīrī's "reḳhtah lines" (*miṣraʿ-e reḳhtah*) with "īhām craft" (*īhām bandī*) in Sarḳhwush, "Kalimāt," 1700, fols. 43b–44a.

92. Inshā and Qatīl, *Daryā*, 1850, 447. See "íhámist" in Siddiqi, "Sauda's Works," 26.

93. On auditory and multilingual approaches, see Orsini and Schofield, "Introduction," 3–5, 7–10. On "performative" definitions of group formation, see Latour, *Actor-Network-Theory*, 35–37.

94. As suggested in Russell, *Essays on Urdu*, 40.

95. See "reading, reciting, and writing of poetry" in Mughal courtly contexts from Sharma, *Arcadia*, 55–60.

96. Pfeifer, *Salons*, 2–13; Brookshaw, "Palaces," 199; Ali, *Literary Salons*, 17–19. For bad behavior in gatherings, see Stroumsa, "Adab al-Mujādala."

97. In Urdu and Persian, recitation is construed with the verbs "to read," as in *shiʿr paṛhnā* or *shiʿr ḳhwāndan*. For a comparative example of poetry's material and recitational histories, see Cohen, *Social Lives of Poems*.

98. On contemporary mushāʿirah performance styles, see Naim, "Audience Interaction"; Qureshi, "Tarannum"; Silver, "Urdu Mushaʿirah."

99. On historical approaches to listening in the early modern world, see Johnson, *Listening in Paris*, 1–6, 53–70; Dell'Antonio, *Listening as Spiritual Practice*, 2–14; Erlmann, "Early Modern Voice." For music as heard, see Botstein, "Toward a History of Listening." On sound and language in modern South Asia, see Huacuja Alonso, *Radio for the Millions*, 7–13, 81–105.

100. For "bimodal oral-written performance," see Ali, *Literary Salons*, 278–79.

101. For "Persographic" networking and history writing, see Naqvi, "Novice Munshi," 482–84, 496–98. For accounts of how socialization, script, and secretaries formed the Persographic world, see Green, "Introduction," 17–29; Spooner and Hanaway, "Persian as Koine," 18–22. On paper's role in Mughal India, see Hasan, *Paper, Performance*, 101–17; Chatterjee, *Negotiating Mughal Law*, 26–33, 162–70.

102. Pritchett, *Nets of Awareness*, 63–76.

103. For surveys and analysis of the taẕkirah corpus of Iran and South Asia, see ʿAbdullāh, *Taẕkirah Nigārī*; Naqvī, *Taẕkirah Nawīsī*; Gulchīn-e Maʿānī, *Tārīḳh-e Taẕkirah*; Pritchett, "Long History 2"; Storey, *Survey*; Naqvī, *Urdū ke Taẕkire*. Also Shiblī Nuʿmānī, *ʿAjam*, 1:1–8.

104. McChesney, "Review of *Majmaʿ al-Shuʿara*," 423. For taẕkirahs as links with "early modern Indo-Persian intelligentsia," see Kinra, *Writing Self*, 251.

105. Pritchett, *Nets of Awareness*, 65. Following Sheldon Pollock, taẕkirahs "do things with the past" by structuring time, as noted in his first example in "Forms of History" in Pollock, "Introduction," 18–19. For taẕkirah-based idiosyncrasies and anxieties circa early 1900s, see Boyk, "Fashionality," 882–85.

106. Iḳhlāṣ, "Taẕkirah," fol. 5b. For plagiarism of Iḳhlāṣ's lines, see Qāqshāl, *Tuḥfat*, 1.

107. For the observation that eighteenth-century sources, in particular, offer profound "historiographical diversity and depth," see Nārāyaṇarāvu et al. *Textures*, 249–51.

108. Hermansen and Lawrence, "Indo-Persian Tazkiras," 150; Kia, *Persianate Selves*, 172. On early modern emotions and literature, see Hasan, *Paper, Performance*, 85–90. For a definition that accounts for the diversity of memory-based associations with the taẕkirah, see *Luġhatnāmah-e Dihḳhudā*, comp. ʿAlī Akbar Dihḳhudā (Tehran: Muʾassisah-e Luġhatnāmah-e Dihḳhudā, 2020 [1399 SH]), s.v. *taẕkirah*, https://dehkhoda.ut.ac.ir/fa/dictionary/detail/85828?title=%D8%AA%D8%B0%DA%A9%D8%B1%D8%A9.

109. Schofield, "Emotions in Indian Music History," 184–85. For further discussion, see Schofield, *Music and Musicians*, 20–25.

110. Thum, *Sacred Routes*, 16–51.

111. Hermansen, "Collective Memory," 6–9, 15–17. Apropos of networking, see also "the hardware of cultural memory" in Green, "The Uses of Books," 246.

112. For women poets from the ʿAbbasid court, see Ibn al-Sāʿī, *Consorts*.

113. ʿAṭṭār Nīshāpūrī, *Auliyā*, 61–75.

114. Faḳhrī Haravī, *Taẕkirah*, 109–42; Szuppe, "Female Intellectual Milieu," 122–25. For a discussion of this work as it frames Persian literary history, see

Bashir, *Market in Poetry*, 47–51. For examples from late-Mughal India, see Muṣḥafī, *Tażkirah*, 1933, 279–82; Lodī, *Tażkirah*, 278–82. For nineteenth-century tażkirahs of women poets, see Āsī, *Tażkirat*; Ṣafā, *Tażkirah*.

115. Sharma, "Poetic Canon of Women," 154–58. Shah Jahan Begam (1803–1901) patronized tażkirah production in the late 1800s, when, based on an Ottoman source, she commissioned a survey of women poets, as noted in Rafīʿ Shīrāzī, *Tażkirat*, 2, 177. See also Sharma, "Poetic Canon of Women," 163; Storey, *Survey*, 1 (2):916. For the Ottoman source, see Żahnī, *Mashāhīr*. This coincided with the release of Rafīʿ Shīrāzī's 1887 edition of Daulat Shāh's *Tażkirat ush-Shuʿarā* (circa 1487), titled *Tażkirah-e Daulat Shāh*.

116. Tandon, "The Marginalised," 69–71. See further discussion in Alam, *Crisis of Empire*, xxiv–xxv; Schofield, "The Courtesan," 152–58; Hasan, *State and Locality*, 71–90. Also, Cherian, "Stolen Skin," 4–6.

117. Tandon considers the presence of marginalized groups as a negotiation formed by "notions of charity" and relational frames defined from above in "The Marginalised," 71–72.

118. Saksena, *History*, 53. Among scholars damning tażkirah writing with faint praise, see Sādiq, *History of Urdu*, 41–42. Also see "obscure poets" in Green, "The Uses of Books," 246.

119. See also "minutiae of local detail" in Hermansen and Lawrence, "Indo-Persian Tazkiras," 150; Pellò, "Poets on the Street," 307–8.

120. Tavakoli-Targhi, "Homeless Texts," 281.

121. For travel and patronage in the "poetic economy," see McChesney, "Barrier Heterodoxy," 236.

122. Zaidī, *Tārīḵh*, 48, 54–74.

123. Pellò, "Poets on the Street," 304–6.

124. O'Hanlon, "World of Paper," 94–96; Hasan, *Paper, Performance*, 4–7, 34–36; also see libraries and letter writing in Bayly, *Empire and Information*, 195–98, 203–4.

125. On the *bayāẓ*, see Pritchett, *Nets of Awareness*, 64; Dānešpažūh, "Bayāż"; Khan, *Broken Spell*, 113; Sharma, *Arcadia*, 58. For a brief summary of how anthology writers employed the *bayāẓ*, see Kārdigar, "Bayāẓī," 2–3.

126. Ġhālib, *Dīwān*, 1969, 12; Ġhālib, *Dīwān*, 1925, 11.

127. Āzād, *Ḥayāt*, 55.

128. Sharma, "Lives of Performers," 293–95.

129. For secretaries shaping knowledge regimes, see Alam and Subrahmanyam, "Munshi." On writers' social mobility, see Chatterjee, "Scribal Elites." On scribal practices mediating the Mughal and colonial states, see Bellenoit, *Formation of the Colonial State*, 13–28.

130. Schwartz, *Remapping Persian*, 91–115. See also Dudney, *Persian World*, 24, 198.

131. Called "fossils from the great sea of conversation" among eighteenth-century gatherings in Kaicker, *The King and the People*, 126.

132. Zaidī, *Tārīḵh*, 72–74.

133. Goitein, "Near-Eastern Bourgeoisie," 585. For a quantitative history utilizing biographical dictionaries, see Bulliet, *Conversion to Islam*, 1–15.

134. On Ḳhwushgo's *safīnah*, see Pellò, "Safina."

135. Kia, *Persianate Selves*, 172.

136. Zaidī, *Tārīḳh*, 99.

137. Beg, Preface to *Yaqīn*, 68–82; Adīb Lakhnawī, Preface to *Fāʾiz*, 90–105; Aḥmad, Preface to *Yakrū*, 51–58; Ṣiddīqī, Preface to *Nājī*, 61–67; Hāshimī, Preface to *Walī*, 53, 61–64; Hāshimī, Preface to *Mubtalā*, 6–9; Sarvar ul-Hudá, Preface to *Tābān*, 23–41; Sarvar ul-Hudá, Preface to *Fuġhān*, 107–10; Ḥasan, Preface to *Ābrū*, 63–64. Only two collected works depict emulative networks across a corpus of ġhazals: Ẓuhūr ud-Dīn Ḥātim's *Dīwānzadah* (in two critical editions) and Zain ud-Dīn ʿIshq's 1784 dīwān (in manuscript form only), as discussed in Dudney, "Shāh Ḥātim"; Dhavan and Pauwels, "Crafting Urdu"; White, "On the Road."

138. Green, "The Uses of Books," 246. Green finds that taẕkirahs feature "obscure poets" lacking dīwāns. Only a minority of poets produced dīwāns. Obscure is the wrong word for a crowded field of dīwān-less writers, famous within their immediate communities in the past.

139. Losensky, *Welcoming Fighānī*, 9. See also Zipoli, *Ǧawāb*, 5–16.

140. Losensky, *Welcoming Fighānī*, 113.

141. Losensky, *Welcoming Fighānī*, 9.

142. Other terms for emulation include *istiqbāl* and *jawāb-goʾī*; however, neither of these terms have appeared in my survey of the taẕkirah corpus and period literary manuals. Delhi's poets of the 1700s only used the term *tatabbuʿ*. *Luġhatnāmah-e Dihḳhudā*, comp. ʿAlī Akbar Dihḳhudā (Tehran: Muʾassisah-e Luġhatnāmah-e Dihḳhudā, 2020 [1399 SH]), s.vv. *tatabbuʿ*, accessed July 20, 2024, https://dehkhoda.ut.ac.ir/fa/dictionary/detail/83807?title=%D8%AA%D8%AA%D8%A8%D8%B9.

143. Subtelny, "Taste for the Intricate," 68.

144. Subtelny, "Taste for the Intricate," 68.

145. The evidence of emulative connections between contemporary Delhi poets far outpaces the taẕkirah corpus's anecdotes. The citations and examples presented here represent about one-tenth of the connections I was able to discover through my own emulation of the Losensky method.

146. For definitions of *ṭarḥ*, see Pritchett, *Nets of Awareness*, 199; Aḥmad Dihlavī, *Farhang*, 3:242. For modern mushāʿirah applications, see Silver, "Urdu Mushaʿirah," 363, 367–69; Mahmudabad, *Poetry of Belonging*, 51–52, 89–110. On the development of poetry through call and response (*sawāl wa jawāb*), see Shiblī Nuʿmānī, *ʿAjam*, 3:17.

147. The comprehensive name for this meter is *hazaj musamman sālim*—"unmodified trilling octuple meter."

148. For further introduction to meter, see Thackston, *Classical Persian*, xiii–xxvi. For an accessible Urdu-related resource, see Frances W. Pritchett, "Urdu Meter: A Practical Handbook (The New Online Version)," last modified October 12, 2023, https://franpritchett.com/00ghalib/meterbk/00_intro.html.

149. Sarḳhwush, "Kalimāt," 1700, fol. 40b.

150. For Nāṣir ʿAlī on his competitions with Ṣāʿib, see his *Dīwān-e Ashʿār*, 282.

151. Nāṣir ʿAlī Sirhindī, 291–92.

152. Ḳhwushgo, "Safīnah," fol. 15a.

153. Naṣrābādī, *Tażkirah*, 691.

154. Ṣā'ib Tabrezī, *Dīwān*, 1988, 4:2140–41.

155. For the dispersed leaf depicted in figure 0.1, see "Leaf with Miniature of a Gathering."

156. Awḥadī Marāġha'ī, *Kulliyāt*, 218–19. For further emulations of this verse, see Asīr Shahristānī, *Dīwān*, 309–10; Ḥazīn Lāhījī, *Dīwān*, 326–27, 395–96; Bedil, *Kulliyāt*, 1961, 1:531–530, 629–30.

157. Convention would translate *shiʿār* as "sign," but in the spirit of emulative rivalry at focus in this book, I instead translate the term as *poetry competition*. For supporting definitions, see *Luġhatnāmah-e Dihḳhudā*, comp. ʿAlī Akbar Dihḳhudā (Tehran: Mu'assisah-e Luġhatnāmah-e Dihḳhudā, 2020 [1399 SH]), s.vv. *mushāʿarah* and *shiʿār*, accessed July 20, 2024, https://dehkhoda.ut.ac.ir/fa/dictionary/detail/340730?title=%D9%85%D8%B4%D8%A7%D8%B9%D8%B1%D9%87 and https://dehkhoda.ut.ac.ir/fa/dictionary/detail/194151?title=%D8%B4%D8%B9%D8%A7%D8%B1.

158. Naim, "Audience Interaction," 109; Spooner and Hanaway, "Persian as Koine," 48.

159. Throughout the text, poems with the same formal parameters (*ham-ṭarḥ*) appear in block quotations to call attention to the shared rhyme and refrains as reflected in their transliterations. I attempt to maintain some formal features in the translations.

160. Frances W. Pritchett, "A Garden of Kashmir: The Urdu Ġhazals of Mīr Muḥammad Taqī Mīr," and "A Desertful of Roses: The Urdu Ghazals of Mirza Asadullah Khan Ghalib," last modified January 5, 2024, https://franpritchett.com/.

161. "*dabārah-e ganjūr*," Ganjoor, accessed July 20, 2024, https://ganjoor.net/about.

162. "*mashābih-yābī*," Ganjoor, accessed July 20, 2024, https://ganjoor.net/simi.

163. All verse cited throughout this book appears from manuscripts and critical editions of dīwāns, tażkirahs, miscellanies, and commonplace books.

164. Ḳhwushgo, "Safīnah," fol. 15a.

165. From their comprehensive perspectives, tażkirahs document poets' networks through a "flat" depiction of literary history, a facet theorized in Latour, *Actor-Network-Theory*, 166–72.

166. For discussion of the mushāʿirah's popularity, see Aḥmad, *Shahr*, 5–8.

167. "World's Largest Mushaira Channel On YouTube," at Mujib Khan, About, Mushaira Media, accessed July 20, 2024, https://www.youtube.com/channel/UC7U_L8YcpotRPcra3MBk5gQ/about. For comparison, the YouTube channel with the greatest number of views (in the hundreds of billions) is that of the T-Series record label that posts Bollywood music videos and Indian pop songs, genres that carry ġhazal-based emotions and aesthetics, noted in "About," T-Series, accessed July 20, 2024, https://www.youtube.com/user/tseries/about.

Chapter 1

1. Ḳhwushgo, *Safīnah*, 1959, 120–21.

2. Ḳhwushgo, 120–21.

3. Afżalī et al., "Mukhātib," 90–91.

4. Keshavmurthy, "Bīdil's Portrait," 8–9.

5. Ḳhwushgo, *Safīnah*, 1959, 123.

6. For courtesans' literary contributions in late 1700s Hyderabad, see Kugle, *When Sun Meets Moon*, 147–65; Schofield, *Music and Musicians*, 79–116. For information on early 1700s Delhi, see Schofield, "The Courtesan," 152–58; Kaicker, *The King and the People*, 186–93.

7. Hindī, *Safīnah*, 90–91. To account for the īhām, alternate translations of the first line read, "When debauchery renounces faith and fortitude and soul, beware!" or "When even a rogue casts aside faith and fortitude and soul, beware!"

8. For Maʿnī Yāb Ḳhān's biography, see Dargāh Qulī Ḳhān, *Muraqqaʿ*, 27; Ārzū, *Tażkirah*, 1:241; Ḳhwushgo, *Safīnah*, 1959, 244. Also, Ahsanuzzafar, *Mirzā Bedil*, 403.

9. Ḳhwushgo, *Safīnah*, 1959, 149. For stories of ʿAṭā's swordsmanship, see Qāsim, *Majmūʿah*, 1:398–399. Also, Ahsanuzzafar, *Mirzā Bedil*, 1:397.

10. Bedil, "Safīnah," fol. 231a. I am deeply thankful to Shaahin Pishbin for carefully retrieving ʿAṭā's invaluable citations from Bedil's *safīnah* after I had first missed them.

11. Muḳhliṣ, *Tażkirah*, 236.

12. Tassy, *Histoire*, 1:251–52; Sprenger, *Catalogue*, 207.

13. For example, ʿAṭā is not included in *The Water of Life* (*Āb-e Ḥayāt*) by Muḥammad Ḥusain *Āzād* (The Liberated) (1830–1910).

14. Muḳhliṣ, *Tażkirah*, 236.

15. Muḳhliṣ, 236. ʿAṭā's connection to Shīʾī Islam appears in an allusion to Wāʿiẓ Kāshifī's martyrology *Rauẓat ush-Shuhadā* in a poem recorded in Ḳhwushgo, *Safīnah*, 1959, 150. Two other couplets from this ġhazal appear in Muḳhliṣ, *Tażkirah*, 236. Another local notable from Amroha named Sayyid Saʿādat ʿAlī Ḳhān *Saʿādat* (The Bliss) (fl. 1740–60) impacted later reḳhtah development, as cited in Mīr, *Remembrances*, 133.

16. Sarḳhwush, *Tażkirah*, 140. For another possible verse from ʿAṭā, see Wālih Dāġhistānī, *Tażkirah*, 3:1474.

17. For Ḳhwushgo's misdirection with "a delicate branch," see Ḳhwushgo, *Safīnah*, 1959, 111. See the further discussion in Pellò, "Poets on the Street," 323.

18. Shād ʿAẓīmābādī, *Navā*, 71–72; Bedil, *ʿUnṣur*, 227; Bedil, *Kulliyāt*, 1962, 2:135.

19. Bedil, *Āwāz-hā*, 57–58, 76.

20. Bedil, *Āwāz-hā*, 93.

21. On Ḳhāksār and his son (appointed as a governor in 1702 and promoted in 1704/5), see Ali, *Nobility*, 70; Ḳhwushgo, *Safīnah*, 1959, 17; Lodī, *Tażkirah*, 207–13; Beale, *Dictionary*, 382–83.

22. On the equivalent stipend ʿAṭā secured from his mother, see Shafīq Aurangābādī, *Chamanistān*, 441.

23. Chānd, "Tārīḳh," fol. 298a.

24. Ahsanuzzafar, *Mirzā Bedil*, 259.

25. On cannabis, see Ḳhwushgo, *Safīnah*, 1959, 110. Imbibing liquor was in the domain of the elite, but Bedil supposedly shook this habit in his youth.

26. Dargāh Qulī Ḳhān, *Muraqqaʿ*, 77–78.

27. Ḳhwushgo, *Safīnah*, 1959, 110; Bedil, *ʿUnṣur*, 98–100.

28. Ḳhwushgo, *Safīnah*, 1959, 110–11.

29. Muṣḥafī, "Tażkirah," fol. 25a. Muḥammad Ḥasan *Qatīl* (The Slaughtered) (d. 1817), who presented Muṣḥafī with initial material for *ʿIqd-e Śuraiyah*, was the conduit for this idea. For Qatīl's wrestling terms, see Qatīl, *Sharbat*, 29–31; Qatīl, "Nahr," fol. 77a. For other instances of wrestlers of speech (*pahlawānān-e suḳhan*), see ʿĀrif ud-Dīn ʿĀjiz (fl. 1750–70), "the Mīrzā Bedil of the Times for *reḳhtah* composition" in Shafīq Aurangābādī, *Chamanistān*, 463, 466; and Imām Baḳhsh Nāsiḳh (1772–1838) in Āzād, *Ḥayāt*, 235.

30. Ḳhwushgo, *Safīnah*, 1959, 71.

31. Bedil, *Ruqaʿāt*, 84; Bedil, *Āwāz-hā*, 117. Also, Ahsanuzzafar, *Mirzā Bedil*, 1:406.

32. Ḳhwushgo, *Safīnah*, 1959, 68; Hindī, *Safīnah*, 90; Ṭabāṭabāʾī, "Naġhmah," fol. 122b.

33. Ḳhwushgo, *Safīnah*, 2010, 201. On the *mustazād* and this poem, see Ṭūsī and Murādābādī, *Miʿyār*, 163. Also see Browne, *Literary History*, 2:43, cited in Rahman, "Mustazād." For Ibn-e Ḥusām's biography, see Daulat Shāh Samarqandī, *Tażkirat*, 225–26. For Ibn-e Ḥusām's competition over this poem, see Hasan, *Falakī*, 42–43. Other *mustazāds* by Bedil appear in his "Safīnah," fols. 200a–212b.

34. For "tough guys' talk/sodomites' speech" (*zabān-e lūṭiyān*), see Mīr, *Nikāt*, 141; Ārzū, "Majmaʿ," binding 2, fol. 493a; and "language of sodomites" in *A Comprehensive Persian-English Dictionary, Including the Arabic Words and Phrases to Be Met with in Persian Literature*, comp. Francis Joseph Steingass (London: Routledge & K. Paul, 1892), s.vv. *ḳhabar, ḳhurmā, salām mufattiḥ, sūr nā, shiyāf, ṭabl, kulāh, gul.* For a poem written in *zabān-e lūṭiyān*, see Najāt Iṣfahānī, *Maśnawī*. On obscenity in Steingass, see Zipoli, "Vocabulary." For Ġhālib on Bedil's singing abilities, "The musician of the heart with my breath's wire, O Ġhālib, / strung the guitar in pursuit of Bedil's song" (*muṭrib-e dil ne mire tār-e nafs se ġhālib / sāz par rishtah piʾe naġhmah-e bedil bāndhā*), see *Dīwān*, 1995, 161. For commentary on Ġhālib's verse, see Frances W. Pritchett, "*muṭrib-e dil ne . . .*" "A Desertful of Roses: The Urdu Ġhazals of Mirzā Asadullāh Ḳhān Ġhālib," accessed June 5, 2024, https://franpritchett.com/00ghalib/029/29_10x.html.

35. Mīr, *Nikāt*, 46–47.

36. Ḳhwushgo, "Safīnah," fol. 78a. Written as *phish* [sic] in Ḳhwushgo, *Safīnah*, 1959, 113; Pellò, "Poets on the Street," 314, 315, 322. See *phus* [sic] in Faruqi, "Burning Rage," 4; Tabor, "Heartless," 84, 92nn15 and 16; and *ventris crepitation* and "owl" in *A Dictionary of Urdu, Classical Hindi, and English*, comp. John Thompson Platts (London: Oxford University Press, 1968), s.vv. *phus* and *push*.

37. Ḳhwushgo, *Safīnah*, 1959, 113. Another anecdote appears with Zaṭallī responding to a line from Bedil who was stumped on a particular line: "Why does the tulip have a scar on his chest?" (*lālah bah sīnah dāġh chūn dārad*). Zaṭallī rejoined in matching rhyme and meter: "Because he has a green pole up his ass" (*chubkī-e sabz zer-e kūn dārad*), as discussed in Faruqi, "Burning Rage," 4–5; Ḥasan Dihlavī, *Tażkirah*, 40. I have lightly modified the translation from Faruqi.

38. As transmitted by the Sufi and poet Gulshan (d. 1728) in Ḳhwushgo, *Safīnah*, 2010, 272. For Zulālī, see Lodī, *Tażkirah*, 62; Losensky, "Zulālī." For Hātifī, see Ḳhwushgo, *Safīnah*, 2010, 797; Huart and Massé, "Hātifī."

39. Ḳhwushgo, *Safīnah*, 1959, 111–12.

40. Ḳhwushgo, *Safīnah*, 1959, 109.

41. For Āzād's biography, see *Āzād Bilgrāmī, Maʾās̱ir*, 2:291–307; Malik, "Āzād"; Bazmee Ansari, "Āzād"; Siddiqi, "Āzād."

42. Beḳhabar was buried near the shrine of Niẓām ud-Dīn Auliyā in Delhi according to Ḳhalīl, *Ṣuḥuf*, 23.

43. Āzād Bilgrāmī, *Sarv*, 330.

44. See *ḳhūn shudan* and *rang kardan* in Bahār, *ʿAjam*, 869 and 1104. To account for multiple meanings among the verse's various idioms, an alternate translation reads, "Even the rags I wear must be styled."

45. Beḳhabar recited a third couplet with wordplay (in this case *īhām*) that apparently did not warrant discussion from Bedil: "No matter how trifling, it is futile to run in all directions. / So split open your chest and find the right of way" (*īn qadr harzih chap-o rāst dawīdan ʿabas̱ ast / chāk kun sīnah-e ḳhwud rā sar-e rāhī dar yāb*). The idiom *sīnah chāk* (to bare your heart) can be interpreted both figuratively and literally, especially when modified with *sar-e rāhī* (right of way, foundling, placenta previa), as noted in Āzād Bilgrāmī, *Sarv*, 330.

46. For Mughal administration in seventeenth-century Orissa, see Sarkar, *Studies*, 198–230.

47. Bedil, *ʿUnṣur*, 248–49.

48. For Wālih's biography, see Afẓalī, "Ġharīb-e Bangāl."

49. Bedil, *ʿUnṣur*, 200. For Wālih's impact on Bedil, see Afẓalī, "Ṭarz-e Shiʿrī."

50. Serial methods provided external means for expanding meaning on old themes. For Bedil's verse that utilized only dotted letters, as presented at the gathering, see Bedil, *ʿUnṣur*, 202. For definitions of scribal punning, see *A Dictionary of Urdu, Classical Hindi, and English*, comp. John Thompson Platts (London: Oxford University Press, 1968), s.v. *tajnīs*; *Luġhatnāmah-e Dihḳhudā*, comp. ʿAlī Akbar Dihḳhudā (Tehran: Muʾassisah-e Luġhatnāmah-e Dihḳhudā, 2020 [1399 SH]), s.v. *raqṭāʾ*, https://dehkhoda.ut.ac.ir/fa/dictionary/detail/165526?title=%D8%B1%D9%82%D8%B7%D8%A7-.

51. To account for the double meaning, an alternate translation reads, "Startle your vision with the funhouse of cannabis (*asrar*)."

52. Bedil, *ʿUnṣur*, 201. Also quoted in ʿAndalīb, *Nālah*, 1:257.

53. Bedil, *ʿUnṣur*, 202.

54. Āzād Bilgrāmī, *Sarv*, 330; Bedil, *Kulliyāt*, 1961, 1:1165.

55. Āzād Bilgrāmī, *Sarv*, 330; Āzād Bilgrāmī, *Maʾās̱ir*, 2:315.

56. Bedil, "Safīnah," fol. 242a. Aḥmad-e Jām's nickname was "The Colossal Elephant" (*Ẕẖandah Pīl*). For his biography, see Mahendrarajah, *The Sufi Saint of Jam*, 9–31.

57. Bedil, "Safīnah," fol. 330a–b.

58. Ḳhwushgo, *Safīnah*, 1959, 150.

59. Bedil, "Safīnah," fol. 443a.

60. Asīr Shahristānī, *Dīwān*, 321. For a recent study of his stylistic complexity and historical significance, see Pishbin, "Jalāl Asīr."

61. For examples of approaches to literature as examples of Mughal decline, see Lehmann, "Mughal Decline"; Petievich, "Declining Mughals"; Tignol, "Nostalgia and the City."

62. Dadlani, *From Stone to Paper*, 83–111; Chatterjee, *Negotiating Mughal Law*, 124–36; see especially Kaicker, *The King and the People*, 302–8 on the long history of popular politics.

63. Ḥasan Dihlavī, *Taẕkirah*, 106. Satires of Kām Bakhsh discussed in Khān, preface to *Zaṭal Nāmah*, 140–48. On the 1707–9 war of succession, see ʿĀlī, "Razmnāmah."

64. Shafīq Aurangābādī, *Chamanistān*, 441.

65. Āzād Bilgrāmī, *Sarv*, 197.

66. Āzād Bilgrāmī, 197–98. Also discussed in Ahsanuzzafar, *Mirzā Bedil*, 457–60.

67. Shāh Nawāz Khān Aurangābādī, *Maʾāṣir*, 1:712. Also, Kaicker, *The King and the People*, 225.

68. Āzād Bilgrāmī, *Sarv*, 197.

69. Āzād Bilgrāmī, 180. Further verse commentary on the overthrow of Farrukh Siyar appears in Khwushgo, *Safīnah*, 1959, 248–49; Mukhliṣ, *Taẕkirah*, 80. Bedil likely returned to Delhi in a hurry, leaving behind his commonplace book in Lahore, where it was copied in 1743. See marginalia in Bedil, "Safīnah," fol. n397a.

70. Ahsanuzzafar, *Mirzā Bedil*, 1:460–462; ʿĀshiqī ʿAẓīmābādī, *Taẕkirah*, 1:270.

71. Kaicker, *The King and the People*, 132; Dargāh Qulī Khān, *Muraqqaʿ*, 73.

72. ʿAbd ul-Ġhanī, *Life of Bedil*, 92nn3; Bedil, *Āwāz-hā*, 57, 76, 92. For poets' commentaries on *waqf*, see Schimmel, *Imagery of Persian*, 123nn47; Bahār, *ʿAjam*, 3:2117. Also discussed in Kozlowski, *Endowments*, 38. For historical considerations of *waqf*, see McChesney, *Waqf in Central Asia*; Dale and Payind, "*Waqf* in Kābul." For poets' commentary on the misuses of *waqf* properties, see Subtelny, *Timurids*, 163–64.

73. Dadlani, *From Stone to Paper*, 102–3.

74. The Qur'an 4:11–14.

75. Singer, *Beneficence*; Memiş, "Benefactresses of Waqf"; Bashir, *Market in Poetry*, 51.

76. Meier, "*Waqf* as a Political Weapon," 93.

77. For examples of poets' tomb-based *waqf* infrastructure, see Homerin, *From Arab Poet*, 65–67, 78–79; Diem and Schöller, *The Living and the Dead*, 191; Losensky, *Welcoming Fighānī*, 44–46; Limbert, *Shiraz*, 219; Sharma, *Arcadia*, 126nn2; Kābulī, *Taẕkirat*, 296–98; Mukhliṣ, *Taẕkirah*, 329; Shād ʿAẓīmābādī, *Ḥayāt*, 149–50; Wālih Dāghistānī, *Taẕkirah*, 1:1005; Naṣrābādī, *Taẕkirah*, 409; Homerin, "Al-Fāriḍ," 87–88nn9; McChesney, *Central Asian Shrines*, 135, 196, 211.

78. Junayd Shīrāzī, *Hazār Mazār*, 477–78; Ibn Baṭṭūṭa, *Travels*, 1962, 2:318nn145; Ingenito, *Beholding Beauty*, 62nn14.

79. Singer, *Beneficence*, 18. For other instances of books secured through *waqf*, see Ibn Baṭṭūṭa, *Travels*, 1962, 2:305nn115 and 307nn121; Simpson and Farhad, *Ibrahim Mirza's Haft Awrang*, 34–35; Brookshaw, *Hafiz*, 161; O'Fahey and Vikør, "*Waqf* of Books."

80. Muḳhliṣ, *Tażkirah*, 95. For the grave of Ḥāfiẓ, see Kābulī, *Tażkirat*, 296–98; Lewisohn, "Rabindranath," 29; Tagore, *Journey*, 50; Marashi, "Imagining," 64.

81. Muḳhliṣ, *Tażkirah*, 95; Ḥāfiẓ, *Dīwān*, 1:38.

82. On Ḥāfiẓ's tomb and his dīwān's uses, see Sarvestani, "Ḥāfeẓiya"; Ḳhurramshāhī, "Fāl-e Ḥāfiẓ." For some historical context regarding such practices of bibliomancy, see Gruber, "Practice of *Fāl*," 31–35.

83. Kozlowski, *Endowments*, 25; Cole, *North Indian Shi'ism*, 51–52; Hindī, *Safīnah*, 52; Muṣḥafī, "Tażkirah," fols. 33b and 54a.

84. Ḳhwushgo, *Safīnah*, 1959, 121; Dargāh Qulī Ḳhān, *Muraqqaʿ*, 57, 219.

85. Ārzū, *Tażkirah*, 1:241.

86. Dargāh Qulī Ḳhān, *Muraqqaʿ*, 84. Extending the metaphor, the poem was "ingested via ear" (*maṯlaʿ bah gosh ḳhwurdah būd*). For the poem that inspired its author, Abū ul-Ḥasan *Āgāh* (The Watchful), see Salmān Sāwajī, *Dīwān*, 386; Ṣāʾib Tabrezī, *Dīwān*, 1986, 2:547.

87. Ārzū, *Tażkirah*, 1:241.

88. Bayly, *Empire and Information*, 180; Green, "The Uses of Books," 243.

89. Ḳhwushgo, *Safīnah*, 1959, 123.

90. Muḳhliṣ, *Tażkirah*, 95.

91. Ḳhwushgo, *Safīnah*, 1959, 111, 123; Muḳhliṣ, *Tażkirah*, 95. For weights and measures after Shah Jahan (r. 1628–58), see Fryer, *Eight Letters*, 205–6; Habib, *Atlas*, xiii–xiv.

92. Dargāh Qulī Ḳhān, *Muraqqaʿ*, 27; Bedil, *Kulliyāt*, 1962, 2:220.

93. For the aural nature of Bedil's lines and the notion of music as a public trust, see Afẓalī et al., "Muḳhātib," 91–92.

94. As a call to war, see Bahār, *ʿAjam*, 2:1457–1458. For *ṣalā-e ʿāmm* as a metaphor, see Ġhālib, *Dīwān*, 1982, 312.

95. ʿAndalīb, *Nālah*, 1:5. See the discussion in Alam, *Political Islam*, 176–78. I thank the anonymous reader who suggested the water and salt referenced the oceans of tears wept by the lover.

96. Ḳhwushgo, *Safīnah*, 1959, 123.

97. Thévenot and Careri, *Travels*, 66–67; Thackston, *Memoirs*, 461; Blake, *Time*, 91–95; Balabanlilar, "Begims," 136.

98. Thackston, *Memoirs*, 139; see also Calabria, "Munificence," 37–42.

99. Dargāh Qulī Ḳhān, *Muraqqaʿ*, 57.

100. ʿAbd ul-Ġhanī, *Life of Bedil*, 14–15.

101. For the sellers "with entertaining speeches and attractive gestures" and "the same zeal of a missionary's sermon" who would ensnare "cuckolds [and] a strange tumult of common and mean folk," see Dargah Quli Khan, *Muraqqaʿ*, 60.

102. Ḳhwushgo, *Safīnah*, 1959, 109. On arsenic as an aphrodisiac, see Liu, *Healing with Poisons*, 137; Hehir and Gribble, *Outlines*, 533.

103. Ḳhwushgo, *Safīnah*, 1959, 113–14. See further discussion in ʿAbd ul-Ġhanī, *Life of Bedil*, 93, 98–99nn1.

104. Ḳhwushgo, *Safīnah*, 1959, 321.

105. Iḳhlāṣ, "Tażkirah," fol. 19a; Muḳhliṣ, *Tażkirah*, 86; Sarḳhwush, *Tażkirah*, 41. Ilqā's notice does not appear in the Manchester (1700) and Berlin (1784) copies of

Sarḳhwush's *Kalīmāt ush-Shuʿarā*. However, Ilqā's partial notice does appear in Sarḳhwush, "Kalimāt," 1800, fol. 10a–b, and in the margins of Sarḳhwush, "Kalimāt," 1826, fol. 5b.

106. Ḳhwushgo, *Safīnah*, 1959, 73–74.

107. Ḳhwushgo, 278. Ilqā suffered fits of holy madness that caused him to quote the Pharaoh's blasphemous phrase, "I am your Lord, the Most High" (*anā rabbukum ul-aʿlā*) (The Qur'an 79:24, Habib and Lawrence trans.), as noted in Muḳhliṣ, *Tażkirah*, 86.

108. Naṣrābādī, *Tażkirah*, 690–91; Ḳhalīl, *Ṣuḥuf*, 101. Central Asian chronicler Malīḥā Samarqandī (fl. 1660–1700) writes that Nāṣir ʿAlī's style flourished in Isfahan and Samarqand, circa 1680–90, in *Mużakkir*, 119, 176, 398, esp. 516. On Malīḥā, see Ambler, "Distant Meanings," 33–45, 80–90; McChesney, "Barrier Heterodoxy," 236–39.

109. Ḳhwushgo, *Safīnah*, 1959, 278.

110. The official in question was Bahadur Shah I's prime minister, Munʿam Ḳhān-e Ḳhānān (d. 1711), as noted in Ḳhwushgo, 54. For Bedil's response to Munʿam's verse, see Bedil, *Kulliyāt*, 1961, 1:951.

111. Lodī, *Tażkirah*, 250.

112. Lodī, *Tażkirah*, 250. As discussed in Pellò, "Portrait and Its Doubles," 25.

113. On his many patrons and travels, see Āzād Bilgrāmī, *Maʾāṡir*, 2:129–31.

114. Ḥusain Dost Sambhalī, "Tażkirah," fol. 136a.

115. Ḥusain Dost Sambhalī, "Tażkirah," fol. 136b. Cf. Ābrū, *Dīwān*, 2000, 317–19.

116. Bedil, "Safīnah," fol. 439a–b; Ḳhwushgo, *Safīnah*, 1959, 4. Their shared patron was Shukrullāh Ḳhān (d. 1698), who exchanged detailed correspondence with Nāṣir ʿAlī, as noted in Lodī, *Tażkirah*, 210–13.

117. Āzād Bilgrāmī, "Yad-e Baiẓā," 29. Also noted in ʿAbd ul-Ġhanī, *Life of Bedil*, 88.

118. Muḳhliṣ, *Tażkirah*, 86.

119. Bedil, *Kulliyāt*, 1961, 1:178–79.

120. For further evidence of Ilqā's emulation of Bedil, see the fourth couplet of the same ġhazal in Bedil, *Kulliyāt*, 1961, 1:178–79.

121. Shafīq Aurangābādī, *Chamanistān*, 442.

122. Muḳhliṣ, *Tażkirah*, 236.

123. Beale, *Dictionary*, 283.

124. On ʿAṭā's purported connection to Zaṭallī, see Qāsim, *Majmūʿah*, 1:398. Tassy, *Histoire*, 1:251–52; Sprenger, *Catalogue*, 207. Also, "in competition with Mīr Jaʿfar" (*dar muqābal-e mīr jaʿfar*) in Muḳhliṣ, *Tażkirah*, 236.

125. The original satire did not survive in Bedil's commonplace book.

126. Ḳhwushgo, "Safīnah," 1768, fol. 98a–b.

127. Muḳhliṣ, *Tażkirah*, 236. As "mongrel speech," see *A Dictionary of Urdu, Classical Hindi, and English*, comp. John Thompson Platts (London: Oxford University Press, 1968), s.v. *khichaṛī*.

128. Muḳhliṣ, 97–98. To account for the multiple meanings in Payām's pen name (in this case the misdirection of *īhām*), an alternate translation reads: "The brains of Majnūn will spill out of the ear canal, / and thus the plaintive sound of my 'Message' has not yet been heard."

129. Wālih Dāġhistānī, *Tażkirah*, 1:1:425. Before writing under "Payām," Sharaf ud-Dīn wrote as *Ḳhirad* (The Wisdom). During Ramẓān, when ending the fast with other poets after a mushāʿirah, Payām kept getting passed over when a dish of lentils circulated. The word for lentils (*dāl*) and the last letter of Payām's former pen name (Ḳhirad) are homonyms: *dāl*. When the lentil dish went around again, he piped up and said, "I will eat the *dāl*." Another poet used this moment to ridicule Payām—then known as Ḳhirad. The witty poet said, "You did well to eat the *dāl* in your pen name." This phrase turned *ḳhirad* into *ḳhar* (the word for donkey), making wisdom into an ass, as recorded in Ḥairat Akbarābādī, *Tażkirah*, 20–21. For Payām's son, the reḳhtah poet Najm ud-Dīn ʿAlī *Salām* (The Compassion) (fl. 1730–50), see Mīr, *Remembrances*, 143; Ḥasan Dihlavī, *Tażkirah*, 79.

130. For Payām and Ārzū's shared links with Agra, see Ārzū, *Muʿāṣirān*, 64; Muḳhliṣ, *Tażkirah*, 97. For his attendance in Ḳhwushgo's gatherings, see *Safīnah*, 1959, 212. A discussion of Payām's reḳhtah compositions appears in chapter 3.

131. Mīr, *Nikāt*, 141; Ārzū, "Majmaʿ," binding 2, fol. 493a. Inshā and Qatīl refer to this group as "hooligans" (*shuhde*) who spoke with unique phrases, in double meanings, and according to odd pronunciations, inhabiting the neighborhood around the Congregational Mosque (*jāmiʿ masjid*). See *Daryā*, 1850, 157–59. Nandini Chatterjee reveals that Zaṭallī and ʿAṭā's register also flourished in local chancelleries in "Translating Obligations," 541–42, 571–72.

132. Qāsim, *Majmūʿah*, 1:42.

133. Faiẓān, "Ġhair Dakanī," 576–77; Qāsim, *Majmūʿah*, 1:399.

134. Shafīq Aurangābādī, *Chamanistān*, 441–42; Qāʾim Chāndpūrī, *Tażkirah*, 30; Mīr, *Nikāt*, 46; Ḥasan Dihlavī, *Tażkirah*, 106; Qāsim, *Majmūʿah*, 1:398–399. Recorded as *ʿAẓam* in Shauq Murādābādī, *Tażkirah*, 17–18, 17nn2, 707.

135. Ḥasan Dihlavī, *Tażkirah*, 106.

136. For description of narrow-waisted, "lion-bodied" (*sher andām*) wrestlers, see Zaḳhmī, "Sharḥ," fols. 4b–5a.

137. This couplet is only found in Ḥasan Dihlavī, *Tażkirah*, 106.

138. The remaining stanza is misattributed to ʿAbd ul-Jalīl Bilgrāmī *Aṭal* (The Stubborn) in Qāsim, *Majmūʿah*, 1:42–43.

139. Muḳhliṣ, *Tażkirah*, 236.

140. Muḳhliṣ, *Tażkirah*, 236. Profiteering from poetry made Bedil nervous, as noted in Lodī, *Tażkirah*, 250.

141. Kaicker, "Promises and Perils," 332. For examples of Bilgrāmī's compositions in Arabic, Braj Bhasha, Hindi, and Turkish, see Āzād Bilgrāmī, *Sarv*, 384–85; Bilgrāmī, "Letters," 135, 206, 208. For his biography, see Siddiqi, "Jalīl."

142. Ḥasan Dihlavī, *Tażkirah*, 106; Qāʾim Chāndpūrī, *Tażkirah*, 30; Shauq Murādābādī, *Tażkirah*, 18. Cf. Shafīq Aurangābādī, *Chamanistān*, 441–42; Shorish ʿAẓīmābādī, *Tażkirah*, 434. For an additional obscene couplet, see Mīr, *Nikāt*, 46; Mīr, "Nikāt," 1852, 35; and as ascribed to Zaṭallī in *Zaṭal Nāmah*, 331.

143. *A Dictionary of Urdu, Classical Hindi, and English*, comp. John Thompson Platts (London: Oxford University Press, 1968), s.v. *pachhāṛ*. For other wrestling-themed couplets, see Mīr, *Kulliyāt*, 1983, 1:178; Muḥibb Dihlavī, *Dīwān*, 180; Walī Dakhanī, *Kulliyāt*, 280.

144. See "cow toss" in *A Dictionary of Urdu, Classical Hindi, and English*, comp. John Thompson Platts (London: Oxford University Press, 1968), s.vv. *gāʾo pachhāṛ, qasāʾiyā dāv.*

145. Called *Qadam Sharīf* or *Qadam Rasūl*, as noted in Sangīn Beg, "Sair," fols. 72b, 78a.

146. Qāsim, *Majmūʿah*, 1:42; Tassy, *Histoire*, 1:252. For ʿAbd ul-Jalīl's familiarity with Bedil's verse, see Āzād Bilgrāmī, *Sarv*, 280.

147. Bedil, *Ruqaʿāt*, 68; Ahsanuzzafar, *Mirzā Bedil*, 1:397.

148. Bedil, *Ruqaʿāt*, 68; Ahsanuzzafar, *Mirzā Bedil*, 1:397.

149. Ḳhwushgo, *Safīnah*, 1959, 150. ʿAṭā's math could be wrong as the chronogram contradicts Ḳhwushgo's date for ʿAṭā's passing (1136 AH) and Iḳhlāṣ's chronogram for ʿAṭā: "Alas, the friend departed" (*āshnā raftah ḥaif*, 1135 AH), Iḳhlāṣ, "Tażkirah," fol. 116a–b. Cf. ʿĀshiqī ʿAẓīmābādī, *Tażkirah*, 1:1096. For discussions of the children's poem, an eighteenth-century rhymed dictionary titled *Ḳhāliq Bārī* and attributed to Amīr Ḳhusrau (1253–1325), see Hakala, *Negotiating Languages*, 36; Losensky and Sharma, *Bazaar*, 58.

150. Ḳhwushgo, *Safīnah*, 1959, 150; Hindī, *Safīnah*, 134–35.

151. Bahār, *ʿAjam*, 2:1175. To account for its multiple meanings, an alternate translation of the couplet reads: "Is it such a calamity to seize conceits from the original ideas of neighbors? / For the parameters of poetry (*zamīn-e shiʿr*), the law of eminent domain has been applied everywhere."

152. Muṣḥafī, "Tażkirah," fol. 23a.

153. Muṣḥafī, "Tażkirah," fol. 25b.

154. Sangīn Beg, *Sair*, 1982, 119. For the legend of Bedil changing his pen name from *Ramzī* (The Cryptic) after reading from Saʿdī's *Gulistan*, see ʿĀshiqī ʿAẓīmābādī, *Tażkirah*, 1:269. For Saʿdī's couplet that inspired him, "When some asked me for a description of him, / what can the disheartened say about the one with no mark? // Lovers are the beloved's murder victims / and not a peep comes from those slaughtered" (*gar kasī waṣf-e ū zi-man pursīd / bedil az be-nishān chih goʾīd bāz // ʿāshiqān kushtigān-e maʿshūq-and / bar niyāyad zi-kushtigān āwāz*), see Thackston, *Gulistan*, 2.

155. For Bedil-reading sessions beyond Delhi, see Schwartz, "Transregional Poet," 91–97; Keshavmurthy, "Circling the Shrines." On other origins in 1920s Kabul and continuing today, see Īrāj, "Bedil Girāʾī," 18–19. For accounts of gatherings circa 1950, see Ḳhalīl, "ʿUrs"; "ʿUrs-e Bedil."

Chapter 2

1. Cf. "favorite place where mystical poets used to meet" in Schimmel, *Pain and Grace*, 48.

2. Taken from an ethical proverb that listening to music "is conditioned by time, place, and companions" (*dar samāʿ zamān-o makān-o aḳhwān sharṭ ast*) in Ġhazālī, *Kīmyā*, 1:497.

3. Shafīq Aurangābādī, *Chamanistān*, 256. There are several alternate translations with the term *maẓmūn*. In the legal sense of the term: "The market for

pawned merchandise (*māl-e maẓmūn*) grows lively with counterfeit goods" or with the poet's self-deprecation based on his pen name: "Maẓmūn's market is flush with counterfeit goods. / You call yourself some kind of poet, so go open a shop."

4. Ḳhwushgo, *Safīnah*, 1959, 166.

5. Ḥāfiẓ, *Dīwān*, 1:22. Shiraz's Ruknābād, which flowed past the tomb of Saʿdī, was an equally inviting natural setting, as described in Ibn Baṭṭūṭa, *Travels*, 2:318.

6. Asher, *Architecture*, 266. See also the Pride of Mosques (*Faḳhr ul-Masājid*), built in 1728 by Faḳhr un-Nisā Begam (fl. 1700–1730) near Kashmir Gate, cited in Stephen, *Archæology*, 270–71; Beale, *Dictionary*, 128; Sanderson, *List of Monuments*, 1:183–84; Sangīn Beg, *Sair*, 1982, 44–45. For consideration of women's patronage for both mosques, see Dadlani, *From Stone to Paper*, 17–18, 71–73.

7. Ḳhān, *Ṣubḥ*, 191–92; Mustaʿidd Ḳhān, *Maʾāṡir*, 539; Sarkar, *History of Aurangzib*, 1:70 and 3:62. For Zīnat un-Nisā's patronage, see Kāẓim, *ʿĀlamgīrnāmah*, 368–69; Mustaʿidd Ḳhān, *Maʾāṡir*, 517. For her role in court politics during Aurangzeb's reign and administering the emperor's funeral arrangements, see Mustaʿidd Ḳhān, 248, 312, 343, 359, 361, 385, 408, 433, 461, 484, 522. On Zīnat un-Nisā's influence during the fraught reign of Jahāndār Shāh (r. 1712–13), see Wāẓiḥ, *Irādat*, 130–31.

8. Cunningham, *Archaeological Survey*, 1:230; Sangīn Beg, "Sair," fols. 43b–44a; Stephen, *Archæology*, 261–63; Aḥmad Dihlavī, *Wāqiʿāt*, 2:127–32.

9. For the poet Jurʾat's praise of Gulshan, see Ḳhwushgo, *Safīnah*, 1959, 206; Iḳhlāṣ, *Hameshah*, 55.

10. See "Advice to a Beloved" in Vanita and Kidwai, *Same-Sex*, 161–68.

11. Ābrū, *Dīwān*, 2000, 140.

12. Ḳhwushgo, *Safīnah*, 1959, 166; Ārzū, *Muʿāṣirān*, 112.

13. Ārzū, *Muʿāṣirān*, 112–13.

14. Ḳhwushgo, *Safīnah*, 1959, 267.

15. Ḥātim, *Intiḳhāb*, 147; Shafīq Aurangābādī, *Chamanistān*, 143; compare Ḥātim, *Dīwānzādah*, 2011, 209; on coffee and cigarettes 409–15; Persian version on coffee: Ḥātim, *Dīwān-e Fārsī*, 237–38. Translation of Urdu version in Hakala and Naru, "Praise of Coffee."

16. Ḳhwushgo, *Safīnah*, 1959, 266–67; also Pellò, "Poets on the Street," 321–22. For the literary inspiration that comes from taking cannabis, see Mīr, *Kulliyāt*, 1983, 1:323–24; Faruqi, *Shor-Angez*, 4:370–79; Frances W. Pritchett, "*sarsarī kuchh sun liyā. . . .*" A Garden of Kashmir: The Urdu Ġhazals of Mīr Muḥammad Taqī Mīr, last modified October 12, 2023, https://franpritchett.com/00garden/06c/0602/0602_11.html.

17. On Zīnat ul-Masājid, see Sangīn Beg, "Sair," fol. 43b; *List of Monuments*, 1:31; Ḳhān, *Āṡār*, 3:78; Aḥmad Dihlavī, *Wāqiʿāt*, 2:127–32; Blake, *Shahjahanabad*, 32, 82, 53, 172.

18. McChesney, *Central Asian Shrines*, 176; Homerin, *From Arab Poet*, 60–62; Aigle, "Among Saints and Poets."

19. Kulke, "ʿInāyat Allāh Khān."

20. Hāshmī Sandīlavī, *Taẕkirah*, 1994, 4:789.

21. Ḥamīd Aurangābādī, *Gulshan*, 42–43. For similar verse as cited from Maẓhar's purported commonplace book, see Qureshī, *Mīrzā Maẓhar*, 331. Compare Āzād's

depiction of the episode in *Ḥayāt*, 60. My thanks to Purnima Dhavan for her correction on my translation.

22. For example, see Ābrū, *Dīwān*, 2000, 260; Nājī, *Dīwān*, 318; Ḥātim, *Intiḳhāb*, 194; Qureshī, Mīrzā Maẓhar, 339.

23. Ḳhwushgo, *Safīnah*, 1959, 165.

24. For ʿĀlamgīr's reign and his impact on literature, see Ansārī, *Fārsī Adab*; Ali, *Nobility*; Truschke, *Aurangzeb*.

25. On Waḥdat's residence in Fīroz Shāh Koṭlā and other particulars, see Ārzū, *Muʿāṣirān*, 112; Ḳhwushgo, *Safīnah*, 1959, 69. The Naqshbandi order began in Central Asia in the middle 1300s and was given a home in India by Shāh Gul's paternal grandfather Aḥmad Sirhindi (1564–1624), the Renewer of the Faith of the Second Millennium (*Mujaddid-e Alf-e S̤ānī*).

26. Ḳhwushgo, *Safīnah*, 1959, 165–66. For other writers who stayed at mosques, including Maẓhar and Waḥdat, see Ḳhwushgo, 69, 211, 302. For Muṣḥafī living at Ġhāzī ud-Dīn madrasah circa 1780, see Muṣḥafī, *Riyāẓ*, 301.

27. Ḳhwushgo, *Safīnah*, 1959, 167.

28. Gulshan and Sadārang likely shared a connection among guilds of devotional singers (*qawwālān*) who staffed listening sessions at various shrines throughout the city. For a history of Sadārang's career and musical innovations, see Brown [Schofield], "Origins of Khayal"; Schofield, "Musicians to the Mughal Emperors." For firsthand accounts of Sadārang, see Nājī, *Dīwān*, 405–6; Dargāh Qulī Ḳhān, *Muraqqaʿ*, 90–91. For Sadārang's legendary passing as it coincided with that of Ummīd (discussed in chapter 3), see Muṣḥafī, "Tażkirah," fol. 8b.

29. Hindī, *Safīnah*, 177.

30. Sarḳhwush was born in Kashmir, the second of son of Muḥammad Zāhid, a supply chain officer under the Mughal courtier, ʿAbdullāh Ḳhān Zaḳhmī, noted in Ḳhwushgo, *Safīnah*, 1959, 71–72; Ārzū, *Tażkirah*, 2:676; and in Shāh Nawāz Ḳhān Aurangābādī, *Maʾās̤ir*, 1891, 3:92; Shāh Nawāz Ḳhān Aurangābādī, *Maʾās̤ir*, 1888, 1:718 and 729. For his multilingual chronograms, see "Kalimāt," 1700, fol. 71a. For Sarḳhwush's emulations of Ṣāʾib Tabrezī, see Lodī, *Tażkirah*, 245; Ṣāʾib Tabrezī, *Dīwān*, 1985, 1:226–27. For background on Sarḳhwush's son Fażlullāh *Ḳhwushtar* (The Jollier) (fl. 1680–1730), see Muḳhliṣ, *Tażkirah*, 135.

31. Naṣrābādī, *Tażkirah*, 690–91; Malīḥā Samarqandī, *Mużakkir*, 516; Ḳhalīl, *Ṣuḥuf*, 101.

32. For Saʿdullāh Ḳhān Square, see Aḥmad Dihlavī, *Wāqiʿāt*, 2:123–24; Dargāh Qulī Ḳhān, *Muraqqaʿ*, 60–61; Blake, *Shahjahanabad*, 57, 118, 162.

33. Ḳhwushgo, *Safīnah*, 1959, 72. On Sarḳhwush's fame in Isfahan, Naṣrābādī, *Tażkirah*, 695; Ārzū, *Tażkirah*, 2:677.

34. Sarḳhwush, "Kalimāt," 1700, fol. 51b. For the amended words, see Sarḳhwush, "Kalimāt," 1826, fol. 47b.

35. Ḳhwushgo, *Safīnah*, 1959, 74. Ārzū later corrected Sarkhwush's line to this: "In remembrance of righteousness, I have grabbed both worlds by the pubic hair" (*ba yād-e ḥaqq zi-har do jahan rum giriftah-īm*), in Ḳhwushgo, "Safīnah," fol. 55b. For Bedil's memorial chronogram for Sarḳhwush, see Bedil, "Safīnah," fol. 442a–b.

36. Ḳhwushgo, *Safīnah*, 1959, 73–74.

37. Sarḳhwush, *Tażkirah*, 132; Ḳhwushgo, *Safīnah*, 1959, 1. Sarḳhwush also relied on Nāṣir ʿAlī for citations of favorite poems included in his tażkirah, see Sarḳhwush, "Kalimāt," 1700, fol. 32b.

38. Āzād Bilgrāmī, *Maʾāṡir*, 2:143; Sarḳhwush, *Tażkirah*, 133. On the Timurid calligrapher Mīr ʿAlī Haravī (1476?–1543) see Sarḳhwush, 133nn5; Bloom and Blair, "Mīr 'Alī Ḥusaynī Haravī"; Soucek, "ʿAlī Heravī."

39. Nāṣir ʿAlī Sirhindī, *Dīwān-e Ashʿār*, 474.

40. Sarḳhwush, *Tażkirah*, 136.

41. For the famous couplet uttered by Sarḳhwush, "Whoever blows out the candle that God lit burns his beard" (*chirāghī rā kih ezid bar furozad / har ān ko puf zanad reshish basozad*), see Sarḳhwush, *Tażkirah*, 136. Also in Faruqi, "Imitation in Sabk-i Hindi," 12. I have slightly modified the translation from Faruqi.

42. Ḳhwushgo, *Safīnah*, 1959, 166–67.

43. Schimmel, *Pain and Grace*, 35–36.

44. Ḳhwushgo, *Safīnah*, 1959, 166. For a Sufi interpretation of the event, see Pellò, "Poets on the Street," 319.

45. Ḳhwushgo, *Safīnah*, 1959, 2–3; Ṣāʾib Tabrezī, *Dīwān*, 1987, 3:1498. See also Pellò, "Poets on the Street," 312.

46. Ḳhwushgo, *Safīnah*, 1959, 2. Translation from Pellò, "Poets on the Street," 312. In rough language, Nāṣir ʿAlī did get his comeuppance after reciting, "A thing which is not seen—I too am that" (*chīzī kih nadīdanī ast ān ham māʾīm*). To Nasir ʿAli, Muḥammad Sanā Ḳhān *Wahshat* (d. 1730?) said, "'Something not seen?' Doesn't that mean the special appendage of women [i.e., the clitoris] (*ʿuẓw-e maḳhṣūṣ-e zanān*)? The good sir clearly means that he is that too," as cited in Ḳhwushgo, *Safīnah*, 1959, 205.

47. ʿĀshiqī ʿAẓīmābādī, *Tażkirah*, 1:251.

48. Ḳhwushgo, *Safīnah*, 1959, 72. Ibn ʿArabī (1165–1240) was the preeminent philosopher of the premodern world whose ideas touched many intellectual traditions. Jalāl ud-Dīn Rūmī (1207–1273) founded a Sufi order in Anatolia. Ṣaḥābī Astarābādī (d. 1602) was a Persian poet famous for his mystical poetry that addressed philosophical questions, as noted in Shiblī Nuʿmānī, *ʿAjam*, 5:196–197; Āzād Bilgrāmī, *Sarv*, 47–48. Mullā Shāh Badaḳhshī (d. 1661) was a leader of a branch of the Qādirī Sufi order based in Lahore. His teacher was Miyān Mīr ʿĀrif (d. 1635), a scholar well connected with the Mughal court, as noted in Algar, "Badaḵšī."

49. Ḳhwushgo, "Safīnah," fol. 54a–b.

50. Sarḳhwush, "Kalimāt," 1700, fols. 51b.

51. Sarḳhwush's disappointment in Gulshan is further reflected in a conversation he shared with Ḳhwushgo when the latter presented to him Gulshan's new poems, presumably composed under Bedil's direction. Sarḳhwush read them. Then, damning Gulshan with faint praise, said, "None are empty of delight. Just like the like poems of Ḥāfiẓ, how can you choose even one?" See Ḳhwushgo, "Safīnah," fol. 109b.

52. Āzād, *Ḥayāt*, 64.

53. Mīr, who had no contact with Maẓmūn, cited Jājmau, a town contiguous with Kanpur, in *Nikāt*, 34. Qā'im Chāndpūrī, who claimed to have encountered the poet several times at gatherings, noted Maẓmūn was from Jāji'o (Jājau) in *Tażkirah*, 52. See also Ahmadabad cited in Ḥamīd Aurangābādī, *Gulshan*, 19.

54. Ḳhwāfī Ḳhān, *Muntaḳhab*, 2:590–91.

55. Mīr, *Nikāt*, 34; Shafīq Aurangābādī, *Chamanistān*, 255. For the many legends on how the Sufi Bābā Farīd received his nickname, see Nizami, *Shaikh Farid*, 25, 27, 116–17. For an overview of his Sufi milieu in the 1200s, see Schimmel, *Dimensions*, 346–52; Schimmel, *Islam*, 25–27.

56. Shafīq Aurangābādī, *Chamanistān*, 255.

57. Gardezī, "Tażkirah," fol. 63a. See also Qā'im Chāndpūrī, *Tażkirah*, 52–53; Mīr, *Nikāt*, 34.

58. Mīr, *Nikāt*, 35; Shafīq Aurangābādī, *Chamanistān*, 260.

59. Ḥamīd Aurangābādī, *Gulshan*, 21. To account for īhāms, an alternate translation incorporating the idiom *bāt nikālnā* ("to make a point"), as is noted in the poem: "You certainly achieved world fame, Maẓmūn, / ever since you made a point as if an *īhām*." Further self-praise for writing īhām appears in Nājī, *Dīwān*, 326.

60. Nājī, *Dīwān*, 365; Qureshī, *Mīrzā Maẓhar*, 310.

61. Qā'im Chāndpūrī, *Tażkirah*, 35. Ārzū, *Mu'āṣirān*, 124. Ārzū, *Tanbīh*, 76.

62. Mīr, *Nikāt*, 34; Qā'im Chāndpūrī, *Tażkirah*, 52; Ḥasan Dihlavī, *Tażkirah*, 146; Qāsim, *Majmū'ah*, 2:197; Żakā, *'Ayyār*, 603; Ārzū, *Tanbīh*, 76. This was also a pun. As a homonym, Maẓmūn's student referenced the unlettered (*be-dānā*) as an auditory allusion to his toothless mouth (*be-dandān*). See Tassy's "poëte sans pepin" in *Histoire*, 2:301. Noted as "Toothless Poet" in Bailey, *History of Urdu*, 45; Pritchett and Faruqi, *Āb-e Ḥayāt*, 116; Saksena, *History*, 49.

63. Ḳhwushgo, *Safīnah*, 1959, 228, 338. For reference to "Miyāñ Maẓmūn," see Tābān, *Dīwān*, 2006, 395–96.

64. Qā'im Chāndpūrī, *Tażkirah*, 52–53.

65. Shafīq Aurangābādī, *Chamanistān*, 254. Compare Ābrū's response to this poem in *Dīwān*, 2000, 224.

66. Shafīq Aurangābādī, *Chamanistān*, 253–61. On the size of Maẓmūn's dīwān, Mīr, *Nikāt*, 34; Shafīq Aurangābādī, *Chamanistān*, 255; Jālibī, *Tārīḳh*, 2:259.

67. For Urdu translation, see 'Aṭā Kākvī, *Tażkirah*. On Shafīq's life, see Riẓvī, *Lachhmī Narāyan Shafīq*. See also Baily, "Review."

68. For 'Ārif's verse, "To the daughter of the vine say, 'Go hook up with him!' / But, alas, 'Ārif the Mystic eats only opium" (*duḳhtar-e raz ko kah-kih us se mile / varnah 'ārif afīm khātā hai*), see Shauq Murādābādī, *Tażkirah*, 56; Mīr, *Nikāt*, 125; Shafīq Aurangābādī, *Chamanistān*, 439. To account for the īhām, an alternate translation reads, "But 'Ārif the Mystic committed suicide."

69. Mīr, *Nikāt*, 123–24; Ḥasan Dihlavī, *Tażkirah*, 23; Żakā, *'Ayyār*, 221–22; Shauq Murādābādī, *Tażkirah*, 56; Shafīq Aurangābādī, *Chamanistān*, 75. Dānā likely took his pen name to echo Maẓmūn's nickname of *shā'ir-e be-dānah* (The Seedless Poet). On Dānā's literary style, see Niẓāmī, *Īhām Go'ī*, 189–90.

70. Ḥasan Dihlavī, *Tażkirah*, 47.

71. Sangīn Beg, "Sair," fol. 35a.

72. For record of Amīr Ḳhān's passing on Friday, January 6, 1747 (December 26, 1746 JD; 23 Żū'l-Ḥijjah 1159 AH), see Shāh Nawāz Ḳhān Aurangābādī, *Maʾāṡir*, 1890, 2:2:841; Beale, *Miftāḥ*, 324–25; Hāshmī Sandīlavī, *Tażkirah*, 1968, 1:257; Alam, *Crisis of Empire*, 288nn139. For examples of chronograms written in his memory, see Tābān Dihlavī, *Dīwān*, 2006, 397; Muḳhliṣ, *Tażkirah*, 77–79.

73. These included Ḥātim and Nājī. On Amīr Ḳhān, see Ḥasan Dihlavī, *Tażkirah*, 146; Hakala, "Coffee in Eighteenth-Century Delhi," 375; Shāh Nawāz Ḳhān Aurangābādī, *Maʾāṡir*, 1890, 2:2:839; Ḳhwushgo, *Safīnah*, 1959, 321. On Amīr Ḳhān's career and patronage, see Malik, *Muhammad Shah*, 184–88, 299–301, 366–68.

74. Upon his death, Amīr Ḳhān's servants refused to bury his corpse until fourteen months' worth of arrears on their salaries had been paid. In violation of Islamic funerary practices, Amīr Ḳhān's body rotted over four days before it was interred in the wayfarers' inn of Rūḥullāh Ḳhān (Sarai Rohilla), situated outside the Lahore Gate of the walled city as noted in Beale, *Miftāḥ*, 325; Pillai, *Diary*, 1914, 3:431; Sangīn Beg, "Sair," fol. 69a.

75. Ḥasan Dihlavī, *Tażkirah*, 146.

76. Jālibī, *Tārīḳh*, 2:259–61. For a brief discussion of Maẓmūn's verse, see ʿAbd ul-Ḥaqq, "Īhām-Goʾī," 11.

77. Żū'l-Faqār, "Īhām-go," 74.

78. Niẓāmī, *Īhām Goʾī*, 156–59.

79. Amrullāh Allāhābādī, *Tażkirah*, 129. To account for īhām, an alternate translation reads, "Do not terrorize metaphor with the renown of the apocalypse."

80. Shafīq Aurangābādī, *Chamanistān*, 257–58. To account for īhām, an alternate translation of the second line reads, "Otherwise, from those words, your literary theme will become a religious principle."

81. Yaqīn, *Dīwān*, 1916, 59–60. To account for īhām, an alternate translation of the second line reads, "Indeed, from those words you only attain a metaphorical beloved." The verse is missing in Yaqīn, *Dīwān*, 1995. See also, "Like your tresses, when this verse was formed in meter, / my heart appeared to be tangled up in it like a *maẓmūn*" (*tujh zulf kā yih miṣrā[ʿ] tab señ huʾā hai mauzūn / jab soñ bañdhā hai us meñ dil ā miṡāl-e maẓmūn*) in Ābrū, *Dīwān*, 2000, 212.

82. Muṣḥafī, *Tażkirah*, 1933, 80.

83. Ḥātim, *Intiḳhāb*, 147. This verse was later cut, as noted in Ḥātim, *Dīwānzādah*, 2011, 209. For Mīr's critique of the term *sabz-rū* (fresh-or green-faced) and Shafīq's correction of the term to *ḳhaṭ kī sabzī* (peach fuzz), see Mīr, *Nikāt*, 80–81; Shafīq Aurangābādī, *Chamanistān*, 143. In Ḥātim's defense, see Ṣāʾib's *sabz-rū* in his *Dīwān*, 1990, 5:2825.

84. Muṣḥafī, "Tażkirah," fol. 41a. For Ḥātim's patronage under ʿUmdat ul-Mulk Amīr Ḳhān, see Hakala, "Coffee in Eighteenth-Century Delhi," 375.

85. Ḥātim, *Dīwānzādah*, 2011, 247.

86. Muṣḥafī, "Tażkirah," fol. 41a.

87. Muṣḥafī, *Tażkirah*, 1933, 81.

88. ʿAṣīm, *Talāmiżah-e Ḥātim*, 30.

89. Muṣḥafī, "Tażkirah," fol. 3a.

90. For the chronogram "Woe is me! One hundred times alas! Shāh Ḥātim is dead" (*āh ṣad ḥef shāh ḥātim murd*) (1197 AH), see Muṣḥafī, "Tażkirah," fol. 41b.

91. Ḥātim, *Dīwānzādah*, 2011, 248.

92. Hakala, *Negotiating Languages*, 8–12.

93. Gramsci, *Quaderni*, 2:1376.

94. Ḥātim, *Dīwānzādah*, 2011, 105.

95. Ḥātim, *Intik̤hāb*, 98. Noted as *kaun hove jo nah hove tū mirā* in Ḥātim, *Dīwānzādah*, 2011, 136.

96. Shafīq Aurangābādī, *Chamanistān*, 256.

97. Ḥātim, *Dīwānzādah*, 2011, 105.

98. Muṣḥafī, *Tażkirah*, 1933, 80.

99. Muṣḥafī, *Tażkirah*, 1933, 80. For Walī on his own fame in the couplet, "Your poems have been famous ever since, O Walī, / they yearned for your words from Arabia to Persia" (*shahrat hūʾī hai jab se tire shiʿr kī walī / mushtāq tujh suk̤han kā ʿarab tā ʿajam hūʾā*), see Walī Dakhanī, *Kulliyāt*, 112; Walī Dakhanī, *Œuvres*, title page. See also Shackle, "Walī."

100. Walī Dakhanī, *Kulliyāt*, 91.

101. Ḥasan Dihlavī, *Tażkirah*, 147. For another ġhazal in Walī's form ending in *be-qarārī hai*, see, Walī Dakhanī, *Kulliyāt*, 297; Shafīq Aurangābādī, *Chamanistān*, 259.

102. Ābrū, *Dīwān*, 2000, 295.

103. Ābrū, *Dīwān*, 2000, 271.

104. Ḥātim, *Intik̤hāb*, 122. See also, Tābān Dihlavī, *Dīwān*, 2006, 192–93; Saudā, *Dīwān*, 231–32.

105. *Dīwānzādah*, 2011, 160. For other instances of writers teasing Walī and criticizing his verse, see Shafīq Aurangābādī, *Chamanistān*, 105–6. Also discussed in Dhavan and Pauwels, "Controversies," 624–43. See also discussion in Faruqi, *Early Urdu*, 132–33.

106. Sāyānī, preface to *Walī*, 9. For discussion of *muʿamalah bandī*, see Shiblī Nuʿmānī, *ʿAjam*, 3:17–18.

107. Pritchett, "Long History 2," 900.

108. Walī Dakhanī, *Kulliyāt*, 347.

109. Ḥamīd Aurangābādī, *Gulshan*, 8; Shafīq Aurangābādī, *Chamanistān*, 104–5. For Walī's praise of Mecca, see Walī Dakhanī, *Kulliyāt*, 363–65.

110. Ḥamīd Aurangābādī, *Gulshan*, 8.

111. Gardezī, "Tażkirah," fol. 66b.

112. Mīr, *Nikāt*, 91. For an alternate version that emerged later in which Gulshan urged Walī to forsake Deccani language, see Shauq Murādābādī, *Tażkirah*, 6. Cf. Day of Judgement theme in Nājī, *Dīwān*, 349.

113. Amrullāh Allāhābādī, *Tażkirah*, 154.

114. Dhavan and Pauwels, "Controversies," 627–28. See also Faruqi, "Long History 1," 845–46; Faruqi, *Early Urdu*, 129–42.

115. Chuġhatā'ī, "Walī Gujarātī," 10. See discussion in Qā'im Chāndpūrī, *Tażkirah*, 22nn1; Ẓahīr ud-Dīn Madanī, *Suḳhanwarān*, 86–87. Further discussion in Faruqi, "Long History 1," 845nn90.

116. Tassy, Preface to *Les Œuvres*, x; Walī Dakhanī, *Œuvres*, 30, 59; Walī Dakhanī, *Kulliyāt*, 199. For court poetry on the Aurangzeb's victory at Satārā, see Musta'idd Ḳhān, *Ma'āśir*, 421.

117. Ishwar Das Nagar, *Futuhat*, 162–63. See also Sarkar, *Studies*, 54.

118. Sarḳhwush, *Tażkirah*, 141. Gulshan later claimed authority on Bedil's verse to deflect criticisms of the poet-saint's supposed mistakes, noting that any errors would later be considered authoritative (*sanad*) by lexicographers (*ahl-e luġhat wa farhang-hā*) after a few hundred years, as noted in Ḳhwushgo, *Safīnah*, 1959, 116.

119. For his contemporaries' diaries, see Maẓhar, *Dīwān wa Ḳharīṭah*, 152.

120. Sarḳhwush, *Tażkirah*, 161; Ṣā'ib Tabrezī, *Dīwān*, 1986, 2:1032.

121. On Asīr's life and literary circles, see Vildānī, preface to *Asīr*, xxii–xxvii, xxx–xl.

122. Asīr Shahristānī, *Dīwān*, 8. From Ṣā'ib, *Dīwān*, 1985, 1:175.

123. Muḳhliṣ, *Tażkirah*, 281; Ārzū, "Majma'," binding 2, fol. 402b.

124. For tażkirah accounts of Wā'iẓ from Sarḳhwush, Ḳhwushgo, and others, see Nāṣirī, preface to *Wā'iẓ*, 61–64.

125. Wā'iẓ-e Qazwīnī, *Dīwān*, 448.

126. Iḳhlāṣ, "Tażkirah," fol. 143b; Ḳhwushgo, *Safīnah*, 1959, 169; Muḳhliṣ, *Tażkirah*, 281; Wālih Dāġhistānī, *Tażkirah*, 1:3:1934; Qudratullāh Gūpāmvī, *Tażkirah*, 639; Hāshmī Sandīlavī, *Tażkirah*, 1994, 4:790.

127. For Kātibī's and Ibn Mubārakshāh's intellectual milieus, see Rouayheb, "Islamic Philosophers"; Rouayheb, "Al-Kātibī al-Qazwīnī."

128. See colophon in Iḳhlāṣ, "Tażkirah," fol. 173a.

129. For a quatrain ridiculing Gulshan's use of China root and its role in his death, see Ḳhwushgo, *Safīnah*, 1959, 246. On China root's uses, see da Orta, *Colloquies*, 381; Winterbottom, "Of the China Root," 30–31.

130. 'Āshiqī 'Aẓīmābādī, *Tażkirah*, 2:1354; Ḳhwushgo, *Safīnah*, 1959, 168; Dard, *Majmū'ah*, 117–18. For intellectual history of Dard and his milieu, see Ziad, "Quest of the Nightingale."

131. Ḳhwushgo, *Safīnah*, 1959, 168; Dargāh Qulī Ḳhān, *Muraqqa'*, 90–91.

132. Ārzū, *Mu'āṣirān*, 112; Ḳhwushgo, *Safīnah*, 1959, 90, 168; Muḳhliṣ, *Tażkirah*, 281.

133. Muḳhliṣ, *Tażkirah*, 281. Gulshan's grave still stands today in the H Block of New Delhi's Connaught Place, at the end of Chelmsford Road (formerly Qutb Road), as described in Farīdī Dihlavī, *Mazārāt*, 121. Municipal development continues to pose risks to his grave, as discussed in Zafarul-Islam Khan, "Return of 123 Waqf Properties—No Reason to Rejoice," *The Milli Gazette*, March 16, 2014.

134. Dargāh Qulī Ḳhān, *Muraqqa'*, 72. Ḳhwushgo noticed a certain Kashmiri poet named Muḥammad Mas'ūd *Rāfi'* (The Exalter) skillfully reciting at Gulshan's 'urs on a one occasion, Ḳhwushgo, *Safīnah*, 1959, 238.

135. Ḳhwushgo, *Safīnah*, 1959, 167.

136. Wālih Dāġhistānī, *Taẕkirah*, 1:3:1934. For a similar sentiment attached to the poetry of Gulshan's teacher Waḥdat, see Alam, *Mughals and the Sufis*, 382. ʿAndalīb's son Dard inflated Gulshan's dīwān to the massive size of 200,000 verses in *Majmūʿah*, 117. See Ḳhwushgo's more reliable estimation at 20,100 verses in *Safīnah*, 1959, 165.

137. Muḳhliṣ, *Taẕkirah*, 281.

138. Shafīq Aurangābādī, *Chamanistān*, 255. Compare the same verse that appears in a *bayāẓ* attributed to Maẓhar in Qureshī, *Mīrzā Maẓhar*, 335. For other similar verses, see Qureshī, 332nn1; Shafīq Aurangābādī, *Chamanistān*, 260. For a ġhazal with the same end rhyme but a distinct meter, see Nājī, *Dīwān*, 148.

139. Ābrū, *Dīwān*, 2000, 79 and compare 115. For Maẓhar's version, see Qureshī, *Mīrzā Maẓhar*, 295. Later emulations, see Fuġhān, *Dīwān*, 152; Saudā, *Dīwān*, 202–3. For likely connection to Wālī, see *Kulliyāt*, 385–86. My thanks to Purnima Dhavan for alerting me to Walī's influence on these poems.

140. Ḥātim, *Dīwānzādah*, 2011, 139; Ḥātim, *Intiḳhāb*, 94.

141. Ḥātim, Ābrū, Nājī, and Maẓhar composed many shared verses during 1723—e.g., poems with the refrain "where'd they go" (*kidhar gaʾe*), see Ḥātim, *Intiḳhāb*, 194; Nājī, *Dīwān*, 318; Qureshī, *Mīrzā Maẓhar*, 339; Ābrū, *Dīwān*, 2000, 260. For Ḥātim's revision and dating the exchange, see Ḥātim, Dīwānzādah, 2011, 351.

142. Ṣāʾib Tabrezī, *Dīwān*, 1991, 6:3203.

143. Walī Dakhanī, *Kulliyāt*, 225.

144. For Ābrū's response, "This line from Walī was excellent to me, O Ābrū: / You ask bit by bit, I answer bit by bit" (*lagā hai ābrū mujh koñ walī kā ḳhūb yih miṣrā / sawāl āhistah āhistah jawāb āhistah āhistah*), see *Dīwān*, 2000, 226. In the same meter with the same refrain but a distinct end rhyme, see ʿIshq, "Dīwān," fols. 542b–543a; Ṣāʾib Tabrezī, *Dīwān*, 1991, 6:3203. See also Shafīq's discussion of Walī's emulators on another Ṣāʾib-inspired ġhazal in *Chamanistān*, 183.

145. For debates on Maẓmūn's death year as noted by Jālibī, *Tāriḳh*, 2:257–258nn. Cf. Ārzū, *Tanbīh*, 76. For conjecture of 1734 and 1744, see Qāʾim Chāndpūrī, *Taẕkirah*, 53. For Tābān's chronogram "Hey, hey, when did Mister Maẓmūn die?" (*kad moʾe he he miyāñ maẓmūn*) (1147 AH), see *Dīwān*, 2006, 395–96. Muḥammad Rafiʿ Saudā (1706/7–1781) also mourned Maẓmūn's passing in a ġhazal cited in this book's introduction, Saudā, *Dīwān*, 343; Āzād, *Ḥayāt*, 64.

146. Shafīq Aurangābādī, *Chamanistān*, 259.

147. Ḥātim, *Dīwānzādah*, 2011, 336. My thanks to David Boyk for his correction on my translation. For Ḥātim's Persian version with a tribute (*taẓmīn*) to Ṣāʾib, see Ḥātim, *Dīwān-e Fārsī*, 218; Ṣāʾib Tabrezī, *Dīwān*, 1991, 6:3297.

148. Nājī, *Dīwān*, 320.

149. Saudā's memorial for Ābrū, see Shafīq Aurangābādī, *Chamanistān*, 9.

150. For discussion of Ṣāʾib's early career in a largely ignored taẕkirah, see Beers, "Khayr al-Bayān," 128–31.

151. Āzād Bilgrāmī, *Sarv*, 112.

152. Ṣāʾib Tabrezī, *Dīwān*, 1988, 4:1886. Also cited in Āzād Bilgrāmī, *Sarv*, 111.

153. Awḥadī Balyānī, *ʿArafāt*, 6:4141–4142; Ārzū, *Taẕkirah*, 3:1410–19; Ḳhwushgo, *Safīnah*, 2010, 643; Muḳhliṣ, *Taẕkirah*, 302–4. For mention of Maʿṣūm in Iran, see Naṣrābādī, *Taẕkirah*, 374–76.

154. Qudratullāh Gūpāmvī, *Tażkirah*, 665; Wālih Dāġhistānī, *Tażkirah*, 3:1753; Hāshmī Sandīlavī, *Tażkirah*, 1994, 5:160; ʿĀshiqī ʿAẓīmābādī, *Tażkirah*, 2:1473–74. For the incorrect attribution of Maʿṣūm's verse to Ṣāʾib, see Muḳhliṣ, *Tażkirah*, 282; Ārzū, *Tanbīh*, 137.

155. Ṣāʾib Tabrezī, *Dīwān*, 1991, 6:3297. My thanks to the anonymous reviewer for catching my previous errors in this verse.

156. Joyā Tabrezī, *Kulliyāt*, 866–67; Joyā Tabrezī, *Dīwān*, 297.

157. Sarḳhwush, "Kalimāt," fol. 52a.

158. Muḳhliṣ, *Tażkirah*, 282; ʿĀshiqī ʿAẓīmābādī, *Tażkirah*, 2:1374. Compare Wālih Dāġhistānī, *Tażkirah*, 3:1934.

159. See *manẓūr-e ṭabʿ-e mushkil pasand* in Muḳhliṣ, *Tażkirah*, 282.

160. Muḳhliṣ, 282–83; Ummīd, "Dīwān," fol. 212b; Ḥazīn Lāhījī, *Dīwān*, 553. For Maẓhar's citation of Muḳhliṣ's version in his verse collection *Ḳharīṭah-e Jawāhir*, see Maẓhar, *Dīwān wa Ḳharīṭah*, 160. For a recent critical edition of Ummīd's dīwān, see Ḳhūrshīd, "Taṣḥīḥ-e Dīwān," though there are some print errors in this text, as noted by White, "On the Road," 22nn118.

161. Ārzū, *Tanbīh*, 136–37.

162. Nudrat Kashmīrī, "Kulliyāt," fol. 152a.

163. Wāʿiẓ-e Qazwīnī, *Dīwān*, 375; Mushtāq Iṣfahānī, *Dīwān*, 103. On Mushtāq's contributions during the late 1700s, see Schwartz, *Remapping Persian*, 88–89. On Mushtāq and the "literary return" movement, see Smith, "Literary Connections," 200–203; Bahār, *Sabkshināsī*, vol. 1, author's preface, *ye*. For a translation of Bahār's preface, see Jabbari, "Introduction," 272.

164. For Ārzū's attempt at a variation of this form in the early 1720s, "Afterall, the scratch of my pen started up the song o' the ringdove" (*gar ṣarīr-e qalamam ḳhāst nawāʾī-e qumrī*), see Ārzū, "Dīwān," fol. 311a.

165. Nājī, *Dīwān*, 320.

166. Saudā, *Dīwān*, 343; Āzād, *Ḥayāt*, 64. For Ḥātim's memorial of Maẓmūn, see *Dīwānzādah*, 2011, 145.

Chapter 3

1. Āzād Bilgrāmī, *Ḳhazānah*, 315–18; Dargāh Qulī Ḳhān, *Muraqqaʿ*, 70–71, 90–91; Shād ʿAẓīmābādī, *Ḥayāt*, 165–66.

2. Three other noted émigrés include: Mirzā Zakī *Nadīm* (The Confidant) (d. 1750), a companion to Ummīd; Sharaf ud-Dīn ʿAlī *Wafā* (The Trust) (fl. 1740–70), who socialized with Ārzū, Wālih, and Ḥākim; and Kāẓim Beg Ḳhān (fl. 1720–90), who reached Delhi from Astarābād in 1741. On Nadīm, see Ārzū, "Majmaʿ," binding 2, fols. 491a–492b. For Wafā, see Ārzū, Majmaʿ," 2, fol. 524b. Wafā's later mentions appear in Āżar Begdilī, *Ātishkadah*, 2:681–82; Ḥairat Akbarābādī, *Tażkirah*, 126–27. Also discussed in Kia, *Persianate Selves*, 181, 187. Kāẓim Beg Ḳhān's arrival was noted by his son ʿAlī Luṭf ʿAẓīmābādī (d. 1866) in "Gulshan," 1801, fol. 140a.

3. While no images of these performers survived, as captured in figure 3.1, a painting from the Richard Johnson collection by the artist Kalyān Dās (aka Chitar-

man II), depicts an elite, wealthy woman dressed as would be expected of any influential woman in Delhi—courtesan or otherwise. Kalyān Dās, "Portrait of a Lady." For background on Kalyān Dās and Richard Johnson, see McInerney, "Chitarman II (Kalyan Das)"; Di Pietrantonio, "Pornography and Indian Miniatures."; Ursula Sims-Williams, "'White Mughal' Richard Johnson and Mir Qamar al-Din Minnat," Asian and African studies blog, accessed June 2, 2024, https://blogs.bl.uk/asian-and-african/2014/04/white-mughal-richard-johnson-and-mir-qamar-al-din-minnat.html.

4. For a discussion of īhām in light of recent scholarship, see Tabor, "Tābān's Magnificence," 227–29.

5. Wālih Dāġhistānī, *Tażkirah*, 1:433.

6. Ḥazīn Lāhījī, *Rasāʾil*, 241–42.

7. Ḥazīn Lāhījī, *Dīwān*, 553.

8. Āzād Bilgrāmī, "Yad-e Baiẓā," 64.

9. Muṣḥafī, "Tażkirah," fol. 33a. For the location of Amīr Ḳhān's home, see Sangīn Beg, "Sair," fol. 35a. On Amīr Ḳhān's later patronage of Ḥāzīn, see Ḳhwushgo, *Safīnah*, 1959, 291–92. After Amīr Ḳhān's death, his home remained a haven for poets, as noted in Mīr, *Remembrances*, 144–45.

10. Ḳhān, "Qabūl," 61.

11. Ārzū, *Tażkirah*, 3:1363. Mercury sulphate or cinnabar (*shangarf* or *shanjarf*) is also a medical substance. For similar usage and discussion of the term *māhī* in other īhām-styled verse, see Wālih Dāġhistānī, *Tażkirah*, 4:1751. For its emulation, see Ummīd, "Dīwān," 1713, fol. 3a; Ummīd, "Dīwān," n.d., fol. 2a.

12. Ārzū, *Tażkirah*, 3:1362–63.

13. Muḳhliṣ, *Mirʾāt*, 2:497.

14. Wālih Dāġhistānī, *Tażkirah*, 3:1938; Qāʾim Chāndpūrī, *Tażkirah*, 78; Ārzū, *Tażkirah*, 3:1362. For other public religious leaders, see Taqī as noted in Dargāh Qulī Ḳhān, *Muraqqaʿ*, 97.

15. Ḥazīn Lāhījī, *Tārīḳh*, 174.

16. Ḥazīn Lāhījī, *Rasāʾil*, 181–83. On medieval *samāʿ*, see Lawrence, "Early Chishti"; Ġhazālī, *Kīmyā*, 1:473–98.

17. Ārzū, *Tażkirah*, 3:1363.

18. Ārzū, 3:1362.

19. Ārzū, "Majmaʿ," binding 2, 400a. For detailed consideration of the Qabuliyans and their milieu, see Tabor, "Tābān's Magnificence," 243–45.

20. Muḳhliṣ, *Tażkirah*, 272; Ḳhwushgo, "Safīnah," fol. 99b.

21. Sharma, *Arcadia*, 126, 222nn2.

22. For Ġhanī's biography and verse samples, see Rāshidī, *Tażkirah*, 2:968–1001. For a critical appraisal of Ġhanī, see Keshavmurthy, "Ḡani."

23. For Joyā's biography and verse samples, see Rāshidī, *Tażkirah*, 1:181–206; Ḳhān, "Joyā."

24. Ḳhwushgo, *Safīnah*, 1959, 201–4; Ārzū, *Muʿāṣirān*, 95; Muḳhliṣ, *Tażkirah*, 181–82; Hadi, *Dictionary*, 572.

25. Iḳhlāṣ, "Tażkirah," fol. 145a. On the fortress, see Aḥmad Dihlavī, *Wāqiʿāt*, 2:594–606; Ḳhān, *Āṡār*, 23–24; Sangīn Beg, "Sair," fol. 86a.

26. Notably, Bedil's challenger Beḳhabar visited with Qabūl, as noted in Āzād Bilgrāmī, "Yad-e Baiẓā," 189. For Ḳhwushgo's visits, see Ḳhwushgo, "Safīnah," fol. 100a.

27. Kaicker, "Market of Shaikh-Dom," 277.

28. Ḳhwushgo, *Safīnah*, 1959, 69, 165. For Shāh Gul's reḳhtah verse, see Jālibī, *Tārīḳh*, 2:123.

29. For a discussion of the confusion over Ishtiyāq's identity, see Jālibī, *Tārīḳh*, 2:266.

30. Ḳhwushgo, *Safīnah*, 1959, 302; Dargāh Qulī Ḳhān, *Muraqqaʿ*, 78–79; Ḥākim Lāhaurī, *Tażkirah*, 112. Maẕhar held his verse recitals every Thursday at the downtown Congregational Mosque. For Inshā's early memory of meeting Maẕhar there, circa 1762, see Inshā and Qatīl, *Daryā*, 1850, 38–39.

31. Dargāh Qulī Ḳhān, *Muraqqaʿ*, 100; Kashmīrī, *Bayān*, 265–66; Sangīn Beg, *Sair*, 1982, 65. For a record of Bāsiṯ and his conflict over musical assemblies, see Muṣḥafī, "Tażkirah," fol. 21a; Ḥārisī, "ʿIbrat Nāmah," fols. 159a–160b. My thanks to Abhishek Kaicker for sharing images from the latter source.

32. Ḳhwushgo, "Safīnah," fol. 99b. For Qabūl's words about himself, "I am neither Sunni nor Shīʿī nor atheist. / Few realize they are all the same path" (*shīʿī-o sunnī-o mulḥid nīstam / kam kasī dānad kih īn ham maslakī ast*), see Ārzū, "Majmaʿ," binding 2, fol. 390a. For a discussion of influential students, see Ḳhān, "Qabūl," 58–61.

33. Iḳhlāṣ, "Tażkirah," fol. 135b. For a discussion of Iḳhlāṣ's historical project, see Kinra, *Writing Self*, 269–74.

34. Iḳhlāṣ, "Tażkirah," fol. 46a–b. On Ḥashmat's sartorial choices, see Ḳhalīl, "Gulzār," fol. 57a. For the verse "The scent of his love abides in poetic speech, Tābān. / Only then did I establish sincere friendship with Mr. Kishan Chand Iḳhlāṣ" (*suḳhan meñ un ke maḥabbat kī bū hai ai tābān / rakheñ haiñ tab to kishan chand jī se ham iḳhlāṣ*), see Tābān Dihlavī, *Dīwān*, 2006, 215. Also discussed in Aḥmad Qamar, "Maʿrufī," 154.

35. Ārzū, "Majmaʿ," binding 2, fols. 389b–392a.

36. One example that uses complex īhāms with scribal terms, "Indeed, you don't recognize the distance between good and bad, for as you say, / fate is written on partridge feathers in chicken-scratch" (*chū nek-o bad nashināsī chih dūr agar goʾī / qażā nawishtah ḳhaṭ-e kabk rā bah pā-e kulāġh*), see Ārzū, "Dīwān," fol. 240a.

37. Ārzū, "Majmaʿ," binding 2, fol. 390a.

38. Muḳhliṣ, *Tażkirah*, 81, 272–73.

39. For further discussion of *īhām-e nātamām*, see Tabor, "Tābān's Magnificence," 245–46.

40. Muḳhliṣ, 272–73; Ḳhwushgo, "Safīnah," fol. 99b.

41. Qabūl's citation of *maḥmil* alludes to Arabic-language terminology for double entendre "as bearing two antithetical meanings" (*al-muḥtimal lil-żiddain*) in Stetkevych, "Snake in the Tree," 4n2. Further discussion is in Ambler, "Distant Meanings," 119nn84. For literary theorization of *īhām* in early modern Persian literature, see Wāʿiẓ Kāshifī, *Badāʾiʿ*, 109–13; and earlier considerations in Waṭwāṭ, *Dīwān*, 359–62; ur-Rāzī, *Al-Muʿjam*, 365–66. My thanks are owed to Alessia Dal

Bianco for sharing her expertise on the early theorists. For eighteenth-century discussions of *īhām*, see Faqīr's treatise as cited in Wālih Dāġhistānī, *Tażkirah*, 3:1751–52. For a discussion of *īhām* in reḳhtah composition, see Inshā and Qatīl, *Daryā*, 1850, 446–51. For the intellectual history of īhām in light of recent scholarship, see Ambler, "Distant Meanings," 114–23.

42. Ārzū, *Dād*, 10.

43. Faruqi, *Urdū Ġhazal*; Pritchett, "Long History 2"; Niẓāmī, *Īhām Goʾī*.

44. Sheftah, *Gulshan*, 419. Also cited in Jālibī, *Tārīḳh*, 2:127.

45. For Ishtiyāq's emulation of Ābrū, see *Dīwān*, 2000, 127, 196; Mīr, *Nikāt*, 28; Shafīq Aurangābādī, *Chamanistān*, 28. On Ishtiyāq's īhām style, see Niẓāmī, *Īhām Goʾī*, 173–75. For his Persian-language emulations, see Rūmī, *Kulliyāt*, 1062; Ḳhwushgo, *Safīnah*, 1959, 212. For other emulations and likely inspiration, see Ṣāʾib Tabrezī, *Dīwān*, 1991, 6:3320.

46. For a discussion of Ḥashmat's instruction, see Tabor, "Tābān's Magnificence," 249–252.

47. For a brief mention of Girāmī's interactions with Rājā Roshan Rāy, see Beale, *Miftāḥ*, 323. For reference to literary production within Roshan Rāy's circles, see Mobad Kashmīrī, "Kulliyāt," fol. 315b; Ḥashmat, "Bayāẓ," fol. 209b.

48. Hindī, *Safīnah*, 165; Qāʾim Chāndpūrī, *Tażkirah*, 78. His skills in magic were likely learned from his father, who also taught them to Iḳhlāṣ and Ḥashmat. On Girāmī's student Mobad and his mastery of geomancy, see Mobad Kashmīrī, "Kulliyāt," fol. 6a. On Girāmī's elite connections, see ʿĀshiqī ʿAẓīmābādī, *Tażkirah*, 2:1333; Shāh Nawāz Ḳhān Aurangābādī, *Maʾāṡir*, 1888, 1:358–61; Muʿtamad Ḳhān Badaḳhshī, *Tārīḳh-e Muḥammadī*, 2 (6):133.

49. Hindī, *Safīnah*, 165; Ārzū, *Tażkirah*, 3:1362.

50. Iḳhlāṣ, "Tażkirah," fol. 145a.

51. Ārzū, *Tażkirah*, 3:1362.

52. For a discussion of Mirzā Kallū's event planning, see Kaicker, "Mughal Habitus," 14.

53. Ḳhwushgo, *Safīnah*, 1959, 234; Dargāh Qulī Ḳhān, *Muraqqaʿ*, 58–59.

54. Mīr, *Nikāt*, 141; Ḥasan Dihlavī, *Tażkirah*, 23. For similar registers in coeval Persian literature sources, see Ārzū, "Majmaʿ," binding 2, fol. 493a; Ḳhwushgo, *Safīnah*, 2010, 608.

55. "Like a candle, O Girāmī, I have no complaint with the other guy. / Whatever I have seen I saw with my own eyes" (*chū shamaʿ shikwah girāmī zi-ġhair nīst marā / har ān chih dīdah-am az chashm-e ḳhwīshtan dīdam*) in Ārzū, "Majmaʿ," binding 2, fol. 401a; Maẓhar, *Dīwān wa Ḳharīṭah*, 152 and 74–75 for a probable emulation.

56. Ārzū, *Tażkirah*, 3:1364; Maẓhar, *Dīwān wa Ḳharīṭah*, 16; Nāṣir ʿAlī Sirhindī, *Dīwān-e Ashʿār*, 193–94.

57. Muḳhliṣ, *Tażkirah*, 318–19. For Maẓhar's unique use of linguistic registers and salon hierarchies in the poem "As soon as he went to the party, my enemy acted the Grand Poo-Bah / [In Persian:] *What hallowed ground*! Hey friends, let's call him our revered guru" (*ab raqīb us bazm meñ jā kar hūʾā pīr-e muġhān / jā-e taʿẓīm ast ai yāro use guru-jī kaho*), see Qureshī, *Mīrzā Maẓhar*, 302.

58. For Yaqīn's earliest datable verse shared with Ḥātim, see Ḥātim, *Dīwānzādah*, 2011, 225; Yaqīn, *Dīwān*, 1916, 32.

59. Ārzū, "Majmaʿ," binding 2, fol. 464a; Mīr, *Nikāt*, 83.

60. Ḳhwushgo, "Safīnah," fol. 188a. On Maẕhar's eventual burial place near Turkman Gate, see Sangīn Beg, "Sair," fol. 33b.

61. For a discussion of Ummīd's biography, see Khwājah, "Ummīd," 12–14. On Ummīd's identity within pan-regional contexts, see Kia, *Persianate Selves*, 190–94.

62. Wālih Dāġhistānī, *Taẕkirah*, 4:2344–46.

63. Āzād Bilgrāmī, *Maʾāsir*, 2:209; Qāqshāl, *Tuḥfat*, 100–101; Luṯf ʿAẕīmābādī, *Gulshan*, 1906, 17–19.

64. On Muhammad Shah's attempt to unseat Niẕām ul-Mulk, see Ḳhwāfī Ḳhān, *Muntaḳhab*, 2:848, 953–55; Shāh Nawāz Ḳhān Aurangābādī, *Maʾāsir*, 1891, 3:843; Richards, *The Mughal Empire*, 278–81.

65. Ārzū, "Majmaʿ," binding 1, fols. 148a–149b; Muṣḥafī, "Taẕkirah," fol. 8b. See further discussion in Kia, *Persianate Selves*, 191. For Ārzū, this was extraordinary as many people with Turkish roots (*muġhal*) had little tolerance for the people of India or anything Indian. See *muġhal bachah* [sic] in Ārzū, *Muʿāṣirān*, 45; Dudney, *Persian World*, 139–40. For Ummīd's reḳhtah/Deccani verse and singing abilities, see Luṯf ʿAẕīmābādī, *Gulshan*, 1906, 22; ʿĀshiqī ʿAẕīmābādī, *Taẕkirah*, 1:125; Inshā and Qatīl, *Daryā*, 1850, 64–65.

66. Dargāh Qulī Ḳhān, *Muraqqaʿ*, 90. For Nājī's pun-filled praise of Sadārang, see *Dīwān*, 405–6. On ḳhayāl and Mughal history, see Brown [Schofield], "Origins of Khayal"; Schofield, "Musicians to the Mughal Emperors."

67. Muṣḥafī, "Taẕkirah," fol. 8b.

68. Qāʾim Chāndpūrī, *Taẕkirah*, 74–75.

69. Ḳhwushgo, *Safīnah*, 1959, 250. For Ummīd's visit to the Rasūl Numā shrine (and location of Ābrū's tomb), see Mīr, *Nikāt*, 28–29.

70. Faqīr also wrote under *Maftūn* (The Charmed), as noted in Dargāh Qulī Ḳhān, *Muraqqaʿ*, 82; Rahman, "Faqīr." On Nadīm, see Ārzū, *Muʿāṣirān*, 119–20. On Ummīd's disposition, see Muḳhliṣ, *Taẕkirah*, 283, 344; Gardezī, "Taẕkirah," fol. 12a.

71. For Ummīd's citations, see Muḳhliṣ, *Mirʾāt*, 2:782; Bahār, *ʿAjam*, 1:606, 2:731; Nudrat Kashmīrī, "ʿAin-e ʿAṯā," fol. 719a.

72. Maẕhar, *Dīwān wa Ḳharīṯah*, 34. For "information gathering" (*ḳhabar giriftan*) as part of the "Language of the Sodomites," see *A Comprehensive Persian-English Dictionary, Including the Arabic Words and Phrases to Be Met with in Persian Literature*, comp. Francis Joseph Steingass (London: Routledge & K. Paul, 1892), s.v. *ḳhabar*. Further emulations are found in ʿIshq, "Dīwān," fol. 204a; Ummīd, "Dīwān," 1713, fol. 8a–b. For the originating form, see Ṣāʾib, *Dīwān*, 1986, 2:681. For analysis of ʿIshq and Ummīd's versions without reference to Maẕhar or Ṣāʾib, see White, "On the Road," 22–23nn118.

73. Ārzū, "Majmaʿ," binding 2, fol. 400b.

74. Ummīd, "Dīwān," n.d., fol. 123b. Incomplete in Ummīd, "Dīwān," 1801, fol. 13a.

75. Anonymous, "Bayāẕ," fol. 1a.

76. Ārzū, *Muʿāṣirān*, 110–11.

77. For Dargāh Qulī Ḳhān's verse from Girāmī "Oh, until you stepped into the garden, / color was never shy before the roses" (*dar chaman tā nihādah ai pā rā / rang bar rū namānad gul-hā rā*), see Dargāh Qulī Ḳhān, *Muraqqaʿ*, 84.

78. Āzād Bilgrāmī, "Yad-e Baiẓā," 196. To account for īhām, an alternate translation reads, "May the of blood of the lovers be on that gleaming white neck of his. / So that even the whiteness therein may have a colorful meaning."

79. On the preciousness of verse in notebooks, see Walī and Jamāl ud-Dīn Muḥammad Sīdī *ʿUrfī* (The Notorious) (1555–1591) and their notion of *bayāẓī* in Walī Dakhanī, *Kulliyāt*, 374; ʿUrfī Shīrāzī, *Qaṣāʾid*, 71; also Kāshānī, *Ḳhulāṣat*, 6(9):208. Further evidence is found among the many puns on the word *bayāẓ* itself: Bedil, *Kulliyāt*, 1:711; Mīr, *Kulliyāt*, 1983, 1:557 line 8541; Ḳhwushgo, *Safīnah*, 1959, 153 and 199. On the *bayāẓ* in Islamic history, see Dānešpažūh, "Bayāż."

80. Dargāh Qulī Ḳhān, *Muraqqaʿ*, 84. Muḳhliṣ, *Mirʾāt*, 2:498. For a verse that Girāmī recited at Ḳhwushgo's gathering, see Ḳhwushgo, "Safīnah," fol. 149a. For one reḳhtah verse from Girāmi, see Mīr, *Nikāt*, 29. For a non-confrontational Qabuliyan, see Kashmiri poet Nūrullāh *Nuzhat* (The Delight) (fl. 1710–30), see Ḳhwushgo, *Safīnah*, 1959, 206.

81. Muḳhliṣ, *Tażkirah*, 114–15.

82. Ṡābit's literary background emerged through his uncle Himmat Ḳhān *Mīran* (d. 1681), a highly stationed Mughal official who also composed in Hindi, as noted in Busch, *Poetry of Kings*, 158; Shafīq Aurangābādī, "Gul-e Raʿnā," 1790, fol. 69a. Ṡābit and Qabūl shared a friendship with Muḥammad Ḥusain *Shuhrat* (The Fame) (d. 1736), an Iranian émigré and medic who frequented the gatherings of Ḳhwushgo, Muḳhliṣ, and Ārzū. For Shuhrat's notices, see Ḳhwushgo, *Safīnah*, 1959, 201–4; Hadi, *Dictionary*, 572.

83. Ārzū, "Majmaʿ," binding 1, fol. 111b; Iḳhlāṣ, "Tażkirah," fol. 40a.

84. Ḳhwushgo, *Safīnah*, 1959, 223. For the model verse from Bedil, see Bedil, *Kulliyāt*, 1:786. Also cited in Āzād, see "Yad-e Baiẓā," 50. For an emulation from Ārzū, see "Dīwān," fol. 240a. Also cited in Iḳhlāṣ, "Tażkirah," fol. 15a–b.

85. Iḳhlāṣ avoids all mention of Istiʿdād in *Hameshah Bahār*. For a record of Istiʿdād, see Ḥākim Lāhaurī, *Tażkirah*, 114; Shafīq Aurangābādī, "Gul-e Raʿnā," 1790, fols. 34b, 72a, 75b; ʿĀshiqī ʿAẓīmābādī, *Tażkirah*, 1:112.

86. ʿĀshiqī ʿAẓīmābādī, *Tażkirah*, 1:112, 897 and 2:1526–7, 1532; Āzād Bilgrāmī, *Ḳhazānah*, 635; Āzād Bilgrāmī, "Yad-e Baiẓā," 220–21.

87. Muḳhliṣ, *Tażkirah*, 115.

88. Ṡābit, "Dīwān," 1738, fols. 21a–39b.

89. Ṡābit, "Dīwān," 1738, fol. 31a. Many thanks are owed to Peter Knapczyk for securing images from this manuscript and to Thomas Parsa for his partnership in reading the Persian with me.

90. While many gestured toward the episode, Shafīq reproduced much of qaṣīdah and provided a detailed commentary about the poem's context in Shafīq Aurangābādī, "Gul-e Raʿnā," 1790, fols. 72a–75b.

91. Ṡābit, "Dīwān," 1738, fol. 31a.

92. For an anecdote about Amīr Ḳhān serving coffee to Muhammad Shah and Nadir Shah, see Ḥairat Akbarābādī, *Tażkirah*, 12.

93. Ārzū, *Taẓkirah*, 1:379; Āzād Bilgrāmī, *Ḳhazānah*, 273; Wālih Dāġhistānī, *Taẓkirah*, 1:634.

94. For Wālih's discussion of Ṣultān and her verse, see Wālih Dāġhistānī, *Taẓkirah*, 2:1029–35 and 4:2557–2562. Wālih never cites Ṭahmāsp Qulī Ḳhān by his reginal title (Nadir Shah), only referring to him as "Iran's Champion" (*qahramān-e īrān*), as noted throughout; see the indices in *Taẓkirah*, 5:2717.

95. Hindī, *Safīnah*, 110–11.

96. Dargāh Qulī Ḳhān, *Muraqqa*ʿ, 106; Kia, *Persianate Selves*, xxii. On Gannā Begam (Lady Sugarcane), see Muṣḥafī, *Taẓkirah*, 1933, 279; Ḳhān, *Ṣubḥ*, 350; Tassy, *Histoire*, 1:488–90; Beale, *Dictionary*, 146; Jones, "Orthography," 226–28; Qāsim, *Majmūʿah*, 2:145–146. She married Mughal premier ʿImād ul-Mulk (1736–1800) and died near Gwalior, where she is purportedly buried.

97. Wālih Dāġhistānī, *Taẓkirah*, 1:293.

98. Wālih Dāġhistānī, 1:299; Ḥātim, *Dīwānzādah*, 2011, 215.

99. Wālih Dāġhistānī, *Taẓkirah*, 1:299. Ḥazīn noted the arrival as a day later in *Tārīḳh*, 281.

100. For a detailed reconsideration of this political event, see Kaicker, *The King and the People*, 18–76.

101. Pillai, *Diary*, 1904, 1:93–95.

102. For Wālih's brother Mirzā Imām Qulī Beg *Ḥashmat* (The Magnificence) (fl. 1710–50), see Muṣḥafī, "Taẓkirah," fol. 32a–b.

103. Wālih Dāġhistānī, *Taẓkirah*, 4:2366–67; Ḳhwushgo, *Safīnah*, 1959, 251–53; Muḳhliṣ, *Taẓkirah*, 344–45; Ḥākim Lāhaurī, *Taẓkirah*, 158–59. For Nadīm's later biography after his return to Iran, see Āẕar Begdilī, *Ātishkadah*, 2:655–56.

104. Kaicker, *The King and the People*, 18–53. I have relied on Kaicker's detailed account throughout this chapter. The only small addition I make to his expertly considered analysis of the occupation and ensuing violence concerns the view of Wālih as found in his taẓkirah. Wālih's description of the event appears in the capsule biography he wrote for his patron Burhān ul-Mulk.

105. Wālih Dāġhistānī, *Taẓkirah*, 1: 300–301.

106. Fraser, *Nadir Shah*, 182–83. On the mosque from where the order was given, see Aḥmad Dihlavī, *Wāqiʿāt*, 2:218–20.

107. Eschewing inflated figures from police, Wālih estimated that twenty thousand died, as noted in *Taẓkirah*, 1:301. See 150,000 dead in Fraser, *Nadir Shah*, 185.

108. Fraser, *Nadir Shah*, 184–85. For mention of Amīr Ḳhān's home, see Pillai, *Diary*, 1914, 3:340–42. On the extent of the violence, see Chānd, "Tārīḳh," fol. 199a; Astarābādī, "Wāqiʾāʿ," fol. 186a.

109. For the location of ʿAndalīb and Dard's home, see Sangīn Beg, "Sair," fol. 34b. On their move, see Firāq Dihlavī, *Maiḳhānah*, 118–19. Further discussion is in Ziad, "Quest of the Nightingale," 58. On Mihrparwar Begam, see Muʿtamad Ḳhān Badaḳhshī, *Tārīḳh-e Muḥammadī*, 2(6):123; Irvine, *Later Mughals*, 1:141.

110. Dargāh Qulī Ḳhān, *Muraqqa*ʿ, 109.

111. Ārzū, *Muʿāṣirān*, 49. Ārzū's response to the cannibalism: "As a yogi with abilities to see the future, why could you have not seen the unfortunate fate of your own mother?"

112. Ḳhwushgo, *Safīnah*, 1959, 221.

113. Muḳhliṣ, "Waqā'iʿ," 36.

114. Ḥazīn Lāhījī, *Tārīḳh*, 281–83.

115. Mīr, *Remembrances*, 126–27.

116. Wālih Dāġhistānī, *Tażkirah*, 1:299. Wālih avoided detailing Burhān ul-Mulk's military failures at Karnal.

117. Dudney, "Decadence," 197, 204.

118. Tābān Dihlavī, *Dīwān*, 2006, 211. Also discussed in Jālibī, *Tārīḳh*, 2:347. Following Kaicker, any political import from these lines would be a humorous commentary on Mughal elites, the court's politicians who increasingly pulled the levers of power after 1707. Nadir Shah beat them to whatever hopes they had in their hearts for the Peacock Throne. For an analysis that focuses on the couplet as tragedy, see Sarvar ul-Hudá, preface to *Tābān*, 35–37.

119. Later tellings misconstrue period verse as illustrative of the event, often subject to imaginative interpretation. See also from Mīr Taqī Mīr's first dīwān noting the city's "every door and wall is now soaked in blood from the [lover's cut] head" (*tar haiñ sab sar ke lahū se dar-o dīwār hanūz*) in *Kulliyāt*, 1983, 1:199.

120. Muḳhliṣ, "Waqā'iʿ," 44.

121. Ṣā'ib Tabrezī, *Dīwān*, 1986, 2:708–9.

122. *A Dictionary of Hindustani Proverbs*, comp. S. W. Fallon, eds. R. C. Temple and Lala Faqirchand Vaish (Benares: E.J. Lazarus, 1886), s.v. *diye*.

123. Ārzū, *Tażkirah*, 1:269. See chapter 1. For a discussion of Payām's death year, see Ḥairat Akbarābādī, *Tażkirah*, 20–21; Qudratullāh Gūpāmvī, *Tażkirah*, 161; Jālibī, *Tārīḳh*, 2:131nn.

124. Muḳhliṣ, "Waqā'iʿ," 42. For a discussion of Payām's verse without reference to Walī or Muḳhliṣ, see Dudney, "Decadence," 195; Hakala, *Negotiating Languages*, 141–45. Hakala cites misattributions of Payām's verse to Mīr in nineteenth-century dictionaries. For the English translation of Muḳhliṣ's account that avoids Payām's verse, see Elliot, *Muhammadan Period*, 8:88–89. Also cited in Hakala, *Negotiating Languages*, 142nn113. For occurrences of *qatl-e ʿāmm* in Persian-language and reḳhtah ġhazals, see Asīr Shahristānī, *Dīwān*, 294; Fayyāẓ Lāhījī, *Dīwān*, 138, 143, 319, 331; Mīr, *Nikāt*, 142.

125. Ḥasan Sijzī Dihlavī, *Dīwān*, 390; Ḳhusrau Dihlavī, *Dīwān*, 283.

126. Mīr, *Nikāt*, 44; Shafīq Aurangābādī, *Chamanistān*, 51; Qā'im Chāndpūrī, *Tażkirah*, 57; Ḥasan Dihlavī, *Tażkirah*, 34; Żakā, *ʿAyyār*, 94; Qāsim, *Majmūʿah*, 1:131. Mīr was the likely source for later works. Payām's position as a student of Bedil and his close links with Muḳhliṣ contributed to the frequency with which his authority stood to be deployed, most notably by Ṡābit in his extended literary battles as cited in Shafīq Aurangābādī, "Gul-e Raʿnā," 1790, fol. 61b. See also Tābān's chronogram for Payām's passing in *Dīwān*, 2006, 394–95.

127. Later misidentified as plagiarism in Qāsim, *Majmūʿah*, 1:131. Also discussed in Jālibī, *Tārīḳh*, 2:132.

128. Payām's emulation demonstrates the resonance of Rūmī's verse within Bedil's circle as noted by Keshavmurthy, "Bīdil's Portrait," 29nn63. For Payām's Persian emulations, see Rūmī, *Kulliyāt*, 1389, 1359; Ḳhwushgo, *Safīnah*, 1959, 212. For

Payām's emulations of reḳhtah poets, see Ābrū, *Dīwān*, 2000, 132; Shauq Murādābādī, *Taẕkirah*, 66.

129. Walī Dakhanī, *Kulliyāt*, 121. The end of this ġhazal features an acrostic verse (*muʿammā*), "The Almighty saw that your figure was as singular as the letter A" (*ḥaqq ne tujh qadd koñ dekh miśl-e alif*), that spells the name of a certain Akmal.

130. For Ṣāʾib's verse "The blossom, like an Anatolian general, turned white in the face / as soon as, like a Qizilbash soldier, the tulip made its appearance" (*shikūfah chūñ sapah-rūm rūʾī gardāndah ast / shudah ast tā chū qizilbāsh jalwah-gar lālah*), see *Dīwān*, 1991, 6:3218.

131. Muʿtamad Ḳhān Badaḳhshī, *Tārīḳh-e Muḥammadī*, 2(6):110–11.

132. Mīr Dard in the 1740s held monthly gatherings, Gulshan's mushāʿirahs were weekly, and Mīr's were weekly, as noted in Mīr, *Nikāt*, 61; Ḳhwushgo, *Safīnah*, 1959, 166; Ḥairat Akbarābādī, *Taẕkirah*, 118.

133. Noted as *zamīn-e ṭarḥī* in Ḥātim, *Dīwānzādah*, 2011, 167. For the pre-1755 version with identical final couplet, see Ḥātim, *Intiḳhāb*, 127. Red is a celebratory color crucial for Nowruz.

134. Ḥātim, *Dīwānzādah*, 2011, 160; Ḥātim, *Intiḳhāb*, 122; Saudā, *Dīwān*, 231–32; Tābān Dihlavī, *Dīwān*, 2006, 192.

135. For Muḥtasham's verse under his pen name Ḥashmat, see Nāṣir, *Taẕkirah*, 1:119. For his connections to Śābit (the anti-Qabuliyan), Matīn (who Śābit hated), and Ārzū's patron Najm ud-Daulah (with whom Muḥtasham died in battle), see Ārzū, *Taẕkirah*, 1:397; Dudney, *Persian World*, 34, 36. For Muḥtasham's other reḳhtah verse under Ḥashmat, see Gardezī, "Taẕkirah," fol. 24a–b; Ḥasan Dihlavī, *Taẕkirah*, 47–48; Mīr, *Nikāt*, 74–75.

136. Ḥātim, *Dīwānzādah*, 2011, 173.

137. For Maẓhar's version, see Gardezī, "Taẕkirah," fol. 61b; Mīr, *Nikāt*, 28; Shauq Murādābādī, *Taẕkirah*, 62; Luṭf ʿAẓīmābādī, *Gulshan*, 1906, 160; Ḥasan Dihlavī, *Taẕkirah*, 148. Also discussed in Qureshī, *Mīrzā Maẓhar*, 297–98.

138. For Muḳhliṣ, see Shafīq Aurangābādī, *Chamanistān*, 285. Also cited in Nasīm, "Adabī," 41.

139. Saudā, *Dīwān*, 240–41.

140. For Bāqir Ḥazīn's biography and verse, see Gardezī, "Taẕkirah," fols. 17b–24a; Qāʾim Chāndpūrī, *Taẕkirah*, 140–41; Ḥasan Dihlavī, *Taẕkirah*, 48; Shauq Murādābādī, *Taẕkirah*, 90–92; Muṣḥafī, *Taẕkirah*, 1933, 79; Qāsim, *Majmūʿah*, 1:200–201; Luṭf ʿAẓīmābādī, *Gulshan*, 1906, 82; Lehmann, "Transition in India," 24. Patna-based taẕkirah writer Shorish ʿAẓīmābādī (d. 1781) documented Bāqir Ḥazīn's death in Bengal, as noted in Shorish ʿAẓīmābādī, *Taẕkirah*, 182–83. Cf. Mīr's exceeding brief mention of Bāqir Ḥazīn in *Nikāt*, 108–9. For Maẓhar-protégé Yaqīn's praise of Bāqir Ḥazīn, see Jālibī, *Tārīḳh*, 2:390.

141. Gardezī, "Taẕkirah," fol. 62a; Shafīq Aurangābādī, *Chamanistān*, 251. For attribution to Amīr Ḳhān, see Luṭf ʿAẓīmābādī, *Gulshan*, 1906, 17. For a discussion of Amīr Ḳhān's ġhazal and proto-nationalism in Urdu but without reference to the events of 1739, see ʿAqīl, *Taḥrīk*, 37.

142. Shafīq Aurangābādī, *Chamanistān*, 121. For a misattribution of this poem to Yaqīn without reference to Amīr Ḳhān, see ʿAqīl, *Taḥrīk*, 38.

143. Gardezī, "Tażkirah," fol. 9b; Shorish ʿAẓīmābādī, *Tażkirah*, 72. For legends about this verse associated with Nadir Shah's occupation, see Hāshimī, *Dabistān*, 121.

144. Wālih Dāġhistānī, *Tażkirah*, 1:299; Ḥātim, *Dīwānzādah*, 2011, 215.

145. Saudā, *Dīwān*, 282–83.

146. Tābān Dihlavī, *Dīwān*, 2006, 230.

147. Gardezī, "Tażkirah," fol. 20b; Shafīq Aurangābādī, *Chamanistān*, 122.

148. Ḥātim, *Dīwānzādah*, 2011, 215.

149. Tābān Dihlavī, *Dīwān*, 2006, 230. For discussion, see Sarvar ul-Hudá, preface to *Tābān*, 118nn3, 118–19.

150. Saudā, *Dīwān*, 282–83.

151. Luṭf ʿAẓīmābādī, "Gulshan," 1801, fol. 12b.

152. Tābān Dihlavī, *Dīwān*, 2006, 230. To account for the īhām, an alternate translation reads: "When he opens the jugular vein will we get some relief from the poet Saudā. / If you now search for someone like this, then I am your phlebotomist."

153. Ḥātim, *Dīwānzādah*, 2011, 215.

154. Shafīq Aurangābādī, *Chamanistān*, 123. For Bāqir Ḥazīn's two additional couplets in this ġhazal, see Gardezī, "Tażkirah," fol. 20b.

155. Ḥātim, *Dīwānzādah*, 2011, 215. To account for the īhām, an alternate translation reads: "While other cities have already given up their hearts to India's Hindu boys, / why should I forsake Ḥātim? I am Shāhjahānābād!"

156. Shafīq Aurangābādī, "Gul-e Raʿnā," 1876, fols. 173a–178b; Ṡābit, "Dīwān," n.d., fols. 91a–92b.

157. Ḳhwushgo, *Safīnah*, 1959, 258.

158. Ṡābit, "Dīwān," 1738, fol. 2a.

159. Āzād Bilgrāmī, "Yad-e Baiẓā," 50; Ārzū, *Tażkirah*, 1:319.

160. Ārzū, *Tażkirah*, 1:319; Ḳhwushgo, *Safīnah*, 1959, 258. For early mention of Aksīr, see Iḳhlāṣ, "Tażkirah," fols. 12b–13a.

161. Āzād Bilgrāmī, *Ḳhazānah*, 244–45; Wālih Dāġhistānī, *Tażkirah*, 1:466; Muʿtamad Ḳhān Badaḳhshī, *Tārīḳh-e Muḥammadī*, 2 (6):108; Ḳhwushgo, "Safīnah," fol. 142a. Also cited in Shafīq Aurangābādī, "Gul-e Raʿnā," 1790, fol. 69b. For Maẓhar's troubles remembering even the year of his birth, see Āzād Bilgrāmī, *Maʾāṡir*, 2:232; Shafīq Aurangābādī, *Chamanistān*, 247. Also discussed in Jālibī, *Tārīḳh*, 2:360–61; Ḳhān, Preface to *Maẓhar*, 12nn1. Shafīq records the qaṣīdah to settle varying accounts of Ṡābit's death year first noted by Shafīq's teacher Āzād, who cited personal correspondence with Maẓhar and the tażkirahs by Ḳhwushgo and Wālih.

162. Shafīq Aurangābādī, "Gul-e Raʿnā," 1790, fol. 69b.

163. Ḳhwushgo, "Safīnah," fol. 178b.

164. Shafīq Aurangābādī, "Gul-e Raʿnā," 1790, fols. 70a–71b; Ṡābit, "Dīwān," n.d., fols. 90a–92b.

165. ʿIshrat, "Safīnah," fol. 153b.

166. While Nūr Bāʾī's portrait has yet to appear, a painting in figure 3.1 by the artist Kalyān Dās (Chitarman II) depicts a similarly wealthy woman.

167. On the wedding, see Anṣārī, "Tārīḳh-e Muẕaffarī," fol. 193b; Ḥazīn Lāhījī, *Tārīḳh*, 283.

168. Fraser, *Nadir Shah*, 197; Muḳhliṣ, "Waqāʾīʿ," 46.

169. Fraser, *Nadir Shah*, 198–99.

170. For Nūr Bāʾī's genealogy, see Schofield, *Music and Musicians*, 61.

171. For the inequities and artistry among courtesans' experiences, see Schofield, "The Courtesan," 160–63; Schofield, *Music and Musicians*, 97–102.

172. Kashmīrī, *Bayān*, 43; Ṣāʾib Tabrezī, *Dīwān*, 1991, 6:3317.

173. Kashmīrī, *Bayān*, 178.

174. Kashmīrī, 44. For a translation that avoids Nūr Bāʾī's double meanings, see Kaicker, *The King and the People*, 53.

175. Ḥairat Akbarābādī, *Taẕkirah*, 38.

176. This may have been Wālih's residence.

177. Dargāh Qulī Ḳhān, *Muraqqaʿ*, 80.

178. Dargāh Qulī Ḳhān, 80; Ḥazīn Lāhījī, *Dīwān*, 493–94.

179. Ṣāʾib Tabrezī, *Dīwān*, 1991, 6:3055.

180. Schofield, "The Courtesan," 152–58; Kashmīrī, *Bayān*, 43. On female sex workers and petty commerce within the Mughal economy, see Moosvi, *Trade in Mughal India*, 150–53.

181. For example, see Raḥmān Bāʾī, a *ḍhāṛhī* from the Muslim caste of professional singers, in Dargāh Qulī Ḳhān, *Muraqqaʿ*, 108. On slavery and concubine traditions in Mughal/Timurid contexts, see Kalb, "Slavery"; Hamid, "Slaves in Name Only."

182. Dargāh Qulī Ḳhān, *Muraqqaʿ*, 105–6.

183. Dargāh Qulī Ḳhān, 107; Ṣāʾib Tabrezī, *Dīwān*, 1986, 2:992. For emulations preceding Ṣāʾib, see Rūmī, *Kulliyāt*, 203; Jahān Malik Ḳhātūn, *Dīwān*, 92.

184. For consideration of early modern portraiture and mirrors, see Pellò, "Black Curls in a Mirror."

185. On the role of *ḍhāṛhīs* in the nineteenth century, see Brown [Schofield], "Social Liminality," 28–30, 34nn109; Crooke, *Tribes and Castes*, 2:276–78.

186. See *chūb-e ustād* (the teacher's rod) in Dargāh Qulī Ḳhān, *Muraqqaʿ*, 108. On the painter Bihzād, see Soucek, "Behzād."

187. Bedil, *Kulliyāt*, 1:218.

188. Iḳhlāṣ, "Taẕkirah," fol. 46b. To account for the īhām, an alternate translation of the first line reads: "Upon seeing your sideburns, O Masīḥā, the beard emotionally announced . . ."

189. ʿIrāqī, *Dīwān*, 166–67.

190. Dargāh Qulī Ḳhān, *Muraqqaʿ*, 110–11. A distant connection appears in the poem, "Since you have taken up a place in my heart, / even the affairs of this worn-out heart turned difficult" (*tā jāʾī giriftah-ī tū dar dil / kār-e dil ḳhastah gasht mushkil*), by Jahān Malik Ḳhātūn *Jahān* (The World) (fl. 1324–93) in her *Dīwān*, 325. On her influence, see Brookshaw, "Odes," 177–78, 185–86. For her dīwān's preface where she aligns her words with past women writers, see Ingenito, "Appendix III," 336.

191. Ḥazīn Lāhījī, *Dīwān*, 363.

192. Schimmel, *My Soul Is a Woman*, 107–17.

193. Losensky, "Poetics and Eros," 753–55; Vanita, *Urdu Rekhtī*, 192–206. For such enactment in Delhi, see Kaicker, *The King and the People*, 132–33.

194. The career and intellectual history of courtesan Māh Laqā Bāʾī *Chandā* (The Moon) (1768–1824) illustrate gendered performance traditions in late 1700s Hyderabad. For the ġhazal as autobiography in her milieu, see Jha, "Poet and Patron," 152–54. For detailed historical considerations of her career and creativity, see Schofield, *Music and Musicians*, 117–46; Kugle, *When Sun Meets Moon*, 211–25.

195. Dargāh Qulī Ḳhān, *Muraqqaʿ*, 107.

196. Dargāh Qulī Ḳhān, 80.

197. Ḥashmat, "Bayāẓ," fol. 209a.

198. Ṭabāṭabāʾī, *Mutaʾak͟hk͟hirīn*, 2:21–23; Mīr, *Nikāt*, 109.

199. Tābān Dihlavī, *Dīwān*, 2006, 402; Tābān Dihlavī, *Dīwān*, 1935, 276. Also, Mīr, *Nikāt*, 109.

200. Mobad Kashmīrī, "Kulliyāt," fol. 319a. On Mobad's manuscript, see Sprenger, *Catalogue*, 504–5.

201. Mobad Kashmīrī, "Kulliyāt," fol. 319a.

Chapter 4

1. For Muṣḥafī's ambivalence and bragging about breaking up secretaries' gatherings in Lucknow, see Muṣḥafī, *Riyāẓ*, 264–65. On Muṣḥafī's comeuppance in another conflict in Lucknow, see Nāṣir, *Tażkirah*, 1:359–74.

2. Ḥairat Akbarābādī, *Tażkirah*, 118. For Mīr's fraught gatherings and others in the late 1740s, see Mīr, *Nikāt*, 61, 132, 141–43.

3. Mīr, *Nikāt*, 140. Mīr only uses this term when critically assessing the verse of other poets, especially when he found it nonsensical. My thanks to David Boyk for suggesting "sardonic neologism."

4. Zipoli, *Ǧawāb*, 6–7. For accusations of Yaqīn plagiarizing from Maẓhar and being romantically involved with other men, see Ārzū, "Majmaʿ," binding 2, fol. 464a; Mīr, *Nikāt*, 83. For Ḥazīn's downfall, see note 82. On plagiarism in Arabic literary theory, see Grunebaum, "Plagiarism."

5. For Shafīq's citation of Kalīm comparing plagiarism to a venereal disease in the context of Yaqīn's plagiarism, see Shafīq Aurangābādī, *Chamanistān*, 169–70.

6. On Mīr's purported affairs with Muḥammad Yār Ḳhāksār (fl. 1730–60), an attendant at the shrine of the Holy Footprint (*Qadam Sharīf*), see Qāʾim Chāndpūrī, *Tażkirah*, 141–42; Muṣḥafī, *Tażkirah*, 1933, 88. Also Mīr's denunciation of Ḳhāksār in Mīr, *Nikāt*, 114; and Ḳhāksār's particulars in Gardezī, "Tażkirah," fols. 25b–26a.

7. Ḥasan Dihlavī, *Tażkirah*, 23. For Iranian émigré Wafā's insult of a sex worker, circa 1749 [1162 AH], see Ārzū, "Majmaʿ," binding 2, fol. 525a. For elite and nonelite women's harsh words directed at men, see Lodī, *Tażkirah*, 280; Wālih Dāġhistānī, *Tażkirah*, 3:1086; Faḳhrī Haravī, *Tażkirah*, 128.

8. Siddiqi, "Sauda's Works," 588.

9. Siddiqi, "Sauda's Works," 590–91 and 591–93. On satirizing family members in Persian literature, see Zipoli, *Irreverent Persia*, 113–16.

10. For the centrality of obscenity in Persian verse of the classical era, see Sprachman, "Hajv and Profane Persian"; Zipoli, *Irreverent Persia*; Ingenito, *Beholding Beauty*, 151–203; Yazdānī, *Fārsī Shāʿirī*, 12–25. Of particular note is Sprachman's anthology *Suppressed Persian*.

11. Faruqi, "Satires of Sauda"; Faruqi, "Burning Rage." Further discussion appears among prefaces to critical editions of eighteenth-century humorists such as Zaṭallī and Chirkīn, as noted in Faruqi, preface to *Chirkīn*; Shāṯir Gorakhpūrī, introduction to *Chirkīn*; Ḵhān, preface to *Zaṭal Nāmah*.

12. Kaicker, *The King and the People*, 99–146. For obscenity in the early modern Persianate world, much scholarship focuses on Urdu literary history, as noted in ʿAbd ul-Ġhafūr, *Ṯanz wa Mizāḥ*, 170–82; Hasan, *Paper, Performance*, 67–98.

13. Satirical writing in Persian was foremost concerned with meter and rhyme, "Persian Satire," 227.

14. Siddiqi, "Sauda's Works," 589.

15. Nudrat Kashmīrī, "Kulliyāt," fol. 53b. For a Persian poem praising reḵhtah attributed to Ḥātim, see Ḥamīd Aurangābādī, *Gulshan*, 4–5.

16. Bahār, *ʿAjam*, 1:491.

17. Siddiqi, "Sauda's Works," 589. To preserve īhām, the translation includes Nudrat's refrain of "reḵhtah." To account for īhām, an alternate translation of the second line reads, "Whenever you have reḵhtah it as if one's heart has been poured out."

18. See "empty ideas" (*ḵhayāl-e pūch*) in S̤ābit, "Dīwān," 1738, fol. 30b; and "frivolous words" (*kalimāt-e pūch*) in Shafīq Aurangābādī, *Chamanistān*, 105.

19. Bedil, *Kulliyāt*, 1961, 1:1109.

20. Instead of *kulāġh* (crow), *wazaġh* (lizard) appears in Siddiqi, "Sauda's Works," 588.

21. For importance of quintains in Delhi, see Umar, *Urban Culture*, 80–83.

22. Siddiqi, "Sauda's Works," 587. For brief considerations of this poem that neglect to mention connection to Bedil, see Aḥmad, *Taẓmīn Nigārī*, 81–82; Anjum, "Saudā ke Maʿrake," 63–64.

23. Bedil, *Kulliyāt*, 1961, 1:1109.

24. Siddiqi, "Sauda's Works," 588. For the idiom "to scatter dust" (*ḵhāk reḵhtan*), see Bahār, *ʿAjam*, 2:761.

25. For "semantic scaffolding" of "the early modern Persian ghazal as a verbal game," see Keshavmurthy, "Poetic Jousting."

26. Other examples appear in Nasīmī, *Dīwān*, 151–52; Fayyāẓ Lāhījī, *Dīwān*, 121–24.

27. Rāshidī, *Taẕkirah*, 4:1599.

28. Dudney, *Persian World*, 110nn19, 156nn47.

29. Nudrat Kashmīrī, "Kulliyāt," fol. 133b.

30. Nudrat Kashmīrī, "Kulliyāt," fols. 1b, 3a, 41b, 130a, 152b.

31. Ḵhwushgo, "Safīnah," fol. 123a; Muḵhliṣ, *Taẕkirah*, 383.

32. Nudrat Kashmīrī, "Kulliyāt," fol. 50b.

33. Cole, "Iranian Culture," 18.

34. Nudrat Kashmīrī, "Tażkirah," fol. 32a.

35. Āżar Begdilī, *Ātishkadah*. On the "stylistics" (*sabk-shināsī*) approach, see Bahār, *Sabkshināsī*, author's preface, volume 1; Jabbari, *Persianate Modernity*, 35–39, 65–69. On Āżar's impact on the "literary return" and conceptualization of "the Indian style" (*sabk-e hindī*), see Smith, "Literary Connections"; Kia, *Persianate Selves*, 122–45; Schwartz, *Remapping Persian*, 35–80. For the problematic "Indian school" (*sabk-e hindī*) moniker and its endurance to the exclusion of much else, see Yarshater, "Indian or Safavid Style"; Bruijn, "Sabk-i Hindi." For critique and reconsideration of this approach, see Faruqi, "Stranger in the City."

36. Nudrat Kashmīrī, "Tażkirah," fol. 71b.

37. For an example of the Majlis-e Taraqqī-e Urdū's censorship regime, see Siddiqi, *Kulliyāt*, 3:156, which appears uncensored in Siddiqi, "Sauda's Works," 56.

38. Mīr, *Nikāt*, 48; Anjum, *Mirzā*, 78–81, 86–89; Chānd, *Saudā*, 39; Jālibī, *Tārīḳh*, 2:655–56. For brief discussion of his early patron imperial eunuch Ḳhwājah Basant, see Siddiqi, "Sauda's Works," 32–33, 369–70. On Mughal eunuchs, see Kalb, "At the Threshold." For discussion of Saudā's marṡiyahs, see Hyder, *Reliving Karbala*, 28–30.

39. Qā'im Chāndpūrī, *Tażkirah*, 86.

40. Qā'im Chāndpūrī, 86; Siddiqi, "Sauda's Works," 28. For discussion of Saudā's connection to and critique of Niʿmat Ḳhān-e ʿĀlī, see Jālibī, *Tārīḳh*, 2:650; Anjum, *Mirzā*, 62–64. On Niʿmat Ḳhān-e ʿĀlī's role as a political satirist, Kaicker, *The King and the People*, 108–17.

41. ʿĀshiqī ʿAẓīmābādī, *Tażkirah*, 1:774.

42. For Widād's biography, see Muṣḥafī, "ʿIqd," fol. 71a. On Saudā's exile to Lucknow, see Haywood, "Sawdā."

43. Saudā, *Dīwān*.

44. Jālibī, *Tārīḳh*, 2:650; Anjum, *Mirzā*, 64; Siddiqi, "Sauda's Works," 201.

45. Saudā, *ʿIbrat*, 48; Siddiqi, "Sauda's Works," 126. Discussed in Faruqi, "Satires of Sauda," 2. See also Jālibī, *Tārīḳh*, 2:665–67.

46. Saudā, *ʿIbrat*, 48. Also Siddiqi, "Sauda's Works," 52–57.

47. One stanza from the episode appears (circa 1806) in Qāsim, *Majmūʿah*, 1:26. Qāsim refers to Nudrat as Hidāyatullāh Nudrat Kashmīrī and assigns authorship to Ārzū, forming the basis for Āzād's invocation of the episode (circa 1880) in Pritchett and Faruqi, *Āb-e Ḥayāt*, 169. So too, Imām Baḳhsh Ṣahbā'ī (1807–57) obliquely referenced their competition in the context of slander (*taʿbīr*) in his 1842 translation of Faqīr Dihlavī's *Ḥadā'iq ul-Balāġhat*, as noted in Ṣahbā'ī, *Tarjumah*, 86. I have slightly modified the translation from Pritchett and Faruqi, *Āb-e Ḥayāt*, 169.

48. Pritchett, "Long History 2," 882–901.

49. Nāṣir, *Tażkirah*, 1:2.

50. Pritchett, "Long History 2," 892.

51. Nāṣir, *Tażkirah*, 1:4.

52. Nāṣir, *Tażkirah*, 1:4.

53. Siddiqi, "Sauda's Works," 622.

54. Shafīq Aurangābādī, *Chamanistān*, 341–42. Also discussed in Āzād Bilgrāmī, *Sarv*, 177.

55. Shafīq may have confused Saudā's quintain-based tributes ridiculing certain shaiḳhs as lampoons of Ḥazīn. See the tribute to ʿIṣmatullāh Buḳhārī (d. 1426) or the story of a shaiḳh marrying a younger woman in Siddiqi, "Sauda's Works," 551–53, 575–81. On ʿIṣmat ullāh Buḳhārī, see Daulat Shāh Samarqandī, *Taẕkirat*, 357–61.

56. Saudā, *ʿIbrat*, 101–2; Anjum, *Mirzā*, 81, also 106.

57. Siddiqi, "Sauda's Works," 573–75; Thackston, *Gulistan*, 47. Siddiqi, "Sauda's Works," 609–12; Muḥtasham, *Haft Dīwān*, 1:467. For Saudā's tribute to Makīn, see Siddiqi, "Sauda's Works," 612–13; Makīn, "Dīwān," fol. 237b. See also Shafīq Aurangābādī, "Gul-e Raʿnā," 1790, fols. 228a–229b.

58. Saudā, *ʿIbrat*, 96; Sarḳhwush, *Taẕkirah*, 134.

59. Sām Mīrzā, *Tuḥfah*, 150; Siddiqi, "Sauda's Works," 546–47. On Nidāʾī in the context of Safavid devotional verse, see Kiyā and Qanbarī Nanīz, "Mashhad ush-Shuhadā," 267–70. For a later legend assigning Nidāʾī's opening couplet to the courtesan Nūr Bāʾī, see Aḥmad Dihlavī, *Wāqiʿāt*, 2:220.

60. Siddiqi, "Sauda's Works," 553–54; Kalīm Kāshānī, *Dīwān*, 268; Ṣāʾib Tabrezī, *Dīwān*, 1990, 5:2579.

61. Siddiqi, "Sauda's Works," 542.

62. Nāṣir-e Ḳhusrau, *Dīwān*, 490–94; Sanāʾī Ġhaznawī, *Dīwān*, 297–301; Rūmī, *Kulliyāt*, 928; Nīyāzkār, *Sharḥ-e Saʿdī*, 1125; Kalīm Kāshānī, *Dīwān*, 317–18. In particular, see the final couplet in ġhazal no. 6780, referencing in a tribute (*taẓmīn*) the final couplet in Saʿdī's contribution to the form, as cited in Ṣāʾib Tabrezī, *Dīwān*, 1991, 6:3309–11.

63. Ḥazīn Lāhījī, *Dīwān*, 540.

64. Siddiqi, "Sauda's Works," 544.

65. Kalīm Kāshānī, *Dīwān*, 255.

66. Ḥazīn Lāhījī, *Dīwān*, 436.

67. Nudrat Kashmīrī, "Kulliyāt," fol. 126b.

68. Siddiqi, "Sauda's Works," 545–46; Ḥāfiẓ, *Dīwān*, 1:24; Ḥazīn Lāhījī, *Dīwān*, 185; Nudrat Kashmīrī, "Kulliyāt," fol. 6a. For other emulations that preceded Ḥāfiẓ, see Rūmī, *Kulliyāt*, 127; Masʿūd Saʿd Salmān, *Dīwān*, 636.

69. Ḥākim Lāhaurī, *Taẕkirah*, 100–101. For similar warm words about Ḥazīn and mention that the poet spent several months in Agra, see Ḥairat Akbarābādī, *Taẕkirah*, 39.

70. Saudā, *Kulliyāt*, 1872, 490. Also discussed in Khatak, *Shaikh Muḥammad*, xiin22.

71. Muḥammad ʿAẓīm *Ṡabāt* will be referred to by his given name, as opposed to his pen name, to avoid confusion with his father Ṡābit. Among the few Indian poets recorded in Riẓā Qulī Ḳhān Hidāyat's highly selective 1876 taẕkirah, Ṡābit and Ṡabāt make brief if noteworthy appearances; see Hidāyat, *Majmaʿ*, 2:296.

72. Wālih Dāġhistānī, *Taẕkirah*, 1:468.

73. Bandah ʿAlī Sabaqat will be referred to by his given names, as opposed to his pen names, to avoid confusion.

74. On Roshan ud-Daulah's extended downfall, see Kaicker, *The King and the People*, 272–87; Irvine, *Later Mughals*, 2:266–71.

75. Ṡābit, "Dīwān," 1738, fol. 2a.

76. Ṡābit's son Muḥammad ʿAẓīm could not accept the position as an ustād as he only recently had begun composing verse, as noted in Ārzū, "Majmaʿ," binding 1, fol. 113b; Wālih Dāġhistānī, *Tażkirah*, 1:468.

77. Other students migrated to Ḥazīn after Shuhrat died, as noted in Ḥākim Lāhaurī, *Tażkirah*, 159.

78. Muṣḥafī, "Tażkirah," fol. 23b.

79. Bāsiṭī, "Bayāẓ," fol. 228a.

80. Shafīq Aurangābādī, *Chamanistān*, 105–6. See further discussion in Dhavan and Pauwels, "Controversies," 642–43.

81. Bāsiṭī, "Bayāẓ," fol. 227b.

82. Wālih Dāġhistānī, *Tażkirah*, 1:647.

83. For a damning instance of Ḥazīn's plagiarism for which Muḥammad ʿAẓīm cites his sources, see Wālih Dāġhistānī, 1:649; Naṣrābādī, *Tażkirah*, 531; Ḥazīn Lāhījī, *Dīwān*, 212. For Ḥazīn's response to the accusations, see Ḥazīn Lāhījī, *Dīwān*, 153.

84. Shafīq Aurangābādī, *Chamanistān*, 259.

85. Muḳhliṣ, *Tażkirah*, 282.

86. Muḳhliṣ, *Tażkirah*, 282; Ummīd, "Dīwān," n.d., fol. 212b. This poem does not appear in the early eighteenth-century recension of Ummīd's dīwān held in the Bodleian Library.

87. Ḥazīn Lāhījī, *Dīwān*, 553. For Wālih's selection of couplets from this ġhazal, see *Tażkirah*, 1:670.

88. Ārzū, "Majmaʿ," binding 2, fol. 400a.

89. Ḥazīn Lāhījī, *Dīwān*, 553.

90. Ārzū, *Tanbīh*, 137. Ārzū overshot his target and mistakenly assigned the couplet to Ṣāʾib. For Maʿṣūm's authorship, see Qudratullāh Gūpāmvī, *Tażkirah*, 665; Wālih Dāġhistānī, *Tażkirah*, 3:1753; Hāshmī Sandīlavī, *Tażkirah*, 1994, 5:160; ʿĀshiqī ʿAẓīmābādī, *Tażkirah*, 2:1473–74.

91. Wālih Dāġhistānī, *Tażkirah*, 1:634; Ḥākim Lāhaurī, *Tażkirah*, 101.

92. Āzād Bilgrāmī, *Ḳhazānah*, 273–76.

93. Saudā, *ʿIbrat*, 101.

94. Nudrat Kashmīrī, "Kulliyāt," fol. 152a.

95. Mikkelson, "Parrots and Crows," 524–25.

96. Nudrat Kashmīrī, "ʿAin-e ʿAṭā," fol. 13b. Thanks are owed to Arthur Dudney for sharing his insights on and images of this manuscript when it was unconsultable.

97. Nudrat Kashmīrī, "ʿAin-e ʿAṭā," fol. 14b.

98. Nudrat Kashmīrī, "ʿAin-e ʿAṭā," fol. 14a.

99. Nudrat Kashmīrī, "ʿAin-e ʿAṭā," fols. 15a, 731a.

100. Ārzū, "Majmaʿ," binding 2, fol. 316ab.

101. Siddiqi, "Sauda's Works," 588.

102. Bedil, *Kulliyāt*, 1961, 1:1109.

103. Bedil, *Kulliyāt*, 1961, 1:375.

104. For Bedil's fixation on the phoenix, see Mikkelson, "Flights," esp. 63–64 for similar considerations of nothingness.

105. Siddiqi, "Sauda's Works," 161; Saudā, *Dīwān*, 232. Later reḳhtah emulations found in Mīr, *Kulliyāt*, 1941, 686; Ġhālib, *Dīwān*, 1992, 94–95.

106. Ḥazīn Lāhījī, *Dīwān*, 294.

107. On friendship and Mughal-era *adab* practices, see Kia, "Indian Friends"; Flatt, "Practicing Friendship"; Keshavmurthy, "Two Interpretive Postures." For Arabic-language settings, see al-Musawi, *Islamic Republic*, 38–40.

108. Andrews and Kalpaklı, *Age of Beloveds*, 27–31.

109. Babayan, *City as Anthology*, 11–17, 112, 137–44.

110. Mikkelson, "Parrots and Crows," 511.

111. Ḥazīn Lāhījī, *Dīwān*, 294. Also noted in Wālih Dāġhistānī, *Tażkirah*, 1:664. To account for the multiple meanings in the first line, an alternate translation reads, "From Naẓīrī's complaint comes the clamor of grief."

112. Naẓīrī Nīshāpūrī, *Ġhazaliyāt*, 60–61.

113. Muḳhliṣ, *Tażkirah*, 329.

114. Ārzū, "Majmaʿ," binding 2, fol. 391a. An early response to Naẓīrī comes from Asīr, Ṣāʾib's colleague in Isfahan whose contribution influenced Qabūl: "Message of your flirtations was not sealed with a kiss . . ." (*az būsah ḳhāṭam naburad ʿarẓ-e nazākat* . . .) in Asīr Shahristānī, *Dīwān*, 197–98.

115. Saudā, *ʿIbrat*, 80.

116. Nudrat Kashmīrī, "Kulliyāt," fol. 69a.

117. Siddiqi, "Sauda's Works," 161; Saudā, *Dīwān*, 232.

118. For other aural ideas, see ". . . When there is no pain in poetry, then it is just murmurings or something" (. . . *chūn dard-e suḳhan nīst digar zamzamah-hā hech*) in Asīr Shahristānī, *Dīwān*, 197–98; and ". . . I am the winds in the instrument; the voice is nothing" (. . . *tūfān-e ṣadāʾīm dar īn sāz-o ṣadā hech*) in Bedil, *Kulliyāt*, 1961, 1:375.

119. Nudrat Kashmīrī, "Kulliyāt," fol. 69a.

120. Siddiqi, "Sauda's Works," 161; Saudā, *Dīwān*, 232.

121. Bedil, *Kulliyāt*, 1961, 1:375.

122. Siddiqi, "Sauda's Works," 161; Saudā, *Dīwān*, 232.

123. Ḳhwushgo, *Safīnah*, 1959, 206–7.

124. Beale, *Dictionary*, 335; Ḳhwāfī Ḳhān, *Muntaḳhab*, 2:791; Hindī, *Safīnah*, 200; ʿĀshiqī ʿAẓīmābādī, *Tażkirah*, 2:1559. For Qamar ud-Dīn Khan's biography, see Beale, *Dictionary*, 313–14.

125. Ḳhwushgo, *Safīnah*, 1959, 207.

126. For Mast's connection to Saʿdī, see Ḳhwushgo, 281.

127. Thackston, *Gulistan*, 43–44; Ḳhwushgo, *Safīnah*, 1959, 207.

128. Kaicker, *The King and the People*, 132–33.

129. For Ḳhwushgo's post-Delhi itinerary to Varanasi and Patna, see Ḥairat Akbarābādī, *Tażkirah*, 79.

130. For later mention of Mast, see Shafīq Aurangābādī, "Gul-e Raʿnā," 1790, fol. 223a–b; ʿĀshiqī ʿAẓīmābādī, *Tażkirah*, 2:1558–59.

131. Wālih Dāġhistānī, *Tażkirah*, 3:1934.

132. For example, see Maẓhar, *Dīwān wa Ḳhariṭah*, 152.

133. See discussion of Gulshan's death and memorialization in chapter 2.

134. Iḳhlāṣ, "Tażkirah," fol. 143b.

135. Iḳhlāṣ, "Tażkirah," fol. 143b.

136. Ḳhwushgo, "Safīnah," fol. 109b. Also Āzād Bilgrāmī, "Yad-e Baiẓā," fol. 196a; Muḳhliṣ, *Tażkirah*, 281. Despite saying that even a selection of Gulshan's weighty dīwān would "require another book all together," Ārzū does not record Gulshan's most famous couplet in "Majmaʿ," binding 2, fols. 402b–403b.

137. For Kātib's and ul-Buḳhārī's backgrounds, see Rouayheb, "Islamic Philosophers."

138. Siddiqi, "Sauda's Works," 591.

139. Siddiqi, "Sauda's Works," 592nn26.

140. Siddiqi, "Sauda's Works," 592.

141. ʿĀlim, "Saudā kā Fārsī Kalām," 340.

142. Bano, "Age of Marriage," 597.

143. For the line in question, "Hey Lolo, you are flopping around. It's in pieces, O Loverboy," (*lolo karāñ chhū lach lach vuh pāre pāre madnā*), see Siddiqi, "Sauda's Works," 590. While Siddiqi finds that "the meaning of this line appears to be unclear," the refrain contains the Kashmiri verb *karun* conjugated in second-person present continuous tense. I thank colleagues who have weathered my questions in attempt to decipher it. None of the vocabulary from this poem appears in *Farhang-e Kulliyāt-e Saudā* [A Lexicon for the Complete Works of Saudā], comp. Mujāhid ul-Islām (Delhi: Educational Publishing House, 2017).

144. Lodī, *Tażkirah*, 66, 72, 280; Faḳhrī Haravī, *Tażkirah*, 128.

145. Ḳhān, *Ṣubḥ*, 350; Muṣḥafī, *Tażkirah*, 1933, 279.

146. Qāsim, *Majmūʿah*, 2:145; Tassy, *Histoire*, 1:490.

147. Wālih Dāġhistānī, *Tażkirah*, 3:1878–79.

148. Wālih Dāġhistānī, *Tażkirah*, 2:895. For further discussion of women in tażkirahs cited here, see Kia, *Persianate Selves*, 184–85; Sharma, "Poetic Canon of Women," 151–58.

149. Wālih Dāġhistānī, *Tażkirah*, 4:2583–84, 2600.

150. Wālih Dāġhistānī, *Tażkirah*, 2:1035.

151. Hindī, *Safīnah*, 90–91. Dargāh Qulī Ḳhān, *Muraqqaʿ*, 108.

152. Siddiqi, "Sauda's Works," 591–93.

153. Nudrat Kashmīrī, "Kulliyāt," fol. 144a.

154. Significantly, Nudrat is the only eighteenth-century poet I have found who attempted to emulate Gulshan's once-famous form.

155. The Qur'an 53:9 (Habib and Lawrence trans.).

156. Kulaynī, *Al-Kāfī*, 5:75.

157. Gould, "Russifying the *Radīf*," 265.

158. Nelson, "Complex Information Processing," 96.

159. For Ġhazālī's ethical formulation on context, see Ġhazālī, *Kīmyā*, 1:497.

160. Dargāh Qulī Ḳhān, *Muraqqaʿ*, 81; Ārzū, "Dīwān," fol. 304a–b.

161. Bedil, *Kulliyāt*, 1961, 1:1162. For Bedil's likely source of inspiration with the same formal parameters, see Rūmī, *Kulliyāt*, 966–67.

162. Tābān Dihlavī, *Dīwān*, 2006, 307.

163. For the many eighteenth-century poems that feature *vāh vāh* as a refrain, see Ummīd, "Dīwān," 1801, fol. 18a; ʿIshq, "Dīwān," fol. 53a–b; Saudā, *Dīwān*, 336–37; Yaqīn, *Dīwān*, 1995, 176; Ḥamīd Aurangābādī, *Gulshan*, 15–16; Mīr, *Kulliyāt*, 1983,

1:254; Tābān Dihlavī, *Dīwān*, 2006, 269–70; Ḥātim, *Dīwānzādah*, 2011, 280–81; Ābrū, *Dīwān*, 2000, 224.

Conclusion

1. Bazm-e Sahārā, "*Mubāḥiṡah: Kyā Āj ke Mushāʿare Urdū Tahżīb ke Zawāl kā Bāʿiṡ Haiñ?*," October 2009.

2. Beg, *Āḳhrī Shamaʿ*. For connections between dramatic or imagined gatherings and nineteenth-century tażkirah writing, see Mahmudabad, *Poetry of Belonging*, 48–64.

3. Taneja, *Jinnealogy*, 36–46.

4. Sarḳhwush, "Kalimāt," 1700, fol. 40b.

5. Mahmudabad, *Poetry of Belonging*, 51–52, 89–110.

6. For an account of improvisation in a *ṭarḥī mushāʿarah*, see Hyder, *Reliving Karbala*, 204–6.

7. Bayly, *Empire and Information*, 194.

8. Karīm ud-Dīn's partners pulled out of his printing venture and subsequently shut him out of the shop where he intended to host poetry gatherings, as discussed in Karīm ud-Dīn Maġhfūr, *Ṭabaqāt*, 400–401, 470; Powell, "Maulawi Karimu'd-Din," 210nn21.

9. Bashir, *Market in Poetry*, 53–58; Kaicker, *The King and the People*, 79. For discussion of Mughal silver flows over the 1600s, see Moosvi, *Trade in Mughal India*, 35–80.

10. For example, Lilti, *World of the Salons*.

11. For *mushāʿare kā shāʿir*, see Naim, "Audience Interaction," 114; Sādiq, *History of Urdu*, 35, 377. For poems complaining about mushāʿirah-based populism, see Josh Malīḥābādī, *Kulliyāt*, 1305–9.

Bibliography

Abbreviations

AH Anno Hegirae
JD Justinian date
PE Pahlavi Era
SH Solar Hijri

Manuscripts

ʿĀlī, Niʿmat Ḳhān. "Razmnāmah-e Bahādur Shāh wa Aʿẓam Shāh," 1838. Ms. or. oct. 607. Staatsbibliothek zu Berlin.

Anonymous. "Bayāẓ," n.d. IO Islamic 454. British Library, London.

Anṣārī, Muḥammad ʿAlī Ḳhān. "Tārīḳh-e Muẓaffarī," 1786 [1200 AH]. Ms. or. fol. 239. Staatsbibliothek zu Berlin.

Ārzū, Sirāj ud-Dīn ʿAlī Ḳhān. "Dīwān-e Ārzū," 1728 [1140 AH]. HL 535/No. 399. Khuda Bakhsh Oriental Public Library, Patna.

——. "Majmaʿ un-Nafāʾis" Binding 1, 1765 [1179 AH]. HL 237/No. 695. Khuda Bakhsh Oriental Public Library, Patna.

——. "Majmaʿ un-Nafāʾis" Binding 2, 1765 [1179 AH]. HL 238/No. 696. Khuda Bakhsh Oriental Public Library, Patna.

Astarābādī, Mahdī Ḳhān. "Wāqiʾāʿ-e Nādirī," 1759 [1173 AH]. DS294 .M312 1759. Library of Congress, Washington, DC.

Āzād Bilgrāmī, Ġhulām ʿAlī. "Yad-e Baiẓā," 1740 [1152 AH]. HL 244/No. 691. Khuda Bakhsh Oriental Public Library, Patna.

Bāsiṭī, Bandah ʿAlī Sher Afgan Ḳhān. "Bayāẓ," 1784 [1199 AH]. MS 646. Rylands Library, Manchester.

Bedil, ʿAbd ul-Qādir. "Safīnah-e Bedil," 1740–1743 [1152–1155 AH]. Add. 16,803. British Library, London.

Chānd, Ḳhwush Ḥāl. "Tārīḳh-e Muḥammad Shāhī ʿUrfā-e Nādir uz-Zamānī," 1834 [1250 AH]. Ms. or. fol. 222. Staatsbibliothek zu Berlin.

Firdausī, Abū'l Qāsim. "Shāhnāmah," 1217 [614 AH]. Magl CI.III.24. Biblioteca Nazionale Centrale di Firenze.

Gardezī, ʿAlī ul-Ḥusainī. "Taẑkirah-e ʿAlī Ḥusain Gardezī," n.d. HL 1785/No. 1787. Khuda Bakhsh Oriental Public Library, Patna.

Ḥārisī, Mirzā Muḥammah. "ʿIbrat Nāmah," n.d. IO Islamic 50(2). British Library, London.

Ḥashmat. "Bayāẓ," n.d. IO Islamic 1488. British Library, London.

Ḥusain Dost Sambhalī. "Tażkirah-e Ḥusainī," 1749 [1163 AH]. Or. 229. British Library, London.
Ikhlāṣ, Kishan Chand. "Tażkirah-e Hameshah Bahār," 1727 [1139 AH]. IO Islamic 3163. British Library, London.
Inshā, Sayyid Inshāʾullāh Ḳhān, and Muḥammad Ḥasan Qatīl. "Daryā-e Laṭāfat," 1825 [1241 AH]. Islamic Manuscripts, Garrett no. 470L. Princeton University Library, Princeton.
ʿIshq, Zain ud-Dīn Ḳhān. "Dīwān-e ʿIshq," 1785 [1199 AH]. Persian MS 219. Rylands Library, Manchester.
ʿIshrat, Durgā Dās. "Safīnah-e ʿIshrat," 1761 [1175 AH]. HL 226/No. 699. Khuda Bakhsh Oriental Public Library, Patna.
Kalyān Dās. "Portrait of a Lady Holding a Rose," circa 1740. J.60,22. British Library, London.
Ḳhalīl, Ibrāhīm Ḳhān. "Gulzār-e Ibrāhīm," n.d. Add. 27,319. British Library, London.
Ḳhwushgo, Bindrāban Dās. "Safīnah-e Ḳhwushgo," 1768 [1182 AH]. HL 225/No. 690. Khuda Bakhsh Oriental Public Library, Patna.
"Leaf with Miniature of a Gathering of Poets [with Rukn ud-Dīn Awḥadī Marāġhaʾī]," circa 1550 [circa 957 AH]. MSP Leaf 27. McGill University Library, Montreal.
Luṭf ʿAẓīmābādī, Mīrzā ʿAlī. "Gulshan-e Hind," 1801 [1215 AH]. Sprenger 345. Staatsbibliothek zu Berlin.
Makīn, Muḥammad Fāḳhir. "Dīwān-e Fāḳhir Makīn," n.d. HL 596/No. 430. Khuda Bakhsh Oriental Public Library, Patna.
Mīr, Mīr Muḥammad Taqī. "Nikāt ush-Shuʿarā," 1852. Sprenger 343. Staatsbibliothek zu Berlin.
Mobad Kashmīrī, Zindah Rām Panḍit. "Kulliyāt-e Mobad Dar Naẓm-e Fārsī," 1767 [1181 AH]. Or. 324. British Library, London.
Muḳhliṣ, Ānand Rām. "Tażkirah-e Waqāʾiʿ-e Ānand Rām Ḥiṣṣh-e Duwīm," n.d. Micro fm 520. Middle East Department, Regenstein Library, Chicago.
Muṣḥafī, Ġhulām Hamadānī. "ʿIqd-e S̱uraiyā," 1829 [1244 AH]. HL 231/No. 709. Khuda Bakhsh Oriental Public Library, Patna.
———. "Tażkirah-e Muṣḥafī [ʿIqd-e S̱uraiyā]," 1785 [1199 AH]. IO Islamic 16727. British Library, London.
Nudrat Kashmīrī, ʿĀlá Fiṭrat ʿAṭāʾullāh. "ʿAin-e ʿAṭā," 1749 [1162 AH]. IO Islamic 1813. British Library, London.
———. "Kulliyāt-e Nudrat," n.d. IO Islamic 257. British Library, London.
———. "Tażkirah-e Nudrat," 1736 [1149 AH]. IO Islamic 2678. British Library, London.
Qatīl, Muḥammad Ḥasan. "Nahr ul-Faṣāḥah wa Chār Sharbat," 1805 [1219 AH]. Garret No. 466. Princeton University Library, Princeton.
S̱ābit, Muḥammad Afẓal. "Dīwān-e S̱ābit," n.d. HL 551/No. 393. Khuda Bakhsh Oriental Public Library, Patna.
———. "Dīwān-e S̱ābit," 1738 [1151 AH]. Or. 281. British Library, London.
Sangīn Beg. "Sair ul-Manāzil," 1821 [1236 AH]. Sprenger 234. Staatsbibliothek zu Berlin.
Sarḳhwush, Muḥammad Afẓal. "Kalimāt ush-Shuʿarā," circa 1700. Persian MS 322. Rylands Library, Manchester.

——. "Kalimāt ush-Shuʿarā," 1784 [1190 AH]. Ms. or. quart. 235. Staatsbibliothek zu Berlin.
——. "Kalimāt ush-Shuʿarā," circa 1800. HL 232/No. 688. Khuda Bakhsh Oriental Public Library, Patna.
——. "Kalimāt ush-Shuʿarā," 1826 [1242 AH]. Sprenger 326. Staatsbibliothek zu Berlin.
Shafīq Aurangābādī, Lachhmī Narāyan. "Gul-e Raʿnā," 1790 [1204 AH]. HL 234/No. 701. Khuda Bakhsh Oriental Public Library, Patna.
——. "Gul-e Raʿnā," 1876 [1293 AH]. IO Islamic 3692. British Library, London.
Ṭabāṭabāʾī, Muḥammad Riẓā Abū'l Qāsim. "Naġhmah-e ʿAndalīb," 1850. Or. 1811. British Library, London.
Ummīd, Muḥammad Riẓā Qizilbāsh Ḳhān. "Dīwān-e Ummīd," n.d. HL 540/No. 396. Khuda Bakhsh Oriental Public Library, Patna.
——. "Dīwān-e Ummīd," 1713–1720. MS. S. Digby Or. 43. Bodleian Library, Oxford.
——. "Dīwān-e Ummīd," 1801 [1215 AH]. HL 541/No. 397. Khuda Bakhsh Oriental Public Library, Patna.
Zaḳhmī, Ratan Singh. "Sharḥ-e Gul-e Kushtī," 1817 [1232 AH]. HL 1940/No. 1916. Khuda Bakhsh Oriental Public Library, Patna.
"The Zinat ul-Masajid, Daryaganj, Delhi," circa 1820–1825. Add. Or. 550. British Library, London.

Primary Sources

ʿAbbāsī, ʿIrfān. *Tażkirah-e Shuʿarā-e Reḳhtī*. Lucknow: Nasīm Būk Ḍīpo, 1989.
Ābrū, Najm ud-Dīn Shāh Mubārak. *Dīwān-e Ābrū*. Edited by Muḥammad Ḥasan. Aligarh: Idārah-e Taṣnīf, 1967.
——. *Dīwān-e Ābrū*. Edited by Muḥammad Ḥasan. New Delhi: Taraqqī-e Urdū Biyūro, 2000.
Aḥmad Dihlavī, Bashīr ud-Dīn Maḥmūd. *Wāqiʿāt-e Dār ul-Ḥukūmat-e Dihlī*. 3 vols. Agra: Shamsī Press, 1919.
Aḥmad, Malikzādah Manẓūr. *Shahr-e Suḳhan*. 2nd ed. Lucknow: Imkān, 2007.
Aḥmad Dihlavī, Sayyid. *Farhang-e Āṣafiyyah*. 4 vols. Lahore: Maṭbaʿ-e Rifāh-e ʿĀmm Press, 1908.
Amrullāh Allāhābādī, Abū ul-Ḥasan Amīr ul-Dīn Aḥmad. *Tażkirah-e Masarrat Afzā*. Edited by Sayyid Shāh Muḥammad Ismāʿil. Patna: Khuda Bakhsh Oriental Public Library, 1998.
ʿAndalīb, Muḥammad Nāṣir Muḥammadī. *Nālah-e ʿAndalīb*. 2 vols. Bhopal: Maṭbaʿ-e Shāh Jahānī, 1891 and 1893 [1308 and 1310 AH].
Ārzū, Sirāj ud-Dīn ʿAlī Ḳhān. *Dād-e Suḳhan*. Edited by Sayyid Muḥammad Akram. Islamabad: Intishārāt-e Markaz-e Taḥqīqāt-e Fārsī-e Īrān wa Pākistān, 1974 [1352 SH].
——. *Majmaʿ un-Nafāʾis: Baḳhsh-e Muʿāṣirān*. Edited by Mīr Hāshim Muḥaddiṡ. Tehran: Anjuman-e Aṡār wa Mufāḳhar-e Farhangī, 2005 [1384 SH].
——. *Tanbīh ul-Ġhāfilīn*. Edited by Sayyid Muhammad Akram. Lahore: Punjab University, 1981 [1401 AH].

——. *Tażkirah-e Majmaʿ un-Nafāʾis*. Edited by Zeb un-Nisā ʿAlī Ḳhān Sultān ʿAlī. 3 vols. Islamabad: Markaz-e Taḥqīqāt-e Fārsī-e Īrān wa Pākistān, 2004 [1383 SH; 1425 AH].

ʿĀshiqī ʿAẓīmābādī, Āqā Ḥusain Qulī Ḳhān. *Tażkirah-e Nishtar-e ʿIshq*. Edited by Sayyid Kamāl Hājj Sayyid Jawādī. 2 vols. Tehran: Miras Maktoob, 2012 [1391 SH].

Āsī, ʿAbd ul-Bārī. *Tażkirat ul-Ḳhawātīn yaʿnī Hindustān aur Fārs kī Bih-Tar aur Mashhūr Shāʿirah ʿAuratoñ kā Żikr maʿ Namūnah Kalām*. Lucknow: Nawal Kishore Press, n.d.

Asīr Shahristānī, Jalāl Muḥammad bin Mīrzā Moʾmin. *Dīwān-e Ġhazaliyāt-e Asīr-e Shahristānī*. Edited by Ġhulāmḥusain Sharīfī Vildānī. Leiden: Brill, 2019.

ʿAṭṭār Nīshāpūrī, Farīd ud-Dīn Muḥammad. *Tażkirat ul-Auliyā*. Edited by Muḥammad Istaʿlāmī. Tehran: Instishārāt-e Zawwār, 2010 [1391 SH].

Awḥadī Balyānī, Taqī ud-Dīn. *ʿArafāt ul-ʿĀshiqīn wa ʿAraṣāt ul-ʿĀrifīn*. Edited by Żabīḥullāh Ṣāḥibkār, Āminah Faḳhr Aḥmad, and Muḥammad Qahramān. 8 vols. Tehran: Miras Maktoob, 2010 [1388 SH].

Awḥadī Marāghaʾī, Rukn ud-Dīn. *Kulliyāt-e Awḥadī Iṣfahānī*. Edited by Saʿīd Nafīsī. Tehran: Amīr Kabīr, 1961 [1340 SH].

Āzād Bilgrāmī, Ġhulām ʿAlī. *Ḳhazānah-e ʿĀmarah*. Edited by Nāṣir Nekobaḳht and Shakīl Islam Beg. Tehran: Piẕhuhishgāh-e ʿUlūm-e Insānī wa Muṭālaʿāt-e Farhangī, 2012 [1390 SH].

——. *Maʾāṡir ul-Karām Mawasūm bah Sarv-e Āzād*. 2 vols. Lahore: Kutubḳhānah Asifiyah, 1913.

——. *Sarv-e Āzād*. Edited by Zuhrah Nāmdār. Tehran: Shirkat-e Sahāmī Intishār, 2014 [1392 SH].

Āzād, Muḥammad Ḥusain. *Āb-e Ḥayāt*. Edited by Abrār ʿAbd ul-Islām. Multan: Bahauddin Zakariya University, 2006.

Āżar Begdilī, Luṭf ʿAlī Beg. *Ātishkadah-e Āżar*. Edited by Mīr Hāshim Muḥaddiṡ. 4 vols. Tehran: Amīr Kabīr, 1999 [1378 SH].

Azraqī Haravī. *Dīwān-e Azraqī Haravī*. Edited by Saʿīd Nafīsī. Tehran: Kitāb Faroshī-e Zawwār, 1957 [1336 SH].

Bahār, Lālah Tek Chand. *Bahār-e ʿAjam: Farhang-e Luġhat Tarkībāt Kināyāt wa Amṡāl-e Fārsī*. Edited by Kāẓim Dizfūliyān. 3 vols. Tehran: Ṭalāyah, 2001 [1380 SH].

Beale, Thomas William. *An Oriental Biographical Dictionary*. Edited by Henry George Keene. London: W.H. Allen, 1894.

——. *Miftāḥ ut-Tawārīḳh*. Lucknow: Nawal Kishore Press, 1872.

Bedil, ʿAbd ul-Qādir. *Āwāz-hā-e Bedil: Naṡr-e Adabī*. Edited by Akbar Bihdarvand. Tehran: Muʾassisah-e Intishārāt-e Nigāh, 2007 [1386 SH].

——. *Chahār ʿUnṣur-e Bedil*. Edited by Ẓiyāʾ ud-Dīn Shifīʿī. Tehran: Alhoda International Cultural, Artistic & Publishing Institution, 2013 [1392 SH].

——. *Kulliyāt-e Abū'l-Maʿānī Mīrzā ʿAbd ul-Qādir Bedil*. Edited by Ḳhalīlullāh Ḳhalīlī. 4 vols. Kabul: Da Pohane Vizārat, da Dūr ut-Taʾlif-e Riyāsat, 1961–1965 [1341–1344 SH].

——. *Ruqaʿāt-e Mīrzā Bedil*. Lucknow: Maṭbaʿah-e Ḥasanī, 1845 [1261 AH].

Bilgrāmī, ʿAbd ul-Jalīl ibn Aḥmad. "Original Letters, from a Father to His Son on Various Subjects." In *The Oriental Miscellany: Consisting of Original Productions and Translations*, edited and translated by Francis Gladwin, 133–287. Calcutta: n.p., 1798.
Dard, ʿAlī Muḥammadī. *Majmūʿah-e Chahār Risālah: Nālah-e Dard, Āh-e Sard, Dard-e Dil, Shamaʿ-e Maḥfil*. Bhopal: Maṭbaʿ-e Shāhjahānī, 1893 [1311 AH].
Dargāh Qulī Ḳhān. *Muraqqaʿ-e Dihlī*. Edited and translated by Ḳhalīq Anjum. Delhi: Anjuman-e Taraqqī-e Urdū Hind, 1993.
Daulat Shāh Samarqandī. *Tażkirah-e Daulat Shāh*. Edited by Muḥammad Rafīʿ Shīrāzī. Bombay: Maṭbaʿ-e ʿAlawī, 1887 [1305 AH].
——. *Tażkirat ush-Shuʿarā*. Edited by Edward G. Browne. Leiden: Brill, 1901.
Faḳhrī Haravī, Muḥammad. *Tażkirah-e Rawżat us-Salāṭīn wa Jawāhir ul-ʿAjāʾib maʿ Dīwān-e Faḳhrī Haravī*. Edited by Ḥuṣām ud-Dīn Rashīdī. Hyderabad, Sindh: Sindhī Adabī Baurd, 1968.
Fayyāẓ Lāhījī, ʿAbd ur-Razāq. *Dīwān-e Fayyāẓ Lāhījī*. Edited by Abū'l Ḥasan Parwīn Pareshānzādah. Tehran: Intishārāt-e ʿIlmī va Farhangī, 1991 [1369 SH].
Firāq Dihlavī, Sayyid Nāṣir Nażīr. *Maiḳhānah-e Dard*. Delhi: Jayyid Barqī Press, 1926 [1344 AH].
Fraser, James. *The History of Nadir Shah, Formerly Called Thamas Kuli Khan, the Present Emperor of Persia*. London: W. Straban, 1742 JD.
Fryer, John. *A New Account of East-India and Persia, in Eight Letters. Being Nine Years Travels, Begun 1672 and Finished 1681*. London: R.R. for Ri. Chiswell, 1698.
Fuġhān, Ashraf ʿAlī Ḳhān. *Dīwān-e Ashraf ʿAlī Ḳhān Fuġhān*. Edited by Muḥammad Sarvar ul-Hudá. New Delhi: Qaumī Kaunsil barāʾe Furoġh-e Urdū Zabān, 2003.
Ġhālib, Asadullāh Ḳhān. *Dīwān-e Ġhālib*. Aligarh: Maktabah-e Jāmiʿah Milliyah Islāmiyah, 1925.
——. *Dīwān-e Ġhālib*. Edited by Ḥāmid ʿAlī Ḳhān. Lahore: Maṭbūʿāt-e Majlis-e Yādgār-e Ġhālib, Punjab University, 1969.
——. *Dīwān-e Ġhālib Kāmil: Nusḳhah-e Raẓā Tārīḳhī Tartīb se*. Edited by Kālidās Guptā Raẓā. 3rd ed. Bombay: Sākār Pablisharz, 1995.
——. *Dīwān-e Ġhālib: Nusḳhah-e ʿArshī*. Edited by Imtiyāz ʿAlī Ḳhān ʿArshī. Lahore: Majlis-e Taraqqī-e Urdū, 1982.
——. *Dīwān-e Ġhālib, Nusḳhah Ḥamīdiyyah*. Edited by Ḥamīd Aḥmad Ḳhān. 2nd ed. Lahore: Majlis-e Taraqqī-e Adab, 1992.
Ġhanī Kashmīrī, Muḥammad Ṭāhir. *Dīwān-e Ġhanī Kashmīrī*. Edited by Aḥmad Karamī. Tehran: Mā, 1983 [1362 SH].
Ġhazālī, Abū Ḥāmid Imām Muḥammad. *Kīmyāʾ-e Saʿādat*. Edited by Ḥusain Ḳhadīwjam. 9th ed. 2 vols. Tehran: Intishārāt-e ʿIlmī wa Farhangī, 2001 [1380 SH].
Gilchrist, John. *Oriental Linguist, Easy and Familiar Introduction to the Popular Language of Hindoostan Vocabulary the Language the Articles War*. Calcutta: Ferris and Greenway, 1798.
Ḥāfiẓ, Shams ud-Dīn Muḥammad. *Dīwān-e Ḥāfiẓ*. Edited by Parwez Nātil Ḳhānlarī. 2nd ed. 2 vols. Tehran: Intishārāt-e Khwārazmī, 1984 [1362 SH].

Ḥairat Akbarābādī, Qiyām ud-Dīn. *Tażkirah-e Maqālāt ush-Shuʿarā*. Edited by ʿAlī Riżā Qazvah. Tehran: Majlis-e Shūrā-e Islāmī, Kitābkhānah, Mūzih wa Markaz-e Asānad, 2017 [1396 SH].
Ḥākim Lāhaurī, ʿAbd ul-Ḥakīm. *Tażkirah-e Mardum-e Dīdah*. Edited by ʿAlī Riżā Qazvah. Tehran: Kutubḳhānah Muzih wa Markaz-e Asnād-e Majlis-e Shorā-e Islāmī, 2011 [1390 SH].
Ḥamīd Aurangābādī, Ḳhwājah Ḳhān. *Gulshan-e Guftār: Shuʿarā-e Urdū kā Qadīmtarīn Tażkirah*. Edited by Sayyid Muḥammad. Hyderabad, Deccan: Maktabah-e Ibrāhīmiyah, 1929.
Ḥasan Dihlavī, Mīr Ġhulām. *Tażkirah-e Shuʿarā-e Urdū*. Edited by Nawwāb Ṣadr Yār Jang Bahādur Maulanā Muḥammad Ḥabīb ur-Raḥmān Ḳhān Ṣāḥib Shirwānī. Delhi: Anjuman-e Taraqqī-e Urdū, 1940.
Ḥasan Sijzī Dihlavī, Najm ud-Dīn. *Dīwān-e Ḥasan Sijzī Dihlavī*. Hyderabad, Deccan: Maktabah-e Ibrāhīmiyah, 1934.
Hāshmī Sandīlavī, Aḥmad ʿAlī Ḳhān. *Tażkirah-e Maḳhzan ul-Ġharāʾib*. Edited by Muḥammad Bāqir. Vols. 1–2. 5 vols. Lahore: Intishārāt-e Dānishgāh-e Panjāb, 1968–1970.
——. *Tażkirah-e Maḳhzan ul-Ġharāʾib*. Edited by Muḥammad Bāqir. Vols. 3–5. 5 vols. Islamabad: Markaz-e Taḥqīqāt-e Fārsī-e Īrān wa Pākistān, 1994 [1372 SH].
Ḥātim, Ẓuhūr ud-Dīn. *Dīwān-e Fārsī-e Ḥātim Dihlavī*. Edited by Muḳhtar ud-Dīn Aḥmad. Rampur: Kitabḳhānah-e Rażā Rāmpur, 2010.
——. *Dīwānzādah*. Edited by Ġhulām Ḥusain Żūʾl-Faqār. Lahore: Maktabah-e Ḳhayābān-e Adab, 1975.
——. *Dīwānzādah*. Edited by ʿAbd ul-Ḥaqq. New Delhi: National Mission for Manuscripts and Dillī Kitāb Ghar, 2011.
——. *Intiḳhāb-e Ḥātim: Dīwān-e Qadīm*. Edited by ʿAbd ul-Ḥaqq. Delhi: Department of Urdu, Delhi University, 1977.
Ḥazīn Lāhijī, Muḥammad ʿAlī. *Dīwān-e Ḥazīn Lāhījī*. Edited by Żabīḥullāh Ṣāḥibkār. 3rd ed. Tehran: Nashr-e Sāyah, 2005 [1384 SH].
——. *Rasāʾil-e Ḥazīn-e Lāhijī*. Edited by ʿAlī Aujabī, Nāṣir Bāqarī Bīdhindī, Iskandar Isfandyārī, and ʿAbd ul-Ḥusain Mahdawī. Tehran: Miras Maktoob, 1998 [1377 SH].
——. *Tārīḳh wa Ṣafarnāmah-e Ḥazīn*. Edited by ʿAlī Dawānī. Tehran: Intishārāt-e Markaz-e Asnad-e Inqilāb-e Islāmī, 1997 [1375 SH].
Hidāyat, Riżā Qulī Ḳhān. *Majmaʿ ul-Fuṣahā*. Edited by Mażāhir Muṣaffā. 2 vols. Tehran: Amīr Kabīr, 2003 [1382 SH].
Hindī, Bhagwān Dās. *Safīnah-e Hindī*. Edited by Sayyid Shāh Muḥammad ʿAṭāʾ ur-Raḥmān ʿAṭā Kākvī. Patna: Idārah-e Taḥqīqāt-e ʿArabī wa Fārsī, 1958.
Ibn al-Sāʿī, Tāj al-Dīn ʿAlī ibn Anjab. *Consorts of the Caliphs: Women and the Court of Baghdad*. Edited by Shawkat M. Toorawa and Julia Bray. New York: New York University Press, 2015.
Ibn Baṭṭūṭa, Muḥammad Ibn ʿAbdallāh. *The Travels of Ibn Baṭṭūṭa, A.D. 1325–1354*. Translated by Hamilton Alexander Rosskeen Gibb. Vol. 2. 4 vols. London: The Hakluyt Society, 1962.
ul-Iḥsānī, Karīmī. *Āl Inḍiyā Mushāʿire*. Muzaffarnagar: Shān-e Hind, 1987.

Iḳhlāṣ, Kishan Chand. *Hameshah Bahār*. Edited by Wahīd Qureshī. Karachi: Anjuman-e Taraqqī-e Urdū Pākistān, 1973.

Injū Shīrāzī, Jamāl ud-Dīn Ḥusain bin Faḳhr ud-Dīn Ḥasan. *Farhang-e Jahāngīrī*. Edited by Raḥīm ʿAfīfī. 2nd ed. 2 vols. Mashhad: Chāpḳhānah-e Dānishgāh-e Mashhad, 1980 [1351 SH].

Inshā, Sayyid Inshāʾullāh Ḳhān, and Muḥammad Ḥasan Qatīl. *Daryā-e Laṭāfat*. Edited by Aḥmad ʿAlī Gūpāmavī. Murshidābād: Āftāb-e ʿĀlamtāb, 1850 [1266 AH].

ʿIrāqī, Faḳhr ud-Dīn. *Dīwān-e Faḳhr ud-Dīn ʿIrāqī*. Edited by M. Darwīsh. Tehran: Sāzmān-e Intishārāt-e Jāvedān, 1983 [1362 SH].

Ishwar Das Nagar. *Ishwar Das Nagar's Futuhat-i-Alamgiri: English Translation and Persian Text*. Edited by Raghubir Sinh and Quazi Karamtullah. Translated by M. F. Lokhandwala and Jadunath Sarkar. Vadodara: Oriental Institute, 1995.

Jahān Malik Ḳhātūn. *Dīwān-e Kāmal-e Jahān Malik Ḳhātūn*. Edited by Pūrānduḳht Kāshānīrād and Kāmil Aḥmadniẕhād. Tehran: Intishārāt-e Zawwār, 1995 [1374 SH].

Josh Malīḥābādī, Shabīr Ḥasan Ḳhān. *Kulliyāt-e Josh Malīḥābādī*. Edited by ʿIṣmat Malīḥābādī. New Delhi: Farīd Būk Ḍīpo, 2007.

Joyā Tabrezī, Dārāb Beg. *Dīwān-e Joyā-e Tabrezī*. Edited by Parvez ʿAbbāsī Dākānī. Tehran: Intishārāt-e Barg, 2000 [1378 SH].

——. *Kulliyāt-e Joyā Tabrezī*. Edited by Muḥammad Bāqir. Lahore: Chāpaḳhānah-e Dānishgāh-e Panjāb, 1959 [1337 SH].

Junayd Shīrāzī, ʿĪsā Abū ul-Qāsim. *Taẕkirah-e Hazār Mazār: Tarjumah-e Shadd ul-Izār, Mazārāt-e Shīrāz*. Edited by Nūrānī Wiṣāl. Shiraz: Kitabḳhānah-e Aḥmadī, 1985 [1364 SH].

Kābulī, ʿAbdullāh. *Taẕkirat ut-Tawārīḳh*. Edited by ʿAlī Riẓā Qujahzādah. Tehran: Kitābḳhānah Muzih wa Markaz-e Asnād-e Majlis-e Shurā-e Islāmī, 2013 [1392 SH].

Kalīm Kāshānī, Abū Ṭālib. *Dīwān-e Abū Ṭālib Kalīm Kāshānī*. Edited by Partuw Baiẓāʾī. Tehran: Kitābfaroshī-e Ḳhayyām, 1957 [1336 SH].

Karīm ud-Dīn Maġhfūr. *Ṭabaqāt-e Shuʿarā-e Hind*. Lucknow: Uttar Pradesh Urdū Akādmī, 1983.

Kashānī, Mīr Taqī ud-Dīn. *Ḳhulāṣat ul-Ashʿār wa Zubdat ul-Afkār*. Edited by Nafīsah Īrānī. 6 vols. Tehran: Miras Maktoob, 2013 [1392 SH].

Kashmīrī, Ḳhwājah ʿAbd ul-Karīm. *Bayān-e Wāqiʿ*. Edited by K. B. Nasīm. Lahore: Idārah-e Taḥqīqāt-e Pākistān, Dānishgāh-e Panjāb, 1970.

Kāẓim, Munshī Muḥammad. *ʿĀlamgīrnāmah*. Edited by Ḳhādim Ḥusain and ʿAbd ul-Ḥayy. Calcutta: Asiatic Society of Bengal, 1868.

Ḳhalīl, ʿAlī Ibrāhīm Ḳhān. *Ṣuḥuf-e Ibrāhīm*. Edited by ʿĀbid Raẓā Bedār. Patna: Kutubḳhānah-e Ḳhudā Baḳhsh, 1978.

Ḳhān, Sayyid Aḥmad. *Ās̤ār us-Ṣanādīd*. Edited by Muḥammad Raḥmatullāh Raʿd. Kanpur: Nāmī Press, 1904.

Ḳhān, Sayyid ʿAlī Ḥasan. *Ṣubḥ-e Gulshan*. Bhopal: Maṭbaʿ-e Shāh Jahānī, 1878 [1295 AH].

Ḳhān, Ṭahmās Beg. *Ṭahmas Nāmah*. Edited by Muḥammad Aslam. Lahore: Punjab University, 1986.

Ḳhusrau Dihlavī, Abū ul-Ḥasan Yamīn ud-Dīn. *Dībāchah-e Dīwān-e Ġhurrat ul-Kamāl*. Edited by Sayyid Wazīr ul-Ḥasan ʿĀbidī. Lahore: Naishnal Kamīṭī barāʾe Sāt Sau Sālah Taqrībāt-e Amīr Ḳhusrau, 1975.

——. *Dīwān-e Kāmal Amīr Ḳhusrau Dihlavī*. Edited by Saʿīd Nafīsī. 2nd ed. Tehran: Sāzmān-e Intishārāt-e Jāvedān, 1982 [1361 SH].

——. *Ḳhāliq Bārī*. Lucknow: Nawal Kishore Press, 1881.

——. *Qirān us-Saʿdain*. Edited by Mīrzā Āqā Kamraʾī. Tehran: Mīrzā Āqā Kamraʾī, n.d.

Ḳhwāfī Ḳhān, Muḥammad Hāshim. *Muntaḳhab ul-Lubāb, Ḥissah-e Duvum*. Edited by Kabīr ud-Dīn Aḥmad and Ġhulām Qādir. Vol 2. 3 vols. Calcutta: Asiatic Society of Bengal, 1874.

Ḳhwushgo, Bindrāban Dās. *Safīnah-e Ḳhwushgo Daftar-e Duvum*. Edited by Sayyid Kalīm Aṣġhar. Tehran: Majlis-e Shawrā-e Islāmī, 2010 [1389 SH].

——. *Safīnah-e Ḳhwushgo Daftar-e Ṡāliṡ*. Edited by Sayyid Shāh Muḥammad ʿAṭāʾ ur-Raḥmān ʿAṭā Kākvī. Patna: Idārah-e Taḥqīqāt-e ʿArabī wa Fārsī, 1959.

Kulaynī, Muḥammad ibn Yaʿqūb. *Al-Kāfī: Maʿ Taʿlīqāt Nāfiʿah Maʾḳhūżah min ʿIddat Shurūḥ*. Edited by ʿAlī Akbar Ġhaffārī. 8 vols. Tehran: Dār ul-Kutub ul-Islāmiyyah, 1957 [1377 AH].

Lodī, Sher ʿAlī Ḳhān. *Tażkirah-e Mirʾāt ul-Ḳhayāl*. Edited by Ḥamīd Ḥasanī. Tehran: Intishārāt-e Rauzanah, 1998 [1377 SH].

Luṭf ʿAẓīmābādī, Mīrzā ʿAlī. *Gulshan-e Hind*. Edited by Muḥammad Shiblī Nuʿmānī and ʿAbd ul-Ḥaqq. Hyderabad, Deccan: ʿAbdullāh Ḳhān, 1906.

Malīḥā Samarqandī, Muḥammad Badīʿ. *Mużakkir ul-Aṣḥāb*. Edited by Muḥammad Taqwī. Tehran: Kitābkhānah Muzih wa Markaz-e Asnād-e Majlis-e Shorā-e Islāmī, 2011 [1390 SH].

Masʿūd Saʿd Salmān. *Dīwān-e Masʿūd Saʿd Salmān*. Edited by Ġulāmriḍā Rašīd Yāsimī. Tehran: Intishārāt-e Pairūz, 1960 [1339 SH].

Maẓhar, Sayyid Shams ud-Dīn Ḥabībullāh Jān-e Jānān. *Dīwān-e Mīrzā Maẓhar Jān-e Jānān wa Ḳharīṭah-e Jawāhir*. Edited by Ġhulām Muṣṭafā Ḳhān and Muḥammad ʿAbd ul-Raḥmān bin Ḥājī Muḥammad Roshan Ḳhān. Hyderabad, Sindh: al-Muṣṭafā Akādmī, 1988 [1408 AH].

Mīr, Mīr Muḥammad Taqī. *Kulliyāt-e Mīr*. Edited by Żill-e ʿAbbās ʿAbbāsī. Vol. 1. New Delhi: Taraqqī-e Urdū Biyūro, 1983.

——. *Kulliyāt-e Mīr Taqi Mīr*. Edited by ʿAbd ul-Bārī Āsī. Lucknow: Nawal Kishore Press, 1941.

——. *Remembrances*. Edited and translated by C. M. Naim. Cambridge, MA: Harvard University Press, 2019.

——. *Tażkirah-e Nikāt ush-Shuʿārā*. Edited by Maḥmūd Ilāhī. Delhi: Jamal Printing Press, 1972.

Muḥibb Dihlavī, Walīullāh. *Dīwān-e Walīullāh Muḥibb*. Edited by Shaguftah Zakariyā. Lahore: Sangat Publishers, 1999.

Muḥtasham, Kamāl ud-Dīn. *Haft Dīwān-e Muḥtasham Kāshānī*. Edited by ʿAbd ul-Ḥusain Nawāʾī and Mahdī Ṣadrī. 2 vols. Tehran: Miras Maktoob, 2001 [1380 SH].
Mukhliṣ, Ānand Rām. *Mirʾāt ul-Iṣṭalāḥ*. Edited by Chander Shekhar, Himdreza Ghelichkani, and Houman Yousefdahi. 2 vols. New Delhi: National Mission for Manuscripts and Dillī Kitāb Ghar, 2013.
——. *Tażkirah-e Shuʿarā*. Edited by Ṣaulat ʿAlī Khān. Tonk: Maulana Abu al-Kalam Azad Arabic and Persian Research Institute, 2017.
Muṣḥafī, Ġhulām Hamadānī. *Kulliyāt-e Muṣḥafī*. Edited by Niśār Aḥmad Fārūqī. 8 vols. New Delhi: Qaumī Kaunsil barāʾe Furoġh-e Urdū Zabān, 2003.
——. *Tażkirah-e Hindī*. Edited by ʿAbd ul-Ḥaqq. Aurangabad: Anjuman-e Taraqqī-e Urdū, 1933.
——. *Tażkirah-e Riyāẓ ul-Fuṣaḥā*. Lucknow: Uttar Pradesh Urdū Akādmī, 1985.
Mushtāq Iṣfahānī, Mīr Sayyid ʿAlī. *Dīwān-e Ġhazalīyāt wa Qaṣāʾid wa Rubāʿīyāt-e Mushtāq*. Edited by Ḥusain Makkī. Tehran: Kitābfaroshī-e Murawwaj, 1941 [1320 SH].
Mustaʿidd Khān, Muḥammad Sāqī. *Maʾāśir-e ʿĀlamgīrī*. Edited by Aḥmad ʿAlī Dām Afāẓatah. Calcutta: Baptist Mission Press, 1870.
Muʿtamad Khān Badakhshī. *Tārīkh-e Muḥammadī*. Edited by Imtiyāz ʿAlī Khān ʿArshī. Vol. 2 (6). 2 vols. Aligarh: Sayyid Nūr ul-Ḥasan, Shuʿbah-e Tārīkh, Muslim Yūnivarsiṭī ʿAlīgaṛh, 1973.
Najāt Iṣfahānī, ʿAbd ul-ʿĀl. *Maśnawī-e Gul-e Kushtī az Mīr Abū ul-ʿĀl Najāt Iṣfahānī maʿ Sharḥ-e Ḥāmal ul-Matan*. Edited by Ratan Singh Zakhmī. Lucknow: Nawal Kishore Press, 1881.
Nājī, Muḥammad Shākir. *Dīwān-e Shākir Nājī Maʿ Muqaddamah wa Farhang*. Edited by Iftakhār Begam Ṣiddīqī. New Delhi: Anjuman-e Taraqqī-e Urdū Hind, 1989.
Nasīmī, ʿImād ud-Dīn. *Dīwān-e Sayyid ʿImād ud-Dīn Nasīmī*. Edited by Ismāʿīl Niżhād-e Fard-e Luristānī. 2nd ed. Tehran: Intishārāt-e Furoġhī, 2004 [1383 SH].
Nāṣir, Saʿādat ʿAlī Khān. *Tażkirah-e Khwush Maʿrakah-e Zebā*. Edited by Mushfiq Khwājah. 2 vols. Lahore: Majlis-e Taraqqī-e Urdū, 1970.
Nāṣir ʿAlī Sirhindī. *Dīwān-e Ashʿār-e Nāṣir ʿAlī Sirhindī*. Edited by Ḥamīd Karamī. Tehran: Ilhām, 2009 [1388 SH].
Nāṣir-e Khusrau. *Dīwān-e Nāṣir-e Khusrau*. Tehran: Muʾassisah-e Intishārāt-e Nigāh, 1994 [1373 SH].
Naṣrābādī, Muḥammad Ṭāhir. *Tażkirah-e Naṣrābādī*. Edited by Aḥmad Mudaqqiq Yazdī. Yazd: Dānishgāh-e Yazd, 1999 [1378 SH].
Naẓīrī Nīshāpūrī, Muḥammad Ḥusain. *Ġhazaliyāt-e Naẓīrī Nīshāpūrī*. Lahore: Shaikh Mubārak ʿAlī, 1935.
Orta, Garcia da. *Colloquies on the Simples and Drugs of India*. Edited by Clements Markham and Francisco Manuel de Melo Breyner, Conde de Ficalho. Translated by Clements Markham. London: Henry Sotheran, 1913.
Pillai, Ananda Ranga. *The Diary of Ananda Ranga Pillai, Dubash to Joseph François Dupleix, A Record of Matters Political, Historical, Social, and Personal, From 1736*

to 1761. Edited by Henry Dodwell. Translated by Frederick Price and K. Rangachari. 12 vols. Madras: Superintendent, Government Press, 1904.
Qāʾim Chāndpūrī, Muḥammad Qayām ud-Dīn. *Tażkirah-e Maḳhzan-e Nikāt*. Edited by Iqtidā Ḥasan. Lahore: Majlis-e Taraqqī-e Adab, 1966.
Qāqshāl, Afẓal Beg Ḳhān. *Tuḥfat ush-Shuʿarā*. Edited by Ḥafīẓ Qatīl. Hyderabad, Deccan: Idārah-e Adab-e Urdū, 1961.
Qāsim, Hakīm Abū'l-Qāsim Mīr Qudratullāh. *Majmūʿah-e Naġhz*. Edited by Mahmūd Shīrānī. 2 vols. New Delhi: Qaumī Kaunsil barāʾe Furoġh-e Urdū Zabān, 2002.
Qatīl, Muḥammad Ḥasan. *Chār Sharbat*. Lucknow: Muḥammadī Press, 1845.
Qudratullāh Gūpāmvī, Muḥammad. *Tażkirah-e Natāʾij ul-Afkār*. Edited by Yūsuf Beg Bābāpūr. Qom: Majmaʿ-e Żaḳhāʾir-e Islāmī, 2008 [1387 SH].
Rafīʿ Shīrāzī, Muḥammad ibn Muḥammad. *Tażkirat ul-Ḳhawātīn*. Bombay: Mīrzā Mahdī Shīrāzī, 1889 [1306 AH].
Rangīn, Saʿdat Yār Ḳhān. *The Faras-Nāma-e Rangīn or The Book of the Horse*. Translated by Douglas Craven Phillott. London: B. Quaritch, 1911.
ur-Rāzī, Shams ud-Dīn Muḥammad ibn Qays. *Ul-Muʿjam fī Maʿāyīr-e Ashʿār ul-ʿAjam*. Edited by Muḥammad Qazwīnī, Sīrūs Shamīsā, and Mudarris Riẓvī. Tehran: Zavvār, 2009 [1388 SH].
Rūmī, Jalāl ud-Dīn Muḥammad. *Kulliyāt-e Shams Tabrezī*. Edited by Badīʿ uz-Zamān Furozānfar. 14th ed. Tehran: Amīr Kabīr, 1997 [1376 SH].
Ṣābir, Mirzā Qādir Baḳhash. *Tażkirah-e Gulistān-e Suḳhan*. Edited by Ḳhalīl ur-Raḥmān Dāʾūdī. 2 vols. Lahore: Majlis-e Taraqqī-e Adab, 1966.
Ṣafā, Muḥammad ʿAbd ul-Ḥayy. *Tażkirah-e Shamīm-e Suḳhan*. Lucknow: Nawal Kishore Press, 1891.
Salmān Sāwajī, Jamāl ud-Dīn Muḥammad. *Dīwān-e Salmān Sāwajī*. Edited by Abū'l Qāsim Ḥālat. Tehran: Mā, 1992 [1371 SH].
Sām Mīrzā. *Tuḥfah-e Sāmī*. Edited by Waḥīd Dastagirdī. Tehran: Aramġhān, 1935 [1314 SH].
Sanāʾī Ġhaznawī, Ḥakīm Abū ul-Majd Majdūd ibn Ādam. *Dīwān-e Ḥakīm Sanāʾī Ġhaznawī*. Tehran: Nashr-e Āzād Mihr, 2002 [1381 SH].
Sangīn Beg. *Sair ul-Manāzil*. Edited by Sharīf Ḥusain Qāsmī. New Delhi: Ġhālib Insṭiṭūṭ Naʾī Dihlī, 1982.
Sarḳhwush, Muḥammad Afẓal. *Tażkirah-e Kalimāt ush-Shuʿarā*. Edited by ʿAlī Riẓā Qazvah. Tehran: Kutubḳhānah Muzih wa Markaz-e Asnād-e Majlis-e Shorā-e Islāmī, 2010 [1396 SH].
Sarvar Taunsvī, Vidyā Prakāsh. *Dillī ke Mushāʿare*. New Delhi: Māhnāmah Shān-e Hind, 1991.
Saudā, Muḥammad Rafīʿ. *Dīwān-e Ġhazaliyāt-e Saudā: Taḥqīq wa Tadwīn*. Edited by Nasīm Aḥmad. Varanasi: Banāras Hindū Yūnīvarsiṭī, 2001.
——. *ʿIbrat ul-Ġhāfilīn*. Edited by Sharīf Ḥusain Qāsmī. New Delhi: Markaz-e Taḥqīqāt-e Fārsī, 2011.
——. *Kulliyāt-e Saudā*. Edited by Muḥammad Anwar Ḥusain Taslīm. Lucknow: Nawal Kishore Press, 1872 [1289 AH].

Ṣā'ib Tabrezī, Muḥammad ʿAlī. *Dīwān-e Ṣā'ib Tabrezī*. Edited by Muḥammad Qahramān. 6 vols. Tehran: Scientific and Cultural Publications, 1985–1991 [1364–1370 SH].
Shafīq Aurangābādī, Lachhmī Narāyan. *Chamanistān-e Shuʿarā*. Edited by ʿAbd ul-Ḥaqq. Aurangabad: Anjuman-e Taraqqī-e Urdū, 1928.
Shāh Nawāz Ḳhān Aurangābādī, Ṣamsām ul-Daulah. *Ma'āṡir ul-Umarā*. Edited by Maulavī Mirzā Ashraf ʿAlī and Maulavī ʿAbd ur-Raḥīm. 3 vols. Calcutta: Asiatic Society of Bengal, 1888–1891.
Shauq Murādābādī, Qudratullāh Ṣiddīqī. *Taẕkirah-e Ṭabaqāt ush-Shuʿarā*. Edited by Niṡār Aḥmad Farūqī. Lahore: Majlis-e Taraqqī-e Adab, 1968.
Sheftah, Muḥammad Mustafā Ḳhān. *Gulshan-e Beḳhār*. Lahore: Majlis-e Taraqqī-e Adab, 1973.
Shorish ʿAẓīmābādī, Ġhulām Ḥusain. *Taẕkirah-e Shorish*. Edited by Maḥmūd Ilāhī. Lucknow: Uttar Pradesh Urdū Akādmī, 1984.
Tābān Dihlavī, ʿAbd ul-Ḥayy. *Dīwān-e Tābān*. Edited by Muḥammad Sarvar ul-Hudá. New Delhi: Qaumī Kaunsil barā'e Furoġh-e Urdū Zabān, 2006.
———. *Dīwān-e Tābān: Mīr ʿAbd ul-Ḥayy Tābān Dihlavī ke Kalām kā Majmūʿah*. Edited by ʿAbd ul-Ḥaqq. Aurangabad: Anjuman-e Taraqqī-e Urdū, 1935.
Ṭabāṭabā'ī, Sayyid Ġhulām Ḥusain Ḳhān. *Siyar ul-Muta'aḳhḳhirīn*. Edited by Ḥakīm ʿAbd ul-Majīd. 2 vols. Calcutta: Editor's Medical Press, 1833.
Tagore, Rabîndranâth. *Journey to Persia and Iraq, 1932*. Kolkata: Visva-Bharati Pub. Dept., 2003.
Tattavī, ʿAbd ur-Rashīd. *Muntaḳhab ul-Luġhāt-e Shāh Jahānī*. Lucknow: Nawal Kishore Press, 1869 [1286 AH].
Thévenot, Jean de, and Giovanni Francesco Gemelli Careri. *Indian Travels of Thevenot And Careri*. Edited by Surendranath Sen. New Delhi: National Archives of India, 1949.
Ṭūsī, Abū Manṣūr Aḥmad ibn ʿAlī Asadī. *Kitāb-e Luġhat-e Furs*. Edited by ʿAbbās Iqbāl. Tehran: Chāpḳhānah-e Majlis, 1940 [1319 SH].
Ṭūsī, Naṣīr ud-Dīn Muḥammad ibn-e Muḥammad, and Muḥammd Saʿdullāh Muftī Murādābādī. *Miʿyār ul-Ashʿār wa Maizān ul-Afkār fī Sharḥ-e Miʿyār ul-Ashʿār*. Edited by Muḥammad Fishārkī. Tehran: Miras-e Maktoob, 2011 [1389 SH].
ʿUrfī Shīrāzī, Jamāl ud-Dīn Muḥammad Sīdī. *Qaṣā'id-e ʿUrfī*. Lucknow: Nawal Kishore Press, 1915.
Walī Dakhanī, Shams ud-Dīn Walī Muḥammad. *Kulliyāt-e Walī*. Edited by Nūr ul-Ḥasan Hāshmī. Lucknow: Uttar Pradesh Urdū Akādmī, 1989.
———. *Les Œuvres de Wali*. Edited by Joseph Héliodore Garcin de Tassy. Paris: Imprimerie Royale, 1834.
Wālih Dāġhistānī, ʿAlī Qulī. *Taẕkirah-e Riyāẓ ush-Shuʿarā*. Edited by Sayyid Muḥsin Nājī Nasrābādī. 5 vols. Iranshahr: Intishārāt-e Asāṭīr, 2005 [1384 SH].
Waṭwāṭ, Rashīd ud-Dīn Muḥammad ibn Muḥammad. *Dīwān-e Rashīd ud-Dīn Waṭwāṭ*. Edited by Saʿīd Nafīsī and ʿAbbās Iqbāl. Tehran: Kitābkhānah-e Bārānī, 1960 [1339 SH].

Wāẓiḥ, Mubārak Allāh. *Tāriḳh-e Irādat Ḳhān*. Edited by Ġhulām Rasūl Mihr. Lahore: Idārah-e Taḥqīqāt-e Pākistān, Dānishgāh-e Panjāb, 1971.
Wāʿiẓ Kāshifī, Kamāl ud-Dīn Ḥusain. *Badāʾiʿ ul-Afkār fī Ṣanāʾiʿ il-Ashʿār*. Edited by Jalāl ud-Dīn Kazzāzī. Tehran: Nashr-e Markaz, 1990 [1369 SH].
——. *Rauẓat ush-Shahudā*. Lucknow: Nawal Kishore Press, 1873.
Wāʿiẓ-e Qazwīnī, Muḥammad Rafīʿ. *Dīwān-e Mullā Muḥammad Rafīʿ Wāʿiẓ-e Qazwīnī*. Edited by Sayyid Ḥasan Sādāt Nāṣirī. Tehran: ʿAlī Akbar ʿIlmī, 1980 [1359 SH].
Yaktā, Sayyid Aḥad ʿAlī Ḳhān. *Dastūr ul-Faṣāḥat*. Edited by Imtiyāz ʿAlī Ḳhān ʿArshī. Rampur: Hindūstān Press, 1943.
Yaqīn, Inʿāmullāh Ḳhān. *Dīwān-e Yaqīn*. Edited by Farḥatullāh Beg. Aurangabad: Anjuman-e Taraqqī-e Urdū, 1916.
——. *Dīwān-e Yaqīn Dihlavī*. Edited by Farḥat Fāṭimah. New Delhi: Anjuman-e Taraqqī-e Urdū Hind, 1995.
Ẓahīr ud-Dīn Madanī. *Suḳhanwarān-e Gujarāt*. Delhi: Qaumi Kaunsil barāʾe Furoġh-e Urdū Zabān, 1981.
Żahnī, Muḥammad. *Mashāhīr un-Nisā*. 2 vols. Istanbul: Dār uṭ-Ṭibāʿat ul-ʿĀmirah, 1877 [1296 AH].
Żakā, Ḳhūb Chand. *ʿAyyār ush-Shuʿarā*. Edited by Sayyid Muḥammad Ṭāriq Ḥasan and Sayyid Nūr ul-Ḥasan Naqwī. New Delhi: Qaumi Kaunsil barāʾe Furoġh-e Urdū Zabān, 2011.
Zaṭallī, Muḥammad Jaʿfar. *Zaṭal Nāmah: Kulliyāt-e Jaʿfar Zaṭallī*. Edited by Rashīd Ḥasan Ḳhān. New Delhi: Anjuman-e Taraqqī-e Urdū Hind, 2003.

Secondary Sources

ʿAbd ul-Ġhafūr, Ḳhwājah. *Ṭanz wa Mizāḥ kā Tanqīdī Jāʾizah*. New Delhi: Modern Publishing House, 1983.
ʿAbd ul-Ġhanī, Muḥammad. *A History of Persian Language and Literature at the Mughal Court*. 3 vols. Allahabad: The Indian Press, 1929.
——. *Life and Works of Abdul Qadir Bedil*. Lahore: Publishers United, 1960.
ʿAbd ul-Ḥaqq, ed. *Daryā-e Laṭāfat* by Sayyid Inshāʾullāh Ḳhān Inshā. Aurangabad: Anjuman-e Taraqqī-e Urdū, 1916.
——. "Urdū Shāʿirī meñ Īhām-Goʾī." *Ham Qalam* 1, no. 10 (1961): 9–16.
ʿAbdullāh, Sayyid Muḥammad. *Shuʿarāʾ-e Urdū ke Tażkire aur Tażkirah Nigārī kā Fann*. Delhi: Maktabah-e Shiʿr wa Adab, 1973.
Adīb Lakhnawī, Sayyid Masʿūd Ḥasan Riẓvī. Preface to *Fāʾiz Dihlavī aur us kā Dīwān* by Ṣadr ud-Dīn Muḥammad Ḳhān Fāʾiz Dihlavī, 3–176. Delhi: Anjuman-e Taraqqī-e Urdū Hind, 1946.
Afẓalī, Ḳhalīlullāh. "Ġharīb-e Bangāl: Nigāhī bah Zindagī wa Āṡar-e Wālih Haravī Shāʿir Barjustah-e Sabk-e Hindī dar Ṣadah-e Yāzdaham." *Pāẕh* 19–20, no. 4 (2015 [1394 SH]): 143–50.
——. "Ṭarz-e Shiʿrī-e Darwesh Ḥusain Wālih wa Barsī Aṡr Guẕārīhā-e Vī Bar ʿAbd al-Qādir Bedil." *Rudakī* 16, no. 45 (2016 [1394 SH]): 7–29.

Afżalī, Ḳhalīlullāh, Mahduḳht Pūr Ḳhāliqī Chatrūdī, and Mariyam Ṣālhī-e Nayā. "Muḳhāṭib az Nigāh-e Bedil Dihlavī." *Adab-e Piẕẖohī* 29 (Autumn 2014 [1393 SH]): 73–96.
Ahmad, Aziz. "Ṣafawid Poets and India." *Iran* 14 (1976): 117–32.
Aḥmad Qamar, Zubair. "Maʿrufī Ajmālī-e Taẕkirah-e Hameshah Bahār." *Nāmah-e Pārsī* 42–43, no. 12 (2007 [1386 SH]): 151–58.
Aḥmad, Shaiḳh ʿAqīl. *Fann-e Taẓmīn Nigārī: Tanqīd wa Tajziyah.* 2nd ed. Delhi: ʿArshiyah Pablīkeshanz, 2017.
Aḥmad, Shamīm. Preface to *Dīwān-e Yakrū* by ʿAbd ul-Wahhāb Yakrū, 4–85. Muzaffarpur: Idārah-e Urdū, 1978.
Ahmed, Shahab. *What Is Islam? The Importance of Being Islamic.* Princeton: Princeton University Press, 2015.
Ahsanuzzafar, Sayyid. *Mirzā Bedil: Ḥayāt aur Kārnāme.* Rampur: Rāmpūr Raẓā Library, 2009.
Aigle, Denise. "Among Saints and Poets: The Spiritual Topography of Medieval Shiraz." *Eurasian Studies* 16, no. 1–2 (2018): 142–76.
Alam, Muzaffar. *The Crisis of Empire in Mughal North India: Awadh and Punjab, 1707–48.* 2nd ed. New York: Oxford University Press, 2013.
———. *The Languages of Political Islam in India, c. 1200–1800.* Ranikhet: Permanent Black, 2010.
———. *The Mughals and the Sufis: Islam and Political Imagination in India, 1500–1750.* Albany: State University of New York Press, 2021.
———. "Trade, State Policy and Regional Change: Aspects of Mughal-Uzbek Commercial Relations, C. 1550–1750." *Journal of the Economic and Social History of the Orient* 37, no. 3 (1994): 202–27.
Alam, Muzaffar, and Sanjay Subrahmanyam. "The Making of a Munshi." *Comparative Studies of South Asia, Africa, and the Middle East* 2, no. 24 (2004): 61–72.
Algar, Hamid. "Badaḵšī, Mollā Shah." In *Encyclopaedia Iranica Online.* Leiden: Brill, 2020. https://doi.org/10.1163/2330-4804_EIRO_COM_6294.
Ali, M. Athar. *The Mughal Nobility under Aurangzeb.* Delhi: Oxford University Press, 1997.
Ali, Samer M. *Arabic Literary Salons in the Islamic Middle Ages: Poetry, Public Performance, and the Presentation of the Past.* South Bend: University of Notre Dame Press, 2010.
ʿĀlim, Muḥammad Sharf. "Saudā kā Fārsī Kalām aur Fārsī Ashʿār kā Taẓmīn." *Ġhālib Nāmah* 22, no. 2 (2001): 333–43.
Ambler, Catherine Henderson. "Masters of the Distant Meanings: Unity and Multiplicity in the Persian Poesis of Freshness." PhD diss., Columbia University, 2022.
Andrews, Walter G., and Mehmet Kalpaklı. *Age of Beloveds: Love and the Beloved in Early Modern Ottoman and European Culture and Society.* Durham: Duke University Press, 2005.
Anjum, Ḳhalīq. *Mirzā Muḥammad Rafīʿ Saudā.* New Delhi: Qaumī Kaunsil barāʾe Furoġh-e Urdū Zabān, 2003.

——. “Saudā ke Maʿrake.” *Nuqūsh* 127, no. 2 (1981): 60–86.
Ansārī, Nūr ul-Ḥasan. *Fārsī Adab ba-ʿAhad-e Aurangzeb*. Delhi: Indo-Persian Society, 1969.
Appadurai, Arjun. “Commodities and the Politics of Value.” In *The Social Life of Things: Commodities in Cultural Perspective*, edited by Arjun Appadurai, 3–63. Cambridge: Cambridge University Press, 2013.
ʿAqīl, Muʿīn ud-Dīn. *Taḥrīk-e Āzādī meñ Urdū kā Ḥiṣṣah*. Lahore: Anjuman-e Taraqqī-e Urdū, 2008.
ʿAṣīm, ʿAbd ur-Rashīd. *Taẕkirah-e Talāmiẕh-e Shāh Ḥātim Dihlavī Talḳhīṣ wa Tartīb*. Multan: Beacon Books, 1994.
Asher, Catherine B. *Architecture of Mughal India*. Cambridge: Cambridge University Press, 1992.
ʿAṭā Kākvī, Sayyid Shāh Muḥammad ʿAṭāʾ ur-Raḥmān, trans. *Taẕkirah-e Chamanistān-e Shuʿarā* by Lachhmī Narāyan Shafīq Aurangābādī. Patna: Idārah-e Taḥqīqāt-e ʿArabī wa Fārsī, 1928 [1388 AH].
Babayan, Kathryn. *The City as Anthology: Eroticism and Urbanity in Early Modern Isfahan*. Stanford: Stanford University Press, 2021.
Bahār, Muḥammad Taqī. *Sabkshināsī Yā Tāriḳh-e Taṭawwur-e Nashr-e Fārsī*. 4th ed. 3 vols. Tehran: Amir Kabir, 1976 [2535 PE].
Bailey, T. Grahame. “Urdu: The Name and the Language.” *The Journal of the Royal Asiatic Society of Great Britain and Ireland*, no. 2 (April 1930): 391–400.
——. *A History of Urdu Literature*. Calcutta: Oxford University Press, 1932.
——. Review of *Camanistan i Shu'arā*, by Lachhmī Narāyan Shafīq Aurangābādī and edited by Abdul Haq [ʿAbd ul-Ḥaqq]. *Bulletin of the School of Oriental Studies, University of London* 5, no. 4 (1930): 927–28.
Balabanlilar, Lisa. “The Begims of the Mystic Feast: Turco-Mongol Tradition in the Mughal Harem.” *The Journal of Asian Studies* 69, no. 1 (2010): 123–47.
Bangha, Imre. “Rekhta, Poetry in Mixed Language: The Emergence of Khari Boli Literature in North India.” In *Before the Divide: Hindi and Urdu Literary Culture*, edited by Francesca Orsini, 21–83. New Delhi: Orient Blackswan, 2010.
Bano, Shadab. “Age of Marriage in Pre-Colonial India.” *Proceedings of the Indian History Congress* 64 (2003): 596–602.
Bashir, Shahzad. *The Market in Poetry in the Persian World*. New York: Cambridge University Press, 2021.
Bayly, C. A. *Empire and Information: Intelligence Gathering and Social Communication in India, 1780–1870*. New York: Cambridge University Press, 1996.
Bazmee Ansari, A. S. “Āzād Bilgrāmī.” In *Encyclopaedia of Islam New Edition Online (EI-2 English)*, edited by P. Bearman. Leiden: Brill, 2012. http://dx.doi.org/10.1163/1573-3912_islam_SIM_0937.
Beers, Theodore S. “Taẕkirah-i Khayr al-Bayān: The Earliest Source on the Career and Poetry of Ṣāʾib Tabrīzī (d. ca. 1087/1676).” *Al-ʿUsur al-Wusta* 24, no. 1 (November 15, 2016): 114–38.
Beg, Farḥatullāh. *Dihlī kī Āḳhrī Shamaʿ*. New Delhi: Urdū Akādmī, 2003.

——. Preface to *Dīwān-e Yaqīn* by Inʿāmullāh Ḳhān Yaqīn, 1–98. Aurangabad: Anjuman-e Taraqqī-e Urdū, 1916.
Bellenoit, Hayden J. *The Formation of the Colonial State in India: Scribes, Paper and Taxes, 1760–1860*. London: Routledge, 2017.
Binbaş, İlker Evrim. *Intellectual Networks in Timurid Iran: Sharaf al-Dīn ʿAlī Yazdī and the Islamicate Republic of Letters*. New York: Cambridge University Press, 2016.
Bishara, Fahad Ahmad, and Nandini Chatterjee. "Introduction: The Persianate Bazaar." *Journal of the Economic and Social History of the Orient* 64, no. 5–6 (2021): 487–512.
Blake, Stephen P. *Shahjahanabad: The Sovereign City in Mughal India, 1639–1739*. New York: Cambridge University Press, 2002.
——. *Time in Early Modern Islam: Calendar, Ceremony, and Chronology in the Safavid, Mughal, and Ottoman Empires*. New York: Cambridge University Press, 2013.
Bloom, Jonathan M. *Paper before Print: The History and Impact of Paper in the Islamic World*. New Haven: Yale University Press, 2001.
Bloom, Jonathan M., and Sheila S. Blair, eds. "Mīr ʿAlī Ḥusaynī Haravī." In *The Grove Encyclopedia of Islamic Art and Architecture*. New York: Oxford University Press, 2009. http://www.oxfordreference.com/view/10.1093/acref/9780195309911.001.0001/acref-9780195309911-e-605.
Bonebakker, S. A. "Tawriya." In *Encyclopaedia of Islam New Edition Online (EI-2 English)*, edited by P. Bearman. Leiden: Brill, 2012. https://doi.org/10.1163/1573-3912_islam_SIM_7460.
Borah, M. J. [M. I.]. "The Nature of the Persian Language Written and Spoken in India during the 13th and 14th Centuries." *Bulletin of the School of Oriental Studies, University of London* 7, no. 2 (1934): 325–27.
Botstein, Leon. "Toward a History of Listening." *The Musical Quarterly* 82, no. 3/4 (1998): 427–31.
Boyk, David. "Nationality and Fashionality: Hats, Lawyers and Other Important Things to Remember." *South Asia: Journal of South Asian Studies* 43, no. 5 (2020): 879–97.
Brookshaw, Dominic Parviz. *Hafiz and His Contemporaries: Poetry, Performance and Patronage in Fourteenth Century Iran*. New York: I.B. Tauris, 2019.
——. "Odes of a Poet-Princess: The *Ghazals* of Jahān-Malik Khātūn." *Iran* 43 (2005): 173–95.
——. "Palaces, Pavilions and Pleasure-Gardens: The Context and Setting of the Medieval Majlis." *Middle Eastern Literatures* 6, no. 2 (July 2003): 199–223.
——. "Sung with Melodious Tunes: Performance Context as Described in the *Ghazals* of Jahān-Malik Khātūn." In *Ghazal as World Literature II*, edited by Angelika Neuwirth, Michael Hess, Judith Pfeiffer, and Börte Sagaster, 87–108. Würzburg: Ergon-Verlag, 2006.
Brown [Schofield], Katherine Butler. "The Origins and Early Development of Khayal." In *Hindustani Music: Thirteenth to Twentieth Centuries*, edited by Joep

Bor, Françoise "Nalini" Delvoye, Jane Harvey, and Emmeie Te Nijenhuis, 159–91. Delhi: Manohar, 2010.
———. "The Social Liminality of Musicians: Case Studies from Mughal India and Beyond." *Twentieth-Century Music* 3, no. 1 (2007): 13–49.
Browne, Edward G. *A Literary History of Persia: From Firdawsí to Sa'dí*. Vol. 2. 4 vols. Cambridge: Cambridge University Press, 1964.
Bruijn, J.T.P. de. "The Name of the Poet in Persian Poetry." In *Proceedings of the Third European Conference of Iranian Studies, Part 2: Mediaeval and Modern Persian Studies*, edited by Charles Melville, 45–56. Wiesbaden: Dr. Ludwig Reichert Verlag, 1999.
———. "Sabk-i Hindī." In *Encyclopaedia of Islam New Edition Online (EI-2 English)*, edited by P. Bearman. Leiden: Brill, 2012. https://doi.org/10.1163/1573-3912_islam_SIM_6377.
Bulliet, Richard W. *Conversion to Islam in the Medieval Period: An Essay in Quantitative History*. Cambridge, MA: Harvard University Press, 1979.
Busch, Allison. *Poetry of Kings: The Classical Hindi Tradition of Mughal India*. New York: Oxford University Press, 2011.
Calabria, Michael. "Mughal Munificence: Care and Concern for the Poor in Islamic Hindustan from Tuladan to the Taj." In *Poverty and Wealth in Judaism, Christianity, and Islam*, edited by Nathan R. Kollar and Muhammad Shafiq, 31–53. New York: Palgrave Macmillan, 2016.
Chānd, Shaiḳh. *Saudā*. Aurangabad: Anjuman-e Taraqqī-e Urdū, 1936.
Chandra, Satish. *Parties and Politics at the Mughal Court, 1707–1740*. 4th ed. New Delhi: Oxford University Press, 2002.
Chatterjee, Indrani. "A Slave's Quest for Selfhood in Eighteenth-Century Hindustan." *The Indian Economic & Social History Review* 37, no. 1 (2000): 53–86.
Chatterjee, Kumkum. "Scribal Elites in Sultanate and Mughal Bengal." *The Indian Economic & Social History Review* 47, no. 4 (October 1, 2010): 445–72.
Chatterjee, Nandini. *Negotiating Mughal Law: A Family of Landlords across Three Indian Empires*. New York: Cambridge University Press, 2020.
———. "Translating Obligations: *Tamassuk* and *Fārigh-Khaṭṭī* in the Indo-Persian World." *Journal of the Economic and Social History of the Orient* 64, no. 5–6 (2021): 541–82.
Cherian, Divya. "Stolen Skin and Children Thrown: Governing Sex and Abortion in Early Modern South Asia." *Modern Asian Studies* 55, no. 5 (2021): 1–49.
Chuġhatā'ī, Muḥammad Akrām. "Walī Gujarātī aur Shāh Sa'dullāh Gulshan." *Urdū Nāmah*, no. 23 (March 1966): 5–11.
Cohen, Michael C. *The Social Lives of Poems in Nineteenth-Century America*. Philadelphia: University of Pennsylvania Press, 2015.
Cole, Juan R. "Iranian Culture and South Asia, 1500–1900." In *Iran and the Surrounding World*, edited by Nikki R. Keddie and Rudi Matthee, 15–35. Seattle: University of Washington Press, 2002.
———. *Roots of North Indian Shi'ism in Iran and Iraq: Religion and State in Awadh, 1722–1859*. New York: Oxford University Press, 1989.

Cook, Michael. "Islam: History's First Shot at a Global Culture?" *Historically Speaking* 5, no. 4 (2004): 7–10.
Crooke, William. *The Tribes and Castes of the North-Western Provinces and Oudh.* Vol. 2. 4 vols. Calcutta: Office of the Superintendent of Government Printing, 1896.
Cunningham, Alexander. *Archaeological Survey of India.* Vol. 1. 11 vols. Simla: Government Central Press, 1871.
Dadlani, Chanchal B. *From Stone to Paper: Architecture as History in the Late Mughal Empire.* New Haven: Yale University Press, 2019.
Dale, Stephen F., and Alam Payind. "The Ahrārī *Waqf* in Kābul in the Year 1546 and the Mughūl Naqshbandiyyah." *Journal of the American Oriental Society* 119, no. 2 (1999): 218–33.
Dānešpažūh, M.-T. "Bayāż." In *Encyclopaedia Iranica Online.* Leiden: Brill, 2020. http://dx.doi.org/10.1163/2330-4804_EIRO_COM_6754.
Dell'Antonio, Andrew. *Listening as Spiritual Practice in Early Modern Italy.* Berkeley: University of California Press, 2011.
Deshpande, Prachi. "The Marathi Kaulnāmā: Property, Sovereignty and Documentation in a Persianate Form." *Journal of the Economic and Social History of the Orient* 64, no. 5–6 (2021): 583–614.
Deweese, Devin. "Islamization in the Mongol Empire." In *The Cambridge History of Inner Asia: The Chinggisid Age*, edited by Allen J. Frank, Nicola Di Cosmo, and Peter B. Golden, 120–34. Cambridge: Cambridge University Press, 2009.
Dhavan, Purnima, and Heidi Pauwels. "Controversies Surrounding the Reception of 'Valī' Dakhanī (1665?–1707?) In Early Tażkirahs of Urdu Poets." *Journal of the Royal Asiatic Society* 25, no. 4 (2015): 625–46.
——. "Crafting Literary Urdu: Mirza Hatim's Engagement with Vali Dakhani." *Modern Asian Studies* 57, no. 3 (2022): 711–39.
Di Pietrantonio, Natalia. "Pornography and Indian Miniature Painting: The Case of Avadh, India." *Porn Studies* 7, no. 1 (2020): 36–60.
Diem, Werner, and Marco Schöller. *The Living and the Dead in Islam: Epitaphs as Texts.* Wiesbaden: Otto Harrassowitz Verlag, 2004.
Dudney, Arthur. *Delhi: Pages from a Forgotten History.* New Delhi: Hay House India, 2015.
——. *India in the Persian World of Letters: Khān-i Ārzū Among the Eighteenth-Century Philologists.* New York: Oxford University Press, 2022.
——. "Literary Decadence and Imagining the Late Mughal City." *Journal for Early Modern Cultural Studies* 18, no. 3 (2018): 187–211.
———. "Why Did Shāh Ḥātim's Collected Works Spawn a Child?" Unpublished paper, last modified April 2010. https://academiccommons.columbia.edu/doi/10.7916/D83N296P/download.
Eaton, Richard Maxwell. *India in the Persianate Age, 1000–1765.* Oakland: University of California Press, 2019.
Elliot, Henry Miers, trans. *The History of India as Told by Its Own Historians: The Muhammadan Period.* Edited by John Dowson. Vol. 8. London: Trubner, 1877.

Erlmann, Veit. “Refiguring the Early Modern Voice.” *Qui Parle* 21, no. 1 (2012): 85–105.
Evilsizor, Kacey. “Poetry and Patronage: Persian Literature during the Mongol Empire.” In *Routledge Handbook of Ancient, Classical and Late Classical Persian Literature*, edited by Kamran Talattof, 335–43. New York: Routledge, 2023.
Faiẓān, Dānish. “Walī ke Ġhair Dakanī Muʿāsir Shuʿarā.” In *Tārīḳh-e Adabiyāt-e Musalmānān-e Pākistān wa Hind: Urdū Adab, Awwal*, edited by Waḥīd Qureshi, 6:570–76. Lahore: Punjab University Press, 1971.
Farīdī Dihlavī, Muḥammad ʿĀlam Shāh Ṣāḥib. *Mazārāt-e Auliyāʾ-e Dihlī*. 2nd ed. Delhi: Jayyid Barqī Press, 1927 [1346 AH].
Farooqi, Mehr Afshan. “The ‘Hindi’ of the ‘Urdu.’” *Economic and Political Weekly* 43, no. 9 (2008): 18–20.
Faruqi, Shamsur Rahman. “Burning Rage, Icy Scorn: The Poetry of Ja’far Zatalli.” Unpublished paper, last modified September 24, 2008. https://franpritchett.com/00fwp/srf/srf_zatalli_2008.pdf.
———. *Early Urdu Literary Culture and History*. New Delhi: Oxford University Press, 2001.
———. “Five (or More) Ways for a Poet to Imitate Other Poets, *or*, Imitation in Sabk-i Hindi.” Unpublished paper, last modified May 2008. https://franpritchett.com/00fwp/srf/srf_imitation_2008.pdf.
———. *Kaʾī Chānd The Sar-e Āsmān*. New Delhi: Pengin Books India, 2006.
———. “A Long History of Urdu Literary Culture, Part 1: Naming and Placing a Literary Culture.” In *Literary Cultures in History: Reconstructions from South Asia*, edited by Sheldon I. Pollock, 805–63. Berkeley: University of California Press, 2003.
———. Preface to *Dīwān-e Chirkīn: Mustanad Kalām* by Bāqir ʿAlī Chirkīn Rūdaulavī, edited by Abrār ul-Ḥaqq Shāṭir Gorakhpūrī, 5–18. Gorakhpur: self-published, 2009.
———. “The Satires of Sauda (1706–1781).” Unpublished paper, last modified September 2010. https://franpritchett.com/00fwp/srf/srf_sauda_2010.pdf.
———. *Sawār aur Dūsre Afsāne*. Allahabad: Shab Ḳhūn Kitāb Ghar, 2003.
———. *Shiʿr-e Shor-Angez: Ġhazaliyāt-e Mīr kā Muḥaqqiqānah Intiḳhāb, Mufaṣṣal Muṭāliʿe ke Sāth*. 3rd ed. 4 vols. New Delhi: Qaumī Kaunsil barāʾe Furoġh-e Urdū Zabān, 2006.
———. “A Stranger in the City: The Poetics of Sabk-i Hindi.” *Annual of Urdu Studies* 19 (2004): 1–93.
———. *The Sun That Rose from the Earth*. Translated by Shamsur Rahman Faruqi. Gurgaon: Penguin Books India, 2016.
———. *Urdū Ġhazal ke Aham Moṛ: Īhām, Riʿāyat, Munāsibāt*. New Delhi: Ghalib Academy, 1996.
Favereau, Marie. *The Horde: How the Mongols Changed the World*. Cambridge, MA: Belknap Press of Harvard University Press, 2021.
Flatt, Emma J. *The Courts of the Deccan Sultanates: Living Well in the Persian Cosmopolis*. New York: Cambridge University Press, 2019.

——. "Practicing Friendship: Epistolary Constructions of Social Intimacy in the Bahmani Sultanate." *Studies in History* 33, no. 1 (2017): 61–81.
Fox, Aaron A. *Real Country: Music and Language in Working-Class Culture*. Durham: Duke University Press, 2007.
Gabbay, Alyssa. *Islamic Tolerance: Amir Khusraw and Pluralism*. London: Routledge, 2010.
Ghougassian, Vazken S., Armen Haghnazarian, and Sebouh Aslanian. "Julfa." In *Encyclopaedia Iranica Online*. Leiden: Brill, 2020. https://doi.org/10.1163/2330-4804_EIRO_COM_10414.
Goitein, Shelomo Dov. "The Rise of the Near-Eastern Bourgeoisie in Early Islamic Times." *Cahiers d'Histoire Mondiale* 3, no. 3 (1957): 583–604.
Gould, Rebecca R. "Russifying the *Radīf*: Lyric Translatability and the Russo-Persian Ghazal." *Comparative Critical Studies* 17, no. 2 (2020): 263–84.
Gramsci, Antonio. *Quaderni del Carcere*. Edited by Valentino Gerratana. 2nd ed. 4 vols. Torino: G. Einaudi, 1977.
Green, Nile. "Introduction: The Frontiers of the Persianate World (ca. 800–1900)." In *The Persianate World: The Frontiers of a Eurasian Lingua Franca*, edited by Nile Green, 1–72. Berkeley: University of California Press, 2019.
——. "The Uses of Books in a Late Mughal Takiyya: Persianate Knowledge between Person and Paper." *Modern Asian Studies* 44, no. 02 (2009): 241–65.
Grewal, Sara Hakeem. "The Ghazal as 'World Poetry': Between Worlding and Vernacularization." *Comparative Literature* 74, no. 1 (2022): 25–51.
Gruber, Christiane. "The 'Restored' Shīʿī *Muṣḥaf* as Divine Guide? The Practice of *Fāl-i Qurʾān* in the Ṣafavid Period." *Journal of Qur'anic Studies* 13, no. 2 (2011): 29–55.
Grunebaum, Gustave E. von. "The Concept of Plagiarism in Arabic Theory." *Journal of Near Eastern Studies* 4, no. 3 (1944): 234–53.
Guha, Sumit. "Empires, Languages, and Scripts in the Perso-Indian World." *Comparative Studies in Society and History* 66, no. 2 (2024): 443–69.
——. "Rethinking the Economy of Mughal India: Lateral Perspectives." *Journal of the Economic and Social History of the Orient* 58, no. 4 (2015): 532–75.
Gulchīn-e Maʿānī, Aḥmad. *Tārīḵh-e Tażkirah-hā-e Fārsī*. 2 vols. Tehran: Kitābkhānah-e Sanānī, 1985 [1363 SH].
Gupta, Ashin Das. "Trade and Politics in Eighteenth-Century India." In *The Mughal State, 1526–1750*, edited by Muzaffar Alam and Sanjay Subrahmanyam, 391–97. Delhi: Oxford University Press, 2000.
Habib, Irfan. *Atlas of the Mughal Empire: Political and Economic Maps with Detailed Notes, Bibliography and Index*. Delhi: Oxford University Press, 1982.
Habib, Rafey, and Bruce B. Lawrence, trans. *The Qur'an: A Verse Translation*. New York: Liveright, 2024.
Hadi, Nabi. *Dictionary of Indo-Persian Literature*. New Delhi: Indira Gandhi National Centre for the Arts: Abhinav Publications, 1995.
——. *Mirzā Bedil*. Aligarh: Aligarh Muslim University, 1982.
Haim, Ofir. "An Early Judeo-Persian Letter Sent from Ghazna to Bāmiyān (Ms. Heb. 4°8333.29)." *Bulletin of the Asia Institute* 26 (2012): 103–19.

Hakala, Walter N. *Negotiating Languages: Urdu, Hindi, and the Definition of Modern South Asia*. New York: Columbia University Press, 2016.
———. "A Sultan in the Realm of Passion: Coffee in Eighteenth-Century Delhi." *Eighteenth-Century Studies* 47, no. 4 (2014): 371–88.
Hakala, Walter N., and M. A. Naru, trans. "A Maṣnavī in Praise of Coffee: [Prepared] at the Bidding of Nawāb 'Umdat al-Mulk Amīr Khān Bahādur by Ẕuhūr Ud-Dīn Ḥātim." *Eighteenth-Century Studies* 47, no. 4 (2014): 425–27.
Hamid, Usman. "Slaves in Name Only: Free Women as Royal Concubines in Late Timurid Iran and Central Asia." In *Concubines and Courtesans: Women and Slavery in Islamic History*, edited by Matthew S. Gordon and Kathryn A. Hain, 190–206. New York: Oxford University Press, 2017.
Hammer-Purgstall, Joseph von. *Geschichte der schönen Redekünste Persiens, mit einer Bläthenlese aus zweyhundert persischen Authern*. Wien: Bey Heubner, 1818.
Hasan, Farhat. "Forms of Civility and Publicness in Pre-British India." In *Civil Society, Public Sphere, and Citizenship: Dialogues and Perceptions*, edited by Rajeev Bhargava and Helmut Reifeld, 84–105. Thousand Oaks: Sage Publications, 2005.
———. *Paper, Performance, and the State: Social Change and the Political Culture in Mughal India*. New York: Cambridge University Press, 2021.
———. *State and Locality in Mughal India: Power Relations in Western India, c. 1572–1730*. New York: Cambridge University Press, 2004.
Hasan, Hadi. *Falakī-i-Shirwānī: His Times Life and Works*. London: The Royal Asiatic Society, 1929.
———. *Mughal Poetry, Its Cultural and Political Value*. Delhi: Aakar, 1998.
Ḥasan, Muḥammad. Preface to *Dīwān-e Ābrū* by Najm ud-Dīn Shāh Mubārak Ābrū, 8–74. New Delhi: Taraqqī-e Urdū Biyūro, 2000.
Ḥasan, Muḥī ud-Dīn. *Dillī kī Begamātī Zabān*. Delhi: Na'ī Awāz, 1976.
Hāshimī, Nūr ul-Ḥasan. *Dillī kā Dabistān-e Shā'irī*. Karachi: Urdū Ikaiḍamī Sindh, 2015.
———. Preface and Introduction to *Kulliyāt-e-Walī* by Shams ud-Dīn Walī Muḥammad Walī Dakhanī, edited by Nūr ul-Ḥasan Hāshimī, 21–64. Lucknow: Uttar Pradesh Urdū Akādmī, 1989.
———. Preface to *Dīwān-e Mubtalā: Ek Īhām-Go Shā'ir Muqallid-e Walī* by 'Abīdullāh Ḳhān Mubtalā, edited by Nūr ul-Ḥasan Hāshimī, 4–9. Lucknow: Dānish Maḥal, 1996.
Haywood, J. A. "Sawdā." In *Encyclopaedia of Islam New Edition Online (EI-2 English)*, edited by P. Bearman. Leiden: Brill, 2012. https://doi-org.proxy.lib.umich.edu/10.1163/1573-3912_islam_SIM_6669.
Hehir, Patrick, and James Dunning Baker Gribble. *Outlines of Medical Jurisprudence for India*. Madras: Higginbotham, 1908.
Hermansen, Marcia K. "Imagining Space and Siting Collective Memory in South Asian Muslim Biographical Literature (*Tazkirahs*)." *Studies in Contemporary Islam* 4, no. 2 (2002): 1–21.
Hermansen, Marcia K., and Bruce B. Lawrence. "Indo-Persian Tazkiras as Memorative Communications." In *Beyond Turk and Hindu: Rethinking Religious

Identities in Islamicate South Asia, edited by David Gilmartin and Bruce B. Lawrence, 149–215. Gainesville: University Press of Florida, 2000.

Hodgson, Marshall G. S. *The Venture of Islam: The Expansion of Islam in the Middle Periods*. 3 vols. Chicago: University of Chicago Press, 1974.

Homerin, Th. Emil. *From Arab Poet to Muslim Saint: Ibn al-Fāriḍ, His Verse, and His Shrine*. 2nd ed. Cairo: The American University in Cairo Press, 2001.

———. "'Umar Ibn al-Fāriḍ, A Saint of Mamluk and Ottoman Egypt." In *Manifestations of Sainthood in Islam*, edited by Grace Martin Smith and Carl W. Ernst, 83–94. Istanbul: The Isis Press, 1993.

Huacuja Alonso, Isabel. *Radio for the Millions: Hindi-Urdu Broadcasting across Borders*. New York: Columbia University Press, 2023.

Huart, Clément, and Henri Massé. "Hātifī." In *Encyclopaedia of Islam New Edition Online (EI-2 English)*, edited by P. Bearman. Leiden: Brill, 2012. https://doi.org/10.1163/1573-3912_islam_SIM_2803.

Ḥusain, Iqbāl. *The Early Persian Poets of India (A.H. 421–670)*. Patna: Patna University, 1937.

Hyder, Syed Akbar. *Reliving Karbala: Martyrdom in South Asian Memory*. New York: Oxford University, 2006.

Ikegami, Eiko. *Bonds of Civility: Aesthetic Networks and the Political Origins of Japanese Culture*. New York: Cambridge University Press, 2005.

Ingenito, Domenico. "Appendix III: Jahān Malik Khātūn's Introduction to Her Dīvān." In *The Beloved in Middle Eastern Literatures: The Culture of Love and Languishing*, edited by Alireza Korangy, Hanadi al-Samman, and Michael C. Beard, 333–37. London: I. B. Tauris, 2017.

———. *Beholding Beauty: Saʿdi of Shiraz and the Aesthetics of Desire in Medieval Persian Poetry*. Leiden: Brill, 2021.

Īrāj, Shahbāz. "Guftgū bā Ustād Wāṣaf Bāḳhtarī, Shāʿir wa Paẕhohashgar-e Afġhān: Bedil Girāʾī dar Afġhānistān." *Shiʿr* 29, no. 9 (2001 [1380 SH]): 16–21.

Irvine, William. *Later Mughals*. Edited by Jadunath Sarkar. 2 vols. Calcutta: M. C. Sarkar & Sons, 1922.

Jabbari, Alexander. "The Introduction to Mohammad-Taqi Bahār's *Sabkshenāsi*: A Translation." *Journal of Persianate Studies* 15, no. 2 (2023): 257–80. https://doi.org/10.1163/18747167-bja10031.

———. *The Making of Persianate Modernity: Language and Literary History between Iran and India*. New York: Cambridge University Press, 2023.

Jackson, Peter. *The Delhi Sultanate: A Political and Military History*. Cambridge: Cambridge University Press, 2000.

Jālibī, Jamīl. *Tārīḳh-e Adab-e Urdū*. Edited by Aḥmad Nadīm Qāsmī. 3 vols. Lahore: Majlis-e Taraqqī-e Adab, 1994.

Jayyusi, Salma Khadra, Renata Holod, Attilio Petruccioli, and André Raymond, eds. *The City in the Islamic World*. 2 vols. Leiden: Brill, 2008.

Jha, Shweta Sachdeva. "Tawa'if as Poet and Patron: Rethinking Women's Self-Representation." In *Speaking of the Self: Gender, Performance, and Autobiography in South Asia*, edited by Anshu Malhotra and Siobhan Lambert-Hurley, 141–64. Durham: Duke University Press, 2015.

Johnson, James H. *Listening in Paris: A Cultural History.* Berkeley: University of California Press, 1995.
Jones, William. "A Dissertation on the Orthography of Asiatick Words in Roman Letters." In *The Works of Sir William Jones*, 1:175–228. London: G. G. and J. Robinson, 1799.
Kaicker, Abhishek. "'Briskness in the Market of Shaikh-Dom': The Commercialization of Piety in Early Eighteenth-Century Delhi." *History of Religions* 61, no. 3 (February 2022): 243–78.
———. "The Colonial Entombment of the Mughal Habitus: Delhi in the Eighteenth and Nineteenth Centuries." Master's thesis, University of British Columbia, 2006.
———. *The King and the People: Sovereignty and Popular Politics in Mughal Delhi.* New York: Oxford University Press, 2020.
———. "The Promises and Perils of Courtly Poetry: The Case of Mir ʿAbd al-Jalil Bilgrami (1660–1725) in the Late Mughal Empire." *Journal of the Economic and Social History of the Orient* 61, no. 3 (2018): 327–60.
Kaifī Dihlavī, Paṇḍit Braj Mohan Dattātriyah, trans. *Daryā-e Laṭāfat* by Sayyid Inshāʾullāh Ḳhān Inshā. Edited by ʿAbd ul-Ḥaqq. Karachi: Anjuman-e Taraqqī-e Urdū Pākistān, 2010.
Kalb, Emma. "A Eunuch at the Threshold: Mediating Access and Intimacy in the Mughal World." *Journal of the Royal Asiatic Society* 33, no. 3 (2023): 747–68.
———. "Slavery in South Asia." In *The Palgrave Handbook of Global Slavery throughout History*, edited by Damian A. Pargas and Juliane Schiel, 517–34. New York: Palgrave Macmillan, 2023.
Karamustafa, Ahmet T. *God's Unruly Friends: Dervish Groups in the Islamic Later Middle Period, 1200–1550.* Salt Lake City: University of Utah Press, 1994.
Kārdigar, Yaḥyā. "Bayāẓī dar Bayāẓ-e Ṣāʾib." *Gardhamāʾī-e Anjuman-e Tarwīj-e Zabān wa Adab-e Fārsī-e Īrān* 8 (2013 [1392 SH]): 1–14.
Keshavmurthy, Prashant. "Bīdil's Portrait: Asceticism and Autobiography." *Philological Encounters* 1, no. 1–4 (2015): 1–34.
———. "Circling the Shrines of a Hundred Mouths." *Paper Cuts Magazine* 14 (Spring 2015). https://desiwriterslounge.net/articles/circling-the-shrines-of-a-hundred-mouths-reading-and-remembering-bedil/.
———. "Ḡani Kašmiri." In *Encyclopaedia Iranica Online.* Leiden: Brill, 2020. https://doi.org/10.1163/2330-4804_EIRO_COM_11355.
———. "On the Benefits of Persian Poetic Jousting." *Seminar*, no. 671 (2015). http://www.india-seminar.com/2015/671/671_prashant_keshavmurthy.htm.
———. *Persian Authorship and Canonicity in Late Mughal Delhi: Building an Ark.* New York: Routledge, 2016.
———. "Two Interpretive Postures and Two Kinds of Friendship in Mughal Commentaries on Saʿdī's Gulistān." *PMLA* 137, no. 2 (March 2022): 246–61.
Keyvani, M. "The Qaside in the Mongol and Timurid Periods." In *Persian Lyric Poetry in the Classical Era, 800–1500: Ghazals, Panegyrics, and Quatrains*, edited by Ehsan Yarshater, 205–92. New York: I. B. Tauris, 2020.

Ḳhalīl, Muḥammad Ibrahīm. "ʿUrs-e Ḥaẓrat Bedil." *Āryānā*, no. 97 (1950 [1329 SH]): 3–23.
Ḳhān, Ġhulām Muṣṭaḥfā. Preface to *Dīwān-e Mīrzā Maẓhar Jān-e Jānān wa Ḳhariṭah-e Jawāhir* by Sayyid Shams ud-Dīn Ḥabībullah Jān-e Jānān Maẓhar, 3–12. Edited by Muḥammad ʿAbd ul-Raḥmān bin Ḥājī Muḥammad Roshan Ḳhān. Hyderabad, Sindh: al-Muṣṭafā Akādmī, 1988.
Ḳhān, Muḥammad Ẓafar. "ʿAbd ul-Ġhanī Beg Qabūl." *Hilāl* 42, no. 1 (1963 [1342 SH]): 55–61.
———. "Dārā Beg Joyā Kashmīrī." *Hilāl* 40, no. 1 (1962 [1341 SH]): 39–49.
Khan, Pasha M. *The Broken Spell: Indian Storytelling and the Romance Genre in Persian and Urdu*. Detroit: Wayne State University Press, 2019.
Ḳhān, Rashīd Ḥasan. Preface to *Zaṭal Nāmah* by Jaʿfar Zaṭallī, edited by Rashīd Ḥasan Ḳhān, 11–50. New Delhi: Anjuman-e Taraqqī-e Urdū Hind, 2003.
Khatak, Sarfaraz Khan. *Shaikh Muḥammad ʿAlī Ḥazīn: His Life, Times & Works*. Lahore: Shaikh Mohammad Ashraf, 1944.
Ḳhurramshāhī, Bahāʾ ud-Dīn. "Fāl-e Ḥāfiẓ." *Ḥāfiẓ* 7, no. 1 (2004 [1383 SH]): 21–26.
Ḳhūrshīd, Nāʿmah. "Tartīb wa Taṣḥīḥ-e Dīwān-e Qizilbāsh Ḳhān Ummīd." PhD diss., University of the Punjab, 2004 [1425 AH].
Khwājah, Mushfiq. "Mīrzā Muḥammad Riẓā Qizilbāsh Ḳhān Ummīd." In *Taḥqīq Nāmah*, 11–45. New Delhi: Qaumī Kaunsil barāʾe Furoġh-e Urdū Zabān, 2011.
Kia, Mana. "Indian Friends, Iranian Selves, Persianate Modern." *Comparative Studies of South Asia, Africa and the Middle East* 36, no. 3 (2016): 398–417.
———. *Persianate Selves: Memories of Place and Origin before Nationalism*. Stanford: Stanford University Press, 2020.
Kinra, Rajeev. *Writing Self, Writing Empire: Chandar Bhan Brahman and the Cultural World of the Indo-Persian State Secretary*. Oakland: University of California Press, 2015.
Kiyā, Ḥusain, and Waḥīd Qanbarī Nanīz. "Mashhad ush-Shuhadā-e Nidāʾī Yazdī wa Maqāʾish-e Ān bā Rauẓat ush-Shuhdā-e Wāʿiẓ Kāshfī." *Adabiyāt-e Pāyadārī* 9, no. 5 (2013 [1392 SH]): 265–90.
Kozlowski, Gregory C. *Muslim Endowments and Society in British India*. Cambridge: Cambridge University Press, 1985.
Kugle, Scott A. "*Qawwālī* between Written Poem and Sung Lyric, Or . . . How a *Ghazal* Lives." *The Muslim World* 97, no. 4 (2007): 571–610.
———. *When Sun Meets Moon: Gender, Eros, and Ecstasy in Urdu Poetry*. Chapel Hill: University of North Carolina Press, 2016.
Kulke, Tillmann. "ʿInāyat Allāh Khān." In *Encyclopaedia of Islam Three Online*, edited by Kate Fleet, Gudrun Krämer, Denis Matringe, John Nawas, and Devin J. Stewart. Leiden: Brill, 2020. https://doi.org/10.1163/1573-3912_ei3_COM_40281.
Latour, Bruno. *Reassembling the Social: An Introduction to Actor-Network-Theory*. New York: Oxford University Press, 2005.
Lawrence, Bruce B. "The Early Chishti Approach to Samaʿ." In *Islamic Society and Culture: Essays in Honor of Aziz Ahmad*, edited by Milton Israel and N. K. Wagle, 69–94. New Delhi: Manohar Publications, 1983.

Lehmann, Frederick. "The Eighteenth Century Transition in India: Responses of Some Bihar Intellectuals." PhD diss., University of Wisconsin–Madison, 1967.
Lehmann, Fritz. "Urdu Literature and Mughal Decline." *Mahfil* 6, no. 2/3 (1970): 125–31.
Lelyveld, David. "*Zuban-e Urdu-e Mu'alla* and the Idol of Linguistic Origins." *The Annual of Urdu Studies* 9 (1994): 57–67.
Lewis, Franklin D. "Reading, Writing and Recitation: Sana'i and the Origins of the Persian Ghazal." PhD diss., University of Chicago, 1995.
———. "The Transformation of the Persian Ghazal: From Amatory Mood to Fixed Form." In *Ghazal as World Literature II*, edited by Angelika Neuwirth, Michael Hess, Judith Pfeiffer, and Börte Sagaster, 121–40. Würzburg: Ergon Verlag, 2006.
Lewisohn, Leonard. "Rabindranath Tagore's Syncretistic Philosophy and the Persian Sufi Tradition." *International Journal of Persian Literature* 2, no. 1 (2017): 2–41.
Lilti, Antoine. *The World of the Salons: Sociability and Worldliness in Eighteenth-Century Paris*. Translated by Lydia G. Cochrane. New York: Oxford University Press, 2015.
Limbert, John W. *Shiraz in the Age of Hafez: The Glory of a Medieval Persian City*. Seattle: University of Washington Press, 2011.
Liu, Yan. *Healing with Poisons: Potent Medicines in Medieval China*. Seattle: University of Washington Press, 2021.
Losensky, Paul E. "Poetics and Eros in Early Modern Persia: *The Lovers' Confection* and *The Glorious Epistle* by Muhtasham Kāshānī." *Iranian Studies* 42, no. 5 (2009): 745–64.
———. *Welcoming Fighānī: Imitation and Poetic Individuality in the Safavid-Mughal Ghazal*. Costa Mesa: Mazda Publishers, 1998.
———. "Zulālī-Yi Ḵh̲wānsārī." In *Encyclopaedia of Islam New Edition Online (EI-2 English)*, edited by P. Bearman. Leiden: Brill, 2012. https://doi.org/10.1163/1573-3912_islam_SIM_8207.
Losensky, Paul E., and Sunil Sharma, trans. *In the Bazaar of Love: The Selected Poetry of Amir Ḳhusrau*. New Delhi: Penguin Books India, 2013.
Mahendrarajah, Shivan. *The Sufi Saint of Jam: History, Religion, and Politics of a Sunni Shrine in Shi'i Iran*. Cambridge Studies in Islamic Civilization. Cambridge: Cambridge University Press, 2021.
Mahmudabad, Ali Khan. *Poetry of Belonging: Muslim Imaginings of India 1850–1950*. New Delhi: Oxford University Press, 2020.
Malik, Jamal. "Āzād Bilgrāmī, Ghulām ʿAlī." In *Encyclopaedia of Islam Three Online*, edited by Kate Fleet, Gudrun Krämer, Denis Matringe, John Nawas, and Devin J. Stewart. Leiden: Brill, 2013. https://doi.org/10.1163/1573-3912_ei3_COM_23979.
———. "Muslim Culture and Reform in 18th Century South Asia." *Journal of the Royal Asiatic Society* 13, no. 2 (2003): 227–43.
Malik, Zahir Uddin. *The Reign of Muhammad Shah, 1719–1748*. New Delhi: Asia Publishing House, 1977.

Manuel, Peter Lamarche. *Cassette Culture: Popular Music and Technology in North India*. Chicago: University of Chicago Press, 1993.
Marashi, Afshin. "Imagining Hāfez: Rabindranath Tagore in Iran, 1932." *Journal of Persianate Studies* 3, no. 1 (2010): 46–77.
Masʿūd, Naiyar. *Marṡiyah Ḳhwānī kā Fann*. Lahore: Maġhrībī Pākistān Urdū Akādmī, 1989.
McChesney, Robert D. "'Barrier Heterodoxy?': Rethinking the Ties between Iran and Central Asia in the 17th Century." In *Pembroke Papers*, edited by Charles Melville, 231–67. 4. Cambridge: University of Cambridge, Centre of Middle Eastern Studies, 1996.
———. *Four Central Asian Shrines: A Socio-Political History of Architecture*. Leiden: Brill, 2021.
———. Review of *Tazkirah-yi Majmaʿ al-Shuʿara-yi Jahangir Shahi*, by Mulla Qatiʿi Haravi. Edited by Muhammad Saleem Akhtar. *International Journal of Middle East Studies* 16, no. 3 (1984): 423–24.
———. *Waqf in Central Asia: Four Hundred Years in the History of a Muslim Shrine, 1480–1889*. Princeton: Princeton University Press, 1991.
McInerney, Terence. "Chitarman II (Kalyan Das)." In *Masters of Indian Painting, 1650–1900*, edited by Milo C. Beach, Eberhard Fischer, and Brijinder Nath Goswamy, 2:547–62. Zürich: Artibus Asiae Publishers, 2011.
Meier, Astrid. "Waqf as a Political Weapon: A Legal Confrontation between Two Christian Institutions in Eighteenth-Century Ottoman Damascus." *Endowment Studies* 4, no. 1–2 (December 21, 2020): 92–124.
Meisami, Julie Scott. *Medieval Persian Court Poetry*. Princeton: Princeton University Press, 1987.
Memiş, Şerife Eroğlu. "Benefactresses of Waqf and Good Deeds: Charitable Women in Ottoman Jerusalem, 1703–1831." *Jerusalem Quarterly*, no. 72 (Winter 2017): 48–57.
Mikkelson, Jane. "Flights of Imagination: Avicenna's Phoenix (ʿAnqā) and Bedil's Figuration for the Lyric Self." *Journal of South Asian Intellectual History* 2, no. 1 (2020): 28–72.
———. "Of Parrots and Crows: Bīdil and Ḥazīn in Their Own Words." *Comparative Studies of South Asia, Africa and the Middle East* 37, no. 3 (2017): 510–30.
Mir, Raza. *Murder at the Mushaira: A Novel*. New Delhi: Rupa, 2021.
Moosvi, Shireen. *People, Taxation, and Trade in Mughal India*. New Delhi: Oxford University Press, 2011.
Mukhia, Harbans. *The Mughals of India*. Malden: Blackwell Publishing, 2004.
al-Musawi, Muhsin J. *The Medieval Islamic Republic of Letters: Arabic Knowledge Construction*. South Bend: University of Notre Dame Press, 2015.
Naim, C. M. "Poet-Audience Interaction at Urdu Musha'irahs." In *Urdu Texts and Contexts: The Selected Essays of C. M. Naim*, 108–19. Delhi: Permanent Black, 2004.
Naqvī, ʿAlī Riẓā. *Taẕkirah Nawīsī-e Fārsī dar Hind wa Pākistān*. Tehran: Intishārāt-e ʿIlmī, 1964 [1343 SH; 1383 AH].

Naqvī Allāhābādī, Sayyid Muḥammad Mubīn. *Tārīḵh-e Reḵhtī: maʿah Dīwān-e Jān Ṣāhib*. Allahabad: Maṭbaʿ-e Anwār-e Aḥmadī, n.d.
Naqvī, Ḥanīf. *Shuʿarā-e Urdū ke Tażkire: Nikāt ush-Shuʿarā se Gulshan-e Be-Ḵhār Tak*. Lucknow: Uttar Pradesh Urdū Akādmī, 1998.
Naqvi, Naveena. "On the Road: The Novice Munshi's View of Inter-Imperial North India." *Indian Economic & Social History Review* 57, no. 4 (2020): 481–501.
Narayana Rao, Velcheru, Sanjay Subrahmanyam, and David Shulman. *Textures of Time: Writing History in South India, 1600–1800*. New York: Other Press, 2003.
Nasīm, A. D. "Adabī Manẓar." In *Tārīḵh-e Adabiyāt-e Musalmānān-e Pākistān wa Hind: Urdū Adab, Duvum*, edited by Sayyid Waqār ʿAẓīm, 7:1–30. Lahore: Punjab University Press, 1971.
Nāṣirī, Sayyid Ḥasan Sādāt. Preface to *Dīwān-e Mullā Muḥammad Rafīʿ Wāʿiẓ-e Qazwīnī* by Muḥammad Rafīʿ Wāʿiẓ-e Qazwīnī, 1–64. Edited by Sayyid Ḥasan Sādāt Nāṣirī. Tehran: ʿAlī Akbar ʿIlmī, 1980 [1359 SH].
Nelson, T. H. "Complex Information Processing: A File Structure for the Complex, the Changing and the Indeterminate." In *Proceedings of the 1965 20th National Conference*, 84–100. ACM '65. New York: Association for Computing Machinery, 1965.
Nīyāzkār, Faraḥ. *Sharḥ-e Ġhazalīyāt-e Saʿdī*. Tehran: Hirmis, 2012 [1390 SH].
Niẓāmī, Ḥasan Aḥmad. *Shumālī Hind kī Urdū Shāʿirī meñ Īhām-Goʾī*. Aligarh: Educational Book House, 1997.
Nizami, Khaliq Ahmad. *The Life and Times of Shaikh Farid-u'd-Din Ganj-i-Shakar*. Aligarh: Department Of History, Muslim University, 1955.
O'Fahey, R. S., and Knut S. Vikør. "A Zanzibari *Waqf* of Books: The Library of the Mundhirī Family." *Sudanic Africa* 7 (1996): 5–23.
O'Hanlon, Rosalind. "Performance in a World of Paper: Puranic Histories and Social Communication in Early Modern India." *Past & Present* 219, no. 1 (2013): 87–126.
Orsini, Francesca, and Katherine Butler Schofield. Introduction to *Tellings and Texts: Music, Literature and Performance in North India*, 1–30. Cambridge: Open Book Publishers, 2015. https://doi.org/10.11647/OBP.0062.
Orsini, Francesca, and Samira Sheikh, eds. *After Timur Left: Culture and Circulation in Fifteenth-Century North India*. Delhi: Oxford University Press, 2014.
Parthasarathi, Prasannan. "South Asia: From Political Economy to Intellectual and Cultural Life." *Journal for Eighteenth-Century Studies* 34, no. 4 (2011): 551–56.
Pauwels, Heidi. "Cosmopolitan Soirées in Eighteenth-Century North India: Reception of Early Urdu Poetry in Kishangarh." *South Asia Multidisciplinary Academic Journal* (October 2014), 1–11. https://doi.org/10.4000/samaj.3773.
Pellò, Stefano. "Black Curls in a Mirror: The Eighteenth-Century Persian Kṛṣṇa of Lāla Amānat Rāy's *Jilwa-yi Ẕāt* and the Tongue of Bīdil." *International Journal of Hindu Studies* 22, no. 1 (2018): 71–103.
———. "A Linguistic Conversion: Mīrzā Muḥammad Ḥasan Qatīl and the Varieties of Persian (ca. 1790)." In *Borders: Itineraries on the Edges of Iran*, edited by Stefano Pellò, 203–40. Venice: Università Ca' Foscari Venezia, Italia, 2016.

———. "Persian Poets on the Streets: The Lore of Indo-Persian Poetic Circles in Late Mughal India." In *Tellings and Texts: Music, Literature and Performance in North India*, edited by Katherine Butler Schofield and Francesca Orsini, 303–25. Cambridge: Open Book Publishers, 2015. http://books.openedition.org/obp/2520.

———. "The Portrait and Its Doubles: Nāṣir ʿAlī Sirhindī, Mīrzā Bīdil and the Comparative Semiotics of Portraiture in Late Seventeenth-Century Indo-Persian Literature." *Eurasian Studies* 15, no. 1 (2017): 1–35.

———. "Safina-ye Ḵošgu." In *Encyclopaedia Iranica Online*. Leiden: Brill, 2020. https://doi.org/10.1163/2330-4804_EIRO_COM_418.

Petievich, Carla R. *Assembly of Rivals: Delhi, Lucknow, and the Urdu Ghazal*. Delhi: Manohar Publications, 1992.

———. "Poetry of the Declining Mughals: The 'Shahr Āshob.'" *Journal of South Asian Literature* 25, no. 1 (1990): 99–110.

———. "*Rekhti*: Impersonating the Feminine in Urdu Poetry." *South Asia: Journal of South Asian Studies* 24, no. 1 (2001): 75–90.

Pfeifer, Helen. *Empire of Salons: Conquest and Community in Early Modern Ottoman Lands*. Princeton: Princeton University Press, 2021.

Pishbin, Shaahin. "Jalāl Asīr and the Persian Poetics of Wonder between Iran and India." PhD diss., University of Chicago, 2025. https://doi.org/10.6082/uchicago.14587.

Pollock, Sheldon I. Introduction to *Literary Cultures in History: Reconstructions from South Asia*, 1–38. Berkeley: University of California Press, 2003.

Powell, Avril A. "Scholar Manqué or Mere Munshi: Maulawi Karimu'd-Din's Career in the Anglo-Oriental Education Service." In *The Delhi College: Traditional Elites, the Colonial State, and Education before 1857*, edited by Margrit Pernau, 202–31. New Delhi: Oxford University Press, 2006.

Pritchett, Frances W. "A Long History of Urdu Literary Culture, Part 2: Histories, Performances, and Masters." In *Literary Cultures in History: Reconstructions from South Asia*, edited by Sheldon I. Pollock, 864–911. Berkeley: University of California Press, 2003.

———. *Nets of Awareness: Urdu Poetry and Its Critics*. Berkeley: University of California Press, 1994.

———. "On Ralph Russell's Reading of the Classical Ghazal." *Annual of Urdu Studies* 11 (1996): 197–201.

Pritchett, Frances W., and Shamsur Rahman Faruqi, trans. *Āb-e Ḥayāt: Shaping the Canon of Urdu Poetry* by Muḥammad Ḥusain Āzād. Delhi: Oxford University Press, 2001.

Qamber, Akhtar, trans. *The Last Musha'irah of Dehli* by Farḥatullāh Beg. New Delhi: Orient Longman, 1979.

Qureshī, ʿAbd ur-Razzāq, ed. *Mīrzā Maẓhar Jān-e Jānān aur Un kā Urdū Kalām*. Bombay: Adabī Publishers, 1961.

Qureshi, Regula. "Tarannum: The Chanting of Urdu Poetry." *Ethnomusicology* 13, no. 3 (1969): 425–68.

Rahimi, Babak. "The Consolidation of Sunni and Shiʿi Legitimacies." In *The Wiley Blackwell History of Islam*, edited by Armando Salvatore, Roberto Tottoli,

Babak Rahimi, M. Fariduddin Attar, and Naznin Patel, 311–27. Hoboken: Wiley Blackwell, 2017.
Rahman, Munibur. "Faqīr Dehlavī, Mīr Šams-al-Dīn." In *Encyclopaedia Iranica Online*. Leiden: Brill, 2020. https://doi.org/10.1163/2330-4804_EIRO_COM_9494.
——. "Mustazād." In *Encyclopaedia of Islam New Edition Online (EI-2 English)*, edited by P. Bearman. Leiden: Brill, 2012. https://doi.org/10.1163/1573-3912_islam_SIM_5634.
Rāshidī, Sayyid Ḥisām ud-Dīn. *Taẕkirah-e Shuʿarā-e Kashmīr.* 2nd ed. 4 vols. Karachi: Iqbāl Akādmī, 1982.
Richards, John F. *The Mughal Empire*. Cambridge: Cambridge University Press, 1993.
——. "The Seventeenth-Century Crisis in South Asia." *Modern Asian Studies* 24, no. 4 (1990): 625–38.
Ridgeon, Lloyd V. J. "The Felon, the Faithful and the Fighter: The Protean Face of the Chivalric Man (Javanmard) in the Medieval Persianate and Modern Iranian Worlds." In *Javanmardi: The Ethics and Practice of Persianate Perfection*, edited by Lloyd V. J. Ridgeon, 1–27. London: Gingko Library, 2018.
Rossi-Landi, Ferruccio. *Language as Work and Trade: A Semiotic Homology for Linguistics and Economics*. Translated by Martha Adams. South Hadley: Bergin & Garvey, 1983.
El-Rouayheb, Khaled. "Al-Kātibī al-Qazwīnī." In *Encyclopaedia of Islam Three Online*, edited by Kate Fleet, Gudrun Krämer, Denis Matringe, John Nawas, and Devin J. Stewart. Leiden: Brill, 2018. https://doi.org/10.1163/1573-3912_ei3_COM_33084.
——. "Two Fourteenth-Century Islamic Philosophers: Ibn Mubārakshāh al-Bukhārī and Mullāzāde al-Kharziyānī." *Oriens* 48, no. 3–4 (2020): 345–66.
Russell, Ralph. *How Not to Write the History of Urdu Literature and Other Essays on Urdu and Islam*. New Delhi: Oxford University Press, 1999.
——. "The Urdu *Ghazal*: A Rejoinder to Frances W. Pritchett and William L. Hanaway, Jr." *Annual of Urdu Studies* 10 (1995): 96–112.
Riẓvī, Sayyid Muḥammad Raẓā Sājid. *Lachhmī Narāyan Shafīq Aurangābādī: Ḥayāt aur Kārnāme*. Lucknow: Sājid Zaidpūrī, 1985.
Sadiq, Muhammad. *A History of Urdu Literature*. Bombay: Oxford University Press, 1964.
Ṣahbāʾī, Imām Baḳhsh, trans. *Tarjumah-e Ḥadāʾiq ul-Balāġhat* by Shams ul-Dīn Faqīr Dihlavī. Lucknow: Nawal Kishore Press, 1880.
Saksena, Ram Babu. *A History of Urdu Literature*. Allahabad: Ram Narain Lal, 1940.
Sanderson, Gordon, ed. *List of Muhammadan and Hindu Monuments: Shahjahanabad*. Vol. 1. 4 vols. Calcutta: Superintendent of Government Printing, 1916.
Sarkar, Sir Jadunath. *History of Aurangzib: Based on Original Sources*. 5 vols. Calcutta: M. C. Sarkar & Sons, 1912–1924.
——. *Studies in Mughal India*. New York: Longmans, Green and Company, 1920.

Sarvar ul-Hudá, Muḥammad. Preface to *Dīwān-e Ashraf ʿAlī Ḳhān Fuġhān* by Ashraf ʿAlī Ḳhān Fuġhān, 10–111. New Delhi: Qaumī Kaunsil barāʾe Furoġh-e Urdū Zabān, 2003.
——. Preface to *Dīwān-e Tābān* by ʿAbd ul-Ḥayy Tābān Dihlavī, 11–88. New Delhi: Qaumī Kaunsil barāʾe Furoġh-e Urdū Zabān, 2006.
Sarvestani, Kurosh Kamali. "Hafez Xiv. Hafez's Tomb (Ḥāfeẓiya)." In *Encyclopaedia Iranica Online*. Leiden: Brill, 2020. https://doi.org/10.1163/2330-4804_EIRO_COM_2596.
Sāyānī, Ḥaidar Ibrāhīm. Preface to *Dīwān-e Walī maʿ Dībāchah* by hams ud-Dīn Walī Muḥammad Walī Dakhanī, edited by Ḥaidar Ibrāhīm Sāyānī, 2–20. Delhi: Junaid Press, 1921.
Schellenberg, Betty A. *Literary Coteries and the Making of Modern Print Culture: 1740–1790*. Cambridge: Cambridge University Press, 2016.
Schimmel, Annemarie. *A Two-Colored Brocade: The Imagery of Persian Poetry*. Chapel Hill: University of North Carolina Press, 1992.
——. *Islam in the Indian Subcontinent*. Leiden: E.J. Brill, 1980.
——. *My Soul Is a Woman: The Feminine in Islam*. Translated by Susan H. Ray. New York: Continuum, 1997.
——. *Mystical Dimensions of Islam*. Chapel Hill: University of North Carolina Press, 1975.
——. *Pain and Grace: A Study of Two Mystical Writers of Eighteenth-Century Muslim India*. Leiden: Brill, 1976.
——. *The Triumphal Sun: A Study of the Works of Jalaluddin Rumi*. New York: State University of New York Press, 1993.
Schofield, Katherine Butler. "Chief Musicians to the Mughal Emperors: The Delhi Kalāwant Birādarī, 17th to 19th Centuries, Rev. 2015." Unpublished paper in Sources for the History and Analysis of Music and Dance in South Asia, last modified October 17, 2015. https://doi.org/10.5281/zenodo.1445754.
——. "The Courtesan Tale: Female Musicians and Dancers in Mughal Historical Chronicles, c.1556-1748." *Gender & History* 24, no. 1 (2012): 150–71.
——. "Emotions in Indian Music History: Anxiety in Late Mughal Hindustan." *South Asian History and Culture* 12, no. 2–3 (2021): 182–205.
——. *Music and Musicians in Late Mughal India: Histories of the Ephemeral, 1748–1858*. Cambridge: Cambridge University Press, 2023.
Schwartz, Kevin L. "The Local Lives of a Transregional Poet: ʿAbd al-Qāder Bidel and the Writing of Persianate Literary History." *Journal of Persianate Studies* 9, no. 1 (2016): 83–106.
——. *Remapping Persian Literary History, 1700–1900*. Edinburgh: Edinburgh University Press, 2020.
Shackle, Christopher. "Walī." In *Encyclopaedia of Islam New Edition Online (EI-2 English)*, edited by P. Bearman. Leiden: Brill, 2012. https://doi.org/10.1163/1573-3912_islam_SIM_7843.
Shād ʿAẓīmābādī, Sayyid ʿAlī Muḥammad. *Ḥayāt-e Faryād*. Azamgarh: Dār ul-Muṣannifīn, 1927.

——. *Navā-e Waṯan.* ʿAẕīmābād (Patna): Maṯbaʿ-e Qaiṣarī, 1884.
Sharma, Sunil. "The City of Beauties in Indo-Persian Poetic Landscape." *Comparative Studies of South Asia, Africa and the Middle East* 24, no. 2 (2004): 73–81.
——. "From ʿĀʾesha to Nur Jahān: The Shaping of a Classical Persian Poetic Canon of Women." *Journal of Persianate Studies* 2, no. 2 (2009): 148–64.
——. "Generic Innovation in Sayfī Buḫārāʾī's Shahrāshūb Ghazals." In *Ghazal as World Literature II*, edited by Angelika Neuwirth, Michael Hess, Judith Pfeiffer, and Börte Sagaster, 141–49. Würzburg: Ergon Verlag, 2006.
——. *Mughal Arcadia: Persian Literature in an Indian Court.* Cambridge, MA: Harvard University Press, 2017.
——. *Persian Poetry at the Indian Frontier: Mas'ûd Sa'd Salmân of Lahore.* New Delhi: Permanent Black, 2000.
——. "Reading the Acts and Lives of Performers in Mughal Persian Texts." In *Tellings and Texts: Music, Literature and Performance in North India*, edited by Katherine Butler Schofield and Francesca Orsini, 283–302. Cambridge: Open Book Publishers, 2015. https://doi.org/10.11647/OBP.0062.10
Shāṯir Gorakhpūrī, Abrār ul-Ḥaqq. Introduction to *Dīwān-e Chirkīn: Mustanad Kalām*, by Bāqir ʿAlī Chirkīn Rūdaulavī, edited by Abrār ul-Ḥaqq Shāṯir Gorakhpūrī, 19–54. Gorakhpur: self-published, 2009.
Shatzmiller, Maya. "The Adoption of Paper in the Middle East, 700–1300 A.D." *Journal of the Economic and Social History of the Orient* 61, no. 3 (2018): 461–92.
Shiblī Nuʿmānī, Muḥammad. *Shʿir ul-ʿAjam.* 3rd ed. 5 vols. Azamgarh: Maʿārif Press, 1920.
Shīrānī, Ḥāfiẕ Mahmūd. *Maqālāt-e Ḥāfiẕ Mahmūd Shīrānī.* Edited by Maẕhar Maḥmūd Shīrānī. 10 vols. Lahore: Majlis-e Taraqqī-e Adab, 1966.
Ṣiddīqī, Iftak̲h̲ār Begam. Preface to *Dīwān-e Shākir Nājī Maʿ Muqadamah wa Farhang* by Muḥammad Shākir Nājī, edited by Iftak̲h̲ār Begam Ṣiddīqī, 21–112. New Delhi: Anjuman-e Taraqqī-e Urdū Hind, 1989.
Siddiqi, Moazzam. "ʿAbd-al-Jalīl Belgrāmī." In *Encyclopaedia Iranica Online.* Leiden: Brill, 2020. https://doi.org/10.1163/2330-4804_EIRO_COM_4305.
——. "Āzād Belgrāmī." In *Encyclopaedia Iranica Online.* Leiden: Brill, 2020. https://doi.org/10.1163/2330-4804_EIRO_COM_6171.
——. "Bīdel, ʿAbd-al-Qāder." In *Encyclopaedia Iranica Online.* Leiden: Brill, 2020. https://doi.org/10.1163/2330-4804_EIRO_COM_6951.
Siddiqi, Mohammad Shamsuddin [Muḥammad Shams ud-Dīn Ṣiddīqī]. "A Critical Edition of Sauda's Urdu Poetical Works Excluding the Marsiyas." PhD diss., University of London, 1967.
——, ed. *Kulliyāt-e Saudā* by Muḥammad Rafīʿ Saudā. 3 vols. Lahore: Majlis-e Taraqqī-e Urdū, 1973–1976.
Silver, Brian Q. "The Urdu Mushāʿirah." In *Gott Ist Schön Un Er Liebt Die Schönheit*, edited by Alma Giese and J. Christopher Bürgel, 363–75. Berlin: Peter Lang, 1992.
Simmel, Georg. "The Sociology of Sociability." *American Journal of Sociology* 55, no. 3 (1949): 254–61.

Simpson, Marianna Shreve, and Massumeh Farhad. *Sultan Ibrahim Mirza's Haft Awrang: A Princely Manuscript from Sixteenth-Century Iran*. New Haven: Yale University Press, 1997.
Singer, Amy. *Constructing Ottoman Beneficence: An Imperial Soup Kitchen in Jerusalem*. New York: State University of New York Press, 2002.
Smith, Barbara Herrnstein. *On the Margins of Discourse: The Relation of Literature to Language*. Chicago: University of Chicago Press, 1978.
Smith, Matthew C. "Literary Connections: Bahār's *Sabkshenāsi* and the *Bāzgasht-e Adabi*." *Journal of Persianate Societies* 2, no. 2 (2009): 194–209.
Soucek, Priscilla P. "ʿAlī Heravī." In *Encyclopaedia Iranica Online*. Leiden: Brill, 2020. http://dx.doi.org/10.1163/2330-4804_EIRO_COM_5195.
———. "Behzād, Kamāl-al-Dīn." In *Encyclopaedia Iranica Online*. Leiden: Brill, 2020. http://dx.doi.org/10.1163/2330-4804_EIRO_COM_6856.
Spooner, Brian, and William L. Hanaway. "Introduction: Persian as Koine, Written Persian in World-Historical Perspective." In *Literacy in the Persianate World: Writing and the Social Order*, 1–69. Philadelphia: University of Pennsylvania Press, 2012.
Sprachman, Paul R. "Hajv and Profane Persian." In *Persian Lyric Poetry in the Classical Era, 800–1500: Ghazals, Panegyrics, and Quatrains*, edited by Ehsan Yarshater, 579–602. New York: I. B. Tauris, 2020.
———. "Persian Satire, Parody and Burlesque: A General Notion of Genre." In *Persian Literature*, edited by Ehsan Yarshater, 226–48. New York: Columbia University, 1988.
———, ed. *Suppressed Persian: An Anthology of Forbidden Literature*. Costa Mesa: Mazda Publishers, 1995.
Sprenger, Aloys. *A Catalogue of the Arabic, Persian and Hindu'stany Manuscripts of the Libraries of the King of Oudh*. Calcutta: Baptist Mission Press, 1854.
Steingass, Francis Joseph. Preface to *A Comprehensive Persian-English Dictionary, Including the Arabic Words and Phrases to Be Met with in Persian Literature*, edited by Francis Joseph Steingass, v–viii. London: Routledge & K. Paul, 1892.
Stephen, Carr. *The Archæology and Monumental Remains of Delhi*. Calcutta: Mission Press, 1876.
Stetkevych, Suzanne Pinckney. "The Snake in the Tree in Abu al-ʿAlaʾ al-Maʿarri's 'Epistle of Forgiveness': Critical Essay and Translation." *Journal of Arabic Literature* 45, no. 1 (2014): 1–80.
Storey, C. A. *Persian Literature: A Bio-Bibliographical Survey*. Vol. 1 (2). London: Luzac, 1972.
Stroumsa, Sarah. "'Ibn al-Rāwandī's *Sūʾ Adab al-Mujādala*: The Role of Bad Manners in Medieval Disputations." In *The Majlis: Interreligious Encounters in Medieval Islam*, 66–83. Wiesbaden: Harrassowitz, 1999.
Subtelny, Maria E. "A Taste for the Intricate: The Persian Poetry of the Late Timurid Period." *Zeitschrift Der Deutschen Morgenländischen Gesellschaft* 136, no. 1 (1986): 56–79.
———. *Timurids in Transition: Turko-Persian Politics and Acculturation in Medieval Iran*. Leiden: Brill, 2007.

Szuppe, Maria. "The Female Intellectual Milieu in Timurid and Post-Timurid Herāt: Faxri Heravi's Biography of Poetesses, *Javāher al-'Ajāyeb*." *Oriente Moderno* 15 (76), no. 2 (1996): 119–37.
Tabor, Nathan L. M. "Heartless Acts: Literary Competition and Multilingual Association at a Graveside Gathering in Eighteenth-Century Delhi." *Comparative Studies of South Asia, Africa and the Middle East* 39, no. 1 (2019): 82–95.
———. "A Local Apocalypse: District Fairs and Poetry Recitation in Rural India." *Journal of Urdu Studies* 1, no. 1 (2020): 67–89.
———. "Tābān's Magnificence Illuminated in Delhi's Early Reḳhtah Scene, 1728–1748." *Journal of Urdu Studies* 4, no. 2 (2024): 226–261.
Tandon, Shivangini. "Friendship and the Social Life of Merchants in South Asia: The Articulation of Homosocial Intimacies in Banarasidas' *Ardhakathanaka*." *South Asian History and Culture* 12, no. 2–3 (2021): 166–81.
———. "The Presence of the Marginalised in the Life Sketches of the Ruling Elites: Slaves, Musicians and Concubines in the Mughal *Tazkiras*." *Social Scientist* 43, no. 5/6 (2015): 65–75.
Taneja, Anand Vivek. *Jinnealogy: Time, Islam, and Ecological Thought in the Medieval Ruins of Delhi*. Stanford: Stanford University Press, 2018.
Tassy, Joseph Héliodore Garcin de. *Histoire de la Littérature Hindoui et Hindoustani*. 3 vols. Paris: Adolphe Labitte, 1870.
———. Preface to *Les Œuvres de Wali* by Shams ud-Dīn Walī Muḥammad Walī Dakhanī, vii–xx. Edited and translated by Joseph Héliodore Garcin de Tassy. Paris: Imprimerie Royale, 1834.
Tavakoli-Targhi, Mohamad. "Homeless Texts of Persianate Modernity." *Cultural Dynamics* 13, no. 3 (2001): 263–91.
Thackston, Wheeler M., trans. *The Gulistan (Rose Garden) of Sa'di*. Bethesda: Ibex Publishers, 2008.
———., trans. *The Jahangirnama: Memoirs of Jahangir, Emperor of India*. New York: Freer Gallery of Art, Arthur M. Sackler Gallery in association with Oxford University Press, 1999.
———. *A Millennium of Classical Persian Poetry: A Guide to the Reading & Understanding of Persian Poetry from the Tenth to the Twentieth Century*. 2nd ed. Bethesda: Ibex Publishers, 2000.
Thum, Rian Richard. *The Sacred Routes of Uyghur History*. Cambridge, MA: Harvard University Press, 2014.
Tignol, Eve. "Nostalgia and the City: Urdu *Shahr Āshob* Poetry in the Aftermath of 1857." *Journal of the Royal Asiatic Society* 27, no. 4 (2017): 559–73.
Toynbee, Arnold. *A Study of History*. 12 vols. London: Oxford University Press, 1939.
Truschke, Audrey. *Aurangzeb: The Man and the Myth*. Gurgaon: Penguin Random House, 2018.
Umar, Muhammad. *Muslim Society in Northern India during the Eighteenth Century*. New Delhi: Munshiram Manoharlal, 1998.
———. *Urban Culture in Northern India during the Eighteenth Century*. New Delhi: Munshiram Manoharlal, 2001.
"'Urs-e Bedil." *Āryānā* 166, no. 14 (1956 [1335 SH]): 3.

ʿUrūj, ʿAbd ur-Rauf, trans. *Daryā-e Laṭāfat* by Sayyid Inshāʾullāh Ḳhān Inshā. Edited by ʿAbd ul-Ḥaqq. Karachi: Āftāb Akaiḍemī, 1962.

Vambéry, A. "Russia's Influence over the Inhabitants of Central Asia during the Last Ten Years." *The Journal of the Society of Arts* 28, no. 1431 (April 23, 1880): 475–85.

Vanita, Ruth. *Gender, Sex, and the City: Urdu Rekhtī Poetry in India, 1780–1870.* New York: Palgrave, 2012.

Vanita, Ruth, and Saleem Kidwai. *Same-Sex Love in India.* New York: Palgrave, 2000.

Vildānī, Ġhulāmḥusain Sharīfī. Preface to *Dīwān-e Ġhazaliyāt-e Asīr-e Shahristānī* by Jalāl Muḥammad bin Mīrzā Moʾmin Asīr Shahristānī, edited by Ġhulāmḥusain Sharīfī Vildānī, ix–xlvii. Leiden: Brill, 2019.

White, James. "On the Road: The Life and Verse of Mir Zeyn al-Din ʿEshq, a Forgotten Eighteenth-Century Poet." *Iranian Studies* 53, no. 5–6 (2020): 789–820.

Winterbottom, Anna E. "Of the China Root: A Case Study of the Early Modern Circulation of Materia Medica." *Social History of Medicine* 28, no. 1 (2015): 22–44.

Yarshater, Ehsan. "The Indian or Safavid Style: Progress or Decline?" In *Persian Literature*, edited by Ehsan Yarshater, 249–88. New York: Columbia University, 1988.

Yazdānī, Ḳhwājah Ḥamīd. *Fārsī Shāʿirī meñ Ṭanz wa Mizāḥ.* Lahore: Shirkat Printing Press, 1989.

Zaidī, ʿAlī Jawād. *Tārīḳh-e Mushāʿarah.* New Delhi: Shān-e Hind, 1989.

Zhang, Zhan. "Two Judaeo-Persian Letters from Eighth-Century Khotan." *Bulletin of the Asia Institute* 31 (2023): 105–33.

Ziad, Homayra. "Quest of the Nightingale: The Religious Thought of Khvajah Mir Dard (1720–1785)." PhD diss., Yale University, 2008.

Zipoli, Riccardo. *Irreverent Persia: Invective, Satirical and Burlesque Poetry from the Origins to the Timurid Period (10th to 15th Century).* Leiden: Leiden University Press, 2015.

——. "Obscene Vocabulary in Steingass's Dictionary." In *The Persian Language in History*, edited by Mauro Maggi and Paola Orsatti, 297–305. Wiesbaden: L. Reichert, 2011.

——. *Technique of the Ǧawāb: Replies by Nawāʾī to Ḥāfiẓ and Ǧāmī.* Venice: Cafoscarina, 1993.

Żū'l-Faqār, Ġhulām Ḥusain. "Īhām-go aur Dīgar Shuʿarā." In *Tārīḳh-e Adabiyāt-e Musalmānān-e Pākistān wa Hind: Ūrdu Adab, Duvum*, edited by Sayyid Waqār ʿAẓīm, 7:64–91. Lahore: Punjab University Press, 1971.

Index

Italic page numbers refer to illustrations.

ʿAbd ul-Jalīl Bilgrāmī, 76–77, 258n137
ʿAbd ur-Rashīd, 14
Āb-e Ḥayāt. *See* Āzād, Muḥammad Ḥusain
Ābrū, Najm ud-Dīn Shāh Mubārak, 99; death of, 118, 267n149; as follower of Maẓmūn, 115; and *īhām*, 82–84; and Ḳhwushgo, 82, 147–48; at Ornament of Mosques, 86–87; and Walī, 106–7
Abū'l Faẓl ibn Mubārak, 199
Adeeb, Shabeena, 2–4
Aḥmad, Nasīm, 184
Aḥmad Sirhindī Mujaddid, 87–88, 261n25
Aḥsan, Ẓafar Ḳhān, 118
Ahsanuzzafar, Sayyid, 61
Aksīr, Ḥakīm Imām ud-Dīn, 143, 156, 157, 158
ʿĀlī, Niʿmat Ḳhān, 184, 255n63, 281n40
Ali, Samer, 10, 242n15
amatory verse, 162–63, 168
ambiguity and ambiguists. See *īhām*; Qabūl, ʿAbd ul-Ġhanī Beg; Qabuliyans
Amīr Ḳhān, ʿUmdat ul-Mulk, 5, 98, 139, 143, 149, 154, 194, 269n9, 273n92, 276nn141–42; death of, 97, 264n72, 264n74, 274n108; and Ḥazīn, 126–28; as literary patron, 98–99, 102, 213, 220, 228, 254n74, 254n84; mushāʿirah with reḳhtah poets, 150–54; and Qabuliyans, 132; ringdove poem, 197
ʿāmm. *See* commoners; publics; social class
amphibology. See *īhām*
ʿAndalīb, Muḥammad Nāṣir, 65–66, 143, 267n136, 274n109; and Bedil, 63, 66, 254n52, 256n95; and Dard, 130, 267n136, 274n109; and Gulshan, 84, 113
Anjām. *See* Amīr Ḳhān, ʿUmdat ul-Mulk
Anjum, Ḳhalīq, 183
Arabic (script), 12–13
Arabic poetry, 31
ʿĀrif, Muḥammad, 97
Ārzū, Sirāj ud-Dīn, 78, 82, 121, 128–29, 137, 156, 213; and "Admonition of Egoists" (*Tanbīh ul-Ġhāfilīn*), 198–99; as Bedil's student, 84, 96, 129; dictionary of, 201; emulations, 222, 273n84; and "A Miscellany of Delicacies" (*Majmaʿ un-Nafāʾis*), 198, 201; on Nadir Shah's incursion, 143–44; and Qabūl, 130–31; and Ummīd, 135. *See also* Ḥazīn, Muḥammad ʿAlī
ʿĀṣīm, ʿAbd ur-Rashīd, 102
Asīr, Jalāl Muḥammad, 58, 111
ʿAṭā, Muḥammad ʿAṭāʾullāh, 43–50; and ʿAbd ul-Jalīl Bilgrāmī, 76–77; Bedil's favorite poems by, 56–58; and Muḳhliṣ, 71–74, 76, 77; and patrons, 71–72; and Payām, 73–74; and Sarḳhwush, 45–46; and satire, 71–77; and verse politics, 59–60
Ātishkadah-e Āżar, 182–83
ʿAṭṭār, Farīd ud-Dīn, 26, 54
audition. *See* sound
Aurangzeb (Mughal emperor), 59, 82, 87
Awḥadī Marāġhaʾī, Rukn ud-Dīn, 34, *35*
Āzād, Muḥammad Ḥusain, 94; "The Water of Life" (*Āb-e Ḥayāt*), 252n13, 263n62, 281n47

Āzād Bilgrāmī, Ġhulām ʿAlī, 50, 60–61, 126, 156; and Ārzū's conflict with Ḥazīn, 199
Āżar Begdilī, Luṭf ʿAlī, 182–83

Bābā Farīd, 94–95
Babayan, Kathryn, 14, 205
Babrī Rindī, Bhañwarī, 26, 44, 49, 217, 227; as student of Bedil, 43
Bahār, Lālah Ṭek Chand, 135
baḥr and *wazn*, 31, 32
Bandah ʿAlī Bāsiṭī Sabaqat, Sher Afgan Ḳhān, 195. *See also* Ṡābit, Muḥammad Afẓal
bāñkah. See rogues and ruffians
Bāqir Ḥazīn. *See* Ḥazīn, Muḥammad Bāqir
Barhah Sayyids, 60–61
Bashir, Shahzad, 7, 231–32
bayāẓ (commonplace book). *See* diaries and diarists
Bayly, C. A., 9
bazaars and markets, 2, 9, 15–16, 59, 67, 141–43; *bāzār-e urdū*, 17; Saʿdullāh Ḳhān Square, 67, 89, 93, 120, 261n32. *See also* "market for speech"
bāz gasht-e adabī, 182, 268n163, 281n35
Bedil, ʿAbd ul-Qādir, 7–8, 11–12, , 222; and ʿAndalīb, 63, 66, 254n52, 256n95; and ʿAṭā, 45–50, 56–58, 72, 76–77; and Beḳhabar, 50–52, 55; complete works (*kulliyāt*) of, 65, 66–67, 70–71; death of, 58, 61; epitaph on grave of, 79; first mushāʿirahs of, 52–56; and "The Four Elements" (*Chahār ʿUnsur*), 52–53; and Gulshan, 88, 93, 111, 112; and literary inheritance of, 62–64; and medical concoctions, 67; and Nasir ʿAlī, 69–70; and patrons, 48, 71; poetic duel at grave of, 171–80; posthumous mushāʿirah, 40–43, 64–65, 79; and satire, 71–77; and Saudā, 190; and Sufism, 209; text and ritual at grave of, 64–68; *ʿurs*, 7–8, 165, 213; and verse politics, 58–61
Beḳhabar, Aʿẓmatullāh Ḥusainī, 50–52, 55, 56, 60–61
Bhañwarī. *See* Babrī Rindī, Bhañwarī
Bībī Zāʾirī, 217
bibliomancy, 63, 65
Blessed Citadel (Red Fort), 1, 10, 141, 158, 197
Braj Bhasha poetry, 10
Burhān ul-Mulk, 140, 145

cannabis, 85
Chahār ʿUnsur. See Bedil, ʿAbd ul-Qādir
Chamanistān-e Shuʿarā. See Shafīq Aurangābādī, Lachhmī Narāyan
Chānd, Shaiḳh, 183
cheering, clapping, and taunting, 3, 54, 137; *āfrīn* ("bravo!"), 23, 127; *vāh vāh*, 222, 285n163
Chishtis, 56, 93, 94, 133. *See also* Sufism and Sufis
chronogram, 60, 61, 68, 70, 77, 102, 168–69
circulation of texts, 5, 8, 16–29 passim, 64–65, 221; ringdove poem, 118–22; role of courtesans in, 158–68; beyond South Asia, 30–31, 69, 189, 243n41, 246n83. *See also* Persianate; tażkirahs
coded verse, 143–50
coffeehouses, 16, 73
commercial language and literature, 14–18, 78, 133, 223; among courtesans, 161–62; satire, 9, 71–73
commoners, 9, 61; protests and slaughter of (*qatl-e ʿāmm*), 142–43, 147, 149. *See also* publics; social class
couplets, 232. *See also* ġhazals
courtesans, 43, 163–64, 166, 168, 217. *See also* Nūr Bāʾī (courtesan)
courtiers, and cultural influence, 81

Dānā, Faẓl ʿAlī, 97
Dard, Ḳhwājah Mīr, 113, 171; and ʿAndalīb, 130, 143; and Gulshan, 113
dargāh. See shrines, tombs, and graves

Dargāh Qulī Ḳhān, 63–64, 137, 144, 163, 165–66, 168; diary of (*Muraqqaʿ-e Dihlī*), 144, 163, 165
Daryā-e Laṭāfat. *See* Inshā, Inshāʾullāh Ḳhān
death anniversaries. See *ʿurs*
Deccan, 61 69, 120, 122, 134, 150, 188, 201
Deccani language, 109, 147
Dhavan, Purnima, 109
diaries and diarists, 24, 27–28, 63–64, 69; *bayāẓ*, *safīnah*, *jung* (commonplace book), 24, 27, 29, 72, 103, 137; *majmaʿ*, *majmūʿah* (miscellany), 25, 65–66
digital humanities approaches, 36–37
Dīwān-e Shams. *See* Rūmī, Maulānā Jalāl ud-Dīn
dīwāns, 29–30, 87, 231. *See also* reḳhtah poetry; *and names of specific poets*
Dīwānzādah. *See* Ḥātim, Ẓuhūr ud-Dīn
doggerel, nonsense, and meaninglessness, 44, 173–74; *khichaṛī* (hodgepodge), 72–73, 74, 84, 257n127; *pūch* (empty words), 172, 175, 176, 178, 210, 280n18
double entendre. See *īhām*
Dudney, Arthur, 17, 145

Eid, 2–3, 140, 148, 153
elites. *See* social class
emulations, 20, 29, 30–31, 111, 146–48, 206, 225–26; and methodology, 33–37; *tatabbuʿ* (following), 29–30, 32, 36, 105, 116, 200. *See also* Losensky, Paul; tribute ġhazals
end rhyme (*qāfiyah*), 31
epics, in Persian, 12

Faiẓān, Dānish, 75
Faiẓī, Abū'l Faiẓ ibn Mubārak, 49, 54–55, 199, 217
Faḳhr ud-Dīn ʿIrāqī, 166–67
fāl, 63, 65
Faqīr Dihlavī, Shams ud-Dīn, 135, 140
Farḥatullāh Beg, 10, 29, 228
Faryād, Ulfat Ḥusain, 9
female poets, 16, 125, 216–17
Fīrozābād, 11–12
Fīroz Shāh's fortress (Feroz Shah Kotla), 87, 120, 129–30, 143, 212, 228
Flatt, Emma J., 10
Fuġhān, Ashraf ʿAlī Ḳhān, 250n137, 267n139

Gardezī, ʿAlī ul-Ḥusainī, 182
gathering, 22–23
gender, 16, 26, 162, 168, 279n194
Ġhālib, Asadullāh Ḳhān, 28, 36, 223
Ġhanī, Muḥammad Ṭāhir, *īhām* style, 129
ġhazals, 11, 18–22; ambiguity, 5, 19, 162, 199; flexible approaches to style in writing, 19, literary-historical approach to interpreting, 205–6; of minor poets, 29–30; and "New Style" (*ṭarz-e tāzah*), 54–55; rhythm and rhyme, 31–34
ghostwriting and plagiarism, 76, 120–21, 138–39, 172, 195–96
Girāmī, Mīrzā, 127–29, 133–34, 136–37; and Ārzū, 129, 137; as dervish, 127–28; and Mobad, 169; and populism, 132–33; as teacher, 169
Goitein, Shelomo Dov, 28–29
Gould, Rebecca R., 19, 221
Gulāb, 125
Gulshan, Saʿdullāh, 100; and Ārzū, 100, 113; and Bedil, 111, 130; and Bedil's *ʿurs*, 112, 211–14; character of, 95; death and grave of, 113, 266n133; dīwān, 213–14; influence as religious figure, 213; most famous verse of, 112–13, 213–14; and Murād, 211; musical abilities, 88, 114; at Ornament of Mosques, 80, 84–86; poems of, 109–14; as poet-saint, 113–14; and Sarḳhwush, 89–94, 111; story of, 87–94; style and influences of, 111–14; *ʿurs* (death anniversary) of, 113, 213; and Walī, 109–10

Hadith, 156, 219
Ḥāfiẓ, Shams ud-Dīn, 63, 82, 180–81, 193; shrine and dīwān of, 63
Hakala, Walter, 17
Ḥākim, ʿAbd ul-Ḥakīm, 125, 199
Ḥakīm Zulālī Ḳhwānsārī, 50
Hameshah Bahār. *See* Iḳhlāṣ, Kishan Chand
Ḥamīd, Ḳhwājah Ḳhān, 108
Hasan, Farhat, 9
Ḥasan, Mīr Ġhulām, 75
Ḥasan Sijzī, 147
Ḥashmat, Muḥammad ʿAlī, 125, 130, 166, 168–69. *See also* Kashmir
Ḥashmat, Muḥtasham ʿAlī Ḳhān, 149
Ḥātim, Ẓuhūr ud-Dīn, 14, 101–3, 107, 149, 153, 154–55; circle of (1737–39), 155–56; and *Dīwānzādah*, 103–5; as follower of Maẓmūn, 115–16; ġhazals of, 118; and Ṣāʾib, 116
Ḥazīn, Muḥammad ʿAlī, 121, 139, 141, 195, 206, 212; and Ārzū, 121, 128, 198–99; in Delhi during occupation, 125, 126–28, 144; on Muḥammad ʿAẓīm's accusation against him, 195–96; new dīwān, 126, 168, 188, 196, 204; and "nothing form," 204–5; and Nudrat, 199–201; ringdove poem, 198; and Saudā, 188–89, 191–92, 194
Ḥazīn, Muḥammad Bāqir, 152–53, 155, 162–63, 167–68; and Maẓhar, 150
Hermansen, Marcia K., 25–26
hierarchy and inclusivity, 5–7, 10–18, 23, 37, 51, 59, 223, 226; in literature and language, 14, 20, 24, 27, 81; in mushāʿirah spaces, 233–35, 271n57; in political orders, 100, 141, 184, 211
Hindi (language), 14, 105–6, 135, 244n51. *See also* Braj Bhasha poetry; reḳhtah poetry; Urdu
Hindu poets, 84–85, 88. *See also* Iḳhlāṣ, Kishan Chand; Ḳhwushgo, Bindrāban Dās; Muḳhliṣ, Ānand Rām; Shafīq Aurangābādī, Lachhmī Narāyan
Hodgson, Marshall, 12
homoeroticism, 49, 73–74, 92, 101, 134, 166, 172; *kaj kulāh* and *bāñkah* (rakish young man), 74, 75, 147, 148, 155
"horde," 17
humor. *See* ribaldry and obscenity; satire and invective
Hyderabad, Deccan, 42, 61, 96, 163, 279n194

Ibn Mubārak Shāh ul-Buḳhārī, 214
ʿIbrat ul-Ġhāfilīn. *See* Saudā, Muḥammad Rafīʿ
īhām, 20, 21, 56, 95, 112, 125–27, 129, 166, 174, 247n90, 257n128; *īhām-e nā tamām*, 120, 130–32, 270n39. *See also* Qabuliyans
ul-Iḥsānī, Karīmī, 10
Iḳhlāṣ, Kishan Chand, 25, 130, 137; and "The Eternal Spring" (*Hameshah Bahār*), 25, 113, 130, 273n85
Ilqā, Muḥammad Ṣādiq, 68, 256n41, 257n107, 257n120; battlefield language of, 70–71; and Nāṣir ʿAlī Sirhindī and Bedil, 69
imitational poetry and imitation. *See* emulations
Indian-language songs (*naġhmāt-e hindī*), 135
Inshā, Inshāʾullāh Ḳhān, 15–16, 17; and "The Ocean of Witticism" (*Daryā-e Laṭāfat*), 15–16, 244n55
ʿIqd-e Ṡuraiyah. *See* Muṣḥafī, Ġhulām Hamadāni
Iranians, 5, 160–61, 182–83, 195, 197–201; as émigré poets 120–21, 125, 134–35, 268n2, 279n7; and military occupation, 139–42. *See also* Nadir Shah
Isfahan, Iran, 14, 110, 112, 119
ʿIshq, Zain ud-Dīn Ḳhān, 136
ʿIshrat, Durgā Dās, 158
Ishtiyāq, Shāh Walīullāh, 130
Islamicate, concept of, 31, 234–35. *See also* Persianate
ʿIṣmatullāh Buḳhārī, 189
Istiʿdād, Ibrahīm, 138–39

Jahān Malik Ḳhātūn, 278n183, 278n190
Jālibī, Jamīl, 99, 131–32, 183
Jān-e Jānān. *See* Maẓhar, Shams ud-Dīn Ḥabībullāh Jān-e Jānān
jashn-e wazn (weighing ceremony), 66–67
Joyā, Mīrzā Dārāb Beg, 119–20, 129. *See also* Kashmir

Kaicker, Abhishek, 142, 231–32
kaj kulāh. See homoeroticism
Kalīmāt ush-Shuʿarā. See Sarḳhwush, Muḥammad Afẓal
Kalīm Kāshānī, Abū Ṭālib, 189–93
Kām Baḳhsh, 59
Kamgo, ʿAbd ur-Raḥīm, 120
Karīm ud-Dīn Maġhfūr, 231
Kashmir, 69, 110, 118–20, 129, 175–76, 179–80; language of, 16, 173, 180, 285n143; people of, 86, 127, 136, 202; poets from, 87, 135, 174, 180, 266n134, 273n80; Tomb of Poets (*mazār-e shuʿarā*), 129
Kātibī ul-Qazwīnī, 112–13, 214
Keshavmurthy, Prashant, 41
Ḳhāksār, Muḥammad Yār, 172
Ḳhāqānī Shirvānī, 56
ḳhāṣṣ. See publics; social class
ḳhayāl (singing style), 135
ḳhayāl-bandī (thought binding or mind bending), 58, 192
Ḳhusrau, Amīr, 13–14, 88, 114, 147, 160, 196, 244nn43–45
Ḳhusrau, Nāṣir, 191
Ḳhwājah ʿAbd ul-Bāsiṭ, 130, 195. *See also* Bandah ʿAlī
Ḳhwushgo, Bindrāban Dās, 29, 33–34, 36, 68, 137–38, 156–58, 212–13; and ʿAṭā, 57–58, 74, 77; as Bedil's biographer, 41, 42, 43, 48, 64–65; on Bedil's salon space, 49–50; and Maẓhar, 134; and Maẓmūn, 96; on Nadir Shah's incursion, 144; at Ornament of Mosques, 84; poem depicting Ornament of Mosques, 81–82; on Qabūl, 130; and Sarḳhwush, 90
Kia, Mana, 12, 25–26
kulliyāt (complete works). *See names of specific poets*

Lahore, 61, 91, 136, 139, 141, 158, 183, 231
Lawrence, Bruce, 25–26
"literary return" (*bāz gasht-e adabī*), 182, 268n163, 281n35
Lodī, Sher ʿAlī Ḳhān, 216
Losensky, Paul, 30
Lucknow, 22, 184, 189
lūṭī. See rogues and ruffians
lyric poetry. *See* ġhazals; reḳhtah poetry

maḥfil, maḥfil-e mushāʿrah, and *majlis,* 22–23
Mahmudabad, Ali Khan, 10–11, 229, 234
majmaʿ and *majmūʿah. See* diaries and diarists
Majmaʿ un-Nafāʾis. See Ārzū, Sirāj ud-Dīn
Makīn, Muḥammad Fāḳhir, 189
Malīḥā Samarqandī, 257n108
malik ush-shuʿarā. See poet laureates
Malikzādah Manzūr Aḥmad, 38; and "The City of Speech" (*Shahr-e Suḳhan*), 38
maʿnī āfrīnī. See meaning, poetic development of
Maʿnī Yāb Ḳhān, 43, 176
"market for speech" (*bāzār-e suḳhan*), 4, 6–7, 9, 11–14, 25, 59, 73, 243n42; poets as flower sellers, 25; and theme, 81. *See also* Ḳhusrau, Amīr
markets. *See* bazaars and markets
Masīḥā, 125, 130, 166, 168–69. *See also* Kashmir
Mast, Abū'l-Faiẓ, 212
Maʿṣūm, Mīr Maʿṣūm, 118–19, 199
Matīn, ʿAbd ur-Riẓā, 138, 156
Maulānā ʿAlī Kosārī Iṣfahānī, 128

Maẕhar, Shams ud-Dīn Ḥabībullāh Jān-e Jānān, 86–87, 118, 125, 130, 136, 150–51; accusations against, 172; and Maẓmūn, 95–96; mentorship, 96; mushāʿirahs of, 270n30; singing poetry, 134. *See also* Ḥazin, Muḥammad, Bāqir
Maẓmūn, Sharaf ud-Dīn, 20–21, 50; death of, 99, 121–22; dīwān, 96–97; emulations, 105–6; followers of, 114–17; and *īhām*, 21, 95, 99; at Ornament of Mosques, 80, 84, 94, 100, 110, 117–18; reḳhtah verse, 105, 121; story of, 94–101; as student of Ārzū, 96–97, 104; use of double entendre, 95
maẓmūn and *maẓmūn āfrīnī*. *See* themes
meaning, poetic development of, 107–8, 131–32, 182. *See also* doggerel, nonsense, and meaninglessness
Mecca, 40, 87, 108, 136, 219
medicine, 41, 61, 64, 67; as literary theme, 60–61, 119, 127, 157–58, 175, 269n11
merchants, 4, 8, 12, 15–16, 86, 115, 184, 232
meter (*baḥr* or *wazn*), 31, 32
Mihrparwar Begam, 143, 274n109
Mikkelson, Jane, 20, 200, 205
Minnat, Gannā Begam, 140, 216
Mīr, Mīr Muḥammad Taqī, 18–19, 20, 100, 109, 144, 171–72; in Delhi during occupation, 125; and Ḥātim, 102; and *murāḳhatah*, 172
misdirection. See *īhām*
Mobad, Zindah Rām Panḍit, 169
Mongols, 13
mosques, 4, 6, 7, 16, 17, 23, 31, 62, 63, 67, 78, 83, 205, 222, 232; Congregational Mosque (*Jāmiʿ Masjid*), 258n131, 270n30; mosque dwellers (*masjidiyān*), 84, 88, 130, 134; and Nadir Shah, 141–42; Pride of Mosques (*Faḳhr ul-Masājid*), 260n6. *See also* Ornament of Mosques
motifs. *See* themes
Mughals, 8, 14
Muḥammad ʿAẕīm. *See* Ṡabāt, Muḥammad ʿAẕīm
Muhammad Shah (Mughal emperor), 58–59, 140, 141, 142; ringdove poem, 197
Muḥtasham Kāshāni, Kamāl ud-Dīn, 189
Muḳhliṣ, Ānand Rām, 63, 121, 134, 137, 146–47, 156; and ʿAṭā, 71–72, 76; on ʿAṭā's writings, 72–74; class status, 143, 144; coded verse, 150; and Qabūl, 131; ringdove poem, 197; and royal wedding 158–60
Murād, Muḥammad, 211
Muraqqaʿ-e Dihlī. *See* Dargāh Qulī Ḳhān: diary of
Muṣḥafī, Ġhulām Hamadāni, 29, 79, 135, 171; and Ḥātim, 101–5; and "Necklace of the Pleiades" (*ʿIqd-e Ṡuraiyah*), 79, 195; and "The Valley of Orators" (*Riyāẓ ul-Fuṣaḥā*), 29
mushāʿirahs (*mushāʿarah*), 7, 38; after massacre, 150–58; and class, 234; contemporary critique of, 223, 232; and contemporary mass media, 231, 233, 234; hierarchical but inclusivist tendency of, 223–24; as *murāḳhatah*, 172; at Ornament of Mosques, 82, 86–87, 105; purpose of, 10; *ṭarḥī*, 229–30. *See also* ġhazals; taẕkirahs; *and names of specific poets*
Mushtāq, Mīr Sayyid ʿAlī, 121
Muzaffarnagar, 236

Nadīm, Zakī, 141–42, 268n2, 274n103; and Ummīd, 135
Nadir Shah, 139–41; coded verse, 143–50; massacre of commoners, 150, 156–57, 158, 195; occupation of Delhi, 124, 139–50; protest against, 142–43; and royal wedding, 158–62
Naim, C. M., 10
Najāt, ʿAbd ul-ʿĀl, 135
Nājī, Muḥammad Shākir, 117–18, 121
Naqshbandis, 88. *See also* Sufism and Sufis

narrative poems (*maśnawī*), 49, 53
Nasīm, Sayyid Ġhulām Nabī, 96
Nāṣir, Saʿdat ʿAlī Ḳhān, 185; and Nudrat and Saudā's literary duel, 186–87
Nāṣir ʿAlī Sirhindī, 32–34, 68–70, 229; and Gulshan, 89, 91–92; and Ṣāʾib, 33–34; and Sarḳhwush, 89–91
Naẓīrī Nīshāpūrī, Muḥammad Ḥusain, 195–96; "nothing form," 206–8
neighborhoods, 16, 30–31; Aḥdī Pūrah, 113; Delhi Gate, 47, 97, 130, 143; ferry landing (*guẕar ghāṭ*), 47; Fīroz Shāh's fortress, 87, 120, 124, 129–30, 143, 220, 224, 228; Kashmiri neighborhood (Kashmīrī Ṭolā), 216; Pahāṛ Ganj, 113, 130, 143, 149; Wakīl Pūrah, 143, 212. *See also* bazaars and markets
"New Writers" (*tāzah-goʾiyān*), 50, 73, 112
"New Writing" (*tāzah goʾī* or *ṭarz-e tāzah*), 44, 53–54, 181. *See also* "literary return"; themes
Nidāʾī Yazdī, 190
Niʿmat Ḳhān-e ʿĀlī, 184, 255n63, 281n40
Niẓāmī, Ḥasan Aḥmad, 99, 131
Niẓām ud-Dīn Auliyā, 93, 133
Niẓām ul-Mulk, 134–35
Nowruz, 140, 145, 149
Nudrat, ʿAṭāʾullāh, 121, 192–93; biography of, 180–82; classical approach of, 180–82; defense of Ḥazīn, 199–201; dictionary of, 200–201; and Gulshan, 218–19; influence on Saudā, 210; literary duel at Bedil's grave, 172–80, 201–3, 210–11; and Nāṣir's retelling of literary duel, 185–87; "nothing form," 207–8; ringdove poem, 200; Saudā's lampoon of daughter, 214–16, 217–18; untitled taẕkirah, 182
Nūr Bāʾī (courtesan), 135, 158–62, 212

obscenity. *See* ribaldry and obscenity
originality. *See* themes
Ornament of Mosques (*Zīnat ul-Masājid*), 81–82, 83, 84–88, 227, 228; as home for poets, 80, 110, 116, 120–22 *See also* mosques
Ottoman poets, 10, 205, 249n115

Pahlawān, 16, 47–48, 76
panegyrics, 48, 49, 69, 137, 138, 156–58
Pauwels, Heidi, 10, 109
Payām, Muḥammad Sharaf ud-Dīn, 73, 138–39, 257n128, 258nn129–30, 275n126, 276n128; and ʿAṭā and Muḳhliṣ, 73–74; death of, 275n123; reḳhtah poems of, 147–48, 155
Pellò, Stefano, 27
pen names (*taḳhalluṣ*), 31–32, 88–89, 241n4. *See also names of specific poets*
Persian (language), 12–13, 32, 36, 183; dictionaries, 14, 180, 200–201
Persianate, concept of, 8–9, 12–13, 37, 114–17, 131, 148, 173, 183, 189, 205, 226, 229–34, 242n13, 244n51, 246n83, 280n12; previous iterations of, 243n41. *See also* Islamicate
Pfeifer, Helen, 10
place and locality, 8, 13, 81–87, 143, 229–30; as linked with language and literature, 17–31 passim, 205–6, 211, 219–21, 224–27
plagiarism and ghostwriting, 76, 120–21, 138–39, 172, 195–96
poet laureates (*malik ush-shuʿarā*), 94, 189, 217; for Urdu poets (*malik ush-shuʿarā-e reḳhtah*), 183
popular sovereignty, 142
praise poems, 12, 106, 108
Pritchett, Frances W., 10, 36, 131, 185
publics, 5, 7, 9, 11, 224, 232; *ʿāmm fahm wa ḳhāṣṣ pasand*, 14–15, 235, 244n50; public gift (*ṣalā-e ʿāmm*), 61–66, 85, 256n94
puns and punsters. See *īhām*

Qabūl, ʿAbd ul-Ġhanī Beg, 87–88, 120, 129–32, 137–38, 207; and Ārzū, 130–31
Qabuliyans, 128–29, 132, 155, 158

Qadam Sharīf. See shrines
qāfiyah (end rhyme), 31
Qā'im Chāndpūrī, Qayām ud-Din, 96, 108
Qamar ud-Dīn Ḳhān, 132
qaṣīdah (panegyrics), 48, 49, 69, 137, 138, 156–58
Qatīl, Muḥammad Ḥasan, 15–17, 79, 195
qatl-e ʿāmm. See commoners
Qizilbāsh Ḳhān, 121, 125, 134–36, 142, 197
Qizilbash soldiers, 59–60, 124, 139–44, 148–49, 157–58, 160
quatrains, 66, 72, 92–93, 188
Queen Regent's Mosque. *See* Ornament of Mosques (*Zīnat ul-Masājid*)
Qur'an: 4:11–14, 45, 62, 167, 218–19, 255n75; 53:9, 285n155; 79:24, 257n107

radīf (refrain), 31, 37, 71
Raḥmān Bā'ī, 125, 165, 166, 217
Rājā Roshan Rāy, 132
Ramjānī, Ḳhwushḥāl, 140, 164, 216
Rāzī, ʿĀqal Ḳhān, 47
reciting as social process, 1–4, 19, 22–24, 37–38, 64–65, 81–84; and historical method, 28–31. *See also* sound
Red Fort (Blessed Citadel), 1, 10, 141, 158, 197
refrain (*radīf*), 31, 37, 71
reḳhtah poetry, 17–18, 20–22, 101, 105, 106–8, 115–16, 135; and class identity, 144; *murāḳhatah*, 172; and Qabūl, 131–32; by 1750, 172. *See also specific poets*
rhyme (*qāfiyah*), 31
ribaldry and obscenity, 44, 74, 77, 86, 89, 173–75, 262n35, 262n46, 253n34, 258n142, 280nn9–12; excrement, 174, 179; flatulence, 132; menstrual blood, 201; pubic hair, 87, 90
rind. See rogues and ruffians
ringdove poem, 117–21, 197–99
Riyāẓ ul-Fuṣaḥā. See Muṣḥafī, Ġhulām Hamadāni
rogues and ruffians (*rindān* and *lūṭiyān*), 15, 40, 43, 74, 90, 129, 168, 205; language of (*zabān-e lūṭiyān*), 15–16, 74–75, 245n60, 253n34
Roshan ud-Daulah, 194
Rūmī, Maulānā Jalāl ud-Dīn, 93, 147, 183, 191; and *Dīwān-e Shams*, 132

Ṡabāt, Muḥammad ʿAzīm, 158, 194–96; accusations against Ḥazīn, 196
Ṡābit, Muḥammad Afẓal, 137–39, 195–96; and Aksīr, 157–58, 195; and Ārzū, 137–39; death of, 143, 156–58, 194
Ṣadāqat, Muḥammad Māh, 166
Sadārang, Niʿmat Ḳhān, 88, 135
Saʿdī, Musharrif ud-Dīn, 79, 160, 191, 196, 211–12; and *Gulistan*, 211; tomb of, 63
Safavids, 59, 134, 205
Ṣahbā'ī, Imām Baḳhsh, 281n47
Ṣā'ib, Muḥammad ʿAlī, 33–34, 111, 116, 120, 146–47, 191; and Ḥātim, 116, 267n147; and Maʿṣūm, 118–19; and Mīr Taqī Mīr, 264n83; and Nudrat, 180–81; and ringdove poem, 121; and royal wedding, 161; and Walī, 116–17
Saʿīdullāh, Mirzā Muḥammad, 63–64, 67
Saksena, Ram Babu, 27
ṣalā-e ʿāmm. See publics; *waqf*
salons, 10, 16, 72–73
Samsām ud-Daulah, 144
Sanā'ī Ġhaznawī, Majdūd ibn Ādam, 191, 242n 282n62
Sarḳhwush, Muḥammad Afẓal, 45–46, 213; and ʿAṭā, 45–46; and Gulshan, 89–94, 111; and Nāṣir ʿAlī Sirhindī, 89–91; and "The Words of Poets" (*Kalīmāt ush-Shuʿarā*), 120
satire and invective, 9, 49, 71–77, 184, 187–89, 201–4, 211–18, 280n9; by ʿAṭā, 71–74; by Nudrat, 174–79; by Saudā, 184, 188–89, 201–4, 214–18

Saudā, Muḥammad Rafīᶜ, 20–21, 121–22, 150, 151–52, 153, 189–93, 209–10; biography of, 183–85; and Ḥazīn, 188–89, 191–92, 194; literary duel at Bedil's grave, 172–80, 201–3; and Nāṣir's retelling of literary duel, 185–87; "nothing form," 207–8; and Nudrat's daughter, 214–16, 217–18; Nudrat's influence on, 210; as poet laureate of reḳhtah, 183; satire and invective by, 184, 188–89, 201–4, 214–18; and Shafīq, 187–88; tributes, 187–92; and "Warning to Egoists" (*ᶜIbrat ul-Ġhāfilīn*), 189–90, 199
Sāyānī, Ḥaidar Ibrāhīm, 107
Schofield, Katherine Butler, 164
Schwartz, Kevin, 28
scribal practices. *See* writing
Shād, Sayyid ᶜAlī Muḥammad, 9
Shafīq Aurangābādī, Lachhmī Narāyan, 96–97, 156–58, 187–88, 210; and "Garden of Poets" (*Chamanistān-e Shuᶜarā*), 97
Shāh ᶜAbbās II (Safavid emperor), 59
Shah Alam II (Mughal emperor), 232
Shāh Gul, 87–88, 130
Shah Jahan (Mughal emperor), 14, 17, 87, 160, 189
Shāhjahānābād, 11–12, 14
Shahr-e Suḳhan. *See* Malikzādah Manzūr Aḥmad
Shāh Walīullāh Dihlavī, 130
Shāᶜir, Gul Muḥammad, 43, 176
Sharma, Sunil, 23
Sher Afgan Ḳhān. *See* Bandah ᶜAlī Bāsiṭī
Shiraz, Iran, 63, 82, 79, 82, 211, 260n5
shrines, tombs, and graves, 12–17, 62–67, 85, 113–14, 133, 137, 155, 174–87, 211–28, 272n69; Shrine of the Holy Footprint, 76–77, 172
Shuhrat, Ḥakīm Shaiḳh Ḥusain, 121
Shukrullāh Ḳhān Ḳhāksār, 47
Siddiqi, Mohammad Shamsuddin, 183
sociability (*suḥbat*), 7–11, 37–39, 41–42, 223–24, 242n14; within texts, 24, 27
social class, 7–10; distinctions of, 14–16, 26, 46, 59
social networks, and tażkirahs, 26–37 passim
sound, 28, 32, 36, 48–49, 132, 225, 247n93, 248n99, 263n146; and audio reproduction, 2, 36; within literary themes, 45, 119, 208, 257n128; noise and cacophony, 174–73; verse singing, 2–3, 132–34, 158–68; *See also* courtesans; Maẓhar, Shams ud-Dīn Ḥabībullāh Jān-e Jānān
soup kitchens, 62–63, 64, 66. See also *waqf*
sources, 22–28, 37–38, 103–4. *See also* emulation
Subtelny, Maria, 30–31
Sufism and Sufis, 13, 56, 64, 87–88, 130
suḥbat. *See* sociability
style and stylishness (*rang*, *rangīn*), 17, 25, 33, 42, 51, 54, 114, 127, 169, 184; in performance, 168; of rakes and rogues, 74, 75. *See also* ġhazal
Sulṭān, Ḳhadījah Begam, 139–40, 217. *See also* Wālih Dāġhistānī, ᶜAlī Qulī

Tābān, ᶜAbd ul-Ḥayy, 145–46, 153, 154–55, 222
Ṭāhir Naṣrābādī, Muḥammad, 257n108, 261n31, 261n33
taḳhalluṣ. *See* pen names
Tanbīh ul-Ġhāfilīn. *See* Ārzū, Sirāj ud-Dīn
Tandon, Shivangini, 26
Tanū, 125, 166–67
tarannum. *See* sound
ṭarḥ, 32, 36, 95–96, 229; definitions of, 250n146; *ham-ṭarḥ*, 78, 251n159; in newspapers, 231; as test of poet, 190. *See also* ġhazals

ṭarḥī mushāʿarah, 104, 229–30, 276n133, 286n6
ṭarz-e qadīm. See themes
ṭarz-e tāzah. See "New Writing"
Tassy, Joseph Héliodore Garcin de, 110, 243n28, 263n62
tatabbuʿ. See emulations
ṭawāʾif. See courtesans
tāzah goʾī. See "New Writing"
Tażkirah-e Ḳhwush Maʿrakah-e Zebā. See Nāṣir, Saʿdat ʿAlī Ḳhān
tażkirahs, 24, 26–28, 79, 87, 97, 156, 232; blossoming of (1730s–50s), 125; and Maẓmūn, 99; and memory or memorialization, 22–25, 37; reḳhtah, 135; and rumor and gossip, 22, 43–44, 134, 195–96; and social networks, 28–37, 246n83. *See also specific poets and writers*
taẓmīn. See tribute ġhazals
themes, 18, 21; *maẓmūn* and *maẓmūn āfrīnī*, 70, 73, 95, 101, 254n50, 265n80; classical, 45, 56, 73, 135, 162–68; development within mushāʿirah setting, 117–21; ringdove poem, 150–55; after massacre of Delhi and Shāhjāhānābād, 146–47, 155; as insult, 176–79, 185–87, 212, 214–19; originality, 73, 81–85, 111–12, 129, 138, 181, 200; on socio-political context, 145–47; *See also* plagiarism and ghostwriting
Timur Gurkānī, 8, 147
Timurid dynasty, 8, 30
tribute ġhazals (*taẓmīn*), 33–34, 177–78, 180–81, 187–93, 200, 203–4, 206
Tuġhluq dynasty, 11, 13

Ummīd, Muḥammad Riẓā Qizilbāsh Ḳhān, 121, 125, 134–36, 142, 197
urdū (horde), 17
Urdu language, 1–10; contemporary, 230–36; digitally recorded, 38; and meter, 32; poetry and poets, 16–17, 22–23. *See also* reḳhtah poetry
ʿUrfī, Jamāl ud-Dīn Muḥammad Sīdī, 49, 273n79
ʿurs (death anniversaries), 66, 40, 213; of Gulshan, 113, 133; of Mīr Musharraf, 133. *See also* Bedil, ʿAbd ul-Qādir
Uṭakkarlais, 172

vāh vāh. See cheering, clapping, and taunting
Varanasi, 136, 200, 212

Waḥdat, ʿAbd ul-Aḥd (Shāh Gul), 87–88, 130
Waḥīd, Ṭāhir, 134
Wāʿiz, Rafīʿ ud-Dīn Muḥammad, 112, 121
Walī, Shams ud-Dīn Walī Muḥammad, 105–8, 148; emulations, 116–17; and Gulshan, 109–10; praise poems, 108; reḳhtah poetry, 110
Wālih, Ḥusain, 53–54
Wālih Dāġhistānī, ʿAlī Qulī, 135, 139–40, 216–17; class status, 143; on Nadir Shah's occupation, 125, 144–45. *See also* Sulṭān, Ḳhadījah Begam
waqf, 62–63, 64, 85–86, 255n72, 255n79
weddings, 158–62, 167
weighing ceremony (*jashn-e wazn*), 66–67
Widād, Sulaimān ʿAlī Ḳhān, 184
women mushāʿirah poets, 16, 125, 216–17
wrestler of speech (*pahlawān-e suḳhan*), 48, 253n29
wrestling, 16, 47–48, 76
writing, 12, 24, 27–28, 32; and scribal practices, 36, 132, 235, 254n50, 270n36; and tażkirahs, 25, 27, 28

Yaktā, Aḥmad Yār Ḳhān, 181
Yaqīn, Inʿāmullāh Ḳhān, 101, 134, 172, 188
YouTube, 233, 234

Zaidī, ʿAlī Jawād, 10, 27, 29. *See also* taẓkirahs
zamīn. See *ṭarḥ*
Zaṭallī, Muḥammad Jaʿfar, 49–50, 72
Żauq, Muḥammad Ibrāhīm, 94, 223
Zīnat ul-Masājid. *See* Ornament of Mosques
Zīnat un-Nisā Begam, Nawwāb-e Qudsiyah (Queen Regent), 82
Ẓuhūrī, Nūr ud-Dīn Muḥammad, 201
Zulālī Ḳhwānsārī, Ḥakīm, 50
Żū'l-Faqār, Ġhulām Ḥusain, 99, 100–101

www.ingramcontent.com/pod-product-compliance
Lightning Source LLC
Chambersburg PA
CBHW032013300426
44117CB00008B/1012
9781469690223